# THE ROMANCE LANGUAGES

# THE GREAT LANGUAGES

GENERAL EDITOR
*L. R. Palmer, M.A., D.Phil., Ph.D.*
Professor of Comparative Philology in the University of Oxford

## THE FRENCH LANGUAGE
By *A. Ewert, M.A., Litt.D.*

## THE GERMAN LANGUAGE
By *R. Priebsch, Ph.D.* and *W. E. Collinson, M.A., Ph.D.*

## THE SPANISH LANGUAGE, TOGETHER WITH PORTUGUESE, CATALAN, BASQUE
By *William J. Entwistle, M.A., Litt.D., LL.D.*

## THE CHINESE LANGUAGE
By *R. A. D. Forrest, M.A.*

## RUSSIAN AND THE SLAVONIC LANGUAGES
By *William J. Entwistle, M.A., Litt.D., LL.D.*, and *W. A. Morison, B.A., Ph.D.*

## THE LATIN LANGUAGE
By *L. R. Palmer, M.A., D.Phil., Ph.D.*

## THE SANSKRIT LANGUAGE
By *T. Burrow, M.A.*

## THE ROMANCE LANGUAGES
By *W. D. Elcock, M.A., L. ès L., D. de L'U. Toulouse*

## THE ITALIAN LANGUAGE
By *Bruno Migliorini, Dott. in Lettere*
(abridged and re-cast by *T. G. Griffith, M.A., B.Litt.*)

*in preparation*

## THE ENGLISH LANGUAGE
By *N. Davis, M.A.*

## THE GAELIC LANGUAGES
By *Kenneth Jackson, M.A.*

## THE SCANDINAVIAN LANGUAGES
By *Einar Haugen, M.A., Ph.D.*

## INDO-EUROPEAN LANGUAGES
By *G. Bonfante, LL.D.*

## THE HEBREW LANGUAGE
By *G. R. Driver, M.A.*

## THE ANATOLIAN LANGUAGES
By *R. A. Crossland, M.A.*

## THE GREEK LANGUAGE
By *L. R. Palmer, M.A., D.Phil., Ph.D.*

# THE ROMANCE LANGUAGES

BY

## W. D. ELCOCK

M.A., L. ès L., Doct. d'Univ.

*Late Professor of Romance Philology*
*and Medieval French Literature*
*in the University of London*

FABER & FABER LIMITED

24 Russell Square

London

*First published in mcmlx*
*by Faber & Faber Limited*
*24 Russell Square, London, W.C. 1*
*Second Impression mcmlxi*
*Third Impression mcmlxiv*
*Fourth Impression mcmlxvii*
*Printed in Great Britain*
*at the University Press, Oxford*
*by Vivian Ridler*
*Printer to the University*

*To*

HILDE-ELISABETH

*in grateful recognition
of unfailing moral and
material sustenance*

# PREFACE

This volume has been committed to print in the belief that its subject, at least in countries of English tradition, has long awaited the attentions of an author.

In my imagination it is the book for which as a student I scoured the library shelves in vain, the book which should have existed but which in fact did not. True, we already had E. Bourciez's *Éléments de linguistique romane*, to which I remain much indebted, and monumental works of German scholarship, but my requirement was for something in no sense monumental and rather more 'elementary' than Bourciez's conception of elements would allow; yet at the same time more comprehensive in that it would relate the story of how Latin became Romance more intimately to the whole European saga, to the familiar background of humanistic studies. In this wider context the approach to Romance philology seemed inviting and accessible.

Conjuring my ghost book into some kind of embodiment has been a rather arduous process, fraught with misgiving and with much deliberation concerning which detail to include and which to discard. Plagiarism, filtered through lecture-notes, has of necessity supplied most of the basic ingredients, but I have tried to acknowledge my debts, and if any scholar whose goods I have purloined should consider that in this respect I have done less than justice, may I herewith crave indulgence?

A more immediate indebtedness is to those in my vicinity. To friends at Westfield College whom I have importuned I would express my gratitude for their willing response: in particular, to Professor D. M. Jones, Dr. J. A. Cremona (now at Cambridge), Dr. P. F. Ganz, and Dr. Kathleen Chesney, all of whom have read portions of my typescript and returned them with illuminating comment. I have sought the advice of Mr. T. F. Mitchell, of the London School of Oriental and African Studies, about transcription from Arabic; and Professor G. Nandris, of the London School of Slavonic and East European Studies, has been constantly available to answer my queries on Rumanian. In addition to their many creative suggestions, Professor Jones, Professor Nandris, and Dr. Cremona have given unstinting help with the correction of proofs.

# PREFACE
The publishers and the general editor of their 'Great Languages'
series, Professor L. R. Palmer, have been most considerate and
obliging. Nor would I forget that the Central Research Fund
Committee of the University of London has accorded me grants to
facilitate travel in Italy and Spain, employed both for declared ends
and for undeclarable gleaning. To all, my heartfelt thanks.

The initial prospect of publication, and the encouragement which
this implies, I owe to one whom I can no longer thank but only
remember with lasting esteem and affection, the late Professor W. J.
Entwistle. It would please me to think that the completed work is
a passably adequate fulfilment of the project to which he gave his
blessing.

W. D. E.

*Hampstead*
*April, 1959*

# CONTENTS

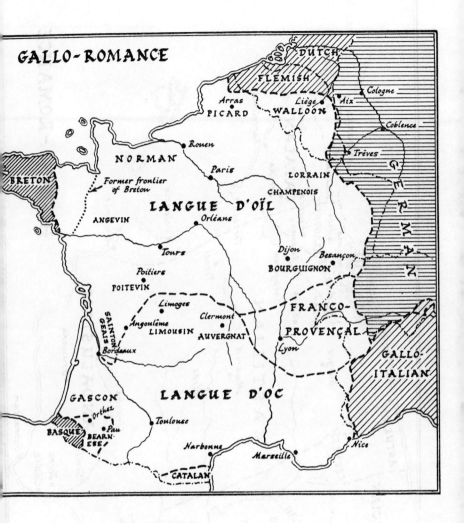

GALLO-ROMANCE

DUTCH

FLEMISH

Arras
PICARD

Liège
WALLOON

Aix
Cologne

Coblence

Trèves

GERMAN

Rouen

NORMAN

Paris

Former frontier
of Breton

BRETON

LORRAIN

ANGEVIN

LANGUE D'OÏL

CHAMPENOIS

Orléans

Tours

Dijon
BOURGUIGNON

Besançon

Poitiers
POITEVIN

Limoges
Angoulême
LIMOUSIN

SAINTON-
GEAIS

Clermont
AUVERGNAT

FRANCO-

PROVENÇAL

Bordeaux

Lyon

GALLO-
ITALIAN

LANGUE D'OC

GASCON

Orthez
Pau
BEARN-
ESE

Toulouse

BASQUE

Narbonne

Marseille

Nice

CATALAN

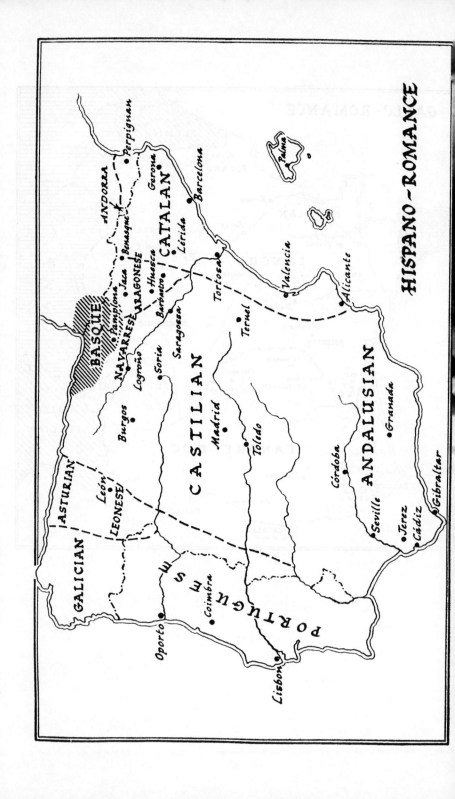

HISPANO~ROMANCE

ITALO- & RHETO-ROMANCE

GERMAN

ROMANSH    Chur    ENGADINISH    LADIN    MAGYAR
                                  FRIULAN
FRANCO-    LOMBARD    VENETIAN    SLOVENE
PROVENÇAL                Trieste
         Milan                Fiume
PIEDMONTESE  GALLO-    Venice    Veglia
Turin                          CROATIAN
      LIGURIAN    ITALIAN    Bologna
                  EMILIAN    Ravenna    SERBIAN
         Genoa  Spezia
              Pisa    Rimini
                   Florence
           TUSCAN    MARCHI-
                     GIANO
CISMONTANO          UMBRIAN

                    Rome
OLTRAMONTANO        ROMAN
                         Benevento
                    ABBRUZZIAN
         GALLURESE    NEAPOLITAN
                                APULIAN
SASSARESE            Naples        Taranto   Lecce
         Nuoro                     LUCANIAN
CATALAN    LOGUDORESE                GREEK
                                CALABRIAN
      CAMPIDANESE

      Cagliari
                    Palermo
                          GREEK
              SICILIAN

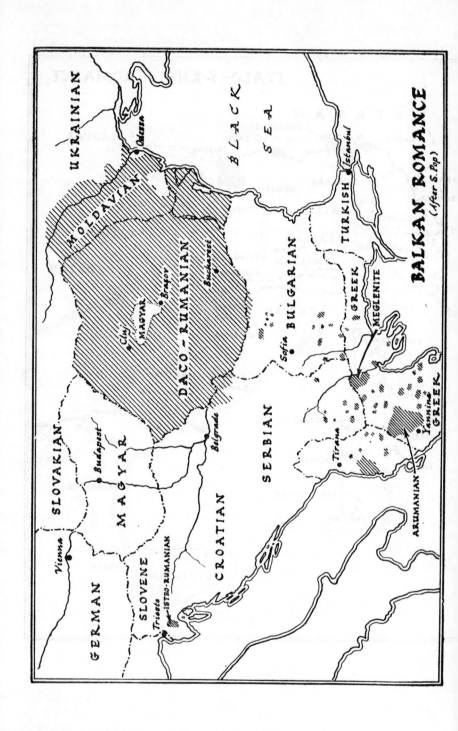

BALKAN ROMANCE *(After S. Pop)*

# I

# THE LATIN FOUNDATION

THE Romance languages might perhaps be defined collectively as a linguistic consequence of the Roman Empire. In furtherance of our purpose, which is to explore in some detail the substance of this definition, it seems appropriate to determine, as a preliminary step, with what languages we shall be concerned and why they are called 'Romance'.

At the height of Roman power a new shade of meaning was conferred upon the word 'Romanus': precisely, in the year A.D. 212, when Caracalla decreed that all free-born inhabitants of the Empire should thereafter be Roman citizens. The wider scope of the adjective called for a new noun, and so, on the readily available models of Italia, Hispania, Gallia, &c., there was coined 'Romania', first attested in the fourth century as a comprehensive name for the whole 'commonwealth', including its large Greek-speaking area. The essentially political nature of the concept of Romania, in its early acceptance, is apparent from the continued use and propagation of the term in the official Greek language of the Byzantine Empire, long after the collapse of the Roman Empire in the west: hence the *Romagna* of Italy, the last part of that country to be held by the Byzantine Exarchate, with headquarters at Ravenna, in its coexistence with the Langobards, whose chief territorial acquisition was by contrast *Langobardia*, i.e. Lombardy (see pp. 257–60).[1]

To the *Romani* in the broad political sense were opposed the *Barbari*, all who lived outside the confines of the Empire (cf. 'Berber'), this word being an early Latin borrowing from the Greeks, for whom it originally meant 'of unintelligible speech'. In the west, as the political situation deteriorated during the later years of Roman rule, the implications of both terms came to be more narrowly linguistic: *Barbari* was increasingly identified with German-speaking

---

[1] The name of Rumania, *Romînia* to the Rumanians, is a 'learned' application of the same word, decided upon in 1859, when Moldavia and Wallachia were united as one country; it has, however, a popular basis in the survival of ROMANUS as Rum. *Rumîn, Romîn*, cf. also the popular *Țara Romînească* (*Țara* from TERRA) for Wallachia.

tribes, while the *Romani* were the speakers of Latin (for whom the Germans had another name, see p. 271, note). 'To speak in the Roman way' then became 'fabulare [or parabolare] ROMA-NICE', this word an adverb derived from the adjective ROMANICUS, which had been generalized to correspond broadly to *Romania* when the adjective *Romanus* was felt to correspond too precisely to *Roma*. Understood as the direct object of the verb, ROMANICE was then launched upon a new semantic career as the substantive designating the 'popular' Latin vernacular, opposed in the Middle Ages to the 'learned' medieval Latin. It is the *rumantsch* or *rumontsch* of the Grisons; with a similar palatalization of the C (see p. 53) it evolved to Old Fr. *romanz* (pronounced *romants*, cf. Eng. *romance*) and this, having the appearance of a nominative case, gave rise to an accusative *roman(t)*. As Old French developed into a literary language the word was applied not only to the language itself but also to any composition in the language: hence the *roman* as a literary genre.[1]

During the Middle Ages the frontiers of Romance became restricted to Europe and even there to specific regions within the expanse of the former Empire. It is nowadays customary to distinguish the following groupings: Gallo-Romance, including *langue d'oïl*, whence modern French, and *langue d'oc*, whence literary Provençal; Hispano-Romance, including Spanish, Portuguese, and Catalan; Italo-Romance, comprising in addition to Italian the speech of Sardinia, of particular interest to linguists on account of the 'archaic' features of its dialects, notably the central Logudorese; Rheto-Romance, now limited to the Romansh and Engadinish of eastern Switzerland, the Ladin of the Dolomites, and Friulan; Balkan Romance, including Rumanian and islets of Romance speech scattered over the Balkan area. This grouping is in no sense rigid: Catalan, for example, though geographically located south of the Pyrenees, shows many of the features of Gallo-Romance; north Italian dialects represent a kind of linguistic half-way house between Gallo-Romance and Italo-Romance; and a similarly intermediate speech between Italo-Romance and Balkan Romance, known as Old Dalmatian, once existed on the eastern seabord of the Adriatic.

*Roman 'urbanity' and 'rusticity'.* Whatever the influences which

[1] For a considerably more detailed examination of these terms, see C. Tagliavini, *Le origini delle lingue neolatine*, 2nd ed., pp. 119–31.

have come to bear on the Romance languages during the course of
their history, their most prominent feature is an abiding Latinity.
From Latium came virtually all their structure and by far the
greater part of their vocabulary. But since they evolved in oral
tradition, free from literary attentions until some centuries after
the fall of Rome, it is of necessity in spoken Latin that one must
seek their true origin. The difference between this and the language
placed on record in the considerable body of Latin literature
which survives should not be exaggerated. It is primarily a stylistic
difference. Literary Latin is itself an expression of speech, but of
a form of speech consciously adapted to a 'noble' style. As in all
languages, a person writing Latin sought in the first place to write
'correctly'. St. Augustine has very aptly stated what this in-
volves: 'What is correctness of speech except the observance of
the usage of others, confirmed by the authority of speakers of old?'[1]
Thus to be 'correct' one must be conservative; and this, in Classical
Latin, required the use of many features of Old Latin, in particular
of forms of declension and conjugation which in contemporary
speech were being discarded in favour of different linguistic possibilities. To convey one's meaning in writing one must think out
a logical sequence of ideas, compensating by the careful arrangement of words and phrases, and by the subordination of clauses
containing notions which are subsidiary to the main line of thought,
for the loss of all the play of voice and gesture which expresses so
much in the normal exercise of speech: hence the complicated
structure of Classical Latin. One must also be judicious in the
choice of words, avoiding those which may have associations unfamiliar or displeasing to the person with whom one seeks at a
distance to establish a link of understanding: hence the absence
from literary texts of many words which must have been in current
use. In forming a literary style it is helpful to consult available
models. This was especially true in the case of early writers confined to a medium which had little behind it in the way of literary
tradition. For early writers in Latin there was an obvious model,
that of Greek, a language with a rich literature far surpassing any
other which they might have known, a language, moreover, which
in its structure, being of kindred Indo-European origin, presented
close affinities with Old Latin. This Greek model was exploited

[1] *De doctrina christiana*, 2. 13. 19; cf. L. R. Palmer, *The Latin Language*
p. 190.

to the full, on an ever-increasing scale as the Roman intelligentsia became more versed in Greek culture.

The combined result was a cleavage between studied literary style and colloquial conversation, a cleavage perhaps more deeply marked than that which exists in the modern languages of Europe: today we are much more subject in our speech to the continual pressure of 'learned influence' than was the average citizen of Rome. Latin writers were fully conscious of the difference, and some of them, Cicero and Quintilian in particular, remarked upon it: for them, written or oratorical style, which doubtless included the more deliberate prose of their normal intercourse, was *sermo urbanus*; the lower stylistic categories were variously assessed, either as 'country speech' *sermo rusticus*, or as 'popular speech' *sermo plebeius*, *sermo vulgaris*, or just as plain 'everyday speech' *sermo cotidianus*, *sermo usualis*. But whether rustic or urbane, it was all Latin.

*Vulgar Latin*, alias *Proto-Romance*. Even though no Latin literature were extant, the wealth of material available for study and comparison in the modern Romance languages is such that it would be no difficult task for the present-day linguist to reconstruct all the essential characteristics of spoken Latin. To quote a very simple illustration: the evidence of Fr. *cheval*, Span. *caballo*, Ital. *cavallo*, would in itself suffice to show that the commonly used word for 'horse' was CABALLO (with V as a possible variant for B). If we knew no more, CABALLO would have to be considered as hypothetical, and the linguist would indicate by the convention of an asterisk that it is a reconstructed form. In fact, although Cicero's word for a horse is ĔQUUS, the Latin CABALLUS does not qualify for an asterisk; apart from its appearance in later and lesser-known texts, it is used occasionally by classical authors, as for instance in Horace's *Satires*, where the meaning is clearly depreciatory, equivalent to our 'nag': briefly, CABALLUS was *rusticus*, whereas ĔQUUS was *urbanus*. Many words quoted in older works on Romance philology are given with an asterisk which may now be removed, archaeological investigations having uncovered Roman inscriptions in which words previously characterized as hypothetical are actually attested. As vocabulary may be reconstructed, so too may syntax and accidence. Thus it would perhaps be true to say that comparative study of the Romance languages, together with their many dialects, represents the surest way of determining the essential characteristics of spoken Latin. Partly for this reason, some scholars, particularly in America, would have us refer to this spoken idiom as 'Proto-Romance', just as Indo-Europeanists designate their purely hypothetical original common language as 'Proto-Indo-European'. This would have the further merit of avoiding any possible confusion of terminology. There is, however, a more commonly accepted term which age has consecrated—Vulgar Latin. Believing that a well-established label should be allowed to remain, we adhere to this term, but on the understanding that it means precisely—the spoken Latin of the Roman Empire.

*Direct evidence for Vulgar Latin.* It is the special privilege of Romance philologists that they are not compelled to rely entirely upon reconstruction. Apart from the massive testimony of Latin literature, various direct sources of information concerning the nature of the spoken language are available for scrutiny. These may be broadly summarized as follows: traces of colloquial usage in the work of Latin writers; the spelling of inscriptions; the remarks of Latin grammarians; the pronunciation of words borrowed from Latin by other languages. These sources are the only ones valid until the end of the third century. Thereafter, the changed prose style of Christian writers provides a much more ample reflection of contemporary vernacular.

In the quest for Vulgar Latin, perusal of classical authors is perhaps the least rewarding line of inquiry. One would expect much from Plautus (254–184 B.C.), the earliest author to have produced a substantial output in the Latin medium, one who was dependent, as a writer of comedies, upon the immediate understanding of an audience. And one would not be entirely disappointed: Plautus affords perhaps a better insight into popular speech than does any other Latin author before the development of Christian literature. In his work, for instance, is already to be found that combination of ECCE with demonstrative pronouns which is such a prominent feature of Romance, e.g. ECCA, ECCUM, ECCOS, ECCISTAM, ECCILLA, ECCILLUM, ECCILLUD, &c.; there, too, is the confusion of relative and interrogative pronouns, e.g. QUI VOCAT? for QUIS VOCAT?; and the assimilation of the neuter declension to the masculine as shown in such forms as COLLUS for COLLUM, DORSUS for DORSUM, NASUS for NASUM, &c. Some of his constructions are distinctly 'vulgar', e.g. the frequent introduction of the personal pronoun with the verb, and the use of the indicative mood where Classical Latin would require the subjunctive. In his adjectives he shows the Romance preference for MINUTUS and GRANDIS, rather than PARVUS and MAGNUS, and approval is commonly expressed by BELLUS, a cognate of BENE and BONUS, later to be as overworked in the Romance of Italy and Gaul as is 'nice' in present-day English. His general vocabulary is characterized by that colloquial fondness for derived forms—substantives being expanded by prefixes and suffixes, and verbs by the use of the frequentative—which accounts for so much in the evolution of the Romance lexicon. In this context one might note his use of VETULUS, which, replacing almost entirely the irregular VETUS, has given in the Romance languages the usual word for 'old'. Yet even Plautus was deeply influenced in his language by the Greek models which he so skilfully adapted to Roman taste and circumstance.[1]

During the classical age it is Cicero, the most classical of writers, who affords, in his letters, the best glimpse of the trends of popular syntax. There he is at pains to explain, to one of his correspondents, that he is deliberately abandoning the more subtle, more ornate, style of his orations and adopting that of everyday speech: 'Quid tibi ego videor in epistolis? nonne plebeio sermone agere tecum? . . . Causas agimus subtilius, ornatius; epistolas vero cotidianis verbis texere solemus' (*Epistolae ad familiares*, 9. 21. 1). In addition to the continual use of ellipsis, one notes in particular in this style that increased reliance upon prepositions which is one of the decisive characteristics of Vulgar Latin, the trend which replaced *aptus alicui rei* by *aptus ad aliquam rem, scribere fratri meo* by *scribere ad meum fratrem, unus eorum* by *unus ex eis*, &c., the trend, in brief, which undermined and finally eliminated the Latin system of declension. In the vocabulary of the letters there appear again the features observed in the comedies of Plautus: much use of BELLUS, and a continual resort to the diminutive suffixes of which Latin possessed such a large variety.

To lesser writers, in particular to the composers of technical treatises, we are indebted for a wide knowledge of the specialized

---

[1] See the analysis of Plautus' language given by L. R. Palmer, op. cit., pp. 74–88. The author here examines J. B. Hofmann's opinion (expressed in *Lateinische Umgangssprache*) that the Roman comic writers reflect contemporary spoken Latin, and reaches a somewhat different conclusion: 'The language of Plautus indubitably contains numerous colloquial elements, but they are among the many ingredients from which Plautus compounded a highly elaborate and artificial language' (p. 88).

vocabulary of trades and callings: to Columella and others for variations on the theme of *De re rustica*, to Vitruvius for the terminology of building, to Vegetius for that of the military art. Circulating among the people, many terms originally associated with particular crafts came to enjoy a wider semantic fortune as part of the basic lexicon of Romance. Nor can one leave the subject of popular idiom in the work of Latin authors without mention of the first novelist, Petronius, believed to be identical with one of the same name whom Tacitus describes as a debauchee acting as adviser to Nero on matters of taste (*elegantiae arbiter*) until A.D. 66, when he contrived an elegant suicide. Best known among the surviving fragments of his voluminous prose is the *Cena Trimalchionis*, in which Professor Palmer detects a 'whiff of the gutter'. It has been suggested that the many mistakes of declension and gender in the conversation of the guests at the banquet are due to a deliberate attempt by the author to satirize the inadequate Latin of Greek-speaking residents in Rome; but most of them have their counterpart in Romance.

For a study of the phonological development of Vulgar Latin, and for that of its morphology too, the most fruitful direct source is the one classed under the general heading of 'inscriptions'. This applies not so much to the prominent inscriptions of public buildings, drawn up by official *scriptores* and couched for the most part in a very conventional Latin, but rather to the humble engravings and scratchings which have been revealed by excavation in every corner of the former Empire, particularly on gravestones. Numbering many thousands, they are now made available in various publications, of which the most important is the monumental *Corpus Inscriptionum Latinarum* (*CIL*), published at Berlin in sixteen volumes from A.D. 1863 to 1943; each volume of this work gathers the harvest of a specific area: thus the seventh concerns Roman Britain, while the fourth is devoted exclusively to Pompeii. The last named is of particular value for its collection of *graffiti*, scratchings on walls such as may be observed in any city at any time. These are of a perishable nature and for their preservation at Pompeii we are indebted to a disaster, the great eruption of Vesuvius in A.D. 79 (described in the *Letters* of the younger Pliny), which buried that city beneath a mass of volcanic ash, and encased the neighbouring Herculaneum in a more unyielding mould of lava. The excavation of Pompeii, now almost complete,

has revealed the astonishing spectacle of a city suddenly arrested
in the midst of the most intimate detail of daily life. Writing on
the wall seems to have been with the Pompeians a quite unin-
hibited practice. There alone, well over 5,000 *graffiti* have been
collected.[1] The variety of their subject-matter would exceed even
the most hopeful expectations: solemn curses, announcements of
gladiatorial combats, dicing sums, accounts, shopping-lists, greet-
ings, and a large proportion of witticisms and eroticisms. At least
one Pompeian was offended by the disfiguration of the city's walls,
and appended in classical metre:

> Admiror, paries, te non cecidisse ruinis
> qui tot scriptorum taedia sustineas.[2]

The exceptional interest of these *graffiti*, which abound in
features characteristic of Vulgar Latin, lies in the fact that they
are almost exactly dated, and thereby show many of the changes
which may be deduced from comparative study to have been
taking place at an earlier time than one might otherwise have suspected. Thus the sonorization of intervocalic plosives, although it
occurs only sporadically, is quite well attested, e.g. PAGATO for
PACATO, LOGUS for LOCUS, and TRIDICUM for TRITICUM ('wheat',
cf. Span. *trigo*). Loss of final M, a feature of phonology which was
bound to play havoc with the declension system, is quite general;
this occasions no surprise: its weakness is already apparent a century earlier, in classical metre, where it is elided before a following vowel, but the later tendency of *sermo urbanus* had been to
restore it, thereby artificially preserving the efficacy of declension. More sporadically attested is the loss of final s, the phonological accident which was to create the deepest rift between
Italian and Rumanian on the one hand, and French, Spanish, and
Portuguese, in which it was retained as essential to the expression
of plurality of substantives, on the other. Also of common occurrence is the phenomenon known to linguists as 'syncope', the loss
of the internal unstressed vowel. One example, from a shopping-
list, will suffice: COLICLO 'small cabbage' (< CAULICULUM), an
instance in which western Romance, though not the east, has

---

[1] Veikko Väänänen, *Le latin vulgaire des inscriptions pompéiennes*, Helsinki,
1937. The author informs us that many more inscriptions have been discovered
at Pompeii since the publication of his book, and that he intends to return to the
subject.
[2] 'I wonder, o wall, that you have not fallen in ruins, since you bear the
noisome scrawl of so many writers.'

preferred the original form to the diminutive (see p. 159). This phenomenon is, however, attested a century earlier by 'cursing tablets'
(*defixionum tabellae*) discovered at Rome, in which ORICLAS—also
in evidence at Pompeii—occurs side by side with ORICULAS (Class.
AURICULAS). To Pompeii belongs the earliest-known example of
the development of a 'prothetic' vowel before 'impure *s*', i.e. *s* plus
consonant: a Greek name beginning with SM is written as ISMURMA.
That the speakers of Latin should have experienced some difficulty in articulating initial SM, which in Latin did not exist, is very
understandable; it is less easy to see why they should thereafter
have begun to pronounce the same short vowel before an s
followed by P, T, or C, but Romance confirms that they did so (e.g.
SCHOLA, Old Fr. *escole*, Span. *escuela*, Ital. *iscuola, scuola*, &c.); in
Spain and Portugal, though not in France and Italy, the habit has
persisted to affect even the most recent borrowings, e.g. Span.
*estación*, Port. *estação*, but Fr. *station*, Ital. *stazione*. Yet another
peculiarity of Vulgar Latin lay in the coalescence into a single
phoneme of an E or I originally in hiatus with a following vowel.
This is well illustrated at Pompeii, e.g. CASIUM for CASEUM 'cheese',
ALIA for ALEA 'die', CERIALIS for CEREALIS, ABIAT for HABEAT, JAMUS
for EAMUS, &c.; a few inverse 'hyper-correct' spellings testify to the
confusion in orthography brought about by this phonemic collision, e.g. MOREOR for MORIOR, PATEOR for PATIOR, &c. In reality,
the phoneme had probably already evolved to the palatal 'yod'
[j],[1] which, on account of its propensity to combine with other
sounds producing different results, was later to play a very important role in the phonological development of Romance. The
diphthongs AE and OE of classical Latin appear frequently written
as simple vowels, e.g. QUERITE for QUAERITE, PHEBUS for PHOEBUS,
&c.; O for AU, often referred to by Latin authors as a 'rusticism'—
it was a characteristic feature of early Umbrian and Faliscan—also
occurs, as in the COLICLO and ORICLAS mentioned above. A new
'secondary' AU was already developing from the combination of A
with a V vocalized in consequence of its coming into contact,
through syncope, with a following consonant, e.g. DEDICAVT,
DONAVT; herein lies the origin of the Romance flexion of third
person singular of the perfect tense (First Conjugation), e.g. Ital.
*cantò*, Span. *cantó*, Port. *cantou*.

---

[1] All phonetic symbols used in the text are those of the International Phonetic
Association.

Groups of consonants show various reductions. Of particular note is the development of -NS- to -S-, e.g. COSIDERATE, MESA, MOSTRAT, ROMANESES, also attested indirectly by a number of instances of 'hyper-correction', e.g. PARIENS for PARIES, FORMONSUS for FORMOSUS. This is a deep-rooted change, apparent in such spellings as COSUL in Latin inscriptions dating from the second century B.C., and which by the time of the Pompeian catastrophe had acquired in the spoken language the universality implicit in the term 'sound-law'; it is confirmed by the evidence of all the Romance idioms. Geminated or 'double' consonants, which phonetically means 'lengthened' consonants, present in orthography a somewhat fluctuating picture, and at times it is difficult to fit the picture to the sound. Though some are due to the assimilation of one consonant to another, many arise simply through the emphasis of affective speech, and their recording has always presented the scribe with a problem. Very common in the writing of Old Latin, they had by the first century A.D. been considerably reduced in the orthography of Rome: thus CAUSSA and DIVISSIO, usual in the first century B.C., had become the more familiar CAUSA and DIVISIO. The general tendency of inscriptions, which probably corresponded to that of speech, was to carry this reduction still farther. Thus at Pompeii we find ACIPE, SULA (the name of the dictator), but, on the other hand, doubtless as an ultra-correction, BASSILICA.

Gravestone inscriptions, both pagan and Christian, contain all the linguistic features of the Pompeian *graffiti*, together with others characteristic of Romance. Many of those assembled in the *CIL* are of uncertain date, but they extend from the early days of the Republic to the fall of the western Empire and beyond. Well known on account of its jest (Here lie two mothers, two daughters, that makes three . . .) is the following, from Pannonia:

> Hic quescunt duas matres, duas filias
> numero tres facunt et advenas II parvolas qui
> suscitabit cuius condicio est Jul. Herculanus. . . .
>
> (*CIL* iii. 3551)

A later one from Gaul runs thus:

> Hic requiiscunt men
> bra ad duus fratres
> Gallo et Fidencio qui fo
> erunt fili Magno. . . .
>
> (*CIL* xiii. 2483)

Taken in conjunction, these two will abundantly illustrate what had happened to the declension system. In the former, the accusative of the feminine plural has taken over the function of nominative, Pannonia thus agreeing on this point with Gaul and Spain. In the latter, *ad duus fratres* and *Magno* both indicate possession: the genitive case of Latin has thus vanished, giving way to the accusative with or without a preposition (in Old French the genitive of proper names or of words referring to persons is still commonly found without a preposition, e.g. *la fille le roi*, while the expression of possession by *à*, as an alternative to *de*, survives in the modern language). As at Pompeii, the form of the masculine accusative singular, its final M gone and the post-tonic U opened to O (though this may be due to rustic persistence of the Old Latin accusative in -OM, cf. second century B.C., HONCE LOUCOM for HUNC LŪCUM), has become identical with that of the classical dative and ablative. It is also the form of modern Spanish, Italian, and Portuguese.

Among other details worthy of note is the disappearance of the 'yod' in QUESCUNT and FACUNT: the former, recalling a Pompeian QUESCE for QUIESCE, derives from the same root as the adjective QUIETUM, which must have become QUETUM in Vulgar Latin in order to give the Old Fr. *coi*, borrowed into English as 'coy' and still present in modern French in the expression 'rester coi'; the latter is the etymological basis of Fr. *font*, and again exemplifies a feature of Vulgar Latin which might be deduced from a comparative study of the Romance languages, viz. the loss of the yod in the third person plural of present indicative verbs, cf. DORMIUNT, replaced in Vulgar Latin by DORMUNT > Fr. *dorment*. The frequent orthographical confusion of I and E, on the one hand, and of U and O, on the other, is a feature which will call for further explanation (see below, p. 43).

Perusing lists of inscriptions, one finds the same 'vulgar' features recurring with an almost monotonous regularity. Here, for instance, is the last line inscribed by a dutiful bereaved husband in Africa, 'Valerius Antoninus ispose rarissime fecit' (*CIL* viii. 3485); the Latin is syntactically correct, but the one word *ispose*, from the dat. SPONSAE, illustrates three of the characteristic phonological developments already observed at Pompeii: reduction of AE to the simple vowel E, of the consonant group -NS- to -S-, and the appearance of a prothetic vowel. The following, an earlier pagan inscription from Naples, introduces a more nostalgic note: 'Antipatra dulcis tua, hic so et non so' (*CIL* x. 2070); as MAGNUM became MAGNO, so the verbal SUM has become the Romance-sounding *so*, just as it appears in Old Italian. Thus inscriptions alone provide quite detailed evidence concerning the tendencies of the spoken tongue, but as yet there is little indication of the considerable local divergences which were to be revealed some centuries later in the first Romance texts.

Latin grammarians are in general disappointing, being even more vague than their Greek counterparts. Their comments are largely subjective. One will tell us that the group -LL- is rendered by some speakers with an *asperum sonum*, a point not without interest in view of its evolution in Sicilian to -*ḍḍ*-, and its curious developments in the Cantabro-Pyrenean area. Another will remark that L before a following consonant is pronounced *pinguius*, from which we may assume that it was the velar L which in later western Romance has commonly vocalized to *u* (e.g. ALTER > Fr. *autre*, Port. *outro*, Span. *otro*). Yet another comments upon popular hesitation between H and F, in which some linguists see an Etruscan influence: recalling that Latin F has become *h* in Castilian and in Gascon, one inclines to value his testimony as being relevant to the discussion of that particular problem (see p. 423). More valuable, however, than all the gleanings from known grammarians, is a single anonymous document, not in itself a work of grammar, which has come to be known as the *Appendix Probi*. This label requires an explanation. Valerius Probus was a grammarian of the first century A.D. who wrote a work entitled *Instituta Artium*. Appended to a manuscript of this work, executed in seventh-century handwriting at the monastery of Bobbio and now kept at Vienna, is a small collection of later compositions. The term *Appendix Probi* first became attached to the whole collection, but it is now generally reserved as a convenient designation for the short word-list which is of particular interest to the student of Romance. This list, in which a correct form is followed by an incorrect form (e.g. VINEA non VINIA), dates approximately from the end of the third century. Its place of origin is difficult to determine: earlier editors placed it in Africa, probably at Carthage, but more recent opinion brings it back to Rome.[1]

[1] The 'Roman' view is supported in particular by W. A. Baehrens, *Sprach-licher Kommentar zur vulgärlateinischen Appendix Probi*, Halle, 1922. All

Scholars writing in English have tended to assume that the author's purpose was to correct faulty pronunciation (thus Studer and Waters: 'The *Appendix Probi* is the fragment of a work which aimed at teaching correct Latin by pointing out common errors in the speech of the uneducated'; and Muller and Taylor: 'This list of mispronounced words accompanied by the correct pronunciation . . .', &c.). But a close examination of the data suggests that his concern was not so much with pronunciation as with spelling. For instance, in corrections such as the following:

| | | |
|---|---|---|
| GYRUS | non | GIRUS |
| CRISTA | non | CRYSTA |
| VIR | non | VYR |
| VIRGO | non | VYRGO |

all that appears to be involved is the orthographical confusion between I and the Greek Y. The many 'hyper-correct' forms here emended also seem to pertain to orthography rather than to pronunciation (see below, FORMOSUS non FORMUNSUS, &c.). Bearing this fact in mind, one can easily account for such a phonetically improbable word as the FRICDA corrected in

FRIGIDA non FRICDA.

We therefore incline towards the idea that the list was compiled by a schoolmaster, much as a teacher of English today might draw up a list of common errors in spelling culled from the exercises of his pupils; but in a Roman class-room, just as they would nowadays, many such errors had their origin in current pronunciation. From their study, although the *Appendix Probi* contains a mere 227 items, it is possible to ascertain various trends of Vulgar Latin. Yet in most respects the conclusions to be drawn from the *Appendix Probi* merely confirm the evidence provided 200 years earlier by the Pompeian *graffiti*.

In selecting examples, which in the original follow no particular order, we have classified them into appropriate categories:

*Vowels*

(*a*) Syncope

| | | |
|---|---|---|
| SPECULUM | non | SPECLUM |
| MASCULUS | non | MASCLUS |

examples quoted are taken from the text as given by Baehrens; it is reproduced in full by Manuel C. Díaz y Díaz, *Antología del latín vulgar*, pp. 55-63.

| VETULUS | non | VECLUS |
|---|---|---|
| VITULUS | non | VICLUS |
| ARTICULUS | non | ARTICLUS |
| OCULUS | non | OCLUS |
| CALIDA | non | CALDA |
| VIRIDIS | non | VIRDIS |

(*b*) Development of yod in the group: consonant+E or I+ vowel (see above, p. 25)

| VINEA | non | VINIA |
|---|---|---|
| CAVEA | non | CAVIA |
| LANCEA | non | LANCIA |
| OSTIUM | non | OSTEUM |
| LILIUM | non | LILEUM |
| ALIUM | non | ALEUM |

(*c*) Change of stressed ŭ to o (see below, p. 43)

| COLUMNA | non | COLOMNA |
|---|---|---|
| TURMA | non | TORMA |
| COLUBER | non | COLOBER |

(*d*) Reduction of pretonic AU to O

| AURIS | non | ORICLA |
|---|---|---|

*Consonants*

(*a*) Loss of final M

| PRIDEM | non | PRIDE |
|---|---|---|
| OLIM | non | OLI |
| IDEM | non | IDE |
| NUNQUAM | non | NUNQUA |
| PASSIM | non | PASSI |

(*b*) Loss of H

| ADHUC | non | ADUC |
|---|---|---|
| HOSTIAE | non | OSTIAE |

(*c*) Reduction of -NS- to -S-

| MENSA | non | MESA |
|---|---|---|
| ANSA | non | ASA |

and corresponding 'hyper-correction'

| FORMOSUS | non | FORMUNSUS |
|---|---|---|
| HERCULES | non | HERCULENS |
| OCCASIO | non | OCCANSIO |

(*d*) Loss of intervocalic v before a back vowel

| | | |
|---|---|---|
| RIVUS | non | RIUS |
| FLAVUS | non | FLAUS |
| AVUS | non | AUS |
| PAVOR | non | PAOR |

(*e*) Confusion between B and V

| | | |
|---|---|---|
| BACULUS | non | VACLUS |
| BRAVIUM | non | BRABIUM |
| ALVEUS | non | ALBEUS |
| PLEBES | non | PLEVIS |
| VAPULO | non | BAPLO |

(*f*) Hesitation between double and single consonants (probably a purely orthographical feature, though the lengthening in ACQUA already suggests modern Italian)

| | | |
|---|---|---|
| CAMERA | non | CAMMARA |
| GARRULUS | non | GARULUS |
| BASILICA | non | BASSILICA |
| AQUA | non | ACQUA |
| DRACO | non | DRACCO |

## *Declension*

(*a*) Elimination of imparisyllabic nouns

| | | |
|---|---|---|
| GRUS | non | GRUIS |
| PECTEN | non | PECTINIS |
| GLIS | non | GLIRIS |

(*b*) Adaptation of third declension adjectives and pronouns to the first and second declensions

| | | |
|---|---|---|
| TRISTIS | non | TRISTUS |
| PAUPER MULIER | non | PAUPERA MULIER |
| ACRE | non | ACRUM |
| IPSE | non | IPSUS |

(*c*) Direct adaptation of feminine nouns of the fourth declension to the first declension

| | | |
|---|---|---|
| NURUS | non | NURA |
| SOCRUS | non | SOCRA |

(*d*) Adaptation of third and fourth declension feminine nouns to the first declension by means of a diminutive suffix

| | | |
|---|---|---|
| AURIS | non | ORICLA |
| FAX | non | FACLA |
| NEPTIS | non | NEPTICLA |
| ANUS | non | ANUCLA |

(*e*) Adaptation of a neuter plural to the first declension

| | | |
|---|---|---|
| VICO CASTRORUM | non | VICO CASTRAE |

(*f*) Elimination of the ablatives NOBIS and VOBIS

| | | |
|---|---|---|
| NOBISCUM | non | NOSCUM |
| VOBISCUM | non | VOSCUM |

(*g*) Alteration of the nominative ending -ES (third declension) to -IS

| | | |
|---|---|---|
| CAUTES | non | CAUTIS |
| TABES | non | TABIS |
| VATES | non | VATIS |
| VULPES | non | VULPIS |
| FAMES | non | FAMIS |
| SEDES | non | SEDIS |

This change, of which the author gives numerous examples, appears at first sight to be simply the result of an assimilation of the nominative flexion to that of the genitive. One wonders, however, whether it does not really represent a loss of clear quality in the articulation of post-tonic E and I before S, leading to the complete disappearance which took place in a large part of western Romania (cf. NAVIS > Old Fr. *nes*), and which is illustrated by the forms which follow (though these might be explained by the analogy of such Latin words as URBS, PLEBS).

(*h*) Reduction of the endings -ES and -IS to -S

| | | |
|---|---|---|
| ORBIS | non | ORBS |
| NUBES | non | NUBS |

(*i*) Loss of the masculine flexion -US

| | | |
|---|---|---|
| FIGULUS | non | FIGEL |
| MASCULUS | non | MASCEL |
| BARBARUS | non | BARBAR |

While the last of these examples might be explained as analogical (cf. CARCER non CARCAR), the two other forms, usually omitted from anthologies, present an interesting problem. They appear to have reached the stage given above via intermediate *FIGELLUS and *MASCELLUS (a common change of suffix, cf. CATULUS non CATELLUS). If this is so, they illustrate the loss of final -S (see above, p. 24), followed by the loss of the post-tonic vowel: an advanced evolution towards Romance, cf. Rum. *mascur*, Rheto-Rom. (Engadine) *maschel*, which is scarcely attested again until the Kassel Glossary (see p. 321).

The *Appendix Probi* thus provides evidence of specific trends in phonological evolution, and also in the morphology of substantives (that of verbs is not exemplified). It also has a particular lexical interest in that it attests forms which have diverged from

the normal trends of development, and which one might otherwise
have to postulate in order to explain their Romance equivalents.
The divergences in Latin are most commonly the result of some
metathesis, assimilation, or dissimilation. Among the more noteworthy are the following:

### PERSICA non PESSICA

Here is confirmation of the consonantal assimilation which took
place in the development of (MALA) PERSICA, the 'Persian apple(s)', to
Ital. *pesca*, Fr. *pêche*. The form with R remained, however, in those
regions which escaped the later linguistic innovations of Rome, e.g.
Prov. *persega*, Cat. *prèssec*, Cast. *prisco*, and Rum. *piersică* (cf. Germ.
*Pfirsich*).[1]

### VETULUS non VECLUS

The author here accepts VETULUS, as used by Plautus (see above,
p. 22) as correct Latin: thus it replaced the irregular VETUS. Also of
interest is the development of the group T'L to CL, confirmed by
VITULUS non VICLUS. The consonantal group of VECLU thereafter
developed in the Romance languages just as did that of OCLU, e.g. Fr.
*vieil*, *œil*; Cast. *viejo*, *ojo*; Ital. *vecchio*, *occhio*. VETUS itself did not
entirely disappear: it is to be found in Italian as *vieto*, in Old French
as *viez*, and in Rheto-Romance (Engadine) as *veider* (< VETEREM). It
also gave rise to other derivative forms: VETERANUS, which survived
peripherally in Italy, e.g. Old Venetian *vetrano*, Old Sicil. *vitranu*, and
in Rumanian as *bătrîn*; and a more rare VETERNUS preserved in dialects
of the Istrian area.

### IUNIPIRUS non IENIPERUS (or IINIPERUS?)

Though editors may vary in their transcription of the first syllable
of the 'incorrect' form, the essential point is that the initial syllable JU-
of Classical Latin was generally replaced in Vulgar Latin by JI- or JE-,
cf. Old Fr. *genoivre* (mod. *genièvre*), Cast. *enebro*, Ital. *ginepro*.

### GRUNDIO non GRUNNIO

Traces in Vulgar Latin of a change from -ND- to -NN- are commonly
attributed to a dialectal influence of Oscan. At Pompeii, which until
80 B.C. was an Oscan town linked to Rome only by alliance, inscriptions
show a similar evolution, e.g. VERECUNNUS for VERECUNDUS. GRUNNIRE is
the basis of Ital. *grugnire*, Prov. *gronhir*, Cast. *gruñir*, Port. *grunhir*; Old
French has both *grognir* and *grondir*, which, with a change of conjugation, have given *grogner* and *gronder* in modern French.

### SIBILUS non SIFILUS

The sporadic alternation of an intervocalic B with F is again an ab-
normality of Vulgar Latin which is traditionally explained by Oscan

---

[1] For further examples of this assimilation, attested at an earlier date, e.g.
DORSUM–DOSSUM, see F. Sommer, *Handbuch der lateinischen Laut- und Formenlehre*, p. 258.

influence. Both forms are represented in Romance. From SIFILARE come Fr. *siffler*, Ital. *zufolare*. Provençal has doublets, *siflar* and *siblar*; so too has Castilian, with *silbar* and *chillar*, the latter appearing from its initial *ch-* to be of Mozarabic origin, and hence identifiable with southern Spain.

PEGMA non PEUMA

PEGMA is a Greek word, of no great importance for Romance. But the example is interesting in that it illustrates the development of another Greek form, SAGMA, which as SAUMA became a household word of Vulgar Latin. The SAUMA was the pack-saddle, hence the Fr. *bête de somme* or *sommier*, Cast. *somero*, Ital. *somaro*, 'donkey'.

| COQUS | non | COCUS |
|---|---|---|
| COQUENS | non | COCENS |
| COQUI | non | COCI |

Other items show the reduction of Q(U) to C, e.g. 'EQUS non ECUS'. This change normally took place in Vulgar Latin only before a back vowel. Such Romance forms as Span. *yegua*, Port. *égua* and Old Fr. *ive* prove that the feminine ĔQUA persisted with its QU intact, being affected only by the general tendency to voice intervocalic plosive consonants; ĔQUUS itself—ECUM would have become a homonym of EGO—was soon lost. Before a front vowel the distinction between QU and C was usually preserved: hence the difference in Old French between the initial consonants of *querre* (< QUAERERE) and *cire* (< CĒRA). Exceptionally, however, in the case of COQUERE the passage of QU to C as here attested must have taken place early, since it is only from COCERE that one can derive Fr. *cuire*, Span. *cocer*, Port. *cozer*, Ital. *cuocere*, &c. The first person singular of the present indicative, COQUO, by becoming *COCO probably supplied the analogue on which the other parts of the verb were remodelled. A trace of the classical form may be seen in the alternative form of Old French, the less common *cuivre*, where the U persists consonified to *v*, cf. SEQUĔRE > Old Fr. *sivre*, and as above, ĔQUA > Old Fr. *ive*, also AQUA > Old Fr. *eve*.

The languages of those countries from which Latin receded abound in Latin loan-words. While these are primarily of interest for the study of the diffusion of Latin vocabulary, they also offer some clues to the chronology of sound-change. Comparison of the Romance languages shows that, except in central Sardinia, the velar C palatalized before a front vowel (cf. above CĒRA > *cire*, and see p. 53); this change must have occurred during the Vulgar Latin period, but its relative lateness is confirmed by Latin loan-words in German, in which the original consonant is preserved, e.g. CELLARIUM, *Keller*; CERĔSEA,[1] *Kirsche*; CISTA, *Kiste*; CYMA,

---

[1] Like PERSICA, originally an adjective derived from a place-name, in this instance Cerasus, situated in the Roman province of Pontus, on the south-

*Keim*; CAESAR, *Kaiser*. These were probably adopted during the imperial age. Before that age had ended German also incorporated *Zins*, from Lat. CENSUS, in which the C had developed to the *ts*-sound of similar words in Old French. Such evidence is sometimes difficult to interpret: for example, in English VALLUM has become 'wall' and VĪNUM 'wine' (cf. Welsh *gwin*), which imply a bilabial pronunciation of the Latin V; on the other hand, French and Italian have kept in general a clearly articulated labio-dental, yet a few words with initial v have developed exceptionally in French as though the sound were bilabial, e.g. VADUM > *gué*, &c. (see p. 255); in Spanish, as in the *Appendix Probi*, v has become confused with the bilabial B. It would certainly seem in this instance that varying pronunciations were current in different parts of the Empire contemporaneously.

The acceptance of Christianity provoked a revolution in Latin prose style. Its general influence on the language has been variously assessed. One author writes:

> Christianity infused hope, optimism, dignity into the speech of the lower classes. Their joy at their new-found spiritual freedom sought and obtained vocal expression. But this vocal expression had perforce to result in an increase of their natural tendencies towards stress and emphasis. Their language broke the bounds of classical restraint, discarded for ever the pitch accent associated with the upper classes, overthrew the barriers of classical literature, and marched on to a new freedom.
>
> (Mario Pei, *The Italian Language*, p. 21)

Such claims seem rather exaggerated. It is unlikely that the vocal enthusiasm of Christians bears any relation to the decline of pitch accent (see p. 39). As for the language breaking the bounds of classical restraint, we do not assume the spoken idiom of the lower classes ever to have been seriously inhibited by such bounds. What Christianity did achieve was a temporary narrowing of the gulf between the spoken language and literary practice. In so far as it affected the former, the influence of Christianity was surely of a learned character, bringing in a mass of new 'technical' terminology, mostly of Greek origin (see p. 199). More remarkable is the approach of written Latin towards everyday speech: the result of a policy deliberately adopted by the Christian fathers.

eastern shores of the Black Sea, whence the cherry-tree is said to have been brought to Italy. Romance forms presuppose the use in Vulgar Latin of both CERĔSEA and CERASEA.

The pioneers in this respect were St. Jerome (A.D. 331–420) and St. Augustine (A.D. 352–430). The former declared: 'Volo pro legentis facilitate abuti sermone vulgato', and in the Vulgate, his translation of the Bible into Latin (A.D. 385–404), he carried this principle into effect, as may be judged from the 'Romance-sounding' quality of such sentences as the following: 'Et dixit ad me: Iste est locus ubi coquent sacerdotes pro peccato, et pro delicto: ubi coquent sacrificium. . . .' St. Augustine, while giving proof of his ability to employ the classical phrase in his *City of God*, addressed to the cultured pagan element who saw in Christianity the cause of all the misfortunes befalling the Empire, in works composed for the propagation of the Gospel disclaimed all literary pretention, and aimed at a like simplicity. To those who criticized Christian writing for its solecisms he retorted: 'A man who is asking God to forgive his sins does not much care whether the third syllable of *ignoscere* is pronounced long or short'; and the new attitude is crisply summarized in his famous axiom: 'Melius est reprehendant nos grammatici quam non intelligant populi.'[1]

If this writing seems already to anticipate the rhythms and manner of Romance—that it does so may be ascertained by a rendering into any Romance language of the above samples from the Vulgate—the reason why is to be found primarily in its syntax. It was still Latin, but a Latin from which the complicated stylistic devices of classical authors had been drastically removed. Simple sentences predominate, standing alone or held together by co-ordinating conjunctions. As co-ordination replaces subordination in the linking of sentences, so in the linking of words analysis tends to replace synthesis. This required an extended use of prepositions, one of the most prominent features of Christian Latin, and with the greater use goes a reduction in the number and variety of prepositions engaged, with the consequence that a few monosyllables, AD, DE, IN, PRO, &c., seem to be much overworked. From no other source could one discover, with such a wealth of evidence, that far back in Roman times the syntax of everyday speech was fundamentally that of Romance.

With regard to other aspects of linguistic evolution, Christian writing serves to confirm earlier testimony: its 'mistakes' are identical with those of inscriptions. Its vocabulary copiously reflects

---

[1] Cf. M. K. Pope, *From Latin to Modern French*, p. 7, and L. R. Palmer, op. cit., p. 190.

the popular tendency to strengthen the body of words by suffixation (see pp. 157–60). Its need to express new concepts was
not always adequately satisfied by importation from Greek. Often
an old Latin word was twisted into a new meaning. As an extreme
example one might quote the term GENTILIS, which originally
meant 'belonging to one of the *gentes*' (i.e. the Roman 'families')
but with political developments in Rome had come to be applied
to 'foreign people' in opposition to the *populus romanus*; now it was
brought into service to translate the Greek ἔθνη, which had
acquired the sense of 'non-Jewish' through its use by Greek-
speaking Jews to translate the Hebrew 'goim' (also, in the first
instance, 'people').

The new literary style gained ground as Christianity attracted
more adherents. Its secularization, of which the outcome was to
be medieval Latin, is apparent at an early date in a work of unusual
interest: a book of travel, the first known account of a Christian
pilgrimage, written by a lady who set out to visit as many as
possible of the places mentioned in the Bible. The single surviving
manuscript, discovered at Arezzo by the Italian scholar Gamurrini
and first published by him in 1887, is of the eleventh century and
probably came from the monastery of Monte Cassino. A doubt
which for long subsisted concerning the identity of the author is
perpetuated in the traditional title, *Silviae vel potius Aetheriae
Peregrinatio ad Loca Sancta* (ed. E. Heraeus, Heidelberg, 1908,
4th ed., 1939); no less uncertain was the date of the original text,
variously placed at between A.D. 380 and 540. The lady was at
first believed to have been Silvia of Aquitaine, a relative of the
Emperor Theodosius; later, she was identified with a certain Abbess
Aetheria. More recent research would incline us to the opinion
that she was a Spanish nun of the name of Egeria, and assesses
the date of her journey as between A.D. 415 and 418. This being at
a time when St. Jerome and St. Augustine were still alive, one
cannot refrain from wondering whether she had deliberately
affiliated herself to their literary as well as their philosophical
school, observing their linguistic precepts and example. Her
descriptions of the way in which she was everywhere received by
the local dignitaries indicate that her standing in the Church was
high. She has all the graces of the distinguished *protégée*. No other
author of her time, or indeed for long afterwards, has succeeded
in conveying in so lively a vein the tones of conversational chatter.

Ample illustration of such characteristics would require quotation at length; we give the following as a minimum:

Cum ergo descendissimus, ut superius dixi, de ecclesia deorsum, ait nobis ipse sanctus presbyter: ecce ista fundamenta in giro colliculo isto, quae videtis, hae sunt de palatio regis Melchisedech. . . .

Nam ecce ista via, quam videtis transire inter fluvium Iordanem et vicum istum, haec est qua via regressus est sanctus Abraam de caede Codollagomor regis gentium revertens in Sodomis, qua ei occurrit sanctus Melchisedech rex Salem. Tunc ergo quia retinebam scriptum esse babtizasse sanctum Iohannem in Enon iuxta Salim, requisivi de eo, quam longe esset ipse locus. Tunc ait ille sanctus presbyter: ecce hic est in ducentibus passibus; nam si vis, ecce modo pedibus duco vos ibi. Nam haec aqua tam grandis et tam pura, quam videtis in isto vico, de ipso fonte venit. Tunc ergo gratias ei agere coepi et rogare, ut duceret nos ad locum.[1]

(Ed. P. Geyer, cit. Rohlfs, *Sermo Vulgaris Latinus*)

Again one observes how near is this prose to Romance, despite its few relics of traditional classicism (e.g. *Cum ergo, ait, nam si vis, ut*). Of particular note are the abundant use of demonstratives, HIC, IPSE, ISTE, and ILLE having little more function than that of definite article, and their continual reinforcement by ECCE. In *hae sunt* the demonstrative serves as a personal pronoun, a not infrequent construction; elsewhere one reads: *ubi ipsi castra posita habebant* (cf. Fr. *où ils avaient posé* . . .). As this last phrase well indicates, in her use of tenses the authoress discards what Romance has discarded and anticipates its new formations. She will often use a present tense to convey immediate futurity, e.g. *duco vos ibi*. Above all, the stilted word-order of conventional Latin prose is seen to be quite remote from current conversational usage. To this enthusiastic sightseer we are much indebted.

Such, briefly, are the direct sources for our knowledge of spoken

---

[1] Translated with due allowance for its 'vulgar' features, this means:

When we had gone down from the Church, as I said above, the holy priest spoke to us:—'You see those ruins in the fold of that hill, they are of the palace of King Melchisedech. . . .

'That path, which you see passing between the river Jordan and the village, that is the way by which holy Abraham came back from the slaughter of Codollagomor, king of the peoples returning to Sodom, where holy Melchisedech the king of Salem met him.'

Then because I remembered that it is written that Saint John had been baptizing in Enon near Salem, I asked of him how far away the place was. Then the holy priest said:—'It is two hundred yards away; if you wish, I will lead you there on foot. The stream which you see in the village, so large and clear, comes from that source.'

Then I began to thank him, and to ask that he should take us to the place.

Latin. To apprehend its entirety one must have recourse to comparative study of the Romance languages as they first appear in writing, and of the formerly neglected dialects in so far as they have been recorded during the past hundred years. From this comparative study the summary of characteristics of spoken Latin which now follows is largely deduced.

## THE PHONOLOGY OF VULGAR LATIN

*Accent and syllable.* With their typically vague terminology, Latin grammarians agree that the accent is the *anima vocis*, the soul of the word. In Old Latin this *anima* consisted primarily of a melodic, or pitch accent, an accent of 'tone'. Since, however, the effort of giving tension to the vocal cords usually induces other tensions, it is probable that the pitch was always accompanied by a certain degree of stress. In the Vulgar Latin with which we are concerned, all trace of distinctions of pitch disappeared, but the vowel which had been so accentuated continued to bear a stress accent, doubtless reinforced by way of compensation; it is this stress accent which we still illogically describe as the 'tonic' accent.

The accent has in general remained stable throughout the long development from Latin to modern Romance: a stability which will be apparent from the following examples of Latin words classified into types according to their syllabic structure and accentuation, together with their modern equivalents in standard French, Spanish, and Italian:

(1) Monosyllables, the only 'oxytone' words in Latin, e.g. MĔL, cf. Fr. *miel*, Span. *miel*, Ital. *miele*.

(2) Disyllables, which are always 'paroxytone', i.e. accentuated on the last syllable but one, in this instance the first, e.g. PŎRTA, cf. Fr. *porte*, Span. *puerta*, Ital. *porta*.

(3) Trisyllables; these are of two types: (*a*) paroxytone words, e.g. MARĪTUM, cf. Fr. *mari*, Span. *marido*, Ital. *marito*, and (*b*) proparoxytone words, e.g. ASINUM, cf. Fr. *âne*, Span. *asno*, Ital. *asino*.

(4) Polysyllables (usually four-syllable words): these bore the stress on the penultimate syllable if it was long, with a secondary accent on the first syllable, e.g. CIVITATEM, cf. Fr. *cité*, Span. *ciudad*, Ital. *città*. If the penultimate syllable was short, as in many words formed in Latin with common

suffixes, the accent fell on the antepenultimate syllable, e.g.
AURĬCULA, but as the well-attested ORICLA shows, words of
this kind were early assimilated to those of type 3 (*a*).

There are in Vulgar Latin a few exceptions, in which the tonic
accent has shifted from one vowel to another: notably, a series of
proparoxytone words (type 3 (*b*)) which have developed in Romance as paroxytone (type 3 (*a*)). The following are among the
most frequently used: INTĔGRUM, TONĬTRUM, CATHĔDRA, COLŬBRA,
TENĔBRAS, PALPĔBRA. The explanation of the shift is here bound
up with the question of vocalic length. All of these words have
a common feature: the second vowel is in each instance short, and
it is followed by a consonantal group of plosive plus R. Since in
the syllabic division of Latin this consonantal group was normally
inseparable (the word INTĔGRUM, for example, was pronounced
IN-TĔ-GRUM), the second syllable, possessing neither a long vowel
nor a closing consonant, was necessarily short, and in Classical
Latin a short penultimate syllable in a word of more than two
syllables could not carry the accent. But this difficulty vanished
with the disappearance of distinctions of vocalic length (see below,
*Vowels*), and thereafter the pronunciation of all these words as
paroxytones, of which there is early evidence, soon came to predominate. Most Romance languages bear witness to this, cf.
Fr. *entier* (Old Fr. *entir*), *tonnerre* (Old Fr. *tonoire*), *chaire* (Old
Fr. *chaiere*), *couleuvre*, *paupiere*; Span. *entero*, *cadera*, *culebra*,
*tinieblas*; Ital. *intero* (*intiero*). The standard accentuation of Ital.
*càttedra*, *tènebre*, *pàlpebra* seems to be due to 'learned' influence;
a popular *palpèbra* is in current use and paroxytonic forms of the
other words are common enough in Italian dialect.

Shift of accent sometimes took place between vowels in hiatus.
In such words as FILIOLUS and LINTEOLUM the original ío and éo
became *ió* and *eó* respectively, and the first element in both combinations thereafter closed to a yod; the terms thus came to conform with the familiar paroxytonic pattern, cf. Fr. *filleul*, *linceul*;
Span. *hijuelo*, *lenzuelo*; Ital. *figliuolo*, *lenzuolo*. A similar shift in
the endings -IETEM and -UERE finally resulted in the complete
elimination of the close vowel; hence PARIĔTEM and BATTUERE
became in Vulgar Latin PARĒTE and BATTERE, cf. Fr. *paroi*, Span.
*pared*, Ital. *parete*, Rum. *părete*, and Fr. *battre*, Span. *batir*, Port.
*bater*, Ital. *battere*, Rum. *a bate*.

In verbs formed with a prefix, the popular tendency, where the prefix was still perceived as such, was to place the accent firmly on the stem, and not on the prefix, as Classical Latin required. Thus in French IMPLĬCAT became *emploie*, and RECĬPIT, *reçoit*. Even a compound of DARE so apparently concealed as PERDIDIT, the perfect of PERDERE, did not escape this tendency: Vulgar Latin said PERDEDIT, pronounced as a paroxytone, and so gave rise to Old Fr. *perdiet*, and a new series of Romance flexions based on the DĔDI pattern (see *Morphology*, p. 137).

Occasional accentual variations in the Vulgar Latin of different regions are to be met with in isolated words. For example, FICA-TUM (see p. 155) must have been accented on the first vowel to give Fr. *foie*, Span. *hígado*, Ital. *fégato*, but on the second to give Rum. *ficat*. Finally, various movements of the accent have taken place in the course of morphological development: in the conjuga-tion of verbs, where it may have shifted from the stem to the flexion or vice versa; in pronouns, which carried the stress some-times on the first syllable and sometimes on the second, and in such small words as IBI and INDE (see *Morphology*).

With reference to the syllabic structure of the word, it may be observed that nearly all these shifts of accent bear witness to a paroxytonizing tendency in Vulgar Latin. So too does the syncope noted in the *Appendix Probi*, whereby proparoxytones, e.g. VIRIDIS, are made to conform to the same paroxytonic pattern. Syncope began early, and the Romance languages show that all of the re-duced forms attested in the *Appendix Probi* were universally em-ployed, cf. Fr. Prov. *vert*, Span. Port. Ital. Rum. *verde*. A close scrutiny of these examples of widespread syncope will, however, reveal that they occurred in general only when one of the con-sonants brought together in consequence of the fall of the un-stressed vowel was either an L or an R (the only other grouping admitted being that of S and T, e.g. POSITA > V. Lat. POSTA). In a large part of Romania, particularly to the east, the process con-tinued no farther, the consonantal groupings which would have resulted being presumably repudiated through local habits of articulation. In most of Gaul, on the other hand, and to a con-siderable extent in Spain, the reduction of proparoxytones by syncope proceeded unchecked. In consequence, as the follow-ing examples will show, the Romance of the west came to be broadly characterized as 'paroxytonic', by contrast with that of the eastern and southern territories (including peninsular Italy and Sardinia):

| | French | Spanish | Sardinian (Logudorese) | Italian | Rumanian |
|---|---|---|---|---|---|
| HŎMINES | hommes | hombres | omines | uomini | oameni |
| DUŎDECIM | douze | doce | doigi | dodici | — |
| FRAXINUM | frêne | fresno | — | frassino | frasin(u) |
| PĔCTINEM | peigne (Old Fr. pigne) | peine | péttene | pettine | pieptene |
| PŪLICEM | puce | pulga | púlige | pulce (Old Ital. pulice) | purece |

The effect of this partial conservation of the Latin proparoxytones has been to give to the speeches of some areas quite different rhythms from those of Spanish and French (the latter of which has, since the Middle Ages, diverged still farther by becoming oxytonic). Largely for this reason—and also on account of the loss in Italian and Rumanian (but not in Sardinian) of the final s—a distinction is sometimes drawn between western Romance (i.e. Gallo- and Hispano-Romance) and eastern Romance (i.e. Italo- and Balkan Romance).

More interesting than the mere attachment of labels is the revelation, thus provided by comparison of the modern languages, of local rifts in the once-postulated linguistic 'unity' of Vulgar Latin, rifts which certainly date back to imperial times but which could not with any certainty be detected from the surviving evidence of those times. A more detailed investigation, based upon the findings of linguistic geography, would show that these rifts followed no such clear-cut frontiers as the modern standard languages appear to imply. For example, a large region in southern France, though within the area of western Romance, would seem to have at first resisted the tendency to continued paroxytonizing by syncope. Thereafter, however, it conformed to the western rhythm by means of a solution of its own, viz. by the apocope of proparoxytones, that is, by dropping their last syllable instead of their penultimate syllable. This is particularly so in Gascony. There, the more usual derivative of TĔPIDUM is tèbe, and of RAPIDUM, rabe (contrast Fr. tiède, Old Fr. rade); HORRIDUM has given orri or orre (Old Fr. ord) and HŎMINEM > òmi, òme; LĔPOREM > lèbe (Fr. lièvre). Yet even within the restricted scope of Gascon the two different solutions are to be found in closely neighbouring localities: as, for instance, in the case of FEMINA, which in one place will be hémno, syncopated, and in another hémi, apocopated.[1]

[1] See G. Rohlfs, Le Gascon, pp. 107-10.

*Vowels.* The vocalic system of Latin underwent considerable modification in the popular speech. From Old Latin the classical norm had inherited only five pure vowels, but each of these had two values according to its length. Therein lies the basis of Latin versification. More than that, distinctions of vocalic length often marked the only phonemic difference between words of varied semantic association, e.g. ŏs 'bone', and ōs 'mouth'. They also played a part in grammatical structure: thus in declension RŎSĂ was nominative whereas RŎSĀ was ablative, while in conjugation only vocalic length served to differentiate between, for example, the present tense forms LĔGĬT, LĔGĬMUS, and the corresponding forms of the perfect, LĒGĬT, LĒGĬMUS. In Vulgar Latin, all these values disappeared. Distinctions of quantity gave way to distinctions of quality.

In principle, short vowels came to be pronounced with a more open quality, while long vowels tended to close. But such changes, which must have taken place gradually over a long period of time, were by no means uniform, and ultimately produced different results in different areas of the Empire. Only in the case of the open vowel *a* do all regions agree in reducing both long and short forms to a single phoneme. The first stage, which may be assumed to represent 'common Vulgar Latin', can be summarized as follows:[1]

$$\begin{array}{ccccccccccc} \breve{a} & \bar{a} & \breve{e} & \bar{e} & \breve{i} & \bar{i} & \breve{o} & \bar{o} & \breve{u} & \bar{u} \\ \diagdown\diagup & & | & | & | & | & | & | & | & | \\ a & & \varepsilon & e & \iota & i & \mathrm{ɔ} & o & \upsilon & u \end{array}$$

From this point certain local divergences appear, particularly in the development of the more close vowels. However, one set of circumstances is applicable to northern and western Romania, to those regions which cradled the future Romance languages of the west, including this time standard Italian (which is basically Tuscan). Over the whole of this large area the **e** and the **ɪ** converged, as did also the corresponding back vowels, **o** and **ʊ**, giving a result which may be tabulated thus:

$$\begin{array}{ccccccc} a & \varepsilon & e & \iota & i & \mathrm{ɔ} & o & \upsilon & u \\ | & | & \diagdown\diagup & & | & | & \diagdown\diagup & & | \\ a & \varepsilon & & e & & i & \mathrm{ɔ} & & o & & u \end{array}$$

To complete the picture we must now take into account the Latin diphthongs. Of the many which had existed in Old Latin only three are preserved in the literary language: AE, OE, and AU.

---

[1] The symbol ɪ represents the open *i* of Eng. *pit*, and similarly ʊ is the open *u* of Eng. *put*.

Spoken Latin continued the process of reduction, with the effect that AE became ɛ and OE became e. There is ample evidence of a contemporary tendency to reduce AU to o (cf. the alternatives CLAUDIUS and CLODIUS), but in this instance the diphthong was preserved, apparently in consequence of learned reaction. Only some centuries after the Vulgar Latin period was AU finally reduced to *o*, via a stage *ou*, as in modern Portuguese (e.g. AURUM > Port. *ouro*); in dialects of southern France it still survives as *au*.

Seven vowels and one diphthong thus represent the range of vocalic possibility in the Vulgar Latin of the west. We should add that this total is valid only when the vowel carries the tonic accent. Unstressed vowels show no difference, in their Romance development, between ɛ and e, or between ɔ and o, and so are only five in number. The diphthong AU, however, despite the evidence of ORICLA, did survive in some areas in a pretonic position, as may be seen from Prov. *aurelha*.

Applying the data given in the above table to specific examples, we may now put forward the following selection comprising all the stressed vowels of western Vulgar Latin, together with corresponding Romance forms from which they could be deduced:

| | Vulgar Latin (phonetic) | | Old French | Spanish | Italian |
|---|---|---|---|---|---|
| MĂRE | mare ⎫ | I | *mer* | *mar* | *mare* |
| CĀRUM | karu ⎭ | | *chier* | *caro* | *caro* |
| CAELUM | kɛlu ⎫ | 2 | *ciel* | *cielo* | *cielo* |
| MĚL | mɛl ⎭ | | *miel* | *miel* | *miele* |
| POENA | pena ⎫ | | *peine* | *pena* | *pena* |
| TĒLA | tela ⎬ | 3 | *toile* (mod. **twal**) | *tela* | *tela* |
| FĬDEM | fede ⎭ | | *foi* (mod. **fwa**) | *fe* | *fede* |
| FĪLUM | filu | 4 | *fil* | *hilo* | *filo* |
| NŎVUM | nɔvu | 5 | *nuef* (mod. **nœf**) | *nuevo* | *nuovo* |
| FLŌREM | flore ⎫ | 6 | *flour* (mod. **flœ:R**) | *flor* | *fiore* |
| GŬLA | gola ⎭ | | *goule* (mod. **gœl**) | *gola* | *gola* |
| MŪRUM | muru | 7 | *mur* (**my:R**) | *muro* | *muro* |
| AURUM | auru | | *or* | *oro* | *oro* |

Beyond the scope of this widespread system are those southern and eastern areas which tended to become of lesser economic and political importance during the later years of the Empire, and hence to escape the influence of the later linguistic innovations. Of the divergent regions, the first to be observed by modern scholarship was Sardinia. All the dialects of this island, with the exception of Sassarese, show a vocalic evolution quite different from that of the west, whereby the loss of Latin distinctions of length had the more straightforward effect of leaving five pure vowels, basically those of Latin. Assuming that the loss of quantities was accompanied everywhere by certain distinctions of quality, we may plot this evolution as follows:

a    ɛ    e    ɪ    i    ɔ    o    ʊ    u
|     \  /      \  /      \  /      \  /
a       ɛ         i         ɔ         u

Thus in Sardinian NĬVEM has become *nive* (contrast Ital. *neve*, Old Fr. *neif, noif*), and CRŬCEM, with a consonantal dissimilation, has become *ruke* (contrast Ital. *croce*, Fr. *croix*); *kadena* (< CATĒNA) and *fele* (< FĔL) have the same stressed vowel, as have also *sole* (< SŌLEM) and *roda* (< RŎTA); in the modern dialects the quality of *e* and *o* is variable, but generally tends to be open.

This evolution was thought for some time to be peculiar to Sardinia. Recent investigations have, however, revealed an identical development in the more remote and archaic dialects of southern Italy, specifically in an area extending along both sides of the frontier between the provinces of Lucania and Calabria, and reaching the Gulf of Taranto.[1] Latin borrowings in the Berber idioms suggest that it was also current in Roman Africa. Its presence may again be detected in some of the earliest Latin loan-words in Basque, e.g. Basque *phike* from Lat. PĬCEM, and *gura* from GŬLA.

Much of the remainder of southern Italy, together with Sicily, bears witness to another type of vocalic evolution: a result comprising the same five pure vowels in Romance, but reached, according to the evidence of derivatives, by a different process, which may be summarized as follows:

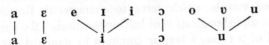

a    ɛ    e    ɪ    i    ɔ    o    ʊ    u
|    |     \  |  /      |     \  |  /
a    ɛ        i         ɔ         u

[1] H. Lausberg, *Die Mundarten Südlukaniens*, Halle, 1939. See also G. Rohlfs, *Historische Grammatik der italienischen Sprache*, vol. i, pp. 42–51; C. Tagliavini, *Le origini delle lingue neolatine*, pp. 186–90; and W. von Wartburg, *Die Ausgliederung der romanischen Sprachräume*, pp. 14–19.

Thus in modern Sicilian *filu*, *nivi*, and *tila*, deriving from FĪLUM, NĬVEM, and TĒLA respectively, all have the same stressed vowel; so too do *luna*, *nuci*, and *vuci*, from LŪNA, NŬCEM, and VŌCEM.

Lastly, there is also an 'eastern' development. This is a kind of half-way house between the 'western' and 'Sardinian' types, in which the front vowels have evolved as in the west, but the back vowels as in Sardinia, thus:

So it comes about that the stressed vowels of Rumanian derive from six stressed vowels in Vulgar Latin, together with the diphthong AU, which survived in the east as in the west: mod. Rum. *cred* and *leg* from CRĒDO and LĬGO have the same vowel (cf. Ital. *credo* and *lego*), but the vowels of *nod* and *gură* from NŌDUM and GŬLA are different (contrast Ital. *nodo* and *gola*, where the vowels are the same).

Latin borrowings in Albanian prove that this Rumanian development was once characteristic of Balkan Romance. Moreover, a similar mixed type is also found in Lucania, in a restricted area adjacent to that of the 'Sardinian' type previously mentioned. All these southern and eastern divergences from the general western type seem therefore to have their origin in the local Latin of southern Italy, and to date from a time when Rome was still expanding her territories and drawing on the south for much of her man-power.

The variety in vocalic evolution which thus emerged from the loss of quantitative distinctions indicates further rifts in the 'unity' of Vulgar Latin. Such differentiation was obviously taking place long before the collapse of the western Empire, and indeed may well have had its origins in the earlier times of Roman expansion. The question now arises: should we place within the period of 'common Vulgar Latin' any of those subsequent developments of the stressed vowels which serve to characterize Romance? Notably, is the diphthongization of half-open vowels—the passage of ɛ to *ie* and of ɔ to *uo*, a feature common to standard French, Spanish, and Italian (see table, p. 44), and, in the case of ɛ > *ie*, also to Rumanian—to be considered as a Vulgar Latin phenomenon?

This is a much-debated point. Some scholars, basing their arguments on the fact that such diphthongization is not universal in Romania (it did not occur in Sardinia and southern Italy, nor in Provençal and Portuguese), and on the fact that where it took place it did so under varying conditions (in French and Italian only before a single consonant, or consonant plus *r* or *l*, but in Spanish and Rumanian before any group of consonants), hold that it must have developed independently in each region. According to W. von Wartburg, for example, its presence in northern France is due to the influence of Germanic stress, and hence it is consequent upon the Frankish invasions (*Die Ausgliederung der romanischen Sprachräume*, pp. 76 ff., and elsewhere). This view seems to us quite untenable: we prefer to see in the initiation of the diphthongs a phenomenon which took place spontaneously in Vulgar Latin, though excluding the conservative south, and subject in the more cultured regions to learned correction.[1]

The varying conditions which have been quoted provide no convincing proof of the contrary. That they exist cannot be disputed, but the basic difference in this respect between French and Italian, on the one hand, and Spanish and Rumanian, on the other, is one of syllabic structure—another cleavage within Vulgar Latin, whereby French and Italian divided a word as FER-RUM (cf. Fr. *fer*, Ital. *ferro*), while Spanish and Rumanian divided it as FE-RRUM (cf. Span. *hierro*, Rum. *fier*). This in no way impinges upon the mechanism of spontaneous diphthongization, namely, the lengthening of a stressed vowel in an open syllable, followed by its segmentation into two different sounds, due to failure on the part of the person speaking to hold the tongue in a fixed position throughout the articulation of the vowel. There is, moreover, fairly clear evidence of the early date of this diphthongization in northern France in the fact of its having taken place in a number of proparoxytone words, presumably before the reduction of those

[1] Cf. Elise Richter, *Beiträge zur Geschichte der Romanismen. Band I: Chronologische Phonetik des Französischen bis zum Ende des 8. Jahrhunderts*, Halle, 1934. For a more recent examination of the problem, see G. Straka, 'Observations sur la chronologie et les dates de quelques modifications phonétiques en roman et en français prélittéraire', *Revue des langues romanes*, 1953, pp. 247–307.
Since the above was written, further contributions to the study of Romance diphthongization have been published by F. Schürr and H. Lausberg (see Bibliography).

words to paroxytones had created a 'block' of two consonants,
e.g. TĔPIDUM > *tiède*, *PĔDICUM > *piège* (the classical PĔDICA
would normally have given *\*pièche*), MĔDICUM > Old Fr. *miege*,
SĔDICUM > *siège*, STĔPHANUM > *Estievne > Étienne*, *JŎVENE
(Class. JŬVENEM) > *\*juovne > Old Fr. *juene* (mod. *jeune*), &c.
Finally, inscriptions dating from the imperial period have provided a few rare but undeniable traces of diphthongization. One
of these, a Roman inscription of *c.* A.D. 120, is so early that its
diphthong has been viewed with suspicion, as a probable 'mistake', yet it is unquestionably there, in the description of a soldier
as NIEPOS CN. DOMITI TROPHIMI: the same text contains NEPOTIS,
where the E, being pretonic, is not diphthongized (*CIL* xv. 1118).
The others were all found in Algeria: MEERITIS, in which the EE
appears to record the intermediate stage of development (*CIL*
viii. 21068); DIEO (*CIL* viii. 9181); UOBIT for OBIIT, in A.D. 419
(C. A. L. Renier, *Inscriptions romaines de l' Algérie*, 3436).

That the beginnings of diphthongization came well within the
imperial period seems, then, to be a most likely hypothesis. Not,
however, until the composition of the first surviving poem in
a Romance tongue, the ninth-century *Cantilène de sainte Eulalie*,
is the phenomenon fully and regularly attested.

Concerning vowels in position other than tonic there is at this
juncture little of importance to say. Pre-tonic, the five primary
vowels regularly survived, though, as the *Appendix Probi* already
shows, they were liable to change their quality in consequence of
assimilation or dissimilation. The diphthong AU in this position
was in some words early reduced to A, e.g. AUGŬSTUM became
*AGŬSTU (cf. Ital. Span. Port. *agosto*, Old Fr. *aoust*, Rum. *agust*);
AUGŬRIUM became *AGŬRIU (cf. Span. *agüero*, Port. *agouro*, Prov.
*aür*, Old Fr. *eür* whence the modern *heur* of *bonheur, malheur,
heureux*). Post-tonic, the vowels underwent little change in Vulgar
Latin apart from the tendency of the U of the masculine flexion,
which had become final after the fall of M, to acquire the more
open quality of *o*.

The outstandingly important feature in the development of the
unstressed vowel, abundantly attested in the *Appendix Probi* and
in the earlier Pompeian *graffiti*, is the closing of I and E, after a
consonant and before a vowel, to a yod; upon this we have already
commented (see p. 25). A U in the same position was frequently
elided, as is shown in the *Appendix Probi* by 'FEBRUARIUS non

FEBRARIUS' (cf. Fr. *février*, Ital. *febbraio*, Span. *febrero*, &c.), and in inscriptions by QUATTOR instead of QUATTUOR (cf. Fr. *quatre*, Ital. *quattro*, Span. *cuatro*, &c.).

*Consonants.* Whereas the reconstruction of vocalic evolution in Vulgar Latin could scarcely be envisaged without the help of comparative study of the modern Romance languages, the development of consonants, for which the Latin alphabet possessed an ample range of symbols, is quite generously attested in contemporary evidence. Most of the prevalent tendencies have thus been already indicated in our brief examination of inscriptions and *graffiti*, and in that of the *Appendix Probi*. It is unnecessary to consider here in greater detail such changes as are common to the whole of Romania (e.g. loss of final M, loss of H, reduction of -NS- to -S-, &c.). A few changes of sporadic occurrence which we might personally incline to attribute to the Vulgar Latin period (e.g. F > *h*, and the cacuminal articulation of -LL- which led to Sicilian -*dd*-, Gascon -*t* and -*tch*, &c.) are considered by many scholars to be of local Romance origin, or due to the influence of a local substratum. There remain, however, certain consonantal developments which are of special interest in that, like vocalic trends, they reveal beyond all possible doubt the differentiation already in progress during the Vulgar Latin period. Notable among these are the treatment of intervocalic voiceless plosives (**p**, **t**, and **k**), the loss or retention of final S, and the widespread palatalization of the velar plosives (**k** and **ǥ**) before a front vowel.

The tendency of intervocalic voiceless plosives to become voiced, through assimilation to the neighbouring vowels, is attested early. Examples from Pompeii have already been noted (p. 24); W. von Wartburg, it is true, casts doubt upon the authenticity of these latter,[1] but quotes from other inscriptions one second-century example, IMUDAVIT for INMUTAVIT (in Spain), and further examples from the third century: PUDORE for PUTORE, LEBRA for LEPRA, MIGAT for MICAT (op. cit., p. 31). There is thus general agreement that the phenomenon dates from within imperial times. Romance derivatives, however, show considerable divergence: one may indeed by this criterion again divide Romania

---

[1] 'Ältere Belege aus Pompei haben sich in der Lesung als nicht sicher erwiesen, so dass ein Hinaufrücken der Erscheinung bis zum Jahre 79 nicht in Frage kommt' (op. cit., p. 31). The examples we have quoted are from Veikko Väänänen (op. cit.), and we know of no reason for supposing that they have been misread.

into east and west, a west in which the intervocalic voiceless plosives have become voiced, and an east in which they have remained intact. This will be appreciated from the following examples, where the Provençal forms may be taken as corresponding to a pre-literary stage in the evolution of northern French:

| | French | Provençal | Spanish | Italian | Rumanian |
|---|---|---|---|---|---|
| RĪPA | *rive* | *riba* | *riba* | *ripa (riva)* | *rîpă* |
| CAPRA | *chèvre* | *cabra* | *cabra* | *capra* | *capră* |
| MUTARE | *muer* | *mudar* | *mudar* | *mutare* | *a muta* |
| FĀTA | *fée* | *fada* | *hada* | *fata* | *fată* |
| AMĪCA | *amie* | *amiga* | *amiga* | *amica* | *amică* |

Once again, the position is much less straightforward in reality than the table would appear to imply. In Italy, as in Sardinia, it is extremely confused, sonorization having often taken place, for no obvious reason. According to a theory of Meyer-Lübke, it occurred primarily in Italian before the accent but not after the accent; but so numerous are the exceptions that the theory can scarcely be considered as valid. In the above list, *mutare* shows preservation of the voiceless plosive before the accent, while many words, e.g. *lago* (< LACUM) and *strada*, from (VIA) STRATA, show sonorization after the accent. On occasion, a *p* after the accent has not only sonorized but even developed further to *v*, e.g. *povero* (< PAUPERUM), and *riva*, which has largely ousted the *ripa* of Old Italian, as given above. Southern Italian, like Rumanian, preserves the voiceless intervocalic plosives much more consistently, and in consequence a majority of scholars nowadays inclines to the view that the many voiced forms of modern standard Italian are due to the strong influence of the dialects to the north of the Spezia–Rimini line, where sonorization is general.

In the western languages this sonorization is a constant feature, though it seems to have progressed slowly before gaining all the dialects. There is indeed still in the Central Pyrenees, extending over both sides of the frontier between France and Spain, a remarkable area of conservation in which, by a strange coincidence, some Latin words have evolved in such a way as to be almost identical with modern Rumanian. Thus in the Bearnese valleys of Aspe and Barétous the modern derivative of PLĬCARE is *pleká*, just as in Rumanian, cf. Fr. *ployer*, Prov. *plegar*, Span. *llegar*, Port. *chegar*, and Ital. *piegare*; a field at Biescas in Upper Aragon is called *as piatras*, showing a development of PĔTRA which is the same as that of Rum. *piatră*. For other examples, cf. Arag. *apella* (< APĬCULA), *saper* (< SAPĒRE), *crapa* (< CAPRA), *mallata* (< MACU-LATA, cf. Cast. *majada*), *matriquera* (< MATRICARIA, cf. Cast. *madriguera*), *afocar* (< AFFOCARE, cf. Cast. *ahogar*), &c.; and Bear-nese *apelho, apríu* (< APRILE), *crapo* (< CAPRA), *maritá* (< MARI-TARE), *nuquero* (< NUCARIA), &c. It has been suggested, by J. Saroïhandy, that this linguistic island owes its existence to an influence of the substratum: in the neighbouring Basque, plosives tend to be aspirated, and therefore, said Saroïhandy, a local ten-dency to aspirate all these intervocalic consonants may have pro-tected them against the sonorization prevalent elsewhere. There is, however, no evidence to adduce in confirmation of this hypo-thesis, and a much more natural explanation, to our mind, lies in accepting them as part of the resistance to change which charac-terizes this mountainous region.

Another aspect of Vulgar Latin, the treatment of final s, is of no less interest for the future of Romance. Its tendency to dis-appear is attested early in Latin inscriptions. From the evidence of early Latin scansion,[1] one may deduce that it was commonly elided before a consonant—this may be seen, for example, in the fact that the syllable NŬS of PLĒNŬS FĬDEI was considered to be short —though it continued to be pronounced before a following vowel: a situation which has its parallel in modern French, e.g. **leplã:t** (les plantes) but **lezami** (les amis) (cf. W. von Wartburg, op. cit., p. 20). In popular speech the tendency towards elision seems to have gone still farther: one may again quote a modern French parallel in the current pronunciation of 'pas encore' as **paãkɔ:R**. In some derivatives the loss of final s is complete throughout the area of eastern Romance; in others, however, particularly in mono-syllabic words, it has left the trace of its presence in the form of an *i*-sound, presumably the result of a partial approach of the tongue to the original point of articulation.

As so often happens, one effect of this popular development was to provoke a 'learned' reaction. By elegant speakers of Latin,

[1] Catullus, born at Verona *c.* 87 B.C., is the last Latin poet whose verse shows an example of this disregard of final s. The practice was remarked upon and described as having become 'subrusticus' by Cicero, in a passage of his *Orator* which must have been well known in the schools of Gaul and Spain: 'Quin etiam, quod iam subrusticum videtur, olim autem politius, eorum verborum, quorum eaedem erant postremae duae litterae quae sunt in *optimus*, postremam litteram detrahebant, nisi vocalis insequebatur. Ita non erat ea offensio in versibus quam nunc fugiunt poetae novi' (Sect. 161).

during the more 'refined' period which began with the closing
years of the Republic, the omission of final s was held to be as
much a vulgarism as is the omission of *h* in present-day English.
In consequence it was either preserved or restored in the western
parts of the Empire, where there was greater scope for education
and social aspirations.

The examples which follow will serve to summarize the more
obvious effects on Romance of this further rift in the structure of
Vulgar Latin:

| | French | Provençal | Spanish | Sardinian (Logudorese) | Italian | Rumanian |
|---|---|---|---|---|---|---|
| FLORES | *fleurs* | *flors* | *flores* | *flores* | *fiori* | *flori* |
| DUOS | *deux* | *dous* | *dos* | *duos* | *due* | *doi* |
| | (Old Fr. *deus*) | | | | | |
| TEMPUS | *temps* | *temps* | *tiempos*[1] | *tempus* | *tempo* | *timp* |
| | | | (Old Span.) | | | |
| CANTAS | *chantes* | *cantas* | *cantas* | *cantas* | *canti* | *cînţi* |
| POS(T) | (Fr. *puis* | *pos* | *pues* | *pus* | *poi* | *poi* |
| | < *POSTIUS*) | | | (Old Sard.) | | |

In the homeland of Latin the hesitations of the spoken tongue
are still perpetuated. North Italian dialects show a partial preservation of final s, notably in verbal forms. In Liguria and Emilia
it is entirely lost, though there is evidence of its presence during
the Middle Ages (for Liguria the modern example of *lünezdí* has
been adduced, with an s remaining from *LUNIS*, created on the
analogy of MARTIS and JŎVIS). Yet final s appears again in the
south, in that Lucanian area previously noted as possessing certain affinities with Sardinia: since final s is regularly preserved in
Sardinian, unquestionably the most archaic of Romance speeches,
we are led to infer that in these areas it corresponds to a phase of
Roman colonization preceding the vicissitudes of its decline, and
its subsequent, geographically circumscribed, restoration.

In conclusion, it must be observed that the affiliation between
the Vulgar Latin loss of final s and its absence from eastern Romance is disputed by some scholars, though for reasons which we
do not find very convincing. It is somewhat arbitrary to admit the
continuity of one phenomenon and deny that of another, when in
both instances the essential conditions for the postulating of such
a continuity, viz. attestation both in Vulgar Latin and in the
Romance languages when they first appear, are entirely fulfilled.

The third feature of consonantal evolution which we have

---

[1] Cf. Old Span. *uebos* < ŎPUS, *cuerpos* < CŎRPUS, *pechos* < PĔCTUS, *peños* <
PĬGNUS, &c. (Menéndez Pidal, *Manual de gramática histórica española*, p. 180).
These relics in Spanish of the neuter singular accusative in -s were afterwards
lost through confusion with the masculine plural.

singled out for special mention, palatalization of the velar plosives k and ǵ before a front vowel, made its appearance later than the other two. During the early years of the Empire k and ǵ continued to have their fully velar pronunciation in current speech, as is proved by Latin borrowings in German (see p. 34). To date the inception of the change, whereby the point of articulation of these consonants began to move towards that of the vowels which followed, is extremely difficult. But it may be inferred from the general development of Romance that by the third century, at the latest, the c of words like CERVUM, CAELUM, CĒRA, CĪRCARE, CIVI-TĀTEM, had in most areas come to be pronounced kj; thereafter, with the point of articulation moving still further forward, the quality of k entirely disappeared, and the sound became tj, which subsequently evolved in medieval Romance either to ts(j) or to tʃ(j). A clue to the timing of kj > tj may probably be found in the fact that kj and tj from other sources became identical in Vulgar Latin during the third century, as is apparent from inscriptions of that time containing such forms as TERMINACIONES (for TER-MINATIONES) and DEFENICIONES (for DEFINITIONES): a confusion which was to become characteristic of medieval Latin orthography; the sound which ultimately evolved was again tsj, as in the German pronunciation given to such words when they were borrowed from Latin (e.g. Germ. *Definition, Martius, Servatius,* &c.).

The medieval scribes of Romance, who in other instances frequently juggled with the letters of the Latin alphabet in an attempt to provide new orthographical devices for the representation of non-Latin sounds, have generally been content to leave a Latin c unchanged, whatever the sound had in fact become. Thus, before the significance of the table which follows can be appreciated, one must know that Fr. *cerf* was pronounced tserf in Old French and has developed to serf in the modern language (since the thirteenth century), that a similar ts evolved in Spanish to *zeta*, whereas, on the other hand, a c before a front vowel in Italian and Rumanian is pronounced tʃ:

| | French | Spanish | Sardinian (Logudorese) | Italian | Rumanian |
|---|---|---|---|---|---|
| CERVUM | *cerf* | *ciervo* | *kerbu* | *cervo* | *cerb* |
| CAELUM | *ciel* | *cielo* | *kelu* | *cielo* | *cer* |
| CĒRA | *cire* | *cera* | *kera* | *cera* | *ceară* |
| CĪRCARE | Old Fr. *cerchier* (mod. *chercher*) | *cercar* | *kirkare* | *cercare* | *a cerca* |
| CIVITĀTEM | *cité* | *ciudad* | — | *città* | *cetate* |

The Logudorese area of Sardinia, which has kept initial **k** intact to the present day, again stands out as the most archaic part of Romania. Old Dalmatian appears to have been similarly conservative in this respect: the dialect of the Adriatic island of Veglia, but lately extinct, preserved the **k** at least before **e**, e.g. CĒNA > Vegl. *kaina*.[1] Elsewhere, palatalization is general. The question now arises: Can we point here once again to a distinction between a western and an eastern Vulgar Latin? Some scholars, who have argued that palatalization in Rumanian took place late and quite independently, would probably answer this question with a negative. But evidence for the early history of Rumanian is very scant: in so far as the evolution of the phenomenon in Rumanian can be observed, it is the same as in Italian; and it is certain that such changes occur in speech long before their appearance in any form of record. We therefore incline to believe that by the fifth century there was already a distinct division between a **ts**-pronunciation in the west, in Gaul and Spain, and a **tʃ**-pronunciation, as consistently preserved in the spoken Latin of the Roman Church, in Italy, and in whichever eastern areas may have provided the Romance-speaking settlers of Rumania (see p. 482). There is, however, as in the case of other phenomena considered, no hard-and-fast line of division. Within the Balkan area the **ts**-type is found in Arumanian, e.g. *tserbu*, *tser*, while outcrops of **tʃ** occur in the west, notably in Rheto-Romance and Picard (see p. 366).

The palatalization of **ǵ** before a front vowel followed a somewhat similar course. As **k** became **kj**, so **ǵ** became **ǵj**, and thereafter the sound was generally dentalized to **dj**; but subsequent development is less easy to trace than in the case of **tj**. In modern Romance one encounters both **dʒ** and **dz**, phonetically parallel with the voiceless **tʃ** and **ts**. The sound **dʒ**, however, occurred in this instance not only in Italian (e.g. *gente* < GENTEM, *genero* < GENERUM), Rheto-Romance, and Rumanian (*gintu*, *ginere*), but also in Old Portuguese and Old French, where it was later reduced to **ʒ** (the Old French pronunciation is preserved in English, in *gentle*, *gender*, &c.). The **dz**-pronunciation is largely restricted to north-Italian dialects, Venetian, Genoese, and Lombard, and to

[1] The standard work on Dalmatian is M. Bartoli, *Das Dalmatische, altromanische Sprachreste von Veglia bis Ragusa und ihre Stellung in der Apennino-balkanischen Romania*, 2 vols., Vienna, 1906. Much of Bartoli's material came from interrogation of the last known speaker of Vegliote.

Istrian, where it has been reduced to z. There is, moreover, a third evolution, characteristic of Castilian Spanish and Sicilian, in which no affricate developed: at a stage which was either **gj** or **dj** the first element disappeared; hence mod. Span. *yerno* and Sicil. *yennaru*. Before an unaccented vowel the second element too has disappeared in Spanish, though it continues to be represented in orthography by a superfluous *h*, e.g. *hermano* < GERMANUM (see p. 420).

Confronted with this repartition, we can scarcely venture to draw conclusions concerning the situation at the time of the Roman collapse. All that we can infer is that local differentiation was already taking place, following perhaps with a certain time-lag upon the differentiation of the voiceless equivalent. But again we can point with certainty to the archaism of Logudorese, which has kept velar **g**, like velar **k**, to the present day, e.g. (in the italianizing script of Sardinia) *ghirare*, *ghelare*, &c. A similar conservatism is attested for the former dialect of Veglia.

## MORPHOLOGY AND SYNTAX

Conventions of linguistic analysis require the study both of the evolution of grammatical forms (Morphology), and also of the arrangement of these forms in the sentence (Syntax). In practice, morphology and syntax are interdependent: from the written evidence of Vulgar Latin it has already been seen, for example, how the weakening of nominal flexions was accompanied by changes in the structure of the sentence, by an increased reliance upon prepositions; to distinguish in such circumstances between cause and effect is virtually impossible. It is thus in conformity with an established method that we consider the two factors under the same heading.

Old Latin had inherited from its Indo-European ancestry a complicated system of flexions. With the diffusion of Latin among populations with which it was at first an acquired tongue, the system of flexions broke down: though again it is difficult to say to what extent the process was conditioned by this extended use, or how far it was an internal and spontaneous Roman development. Whatever the cause, during the period of Vulgar Latin the previously flexional (or synthetic) language changed its character to become predominantly analytic. By the time of imperial collapse the newly evolved linguistic system which forms the common basis of the Romance languages was already in everyday use; and many of the morphological and syntactical features by which those languages are now distinguished can certainly be traced back to local differentiation within Vulgar Latin.

The characterization of general trends which now follows is again deduced, for the most part, from comparative study, though, as before, supporting evidence may on occasion be available from contemporary sources.

*Substantives.* Gender, case, and declension all underwent profound changes, tending in each instance towards reduction and simplification.

The three genders, which had long since become nothing more than grammatical categories, were reduced to two, masculine and feminine. Neuters, in the course of their elimination, were in the singular form absorbed almost completely into the masculine category. The few rare exceptions which appear as feminine in Romance are confined to certain regions, and thus point to hesitation in Vulgar Latin usage. In French the most notable example is *la mer*, from MARE, which also emerged as feminine in Old Spanish, in Provençal and Catalan, and in the Rum. *marea* (contrast Ital. *il mare*, and mod. Span. *el mar*); this has been explained as being due to the frequent linking of MARE with the fem. TERRA. The neuter monosyllables MĔL, SAL (in Class. Lat., masc. or neuter), and LAC (in V. Lat. LACTE) are regularly masculine in parts of Romania (e.g. Fr. *miel, sel, lait*; Ital. *miele, sale, latte*; Port. *mel, sal, leite*) but were adopted as feminine in an area comprising Spain (Span. *miel, sal, leche*), Gascony, and parts of Provence and northern Italy; in Rumanian *miere* and *sare* are likewise feminine, but *lapte* is masculine. It must be noted that these words all derive from the Latin third declension. There is no such fluctuation with regard to neuters of the second declension: adaptation of the nominative flexion -UM to the masculine -US is a tendency apparent in the work of the oldest Latin writers (see p. 21), and which was checked in the literary language only by classical conservatism.

As was natural, the forms of the neuter plural for the most part followed suit. There remained, however, in Vulgar Latin, a small number of neuter plurals, designating objects which could be taken in pairs or with a general collective sense, which on account of this fact, and of their final -A, were taken to be feminine. Examining the fate of these words, one observes a difference in treatment which seems once again to point to the early cleavage between eastern and western varieties of spoken Latin.

In Spanish, and with very few exceptions in Old French, such words had been fully adapted to singular meaning, and were used functionally as singulars in the sentence, when vernacular texts first appeared. Examples are as follows:

|  | French | Spanish |
|---|---|---|
| ARMA | *arme* | *arma* |
| BRACHIA | *brasse* | *braza* |
| (cf. BRACHIUM | *bras* | *brazo*) |
| CORN(U)A | *corne* | *cuerna* |
| (cf. CORNUM | *cor* | *cuerno*) |
| FŎLIA | *feuille* | *hoja* |
| GAUDIA | *joie* | — |
| (cf. GAUDIUM | Old Fr. *joi* | *gozo*) |
| GRANA | *graine* | *grana* |
| (cf. GRANUM | *grain* | *grano*) |
| LIGNA | Old Fr. *legne* | *leña* |
| ŎPERA | *œuvre* | *obra* |
| (cf. ŎPUS | Old Fr. *ues* | Old Span. *huebos*) |
| VASCĔLLA | *vaisselle* | *vajilla* |
| (cf. VASCĔLLUM | *vaisseau*) | |
| VŌTA | (VŌTUM > *vœu*) | *boda* |

With reference to the chronology of this development, it is true that Old French still reveals traces of the use of such words with plural meaning, as for instance in the following line from the *Chanson de Roland*:

> Cinquante care que carier en ferez.
> (Ed. F. Whitehead, l. 131)

The word *care* here derives from CARRA and obviously has plural meaning. Such examples are, however, quite rare, and their preservation may well be due to the learned influence of medieval Latin. Singular usage is, on the other hand, attested in Latin texts of the second and third centuries: the 'Itala' Bible contains RETIAM as the accusative of RETIA 'nets'; an African inscription shows ASTRAM (*CIL* viii. 9725). We may therefore conclude that in the Vulgar Latin of Spain and Gaul these neuter plurals in -A had been generally converted into feminine singulars, and had then come to have new analogical plurals in -S.[1]

---

[1] Some pairs of Romance words suggest that a lingering sense of the former plural function of these Latin neuters motivated the occasional use of the

In Italian, neuter plurals in -A have similarly become feminine, but here there is the significant difference that they have retained plural meaning and continue to function as plural forms corresponding to the original singulars, which are masculine. Thus, when used with the definite article, they take the feminine plural form *le* (< ILLAE, see p. 88), e.g.

|  | Singular |  | Plural |
|---|---|---|---|
| CĬLIUM | *il ciglio* | CĬLIA | *le ciglia* |
| CORNUM | *il corno* | CORN(U)A | *le corna* |
| GENŬCULUM | *il ginocchio* | GENŬCULA | *le ginocchia* |
| LABRUM | *il labbro* | LABRA | *le labbra* |
| DĬGITUM | *il dito* | DĬGITA | *le dita* |
| LINTEŎLUM | *il lenzuolo* | LINTEŎLA | *le lenzuola* |
| ŌVUM | *l'uovo* | ŌVA | *le uova* |

The anomalous character of these plurals has led in some instances, in the modern language, to the creation of analogical forms of masculine plural, e.g. *i diti*, *i labbri*, *i lenzuoli*, but the etymological forms continue to be employed whenever the objects so designated are referred to collectively.

Rumanian agrees with Italian in preserving some of these words as masculine in the singular and feminine in the plural, but in general it has made them less startling by assimilating the plural form to that of normal feminine plurals. Thus Rum. *lemn* 'wood' (< LIGNUM) and *scaun* 'chair' (< SCAMNUM), both masculine, have fem. pls. *lemne* and *scaune*; together with the definite article, attached in Rumanian to the end of the word (see p. 89), we have sing. *lemnul*, *scaunul*, pl. *lemnele*, *scaunele*. The old neuter flexion still remains in *ouă* (< ŌVA), the fem. pl. of masc. sing. *ou* (< ŌVUM). There is, then, in the treatment of these neuter plurals, a fundamentally complete concordance between Rumanian and Italian, which, in view of their early separation in history, may be supposed to have its origin in the common Vulgar Latin of eastern Romania.

Words which in Latin were masculine or feminine have normally retained their original gender. A small category of exceptions comprises names of trees, e.g. PŌPŬLUS, FRAXĬNUS, PĪNUS, ALNUS,

feminine as an augmentative. Thus in Spanish a *huerta* is bigger than a *huerto* (< HORTUM) and a *hoya* (< FOVEA) than a *hoyo*. Similarly in Italian a *capanna* is bigger than a *capanno*, a *carretta* than a *carretto* 'wheelbarrow', a *coltella*, 'kitchen-knife', than a *coltello*. Old Fr. *pree* (< PRATA), still preserved in place-names, e.g. *Prée-Vallée*, stood in the same relation to *pré* (< PRATUM).

ŬLMUS; these were feminine in Latin, but the logic of everyday speech made them masculine, as may be seen from their Romance derivatives. In a few southern areas FĪCUS 'fig-tree', still appears as feminine, and in Spain FĀGUS, the 'beech', was adapted to feminine form, cf. Span. *haya* (but Old Fr. *fou*, masc.). The word ARBOR itself also became generally masculine, cf. Fr. *arbre*, Span. *árbol*, Ital. *albero*, Rum. *arbure*, though the original feminine gender survives in two areas of 'early Vulgar Latin', viz. Portugal, with *árvore*, and again Sardinia, cf. Log. *arbure*. Semantic association with the 'tree' category has been advanced as an explanation of this particular shift of gender; more probably it occurred through grammatical association with other nouns in -OR (we recall from school-days the jingle: 'AEQUOR, MARMOR, COR decline—neuter, ARBOR feminine'). Another class of words, abstract nouns with an accusative ending -OREM, passed in the inverse direction from masculine to feminine, but only in Gallo- and Rheto-Romance, and sporadically in Balkan Romance. Thus Fr. *la douleur, la couleur, la saveur*, from DOLŌREM, COLŌREM, SAPŌREM, present a contrast with Span. *el dolor, el color, el sabor*, and Ital. *il dolore, il colore, il sapore* (Fr. *labeur, honneur, amour* were similarly feminine in the medieval language, but have been restored to masculine as a consequence of the confusion introduced by sixteenth-century French humanists). The change was doubtless due to the fact that abstract nouns generally tended in Latin to be feminine, and there was perhaps a formal association to feminines in -ŪRA, though this does not explain why it should have been so limited in geographical extent. Its presence in the east seems to confirm its antiquity: Rumanian did not retain COLŌREM or SAPŌREM, but DOLŌREM survives in dialect as *duroare* (fem.), and likewise feminine, in the standard language, are *sudoare*, 'sweat', from SUDŌREM (cf. Fr. *la sueur*, Span. *el sudor*, Ital. *il sudore*), and *lîngoare, lungoare*, from LANGUŌREM, which has acquired the meaning of 'fever, typhoid'.

A number of further changes occurred in isolated words from the Latin third declension, which, on account of their flexions, could not be clearly identified either with feminines in -A(M) or with masculines in -U(M). Some of these appear with fluctuating gender even in Classical Latin. In general, though not always, Italian has preserved the Latin gender, presumably on account of the ever-present influence of Classical Latin in the development of literary Italian, while the hesitations of popular speech are reflected in French, Spanish, and Rumanian. The change may have been effected in either direction: thus FLŌREM, masculine in Latin (cf. Ital. *il fiore*), appeared as feminine in Fr. *la fleur* and Span. *la flor*, as also in Rum. *floarea* and even in certain Italian dialects; on the other hand, VALLEM, feminine in Latin (cf. Ital. *la valle*), is masculine in Fr. *le val* and Span. *el valle*, though feminine in Rum. *valea*, and in a large area which comprises southern France and extends over the Pyrenees into northern Spain, whence the French names *Laval*, *Bonneval*, &c. Similar variations may be observed in the Romance derivatives of CALLEM, CANALEM, CARCĔREM, CĬNĔREM, FĪNEM, PAR(I)ĔTEM, PŎNTEM, PŪLĬCEM, PŬLVĔREM, RŬMĬCEM, and SANGUĬNEM. From the present sporadic distribution of these words, as between masculine and feminine, one can draw no general inference concerning linguistic zones within the wide frontiers of Vulgar Latin; one can only observe its uncertainties.

Reduction of the case-system finally brought about its almost complete elimination. If, in giving Latin etyma, it is usual to quote the accusative, this is because the accusative case alone was normally the source of the modern Romance substantive. Inscriptions, from the first century onwards, all tell the same story of confusion in case-endings, while literary Latin continually reflects a growing tendency to define case-relationships by means of prepositions. Though the abandonment of archaic flexions was doubtless gradual, with the people continuing to understand them, at least in their more distinctive forms, for some time after they had fallen out of favour in the medium of everyday speech, yet one may safely assume that by the fifth century this medium retained only two cases, nominative and accusative, in functional use, together with a few survivals of the dative.

The ablative was probably the first to lose its identity, its form being readily merged with that of the accusative. Relics of its plural in -s, used with locative meaning, still exist in the names of French towns, e.g. *Rheims*, *Poitiers*, &c. (see p. 193). There are also a few traces of the singular, as, for instance, in the universally employed COMO, for QUOMODO, already attested at Pompeii in its apocopated form: thence came Old Fr. *com*, Rum. *cum*, Span. Port. Old Ital. *como*, while compounded with ET it gave Fr. *comme*, Ital. *come*, and with AC or AD, Prov. and Old Port. *coma*; compare too Old Fr. *illuec* (< ILLO LŎCO) and *tempre(s)* 'betimes' (< TEMPORE). The genitive is to be found in similarly fossilized relics,

notably in the names of the week-days (e.g. Ital. *lunedì* < LUNAE
DIEM, &c., see p. 169), in a few plant-names (e.g. Fr. *joubarbe* <
JŎVIS BARBA), and in miscellaneous place-names from which the
first part has disappeared, e.g. SANCTI EMERITI > Old Span. *San-
temder*, mod. *Santander*. Its plural form survives in derivatives of
(FESTA) CANDELARUM 'Candlemass' (Old Fr. *chandeler*), or *CANDE-
LORUM (Prov. *candelor*, Fr. *Chandeleur*), or CEREORUM (north Ital.
*ceriöla, seriöra*, &c.);[1] in various place-names, e.g. Fr. *Villefavreux*
(< VILLA FABRORUM); and in a number of medieval phrases, in
which, however, the learned influence of scribal Latin may be
legitimately suspected, e.g. Old Fr. *al tems ancïenur* (*Vie de saint
Alexis*), *la gent paienur* and *la geste Francor* (*Chanson de Roland*),
*un cheval milsoldor* (< MILLE SOLIDORUM), and Old Ital. *lo fogo
infernor*,[1] &c. In these last examples the genitive plural has
obviously come to be construed as an adjective; only the pronominal ILLORUM and IPSORUM retained in any way the function of
indicating possession (see below, p. 83). Survival of the dative is
also confined to pronouns, e.g. CUI, ILLI, ILLUI, *ISTUI (pp. 80, 92),
except that a dative feminine singular still persists in the east
(e.g. Rum. *capre* < CAPRAE, see p. 89).

As the number of cases in current use diminished, so too did the
number of declensions. The tendency for feminine substantives
of the fifth declension to be assimilated to the more numerous first
declension feminines is apparent even in the work of classical
authors, in their hesitation, for instance, between MATĔRIES and
MATĔRIA, between LUXŬRIES and LUXŬRIA. In popular speech the
transfer rapidly became almost complete. Thus RABIES and GLACIES
changed to RABIA and GLACIA, as all their Romance derivatives
show. FACIES, though ousted by FACIA over the greater part of
Romania (cf. Fr. *face*, Ital. *faccia*) was sufficiently resistant to
have left its trace in Span. *haz*, Prov. *fatz*. Otherwise, only RES,
FĬDES, and DIES, all very commonly used words, were retained and
assimilated to the third declension; of these DIES, moreover, was
in competition with a rival form DIA (cf. Span. *día*, Old Ital. *dia*,
Old Fr. *die*, but also Old Ital. and Old Fr. *di*, and Rum. *zi*): both
were to be ousted over a large part of Romania by the adjectival
DIURNUM, employed as a noun (Fr. *jour*, Ital. *giorno*).

The first declension was further reinforced by the previously

---

[1] See G. Rohlfs, *Historische Grammatik der italienischen Sprache*, vol. ii,
p. 23.

mentioned neuter plurals in -A, by a few words adapted from the third declension (e.g. TEMPESTA for TEMPESTAS), and by fourth declension words with feminine meaning, notably NURUS and SOCRUS which as NURA and SOCRA (see p. 31, *App. Probi*) became Span. *nuera, suegra*, Ital. *nuora, suocera*. The remaining fourth declension words were readily identified with the masculine second declension.

The third declension survived with characteristic forms, though most of its words were made to conform to a parisyllabic pattern with a nominative in -IS: this was usually effected in the manner revealed by the *Appendix Probi* (GRUS non GRUIS, PECTEN non PECTINIS, &c., see p. 31), but at least one common word shows a similar result attained in the Vulgar Latin of Italy and Gaul by reduction of the accusative, viz. SANGUINEM, reduced to SANGUE(M), whence Ital. *sangue* and Fr. *sang*; Span. *sangre*, on the other hand, deriving with a consonantal dissimilation from the older SANGUINEM, is typical of the conservatism of Latin in Spain. Such words as remained imparisyllabic in Vulgar Latin were later to appear as a class apart in the declension of Old French and Provençal.

Excluding these imparisyllabics, and a few other anomalies which similarly eluded the normalizing attentions of popular speech, we find that in 'common Vulgar Latin' there remained of the complicated Old Latin system only the three two-case declensions represented in the following categories:

|     |      | Singular   | Plural  |
| --- | ---- | ---------- | ------- |
| I   | Nom. | CAPRA      | CAPRE   |
|     | Acc. | CAPRA(M)   | CAPRAS  |
| II  | Nom. | MURUS      | MURI    |
|     | Acc. | MURU(M)    | MUROS   |
| III | Nom. | MONTIS     | MONTES  |
|     | Acc. | MONTE(M)   | MONTES  |

Even this simplified system was to enjoy no universal favour. After the fall of M, which had brought about such confusion in the singular, came the added difficulty of a compromised final s. The west, probably on account of its stronger scholastic influences, reacted vigorously in face of this threat to the clarity of the spoken tongue, and final s was everywhere restored or maintained. In the feminine declension the -AS form of the accusative plural was extended and finally eliminated the -E (-AE) of the nominative, a development well attested in inscriptions (see p. 26, *Hic quescunt duas matres...*, &c.). On the other hand, masculine plurals of Class II preserved, at least in Gaul, their distinctive forms, and to them were assimilated the masculine words of Class III, MONTES being changed to \*MONTI. Such is the Gallo-Roman basis of the declension system which was later to appear as a distinctive feature of Old French as follows:

|     |              | Singular | Plural |
|-----|--------------|----------|--------|
| I   | Nom. } Acc.  | *chevre* | *chevres* |
| II  | Nom.         | *murs*   | *mur*  |
|     | Acc.         | *mur*    | *murs* |
| III | Nom.         | *monz*   | *mont* |
|     | Acc.         | *mont*   | *monz* |
|     |              | (*z = ts*) |       |

Among words which in Old French do not fit into this simple division into two categories are the few surviving feminines from the third declension. These preserved their final *s* in both cases of the plural, while in the nominative singular some writers use a final *s* whereas others do not. For these feminines there thus emerged a declension as follows:

|      | Singular | Plural |
|------|----------|--------|
| Nom. | *flour(s)* | *flours* |
| Acc. | *flour*  | *flours* |

Whether the *s* of nom. sing. *flours*—as used, among others, by Chrestien de Troyes—is a direct survival from FLORIS, or whether it was lost and later restored by analogy with the masculine forms, is almost impossible to determine. Masculine anomalies include two series of etymological forms which one would have expected to be assimilated already in Vulgar Latin. The first comprises words having a Latin nominative singular ending in -ER (PATER, FRATER, MAGISTER, and such adjectives as PAUPER, NOSTER) which appear at first in Old French with no *s*-flexion. The second series consists of Latin neuters in -US (e.g. TEMPUS, CŎRPUS, LATUS, PĔCTUS), which, although assimilated to masculine gender yet preserved their *s* in both nominative and accusative (Old Fr. *tems*, *cors*, *lez*, *piz*); such words combine with those of which the stem ends in *s*, whereby the value of flexional *s* is destroyed (e.g. NASUS), to form an indeclinable class in Old French.

That the Vulgar Latin here revealed was common to the whole of Gaul is apparent from the fact that Old Provençal emerged in the eleventh century as a literary language with an identical system, the same types of declension (Class I, *cabra*, *cabras*), and the same few anomalies (cf. indeclinable *temps*, *cors*, *latz*, *pieitz*). The vitality of the system seems to decline as we proceed south. There are few traces of it in Old Gascon, and it is quite absent from Catalan: one of the features which mark off medieval Catalan from the Provençal which it otherwise so closely resembles. Like Catalan, and Portuguese too, Castilian appeared as a literary language without declension, its one form of the noun consistently representing the Latin accusative, viz.

|     | Singular | Plural |
|-----|----------|--------|
| I   | *cabra*  | *cabras* |
| II  | *muro*   | *muros* |
| III | *monte*  | *montes* |
|     | (*flor*) | (*flores*) |

In Old Spanish, as in Gallo-Romance, neuter accusatives in -us survived as a class apart (see p. 52, note).

Although south of the Pyrenees the nominative thus disappeared at an early and unspecified date, whereas in northern France a two-case declension persisted and indeed remained in use until the thirteenth century, yet the above comparison shows in respect of declension a close morphological affinity between the two areas, which during the Vulgar Latin period was probably an identity. There was, in fact, a common western trend. In eastern Romance, however, developments were considerably different.

As we have seen, the common eastern trend in phonetic evolution involved loss of final s. In consequence, when Italian appeared as a written language, having like Spanish but a single case, it did so with plural forms assimilated to those of the Latin nominative. The three main types of Vulgar Latin thus emerged in Italian as follows:

|     | Singular | Plural |
|-----|----------|--------|
| I   | *capra*  | *capre* |
| II  | *muro*   | *muri* |
| III | *monte*  | *monti* |

And likewise in Rumanian (LUPUS being here substituted for

MURUS which did not everywhere survive in the simple form):

|     | Singular | Plural |
|-----|----------|--------|
| I   | *capră*  | *capre* |
| II  | *lup(u)* | *lupi* |
| III | *munte*  | *munţi* |

This identity must surely point to a stage in development which had already been reached in the Vulgar Latin of the east before the two areas were separated by invasions.

The last category in Vulgar Latin declension, comprising words of the third declension which remained imparisyllabic, is fully attested only in Gaul, since only in a two-case declension in Romance could the effects of the anomaly be apparent. These words designate human beings and the persistence of the original nominative form is undoubtedly due to its frequent use as a vocative. Most of them had a shifting accent: hence the considerable difference between nominative and accusative forms in their French and Provençal derivatives. The group includes in particular a large number of words designating agents, words formed on verbal stems, usually those of the first conjugation, e.g. IMPERATOR from IMPERARE, less commonly on those of other conjugations, e.g. TRADITOR from *TRADĪRE. They are nearly all masculine: the only exception in French is SŎROR, to which may be added MŬLIER in Provençal.

The list given below contains typical examples of this category, together with the forms which appeared in Old French. Only the singular is quoted, since in the plural there is no irregularity. It will be observed that some of these words, again owing primarily to their vocative use, have been retained in modern French in the form deriving from the Latin nominative (e.g. *traître, prêtre, pâtre, sœur*):

|      |           |              |
|------|-----------|--------------|
| Nom. | IMPERATOR | *empere(d)re* |
| Acc. | IMPERATŌREM | *empere(d)or* |
| Nom. | PISCATOR  | *peschiere* |
| Acc. | PISCATŌREM | *pescheor* |
| Nom. | TRADITOR  | *traître* |
| Acc. | TRADITŌREM | *traitor* |
| Nom. | ĪNFANS    | *enfes* |
| Acc. | INFANTEM  | *enfant* |
| Nom. | LATRO     | *le(d)re* |
| Acc. | LATRŌNEM  | *larron* |

| Nom. | NĔPOS | *nies* |
|---|---|---|
| Acc. | NEPŌTEM | *nevou, neveu* |
| Nom. | PRESBYTER | *prestre* |
| Acc. | PRESBYTERUM | *presveire, presvoire* |
| Nom. | ABBAS | *abes* |
| Acc. | ABBATEM | *abé* |
| Nom. | ANTECĔSSOR | *ancestre* |
| Acc. | ANTECESSŌREM | *ancessor* |
| Nom. | PASTOR | *pastre* |
| Acc. | PASTŌREM | *pastor* |
| Nom. | SŎROR | *suer* |
| Acc. | SORŌREM | *seror* |

Two common words belonging to the same category of imparisyllabics, but which in Latin had a stable accent, retained this characteristic in Old French:

| Nom. | HŎMO | *uem, on* |
|---|---|---|
| Acc. | HŎMINEM | *ome* |
| Nom. | CŎMES | *cuens, cons* |
| Acc. | CŎMITEM | *conte* |

The vitality of this anomalous declension in the Vulgar Latin of Gaul is further confirmed by the evidence of Old Provençal, which shows a similar range of examples, and a much extended use of the 'agent' flexions:

| Nom. | IMPERATOR | *emperaire* |
|---|---|---|
| Acc. | IMPERATŌREM | *emperador* |
| Nom. | AMATOR | *amaire* |
| Acc. | AMATŌREM | *amador* |
| Nom. | *INGANNATOR | *enganaire* |
| Acc. | *INGANNATŌRE(M) | *enganador* |
| Nom. | SERVĪTOR | *servire* |
| Acc. | SERVITŌRE(M) | *servidor* |
| Nom. | *TONDĒTOR | *tondeire* |
| Acc. | *TONDETŌRE(M) | *tondedor* |
| Nom. | ĬNFANS | *enfas* |
| Acc. | INFANTEM | *enfant* |
| Nom. | LATRO | *laire* |
| Acc. | LATRŌNEM | *lairon* |
| Nom. | NĔPOS | *neps* |
| Acc. | NEPŌTEM | *nebot* |
| Nom. | ABBAS | *abas* |
| Acc. | ABBATEM | *abat* |

| Nom. | SŎROR | *sor* |
| Acc. | SORŌREM | *seror* |
| Nom. | MŬLIER | *molher* (accented *mólher*) |
| Acc. | MULIĔREM | *molher* (accented *molhér*) |
| Nom. | DRACO | *drac* |
| Acc. | DRACŌNEM | *dragon* |
| Nom. | HŎMO | *hom* |
| Acc. | HŎMINEM | *home* |
| Nom. | CŎMES | *coms* |
| Acc. | CŎMITEM | *conte* |

When, during the declining years of the western Empire, the Vulgar Latin vocabulary began to absorb words of Germanic origin, many of these were adapted in Gaul to the anomalous declension, particularly after the pattern of Lat. LATRO, LATRONEM. Thus in Old French there appeared: *ber, baron*; *gars, garçon*; *fel, felon*. Similarly in Provençal: *bar, baron*; *gartz, garson*; *fel, felon*. The popular COMPANIO, coined on a Gothic model (see p. 210), belonged to the same category, cf. Old Fr. *compain, compagnon*; Prov. *companh, companhó*.

To what extent this imparisyllabic declension was in use elsewhere than in Gaul is difficult to estimate. Presumably, for so long as declension survived at all in other Roman territories, some similar forms must have persisted there too. Such, at least, is the inference to be drawn from the presence, in the later Romance of those territories, of a few isolated remnants of the Latin nominative. Italian has *uomo, moglie, ladro, prete*, and *sarto* (< SARTOR). Rumanian has *om, drac, preot*, and *împǎrat* (< IMPERATOR), though the last-named may be of learned origin. In Spanish such forms are rare: *sastre* (< SARTOR) and *juez* (< JUDEX) are original nominatives, though once again the latter suggests the influence of a learned context; Old Span. *preste* was probably a temporary borrowing from north of the Pyrenees. A few words of the -O, -ONEM type are quoted by Menéndez Pidal (*Gramática histórica*, p. 174): CURCULIO > *gorgojo* 'grub, weevil', AVIS STRUTHIO > *avestruz* 'ostrich' (STRUTHIO is a Greek etymon, cf. Ital. *struzzo*), COMPANIO > *compaño* (together with COMPANIONEM > *compañón*), TITIO > *tizo* (together with TITIONEM > *tizón*), BUBO > *buho* (together with Arag. *bobón*). Preservation of the nominative of these last two words appears to be due to popular acceptance of the -ON of the accusative as an augmentative suffix. One other word was widely kept in a non-French area in both nominative and accusative forms: it is SERPENS, SERPENTEM (Span. *sierpe, serpiente*; Port. *serpe, serpente*; Cat. *serp, serpent*), perhaps an example of Biblical influence.

Such was the fate of the declension system in Vulgar Latin. Its decline was inevitably accompanied by considerable changes in the structure of the sentence. Not only did the expression of case-relationships thereafter depend to a great extent upon the use of prepositions, a fact which gave to the preposition a much more preponderant syntactical importance and led to the creation of a variety of new ones in Romance, but also the whole word-order of the sentence was bound to become more fixed. In Old French, as in Provençal, it was still possible to follow the liberty of Latin in the positioning of subject and object: the object could and often did precede the subject. But once the two-case system had disintegrated, or rather, as one of the prerequisites of its disintegration, there appeared in French the same conventional word-order with which the other Romance languages had emerged, the beginnings of which go far back into Vulgar Latin. Only by their position in the sentence with relation to the verb could subject and object then be distinguished.

*Adjectives.* The declension of adjectives followed in Vulgar Latin the same course as that of nouns. In every part of the Empire, fem. BŎNA and masc. BŎNUS declined in just the same way as CAPRA and MŪRUS. A neuter BŎNU(M) also survived, to be used either adverbially, i.e. as in Fr. *sentir bon*, or predicatively after a neuter subject, e.g. (ECCE)HOC EST BONUM > Old Fr. *ço est bon*. Adjectives with a masculine nominative singular in -ER, e.g. PAUPER, TENER, ALTER, &c., were retained in Gaul, like nouns in -ER, with no nominative -*s*. Of third declension adjectives, many were early adapted to the standard type of BONUS; this is well attested in the *Appendix Probi* (see p. 31), and even the classical language shows hesitation between such forms as IMBECILLIS and IMBECILLUS, PROCLIVIS and PROCLIVUS. Others, however, including some of the most commonly used, e.g. GRANDIS, FORTIS, kept their separate declension, as is obvious from the fact that they appeared in the Romance languages with identical forms for masculine and feminine, in southern areas with the post-tonic E of FORTEM. Here they still constitute a class apart, with only one form in the singular and one in the plural, e.g. Span. *grande, fuerte*; Ital. *grande, forte*.

Old French usage in this respect was similar, acc. *grant* and *fort* serving at first for all genders, and although these words were later made to conform to the standard French type, by the addition to the feminine of an analogical *-e*, relics of the earlier forms still persist in *grand'mère, grand'faim, grand'route*, &c., in such place-names as *Rochefort*, and in adverbs created in the usual Vulgar Latin way with the fem. MENTE, e.g. *ardemment, constamment* (< ARDENTE MENTE, CONSTANTE MENTE); with these latter may be contrasted *bonnement* (< BŎNA MENTE), and the analogical *fortement*, in Old French *forment* (< FORTE MENTE).

The popular rejection of synthetic forms which characterizes declension is again revealed in the comparison of adjectives. It will be recalled that in Classical Latin the comparative has the flexions masc. and fem. -IOR, acc. -IOREM, and neut. -IUS. Already in the work of Plautus, however, there are instances of an analytic alternative, the comparative being conveyed by the use of MAGIS, less frequently PLŪS, preceding the adjective in its simple form, e.g. MAGIS APTUS, PLUS INFESTA. Occasionally MĔLIUS was used in the same way, as appears from such Old French evidence as 'Des melz gentils de tuta la cuntretha' (*Vie de saint Alexis*), but the choice crystallized around PLŪS and MAGIS. Of these MAGIS was the earlier in general favour and it is therefore not surprising that this should have been the one to persist in many of the areas of earlier colonization (e.g. Span. *más*, Port. *mais*, Cat. *més*, Rum. *mai*). The whole Italian region has, however, preferred PLŪS (Ital. *più*, Sicil. *cchiù*, and even Sard. *prus*). In Gaul both forms were used: the south, ever a meeting-place of Latin currents, shows in Provençal texts both *plus* and *mais*; in the north, Old Fr. *plus* was soon predominant.

While this became the normal way of expressing comparative sense in Vulgar Latin, the abandonment of synthetic forms was not complete. A few very common comparatives, which in Latin were 'irregular' and were in fact for the most part quite different words from those for which they served as comparative, persisted generally in the west. Thus MĔLIOR > Old Fr. *mieldre*, MELIŌREM > Fr. *meilleur*, Span. *mejor*, Ital. *migliore*; PĔJOR[1] > Fr. *pire*, PEJŌREM > Old Fr. *peour*, Span. *peor*, Ital. *peggiore*; MAJOR > Fr. *maire*, MAJŌREM > Old Fr. *maour*, Span. *mayor*, Ital. *maggiore*; MĬNOR >

---

[1] In Latin dictionaries this word is given as PĒJOR, but Romance presupposes forms with Ĕ; it seems that in reality the Latin pronunciation was PĔJJOR, the double consonant accounting for the metrical length of the first syllable.

Fr. *moindre*, MINŌREM > Old Fr. *menour*, Span. *menor*, Ital. *minore*. Similarly with corresponding neuter forms, which, on account of their predicative use, have partially survived as adverbs: MĔLIUS > Fr. *mieux*, Ital. *meglio*; PĔJUS > Fr. *pis*, Ital. *peggio*; MAJUS > Ital. *maggio*; MĬNUS > Fr. *moins*, Span. *menos*, Ital. *meno*. SENIŌREM also continued to exist, though chiefly as a substantive, as appears from Fr. *seigneur*, Span. *señor*, and Ital. *signore*; its nominative SENIOR persisted in Gaul, occurring in the *Strassburg Oaths* as *sendra* (see p. 343), but otherwise only as *sire*, which leads us to infer that in northern Gaul, probably on account of its use as a form of address, SENIOR was reduced to \*SEIOR, cf. acc. \*SEIORE(M) > Fr. *sieur*. In the Provençal of the south a regular nom. *sénher*, together with acc. *senhór*, shows that SENIOR was there preserved. JUNIOREM similarly persisted in Italy and in Gaul, cf. Old Ital. *gignore* 'apprentice', and Old Fr. nom. *joindre*, acc. *joignour*, the former of which developed to *gindre* 'baker's boy'.

Apart from these words which had lost contact with their original positive form, survivals of the Latin synthetic comparative are confined to Gaul. The few which are to be found in medieval Italian, e.g. *genzore, forzore, plusori* are borrowings from Provençal literature. In Gaul, however, such survivals were fairly numerous, especially in the south: a fact which seems to testify, like the persistence of a two-case declension, to the exceptionally strong influence exercised in that part of the Empire by the standards of cultured Latin, as taught in the schools. They include: GRANDIOR and GRANDIOREM (Old Fr. *graindre, graignour*), ALTIOR (Prov. *áusser*) and ALTIOREM (Prov. *alzor*, Old Fr. *halzor*), FORTIOREM (Prov. *forsor*, Old Fr. *forçor*), SORDIDIOR (Prov. *sordéjer*) and SORDIDIOREM (Prov. *sordejór*, Old Fr. *sordeior*), \*PLUSIORI for PLURIORES (Prov. *plusor*, Old Fr. *pluisour*). Two which enjoyed particular favour in the south were \*BELLATIOR, a comparative of \*BELLATUS, formed on BELLUS, whence Prov. nom. *belláire*, acc. *bellazor* (also found in the Picard area of northern France, as in the description of St. Eulalia, 'Bel auret corps, bellezour anima'); and \*GENITIOR, comparative of GĔNITUS 'well-born', in Prov. nom. *génser*, acc. *gensór*. Both belonged to the language of courtly flattery.

To introduce the complement of a comparative Latin used two constructions, one synthetic, e.g. *doctior Petro*, and one analytic, e.g. *doctior quam Petrus*. In popular speech the choice obviously went to the second, and the desire to indicate the differentiation more emphatically gave rise to the use of DE as an alternative to QUAM. Both of these possibilities survived in Romance.

The popular mind seems to have experienced no need to distinguish between the best of three. So at least it would appear from the disappearance of the Latin superlative. The only forms to remain were MAXIMUM (Old Fr. *maisme*, Ital. *massimo*), MINIMUM (Old Fr. *merme*, Ital. *menomo*), PESSIMUM (Old Fr. *pesme*, Ital. *pessimo*), PROXIMUM (Old Fr. *proisme*, Ital. *prossimo*), and perhaps OPTIMUM (Ital. *ottimo*); and even these were used with absolute, and not comparative meaning. All other traces of a synthetic superlative in Romance are of learned origin, the creation of medieval schoolmen, who seem to have found particular pleasure in restoring the lost -ISSIMUS, if one may judge from the proliferation of *-isme*, *-ísimo*, and *-issimo* in medieval French, Spanish, and Italian respectively.

The absolute superlative was in general conveyed, as already in Ciceronian usage (e.g. *vir multum bonus*), by the hard-worked adverb MULTUM (Old Fr. *mout*; Span. *mucho, muy*; Port. *muito*; Ital. *molto*; Rum. *mult*). A less popular alternative was VALDE, 'very'; the eighth-century glossing of OPTIMUM by VALDE BONUM (*Reichenau Glossary*, see p. 315) shows that this term continued to enjoy some currency in the Gallic area and it has survived in a few compounded words, e.g. Old Fr. *vaupute*, < VALDE PŪTIDA, and the dialectal *vaudoux*, < VALDE DULCEM. Yet another possibility, which must have developed late, was supplied by TRANS. Traces of this are found in Italian, e.g. *tra-antico*, 'very old', *tra-avaro*, 'very miserly', but only in France has it met with general favour. Rather infrequently employed in Old French instead of *mout*,—it occurs in the *Chanson de Roland* (*Si li truvez ki tresbien li aiut*, ed. Whitehead, l. 781)—, *très* gradually ousted its rival to become one of the most distinctive features of French vocabulary.

*Numerals.* Cardinal numbers from one to ten were consistently preserved in Vulgar Latin, the first three continuing to decline. Of particular interest is the extended use of ŪNUS, which, while at the same time serving as a numeral, came in the Romance languages to have the new grammatical function of indefinite article. The origins of this development may be observed in Latin texts in which ŪNUS sometimes has the meaning of 'a certain', where it is in fact an alternative expression for QUĪDAM. With this sense it could have a plural and in Vulgar Latin was commonly so used:

hence Span. *unos, unas* 'some', and Old Fr. *uns, unes,* this latter normally employed only with reference to objects considered collectively or in pairs, e.g. Old Fr. *uns dens, unes bottes.* The attenuation of meaning whereby it then became in the singular the indefinite article, a development common to the whole of Romania and thus probably of much earlier generalization than any written evidence would suggest, is a phenomenon to be found again in the growth of a definite article from the demonstrative ILLE.

Further innovations took place in the declension of DUO. With an analogical masculine DUI, attested in the third century, and an analogical neuter DUA, the Vulgar Latin forms must have been as follows:

| Nom. | DUI | DUAE | DUA |
| --- | --- | --- | --- |
| Acc. | DUOS | DUAS | DUA |

The accusative of the feminine being in the west extended to fit both cases, Old French appeared thus:

| Nom. | *dui, doi* | *doues* | *doue* |
| --- | --- | --- | --- |
| Acc. | *dous, deus* | *doues* | *doue* |

Of these, the form *doues* occurs only in eastern French texts; elsewhere the masc. *dous* was used as feminine.

The Vulgar Latin accusatives persisted in Old Span. masc. *dos,* fem. *duas, dues,* reduced since the thirteenth century to the invariable *dos*; Portuguese still has masc. *dous (dois),* fem. *duas.* Sardinia preserves the exact Vulgar Latin forms, masc. *duos,* fem. *duas,* neut. *dua* (M. L. Wagner, *La lingua sarda,* p. 327). Where the eastern type of declension prevailed, Rumanian has *doi* and *două,* while Old Italian appeared with *duo, dui, duoi, due, dua,* all liable to be employed in any context for 'two'; the modern language has selected *due.*

Concurrently with DUO, the Latin dual AMBO was widely used, again with analogical flexions (cf. Old Fr. Prov. and Cat. *am*; Old Span. *amos, amas*; Sard. *ambos, ambas*; Old Ital. *ambi, ambe*; Rum. *îmbi*).[1] The two words were also compounded, giving rise to a Vulgar Latin declension:

| Nom. | AMBI DUI | AMBAE DUAE |
| --- | --- | --- |
| Acc. | AMBOS DUOS | AMBAS DUAS |

[1] In Rumanian orthography the symbols *â* and *î* represent the same sound, a middle vowel. The former usually corresponds to a Latin A, but in the initial position *î* is normally used, as in the above example. A recent spelling reform generalizes *î* at the expense of *â*; for this reason we have used *î* throughout the text.

These appeared in Old French as follows:

| | | |
|------|----------|----------------|
| Nom. | *andui* | *ambesdou(e)s* |
| Acc. | *ansdous* | *ambesdou(e)s* |

Provençal had a similar declension, and both idioms developed a mixed form *ambedui*. Other forms are to be found all over the Romance area, e.g. Old Span. *amos dos*, Ital. *ambedue*, Rum. *amîndoi*, &c.

TRES remained as in Classical Latin, with only one form for two cases and genders, but with a neuter TRIA, which survived in Gaul, appearing in Old French as the dicing-term *treie*, cf. Eng. 'a game of tray'. The other numerals up to ten, invariable in Latin, continued so in popular speech, being affected only by minor phonetic changes, e.g. V. Lat. QUATTOR for QUATTUOR, CINQUE for QUINQUE, the latter showing a dissimilation of the first U, to which the palatalization of the initial C in Romance languages bears ample witness, e.g. Fr. *cinq*, Span. *cinco*, Ital. *cinque*, Rum. *cinci*.

Numbers which follow show rifts in the general linguistic pattern. Rum. *unsprezece*, *doisprezece*, &c., reveal a type UNUS SUPER DECEM, DUO SUPER DECEM, &c. It has been suggested that this construction is due to a post-Latin influence of Slavonic languages, but it could quite obviously have existed as current Vulgar Latin in the eastern area. Elsewhere, UNDECIM, DUODECIM, TREDECIM, QUATTUORDECIM, QUINDECIM persisted, and SEDECIM in Italy and Gaul. The remainder of the series of the 'teens' reflects the popular tendency to decompose such compounds. In Gaul and Italy from seventeen, in Spain from sixteen, new forms developed, in Gaul and Spain with DECEM ET . . . (Old Fr. *dis e set*, Span. *diecisiete*, Old Port. *dez e sete*), and in Italy, it would appear, with DECEM AC . . . (Ital. *diciassette*, &c.). In Portuguese a form *dezassete* has displaced the old *dez e sete*, but whether this has always existed as an alternative derived from DECEM AC . . ., or whether it is of more recent formation, seems impossible to decide.

Numbers denoting compounds of ten all lost in Vulgar Latin their intervocalic G. Most Romance derivatives of VĪGĬNTĪ, e.g. Old Fr. *vint*, Old Span. *veínte*, Port. *vinte*, dialectal Ital. *vint*, *vinti*, suggest that the stressed ĭ was closed under the influence of the neighbouring vowels: Old Span. *veínte* (mod. *veinte*) presumably developed with dissimilation of the vowels of V. Lat. *VIÍNTI*. A comparable V. Lat. *TRIÍNTA* would explain Port. *trinta* and

Old Span. *treínta* (mod. *treinta*), but in Gaul and Italy TRĪGĬNTA evolved more regularly to *TRENTA. In Italy, it would seem, the analogy of this *TRENTA affected the outcome of VĪGĬNTĪ, giving rise to the standard *venti*. The remaining compounds of ten reveal a more clear-cut differentiation between the Vulgar Latin of Spain and that of Gaul and Italy: in the former, the earlier type, the accent is kept on -ĬNTA (> -*énta*), whereas the later affinities between Gaul and Italy are shown in the common tendency to throw back the accent on to the preceding A, e.g. QUADRAGĬNTA > *QUADRÁINTA > QUARRANTA; hence the series:

|  | Spanish | Portuguese | Old French | Italian |
|---|---|---|---|---|
| QUADRAGĬNTA | *cuarenta* | *quarenta* | *quarante* | *quaranta* |
| QUINQUAGĬNTA | *cincuenta* | *cinquenta* | *cinquante* | *cinquanta* |
| SEXAGĬNTA | *sesenta* | *sessenta* | *seisante* | *sessanta* |
| SEPTUAGĬNTA | *setenta* | *setenta* | *setante* | *settanta* |
| OCTOGĬNTA | *ochenta* | *oitenta* | *oitante* | *ottanta* |
| NONAGĬNTA | *noventa* | *noventa* | *nonante* | *novanta* |

It will be observed that for 'ninety' there existed in Vulgar Latin an alternative form, probably introduced at the stage of *NOVA-GINTA, due to the influence of NŎVEM; the presence in Provençal and Catalan, in Sardinian and in north Italian dialects, of *noranta*, points to yet another Vulgar Latin creation, for which QUARRANTA may have served as model.

In northern Gaul the pattern of Vulgar Latin numerals was to be broken by the intrusion of the vigesimal system, with *quatre-vingts*, *quatre-vingt-dix* and the analogical *soixante-dix* surviving into modern French. Generally assumed to be a relic of the Celtic substratum (cf. p. 192), the system provided in Old French a complete set of alternatives, e.g. *deux vins chevaliers*, and extended to numbers over a hundred, whence at Paris *l'Hôpital des Quinze Vingts*. Its surprising persistence in the three present-day numerals meets with no obvious explanation: possibly they drew some psychological support from the existence of compound forms for 'seventeen, eighteen, nineteen'. It is not usual in Provençal. Traces of it occur in Sicily and southern Italy, but it was presumably carried thus far afield by the Norman occupation of that area in the eleventh century.

To the east of Romania, the Latin pattern was discarded in favour of an analytic 'two tens, three tens', &c., system, as is shown by Rum. *douăzeci*, *treizeci*, &c. These forms, like the no less divergent 'teens', may have been favoured by a precedent in the non-Latin speeches of the area, as has indeed been suggested. On the other hand, their exact resemblance to multiples of a hundred in the west (see below) makes the assumption of a 'substratic' influence appear unnecessary.

CENTUM was generally retained, but in Rumanian has given way to a Slav. *sutӑ*. A few of its multiples as used in Classical Latin survived into Romance despite the popular tendency to decompose them. DUCENTOS and TRECENTOS appear in Old Spanish as *dozientos*, *trezientos*, and are still current in Port. *duzentos*, *trezentos*; the nominative is found in Prov. *dozent*, *trezent*; Italian has a form *dugento*. QUINGENTOS also persisted in the Iberian Peninsula, cf. Span. *quinientos*, Port. *quinhentos*. But the characteristic decomposed numbers must have established an early popularity, cf. Fr. *deux cents*, Ital. *duecento*, Span. *doscientos*, *-as*, &c.

Lat. MILLE underwent no change: it is still *mille* in Italian, and an invariable *mil* in France and Spain. Its plural MILIA was less stable. In the east, understood as a feminine singular, it supplanted MILLE (Rum. *mie*). It occurs in Old French as *milie*, and survives in Sardinia (Log. *midza*) and parts of southern Italy. The mod. Ital. pl. *mila* and Fr. *mille* are certainly due to learned influence; probably so too are the various forms of the word with the meaning 'mile', cf. Span. *milla*, Port. *milha*, Ital. *miglia*.

The Latin ordinals from 'first' to 'tenth' were generally preserved in the popular speech. As the table which follows will show, modern Italian has kept them almost unchanged. There were, however, certain Vulgar Latin alternatives which have been partially incorporated into other Romance languages (given below in brackets). That these should have been to some extent held in check is probably due to the same learned influence which, as we shall see, has played a large part in the creation of the Romance systems from 'eleventh' onwards: where dates are expressed by cardinal numbers, the ordinals are not very commonly used.

|  | Italian | Old French | Provençal | Spanish | Portuguese |
|---|---|---|---|---|---|
| PRIMUM | primo | prim (*premier*) | prim (*premier*) | (*primero*) | (*primeiro*) |
| SECUNDUM | secondo | segont | segont | segundo | segundo |
| TERTIUM | terzo | tierz | tertz | (*tercero*) | (*terceiro*) |
| QUARTUM | quarto | quart | quart | cuarto | quarto |
| QUINTUM | quinto | quint | quint | quinto | quinto |
| SEXTUM | sesto | siste | sest (*seizen*) | sésto | sexto |
| SEPTIMUM | settimo | sedme | (*seten*) | séptimo | sétimo |
| OCTAVUM | ottavo | (*oidme*) | (*ochen*) | octavo | oitavo |
| NONUM | nono | (*nuefme, nueme*) | (*noven*) | (*noveno*) | nono |
| DECIMUM | decimo | dime, disme | (*detzen*) | décimo | décimo |

Here the learned influences are clearly apparent (e.g. Span. *octavo*, *décimo*), as are also the popular variants of Vulgar Latin. Side by side with PRĪMUM (still preserved in Fr. *printemps* < PRĪMUM TEMPUS), there had developed a widely used PRIMARIUM. A similarly formed TERTIARIUM gained currency only in the Iberian Peninsula. On the model of SEPTIMUM, northern Gaul had created *OCTIMUM and *NOVIMUM. Southern Gaul made new ordinals, from 'sixth' onwards, by adopting the suffix -ĒNUS from the Latin series of distributive numerals: Prov. *seten* from SEPTĒNI, and *noven* from NOVĒNI, are entirely etymological. The use of this suffix extended into Spain, where *cuatreno*, *cinqueno*, *seiseno*, and *seteno* all existed in the old language; if, in the first ten, only *noveno* has survived, it is because this suggested a closer link with *nueve* than did *nono*, which Portuguese has nevertheless preferred. Similar forms with -*en*, e.g. *cinquen*, *sexen*, *seten* are also found in medieval texts in northern Italy.

In the east, the above mentioned PRIMARIUM survives in a few expressions, e.g. Rum. *cale primară*, the first visit after a wedding to a newly-married couple, and *văr primar*, 'first cousin'. Otherwise, the whole Latin system has disappeared. More currently employed for 'first' was a form *ANTANEUM (> *întîi*), and the remaining ordinals were constructed by means of the corresponding cardinal preceded by the possessive article masc. *al*, fem. *a*, and followed by the suffix masc. -*le*(*a*), fem. -*a*; thus 'third' is masc. *al treile*(*a*), fem. *a treia*.

From 'eleventh' onwards the Latin ordinals seem to have fallen largely out of use. When a need for them was felt in Romance, they were re-created with the help of literary Latin. Thus in Italian the learned suffix -*esimo* was attached to the cardinals, e.g. *undicesimo*, *ventitreesimo*, &c., while modern Spanish employs purely learned forms, e.g. *undécimo*, *vigésimo*, *cuadragésimo*, &c. There do, however, exist in Spanish the forms *veinteno* and *treinteno*, comparable with *noveno*, formed, that is, with the -ĒNUS suffix which continued to be used with all these numbers in Provençal. Northern France found its own solution by attaching -*i*(*s*)*me* as a suffix (< -ECIMUM) to corresponding cardinals, e.g. *onzi*(*s*)*me*, *dozi*(*s*)*me*; interference of the learned -ĒSIMUM was probably responsible for the -*ie*(*s*)*me* by which -*i*(*s*)*me* was replaced during the thirteenth century. From this decay of the 'post-ten' ordinals in Vulgar Latin, one form survived to show all the features of popular evolution: it is QUADRAGĒSIMA, identified by the Church with Lent, cf. Fr. *carême*, Ital. *quaresima*, Span. *cuaresma*, Rum. *păresemi*.

The Latin distributives SĬNGULI, BĪNI, TERNI, QUATERNI, QUĪNI, SĒNI all persisted in popular speech, but to judge from their sporadic occurrence in Romance, and from the specialized usages in which they appear, it would seem that their meaning was often misunderstood and obscured. SĬNGULI generally acquired the sense of 'single', with which indeed it is already used by Cicero (Old Fr. *sangle*, often 'alone', cf. also *bière sangle* 'small beer'). BĪNI gave rise to an Old Fr. *bin et bin* 'two by two'. QUATERN(I) underwent a fully popular development to become Old Fr. *caer*, mod. *cahier*, cf. Span. *cuaderno*, Ital. *quaderno*, the meaning 'note-book' deriving from that of 'four-fold sheet'. Others appear in games, as in the gambling-scenes of the Picard *Jeu de saint Nicolas*, where the players, each throwing three dice with one cast, call *ternes* 'double-three', *quaernes* 'double-four', *quinnes* 'double-five', and *sines* 'double-six'. In view of the age-old popularity of dice-throwing there seems no reason to doubt that these are genuine survivals of Vulgar Latin; they may be feminines, agreeing with an implied VĬCES.

*Personal pronouns.* Apart from the reflexive SĒ, Classical Latin used personal pronouns only for the first and second persons, and in the nominative only for emphasis, the concept of person being already conveyed in the flexions of the finite verb. Popular speech, with its natural inclination to exploit all possibilities of emphasis, brought them into play more often, and also created a third in the series by employing the demonstrative ILLE, in some areas IPSE, in this particular capacity. Used pronominally ILLE thus became a personal pronoun; in its continuing adjectival use it evolved into the definite article (see p. 87). During the later years of the Empire ILLE was sufficiently well established in its function as a personal pronoun to be recognized as such by Latin grammarians, but it differed from the earlier personal pronouns in that it continued to inflect for gender, whereas they did not. In consequence, the third person presents in Romance a more complex picture than do the other two. This complexity is moreover increased by an instability of stress, as between the first syllable and the second, which has its origin in the structure of the spoken sentence. Most pronouns were liable to be affected by this syntactical influence, appearing in Romance with both 'tonic' and 'atonic' forms.

Latin ĔGO was generally reduced to EO; only Old Sardinian, among the Romance languages, appeared with *ego* intact, the *g* being still sounded to this day in the dialect of Nuoro (M. L. Wagner, op. cit., p. 327). With a tonic accent on the first vowel this EO has developed into Ital. *io*, Rum. *eu*, Port. *eu*, Prov. *eu*, *ieu*. On the other hand, both Span. *yo* and Old Fr. *jo* indicate a shift of stress from the first vowel to the second. At what period this accentual differentiation took place is difficult to assess. One cannot draw any valid conclusion concerning French from the orthography *eo* and *io* found in the ninth-century *Strassburg Oaths*. It would seem, from the occurrence of its derivatives in two separate areas in Romance, that EÓ was a possibility already inherent in Vulgar Latin.

The accusative MĒ persisted everywhere, but in many regions side by side with a MI from MIHI. This latter, except in Old Sardinian and in Rum. *mie*, lost its dative function to become an alternative accusative; thereafter either ME or MI could be employed as accusative or dative, as occasion required (cf. the use of *me*, *you*, &c., in modern English). Eventually, where both were used, syntactical distinctions emerged, one form being reserved for the atonic position before the verb, and the other for the tonic position. But this medieval allotment of function must have followed upon a long period of confusion in Vulgar Latin, since Spanish and Italian appeared with exactly opposite solutions, the atonic forms being Ital. *mi* and Span. *me*, whereas the tonic forms are Ital. *me* and Span. *mi*.[1] In the north-central area of Gaul the confusion ended differently, with the complete elimination of MI; atonic and tonic forms were both developed from the single form ME, which appears in French as *me* and *moi*. The original MI did, however, persist in the east of Gaul, in the later Picard–Walloon area and Lorraine.

[1] We should perhaps add that Ital. *mi* does not necessarily derive from MIHI; it could be the result of unemphatic ME, since the closing of pretonic *e* to *i* is a normal Italian development (see p. 464). In Old Italian the distinction of usage, as between *mi* and *me*, is not always precisely made, though it is clear enough in the following lines by Giacomino Pugliese:

> 'Madonna, non ti pesa fare
> fallimento o villania:
> quando mi vedi passare
> sospirando per la via . . .
> a voi ne torna bassanza,
> ed a me ne crescie vergogna, amore.'

(*Early Italian Texts*, ed. C. Dionisotti and C. Grayson, p. 105)

In southern Italy and Sicily there is a form *meve*, which points to a V. Lat. MIBI, assimilated to TIBI and SIBI. This alternative possibility must have formerly been more widespread, since MIBI is in fact attested in the medieval Latin of northern Spain, and appears in Mozarabic as *mibi* (see p. 404). Yet another alternative, found in Balkan Romance, in Rum. *mine* and at Veglia as *main*, exists in southern Italy, beside *meve*, as *mene*. This would seem to be a relic of the interrogative MENE of Latin.

A further feature of Vulgar Latin was the popularity of the appended CUM, as in MECUM. This appeared in Italian as *meco*. But even within the time of the Empire the appending of a preposition must have come to be felt as anomalous, with the result that the common people placed a redundant preposition in front, giving rise to a type CUM MECUM, sufficiently widespread to have appeared in Span. *conmigo*, Port. *comigo*, Old Ital. *conmeco*, and at the island of Veglia as *konmaik*.

In the second person, the nominative TŪ remained, with fronting of the U in those areas where this was usual. Some regions, notably northern Italy, show a tendency to replace it by the accusative TĒ, but this was probably late. TĒ and TIBI evolved in form and usage in exactly the same way as MĒ and MIHI, as did also the third person reflexive SĒ and SIBI. Where MIHI was assimilated to the other datives to give *meve*, there TIBI and SIBI have become *teve* and *seve*; but the much more usual tendency was for TIBI and SIBI to be assimilated to MIHI, whence the common Romance forms *ti* and *si*. Where MENE was preserved, there too are TENE and SENE. Combination with CUM was again very frequent, cf. Span. Port. *contigo*, *consigo*; Ital. *teco*, *seco*; Old Ital. *conteco*, *conseco*.

The plural forms of the first two persons, nominative and accusative NOS and VOS, were unchanged in Vulgar Latin, except in so far as they were affected by general phonetic evolution, cf. Old Fr. *nos*, *vos*; Old Span. *nos*, *vos*; Ital. *noi*, *voi*; Rum. *noi*, *voi*. In some western areas, where final s remained, the initial v of VOS underwent the change to B attested in the *Appendix Probi*, e.g. Log. *bos*; a similar bilabial pronunciation brought about the eventual reduction of Span. *vos* to *os*, in Catalan *us*; occasionally *os* is also met with in Old French texts, but here it seems to be due to enclisis, e.g. *jos* for *je vos*. In the spoken language these forms were commonly made more emphatic by the addition of ALTERI, -OS, whence Fr. *nous autres*, Span. *nosotros*, &c. It may be for this reason that French failed to develop tonic forms *\*neus* and *\*veus*, which one would normally have expected to correspond to *nous* and *vous* as *moi* and *toi* correspond to *me* and *te*. Combination with CUM was also current, e.g. Old Span. *connusco*, *convusco*, Ital. *nosco*, *vosco*, &c.

As the *Appendix Probi* indicates, with NOBISCUM non NOSCUM, the datives NOBIS and VOBIS must have early disappeared from everyday use. It has been suggested that relics of them are to be found in Sardinian, which, side by side with *nos* and *bos*, employs before a consonant *nosi* and *bosi* ('Sarà lecito considerare queste forme in -*i* finale come resti di *nois* = NOBIS con metatesi dovuta all'analogia di *mi*, *ti*.' M. L. Wagner, op. cit., p. 328); but these forms could quite easily have been created on the analogy of *mi* and *ti* directly from *nos* and *bos*.

The declension of ILLE persisted much more fully in Vulgar Latin than that of any substantive. It was, moreover, considerably influenced, in both nominative and dative, by the declension of the relative pronoun, thus developing forms unknown to the classical language. Neither Ital. *egli* nor Fr. *il* could derive directly from ILLE; both could be accounted for by a form *\*ILLĪ*, Fr. *il* being the result of modification of the stressed vowel under the influence of the following vowel (*Umlaut*). This *\*ILLĪ* must have existed in Vulgar Latin, and although other explanations have been suggested, certainly the most likely is to be found in the influence of QUĪ. In the masculine dative, only a parallel influence of CUI can account for the form ILLUI, derivatives of which appeared in Romance together with those of the classical ILLI. Still more curious is the growth of a feminine dative ILLAEI, reproducing the rhythm of ILLUI, and created from a combination of ILLI with the usual feminine flexion -AE. Geographically, the new datives are confined to Gaul, Italy, and the east. Old French has masc. *lui*, side by side with *li* from ILLI, and in the feminine it had *lei*, which occurs in the *Cantilène de sainte Eulalie*, but this was early absorbed into *li*; elsewhere are the corresponding forms: Prov. masc. *lui*, fem. *liei*; Ital. masc. *lui*, fem. *lei*; Rum. masc. *lui*, fem. *ei*. There is no trace of these creations in the Iberian Peninsula, in Sardinia, or in the dialects of Sicily and Calabria. That they originated well within the Vulgar Latin period is, however, quite obvious from their presence both in the east and in the west.

Other forms of the declension of ILLE evolved quite normally, though with varying stress. In the nominative, an emphatic form, the stress remained everywhere on the first syllable. The *el* of Spanish and Rumanian derives directly from ILLE, though the existence in Old Spanish of *elli* side by side with *elle* suggests that *ILLĪ may have been used in Spain concurrently with the classical form. The feminine nominative ILLA developed with no change, other than phonetic, cf. Fr. *elle*, Span. *ella*, Ital. *ella*, Rum. *ea*. The accusative, as the atonic form preceding the verb, shows in both masculine and feminine a general shift of accent on to the second syllable. Thus a Vulgar Latin ILLÚ(M) appeared almost everywhere as *lo*, later reduced in French to *le* and in Portuguese to *o*; *la* from ILLA(M) was universal in the west, and apart from the Portuguese reduction to *a* it is still in general use. The corresponding tonic form of the accusative singular, with the accent placed as in Classical Latin on the first syllable, seems to have virtually disappeared in popular speech: in the disjunctive function both Italian and Old French employed the new datives, Ital. *lui* and *lei*, Old Fr. *lui* and *li* (later replaced in the feminine by *elle*), while Spanish appeared with forms identical with the nominative, Old Sp. *elle*, mod. *él* and *ella*.

The old dative ILLI, common to both genders, persists as *le* in Spanish and as *li* in Sardinian; it is also the probable origin of the Ital. dat. *gli*, which in popular usage is both masculine and feminine, though a fem. *le* has been developed in the standard language.

The neuter ILLUD appears to have survived in Vulgar Latin: there is a neuter *ello* in Spanish, and an *el* used as nominative in Old French, particularly in western dialect (e.g. Si cum el est leis et dreiture, *Roman de Troie*). Ital. *ello* may be either this or a stressed accusative; in Vulgar Latin ÍLLU(D) and ÍLLU(M) would have become identical.

In the plural, the nominative masculine ILLI was preserved in Gaul and Italy, to appear in Old French and Old Italian with forms identical with those of the corresponding singular, viz. Old Fr. *il*, Ital. *egli*; only late in the Middle Ages were these differentiated from the singular, the former to *ils*, by addition of the normal plural flexion of nouns, and the latter, in a more unusual way, to *eglino*, by the addition of a plural flexion -*no*, borrowed from the finite verb. ILLAE became Ital. *elle*, later similarly altered to *elleno*. As in the singular, there was an atonic accusative with a shift of accent: in the west ĬLLÓS and ĬLLÁS, which converged as *les* in French, and in Spanish gave *los* and *las* respectively; in the east, where the nominative form was generalized, ĬLLÍ and ĬLLÁE, cf. Ital. *li*, *le*; Rum. *i*, *le*. In contra-distinction to the singular, a tonic accusative plural persists in Old Fr. *els*, mod. *eux*, from ÍLLOS, which had a feminine counterpart *eles*, mod. *elles*. Spanish employs *ellos* and *ellas* as both nominative and tonic accusative.

The most noteworthy feature of the plural is the survival of the genitive ILLŌRUM. Its feminine ILLARUM disappeared in Vulgar Latin, leaving no trace, and, presumably on account of its distinctive form, ILLŌRUM as a pronoun came to be the invariable plural counterpart of the dative ILLUI, ILLAEI. Where these were adopted, ILLORUM has remained, cf. Fr. *leur*, Ital. *loro*, Rum. *lor*. In the modern languages there is some extension of the area of ILLORUM beyond that of ILLUI, as, for instance, in southern Italy, and in Cat. *llur*, Arag. *lur*, but these are probably of medieval diffusion. The earlier and more 'correct' Vulgar Latin of Spain and Sardinia, as is apparent from the dat. pls. *les* and *lis*, acknowledged in this function only the classical ILLIS. Elsewhere, ILLIS was either discarded or merged with other forms.

Sardinia alone, while using ILLE for atonic forms, has a parallel series of tonic forms derived from IPSE, viz.: masc. nom. *isse*, acc. *issu*; fem. nom. and acc. *issa*; pl. *issos*, *issas*; the form *issoru*, which is also found there, functions as a possessive rather than a personal pronoun.

Finally, it is to be noted that the medieval languages emerged with certain adverbs used pronominally. This usage must have had its origin in Vulgar Latin, where INDE and IBI came to replace in some measure the lost genitive and locative cases. Again, they appeared with proof of local fluctuation in the Latin accent. The west continued to place the accent on the first syllable, cf. Fr. *en* and *y*, Cat. *en* and *hi*, Old Span. *en* and *y*, whereas Ital. *ne* and *vi* show displacement on to the second syllable. Italian was later to supplement its system of personal pronouns by using *ci*, from ECCE HIC, and *vi*, as atonic accusative forms corresponding to *noi* and *voi* respectively. This, however, came about only in medieval times, as a curious analogical accident: the oldest Italian texts contain forms *ne* and *ve*, due to the influence of *me*, *te*, and *se* on atonic *no* and *vo*; through the correspondence of *me*, *te*, and *se* to *mi, ti,* and *si,* the plural *ve* then developed an alternative form *vi,* phonetically identical with the *vi* from IBI, which could be interpreted as '(you) there'; in consequence, *ci* replaced *no, ne, ni* as '(us) here'.

*Possessive pronouns.* The possessive pronouns of Classical Latin were as follows: MĔUS, TŬUS, SŬUS, NŎSTER, VĔSTER. Of these, VĔSTER has left no trace in Romance; all known derivatives come from VŎSTER, which was used by Plautus and is in fact attested in Latin at an earlier date than VĔSTER, this latter appearing to be a local development of the second century B.C. which popular speech did not generally favour (see F. Sommer, *Handbuch der lateinischen Laut- und Formenlehre,* 2nd and 3rd ed., pp. 414–15).

All of the possessive pronouns here listed were regularly declined, but in contrast to the personal pronouns they survived in Vulgar Latin only in a two-case declension, which, like that of nouns and adjectives, persisted in the medieval languages of France. A relic of the old vocative MI is perhaps to be found, combined with DŎMINUS, in the Prov. *midons*; used most frequently in courtly verse when the poet was speaking of a lady, this gave rise to an analogical *sidons* 'his lady'.

Innovation in Vulgar Latin, and consequent local divergence, is most obvious in the manner of expressing possession by the third person plural. The Iberian Peninsula continued to observe the archaic usage of Classical Latin, employing SUUS for the plural as well as for the singular, with the result that in modern Spanish it is impossible to tell, except from the context, whether *su cuadro* means 'his picture', 'her picture', 'its picture', or 'their picture'; in order to specify one must add the preposition *de* with a disjunctive personal pronoun, i.e. *su cuadro de él, de ella,* &c. In respect of number, though not of gender, this linguistic inconvenience was eliminated during Roman times by the inhabitants of a large part of the Empire. In those same regions where ILLŌRUM came to function as a dative plural personal pronoun, it was also employed as a third person plural possessive, both pronominal and adjectival (cf. Fr. *leur,* Ital. *loro,* Rum. *lor*). Generally, it remained invariable, though in medieval French it eventually received an analogical final *-s* to mark agreement with a plural substantive; it still has no feminine flexion. In Sardinia, *issoru,* from IPSŌRUM, was the form adopted.

Further differentiation occurred in the Vulgar Latin development of MĔUS, TŬUS, and SŬUS. In the first place, we may note that they were propagated in a double series, representing tonic and atonic forms of possessive. The contracted atonic series is attested early, as early in fact as the surviving fragments of Ennius (239–169 B.C.). It seems to have been at first confined to a third person form, possibly of different origin from that of the usual Latin possessives, which latter then provided a pattern for its completion. The grammarian Virgilius, who lived in Gaul during the sixth century A.D., bears witness to its currency: 'Sunt et alia pronomina quae in latinitate ussitate (*sic*) non habentur et tamen indubie recipiuntur ... ut *mus* ... *mum* ... *mi* ... *mos* ... *ma* ... *mas* ... et *tus* pro *tuus*.'[1] In Gaul this series was to survive in full: ultimately it provided the possessive adjectives of modern French, whereas the tonic form provided the possessive pronoun, though in medieval French there is no such clear distinction. To what extent the series was 'received' outside Gaul is, however, not entirely clear. It is found in Old Catalan, closely related to Provençal, but has disappeared from the modern language, apart from occasional dialectal usage. It was certainly present in the Vulgar Latin of northern Italy: such forms as *to amigo*, *so mario*, used as in French with no preceding definite article, are common enough in the Old Italian texts of that area; but it has been eliminated from modern standard Italian. There are traces of it in Old Portuguese, as also in Rumanian. In Spain, where the modern language currently employs an atonic series, e.g. *mi amigo*, *tu marido*, &c., it is less characteristic of the old language,[2] which uses adjectivally the tonic form, frequently preceded by the definite article. This is, of course, the normal practice of modern Portuguese, e.g. *o seu amigo*, of modern Catalan, e.g. *el seu amic*, and of modern Italian, e.g. *il suo amico*; a practice still usual in the dialects of northwestern Spain. The modern Spanish atonic forms would certainly appear from the quality of their vowels to be back-formations, developed no doubt in the first instance before a following vowel, from the Old Spanish tonic *mío*, *tuo*, and *suo* (the two latter since changed on the analogy of *cuyo* to *tuyo* and *suyo*). From all this one may conclude that the contracted forms did not everywhere meet with the same favourable reception as in Gaul, many areas

---

[1] *Virgilii Maronis grammatici Opera*, ed. I. Huemer, Leipzig, 1886, p. 47. This Virgilius seems to have lived in Toulouse, see E. Ernault, *De Virgilio Marone, grammatico tolosano*, Paris, 1886.

[2] Such forms do exist, cf. 'Pedir vos a poco por dexar so aver en salvo' (*Poema del Cid*, ed. Menéndez Pidal, l. 133).

preferring to adhere to the more emphatic forms of Classical Latin, even in the atonic position.

The evolution of the tonic forms shows a rift in the linguistic pattern, especially manifest in southern Gaul. There, TĔUS and SĔUS were current, created on the analogy of MĔUS, cf. Prov. *tieus, sieus*. These forms were also used south of the Pyrenees, cf. Cat. *teu* and *seu*, with analogical fem. *teva* and *seva* (the *v* represents a bilabial fricative), and gave rise to the mod. Port. *teu* and *seu*, which appeared in the old language side by side with *tou* and *sou*. The existence of a similar area of TĔUS and SĔUS in the dialects of southern Italy confirms that they are a Vulgar Latin development.

Elsewhere, MĔUS, TŬUS, and SŬUS were generally preserved, but with variation in the quality of the stressed vowels. In northern France, despite the maintenance of a two-case declension, the nominative MĔUS appears only in the *Strassburg Oaths*, as *meos*, but there must have existed at least in the Picard area a form *\*mieus*, with a normally diphthongized vowel, for only the analogy of such a form could account for the usual Picard feminine *mieue, miue*. The diphthong which one would expect is present in the accusative *mien*, eventually to be the analogue of all modern forms; but the Old Fr. fem. *meie, moie*, shows a vocalic evolution which presupposes a Vulgar Latin closing of the stressed vowel of MĔA. The stressed vowel of TŬUM and SŬUM must, on the other hand, have been shifted to the half-open position in the Vulgar Latin which produced Old Fr. *tuen* and *suen*, a development also to be found in the Ital. *tuoi, suoi*, where a diphthong presumably common at first to all forms is preserved before the *i* of the plural. The feminines TŬA and SŬA, however, show in Old French a perfectly normal evolution to *toue* and *soue*. Old Spanish, like Sardinian, kept in this instance the close quality of the vowels used in Classical Latin. The vocalic contrast between the first person and the other two also remains in Rum. *meu (mieu)*, fem. *mea, tău*, fem. *ta, său*, fem. *sa*, though how TŬUM and SŬUM became *tău* and *său* is somewhat obscure.

In the development of the plural possessives NŌSTER and VŌSTER the principal area of divergence is for once the Iberian Peninsula. Whereas these forms were generally maintained in both the tonic and atonic positions in the Vulgar Latin of other regions, here there was a rival type *\*NOSSU(M)* and *\*VOSSU(M)*, created on NOS and VOS; this type survives in Port. *nosso* and *vosso*, and it appeared in Old Span. *nuesso* and *vuesso*, existing side by side with the *nuestro* and *vuestro* which afterwards prevailed. Perhaps one may see in these forms the origin of the Picard *nos* and *vos*, with *no* and *vo*, due to back-formation. The *noz* of Old French, mod. *nos*, must, however, be an atonic evolution of *nostres* from NOSTROS.

*Demonstrative pronouns.* In this category Classical Latin was particularly well endowed. In order to point out something near the speaker, i.e. corresponding to the first person, it employed HIC, HAEC, HOC; to point out something near the person spoken to, i.e. corresponding to the second person: ISTE, ISTA, ISTUD; and for something more remote, i.e. corresponding to the third person: ILLE, ILLA, ILLUD. Used in all the above circumstances, but with reference to something previously mentioned, it had IS, EA, ID; and formed upon this, to convey identity: IDEM, EADEM, IDEM. It could specify self by means of IPSE, IPSA, IPSUM, and to do so more emphatically it could have recourse to the superlative IPSISSIMUS. All these forms were, of course, fully declined.

That some of these demonstratives were rejected in popular speech, and the precise shades of meaning in some instances confused, is no more than we should expect. IDEM, &c., vanished without trace; so too did IS, EA, ID, except that a relic of the neuter persists in Ital. *desso*, from the compound ID IPSUM. But whatever changes took place, Vulgar Latin nevertheless remained very rich in demonstratives. To point out is indeed one of the primary psychological requirements for which a spoken language must make special provision. Often the speaker wishes to point out emphatically, and this need for emphasis led to the creation of various compounds, like the ID IPSUM mentioned above, in which two originally different demonstrative elements were linked together. The phenomenon may be observed in the 'this here' and 'that there' of popular English, and similarly in modern French, in popular constructions with *voilà*, e.g. 'une femme comme voilà l'Adèle'; 'comme voilà ceux qu'on voit dans les églises'. Retaining many of the old words, and creating new ones, Vulgar Latin evolved a store of demonstratives even more plentiful than that of the classical standard, and one within which local selection and differentiation must have begun very early.

Of those demonstratives which remained in an uncompounded form, the neuter HOC enjoyed special favour in Gaul. There alone, in contrast to the SIC used elsewhere, HOC was adopted as the affirmative particle, whence the terms *langue d'oc* and *langue d'oïl*; the latter, it is true, is an example of compounding, but one in which it would appear that an originally independent *o* was added to an *il* functioning as the personal pronoun, for *o je* and *o tu* were also used. It is commonly found in early French texts, e.g. *in o quid* (*Strassburg Oaths*), *por o* (*Cantilène de sainte Eulalie*), and in further conjunction with prepositions it gave rise to Old Fr. *senuec* < SINE HOC, *poruec* < PRO HOC, and *avuec*, mod. *avec* < AB HOC (or possibly < APUD HOC). In Provençal it is still *o* or *oc*. Elsewhere, it does not normally occur alone, though Italy shared with Gaul the compound ECCE HOC, cf. Ital. *ciò*, Cat. *això*, Old Prov. *czo*, Old Fr. *iço, ço*, whence modern *ce*. PER HOC was common to Italy and Spain, cf. Ital. *però*, Span. *pero*.

Other relics of this pronoun were preserved in ECCE HIC, cf. Fr. *ici*, Ital. *ci*, and its variants ECCU HIC, cf. Ital. *qui* and *ACCU HIC, cf. Span. *aquí*; likewise in ECCE HAC, cf. Fr. *ça*, ECCU HAC, cf. Ital. *qua*, and *ACCU HAC, cf. Span. *acá*; and also in certain phrases of time such as HAC NOCTE, cf. Old Fr. *anuit*, Span. *anoche*, HANC HORAM, cf. Fr. *encore*, Ital. *ancora*, and HOC ANNO, cf. Old Fr. *ouan*, Span. *ogaño*, Old Ital. *uguanno*.

ĬSTE, in its uncompounded form, was probably less common in northern Gaul than elsewhere. That it did not entirely disappear is shown by occasional usage in the earliest Old French texts, e.g. *d ist di in avant* (*Strassburg Oaths*), *mi parent d este terre* (*Vie de saint Alexis*), but in general favour it soon fell victim to the compound ECCE ĬSTE. Its ultimate fate in Provençal (*est, esta*) and in Old Italian was similar, the whole Italo-Gallic area showing again in this respect a certain conformity of evolution. But in the Iberian Peninsula ĬSTE continued to be fully functional, cf. Span. *este, esta, esto*, Port. *este, esta, isto*, as also in the east (Rum. *ăst, asta*, &c.).

Meanwhile ĬLLE, used adjectivally, became everywhere specialized in its new function of definite article, an attenuation of its former demonstrative role due to that over-use so well attested in the *Peregrinatio ad loca sancta*. In some areas IPSE tended to follow the same course, appearing as a rival form of definite article. Medieval Latin texts of the seventh and eighth centuries, even those of northern France, show IPSE and ILLE both used in this way, with no apparent difference of meaning; but medieval Latin had by then become so stereotyped that one cannot draw from this fact the inference that local choice in popular parlance had not already been made. Sardinia preferred IPSE, as appears from Log. (*i*)*ssu*, *-a*, *-os*, *-as*; in parts of southern France and Catalonia the rivalry persisted until the time of vernacular literature, a fact which is reflected in the retention of derivatives of IPSE as definite article in the present-day Catalan dialect of Majorca, as masc. sing. and pl. *es*, fem. *sa*, *ses*, forms which also survive in two small and once isolated areas of the Costa Brava, one around Rosas and Cadaqués, the other around Palamós and San Feliu de Guíxols.

In general, ILLE prevailed, but with fluctuations of accent as in the derivatives of IPSE quoted above. The inhabitants of Gaul, when using ILLE as definite article, consistently placed the accent on the second syllable; hence the Old French declension:

|  | Singular | Plural |
|---|---|---|
| Masc. Nom. | *li* | *li* |
| Masc. Acc. | *lo, le* | *les* |
| Fem. | *la* | *les* |

Here the only peculiarity is in the masc. nom. sing. *li*, which, like the personal *il*, must derive from an \*ĪLLĪ, influenced by QUĪ. Provençal forms reveal the same Vulgar Latin accentuation; the alternative masculine nominative singulars, *le* and *lo*, appear to come directly from ILLE and an analogical ILLUM:

|  | Singular | Plural |
|---|---|---|
| Masc. Nom. | *le, lo* | *li* |
| Masc. Acc. | *lo* | *los* |
| Fem. | *la* | *las* |

This type of accentuation extended over the Pyrenees into Aragon and Navarre, and into the north-west of the Iberian Peninsula, whence it gave rise to mod. Port. *o*, *os*, *a*, *as*. On the other hand, the wide area of accentuation in all forms on the second syllable is broken by the intervening or adjacent territories which became Gascony and Castile. The latter, like central Italy, preferred to accentuate the masculine nominative singular on the first syllable, cf. Span. *el*, *los*, *la*, *las*, and Ital. *il* (*lo*), *i* (*gli*), *la*, *le*. In southern parts of Gascony, particularly in the Bearnese *Vallée d'Aspe*, there remain forms accentuated throughout on the first syllable: masc. *et* or *etch*, pl. *es* or *ets*, fem. *era*, pl. *eras*, *eres* (in this region Latin LL regularly becomes *t* or *tch* when final, *r* when intervocalic). No other part of Romania, to our knowledge, has been so faithful in this respect to the classical tradition.

Rumania also derives its article from ILLE, with the accent on the second syllable, but—and this has created what is perhaps the most striking difference between Rumanian and other Romance languages—the article is there agglutinated to the end of the word. Albanian and Bulgarian share this feature, a fact which has led scholars to suppose that the Rumanian phenomenon is due to their influence; but in Latin the word-order DŎMINUM ILLUM was no less acceptable than ILLUM DŎMINUM. Thus the more obvious inference is that in the Vulgar Latin of the east an early choice was made between these two alternative Latin possibilities, a choice which may well have been determined by the linguistic structure of a pre-Romance, probably Illyrian, substratum. A further peculiarity of Rumanian is that it has retained ILLE as definite article with those same case-endings of Vulgar Latin which in the west have survived only when ILLE was used as personal pronoun. The effect of the agglutinated article was thus to produce declensions, as follows:

|               | Masculine |          | Feminine |          |
|---------------|-----------|----------|----------|----------|
|               | Singular  | Plural   | Singular | Plural   |
| Nom. and Acc. | *domnul*  | *domnii* | *casa*   | *casele* |
| Gen. and Dat. | *domnului*| *domnilor*| *casei* | *caselor*|

Similar endings were extended by analogy to the indefinite article, viz. *unui*, *unei*, though this precedes the noun as in the west.

With the development of its new function, ILLE was almost eliminated as an active demonstrative. A few traces of its former usage still linger in Old French, in such expressions as *le jor*, meaning 'that day', and one similar relic, *de la sorte*, has even persisted into Modern French. But in general it made way already in Vulgar Latin for more full-bodied successors. In those areas where it was not similarly compromised, IPSE found a new lease of life as a pure demonstrative, losing its meaning of 'self' to compounds of which it is a part (see below, *METIPSE). In the Iberian Peninsula, after the loss of HIC, HAEC, HOC, the forms of ISTE moved up one, so to speak, to take over the function of demonstratives corresponding to the first person, and IPSE was brought in to fill the gap, as demonstrative corresponding to the second person, cf. Span. *ese*, *esos*, *esa*, *esas*, neut. *eso*; Port. *esse*, *esses*, *essa*, *essas*, neut. *isso*. It occurs in Provençal as *eis* or *eps* (in the oldest texts), fem.

*eissa*, *epsa*, and has survived into modern Italian, though with less fortune than rival demonstratives, being employed only in the singular, *esso*, *essa*, and having changed its function to that of an alternative form of personal pronoun. The relics of IPSE in Old French usually show it in conjunction with ILLE, e.g. *en es le pas* (< IN IPSUM ILLUM PASSUM, cf. p. 251), *en es l'eure*, and in the work of the Anglo-Norman Philippe de Thaün one may read: *par esse la chariere*. Its Vulgar Latin use as a demonstrative is also apparent in certain compounds with a negative or a preposition, to which the Romance languages bear witness, e.g. NE IPSE, cf. Old Fr. *neës*, NE *IPSĪ, cf. Old Fr. *neïs*, and the same combinations with UNUS, cf. Old Fr. *nesuns*, *nisuns*, Ital. *nessuno*, also ANTE IPSUM, cf. Old Fr. *ançois*.

As we have indicated, any weakening or loss of uncompounded demonstratives in Vulgar Latin was more than made good by a proliferation of compounded forms. In addition to ID IPSUM, and the IPSUM ILLUM mentioned above, both ILLUM IPSUM and ISTUM IPSUM were current. The latter, well and early attested in Latin, as when Cicero wrote *ista ipsa lege*, was particularly favoured in Italy, where it still survives as *stesso*, *stessa*, the sense of 'self, self-same' having here predominated. The former is associated with Rhetia and Spain: it is found in the tenth-century Navarrese–Castilian *Glosas Emilianenses* and *Glosas Silenses* (see p. 405), which contain respectively the glosses *tu eleisco jes* and *per sibi eleiso*, and also in Old Catalan as *elex*, but thereafter it disappeared. IPSUM ILLUM, as well as in Gaul, appears in the east, cf. Arum. *usul*. These rather clumsy compounds were, however, all outdone in popularity by combinations formed with the Latin interjection ECCE, already so abundantly attested in the work of Plautus (see p. 21).

ECCE has indeed a most remarkable history in Romance. In Gaul it survived separately, and being understood in Old French as a form of imperative, e.g. *es le vos*, it even came to have an analogical plural, as in *estes le vos*. It appears in Catalan as *eis*, in Old Spanish as *ex*. In the form ECCUM, an early compound of ECCE and *HOM, this latter being the accusative pronoun found in HUNC (< *HOMCE), it persists as Ital. *ecco*. It combined with HIC, HAC, and HOC (see above, p. 87); in Portugal, Catalonia, Sardinia, Sicily, and southern Italy with ĬPSE; and everywhere in Romania with ĬSTE and ĬLLE, wherein lies the origin of many of the demonstratives of the Romance languages, including those of modern French.

Scrutiny of these languages as they emerged compels us to make a distinction in the forms in which ECCE was adopted, a distinction which once again points to regional differentiation within the period of Vulgar Latin. Gaul seems to have been almost alone in preferring ECCE in its classical form, a choice which must be assumed from the fact that Gallic developments all show palatalization of the C, which occurred only before a front vowel. A similar palatalization is found in Ital. *ciò* and *ci*, compounds of ECCE with HOC and HIC, but in other Italian compounds there is no such palatalization: *questo* and *quello* require derivation from ECCU ISTUM and ECCU ILLUM. The currency of ECCU in the Italian area is amply confirmed by Old Sardinian, which possesses a complete series in which the U of ECCU predominated, with the following results: ECCU ISTE >*ecuste, icuste, custe*; ECCU IPSE > *ecusse, icusse, cusse*; ECCU ILLUM > *icullu, cullu*, mod. *kuḍḍu* (M. L. Wagner, op. cit., p. 330). Forms similar to these exist in Apulia, though most of southern Italy and Sicily has preserved the I-vowel, e.g. mod. Sicil. *chistu, chissu*, and *chiḍḍu* (G. Rohlfs, op. cit., vol. ii, p. 246). Yet a third type, *ACCU, must be postulated in order to explain the derivatives found in Spanish and Provençal, and also in Rumanian. Though unattested in Latin, this type must have been an early alternative, as appears from its distribution in the extreme east and the extreme west: it probably evolved from a fusion with ECCU of a common conjunction, either AC or ATQUE.

In the west, it is Provençal which preserves most fully the progeny of *ACCU. Here, almost alone, is *ACCU HOC, as *aco, aquo*. Here is the complete two-case series from *ACCU ISTE and *ACCU ILLE. But also within the Provençal area are the derivatives of ECCE ISTE and ECCE ILLE, as in northern France, with the result that Old Provençal texts appear with a plethora of demonstratives, which may be summarized as follows:

From ECCE ISTE:

| | Masculine | | Feminine | |
|---|---|---|---|---|
| | Singular | Plural | Singular | Plural |
| Nom. | *cest* | *cist* | *cesta* | *cestas* |
| Acc. | *cest* | *cestz* | *cesta* | *cestas* |

From ECCE ILLE:

| | Masculine | | Feminine | |
|---|---|---|---|---|
| | Singular | Plural | Singular | Plural |
| Nom. | *cel (celh)* | *cil (cilh)* | *cela* | *celas* |
| Acc. | *cel* | *cels* | *cela* | *celas* |

From *ACCU ISTE:

| | | | | |
|---|---|---|---|---|
| Nom. | *aquest* | *aquist* | *aquesta* | *aquestas* |
| Acc. | *aquest* | *aquestz* | *aquesta* | *aquestas* |

From *ACCU ILLE:

| | | | | |
|---|---|---|---|---|
| Nom. | *aquel (aquelh)* | *aquil (aquilh)* | *aquela* | *aquelas* |
| Acc. | *aquel* | *aquels* | *aquela* | *aquelas* |

NOTE. Forms *cist, cilh, aquist, aquilh*, due to *Umlaut* caused by the final ī of V. Lat. *ĬSTĪ, *ĬLLĪ, are occasionally found in the nominative singular, used both as masculine and feminine.

Provence thus appears as the meeting-ground of the two different types. To the south, only *ACCU is to be met with, as it appears in Span. *aquel, aquella*, &c. Old Spanish also used *aqueste*, e.g. 'Conpeçaremos aquesta lid campal' (*Poema del Cid*, l. 1111), but this disappeared in face of the Castilian maintenance of un-compounded ĬSTE. Both Portuguese and Catalan, however, have preserved *ACCU ĬSTE, *ACCU ĬPSE, and *ACCU ĬLLE, cf. Port. *aqueste, aquesse, aquele*, Cat. *aquest, aqueix, aquell*.

To the north, Old French emerged with declensions proceeding from ECCE *ĬSTĪ, ECCE *ĬLLĪ, &c., characterized by dative singulars similar to those of the uncompounded *ĬLLĪ used as a personal pronoun. There also exist plural forms in *-or*, but since these are late and of rare occurrence it seems probable that they were created on the analogy of *lor*; it would be hazardous to postulate a survival of *ECCE ISTORUM and *ECCE ILLORUM. The Old French paradigms are as follows:

From ECCE *ĬSTĪ:

| | Masculine | | Feminine | |
|---|---|---|---|---|
| | Singular | Plural | Singular | Plural |
| Nom. | *icist* | *icist* | *iceste* | *icestes (icez)* |
| Acc. | *icest* | *icez* | *iceste* | *icestes (icez)* |
| Dat. | *icesti, icestui* | *(icestor)* | *icestei, icesti* | *(icestor)* |

Neuter
*icest*

From ECCE *ĬLLĪ:

| | Masculine | | Feminine | |
|---|---|---|---|---|
| | Singular | Plural | Singular | Plural |
| Nom. | *icil* | *icil* | *icele* | *iceles* |
| Acc. | *icel* | *icels* | *icele* | *iceles* |
| Dat. | *iceli, icelui* | *(icelor)* | *icelei, iceli* | *(icelor)* |

Neuter
*icel*

In the east, the corresponding forms of modern Rumanian show a close morphological affinity with those of Old French. As usually classified, they are:

From *ACC'ISTE:

|  | Masculine | | Feminine | |
| --- | --- | --- | --- | --- |
|  | Singular | Plural | Singular | Plural |
| Nom. Acc. | *acest* | *acești* | *aceasta* | *aceste* |
| Gen. Dat. | *acestui* | *acestor* | *acestei* | *acestor* |

From *ACC'ILLE:

|  | Singular | Plural | Singular | Plural |
| --- | --- | --- | --- | --- |
| Nom. Acc. | *acel* | *acei* | *acea* | *acele* |
| Gen. Dat. | *acelui* | *acelor* | *acelei* | *acelor* |

The supposition of *ACCU as the first element in these forms seems usually to be taken for granted. Unlike Spanish, however, Rumanian shows palatalization of the c, to the affricate tʃ; it is therefore difficult to postulate more than *ACC', which might have been abbreviated in the Vulgar Latin of the east from either *ACCU or *ACCE. A further point of interest concerning the east lies in the linking there of ALTER with demonstrative pronouns, as in the west it became linked with personal pronouns. With the definite article also entering into the combination, this gave rise to a new series of Rumanian demonstratives, masc. *acestlalt*, *acestuilalt*, &c., fem. *aceastălaltă*, *acesteilalte*, &c.

Within the Vulgar Latin of Italy there evolved a local peculiarity consequent upon the insertion of an ethic dative between ECCU and ISTU: the resultant *ECCU-TI(BI)-ISTU emerged in medieval Italian texts as *cotesto* or *codesto*. Standard Italian came in this way to possess a series of three demonstratives: *questo*, *codesto*, and *quello*. It will be recalled that Sardinian and the languages of the Spanish Peninsula likewise possess a series of three. Despite the diverse origin of all these forms, and the Vulgar Latin confusion which such diversity implies, the series of three continues to correspond to the same psychological conception of position, with reference to the three grammatical persons, upon which we remarked in distinguishing between the usage of Classical Latin HIC, ISTE, and ILLE. So true to the fundamental outlook of Latin have the southern Romance languages remained. In Old French, on the other hand, when in the ninth century it first appeared, the threefold conception had vanished in favour of the twofold 'this here and that there' conception familiar to us in the Germanic languages. One inclines to wonder whether the absence of a middle term in Old French may not be due to a concealed influence of Frankish; yet Rumanian, almost entirely free from Germanic contact, also has the twofold conception.

Syntactically, the dual function of the demonstratives as both adjective and pronoun has been maintained in both Spain and Italy. That this duality was not compromised in the Vulgar Latin of Gaul is apparent from the fact that it is also characteristic of Old French. The distinction made in modern French, where the derivatives of ECCE ISTE are adjectives, while those of ECCE ILLE are pronouns, a change of function which motivated the appending of *ici* and *là* to mark the former difference between proximity and remoteness respectively, dates only from the end of the Middle Ages.

Within the range of demonstrative concept we may finally include the expression of identity, the words for 'same, self-same'. As we have seen, IDEM disappeared, and IPSE uncompounded assumed rather different functions. In their place there came into use forms in which IPSE was reinforced by the MET of the Latin EGOMET IPSE, ILLEMET IPSE, &c.; a form *METĬPSE, and a still further reinforced *METĬPSIMUM, in which the second element is a contraction of the superlative IPSISSIMUM. Such are the etyma which must be postulated in order to account for almost all the words for 'same' which are current in Romance, except in the east, and other than the Ital. *stesso* (see above, p. 90). Once again geographical areas of preference appear. *METĬPSE belonged especially to southern Gaul: hence Prov. *mezeis, mezeissa* (intervocalic -T- in Provençal > -d- > -z-), and mod. Gascon *madech*. A type *METTĬPSE, with a lengthened T, seems to be a necessary postulation in order that we may explain the alternative Provençal form *mateis*, and mod. Cat. *mateix*. Elsewhere *METIPSIMUM predominated, but again in two forms, this time with a vocalic alternation. The tonic *e* which would normally derive from the Ĭ of ĬPSE appears in Ital. *medesimo*, in Old Fr. *meësme*, whence mod. *même*, in a Prov. *medesme* which may have been an early borrowing from the north, and also in Port. and Old Span. *mesmo*. Both Old French and Old Spanish, however, with *meïsme* and *meísmo* respectively, show concurrent forms with a tonic *i*; these are probably due to a Vulgar Latin original type into which had been incorporated an *ĬPSĪ, influenced by QUĪ, comparable, that is, with *ĬLLĪ and *ĬSTĪ. In modern Spanish it is this form which, as *mismo*, has remained.

*Relative and interrogative pronouns.* Classical Latin possessed two series for relatives and interrogatives, identical except in the first two cases of the singular, which declined as follows:

Relative:

|  | Masculine | Feminine | Neuter |
|---|---|---|---|
| Nom. | QUĪ | QUAE | QUŎD |
| Acc. | QUEM | QUAM | QUŎD |

Interrogative:

|  | Masculine | Feminine | Neuter |
|---|---|---|---|
| Nom. | QUIS | QUAE, (QUIS) | QUĬD |
| Acc. | QUEM | QUAM | QUĬD |

These seem predestined to confusion, and in fact the earliest authors frequently used QUI for QUIS, while QUOD was gradually ousted by QUID. In the single series which then remained, further reduction came about through the extension of the masculine forms to include the feminine. Inscriptions of the third and fourth centuries bear ample witness to this change, e.g. FILIA QUEM RELIQUIT (*CIL* v. 5933). The nominative plural QUI was identical in form with the singular: this doubtless provided the psychological motive for the general elimination of QUOS. Thus towards the end of the Empire there remained in Vulgar Latin, as nominative and accusative, only the following:

| Nom. Masc. and Fem. | QUĪ | Neut. QUĬD (> QUED) |
|---|---|---|
| Acc. Masc. and Fem. | QUĒM | |

The survival of these three forms is fully confirmed by Romance, except that there is no trace of QUĪ in the east. In the west QUĪ appears as Fr. *qui*, Ital. *chi*, and Old Span. *qui*, the last of which yielded to *que* in the fourteenth century. QUEM and QUĬD are the only Latin forms which were preserved everywhere in Romania. In atonic usage they merged in the medieval languages of the west, cf. Fr. and Span. *que*, Ital. *che*, but Rumanian preserves the distinction with *ce* from QUID, and *cine* from QUEM; the latter probably owes its final *e* to the analogy of MENE, TENE, SENE (see p. 79). That a similar distinction formerly existed in the Vulgar Latin of the west is proved by the fact that QUID emerged in the earliest Old French texts as *qued*, and by the existence of tonic forms of both QUID and QUEM. Here, however, there is a local difference: Old French appeared with a tonic neuter *quei, quoi*, from QUID, whereas Sardinia and the Iberian Peninsula show a tonic masculine from QUEM, cf. Sard. *chen*, Span. *quien*, Port. *quem*.

Two other cases of the relative and interrogative survived in Vulgar Latin: the genitive CŪIŬS and the dative CUĪ. Here again there was a local difference of choice. Sardinia and the Iberian Peninsula kept CŪIŬS, cf. Sard. *cuiu*, Span. *cuyo*, Port. *cujo*, all with the normal flexions for gender and number.[1] The rest of Romania rejected CŪIŬS but preserved CUĪ, cf. Old Fr. *cui*, Ital. *cui*, Rum. *cui*. This *cui* persists in French, though now identical in form with the nominative *qui*. It was adapted to serve as tonic corresponding to masculine and feminine *que* from QUEM, just as *quoi* served as tonic to the neuter *que* from QUĪD. It occurs after prepositions, e.g. *avec qui*, cf. Ital. *con cui*, and being a strong form of oblique case it was also used in interrogative sentences, e.g. *Qui voyez-vous?* In this way there developed in French, in the accusative, a new distinction between relative and interrogative forms.

As we know from English, the relative pronoun may often be entirely dispensed with in the spoken sentence. Therein, perhaps, lies the explanation for the disappearance of so many of its forms in the popular speech of the Roman Empire. But occasions do arise when it must be used and emphasized. This need, partially satisfied by means of the tonic forms mentioned above, also provoked an extended use of QUALIS. In the east, QUALIS was adopted to make good the loss of QUI, giving rise to the pronominal *care* of Rumanian, e.g. *Care începe multe* . . . 'He who begins many things . . .' It came there to have a new analogical declension, viz., dat. *cărui, cărei*, pl. *cari, căror*. This particular requirement is met in the modern Romance languages of the west by a demonstrative or personal pronoun placed before the relative, e.g. Fr. *celui qui*, Span. *él que*. But ILLE QUALIS (QUALE) has also been pressed into service in the west, when greater precision was sought (cf. Fr. *lequel*, Span. *el cual*, Ital. *il quale*. The fortunes of this combination are usually attributed to the favour which it enjoyed with medieval notaries, but before it became embedded in medieval Latin it must have gained currency as a creation of popular speech. In an adjectival function, QUALIS has persisted everywhere.

---

[1] This use of CŪIŬS, i.e. as an inflected possessive adjective, is attested in the work of early Latin writers, chiefly Plautus and Terence. Thereafter it became rare and was probably considered to be rustic. Virgil uses it interrogatively once in the Eclogues: 'Dic mihi, Damoeta, cuium pecus?'

Gascony and Catalonia have an unusual form believed to derive from the Lat. QUI(S)NAM. The QUINA of Vulgar Latin, being taken as a feminine, gave rise to an analogical masculine, whence the modern forms, common to both areas, masc. *quin*, fem. *quina*. In Catalonia these are used adjectivally, in questions or exclamations, e.g. *Quina hora és? Quin dia!*, but in Gascony they are also used pronominally, e.g. *Quin disét?* 'What do you say?' There are in addition alternative Gascon forms *quinh*, *quinha*, which suggest a V. Lat. *QUINIA, due perhaps to the analogy of QUISPIAM and QUONIAM. It may be on account of the influence of these much-used forms that in Gascony, contrarily to what happened in Castile, the relative *qui* has tended to oust *que* as accusative, e.g. *so qui bouy croumpà* 'that which I wish to buy'.

French alone has diverted an adverb *dont*, from DE UNDE, to serve as a genitive of the relative pronoun, thereby making good the loss of CŪIŬS.

*Indefinite pronouns and adjectives.* Under this heading it is customary to assemble a miscellaneous collection of words conveying such notions as 'other', 'each', 'all', 'certain', 'some', 'none', &c. Most of them function, in identical or kindred form, both as pronoun and as adjective. The repertoire is plentiful in Classical Latin and it continued to be so, though with various modifications, in late Vulgar Latin. Of those encountered in Latin texts, some vanished without trace, e.g. UTER, QUIDAM, QUISPIAM, &c.; others survived partially, or in an altered form; a few, e.g. ALTER, persisted almost unchanged.

In the classical language ALTER meant 'other of two', ALIUS 'other of many', and CETERUS was 'other' in the sense of 'that left over, the remainder'. Vulgar Latin required no such fine distinctions: CETERUS disappeared, and so too did ALIUS, apart from a relic of the neuter ALIUD, which was reduced to ALID (attested with masculine ALIS in inscriptions and in the work of Lucretius, see F. Sommer, op. cit., p. 442), to become eventually Old Fr. *el*, Old Span. Prov. and Port. *al*, 'something else', or used adverbially, 'otherwise'. The field was thus left free for ALTER, cf. Fr. *autre*, Span. *otro*, Ital. *altro*, Rum. *alt*. A Vulgar Latin form ALTERI, probably a nominative masculine singular due to the analogy of QUI, must have developed in southern areas to give Old Span. *otri*, Old Port. *outri*, and Ital. *altri*; there is no trace of this in northern Gaul, where ALTER became Old Fr. *altre*, at first

without flexional *s*. Gaul and Italy, however, shared a dative AL-
TERUI, due to the analogy of CUI, cf. Fr. *autrui*, Ital. *altrui*. An adjec-
tive ALIENUS, originally formed on ALIUS, persisted in the Iberian
Peninsula, cf. Span. *ajeno*, Port. *alheio*, Old Cat. *allè*, and also in
Sardinia, cf. Log. *andzenu*, Campidanese *allenu*.

QUISQUE, the usual Latin word for 'each', has left a trace in
Sardinia, in Old Log. *kis*, but otherwise it survived uncompounded
only in southern Gaul, appearing in Provençal texts as masc.
*quecs*, *quec*, fem. *quega*, *quegas*. Lat. UNUSQUISQUE occurs in the
same regions, cf. Old Log. *uniskis*, *unukis*; Prov. masc. *usquecs*,
fem. *unaquega*. The more common practice of Vulgar Latin was,
however, to reverse the two elements of this compound form,
making QUISQUE UNUS. This appears in Gascon texts as *quiscun*,
together with QUISQUE ET UNUS, as *quisquedun*. The Old Ital.
*cescheduno* suggests a Vulgar Latin type in which consonantal dissimilation had taken place, giving *CISQUE ET UNUS, cf. CINQUE
for QUINQUE, p. 73. The fourth century, however, witnessed the
propagation of a quite different term with the same meaning,
viz. CATA UNUS; this embodies a borrowing from Greek, the prep.
κατά, with distributive sense. Used adjectivally, CATA is frequently
attested in Christian Latin, e.g. *Et faciet sacrificium super eo cata
mane* . . . (Vulgate), *semper cata Pasca* . . . (Peregrinatio ad loca
sancta), *ut cata mansiones monasteria sint* (ibid.). Whether it owed
its popular currency to Greek influence in the language of religion,
or to the jargon of the market-place, is not easy to decide; one
imagines it as pertaining rather to the latter, where in combination
with numbers it would have afforded convenient substitutes for
the awkward Latin distributives (see above, p. 77). In the west
CATA was commonly linked with UNUS, thus giving a pronoun;
from CATA UNUM, to quote the more usual accusative form, derive
Old Fr. *chaün*; Old Ital. *catuno*, *caduno*; Prov. *cadaün*, *cadun*;
Span. *cada uno*; Port. *cada um*. The invariable *cada*, common
enough in Old Provençal, e.g. *cada jorn*, *cada nuech*, and still
universally employed as an adjective in Spain, seems more probably, at least in the latter territory, to be a medieval back-formation
from the pronominal expression. Inevitably, CATA UNUS and QUIS-
QUE (ET) UNUS became involved with one another. Thus we may
read in the *Poema del Cid*:

> Quis cada uno dellos bien sabe lo que ha de far.
>
> (Ed. Menéndez Pidal, l. 1136)

Modern Gascon has a similar form *quiscadû* (S. Palay, *Dict. du béarnais et du gascon modernes*); the maintenance of *i* in these forms is doubtless not learned but due to the influence of QUĪ. A more complete blending of the two types appears in Old Span. *cadascuno, cascuno,* and similarly in Old Fr. *chascun,* whence the mod. *chacun,* from which French eventually derived by back-formation the adjectival *chaque.* The mod. Ital. *ciascuno* is frequently described, on account of its initial affricate, as a borrowing from French, an explanation which should presumably be held to include, for the same reason, the Old Ital. *ciascheduno*; but the very existence of this latter makes it seem more probable that both are in reality the product of a native mixture of CATA UNUS with *CISQUE (ET) UNUS.

Three words were used in Latin to convey the meaning 'all': TŌTUS 'the whole', OMNIS 'every one', and CUNCTI 'all together'. Of these, CUNCTI disappeared, and TŌTUS prospered at the expense of OMNIS. Though there are traces of the latter in Provençal, where it became involved in homonymic clash with derivatives of HOMO, HOMINEM—which suggests, by the way, a good reason for its failure to be established elsewhere—only in Italy did it have any lasting Romance descendance. There, OMNE and OMNIA produced Old Ital. *onne* and *ogna* respectively; that OMNIS should have become *ogni* with palatalized *n,* the single form which survives in the modern standard language, may well be due to the influence of OMNIA > *ogna,* though the group of *n* plus yod which creates the palatalized consonant could also occur wherever OMNI(S) was followed by a vowel, as in the mod. *ognuno, ogn'uomo, ognora* (< OMNI HORA). TŌTUS, on the other hand, was universally accepted, but with local differentiation. Only the *todo* of Spanish and Portuguese can derive in direct phonological tradition from the classical type. Most other forms, e.g. Fr. *tout,* Prov. *tot,* Rum. *tot,* presuppose *TOTTUS, with lengthened T, while Ital. *tutto* corresponds to *TŪTTUS (this appears as *tutti* in the eighth-century Kassel Glossary, see p. 317). A similar *TUTTI, of which the final vowel became a yod in such combinations as *TUTTI ILLI, *TUTTI HOMINES, seems to have been known in Gaul, since this wouln provide the more obvious explanation for the anomalous masc. nom. pl. *tuit* of Old French, *tuch* in Provençal.

In order to specify 'a certain (thing or person)' Classical Latin usually had recourse to QUIDAM, which in the popular speech was entirely rejected. As we have seen, UNUS could be used in the same way, but this was not strong enough to serve as a complete replacement for QUIDAM. Another alternative did, however, exist in Latin: CERTUS, as sometimes employed by Cicero, e.g. *insolentia certorum hominum*. This CERTUS was retained in Italy and the Iberian Peninsula, cf. Ital. *certo*, Span. *cierto*, Port. *certo*, but Gaul preferred in general a derivative *CERTANUS, cf. Fr. *certain*. As so often, southern Gaul appears as the meeting-place of two different currents, Provençal having both *cert* and *certà*, as does also Catalan. Italy seems to have been alone in attaching CERTUS to UNUS, as in *certuno*.

For 'some, somebody' Latin used ALIQUIS, which has disappeared except in the neuter.[1] Here Latin had two forms, a pronominal ALIQUĬD and an adjectival ALIQUOD. Span. and Port. *algo* clearly represent the latter, but Old Fr. and Prov. *alque(s)* could be derived from either: the fact that QUĬD alone survived in Gaul, in preference to QUOD, tends to suggest that the real basis there is ALIQUĬD. In Italy, all trace of this word, in an uncompounded form, has vanished. The propensity of the Vulgar Latin of Italy to combine these words, in an adjectival form, with UNUS, there created in its stead, from ALIQUIS UNUS, a form *ALICUNUS, cf. Ital. *alcuno*, which then spread to all the western Empire, cf. Fr. *aucun*, Cat. *algú*, Span. *alguno*, Port. *algum*. In Old French, since the meaning 'something' was expressed by *aucune chose*, the originally pronominal *alques*, *auques* came to be used largely as an adverb, whence its analogical 'adverbial *s*'. The modern negative sense of *aucun* is, of course, a recent development confined to French.

Among all these indefinite pronouns and adjectives it is the negatives which produced, already in Vulgar Latin, the most bewildering variety. The classical language was in this instance quite precise: 'nobody' was NEMO, and 'nothing' was NIHIL. Of these, NIHIL vanished entirely (it has been suggested as the origin of the

[1] It is commonly stated that the masc. ALIQUEM survives in Span. *alguien*, Port. *alguém*, but this is impossible: ALIQUEM, accented on the first syllable, would normally have given *algue*. Both forms are in fact later creations: Port. *alguem* is attested in the thirteenth century and Castilian *alguien* only in the fifteenth. In Old Spanish usage *alguno* is both adjective and substantive, its replacement in the latter function by *alguien* being due to a fusion of *alguno* and *quien*; Port. *alguém* developed in the same way from *algum* and *quem*. The medieval period also saw the growth of corresponding negative forms from *ninguno*, viz. Span. *ninguien* and Port. *ninguém*, the former of which has fallen out of use whereas the latter has prospered (see Corominas, *Diccionario crítico etimológico de la lengua castellana*, under the rubric *alguno*).

modern Provençal negation *nieu*, but this looks more like 'not I').
NEMO persisted in the south and east: it is found as *nimo* in Old
Italian, and is still used as *nemos*, with an analogical *s*, in Sardinia;
Rumanian has both the sing. *nime* and the pl. *nimeni*, from NEMINI.
No trace of it was left in Spain or in Gaul.

The most propagated form of negative in the west was NULLUS,
cf. Fr. *nul*, Old Ital. *nullo*, Old Span. *nullo*. Beside this there seems
to have existed in northern Gaul a more emphatic form NE ULLUS,
cf. Old Fr. *neüls*; ULLUS itself otherwise disappeared. Modern
Italian uses pronominally *nulla*, which might correspond to the
Lat. neut. pl. NULLA, but more probably developed as a feminine
singular agreeing with RES. There is also evidence of a form
*NULLIUS, due perhaps to the analogy of such neuter plurals as
OMNIA, cf. Old Port. *nulho*, Prov. *nulh*. Commonly used were
various combinations in which a negative preceded UNUS; thus
NE UNUS appears in Old Fr. *neüns*, while NEC UNUS or NEQUE UNUS
must be postulated in order to explain Old Fr. *necun*, *negun*; Old
Ital. *negun*; Prov. *negu*; Old Port. *ne(n)gum*; Span. *ni(n)guno*; and
Rum. *niciun*. Another such combination was NE IPSE UNUS, whence
Old Fr. *nesuns*, *nisuns* (see p. 90), Prov. *neisu*, and the modern
Italian for 'nobody' *nessuno*; this is quite absent from Spain and
Rumania. The Latin adverb VERE 'truly', used in a negative sense
and combined with UNUS, afforded yet a further possibility of
negation, cf. Ital. *veruno*, Rum. *vreun* (for the negative development cf. mod. Fr. *rien*, *aucun*, *personne*, &c.). Negative periphrases
of Latin may also be detected in the modern Rumanian for
'nothing', *nimic*, from NE MICA, and in the Old Lombard *negota*
from NE GUTTA. These developed in the first place through the
use of the second part of the periphrasis after a verb, to emphasize
negation, a device of popular speech which is already to be observed in the comedies of Plautus and Terence, and which was
to give rise to the negative particles of Romance, cf. Old Fr. *ne . . .
mie*, *ne . . . pas*, *ne . . . goutte*, *ne . . . rien*, *ne . . . giens* (< GĔNUS,
cf. Cat. *gens*), &c. To the same category belongs the still problematic
Ital. *niente*, Old Fr. *nient*, mod. *néant*, which has been variously
derived from NE INDE, NEC ENTEM, and NE GENTEM.

Another such trick of emphasis produced the Spanish negatives,
*nada* 'nothing', and *nadie* 'nobody'. In Vulgar Latin RES NATA or
CAUSA NATA meant '(not) a thing born', while HOMINEM NATUM
became '(not) a man born'; the latter is anticipated by the Plautine

NATUS NEMO. Of these, the feminine NATA developed directly to the invariable *nada*; meanwhile, NATUM, presumably in consequence of that influence of QUI which affected so many masculine singular forms, appeared in Old Spanish as *nadi*: as *qui* gave way in medieval Spanish to *quien*, *nadi* was altered to *nadien*, whence comes the modern *nadie*.

Among other isolated remnants of the Latin indefinite pronouns one may note Ital. *cheche* from QUIDQUID; and although QUIVIS and QUILIBET vanished, a semantically kindred QUOD VELLES, used by Cicero, appeared in Old Italian as *covelle*: the same notion was later to produce *cualquiera* in Spanish, and *qualsivoglia* in Italian.

The term 'indefinite' is usually extended to include a small number of words which in Latin are predominantly adjectival, but which in a neuter form could be employed either as substantives or as adverbs. Such are MULTUS and PAUCUS, both of which survived everywhere in the west, and the former also in the east (Rum. *mult*). In Italy and Spain these words retained their adjectival function, with a normal declension, cf. Span. *mucho*, Port. *muito*, Cat. *molt*, Ital. *molto*; Span. *poco*, Port. *pouco*, Cat. *poc*, Ital. *poco*. In Gaul, however, the adjectival function was rejected: Old Fr. *mout* and *peu* appear only as invariable, used as substantive or adverb, in the earliest texts, though a few very early Norman texts have *mulz*, as in *mulz jurs*, *mulz ans*; in Provençal *molt* is normally invariable, though *pauc* is occasionally found as an adjective, e.g. *us paucs aigneus* 'a little lamb' (Guiraut de Bornelh). To the same category belong TANTUS, QUANTUS, and ALIQUANTUS (cf. Old Fr. *auquant*, Old Span. *alguanto*, Ital. *alquanto*); these enjoyed an extended usage through their absorption of the functions of TOT, QUOT, and ALIQUOT, all of which disappeared. Contrarily to the preceding words, they continued to decline and function as adjectives in Gaul as elsewhere, cf. Fr. *toutes et quantes fois*. A problem is set by Fr. *maint*. Some scholars have deemed it to be Celtic, and others have sought in it an affinity with Germ. *manch*, Eng. *many*, but the possibility of its origin in Vulgar Latin is not to be excluded. In addition to *maint*, Old French has *tamaint*: seeking for parallel forms in other Romance languages, one finds Old Ital. *manto* and *tamanto*, while in the Iberian Peninsula the word for 'size' is Span. *tamaño*, Port. *tamanho*. These latter derive from TAM MAGNUS, a combination which makes one wonder whether the other forms may not represent a crossing of TANTUM with MAGNUM, *MANTU in Italy, *MANCTU in Gaul.[1]

Purely adjectival are TALIS and QUALIS, both of which were widely used in Vulgar Latin. The latter, originally an interrogative adjective, 'of what kind?', was later to have its usage considerably increased through association with the derivatives of QUID, whence come Fr. *quelque*, Ital. *qualche*, Span. *cualque* (now archaic); this, however, was a late medieval development, a syntactical combination arising from such phrases as Fr. *quel que soit*, Ital. *qual che sia*.

A further indefinite pronoun came into existence through the practice of using HOMO in an indefinite sense. In the modern standard languages only Fr. *on* continues to be so employed, but a similar application of *uomo*, *omo*, *om* is found in Old Italian texts, and so too with Old Port. *ome* and Old Span. *omne*, e.g. 'pero digo yo a esto que pues que omne non puede escusar la muerte nin foyr della . . .' (*La Crónica General*). It is difficult to say even approximately at what date this began, but the widespread character of the phenomenon seems to point to a Vulgar Latin origin.

*Conjugation.* Like declension, though with less drastic results, conjugation was shorn of many of its intricacies in the popular speech of the whole Empire. Among the earliest and most noteworthy developments was the complete elimination of deponent verbs, generally effected by a simple adjustment of deponent forms to those of the active voice. Evidence for this dates back to Plautus, who uses, for example, LUCTO for LUCTOR, SORTIO for SORTIOR, HORTO for HORTOR, &c.; the Romance languages bear witness to a similar replacement of PRECOR by *PRECO, MORIOR by *MORIO, SEQUOR by *SEQUO, &c. Infinitives followed suit, LUCTARI becoming LUCTARE, cf. Fr. *lutter*, Span. *luchar*, Ital. *lottare*, Rum. *a lupta*, and MORI becoming first MORIRI, as found in the work of Plautus and Ovid, and then MORIRE, not attested until after the Vulgar Latin period (it occurs in the writing of Gregory of Tours, see p. 305), cf. Fr. *mourir*, Span. *morir*, Ital. *morire*, Rum. *a muri*. A few deponent verbs, instead of conforming to this pattern, were remodelled by recourse to the popular device of creating new infinitives on the stem of the past participle (see below, p. 115): thus from UTOR, UTI, ŪSUS SUM, and OBLIVISCOR, OBLIVISCI, OBLĪTUS

---

[1] According to the latest opinion the origin of *maint* is definitely Germanic, see Gunnar Tilander, '*Maint*'. *Origine et histoire d'un mot* (Stockholm: Kungl, 1955, 65 pages).

SUM, were fashioned *USARE and *OBLITARE, cf. Fr. *user*, Prov. Span. Port. *usar*, Ital. *usare*, and Fr. *oublier*, Prov. *oblidar*, Span. *olvidar*, Rum. *a uita*; likewise, the semi-deponent AUDEO, AUDĒRE, AUSUS SUM gave rise to *AUSARE, cf. Fr. *oser*, Prov. *ausar*, Span. *osar*, Ital. *osare*.

The regularization of deponent verbs was followed or accompanied by a gradual elimination of all the inflected forms of the passive voice. Only the analytic perfect and pluperfect were retained, e.g. AMATUS SUM, AMATUS FUI (the latter in preference to the AMATUS ERAM more favoured in Classical prose), and these, the meaning of the past participle changing from past passive to present passive, assumed in Vulgar Latin the functions of the disappearing AMOR, AMABAR, functions which they have continued to fulfil in all the Romance languages. Written evidence affords little indication of the approximate date of these changes, which in any event must have taken place slowly over a long period of time. Medieval writers continued to use the old synthetic forms. Because of this, some scholars have placed the phenomenon at a later date than we can admit; thus K. Nyrop: 'Ce nouveau passif analytique date probablement du VIe ou du VIIe siècle; remarquons qu'on n'en découvre aucune trace dans le latin de Grégoire de Tours' (*Grammaire historique de la langue française*, vol. ii, p. 2). But the Latin of Gregory of Tours is no safe criterion (see p. 307), and the total absence of any trace of the synthetic forms in Romance suggests that they had ceased to be current in the conversational medium by the fifth century at the latest.

We have already had occasion to observe how, in rejecting one form, Vulgar Latin frequently made good the loss not by a single alternative, but by several. This is true with reference to the passive voice. Though the first and most obvious replacement for DICITUR was DICTUS EST, cf. Fr. *il est dit*, precisely the same meaning could also be conveyed in Vulgar Latin by HOMO DICIT, cf. Fr. *on dit*, and by SE DICIT, cf. Span. *se dice*, Ital. *si dice*, Rum. *se zice*. The reflexive construction, quite usual in classical prose with some normally intransitive verbs when the subject was a person, e.g. SE CONVERTIT, and found as a poetic licence with transitive verbs if the subject was not a person, cf. Virgil, 'Clamor se tollit in auras' (*Aeneid*, Bk. 11, l. 455), must in particular have enjoyed a wide and growing popularity: it is one of the most noteworthy features in the earliest texts of all Romance-speaking countries and has continued in favour.

In the active voice, all indicative tenses were preserved, except for the future, of which the simple form vanished completely, while the future perfect survived only in a western area comprising the Iberian Peninsula and Gascony (see p. 144). Present, imperfect, perfect, and pluperfect all appeared in medieval Romance. It would probably be true to say that the same four tenses persisted in Vulgar Latin in the subjunctive mood, but two of them were soon in difficulties. The imperfect subjunctive is still used in Sardinian, and has perhaps left a relic in the so-called 'personal infinitive' of Portuguese (see p. 144, and cf. J. J. Nunes, *Gramática histórica portuguesa*, 3rd ed., p. 283, note), while the perfect subjunctive survived in the east, giving rise to flexions *-rimu, -riş, -ri, -rimu, -ritu, -ri* (cf. Latin AMAVERIM, -ERIS, -ERIT, -ERIMUS, -ERITIS, -ERINT): these are now encountered only in Macedo-Rumanian, though similar forms occur in the earliest texts from north of the Danube. In general, however, the phonetic attrition of popular speech made the perfect and imperfect subjunctive so liable to confusion with other tenses that they were gradually discarded, the functions of both being taken over in the west by the pluperfect subjunctive, with its unmistakable flexions and its everyday currency. In the process, the pluperfect subjunctive lost in western usage its own pluperfect functions, a fate which readily befell the pluperfect indicative too (see below, pp. 142-4). Gaps were thus created in the verbal system, in the expression of the past as in that of the future, but if such gaps were allowed to develop it was because the means of filling them were already at hand, because indeed the old tenses were being forgotten in face of the growing popularity of new compound formations. Setting aside for detailed consideration the simple tenses widely preserved in Romance, we may now explore the subconscious inventiveness by which all losses were more than made good.

Psychological reasons partly account for the general disappearance of the Latin future. One can indeed manage quite well without a future: it suffices to envisage a present, as with reference to the immediate future we commonly do in English. Among relatively primitive peoples a more remote future is seldom contemplated. The frequent use in later Latin texts of the present tense where Classical Latin would require the future suggests that a similar outlook (or lack of outlook!) prevailed among the common people of the Empire. In the Romance of a large part of southern Italy, and even in some regions of central Italy, there is to this day no future tense, the present being always employed in its stead (G. Rohlfs, op. cit., vol. ii, p. 382). In addition to this, the future tenses of Classical Latin were formally weak: in the first and second conjugations they closely resembled the imperfect, in the first the perfect too (cf. AMABIT, AMAVIT), while in the third and fourth they were almost identical with the present, cf. present DICIT, LEGIT, future DICET, LEGET. Thus, in conjugation as in declension, phonetic inadequacy played a part in the discarding of forms which were not vitally important for conversational purposes. Futurity could not, however, be totally eliminated: it is implicit in verbs expressing intention or obligation, like the English 'will' and 'shall', and in Latin in such verbal combinations as DEBEO CANTARE, VOLO CANTARE, and in the familiar HABEO AD CANTARE, HABEO CANTARE, or CANTARE HABEO.

All of these are represented in the new future tenses of Romance. DEBEO CANTARE appeared as a future in Sardinia, in Log. *depo kantare*; VOLO CANTARE is the basis of the Rumanian future, *voi cînta*, &c.; HABEO AD CANTARE occurs in Sardinia, in Log. *apo a kantare*, and was also formerly used in Rumania. These are evidently the older devices, and they have remained in a state of future periphrasis, instead of congealing into new tenses with stem and flexions. The inhabitants of the Iberian Peninsula came to use indifferently HABEO CANTARE or CANTARE HABEO. Both constructions are still in evidence in the twelfth-century *Poema del Cid*, though the latter is more usual, and both could still be used as periphrases, e.g.

> El Campeador a los que han lidiar tan bien los castigó.
> (Ed. Menéndez Pidal, l. 3523)

> Pedir vos a poco por dexar so aver en salvo
> (ibid., l. 133)

cf. mod. Span. *pedirá*, *lidiarán* (*lidiar* < LITIGARE). From the second example it will be noted that, when HABEO followed the infinitive, a pronoun could come between the two parts of the periphrasis. The area where this was possible extended in medieval times to include Provence, cf. Prov. *cantar los ai*. In Spanish the forms of HABEO eventually came to be agglutinated as flexions, but in Portuguese the periphrasis has survived as such to this day: one may still use either *dará-me* or *dar-me-á*, the latter being considered more 'literary'. The later Vulgar Latin which is the basis of standard French and Italian must have evinced a definite preference for CANTARE HABEO. In their earliest manifestations, dating in the case of French from the *Strassburg Oaths* of A.D. 842 (*salvarai, prindrai*), both languages show the present tense of HABEO, in a phonetically reduced form, firmly agglutinated as a new type of flexion with the infinitive as stem.

Amid the general collapse of the Latin synthetic future there survived in isolation that of the verb 'to be', which doubtless owed this exceptional favour to its growing use in an auxiliary function. The Latin ĔRO, ĔRIS, ĔRIT, ĔRIMUS, (ĔRITIS), ĔRUNT developed in northern Gaul to Old Fr. *ier, iers, iert, iermes,* (second plural not attested), *ierent*; in Provençal similar forms are attested only in the singular: *er, ers, er(t)*. That these forms must have survived for a while in Spain is implied by the fact that Castilian, differing in this respect from most other Spanish dialects, adopted the second person singular into the present tense as *eres*, in place of Lat. ĔS. North Italian texts show a few similar relics. Some early Italian authors, including Dante and Boccaccio, also use with the meaning 'will be' a form *fia* from FIAM, the synthetic future of the verb FIERI; popular recourse to this verb as an alternative for 'to be' is attested in the east, where it gave the Rumanian infinitive *a fi*, though the corresponding Rumanian tenses have now been largely supplanted by those drawn from ESSE. Such lingering remains of classical usage in no way prevented Vulgar Latin from creating *ESSERE HABEO, after its established pattern, thus providing the verb 'to be' with a future tense in conformity with those of other verbs.

Throughout that part of Romania which made a simple future from CANTARE HABEO, the past aspect of the future soon came to be conveyed by a combination of CANTARE with the past tense of HABĒRE. The resultant tense has become the 'conditional' of the Romance languages, a mood for which Latin made no specific provision. In selecting the appropriate past tense of HABĒRE, speakers hesitated between the imperfect and the perfect, the original shade of difference in meaning being obscured when the emphasis was thrown on to the infinitive of the other verb. The former soon predominated in Gaul and the Iberian Peninsula: thus the *-ait* of Fr. *chanterait* (in Old Fr. *-eiet*) and the *-ía* of Prov. and Span. *cantaría* derive from HABĒBAT, reduced first through consonantal dissimilation to \*HABÉAT, and then, through loss of its initial syllable in flexional usage, to -ÉAT. A similar reduction in Portuguese has not precluded the possibility of an intercalated pronoun, e.g. *dir-se-ia* 'it would be said'. It is in Italy that hesitation between imperfect and perfect must have persisted for some time. The central area, including Tuscany, eventually opted for HABUIT, which appeared in Old Italian as *-abbe*; this was later altered under the influence of the 'DĔDI-perfects' (see below, p. 137) to *-ebbe*, whence the modern conditional *canterebbe*. North Italian dialects still have flexions deriving from the imperfect, and some areas have created a hybrid system; the *cantaria* found in many of the southern regions, previously mentioned as having no future tense, is probably a medieval importation.[1]

With three past tenses of the indicative remaining intact, the expression of past time in Vulgar Latin cannot be said to have been jeopardized in the same way as was the expression of futurity. That new past tenses should have nevertheless developed seems in this instance to be the result of syntactical accident rather than the subconscious fulfilment of a linguistic need, though it is possible that a sense of need may have been stimulated through the declining efficacy of corresponding tenses in the subjunctive; perhaps the loss in that mood of an adequate expression of pluperfect meaning was responsible for compromising the function of the pluperfect indicative. But even in this event, only a pluperfect was required in order that the Latin indicative system should be restored in full. In fact, the exuberance of popular speech created not only a pluperfect but also the tense known in the manuals of grammar as 'past indefinite', and with them a whole gamut of new possibilities.

Once again the origins of the innovation may be traced back to Plautus, who frequently used a past participle adjectivally in conjunction with the verb HABĒRE, in expressions of the type HABEO CULTELLUM COMPARATUM, literally 'I have a knife bought'.

---

[1] In early Rumanian there existed a conditional tense formed in the same manner as the future, with the infinitive of the verb and, in this instance, the imperfect of VOLĒRE, e.g. *cînta-vrea*. In the modern language, however, this tense has been replaced by *aş cînta, ai cînta, ar cînta, am cînta, aţi cînta, ar cînta*. Authorities on Rumanian are of divided opinions concerning the origin of the auxiliary. Some, including perhaps the majority, hold that it represents in an abbreviated form the earlier *vrea*, &c. Others seek to derive it from various tenses of HABĒRE. Meyer-Lübke suggests a Greek influence, but this view finds little support.

The construction, not uncommon in the work of Cicero where he seeks to stress the completion of an action, became increasingly employed by Christian writers, as in Egeria's CASTRA POSITA HABEBANT (see p. 38). At this stage the new compound tenses were already in being. In the Iberian Peninsula HABĒRE was rivalled in the sense of 'to have' by TENĒRE. There one could say, with the approach of the participle to the verb, either HABEO COM-PARATUM CULTELLUM or TENEO COMPARATUM CULTELLUM. Spanish, while adopting *tener* as its usual verb for 'to have', has nevertheless retained *haber* as the appropriate auxiliary for use in compound tenses; Portuguese, on the other hand, after long hesitation be-tween *haver* and *ter* (loss of intervocalic *n* is a feature of Portuguese phonology) has finally opted for the latter: thus 'I have bought a knife' is in Spanish *he comprado un cuchillo*, but in Portuguese *tenho comprado um cutelo*. All other Romance languages, including Rumanian, have preserved compound tenses formed with HABĒRE.

The passive voice, with AMATUS SUM, &c., already provided the example of compound tenses formed with ESSE. In most areas this usage was extended to include all compound tenses in which the past participle referred back to the subject, i.e. reflexives and in-transitives, cf. Fr. *je suis entré*, Ital. *sono entrato*, from INTRATUS SUM. In the Iberian Peninsula, however, the compound tenses of all active verbs, whether transitive, reflexive, or intransitive, were constructed with the verb 'to have', e.g. Span. *he entrado*, Port. *tenho entrado*, the auxiliary 'to be', for which STARE now appeared as a near alternative to V. Lat. *ESSERE, being strictly confined to the passive voice. There is no evidence in Roman times for the reversal of word-order whereby AMATUS SUM and INTRATUS SUM became SUM AMATUS and SUM INTRATUS; it is presumably due to the analogy of HABEO COMPARATUM.

This word-order seems to have precluded any possibility of fusion of the two elements of compound past tenses such as oc-curred in the evolution of the future and the conditional. The auxiliaries continued to conjugate fully and any of their tenses might be used in conjunction with the past participle. In conse-quence, the Romance languages were to emerge possessed of a range of tenses with past aspect considerably exceeding that of Classical Latin. In at least one Romance language, French, the plethora of past tenses has proved too much for everyday usage, with the result that a further two of the surviving simple forms of

Latin have been virtually discarded: the old perfect, e.g. *je chantai*, and its corresponding subjunctive, the old pluperfect-become-imperfect, e.g. *je chantasse*. Spanish and Italian still contrive to find a use for them all.

Such was the proliferation of tenses. It is in essence a syntactical development. Their neat division into the four different conjugations of Classical Latin, together with various 'irregular and defective' verbs, is largely the result of a grammarians' tidying-up process, and in so far as it was observed in popular speech, its outlines became somewhat blurred. One has only to think of popular English to realize how easily interchangeable verbal forms may be. An examination of the infinitive, of the gerund and participles, and of the simple tenses of the finite verb, will show that this division had little reality in the vernacular of the Empire.

*Nominal and adjectival forms of the verb.* The apparatus of the verb comprised in Latin several forms which lay outside the normal scope of conjugation, forms which were used in the sentence with a nominal or adjectival function, though still retaining certain verbal attributes. This Indo-European inheritance, amplified in some respects by the creations of Old Latin, was considerably modified.

Of the infinitives, while the present survived and prospered, the perfect was completely eliminated: for 'to have sung', instead of CANTAVISSE Vulgar Latin used most commonly HABĒRE CANTATUM, in Lusitania TENĒRE CANTATUM, or in the east, with the verb adopted as 'to be', FIERI CANTATUM, cf. Rum. *a fi cîntat*. Past and present participles were retained, but the future participle, e.g. CANTATŪRUS, shared the fate of the future tenses; a few relics of it remain fossilized in substantives, e.g. ADVENTŪRA 'things to come', cf. Fr. *aventure*, and VENTŪRA, which has acquired in Spanish and Portuguese *ventura* the sense of 'good fortune'.

The supine, a nominal form of which Classical Latin possessed only an accusative and a dative, e.g. CANTATUM, CANTATU, resembled too closely the past participle to prosper independently (though there are relics of its survival in Rumanian). In the classical language it was already of limited usage, and was often replaced by other constructions, preferably gerundial. Thus for VENIO LECTUM 'I come to read', the later inclination was towards VENIO AD LEGENDUM, but since the gerund also fell out of favour, Vulgar Latin replaced both by VENIO (AD) LEGERE, cf. Fr. *je viens lire*; the dative of the supine was employed in Latin only after an adjective, e.g. FACILE DICTU, and this meaning too could be rendered by FACILE AD DICENDUM, or in V. Lat. FACILE (AD) DICERE, cf. Fr. *facile à dire*.

Of the gerund, a verbal noun, e.g. CANTANDUM, and the gerundive, or verbal adjective, which developed from it in Old Latin, e.g. CANTANDUS, there remained in Vulgar Latin usage only a single form—an ablative of the gerund which became in effect a new present participle, ousting the latter, e.g. CANTANTEM, from its verbal function and confining it to a purely adjectival role. Both the gerund, in its other uses, and the gerundive were commonly replaced in Vulgar Latin by the infinitive; thus TE HORTO AD LABORANDUM (gerund, cf. examples given above) became TE HORTO AD LABORARE, cf. Fr. *je t'exhorte à travailler*, and PUEROS UXORI DEDIT EDUCANDOS (gerundive) became PUEROS UXORI DEDIT AD EDUCARE, cf. Fr. *il donna à sa femme les enfants à élever*.

The surviving ablative gerund had in Latin three types of flexion: -ANDO, -ENDO, and -IENDO. The last of these, presumably under the influence of the -IRE infinitive, was modified to -INDO. Portuguese, Gascon, Catalan, and Sardinian appeared as Romance idioms still possessing all three, cf. Port. *cantando, escrevendo, partindo*; Cat. *cantant, perdent, escrivint*; Sard. *filande, legende, buḍḍinde* (different dialects have post-tonic vowels *e, o*, and *u*, cf. M. L. Wagner, op. cit., pp. 376–7). Though islets of -INDO are still found elsewhere, e.g. Piedmontese *drumint* 'sleeping', the remainder of western Romania has in general eliminated this type, probably already in later Vulgar Latin, in favour of the other two. In Castilian, -ANDO is still -*ando*, cf. *cantando*, and -ENDO is presumably the basis of the -*iendo* found with all verbs other than the -ARE type, e.g. *escribiendo, pudiendo*, &c. These are certainly the forms which have persisted in Provençal and Italian, cf. Prov. *cantan (chantan), escriven*, Ital. *cantando, scrivendo*. Within Italian dialects there is a tendency to reduce these to a single form: in the north -*ando* is generalized at the expense of -*endo*, whereas the reverse is true of the south. A similar tendency, assisted by the early phonetic coalescence of *en* and *an* before a consonant, must have prevailed in northern Gaul during the pre-literary period of French, for of all the standard Romance languages French alone appeared with a single type of gerund, ending in -*ant*. In the east, Rumanian preserves two forms, but with an individual choice of -ANDO and -INDO, cf. *avînd* 'having', and *fiind* 'being'.

Wherever in the Romance area the post-tonic *e* and *o* have fallen, as in French, Provençal, and Catalan, the gerund appeared as identical in form with the present participle, though the latter as an adjective could have a plural. In Old French they were completely merged; there remain, however, some traces of the Latin forms in which the characteristic -ND- of the gerundive was preserved by the following -A of neuter plurals interpreted as feminine singular substantives, e.g. *viande* < VIVENDA, in Old Fr. 'food', and *offrande* < OFFERENDA. In Spanish and Italian there is no such confusion, and the Latin present participles enjoy a separate existence as commonly used adjectives, e.g. Span. *agua corriente*, *caliente*, *hirviente*, &c. Some Romance idioms, notably Rheto-Romance, Sardinian, and Rumanian, reveal a tendency for the gerund to oust the present participle even from its adjectival function, e.g. Sard. *ábba buḍḍinde* 'boiling water'.

In all this conflict of nominal and adjectival forms, the present infinitive was the one which emerged with a greater range of functions. Not only did it replace the supine and the gerundive, and in some instances the gerund, but it also kept and extended many of its other usages. In Latin it frequently appears as a substantive, e.g. LABORARE EST ORARE, and thus employed it came in the popular tongue to have a definite article like any other substantive. In modern Spanish and Italian it is still so used, while French bears witness to its former currency with such words as *le manger, les vivres, le plaisir*, &c. The early comic writers in Latin often employ the infinitive colloquially in exclamatory or imperative phrases; hence the syntax of modern official prohibitions, e.g. Ital. *Non sputare nella carrozza*, Fr. *Ne pas marcher sur le gazon*. This negative imperative usage is found in Old French, and it is still current in modern Italian, in a familiar context, that is, in the function of a second person singular. Yet a further use of the infinitive is attested in texts from the third century onwards: as a substitute for a clause in a dependent question, e.g. NESCIO QUID DICĔRE for the classical NESCIO QUID DICAM, cf. Fr. *je ne sais que dire*, Span. *no sé qué decir*, &c.

Of infinitive types, those in -ĀRE and -ĪRE were to prove the most stable, persisting everywhere; both, but particularly the former, were continually augmenting their stock. The representatives of the Latin second and third conjugations were, on the other hand, frequently confused in everyday speech. Over the greater part of Spain, where the consequences of this uncertainty are most obvious, the ending -ĔRE was completely absorbed into -ĒRE, producing a single type -er(e), so that Spanish and Portuguese emerged with only three types of infinitive, e.g. *cantar, vender, partir* (all common to both languages). This, however, is one respect in which the territory which was to become Catalonia shows an early and significant difference of treatment, retaining the four distinct types in common with most of the rest of Romania. In fact, in Catalan they became five: the suffix of verbs in -ĔRE, which were of course stressed on the stem, was reduced either by apocope to -er or by syncope to -re, according to the nature of the preceding consonant. Thus Cat. *córrer* < CURRĔRE, *plànyer* < PLANGĔRE, *créixer* < CRESCĔRE constitute in the medieval language a different category from *beure* < BIBĔRE, *perdre* < PERDĔRE, &c. The difference is nowadays somewhat obscured by the fact that final *r* has ceased to be pronounced. The other three evolved normally with the stress on the ending, e.g. *plorar* < PLORARE, *venir* < VENĪRE, *haver* < HABĒRE, though the last of these represents a class now much diminished numerically on account of the continual attraction of the type in -*re*, e.g. VIDĒRE > Old Cat. *veser*, mod. *veure*, JACĒRE > Old Cat. *jaser*, mod. *jaure, jeure* (A. Badía Margarit, *Gramática histórica catalana*, pp. 297–8). The four endings of the Latin infinitive have also persisted in French, cf. *chanter, partir, devoir, rendre*; in Provençal, cf. *cantar, partir, dever, rendre*; in Italian, cf. *cantare, partire, dovére, pérdere*; and in Rumanian, cf. *cînta(re), dormi(re), vedea(re), merge(re).*[1] Macedo-Rumanian, however, possessing only the first three of the Rumanian types, bears witness to a development in the east similar to that of the Iberian Peninsula.

Despite this fairly consistent preservation of types, the number of infinitives of which the ending was changed from -ĔRE to -ĒRE or vice versa suffices to show that the tendency to confuse them was by no means confined to those areas in which they have merged their identity. Notable converts to the -ĒRE type are SAPĔRE and

---

[1] In Rumanian the infinitive used as a noun has retained its full Latin ending, whereas used in the infinitive function it has lost its final syllable: thus *cîntare* 'singing', but *a cînta* 'to sing', *mergere* 'going', but *a merge* 'to go', &c. It differs from the substantival infinitive of all other Romance languages in that it takes a feminine article, e.g. *cîntarea*, 'the singing', *averea*, 'the wealth'.

CADĔRE, in Vulgar Latin SAPĔRE, cf. Fr. *savoir*, and CADĒRE, cf. Old Fr. *cheoir*, mod. *choir*. Much more numerous, except in the Latin of Spain, are those which moved in the inverse direction, e.g. RESPONDĔRE, TONDĒRE, RIDĒRE, TORQUĒRE, cf. Fr. *répondre, tondre, rire, tordre*, Ital. *rispóndere, tóndere, rídere, tórcere*. MOVĒRE shows a similar change in Ital. *muovere* but not in Fr. *mouvoir*.

A particular source of disturbance, which in common Vulgar Latin brought many recruits to the -ĪRE class, lay in the phonetic coincidence of the endings -IO and -EO of the first person singular present indicative, once the front vowel had become a yod (see above, p. 25). If the yod was not then eliminated, as happened in the case of some verbs, e.g. *DORMO for DORMIO, it induced a general adaptation of the corresponding infinitives to the type in -ĪRE. Thus CAPIO, CAPĔRE, produced CAPĪRE, cf. Ital. *capire*, Fr. *chevir*, and FUGIO, FUGĔRE, produced FUGĪRE, cf. Ital. *fuggire*, Fr. *fuir*, Span. *huir*, Rum. *a fugi*; similarly FLOREO, FLORĒRE, IMPLEO, IMPLĒRE, and PUTEO, PUTĒRE gave rise to FLORĪRE, cf. Old Fr. *flourir*, Ital. *fiorire*, Prov. *florir*, Rum. *a înflori*, IMPLĪRE, cf. Old Fr. *emplir*, Ital. *empire* (*empiere*), Span. *henchir*, and PUTĪRE, cf. Old Fr. *puir*, Ital. *putire*, Old Span. *pudir*, Rum. *a puţi*. Considerable local variety is apparent in the development of these forms. Rumanian, for instance, though participating in the adoption of FLORĪRE and PUTĪRE, has kept IMPLĒRE, as *a împlea*. In the west, the speeches of the Iberian Peninsula adapted RIDEO, RIDĒRE to RIDĪRE, cf. Span. *reír*, Port. *rir*, whereas we have seen RIDĒRE in use in Italy and Gaul. On the other hand, from TENEO, TENĒRE, and GAUDEO, GAUDĒRE the Vulgar Latin of Gaul created TENĪRE and GAUDĪRE, cf. Fr. Prov. and Cat. *tenir*, Fr. *jouir*, Prov. *gauzir*, but Span. *tener*, Port. *ter*, Ital. *tenére, godére*.

The commonest irregular infinitives of Latin were early regularized by attachment to the different recognized types. ESSE became *ESSĔRE, POSSE and VELLE became POTĒRE and VOLĒRE, while the compounds of FERRE were adopted into the -ĪRE class, SUFFERRE and OFFERRE becoming SUFFERĪRE and OFFERĪRE, cf. Fr. *souffrir, offrir*, &c. These creations were almost universally accepted, the only notable differences being in Sardinia, which preferred the -ĔRE type.

A particular feature of the Vulgar Latin infinitive was the popularity of the inchoative suffix -ESCERE. In Spain this was normally assimilated to the infinitive in -*er*, e.g. FLORESCERE, which ousted FLORĒRE to become Span. *florecer*, Port. *chorecer*. Elsewhere, the analogy of FLORĒRE / FLORĪRE gave rise to a type FLORISCERE. As an infinitive this is not widespread in Romance—it occurs in southern Italy, e.g. in Calabrian *addormiscere, guarniscere, temiscere*, &c.—but the so-called 'inchoative infix' ESC/ISC was to play an important part in the evolution of the tenses of -ĪRE verbs (see p. 123).

More significant in the history of the infinitive are the suffixes which contributed to increase the stock of -ARE verbs. In the classical language it was already customary to build such forms upon nouns and upon adjectives of the first and second declensions, e.g. PLANTA—PLANTARE, MATURUS—MATURARE. Vulgar Latin extended the process to third declension adjectives, formerly more liable to be adapted to the verb in -ĪRE. Thus from MOLLIS came *MOLLIARE, cf. Fr. *mouiller*, Prov. Port. *molhar*, Span. *mojar*, Rum. *a muia*; from LEVIS, ALLEVIARE, cf. Fr. *alléger*, Span. *aliviar*, Log. *allebiare*, &c. Thereafter the new suffix -IARE was added to a multitude of adjectives of the first declension and past participles, becoming a most characteristic means of creating verbs in Vulgar Latin, e.g. ALTUS—*ALTIARE, cf. Fr. *hausser*, Span. *alzar*, Ital. *alzare*; BASSUS—*BASSIARE, cf. Fr. *baisser*, Prov. *baisar*, Span. *bajar*, Cat. Port. *baixar*; DIRECTUS—*DIRECTIARE, cf. Fr. *dresser*, Prov. Cat. *dressar*, Span. (*a*)*derezar*, Ital. *dirizzare*; ACUTUS—ACUTIARE, cf. Fr. *aiguiser*, Span. *aguzar*, Ital. *aguzzare*; CAPTUS—CAPTIARE, cf. Fr. *chasser*, Prov. Cat. *casar*, Span. *cazar*, Ital. *cacciare*, Rum. *a acaţa*.

Another Latin suffix which became widely employed was -ICARE, e.g. CABALLICARE (attested in the Salic Law, see p. 308), cf. Fr. *chevaucher*, Span. *cabalgar*, Ital. *cavalcare*, and CARRICARE, cf. Fr. *charger*, Span. *cargar*, Port. *carregar*, Ital. *caricare*. Rather similar, and sometimes confused with -ICARE, was a suffix of Greek origin, adopted as -IZARE, or more popularly, as -IDIARE. The currency of this Greek form seems to have been due to the adaptation of verbs in -ίζειν into Latin in translations, and particularly in Christian literature; BAPTIZARE (see p. 38) is a typical example. The more popular form appears in Old French as *-eier*, in modern French as *-ayer* (*bégayer*), *-eyer* (*grasseyer*), and *-oyer* (*nettoyer, guerroyer*); in Provençal it is *-eiar*, as in *peleiar*, and in Spanish *-ear*, cf. *pelear*, verbs of which the root is PĬLUS, and which mean literally 'to tear out the hair', hence, 'to fight, quarrel'. Many

modern verbs in -*eggiare* bear witness to the extensive use of the
suffix in the Vulgar Latin of Italy, e.g. *corteggiare*, *biondeggiare*,
*amareggiare*, &c. In the east it gave rise to a verbal infix (see p. 126).

Various other suffixes, e.g. the frequentative -ITARE, as in VANI-
TARE, and the diminutive -ULARE, as in TREMULARE and TURBULARE,
contributed yet more verbs to the -ARE stock. Even present participles afforded new stems for -ARE verbs, e.g. *LEVANTARE and
*CREPANTARE, cf. Span. Port. *levantar*, *quebrantar*, Old Fr. *cra-
venter*, and *EXPAVENTARE, which Gaul shared with Italy, cf. Ital.
*spaventare*, Old Fr. *espoenter*, remodelled as *épouvanter*. Past participles, since they were a basis for verbs both in -IARE and -ARE (for
the latter, see above, *USARE, *OBLITARE, p. 104, and cf. CANERE—
CANTARE, RUERE—*RUTARE, Fr. *ruer*), sometimes provoked double
forms with different meanings: thus beside the CAPTIARE mentioned above, CAPTARE also persisted, cf. Old Span. *catar* (as in
the second line of the *Poema del Cid*: 'Tornaua la cabeça e estaua
los catando'), Ital. *cattare*, Rum. *a căuta*, and from ACCAPTARE Fr.
*acheter*, Ital. *accattare*.

In these ways Vulgar Latin brought a continual stream of reinforcements to the -ARE class, founding a tradition of verb-
construction which—with some concessions to -ĪRE, particularly
favoured in the east—has persisted throughout the history of the
Romance languages.

Of the participles, while the present followed a course of
development similar to that of the gerund (for the type with an
-ISC- infix, confined to Gaul, see below, p. 125), the past shows
greater complication. This is largely because of the existence of
two differently accented types. Some past participles have the
stress on the flexion: these are traditionally known as 'weak' forms;
and some, correspondingly known as 'strong' forms, are stressed
on the stem. In the classical language strong past participles
normally occur in conjunction with the strong -ĔRE infinitive, e.g.
PERDĔRE—PERDITUS, ABSCONDĔRE—ABSCONDITUS, TENDĔRE—TEN-
TUS, FALLĔRE—FALSUS, FINDĔRE—FISSUS; it will be noted that they
end in -ITUS, -TUS, or -SUS. Weak past participles correspond to
weak infinitives, e.g. AMARE—AMATUS, DELĒRE—DELĒTUS, AUDĪRE—
AUDĪTUS. There are, however, some weak infinitives, mostly of
the -ĒRE and -ĪRE types, of which the past participle is strong, e.g.
CREPARE—CREPITUS, TORQUĒRE—TORTUS, MOVĒRE—MOTUS, SEN-
TĪRE—SENSUS, SALĪRE—SALTUS. The important distinction between

strong and weak forms is one which will again be encountered in a consideration of the perfect tense, with which the past participle stands in close formal relationship.

Popular language generally favoured the more distinctive weak forms. The ending -ATU remained stable, like the infinitives in -ARE, and is abundantly represented in all Romance languages, cf. Fr. *chanté*, Prov. Cat. *cantat*, Span. Port. *cantado*, Ital. *cantato*, Rum. *cîntat*. Similarly -ĪTU remained, and moreover extended its scope by attracting most of the strong forms of which the corresponding infinitive ended, or in Vulgar Latin came to end, in -ĪRE, e.g. SENTĪTU for SENSU, cf. Fr. *senti*, Span. *sentido*, Ital. *sentito*, Rum. *simṭit*, &c., SALĪTU for SALTU, cf. Fr. *sailli*, Span. *salido*, Ital. *salito*, Rum. *sărit*, &c. On the other hand, -ĒTU became an early casualty: it has completely disappeared from Romance except for a few adjectival relics, e.g. QUIĒTU, QUĒTU, from QUIESCERE (see p. 27). This loss was made good by popular creation of a new type of past participle in -ŪTU, an ending which occurs in Classical Latin only in a few forms in which the U is properly part of the verbal stem, e.g. STATŪTUS, from STATUERE, CONSŪTUS, from CON-SUERE, TRIBŪTUS, from TRIBUERE, and similarly VOLŪTUS and SOLŪ-TUS. While these exceptional instances may have provided the first pattern, the real fortune of the new type was due to its phonetic correspondence with the common perfect in -UI (see below, p. 140). Once established it rapidly gained ground. Verbs with an -UI perfect and a strong past participle in -ITUS were probably the first to be affected: hence *HABŪTU for HABITUM, *DEBŪTU for DEBITUM, *VA-LŪTU for VALITUM, *PLACŪTU for PLACITUM, *PARŪTU for PARITUM, &c. They would then be followed by all the verbs which developed an -UI perfect in Vulgar Latin; hence *BIBŪTU (perfect *BIBUI for BIBI), *CURRŪTU (*CURRUI for CUCURRI), *CADŪTU (*CADUI for CECIDI), *VINCŪTU (*VINCUI for VĪCI), *LEGŪTU (*LEGUI for LĒGI), &c. Such was the popularity of the new participial suffix that it there-after extended in many areas to verbs of which the perfect re-mained true to a different type; this is particularly noticeable in French, in verbs with a perfect of the *-is* type but a past participle which presupposes Vulgar Latin forms such as *PERDŪTU, *VEN-DŪTU, *VIDŪTU, *RENDŪTU, *FINDŪTU, *PENDŪTU, *TENDŪTU, *TONDŪTU, &c. Comparison of the modern Romance languages shows the -ŪTU forms to be especially favoured by French and Rumanian (e.g. *vîndut*, *pierdut*, &c.), but the development was obviously common to the whole area of Vulgar Latin. Old Spanish frequently has past participles such as *metudo, temudo, sabudo, perdudo,* &c.; they were eliminated in the fourteenth century, leaving Spanish with only two weak endings, *-ado* and *-ido.* Portuguese dispensed with *-udo* forms about a century later. The ending is still common in Italian, e.g. *avuto, caduto, creduto,* &c., and the fact that in such words as *cresciuto* and *conosciuto* it has been added to infinitive stems may be taken to indicate that during the Middle Ages it was still gaining ground.

The prevalence of -ŪTU contributed much towards the elimination of the strong past participles of Latin. Yet they were by no means completely effaced. Many lingered on to emerge in medieval Romance side by side with the remodelled weak forms, and some of those most commonly used in Vulgar Latin have never been ousted, or indeed seriously threatened, e.g. FACTU, cf. Fr. *fait,* Span. *hecho,* Port. *feito,* Ital. *fatto,* Rum. *faptu* (but mod. *făcut*); DICTU, cf. Fr. *dit,* Span. *dicho,* Port. *dito,* Ital. *detto,* Rum. *zis*; MORTU, for Class. MORTUUM, cf. Fr. *mort,* Span. *muerto,* Port. Ital. *morto,* Rum. *mort*; SCRIPTU, cf. Fr. *écrit,* Span. *escrito,* Ital. *scritto,* Rum. *scris* (< SCRIPSU); RUPTU, cf. Span. *roto,* Ital. *rotto,* Rum. *rupt,* but Fr. *rompu* (except in *route* < RUPTA); POSITU, cf. Span. *puesto,* Port. Ital. *posto,* Rum. *pus*; VISTU for VISUM, cf. Span. Port. *visto,* Ital. *visto* (but also *veduto*). Of all parts of Romania, Italy proved most amenable to the retention of strong forms, and it is noteworthy that, whereas the Iberian Peninsula generally preferred forms in -TUM, Italy no less readily kept those in -SUM, cf. mod. Ital. *riso, chiuso, corso, sparso, raso, mosso, perso, ascoso.* Some of these indeed reveal a tendency in the Vulgar Latin of Italy to change -TUM forms into -SUM forms: thus MOSSU for MOTUM, ABSCONSU for ABSCONDITUM, PERSU for PERDITUM. In this respect the Vulgar Latin of Gaul presents a contrast, inclining most prominently towards general adaptation of the strong forms to the three weak types.

There even appears sporadically in Old French a fourth weak type, ending in *-eit,* as, for example, in *toleit* (e.g. 'A lur chevals unt toleites les seles', *Chanson de Roland,* ed. Whitehead, l. 2490), which exists side by side with both the adapted *tolu* and the strong *tout,* from TOLTU; this derives from the endings -ECTUM and -ĬCTUM, found in a few Latin past participles, e.g. COLLECTUM > Old Fr. *coilleit,* and BENEDĬCTUM > Old Fr. *bene(d)eit.* Yet despite this propensity for the remodelled weak form, Old French still contained a number of strong forms, in addition to those quoted above; some have remained functional to this day, while others survive in adjectival or otherwise fossilized usage, e.g. *cuit* < COCTU, *teint* < TINCTU, *joint* < JUNCTU, *né* < NATU, *tort* < TORTU, *ouvert* < *OPERTU (due to Vulgar Latin confusion of APERIRE and OPERIRE), *pris* < PRESU, for PREHENSUM, *mis* < MISSU, *clos* < CLAUSU (as in *à huis clos*), *épars* < SPARSU, *res* < RASU (as in *rez-de-chaussée*). A few former past participles which in Old French are already substantives bear witness to an early tendency in northern Gaul to convert other strong forms to the strong proparoxytonic type in -ITU, e.g. *fente* < FÍNDITU (Class. FISSUM), *meute* < MÓVITU (Class. MOTUM), *pente* < PÉNDITU (Class. PENSUM), *tente* < TÉNDITU (Class. TENTUM); this evidently served as an intermediate stage in the passage of FISSUM to FINDÚTU, of MOTUM to MOVÚTU, &c.

*Simple tenses.* Much of the difference between corresponding tenses in the Romance languages is due solely to local phonological evolution. In the present tense, both indicative and subjunctive, changing stress produced varying vocalic phonemes within the stem. The forms of the first and second persons plural, like most infinitives, were usually stressed on the flexion, whereas the stem itself bore the stress in the forms of other persons. Hence, in French for example, such results as *mourir, je meurs, tu meurs, il meurt, nous mourons, vous mourez, ils meurent*. Similar developments in other languages will be observed in the tables given below. This is the phenomenon known as 'apophony', a phenomenon which doubtless has its origin in regional Vulgar Latin, but which is not attested until the appearance of vernacular texts. A further disturbing influence was exercised by the yod: though completely eliminated in Vulgar Latin from the third person plural, whence FACUNT for FACIUNT, &c. (see above, p. 27), it persisted in a number of present tenses in the first person singular. Thus the Old French form corresponding to (*je*) *meurs* is *muir* from *MORIO; Fr. *je puis*, from *POTEO, still survives side by side with the analogical *je peux*. This applies in the same way to the present tenses of other Romance languages, though the verbs in which the yod was retained vary in the different regions, cf. TENEO > Span. *tengo*, VIDEO > Old Ital. *veggio*, &c. The loss of final s in eastern Vulgar Latin (see p. 51) is yet another purely phonetic factor which serves to create, in conjugation as in declension, an impression of considerable difference as between French and Spanish on the one hand, and Italian and Rumanian on the other. In the present context, such phonological developments will be considered as incidental, in order that we may concentrate attention upon those morphological changes which can be attributed to the Vulgar Latin period.

Rumanian alone, of all the modern Romance languages, preserves four distinct types of present indicative corresponding to the four types of Classical Latin. This may be seen from the following tables:

| CANTARE | TENĒRE | PERDĔRE | DORMĪRE |
|---|---|---|---|
| CANTO | TENEO | PERDO | DORMIO |
| CANTAS | TENES | PERDIS | DORMIS |
| CANTAT | TENET | PERDIT | DORMIT |
| CANTĀMUS | TENĒMUS | PERDĬMUS | DORMĪMUS |
| CANTĀTIS | TENĒTIS | PERDĬTIS | DORMĪTIS |
| CANTANT | TENENT | PERDUNT | DORMIUNT |

### Rumanian

| a cînta | a ţinea | a pierde | a dormi |
|---|---|---|---|
| cînt | ţin | pierd | dorm |
| cînţi | ţii | pierzi | dormi |
| cîntă | ţine | pierde | doarme |
| cîntăm | ţinem | pierdem | dormim |
| cîntaţi | ţineţi | pierdeţi | dormiţi |
| cîntă | ţin | pierd | dorm |

The particular conservatism of Rumanian lies in the fact that the third type is accented throughout on the stem, just as in the Latin tense, where PERDĬMUS and PERDĬTIS, like the infinitive PERDĔRE, are proparoxytonic. This is apparent from the diphthongization of *pierdem*, *pierdeţi*. In modern colloquial Rumanian the second and third types are in reality confused. In western Romania, including Italy, a similar confusion must have taken place within the time of Vulgar Latin, with the result that the second and third types became identical, PÉRDĬMUS and PÉRDĬTIS changing to PERDÉMUS and PERDÉTIS. The present indicatives of Spanish still reflect quite faithfully the types of western Vulgar Latin:

| I | II | | III |
|---|---|---|---|
| canto | tengo | pierdo | duermo |
| cantas | tienes | pierdes | duermes |

| canta | tiene | pierde | duerme |
|-------|-------|--------|--------|
| cantamos | tenemos | perdemos | dormimos |
| cantáis | tenéis | perdéis | dormís |
| cantan | tienen | pierden | duermen |

This three-type present indicative is also characteristic of Portuguese and Catalan, and north of the Pyrenees it survives in Bearn. The remainder of Gaul, however, must have witnessed an early replacement of the third type flexions -ĪMUS and -ĪTIS by the -ĒMUS and -ĒTIS of the second type, the three types of Vulgar Latin being thus reduced to two. The Provençal flexions are accordingly: I. -, -as, -a, -am, -atz, -an (-en, -on), II. -, -es, -, -em, -etz, -en (-on); for forms with the inchoative infix, see below, pp. 124–5. Loss of -s in the flexion of the first person plural is a phenomenon not confined to Provençal (see below, Norman -um, etc.); it presumably has its origin in a popular inclination to restrict -s to forms of the second person. As for the varying flexions of the third person plural, they show that -UNT was by no means lost, but lingered on as a possible alternative, favoured in one local speech and discarded in another (see pp. 380–1).

The Latin basis of the Old French present indicative is exactly the same as for Provençal, except for a curious innovation in the first person plural. The earliest flexions, before analogical interference, were as follows: I. -, -es, -e(t), -ons, -ez, -ent, II. -, -s, -t, -ons, -eiz, -ent. The continuing process of phonetic attrition has now completely destroyed these flexions in four out of six persons, with the result that in modern French, alone in this respect among the standard languages, a subject, personal pronoun or other, must always be used with the verb. Yet all of these have developed normally from the familiar flexions of Latin, all, that is, with the mysterious exception of -ons. This intrusion is not confined to northern Gaul. In a form similar to the Norman cantum it recurs in north-west Italy, e.g. Piedmontese cantuma, venduma, whence it was carried to the Gallo-Italian colonies of Sicily, and as -om it extends into parts of Emilia and Lombardy (G. Rohlfs, op. cit., vol. ii, p. 293). It is also found in parts of the Rheto-Romance area, e.g. chanton in the Ladin of the Dolomites (W. Theodor Elwert, Die Mundart des Fassa-Tals, p. 147). How and why this type should have come to replace -AMUS and -EMUS, supported as they were by -ATIS and -ETIS, constitutes one of the unsolved problems of Romance philology. It must go back to Vulgar Latin, and thus presupposes a form -UMUS. The only verb in Latin with such an ending, stressed, is sŭMUS; compounds of sŭMUS, e.g. POSSŭMUS, together with VOLŭMUS and NOLŭMUS, have a similar ending but without the stress, and these forms, in so far as they survived, were early adapted to the type in -EMUS, e.g. POTEMUS, VOLEMUS. Could a single auxiliary verb have exerted such an influence as to create a new flexion which replaced all others? Such is the problem. If the phenomenon is purely Latin it can scarcely be explained in any other way. But one is indeed tempted to wonder whether the development may not have been favoured by some undetermined element in the substratum.

Though so 'progressive' in other respects, Old French retained from Vulgar Latin a few exceptional archaisms. In face of the general western suppression of proparoxytonic first and second persons plural, northern Gaul kept FÁCIMUS, FÁCITIS, and DÍCIMUS, DÍCITIS, the origin of Old Fr. *faimes*, *faites*, and *dimes*, *dites*; whereas the first persons have long since succumbed to the regularizing tendency, giving *faisons* and *disons*, the etymological forms of the second person have persisted as anomalies to this day. The -UNT ending, otherwise lost in this region, persisted when the fall of an intervocalic consonant brought it into contact with a preceding A, as in *font* < FAC(I)UNT, and *vont* < VADUNT.

Italy preserved in general the three types of Vulgar Latin. These are apparent, though with flexions considerably changed by analogical substitution, in the accepted forms of the modern standard language:

| I | II | III | |
|---|---|---|---|
| canto | tengo | perdo | dormo |
| canti | tieni | perdi | dormi |
| canta | tiene | perde | dorme |
| cantiamo | teniamo | perdiamo | dormiamo |
| cantate | tenete | perdete | dormite |
| cantano | tengono | perdono | dormono |

Here, as in French, a single form has been generalized in the first person plural, but in this instance it is the Lat. -EAMUS, -IAMUS, borrowed from the present subjunctive, a loan presumably motivated by the frequent use of this subjunctive form as an imperative. This, however, is a Tuscan peculiarity, which does not accurately reflect the situation pertaining in the Vulgar Latin of Italy. Flexions *-amo*, *-emo*, and *-imo* are of common occurrence in Old

Italian texts, and are still in use in the dialects of the Marches, of Umbria and of Latium, e.g. at Assisi, *lavamo, vedemo, partimo*. Farther south, in consequence of the local evolution of stressed Ē, *-emo* has in some regions coalesced with *-imo*, while the north tends to extend *-emo* at the expense of *-amo*. The dialectal picture is in this respect one of considerable variety. More significant, however, from our standpoint, since it is a feature of the oldest texts and also of Rumanian, is the generalization of the flexion *-i* in the second person singular. This might be explained phonetically as a normal outcome of -ES and -IS, but in view of its widespread character, and of the fact that it has also replaced -AS, one is more inclined to infer the development of an early phonetic distinction between the flexions of the three persons singular, assisted by borrowing from the -IS form. The third person plural shows an extension of -UNT at the cost of -ENT. Early texts have *-on*, the later *-ono* and the *-ano* of *cantano* having acquired a final *o* on the analogy of the first person, singular and plural.

Of all the innovations in the active verb of Vulgar Latin, perhaps the most noteworthy is the extension of the ESC/ISC infix; and there is no morphological feature in which the different phases of Vulgar Latin are better illustrated. In Sardinia, Veglia, and the Abruzzi of southern Italy, all of them regions occupied early and lying outside the mainstream of later communications, there was no extension of this infix. With reference to Spain and Portugal, one cannot speak of an infix proper; all that one can observe is a tendency to make much greater use of the inchoative suffix -ESCERE. From this greater use there then developed elsewhere the habit of inserting the infix; it occurs, however, only in connexion with -IRE verbs, and is limited to certain parts of those verbs. In its earlier form it is -ESC-, which probably developed from -ĬSC-. This type is found in the present-day speeches of Bearn and Catalonia in the west, in a large central area comprising south-east France, with Dauphiny and Savoy, and the Rheto-Romance domain, in parts of southern Italy (e.g. Neapolitan *fenesco*), and in Balkan Romance. The -ISC- form, due to the influence of -ĪRE, clearly represents a late Vulgar Latin overlay, which developed in Italy and extended thence into southern and northern Gaul.

In the Iberian Peninsula the vitality of -ESCERE as a verbal suffix continued long after its original inchoative meaning had been forgotten, producing there a considerable number of verbs in *-ecer* which have been completely assimilated into the normal conjugation in -*er*. Such are Span. and Port. *merecer* and *padecer* from \*MERESCERE and \*PATESCERE, formed with the suffix from the original MERĒRE and \*PATĪRE (for deponent PATI; cf. Old Span. *padir*). Continuing usage is apparent in *agradecer*, formed on the root of GRATUM, which exists in both languages side by side with *agradar*; and also in the attachment of the suffix to verbs of Germanic origin, e.g. Span. *guarnecer*, formed on *guarnir* (< WARNJAN, see p. 210). A trace of the inchoative origin of these verbs remains in Spanish in the -*zc*- used before *o* and *a*, as in *agradezco, agradezca* (< -ESCO, -ESCA). The source of -*zc*- was, however, quite lost from memory, as appears from the fact of its analogical introduction into all Spanish verbs of which the infinitive ends in -*cer* or -*cir* preceded by a vowel, e.g. *lucir—luzco, conducir—conduzco*, &c. In Portuguese, with its *agradeço, agradeça*, the assimilation was complete, leaving no trace.

As characteristic of the -ESC- influence we may select two languages located at the extremes of its present geographical distribution, Catalan and Rumanian. In each, the incidence of the infix is exactly the same: it occurs in the first three persons singular and the third plural of the present indicative and subjunctive, and in the second person singular imperative, parts of the verb which in Latin were stressed on the stem. It is, of course, confined to -ĪRE verbs, and in each language affects the majority of the verbs of that conjugation. Comparison of the present indicatives of the verb 'to suffer' will serve to illustrate this morphological identity:

| Catalan | Rumanian |
|---------|----------|
| *patir* | *a păţi* |
| *pateixo* | *păţesc* |
| *pateixes* | *păţeşti* |
| *pateix* | *păţeşte* |
| *patim* | *păţim* |
| *patiu* | *păţiţi* |
| *pateixen* | *păţesc* |

This development may then be taken as representing an intermediate period in Vulgar Latin. To Catalonia it must have come from the north, for Catalan still contains inchoative verbs which seem to date from an earlier time, when the Latin of the region was essentially the same as that of the rest of the Peninsula; thus *mereixer* from MERESCERE, which kept its proparoxytonic accentuation, cf. CRESCĔRE > *créixer*, p. 113. Like those of Spanish, these verbs retain their inchoative stem throughout the conjugation. In Old Catalan, both this type and the -ĪRE type with infix have a first person singular ending in *-esc*, i.e. *meresc, patesc*, the later *mereixo* and *pateixo* being due to the analogical influence of other persons, in which -SC- before a front vowel became the voiceless alveolar fricative. Finally, it should be mentioned that Old Catalan literature contains a number of forms with the -ISC- infix, which survives to this day in Valencian: these probably represent a still later influence from the north, that of medieval Provençal.

Verbs with the -ISC- infix are characteristic of the -ĪRE conjugation in standard French, Provençal, and Italian. Present indicative forms are as follows:

| French | Provençal | Italian |
|---|---|---|
| *finir* | *florir* | *finire* |
| *finis* | *florisc* | *finisco* |
| *finis* | *floris* | *finisci* |
| *finit* | *floris* | *finisce* |
| *finissons* | *florem* | *finiamo* |
| *finissez* | *floretz* | *finite* |
| *finissent* | *florissen, (-on)* | *finiscono* |

That this -ISC- is a late replacement for -ESC- is apparent from the fact that the parts of the verb so affected are basically the same as in Catalan and Rumanian. In Italian they are exactly the same. Gaul, however, practised a slightly further extension. In both Provençal and French the infix was carried into the present participle, e.g. Prov. *florissen*, Fr. *fleurissant*. In French alone it also extended to the imperfect, e.g. *fleurissait, finissait*, &c. From the paradigms given above French would also seem to be alone in having adopted the infix into the first and second persons plural of the present indicative, but dialectally this same analogical extension is to be found in both the Provençal and the Italian areas.

Were it necessary to adduce further evidence of the genuinely Vulgar Latin origin of the ESC/ISC infix, this might be sought in the significant fact that the relatively few verbs of the -ĪRE class which have escaped its intrusion, e.g. PARTĪRE, VENĪRE, DORMĪRE, TENĪRE, MORĪRE, &c.—verbs of everyday usage—are very much the same in all the regions of Romance, from Bearn to Rumania, in which it occurs.

Rumanian presents an additional complication in the form of another infix, of different origin, which became attached in like manner to the present tenses and the imperative of -ARE verbs. It is -*ez*-, developed from the Vulgar Latin verbal suffix -IZARE, -IDIARE, of Greek origin (see p. 115). The two types which thus evolved in the -ARE conjugation may be illustrated by comparison of the present indicative of *a lăuda* 'to praise' < LAUDARE, which does not take the infix, with that of *a lucra* 'to work' < LUCRARE (cf. Span. *lograr* 'to succeed'), which does:

| | |
|---|---|
| *laud* | *lucrez* |
| *lauzi* | *lucrezi* |
| *laudă* | *lucrează* |
| *lăudăm* | *lucrăm* |
| *lăudaţi* | *lucraţi* |
| *laudă* | *lucrează* |

This infix, like -*esc*-, continued to gain ground during the post-Vulgar Latin period: both were introduced into the present tenses of verbs of Slavonic origin. In the modern language, whereas the majority of the -ÎRE verbs have the -*esc*- infix, approximately half of the -ARE verbs have the -*ez*- infix (S. Pop, *Grammaire roumaine*, p. 285). The sporadic occurrence of a similar infix in Italian dialects confirms the Vulgar Latin ancestry of -*ez*-; Old Venetian, for example, possesses forms *vendegea*, &c., which presuppose the existence of a Vulgar Latin present indicative of the type: *VIN-DICEJO, *VINDICEJAS, *VINDICEJAT, VINDICAMUS, VINDICATIS, *VIN-DICEJANT (G. Rohlfs, op. cit., vol. ii, p. 285).

With the addition of 'infix' forms the final result of Vulgar Latin evolution in the east was to increase the number of present indicative types from four to six, in contrast to the western tendency to reduce them.

Irregular verbs were in general regularized, in the tenses as in the infinitive. Thus in place of Class. Lat. VOLO, VIS, VULT, VOLU-MUS, VULTIS, VOLUNT, Vulgar Latin created VOLEO, VOLES, VOLET, VOLEMUS, VOLETIS, VOLENT; and the present indicative of POSSE, originally a compound of ESSE, instead of being POSSUM, POTES, POTEST, POSSUMUS, POTESTIS, POSSUNT, was in most areas detached from its parent verb and assimilated, like that of VELLE, to the -ÉRE conjugation, giving POTEO, POTES, POTET, POTEMUS, POTETIS, POTENT: modern Italian, with *posso*, *possiamo*, *possono*, shows an exceptional retention of the old forms. If one of the commonest of all verbs, the verb 'to go', still remains anomalous in western Romance, it is because of a curious lexical mixture which occurred in Vulgar Latin. The phonetic weakness in the conjugation of IRE first induced a mingling of its forms with those of VADERE: this is the stage attested in Spanish. At the same time Vulgar Latin created another verb, *ANDARE, presumed to be a reduced form of *AMBITARE 'to go around', formed on the past participle AMBITUS. In Spanish, as *andar*, this verb continued to enjoy a quite separate existence; but in the late Vulgar Latin of the Italian and Provençal areas (cf. Ital. *andare*, Prov. and Cat. *anar*) it became mixed with IRE and VADERE, tending to oust still further the tenses of the former. Northern Gaul witnessed a similar development. There, however, the third verb was the mysterious ALARE (see Reichenau Glossary, p. 314). Many are the hypotheses which have been advanced in an attempt to explain this new creation for 'to go'. According to the one most in favour it is a shortened version of AMBULARE (which normally becomes Old Fr. *ambler*), due to the use of AMBULATE (A'LATE!) as a military command. Scarcely less plausible, to our mind, is the suggestion that it derives from ALLATUM, the past participle of AFFERRE, and that it acquired its present meaning through the reflexive usage which persists in *s'en aller* (cf. Old Fr. *se traire* 'to betake oneself', from SE *TRAGERE, V. Lat. for SE TRAHERE). In the present indicative, while Spanish derives consistently from VADERE, the first and second person plural show in Portuguese relics of IRE, and in other languages the intrusion of the third verb:

| Spanish | Portuguese | Provençal | French | Italian |
|---------|------------|-----------|--------|---------|
| *voy* | *vou* | *vau, vauc* | *vais* (Old Fr. *vois*) | *vado, vo* |
| *vas* | *vais* | *vas* | *vas* (Old Fr. *vais*) | *vai* |
| *va* | *vai* | *va, vai* | *va* (Old Fr. *vait*) | *va* |
| *vamos* | *imos* | *anam* | *allons* | *andiamo* |
| *vais* | *ides, is* | *anatz* | *allez* | *andate* |
| *van* | *vam* | *van* | *vont* | *vanno* |

It will be observed that in the first person VADO was generally reduced to *VAO (cf. Provençal and Portuguese), then to *VO (cf. Italian); Spanish and Old French forms are due to the addition to *VO of an analogical yod. In the third person plural VADUNT was similarly reduced to *VAUNT (cf. French), and then to *VANT.

The inhabitants of eastern Romania solved the problems inherent in the verb 'to go' by the simple expedient of adopting with this meaning a quite different verb, the Lat. MERGERE 'to plunge', cf. Rum. *a merge*.

Of the auxiliary verbs, HABĒRE shows in its present tense certain phonetically reduced forms, due to pretonic usage, which must have been in Vulgar Latin: \*AJO, \*AS, \*AT, and in the third person plural, \*AUNT (cf. Fr. *ont*) or \*ANT (cf. Span. *han*, Ital. *hanno*). These are not unduly complicated. The present tense of ESSE, however, already anomalous in Latin, calls for special attention on account of the rich variety of analogical creations to which this anomaly gave rise. Typical Romance developments are as follows:

|        | French   | Provençal | Catalan   | Portuguese |
|--------|----------|-----------|-----------|------------|
| SŬM    | suis     | soi       | só, sóc   | sou        |
| ĔS     | es       | est       | ets       | es         |
| EST    | est      | es        | és        | e          |
| SŬMUS  | sommes   | em        | som, sem  | somos      |
| ESTIS  | êtes     | etz       | sou, seu  | sois       |
| SUNT   | sont     | son       | són       | são        |

|        | Spanish  | Italian   | Rumanian  |
|--------|----------|-----------|-----------|
| SŬM    | soy      | sono      | sunt      |
| ĔS     | eres     | sei       | eşti      |
| EST    | es       | è         | este      |
| SŬMUS  | somos    | siamo     | suntem    |
| ESTIS  | sois     | siete     | sunteţi   |
| SUNT   | son      | sono      | sunt      |

From this table it appears that in Gaul and Spain the V. Lat. SO was rivalled by forms \*SUJO, \*SOJO, adapted to the yod type of first person singular; in parts of Italy, the final consonant of SO(M) tended to be preserved as *n*, probably, as Rumanian suggests, under the influence of SUNT. In the second person singular, only French and Portuguese, among the standard languages, have preserved the Lat. ĔS. Spanish, as we have seen (p. 107), borrowed from the future. Old Italian, exhibiting a tendency to generalize the initial s of SUM, SUMUS, SUNT, appeared with *siei*, which suggests a Lat. \*SĔS. Both Catalan and Rumanian have converted the plural ESTIS to singular usage. In the case of Prov. *est*, it has been suggested that the *t* developed from the interrogative ES TU ?, but influence of ESTIS, which Provençal has kept with plural sense, offers perhaps a more tenable supposition. The climax of analogical creation appears in the forms of the first and second persons plural, as a consequence of popular attempts to reconcile SŬMUS with ESTIS. The whole of the Iberian Peninsula, together with Aquitaine, adopted SŬMUS, \*SŪTIS. Northern Gaul, on the other hand,

together with Rhetia, favoured *ESSIMUS, ESTIS (or *ESSITIS): hence
the Old Fr. *esmes*, which seems to have combined with Old Fr.
*sons*, from SŬMUS, to give the mod. *sommes*. Italy and southern
Gaul, with parts of the Catalan area, bear witness to the existence
of a third type, *SĪMUS, *SĪTIS. This may be due to the Latin
subjunctive, but the short vowel (contrast Class. Lat. SĪMUS,
SĪTIS) also suggests the possibility of an early throw-off from
*ESSIMUS, *ESSITIS. In Old Italian these forms occur as *semo*, *sete*,
in Catalan as *sem*, *seu*, while Prov. *em* is an original *sem* developed
in accordance with the tendency of Provençal, contrasting in this
respect with Italian, to suppress initial *s* in favour of initial *e*.
In the second person, the Ital. *sete* had an early rival in *siete*,
which has since prevailed: this supposes a Vulgar Latin *SĔTIS,
in harmony with the singular *SĔS; mod. *siamo*, as used in the first
person in place of *semo*, is of course due to the Tuscan borrowing
of present subjunctive forms for all first persons plural. By contrast with these forms, those of the third person, both EST and SUNT,
have remained relatively stable. As the paradigm of Rumanian
shows, the vitality of SUNT in the east was such that it tended to
be generalized as a new and presumably more satisfactory stem.

The present subjunctive has always been liable to confusion
with the present indicative. Linguistically, the subjunctive mood
is not indispensable, and its fate in various languages, including
English, has depended upon a vacillation between the popular
tendency to forget it and the subconscious reaction of the purist,
insisting upon the value of its use to convey an element of uncertainty in opposition to a straightforward statement of fact. In the
east, where learned Latin ceased at an early date to have any
appreciable influence, the present subjunctive became entirely
assimilated to the present indicative, except in the third person,
the same form serving as both singular and plural. It is normally
preceded in Rumanian by *să*, from the Latin conjunction SĪ, in
Vulgar Latin SE 'if', e.g. *să cînte*, *să lucreze*, *să țină*, *să piardă*, *să
doarmă*, *să pățească*; in Macedo-Rumanian the -*a* flexion has spread
to all conjugations.

In the west, the Latin system was more generally preserved.
Basically, it resolved itself in Vulgar Latin into two types, the
one corresponding to the first conjugation in -EM, &c., and the
other to -AM, &c. The persistence in many verbs of the yod deriving
from -EAM and -IAM gave rise, however, to a third type in *-JAM,

&c.; this is of particular importance in Gaul and Italy for its contribution to the flexions of the first and second persons plural, but otherwise it is identifiable, apart from phonological complications which it induced in the stem, with the type in -AM. The Spanish forms, compared with those of Classical Latin, may again be used as touchstone; it will be observed that here the yod is represented by *g* in the derivatives of TENEAM, &c., whereas it has completely disappeared in those of DORMIAM, &c.:

| CANTEM | TENEAM | PERDAM | DORMIAM |
|---|---|---|---|
| CANTES | TENEAS | PERDAS | DORMIAS |
| CANTET | TENEAT | PERDAT | DORMIAT |
| CANTEMUS | TENEAMUS | PERDAMUS | DORMIAMUS |
| CANTETIS | TENEATIS | PERDATIS | DORMIATIS |
| CANTENT | TENEANT | PERDANT | DORMIANT |

Spanish

| I | II | | |
|---|---|---|---|
| cante | tenga | pierda | duerma |
| cantes | tengas | pierdas | duermas |
| cante | tenga | pierda | duerma |
| cantemos | tengamos | perdamos | dormamos |
| cantéis | tengáis | perdáis | dormáis |
| canten | tengan | pierdan | duerman |

The forms of Portuguese are similar to those of Spanish. Those of Provençal are also similar, except that the general loss of post-tonic vowels other than A resulted in an -EM type as follows: *cant, cantz, cant, cantém, cantétz, cánten.* Old French appeared with the same two types: thus *je chant* but *je perde*. In northern Gaul, however, the type in *-JAM also persisted strongly, and as the evidence of derivatives shows, its yod sometimes became attached to verbs originally belonging to the other two categories. Some common verbs thus emerged in Old French with more than one form of present subjunctive: whereas DONEM regularly became *don*, the coexistent *doigne* presupposes a Vulgar Latin type *DON-JAM; and while ALLET gave *aut*, attested in the *Chanson de Roland*, a much more favoured *ALL-JAT became *aille*. A further complication was introduced into Old French by a locally divergent development of the yod, which tended to consonify after *l*, *n*, and *r*, thus producing such additional alternatives as *donge, alge,* &c. But these are details of a phonological character. It is to the first and second persons plural that one must look to find the decisive interference of the

yod type in the morphological system. There, while -EMUS and
-AMUS completely disappeared, as in the indicative, to be represented in Old French by -ons, *-JAMUS and *-JATIS survived,
giving -iens and -iez, of which the former was subsequently changed
to -ions under the influence of the more usual flexion.

Old Italian shows a completely normal development of the two
principal Vulgar Latin types. In medieval times, however, the
cante of all three persons singular was replaced by canti, presumably through the influence of the second person singular of
the indicative; the changed vowel becoming characteristic of the
subjunctive then extended to the third person plural. As for the
first and second persons plural, Old Italian texts contain -emo, -ete,
and -amo, -ate, which still persist in Italian dialects, but the
modern standard language shows exactly the same phenomenon as
Old French, viz. generalization of the flexions deriving from *-JAMUS
and *-JATIS. The forms now accepted are therefore as follows:

| | |
|---|---|
| canti | perda |
| canti | perda |
| canti | perda |
| cantiamo | perdiamo |
| cantiate | perdiate |
| cantino | perdano |

The inchoative infix extended to the present subjunctive in
those same areas in which it penetrated the indicative, and with
corresponding variation in the quality of the stressed vowel, i.e.
as -ESCA, cf. Span. merezca, Cat. pateixi (Old Cat. patesca) and as
-ISCA, cf. Fr. finisse, Ital. finisca.

Irregular verbs followed in the subjunctive the same pattern of
regularization as in the indicative. HABEAM, &c., produced *AJA,
&c., in the west, cf. Fr. aie, Span. haya, though Italian, with abbia,
has kept a fuller form. SIM, &c., was everywhere regularized to
sĭA, etc., cf. Old Fr. seie, Ital. sia, but in the Iberian Peninsula this
became confused with *SEDJA, the Class. SEDEAM, as appears from
Port. seja, and from the Old Span. seya, now reduced to sea.
On Italian soil, but not in Spain, DEM and STEM were likewise
converted to *DEA and *STEA, cf. Ital. dia, stia, but Span. dé, esté.
Noteworthy too is the apparent loss of yod in the Span. haga from
*FACA(M), as contrasted with Port. faça, Fr. fasse, Ital. faccia.

In the imperative mood, while the future CANITO, CANITOTE, &c.,
disappeared early with most of the other future forms, the present

was generally retained in Vulgar Latin. The proparoxytonic plural of the Classical third conjugation, e.g. PERDITE, became paroxytonic, e.g. PERDÉTE, the four types being thus reduced to three, as in the present indicative. Modern standard Italian, except for the change of -e to -i, as in *vendi* for VENDE—which however still persists as *vende* in many parts of Italy—has exactly the same forms as common Vulgar Latin, viz.:

|  |  |  |
|---|---|---|
| *canta* | *vendi* | *dormi* |
| *cantate* | *vendete* | *dormite* |

Spanish is similar, but shows inversely the extension in the singular of -e to the -ĪRE type, eliminating the -i form of the old language, viz.:

|  |  |  |
|---|---|---|
| *canta* | *vende* | *duerme* |
| *cantad* | *vended* | *dormid* |

The singular imperative was likewise preserved in Gaul and in the east, cf. Old Fr. *chante, dor(m)*; Prov. *canta, dor(m)*; and Rumanian, with three types, *cîntă, vinde, dormĭ*. In these regions, however, the plural forms were assimilated to those of the second person plural of the present indicative, cf. Fr. *chantez*, Prov. *cantatz*, Rum. *cîntaţi*, &c. Whether this assimilation, attested in the east as in the west in the earliest available vernacular texts, may rightly be attributed to a confusion of forms within the period of Vulgar Latin, cannot be determined with certainty; it is to be noted that in both regions a similar confusion of the singular imperative with the second person singular of the present indicative occurred at a much later date.

The inchoative infix is found in the singular imperative of those verbs of the -ĪRE class in which it had become a normal feature of the present indicative and subjunctive, e.g. Fr. *finis*, Ital. *finisci*, Rum. *păţeşte*; so too in Rumanian is the -ez- infix of -ARE verbs, e.g. *lucrează*. Among anomalous forms, the monosyllabic imperatives of Latin—DIC, DUC, and FAC—were widely preserved, cf. Rum. *zi, du, fă*; Ital. *di, fa*; Old Fr. *di, fai*, &c. A special peculiarity of Gaul and Italy may be seen in the absence from the earliest texts of normally evolved imperative forms for the four verbs *ESSERE, HABĒRE, SAPĒRE, and VOLĒRE; both singular and plural had been replaced by the corresponding forms of the present subjunctive, cf. Fr. *sois, soyez*; *aie, ayez*; *sache, sachez*; *veuille, veuillez*; Ital. *sii (sie), siate*; *abbi, abbiate*; *sappi, sappiate*; *vogli, vogliate*.

This was presumably a making good of Latin deficiencies by an extended use of the hortative subjunctive from which a so-called imperative was supplied for other persons of the verb.

For the imperfect indicative, Classical Latin had three types of flexion: -ABAM, -ĒBAM, the latter common to the second and third conjugations, and -IĒBAM. To -IĒBAM there corresponded in popular speech, as appears from the evidence of Romance, a form -ĪBAM; this form was in fact a feature of Old Latin and it is occasionally attested in the work of Classical authors, e.g. Catullus, Virgil, and Ovid. The three types are fully represented, with analogical adaptation in the flexions of the first and second persons singular, in modern standard Italian:

| | | |
|---|---|---|
| cantavo | tenevo | dormivo |
| cantavi | tenevi | dormivi |
| cantava | teneva | dormiva |
| cantavamo | tenevamo | dormivamo |
| cantavate | tenevate | dormivate |
| cantavano | tenevano | dormivano |

While the adaptation of the second person singular to an -i form is ancient, the first person is more commonly represented in Old Italian, including the language of Dante and Boccaccio, by etymological cantava, teneva, dormiva; in many parts of Italy, these are still in use.

Outside Italy, forms closely resembling those of Vulgar Latin are to be heard in the Central Pyrenean area, a region already noted as being quite exceptionally conservative. There, in northern Aragon, one meets again with cantaba, teneba, dormiba; similar forms occur farther west, in the Cantabrians, and also to the north, sporadically distributed in the patois of Bearn and Gascony (e.g. Bearn, candabi, prenèbi, audibi, see G. Rohlfs, Le Gascon, pp. 148–9). With reference to Aragonese, it has been suggested, on account of the absence of such forms as teneba and dormiba from medieval texts, that they were re-created on the analogy of cantaba (A. Kuhn, 'Der hocharagonesische Dialekt', p. 132). The standard of early Aragonese texts is, however, for the most part that of the plain, closely related to Castilian. The inhabitants of the areas mentioned seem more probably to have inherited their -eba and -iba directly from Latin, though the persistence of so ancient a tradition may well have been assisted by learned influence within the Vulgar Latin period.

Other parts of western Romania, while preserving -ABA, bear witness to a very early Vulgar Latin reduction of -EBA to -EA and -IBA to -IA. This is indeed characteristic of most areas occupied during the first phase of Roman colonization, including Sardinia and a large part of Italy. Lombardy and Piedmont and regions in central Italy still distinguish between -éa and -ía, flexions commonly attested in medieval Italian. Southern Italy and Sardinia, Spain and Provence, all show a coalescence of the two types in -EA and -IA into a single form in -ía. Normal phonetic evolution would in these areas tend towards such a result. In southern Italy the Latin stressed Ē became i (see p. 45), a fact which in Sicily, where the intervocalic consonant was retained as in Tuscan, resulted in the coalescence of both forms as -iva, cf. Sicil. vidiva, standard Ital. vedeva; in Spain and Provence a stressed E has closed to i in hiatus with a following vowel, cf. MĒA > Span. mía. Northern Gaul, on the other hand, eliminated -IA in favour of -EA, probably within the period of Vulgar Latin. In the east, Rumanian shows a similar diffusion of Vulgar Latin types, cf. cînta < CANTABAT, vedea < VIDEBAT, auzia < AUDIBAT. Here it will be noted that the fall of the intervocalic consonant has become general, with a resultant coincidence in the derivatives of CANTABAT and CANTARE which the linguistic sagacity of the west contrived to avoid. Presumably through the analogy of cînta, both vedea and auzia came to be accented on the final vowel, with the effect that here too -ea and -ia have now merged in pronunciation as a single type of flexion.

The development of the imperfect is characterized in the Iberian Peninsula and Aquitaine by an analogical shift of accent in the first and second persons plural. The forms of modern Spanish are thus as follows:

| | |
|---|---|
| cantaba | vendía |
| cantabas | vendías |
| cantaba | vendía |
| cantábamos | vendíamos |
| cantabais | vendíais |
| cantaban | vendían |

A similar placing of the stress on the same vowel throughout the tense is found in present-day speech in parts of Tuscany, e.g. cantávamo, cantávate, finívamo, finívate (G. Rohlfs, Hist. Gram. ital. Sprache, vol. ii, p. 331). Old Provençal, on the other hand, has the same Latin accentuation as standard Italian, e.g. *cantavám*, *cantavátz*, *partiám*, *partiátz*. To assess a date for the beginnings of this fluctuating usage, to say whether it could be attributed to the hesitations of Vulgar Latin, is more than any available evidence would permit.

French has dispensed with the -ABA type, thereby becoming the only modern Romance language with a single series of flexions for the imperfect indicative, though it is also the only one to have preceded these flexions, in the case of -ĪRE verbs, by the -ISC infix. The -ABA type is nevertheless present in medieval French, in two forms: in the -ABA > *-eve* development which appears as characteristic of regions to the east of the Paris basin, still persisting as *-ef* in the Walloon of the Meuse valley, and in the -ABA > *-oue* development, the so-called 'Norman imperfect'. CANTABAM thus survived in the Vulgar Latin of northern Gaul, at least in the first three persons singular and the third person plural. What happened there to the first and second person plural forms, CANTABAMUS and CANTABATIS, is not easy to determine. The earliest Old French texts have *chantiiens*, *chantiiez*, with flexions exactly similar to those of *vendiiens*, *vendiiez*. One can only conclude that at some unspecified time before the ninth century there developed *CANTEAMUS, *CANTEATIS, with flexions borrowed from the -EA type. This latter evolved normally into Old French, as follows:

> *vendeie*
> *vendeies*
> *vendei(e)t*
> *vendiiens*
> *vendiiez*
> *vendeient*

A single 'irregular' imperfect, that of the verb 'to be', survived from Latin to all the Romance languages. As the following paradigms will show, its forms were preserved in oral tradition, apart from analogical adaptations such as affected all verbs, with a quite remarkable fidelity:

|  | Old French | Spanish | Italian | Rumanian |
|---|---|---|---|---|
| ĔRAM | *iere* | *era* | *ero* | *eram* |
| ĔRAS | *ieres* | *eras* | *eri* | *erai* |
| ĔRAT | *iere(t)* | *era* | *era* | *era* |
| ĔRAMUS | *eriens* | *éramos* | *eravamo* | *eram* |
| ĔRATIS | *eriez* | *erais* | *eravate* | *eraţi* |
| ĔRANT | *ierent* | *eran* | *erano* | *erau* |

In French, when the infinitives *estre* < \*ESSERE and *ester* < STARE became confused, the old imperfect from ERAM gave way to *esteie*, a STABAM adapted to the -EA type. Elsewhere, ERAM and STABAM continued to enjoy an independent existence, cf. Span. *estaba*, Ital. *stava*.

The evolution of the perfect tense is more complicated. This is because of the presence in Latin of three structurally different kinds of perfect: 'weak', 'strong', and 'reduplicated'. Division into 'weak' and 'strong' has already been encountered in our examination of the various categories of past participle (see p. 116). Weak forms, i.e. forms in which the accent falls upon the flexion throughout the tense, belonged in general to the first, second, and fourth conjugations of Latin, with first person singular endings -AVI, -ĒVI, and -ĪVI. Of these -ĒVI, e.g. DELĒVI, disappeared early, in common with the past participle in -ĒTUS, while the other two types persisted with elimination of the intervocalic v, i.e. as -AI and -II. The reduction of -ĪVI, ancient in Latin, probably provided the model for the reduction of -AVI. Corresponding mainly to the -ĔRE conjugation, though including also in Classical Latin many of the -ĒRE verbs, was the strong form, in which the accent alternated between stem and flexion; the first person singular of the strong form ended in either -UI, or -SI, or -I, e.g. VALUI, CLAUSI, VIDI. Many such perfects retained in Vulgar Latin their fluctuating stress and in consequence they are the source of the 'irregular' perfects familiar in the grammar of modern Romance languages. Reduplicated perfects, e.g. CECIDI, MOMORDI, SPOPONDI, TETIGI, &c., very common in Old Latin, were already much reduced in number in the language fixed as Classical Latin; with the exceptions of DĔDI and STĔTI they soon vanished entirely from popular usage. Late but effective evidence of the various ways in which they were replaced is provided by the Reichenau Glossary (see p. 316).

The two surviving types of the weak category were universally preserved in Romania; medieval Romance presupposes the following Vulgar Latin paradigms:

| | |
|---|---|
| CANTAI | DORMII |
| CANTASTI | DORMISTI |
| CANTAUT, -AT | DORMIUT, -IT |
| CANTAMUS | DORMIMUS |
| CANTASTIS | DORMISTIS |
| CANTARUNT | DORMIRUNT |

Only in the third person singular may one observe a noteworthy regional variation due to the uncertainties of early Vulgar Latin. The development of -AVIT to -AUT, with vocalization of the v as attested in the Pompeian *graffiti* (see p. 25), must have been fairly general, as is shown by the *-ou, -o* now used in the Romance of Italy and the Iberian Peninsula. A different solution, the reduction of -AVIT to -AT, nevertheless prevailed in the peripheral areas represented by Rumanian and Old French, cf. Rum. *cîntă*, Fr. *chanta*, though the presence of forms with *-ot* in medieval French texts of eastern provenance indicates that the total elimination of the v in the third person singular was not common to the whole of northern Gaul. The parallel elimination of the v of -IVIT was more widespread. It is indeed only in the Iberian Peninsula and southern Italy that the v vocalized, giving the evolution -IVIT > -IUT. This at first retained its Latin accentuation as -íUT, but in Spanish the analogy of -AUT > -ó has given rise to -ió, with a shift of accent.

A more remarkable innovation in the Vulgar Latin of the west was the construction of a third weak type, with ĕ as the characteristic vowel, which served to compensate for the loss of -ĒVI. This derived from the reduplicated DĔDI, or more precisely from those compounds of DĔDI in which popular speech placed the accent on the stem instead of on the prefix, e.g. PERDĔDI for PERDIDI, VENDĔDI for VENDIDI, &c. The D of the flexion being lost through consonantal dissimilation, there evolved a type of perfect PERDĔI, VENDĔI, &c. In the Romance of southern Gaul, where this development is best represented, the new series of flexions was so favoured that it almost completely ousted the type in -AI, now found only in peripheral patois. Thus literary Old Provençal recognizes only two types of weak perfect, as follows:

|  I |  | II |
|---|---|---|
| *cantei* | *vendei* | *parti* |
| *cantest* | *vendest* | *partist* |
| *cantet* | *vendet* | *partit* |
| *cantem* | *vendem* | *partim* |
| *cantetz* | *vendetz* | *partitz* |
| *canteron* | *venderon* | *partiron* |

Consistently with its origin, the *e* of the flexion is normally pronounced as the half-open front vowel.

In this elimination of the -AI type Provençal is alone. The Vulgar

Latin of the Iberian Peninsula comprised three types, still preserved in Portuguese, which emerged as a literary language with
the following paradigms:

| | | |
|---|---|---|
| cantei | vendi | parti |
| cantaste | vendeste (-iste) | partiste |
| cantou | vendeu | partiu |
| cantamos | vendemos | partimos |
| cantastes | vendestes | partistes |
| cantaron | venderon | partiron |

These forms have persisted, except that the ending of the third
person plural has now passed from -on to -ão, giving cantarão,
venderão, partirão. Intrusion of the -ĕi type affected the first
person singular of the -ai type, but there it has stopped. As
though by way of compensation, the first two persons of the type
in -ĕi have been influenced by that in -ii. If we make due allowance for these slight analogical modifications, the weak perfects as
recorded in Old Portuguese may be taken as representing faithfully a much earlier linguistic situation which was common to all
the Vulgar Latin of the west.

In modern Spanish, whereas the first type has remained intact,
the second and third have become completely merged, thus leaving
in the language—as in Provençal but with a different solution—
only two kinds of weak perfect, viz.:

| I | II | |
|---|---|---|
| canté | vendí | partí |
| cantaste | vendiste | partiste |
| cantó | vendió | partió |
| cantamos | vendimos | partimos |
| cantasteis | vendisteis | partisteis |
| cantaron | vendieron | partieron |

Here, the type in -ii has in general prevailed over that in -ĕi, the
latter surviving only in the third person plural. In medieval
Spanish, however, vendiemos and vendiestes, from the -ĕi type,
were still quite commonly used, as were also the analogical par-
tiemos, partiestes. Replacement of the old second person plural
forms cantastes, vendiestes, partistes, by cantasteis, vendisteis, par-
tisteis is a relatively modern phenomenon, due to the influence of
the present indicative.

In northern Gaul, where -ĕi would have developed to -i in the
normal process of local phonetic evolution (presumably through

a triphthong *iei*), the -ĔI type was similarly mingled at an early date with the type from -ĪI; a distinction nevertheless persisted in the forms of the third person, both singular and plural. Thus the weak perfects of Old French which corresponded to those of Portuguese and Spanish were at first as follows:

| | | |
|---|---|---|
| *chantai* | *vendi* | *dormi* |
| *chantas* | *vendis* | *dormis* |
| *chanta* | *vendiet* | *dormit* |
| *chantames* | *vendimes* | *dormimes* |
| *chantastes* | *vendistes* | *dormistes* |
| *chanterent* | *vendierent* | *dormirent* |

For a while the flexions -*iet* and -*ierent* enjoyed considerable popularity in Old French, at least as literary forms, and occasionally they gave rise to analogical flexions for other persons, as for instance a second person singular in -*ies*. In particular, they became attached to verbs of which the stem ended in a dental consonant, e.g. *abatiet*; for a poet requiring an assonance on *ie* this constituted a useful alternative for *abatut* (see p. 235, *Chanson de Roland*, third line). From the thirteenth century they ceased to be used.

Standard Italian, like Portuguese, has kept the three types intact. In its -AI and -ĪI types it remains very close to Vulgar Latin. CANTAVIT became Old Ital. *cantao*, still current in the south, together with *partio* from PARTIVIT. The type deriving from compounds of DĔDI has an additional complication due to the intrusion of STĔTI, though this phenomenon is probably to be attributed to a period later than that of Vulgar Latin. The intrusion must have developed as a consequence of the early presence in Italian vernacular of two forms of the perfect of *dare*, the etymological *diedi* and a *detti* due to the analogy of *stetti* (from V. Lat. *STETUI, see below, p. 141). It would appear that, with normal diphthongization of the stressed vowel and partial retention of the otherwise dissimilated second D, the original paradigm was as follows: *\*vendiedi*, *vendesti*, *\*vendiede*, *vendemmo*, *vendeste*, *\*vendiedero*, and that, at this stage, the analogical *vendetti*, *vendette*, *vendettero* came into existence, the original forms being then levelled out to *vendei*, &c., on the pattern of the types in -AI and -ĪI. Modern Italian paradigms indicate very little difference from the perfect tense as it must have sounded in Italy during later Roman times:

| | | |
|---|---|---|
| *cantai* | *vendei, -etti* | *partii* |
| *cantasti* | *vendesti* | *partisti* |

| cantò | vendè, -ette | partì |
| cantammo | vendemmo | partimmo |
| cantaste | vendeste | partiste |
| cantarono | venderono, -ettero | partirono |

The new type of perfect created from the compounds of DĔDI was most favoured in the west. In the east it was rivalled, and probably preceded, by a fourth weak type with U as its characteristic flexional vowel. This developed in consequence of a shift of accent in strong perfects of the -UI class. Perhaps in the first instance on the model of FUI, the auxiliary HÁBUI became HABÚI, cf. Rum. *fui, fuşi, fu, furăm, furăţi, fură; avui, avuşi, avu, avurăm, avurăţi, avură.* Modern Rumanian shows all other Latin perfects in -UI to have followed in the same path.

As the reader familiar with French will have doubtless already remarked, this fourth type of weak perfect is no less characteristic of French than of Rumanian. The inhabitants of northern Gaul, like those of the east, must have used a Vulgar Latin tense: VALÚI, VALÚISTI, VALÚIT, VALÚIMUS, VALÚISTIS, VALÚERUNT. Moreover, northern Gaul favoured the adaptation to this type, in association with past participles in -UTUS, of a large number of verbs from other categories, including most of the reduplicated perfects of Latin. The familiar *-us* type perfects of modern French presuppose the existence in Vulgar Latin of such forms as *CREDUI, *CURRUI, *CADUI, *LEGUI, *FALLUI, *MORUI, &c. In fact, all of these must have been in general use throughout the Empire, but as strong forms; the shift of accent and creation of a new weak perfect on the pattern of the VALÚI, &c., quoted above is apparent only from French and Rumanian. Elsewhere they either retained their character of strong perfects, with varying phonetic development (see below), or were assimilated to other types.

The French and Rumanian developments are not in this respect identical, inasmuch as the shift of accent did not occur in northern Gaul without exception: a number of common verbs, including the auxiliary HABUI, remained entirely true to the accentuation of the strong category (see below). Yet it seems reasonable to assume that they are interrelated, that they represent peripheral survivals of a Vulgar Latin tendency elsewhere rejected. It would be too much to expect of a language in spontaneous evolution that it should achieve a widely accepted harmony of four weak perfects, each with its own characteristic flexional vowel.

Of the strong perfects, accented in Vulgar Latin on the stem in the first person singular and third persons singular and plural, those in -UI and -SI prospered, largely at the expense of those in -I. Perfects in -UI which remained strong in northern Gaul gave different results in Old French according to the nature of the stem. As being typical one might quote SÁPUI, SAPÚISTI, &c., which became *soi, soüs, sout, soümes, soüstes, sourent* (cf. HABUI, PLACUI, TACUI), and DÉBUI, DEBÚISTI, &c., in Old Fr. *dui, deüs, dut, deümes, deüstes, durent* (cf. *LEGUI, *BIBUI, *CADUI, *COGNOVUI). The originally weak forms were to provide the model in the levelling-out which ultimately occurred. In southern Gaul the initial phoneme of -UI was consonified, and then evolved to -*gu*-, unvoiced to -*c* when it became final through the fall of a post-tonic vowel. This was to constitute one of the most distinctive features of Provençal, e.g.

| COOPERUI | cubérc | DEBUI | dec |
| COOPERUISTI | cuberguíst | DEBUISTI | deguíst |
| COOPERUIT | cubérc | DEBUIT | dec |
| COOPERUIMUS | cuberguém | DEBUIMUS | deguém |
| COOPERUISTIS | cuberguétz | DEBUISTIS | deguétz |
| COOPERUERUNT | cubérgron | DEBUERUNT | dégron |

The Vulgar Latin of Italy shows a similar inclination towards strong perfects of the -UI type. In the central area, however, the U was ultimately lost through assimilation to the preceding consonant when it came after the accent, e.g. *STETUI > *stetti*, *CADUI > *caddi*, HABUI > Old Ital. *abbi*, and by complete elimination before the accent, e.g. *CADUISTI > *cadesti*, &c. The Iberian Peninsula, on the other hand, true to its earlier standards, gave no welcome to the proliferation of -UI. In many verbs it was replaced by -II, less commonly by -AI. In the few common verbs in which it remained the U was attracted to the vowel of the stem, e.g. SAPUI > *SAUPI > Old Span. *sope*, HABUI > Old Span. *ove*, POTUI > Span. *pude*, &c.

The strong perfect in -SI, sometimes described with reference to its Indo-European origin as the 'sigmatic' perfect, also grew in favour in those areas of which the Vulgar Latin belongs to a later period than that of Spain. Italy, Gaul, and the east all bear witness to the analogical creation of such forms as PRE(N)SI, TENSI, CURSI, &c., on the model of Lat. ARSI, CLAUSI, MISI, &c. In this development one may again observe the close affinity between perfect tense and past participle; the original point of contact which led to the approximation of the two series as quoted lay in the fact that both had a strong past participle in -sus, e.g. CURSUS, ARSUS. To the same sigmatic type belong the many strong perfects in -XI, e.g. DIXI, DUXI, which in turn also gave rise to analogical formations such as LEXI for LĒGI, and ELEXI for ELĒGI: these were linked by possessing in common the strong past participle in -TUS. At least one of the -UI verbs, Class. Lat. POSUI, joined the sigmatic type as POSI, a form frequently attested in inscriptions. As typical Romance developments, including examples of the few which have survived in the Iberian Peninsula, we might mention the following:

| | Old French | Proven-çal | Spanish | Portu-guese | Italian | Rumanian |
|---|---|---|---|---|---|---|
| MISIT | *mist* | *mes* | *miso* (mod. *metió*) | .. | *mise* | (*trimise*) |
| DIXIT | *dist* | *dis* | *dijo* | *disse* | *disse* | *zise* |
| POS(U)IT | .. | *pos* | *puso* | *pos* | *pose* | *puse* |

Of strong perfects in -I, only four survived the Vulgar Latin tendency to adapt them to other types. These —VĒNI, VĪDI, FĒCI, and FŪI—have in general persisted into modern Romance.

Intimately related to the perfect, and therefore tending to follow a similar trend in popular development, are all the other simple tenses of the past. This is especially true of the pluperfect subjunctive, preserved in the west with imperfect meaning, thus serving syntactically as the subjunctive form corresponding to both perfect and imperfect indicative, and maintained in the east, with terms reversed, as a full pluperfect but of the indicative mood. With its forms reduced in exactly the same manner as those of the perfect, and similarly including a new creation based on DĔDI, it presents in Vulgar Latin the following three types:

| | | |
|---|---|---|
| CANTA(VI)SSEM | *VENDE(DI)SSEM | PARTI(VI)SSEM |
| CANTA(VI)SSES | *VENDE(DI)SSES | PARTI(VI)SSES |
| CANTA(VI)SSET | *VENDE(DI)SSET | PARTI(VI)SSET |
| CANTA(VI)SSEMUS | *VENDE(DI)SSEMUS | PARTI(VI)SSEMUS |
| CANTA(VI)SSETIS | *VENDE(DI)SSETIS | PARTI(VI)SSETIS |
| CANTA(VI)SSENT | *VENDE(DI)SSENT | PARTI(VI)SSENT |

The Vulgar Latin of Gaul was more conservative than that of the rest of the Empire in so far as it kept the accent on the flexion in the first and second persons plural, cf. Old Fr. *chantissons*, *chantisseiz* (with an *-iss-* which was probably due to the analogy of the -ISSEM type), and *partissons*, *partisseiz*; likewise Old Prov. *cantessém*, *cantessétz*, and *partissém*, *partissétz*. Elsewhere, the accent in these persons was thrown back on to the characteristic vowel of the stem, cf. Span. *cantásemos*, *cantaseis*, and *vendiésemos*, *vendieseis*, and Ital. *cantassimo*, *cantaste*; *vendessimo*, *vendeste*; *partissimo*, *partiste*. With regard to subsequent preservation of types, they are faithfully represented in Ital. *cantassi*, *vendessi*, *partissi*, as also in Portuguese *cantasse*, *vendesse*, *partisse*. Southern Gaul, as in the case of the perfect, eliminated the first type in favour of the second; thus Provençal possessed only *cantés* (*vendés*) and *partís*. In Spanish the second and third types have merged, the forms of the second having in this instance predominated: hence *cantase*, *vendiese*, *partiese*. Old French shows a trace of the second type in the form *perdesse* which occurs in the *Cantilène de sainte Eulalie*, of Picard provenance, but this must have been early assimilated to the *-isse* type, thus leaving *-asse* and *-isse*, as in *chantasse*, *partisse*. Here, however, as in Rumania, was the domain of the weak perfect in -UI, and in consequence of a fourth Vulgar Latin type in -USSEM, cf. Fr. *valusse*. Among the Romance languages Rumanian alone has kept four distinct types (as pluperfect indicative), e.g. *cîntasem* 'I had sung', *văzusem* 'I had seen', *merse(se)m* 'I had gone', and *auzisem* 'I had heard'.

The pluperfect indicative, completely ousted in the east by the forms of the subjunctive, survived in many parts of the west, with varying usage. With the now familiar formal reductions, CANTA-VERAM, *VENDEDERAM, and PARTIVERAM became in V. Lat. CAN-TARA(M), VENDERA(M), PARTIRA(M). In Portuguese these have persisted through 2,000 years of linguistic history with no change of meaning and no significant alteration of form: hence Port. *cantara* 'I had sung', *vendera* and *partira*. In Spanish the three types have again been reduced to two, the second absorbing the third, as *cantara*, *vendiera*, *partiera*, and in usage the tense has become an imperfect subjunctive, coalescing in this respect with *cantase*, *vendiese*, *partiese*—an unusual instance of grammatical pleonasm. The two types of Provençal, *cantera*, *vendera*, and *partira*, have conditional meaning, and so too have the forms which have been preserved in a large part of southern Italy, *cantara* there corresponding in sense to the Tuscan *canterei*; similar examples of this tense are, moreover, sometimes encountered in the work of early

Tuscan poets, especially *fora* from FUERAM. In northern Gaul it was less favoured: instances of its use occur only in the earliest Old French texts, up to and including the eleventh-century *Vie de saint Alexis*, and there it has lost its pluperfect meaning to become an unsuccessful rival of the perfect indicative. Thus do the Romance languages reflect the popular uncertainty prevailing in the use of this tense in spoken Latin, the hesitations which paved the way for the supremacy of the unequivocal compound pluperfect.

Survival of the future perfect of Latin is confined to the Iberian Peninsula, where it has come to have the function of future subjunctive, and to adjacent parts of southern Gaul. CANTAVERO, *VENDEDERO, and PARTIVERO followed the usual pattern of reduction, giving CANTARO, VENDERO, and PARTIRO. All of these have been kept in Portuguese, as *cantar*, *vender* and *partir*. In passing, we should note the existence in Portuguese, alone among the Romance languages, of a 'personal infinitive', i.e. an infinitive which has come to take the flexions of the present tense of the finite verb, e.g. *o prepararmos um volume* 'the fact that we are preparing a volume', -*mos* being the first person plural flexion added to the infinitive *preparar*. This linguistic idiosyncrasy must have developed in consequence of the identity in form, after the fall of post-tonic vowels, between the present infinitive and the first person singular of the Latin future perfect (or possibly imperfect subjunctive, see p. 105). The future perfect-become-future subjunctive has in Spanish been reduced to two types, *cantare* and *vendiere*, *partiere*; Old Spanish had an etymological -*o* as flexion of the first person singular, but this was subsequently changed to -*e* under the influence of other persons. The use of the tense is well illustrated in the *Poema del Cid*, e.g.

> El que aquí muriere lidiando de cara.
>
> (l. 1704)
>
> Si nos muriéremos en campo, en castillo nos entrarán
> Si venciéremos la batalla, creçremos en rictad.
>
> (ll. 697–8)

Before the end of the Middle Ages its popularity had begun to decline, and nowadays it survives only in a few set expressions, e.g. *sea lo que fuere*. On the northern slopes of the Pyrenees, the same tense is found in Bearn, used as a conditional, and in at least one valley, that of Barèges, it appears to have blocked the penetration of the new Vulgar Latin conditional created from CANTARE HABĒBAM (G. Rohlfs, *Le Gascon* p. 147).

Mention has already been made (p. 105) of the isolated survival of the Latin imperfect subjunctive in the archaic Logudorese of Sardinia (cf. G. Rohlfs, *Hist. Gram. ital. Sprache*, vol. ii, p. 353), and of the Latin perfect subjunctive in the east. Such remnants do not invalidate the usual assumption that these tenses had already been largely dispensed with in the spoken Latin of the Empire.

*Invariable parts of speech.* Adverbs, prepositions, conjunctions, and interjections, too, all play their essential part in human utterance. With the development of the complex sentence—'a comparatively recent growth in linguistic history' (L. R. Palmer, *The Latin Language*, p. 328)—conjunctions in particular became increasingly indispensable to its structure. None of these words, however, partakes in the flexional changes associated with declension and conjugation; in consequence they have no 'grammar' of their own, no morphology in the technical sense of the word. If they are considered in the present context it is because of their syntactical importance, and their traditional status as 'parts of speech'.

Adverbs, it is true, modifying the verb as the adjective qualifies the noun, come within the grammatical range of 'comparison'; but in Vulgar Latin comparison of the adverb is identical with the analytical comparison of the adjective, a mere preceding of the appropriate form by PLUS or MAGIS. The synthetic comparatives of Latin, and their few remnants in Romance, are in reality neuter adjectives, and derive from the common practice of using the adjective predicatively (see p. 70).

In the formal development of the adverb the most notable innovation of western Vulgar Latin was the creation of the periphrasis formed from the ablative MENTE preceded by an adjective which agreed with its feminine gender. This is attested in Classical Latin: thus Ovid uses MENTE FERANT PLACIDA, and Quintilian juxtaposes the adjective to the noun in BONA MENTE FACTUM, cf. Fr. *bonnement*, Span. *buenamente*, Ital. *buonamente*. The congealing of the periphrasis in such a way that *mente* became an adverbial suffix indicating manner probably took place very gradually. In Old Italian and Provençal it was unnecessary to express the *mente* in the former of two adverbs, e.g. Old Ital. *villana ed aspramente*, and this construction still persists in modern Spanish and Portuguese, e.g. Span. *clara y distintamente*. In Old Spanish and Proven-çal the *mente* was sometimes attached only to the first adverb, e.g. Prov. *francamen e corteza, cruelmen e amara*. Such constructions were more rare in Old French; Meyer-Lübke and E. Bourciez quote from the *Chanson de Roland* the example of *humle et dulcement*, but in its context this reads as follows:

> Vers Sarrazins reguardet fierement
> E vers Franceis humeles e dulcement.
>
> (Ed. Whitehead, ll. 1162–3)

The *s* of *hum(e)les* seems here to be essential to the scansion, the adjective therefore agreeing with the subject of the sentence and not with the *-ment* of *dulcement*; but the author may well have misunderstood a construction which in his time was already archaic. The agglutination was consummated in Old French by the appearance of such analogical creations as *sifaitement*, and also by the failure to adapt to the feminine type in *-e*, at the time when other adjectives from the Latin third declension were so adapted, those forms which originated from the adjectival present participle, e.g. *constamment*, &c. (see p. 69).

The -MENTE adverb, as it grew in favour, gradually ousted from the Vulgar Latin of the west the Classical types in -E and -ITER (cf. the glossing of SINGULARITER by SOLAMENTE in the Reichenau Glossary). A few frequently used adverbs in -E nevertheless remained: notably MALE and BĔNE, the latter everywhere preserved, cf. Fr. Span. *bien*, Port. *bem*, Ital. *bene*, Rum. *bine*; TARDE, cf. Fr. Prov. *tard*, Span. *tarde*, Ital. *tardi* (for the change of *e* to *i*, see below); PURE in Italy and southern Gaul, cf. Ital. *pure*, Prov. *pur*; to these may be added the ROMANICE which is the origin of 'Romance', see p. 18. In the east there was no comparable extension of the use of MENTE, a fact which may be noted as marking yet another major difference between the Vulgar Latin of the east and that of the west. Rumanian has the solitary example of *aĭminterea*, from ALIA MENTE 'otherwise'. In southern Italy the adverbs in *-mente* seem to be a late importation from the north, and on the eastern seaboard of the Adriatic, in Old Dalmatian, they were equally unknown. The modern Rumanian adverb is most commonly formed by means of the suffixes *-eşte* and *-iş*, which appear to represent -ĪSCE and -ĪCE, e.g. *bătrîn* 'old', *bătrîneşte* 'in the old way'; *cruce* 'cross', *cruciş* 'crosswise'; *faţă* 'face', *făţiş* 'openly'. Many other devices are however available: according to S. Pop

(*Grammaire roumaine*, p. 413), any part of speech except the article can in Rumanian be pressed into service as an adverb.

Certain other endings acquired in the west, through analogical transference, the status of adverbial suffix. In the French and Spanish areas the -s of many Latin adverbs, e.g. PLUS, MAGIS, FORIS, INTUS became attached to forms in which it was not etymological. This so-called 'adverbial *s*' appears, for example, in Old Fr. *onques* from UNQUAM, and *sempres* from SEMPER; it survives in modern French, though it has long since ceased to be functional, in *volontiers* from VOLUNTARIE, and probably in *lors*, *alors*, formed by agglutination of the article to Old Fr. *or(e)s* from HORA, though here there might conceivably be an influence of the plural HORAS. In Provençal the adverbial *s* is equally common, e.g. *oncas*, *sempres*, *alques*, and (presumably) *aoras*, *quoras*. Spanish has a similar *s* in *entonces* from *INTUNCE (see below), lacking in the *entonce* of Old Portuguese, as also in *mientras* (see below). The phenomenon seems therefore to have originated in the Vulgar Latin of the west. Italian, which in view of its loss of final *s* can supply no further evidence, has a similar development with final -I, the etymological *i* of *fuori*, *oggi*, &c., having given rise to *domani* for *domane*, *avanti*, *anzi*, *volentieri*, *tardi*, *quindi* (see below), &c., but this may be of later date.

As may have been suggested by some of the examples quoted above, the loss of many adverbs familiar in Classical Latin was compensated in Vulgar Latin by the creation of new adverbial periphrases. These consisted for the most part of a combination of preposition and adverb, e.g. AD SATIS (Fr. *assez*, Ital. *assai*), *IN SĬMUL (Fr. *ensemble*, Prov. *ensems*, Old Span. *ensiemo*, Ital. *insieme*), SUBĬNDE (Fr. *souvent*, Prov. *soen*) which replaced SAEPE, DE ŬNDE (Fr. *dont*, Span. *donde*), DE ŬBI (Ital. *dove*), DE MANE (Fr. *demain*, Ital. *domani*), IN TUNC (Port. *então*, Old Span. *enton*) which compounded with a Latin adverbial E to give *INTUNCE (Span. *entonces*). Sometimes two adverbs of similar meaning were linked together: thus DUM INTERIM, whence Ital. (*do*)*mentre*, Span. (*de*)*mientras*; in Gaul the combination was preceded by IN, whence Old Fr. *endementiers*, Prov. *endementres*. Noteworthy too are the various adverbial combinations with ECCE, viz. ECCE HIC, ECCE HAC &c. (see p. 87), to which may be added *ECCU INDE (Ital. *quindi*) and *ECCU IBI (Ital. *quivi*). The term VĬCEM (Fr. *fois*, Span. *vez*) also entered in French and Spanish territory into a multitude of adverbial phrases (cf. p. 316, Reichenau Glossary). Common to Gaul and Italy was the creation of a set of adverbial periphrases in which a noun or verbal stem with the suffix -ONE was used in the plural, preceded by AD, to indicate positions of the body; in French the AD survives as *à*, but in corresponding Italian expressions it is sometimes omitted and sometimes replaced by *in*, e.g. Ital. (*a*) *cavalcioni*, 'astride', *boccon* , 'flat on one's face' as in *cadde bocconi*, (*in*) *ginocchioni*, 'kneeling'; Old French *a chevauchons*, *a genouillons*, and modern *à califourchon(s)*, *à reculons*, *à tâtons*. Similar forms exist in Provençal, but not in Spanish, except for *a reculones* which is a borrowing from French. The construction is attested, but without the suffix, in the gloss of PRONUS by QUI A DENTES IACET, cf. Old Fr. *adenz*, in the Reichenau Glossary (see p. 316).

As in the case of adverbs, many of the prepositions of Classical Latin enjoyed no currency in popular speech. Syntactically, however, the preposition came to have a greater importance than ever before, a number of common forms being called upon to serve a multitude of purposes. Widely preserved over most of Romania were AD, CONTRA (Rum. *către*), DE, IN, INTER (Fr. Span. *entre*) or INTRA (Rum. *între*, Ital. *tra*), SŬPER (Old Fr. *soure*, Span. *sobre*, Rum. *spre*) or SUPRA (Ital. *sopra*) and VERSUS (Fr. *vers*, Prov. *ves*, *vas*, Old Span. *vieso*, Ital. *verso*). PER and PRO, though much used (Fr. *par* and *pour*), tended to eliminate one another: thus PER was lost in the Iberian Peninsula (Span. *por* < PRO, and *para*, Old Span. *pora* < PRO AD), but in general triumphed over PRO in Italy and the east (Ital. *per*, Rum. *pre*, *pe*). TRANS was particularly favoured in the Iberian Peninsula and southern Gaul (Span. Port. Prov. *tras*), and was preserved in northern Gaul (Fr. *très*) largely through its use as a verbal prefix, e.g. TRANSPASSARE, whence it came to be an adverb with a quite different meaning. CĬRCA was also an 'Iberian' choice (Span. Port. *cerca*). To the Italo-Gallic area, on the other hand, belong ŬLTRA (Fr. *outre*, Prov. Cat. *oltra*, Ital. *oltre*), and JŬXTA (Old Fr. *jouste*, Prov. *joste*, Ital. *giusta*, Log. *yusta*). EXTRA persisted in Gaul (Old Fr. *estre*, Prov. *estra*) and INFRA in southern Gaul and Italy (Prov. *enfra*, Ital. *fra*). CUM survived in most of Romania (Span. Ital. *con*, Rum. *cu*), but is conspicuously absent from Gaul, where it gave way to APUD (Old Fr. *od*, *o*; Prov. *ab*, *am*; Cat. *amb*). ANTE and POS(T) were kept in the south (Span. *antes*, *pues*, Ital. *anti*, *poi*) but tended to be used as

adverbs, in which function they were rivalled by the derivatives
*ANTIUS (Old Fr. *ainz*, cf. Ital. *anzi*) and *POSTIUS (Fr. *puis*, Port.
*pois*). Two Latin adverbs came to be widely employed as prepositions: SŬBTUS (Fr. *sous*, Prov. *sots*, Old Span. *soto*, Ital. *sotto*, Rum.
*supt*), and SŪSUM, for classical SŪRSUM (Fr. Prov. Cat. Rum. *sus*,
Ital. *suso*, *su*, Span. Port. *suso*); French *sur* is a medieval development due to a combination of *sour(e)* and *sus*, though the latter
survives in its old form in *au-dessus* and *susdit* (cf. Span. *susodicho*).

In Vulgar Latin the range of prepositions was greatly extended
by the creation of compound forms, the favour which these enjoyed contributing to oust many of the simple forms. This was
a process destined to continue throughout medieval Romance.
We quote only a small selection as being typical formations which
appear to date from the earlier period: AB ANTE (Fr. *avant*, Ital.
*avanti*), DE USQUE (Fr. *jusque*), IN VERSUS (Fr. *envers*), IN CONTRA
(Old Fr. *encontre*, cf. p. 317, Reichenau Glossary), DE INTUS (Fr.
*dans*), DE RĔTRO (Fr. *derrière*), SUB LONGE (Fr. *selon*), DE TRANS
(Span. *detrás*), DE IN ANTE (Old Span. *denante*, mod. *delante*),
DE POST (Ital. *dopo*). A certain mystery surrounds the much-used
Italian *da*, attested in inscriptions since the seventh century: for
some scholars it is Latin DE AB, or possibly DE AD, while others see
in it a Vulgar Latin borrowing from Oscan DAT (cf. Rheto-Rom.
*dad*).

Few of the conjunctions with which we learned in the class-room
to embellish our 'Ciceronian' prose find any support in Vulgar
Latin parlance. ENIM and NAM, IGITUR and ITAQUE—the stock-in-
trade of the public orator—vanished utterly. Only the most
simple, the most essential, have survived.

Co-ordinating conjunctions emphasize the differences between
eastern and western selection. ET was universally employed (Fr.
*et*, Prov. Ital. Port. *e*, Span. *y*, and early Rum. *e*), but it had a rival
in SIC. Over the large central area of Romania this rivalry was
presumably terminated by the crystallization of function which
made of SIC the sole affirmative particle. In Old French, however,
SIC appeared as *si*, used both as an adverb and as an alternative
means of linking co-ordinate clauses. Rumanian, on the other
hand, though *e* appears with limited usage in its earlier texts, has
given the primacy to *şi*, now its normal word for 'and'. In further
instances the division is more clear-cut. To convey negative co-
ordination NĔC served in the west (Fr. *ni*; Prov. *ne*, *ni*; Span. *ni*;

Port. *nem*; Ital. *nè*), but in the east, NĔQUE (Rum. *nici*). To express disjunction, AUT (Fr. *ou*, Span. Ital. *o*) was preferred in the west to VEL, SIVE, and SEU; the eastern choice fell upon SEU, cf. Rum. *sau*. With the meaning 'but', MAGIS (Fr. *mais*, Prov. Span. *mas*, Ital. *ma*) prevailed in the west over SED and AT; alternatives have evolved in some areas from PER HOC (Span. *pero*, Ital. *però*). Rumanian has none of these, and conveys 'but' by means of words which reveal a quite different Vulgar Latin usage, viz. *iar*, *iară* < EA RE, and *însă* < IPSA (RE), also by a *dar*, *dară*, of uncertain origin.

Among subordinating conjunctions QUUM (or CUM) was completely lost, whereas QUANDO everywhere remained (Fr. *quand*, Prov. *can*, Span. *cuando*, Ital. *quando*, Rum. *cînd*). Conditional clauses continued to be introduced by SĪ, though the vowel of the Classical form tended to open in popular speech, producing SE: thus the *si* of Spanish and Catalan suggests direct descent from SĪ, but SE must be postulated—it is attested in Gaul in the sixth century—in order to account for Old Fr. *se* (later altered to *si*), Ital. *se*, and Rum. *să*. With causal sense, Gaul preserved QUARE (Fr. Prov. Cat. *car*); a rather similar *ca* is found in Old Spanish, e.g.

Albricia, Albarffanez, ca echados somos de tierra!

(*Poema del Cid*, l. 14)

and it also occurs in medieval texts from southern Italy, Lombardy, and Sardinia, but there is some doubt as to whether this represents QUA(RE) or QU(I)A. The adverbial QUOMO(DO) was also pressed into service as a conjunction (see p. 60). Of those which vanished, perhaps the most noteworthy, considering its vitality in Classical Latin, is ŬT. Phonetically inadequate, and prone to confusion with AUT, it was replaced in the popular sentence by QUO, QUOD, QUID, &c., all of which merged, though by what stages is not entirely clear, into a universally employed *QUE (Fr. Span. *que*, Ital. *che*, Rum. *că*). This must have happened in speech at a considerably earlier date than any written evidence would suggest. *QUE thereafter became the hinge upon which new forms of conjunction were constructed, a process of word-building which continued throughout the Middle Ages, giving rise in the various Romance languages, particularly in French, to a whole range of new possibilities for the expression of shades of meaning in subordination.

Interjections, belonging to the realm of affective speech, seldom follow the normal patterns of linguistic evolution. Such as have their origin in a logical meaning are usually oaths, which tend both to assume a euphemistic disguise and in themselves to be abbreviated or otherwise distorted. Those which are mere noises, however intimately connected with the beginnings of speech, can scarcely be said to have a traceable linguistic history. The author of the fourteenth-century *Leys d'Amor*, a treatise expounding the 'poetic art' of the troubadours of Provence (see p. 394), made an interesting attempt to classify them according to the specific emotions which they express. They may however, like gesture, vary in significance from country to country. Here we will be content with the observation that one such noise, the exclamation 'Ba!' became in the Italo-Gallic and Rheto-Romance areas the root of a new verb *BATARE, cf. Ital. *badare*, Rheto-Rom. (Engadine) *bader*, Old Fr. *baer*, of which the participles, *béant* and (*bouche*) *bée*, are still extant. From the fundamental meaning of 'to be open-mouthed', *BATARE developed in dialectal usage a rich semantic history; scarcely less favoured was its derivative *BATACULARE 'to yawn', cf. Fr. *bâiller*, Prov. *badalhar*.

## VOCABULARY

The principle that each word has its own individual history, implicit in the teaching of Gilliéron and formulated in print by his pupil Karl Jaberg, now commands almost universal acceptance. This means in practice that in analysing vocabulary we cannot make formal categories, as we do with grammar. With reference to meaning, words may of course be grouped within certain semantic fields, according to their associations, but such grouping can only be attempted with the knowledge that it is impossible to fix clearly definable limits: indeed much of the interest of semantic studies lies in the continual shifting of contours in the relationship between sound and sense. Sound and sense cannot profitably be divorced; so every word used in Vulgar Latin must be explored, together with its various derivatives, in all its formal and semantic ramifications, including those of the derivatives.

To study the linguistic destiny of a single Latin word during 2,000 years of usage in the wide domains of Romania may be a very arduous and complicated task. Detailed monographs devoted to this end are now quite plentiful. By way of example we might refer the reader to the recent essays of Yakov Malkiel concerning the manifold progeny of PĔDEM (*Studies in the Reconstruction of*

*Hispano-Latin Word Families*). Pursuing his search in Spain and throughout Romania, the author here shows, *inter alia*, that the use in Vulgar Latin of such forms as *EXPEDARE, *SUPPEDARE, and *APPEDARE must necessarily be postulated on the evidence of their derivatives in medieval and modern Romance.

If the study of a single basic word can range so far, all the more forbidding is the attempt to comprise in one large work of scholarship the whole lexical treasury of a language; but this is the ideal which the dictionary-maker must set before him. It is small wonder that until the sixteenth century, when the printing press was there to offer its practical aid to those for whom such an enterprise was a goad to activity, there should have been little advance in this respect upon the limited word-lists of Classical Antiquity. Medieval glossaries, though obvious antecedents, are far from being dictionaries in the modern sense of the word. Only the labours of the last few centuries have made of the dictionary, in the civilization of our day, almost a household article.

The scope of the English dictionary seems at first to be almost infinite, but upon closer acquaintance we soon realize that it contains a vast number of items which have no part in everyday vocabulary, items which are learned and literary creations pertaining only to very specialized interests. For many of these we shall have no use in a lifetime of talking. The basic lexicon which suffices for our daily communication is in fact more closely circumscribed than we realize. No less circumscribed was that of the ordinary citizen of the Roman Empire, or indeed of Romance-speaking peasants and artisans at any time during their long history.

For the survey of modern French dialects comprised in the *Atlas linguistique de la France* (by Gilliéron and Edmont), a questionnaire eliciting some 2,000 words was found to be sufficiently detailed to include in its scope the characteristic lexicon of a rustic community. A 'normal' questionnaire of the same length was equally adequate for the more technically advanced *Linguistic Atlas of Italy and southern Switzerland* (this normal questionnaire was used in 354 localities, a reduced questionnaire in 28 localities, and a lengthened questionnaire in 29 localities, see K. Jaberg and J. Jud, *Der Sprachatlas als Forschungsinstrument*, p. 175).[1]

[1] The publication of a new linguistic atlas of France, planned on a regional basis by the late A. Dauzat, is at present in progress. The following sections have

Questionnaires devised for this purpose usually begin with the topography of the village and then go the round of the house—its construction, domestic equipment, and operations; thence into the outbuildings and lands, to include the description of all rustic occupations and implements, together with the nomenclature of plants and animals and of all natural phenomena; finally they return to the life of the human being, personal relationships, ailments, superstitions, and simple emotions. Within this range of experience one may identify most of the lexicon of Vulgar Latin. Largely beyond the scope of village life, and consequently tending to be imposed from without, are the additional semantic fields of warfare and administration. Prominent in Latin terminology from the very nature of Roman occupation, these were most obviously exposed to the influence of later Germanic and Arabic invaders.

Having thus attempted to bring within a comprehensive range the inherently vast subject of Vulgar Latin vocabulary, and incidentally to indicate methods of investigation, we must now further restrict our comment to an examination of the most essential differences between the vocabulary of Latin literature and that of the spoken idiom as revealed by comparison of the Romance languages.

In the first place, it is obvious that the ordinary citizen had no great use for the redundant embellishments of rhetoric or for subtle gradations of meaning. Where two or more words conveyed approximately the same notion, one would suffice. The variety of synonyms so skilfully deployed by Latin authors had therefore no counterpart in popular speech. To express, for example, the general concept of 'beautiful', FORMOSUS prevailed in more peripheral areas, cf. Span. *hermoso*, Port. *formoso*, Rum. *frumos*, whereas BELLUS eliminated all rivals in Italy, cf. Ital. *bello*, and northern Gaul, cf. Fr. *bel*, *beau*. Provençal, as is consistent with its position as the meeting place of both earlier and later linguistic currents, has both *bel* and *formos*. In this division of territory all other Latin words, such as LEPIDUS and VENUSTUS, were excluded, and have

so far appeared in whole or in part: *Atlas linguistique et ethnographique du Lyonnais* (P. Gardette); *Atlas linguistique et ethnographique de la Gascogne* (J. Séguy); *Atlas linguistique et ethnographique du Massif Central* (P. Nauton). From Liège have come two volumes of an *Atlas linguistique de la Wallonie* (L. Remacle and E. Legros).

Linguistic atlases of Catalonia (A. Griera) and Rumania (S. Puşcariu, S. Pop and E. Petrovici) appeared in part during the thirties but were left unfinished on account of political conditions. Other projects are afoot.

vanished from circulation. In like manner, over the greater part of Romania—though in some instances relics of the less favoured words may still be encountered in the remoter dialects—TERRA was preferred to TELLUS, MARE to AEQUOR, STELLA to SIDUS, PLAGA to VULNUS, SANGUIS to CRŬOR, CAMPUS to AGER, JOCARE to LUDĔRE, PORTARE to FERRE, PLORARE (Fr. *pleurer*, Prov. *plorar*, Span. *llorar*, Port. *chorar*) or PLANGĔRE (Ital. *piangere*, Rheto-Rom. *plaunger*, Sard. *pranghere*, Rum. *a plînge*) to FLĒRE, APPREHENDĔRE to DISCĔRE, CONVENIT to OPORTET, &c.

The social status of the choosers—soldiers and tradesmen, artisans and peasants—is frequently reflected in the choice. Rustic associations, the same which favoured the survival of CABALLUS rather than ĔQUUS, probably account for the replacement of FELES by CATTUS,[1] of ŌS by BŬCCA, of ĔDĔRE by MANDUCARE, of ONERARE by CARRICARE; and adjectives so rich in Romance progeny as BASSUS and GROSSUS certainly had no place in elegant Latin. CRŪS was replaced in the early Vulgar Latin of the west by PERNA (Span. *pierna*, Port. *perna*), which for Horace meant a 'ham', while in Neapolitan dialect the leg is *cossa*, which shows CŎXA 'hip', cf. Fr. *cuisse*, similarly extended to include the whole limb. The later Vulgar Latin of Italy and Gaul witnessed the replacement of all these terms by a word CAMBA, cf. Prov. *camba*, Cat. *cama*, or GAMBA, cf. Fr. *jambe*, Ital. *gamba*, from the Greek καμπή, adopted during the fourth century from the technical jargon of the veterinary surgeon.

A similar technical influence of Greek, operating this time in the kitchen, brought about the decline of JĔCUR, the Classical word for 'liver'. In culinary terms JĔCUR became FICATUM. A clue to the change may be found in one of Horace's satires, where the poet describes a dish in an over-sumptuous banquet as:

Pinguibus et ficis pastum iecur anseris albi.
(*Satires*, Bk. 2, No. 8, l. 88)

The translation of John Conington (London, 1902)—

a goose's liver, crammed
To twice its bulk, so close the figs were jammed—

---

The full story of CATTUS, believed to have been an import from north Africa, probably remains to be told. From Isidore of Seville (see below, p. 304) it called forth the following etymological extravaganza: '. . . vulgus cattum a captura vocant. Alii dicunt, quod cattat, id est videt. Nam tanto acute cernit ut fulgore luminis noctis tenebras superet. Unde a Graeco venit catus, id est ingeniosus, ἀπὸ τοῦ καίεσθαι (*Etymologiae*, xii. 2. 38). The passage is of interest for the attestation of CATTARE 'to see'.

is based upon what seems to be a common misapprehension. The word *pastum* must be taken literally: the liver was not necessarily stuffed with figs, but fed on them; in other words, the live goose, closely confined, was fattened with figs until its liver became abnormally distended. This is the technique still used in the preparation of *foies gras*, though the fattening is now done chiefly with maize.[1] Before it became Roman, the practice was Greek, and FICATUM is in fact a translation of the Greek word συκωτόν, 'fattened on figs', applied both to animals, especially pigs, and to their liver; modern Greek uses for 'liver' the diminutive συκῶτι. If it is rather strange that in this instance the Romans should have preferred a literal translation to a direct borrowing, it is more peculiar that the word should have been adopted with a proparoxytonic accent, as FÍCATUM, or alternatively FÍCATUM, cf. Fr. *foie*, Prov. *fege*, Gasc. *hidge*, Span. *hígado*, Ital. *fégato*. Possibly, in attempting to reproduce the oxytonic accent of the Greek word, they put a heavy secondary stress on the first syllable, which thereafter became primary. In limited areas of Romania the modern derivatives point to the FICÁTUM which one would expect to have been the normal form, cf. southern Sard. *figáu*, Friulan *figá*, Rheto-Rom. (Engadine) *fió*, Rum. *ficát*.

Whereas the favoured synonyms for 'leg' and 'liver' were Greek in origin, doubtless because in that cosmopolitan Empire such specialists as the horse-doctor and the head cook were Greek in fact, the more prevalent alternative for 'head' seems to have been a Latin creation. From the fourth century on, CAPUT, cf. Fr. *chef*, Prov. *cap*, Ital. *capo*, Rum. *cap*, was rivalled by TESTA, 'a piece of baked earthenware, an earthen pot', cf. Fr. *tête*, Prov. *testa*, Ital. *testa*, Old Span. *tiesta*, Rum. *ţeastă*. A less widespread rival, CONCHA 'a mussel shell', cf. Sard. *conca*, again recalls Greek. It is generally assumed that these came into their new semantic function as playful alternatives, of the kind which abound in the slang of all languages. We nevertheless suspect that the specialist, be

[1] Columella mentions only pearl-barley and wheat-flour (*polentam et pollinem*) as necessary for the cramming of geese. Figs are included among the foods which appeal to pigs, but are specially recommended only with reference to thrushes: 'Dried figs, carefully crushed and mixed with fine flour, ought always to be provided, so abundantly indeed that some is left over. Some people chew a fig and then offer it to the thrushes; but it is scarcely expedient to do this where the number of thrushes is large, because people to chew the figs cost a good deal to hire and themselves eat an appreciable quantity because of the pleasant taste' (*De re rustica*, Bk. viii, chap. x, transl. E. S. Forster and E. Heffner, Loeb Classical Library).

he the grave-digger or the medicine man, may here too have been the source of the innovation. The metaphorical meaning of TESTA, as used by Ausonius and Prudentius, is 'cranium', and this is the meaning of *ţeastă* in Rumanian, where the normal word for 'head' is still *cap*. In this original semantic distinction, as between 'head' and 'cranium, skull' (cf. also Old Fr. *test* < TĚSTUM), may perhaps be found the explanation for the long coexistence of the two words as synonyms in the Romance of Italy and Gaul, cf. Old Fr. *teste* and *chef*, Ital. *testa* and *capo*. Old Spanish shows a similar semantic identity between *tiesta* and *cabeza*, the latter from a derivative CAPĬTIA by which CAPUT was early replaced, in the literal use, over most of the Iberian Peninsula, cf. *Poema del Cid*:

> Tornava la cabeça . . . . (l. 2)
> . . . engrameo la tiesta. (l. 13)

Sometimes the special vocabulary of children has ousted words from their place in traditional usage. PATER and MATER have been retained in the west, but the equivalent terms in Rumanian are *tată* and *mamă*. Ital. *nonno, nonna* 'grandfather, grandmother', likewise derive from childish utterance. In Sicilian the same meanings are expressed by *nannu* and *nanna*. To V. Lat. NONNA and NANNA, created from this source, may be added NĬNNA, with another vocalic variation, cf. Span. *niña*, Cat. *nena*. All three forms have a varied progeny in Romance: the first appears in Fr. *nonne*, whence Eng. 'nun'.

In many of the above examples of synonymic clash the ultimate choice reveals an inclination towards regular types. First or second declension nouns were preferred to those of the third declension, and verbs which conjugated regularly to those which fell out of line. This regularizing tendency is indeed a feature of Vulgar Latin, as we have already remarked apropos of morphology.

Another closely allied factor which may have influenced choice is to be found in the actual structure of the word, the one with more phonetic substance, more 'body', being generally retained to the detriment of the one with less. This was especially so when the smaller word became in the course of phonetic evolution a homonym or near-homonym of some other word of entirely different origin and meaning. Thus the reduction of AU to O, in conjunction with the adaptation of neuter nouns to masculine flexions, might well have produced identity in the accusative between ŌS, ŌRIS 'mouth', and AURIS 'ear': an intolerable confusion which the early use of ORICLA (see p. 25) and the propagation of BŬCCA helped to avoid. The merging of final s and x, as attested in the 'MILES non MILEX' of the *Appendix Probi*, would have resulted in an approximation of sound between CRŪS and CRŬX. Fall of the unstressed medial vowel and a simple consonantal metathesis would have turned ONERARE into ORNARE. Both CRŪS and ONERARE are among the words previously quoted as 'rejects'.

When a word tended to lose its intelligibility in consequence of normal phonetic evolution, and there was no synonym at hand to replace it, speakers sometimes had recourse to a 'therapeutic' process of word derivation, a kind of subconscious 'patching-up' of the casualty. There is in all languages a natural propensity, which the more sophisticated speaker eschews, to lengthen words by means of suffixes (as in English 'dear' has produced 'darling'). Spoken Latin was no exception and indeed made a lavish use of its manifold possibilities of suffixation, the diminutive being especially favoured, and to a lesser extent the augmentative. With everyday currency the value of the suffix often became obscured, and in the Romance derivatives of words so lengthened has usually disappeared. In some instances one may well wonder whether it ever possessed a genuine sense-value: why, for example, should the sun (SŌLEM) have come to be described in Gaul as 'the little sun' (SOLĬCULUM)? Not, one imagines, with reference to its small size, or even affectively, in terms of endearment. Rather, it is a result of the subconscious activity of the regularizing and 'therapeutic' instincts of the speaker, harnessed to the will for clarity.

Derivation was thus a linguistically useful process, both as an expedient whereby irregular words could be made regular, and because the derivative was more resistant to phonetic attrition than the original word. The latter might be reduced to a single syllable, or even, as sometimes happened in Old French, to a single phoneme. The incidence in linguistic evolution of this kind of phonetic attrition and the homonymic clash to which it frequently gave rise was first emphasized by Gilliéron, in what at the time was one of the most revolutionary contributions to the study of Romance philology: *Généalogie des mots qui désignent l'abeille* (Paris, 1918).[1] Pondering over one of the earliest maps of

[1] This was followed in 1921 by *Pathologie et thérapeutique verbales*. Here, as the title indicates, the lessons drawn from the earlier study were expanded into a new linguistic doctrine.

the *Linguistic Atlas of France* to be fully established (the maps are in alphabetical order), he began that thought-process of linguistic excavation which leads back from modern dialect to Vulgar Latin. From the moment when intervocalic P lost in certain parts of the Empire its character of voiceless plosive, APIS was already a compromised word. It was dangerously close to AVIS 'bird', and even to AVUS 'grandfather'. Derivation came to the rescue of all three, producing APĬCULA (Fr. *abeille*, Prov. *abelho*, Span. *abeja*, Port. *abelha*, Ital. *pecchia*), AVICĔLLUM (Old Fr. *oisel*, Prov. *auzel*, Ital. *uccello*), and AVIŎLUM (Fr. *aïeul*, Prov. *aviol*, Span. *abuelo*).

The prevalence of the derived form over the original word must not, however, be envisaged as the result of an act of substitution. Both forms often lingered side by side, the derived form, as the more ample and therefore the more satisfactory, usually tending to assume a gradual ascendancy. Above all, the geographical factor must be taken into consideration: within a relatively limited domain, one locality may prefer one derivative while a neighbouring locality prefers another, and a third locality may for some reason adhere to the original form. Returning to the bee, we find in fact that in northern France, the initial danger of homonymic clash between the designations of the bee and the bird having been averted in the Vulgar Latin of the area by the general adoption of AVICĔLLUM with the latter meaning, the original Latin APIS, APEM was permitted to survive, appearing in Old French as *es*, *e(f)*; a similar situation pertained in parts of Italy, cf. Ital. *ape*. There seems indeed to have been a time during which AVICĔLLUM and APEM were the favoured forms in the Vulgar Latin of a large part of Italy and Gaul, while in that of the Iberian Peninsula the inhabitants had opted inversely for AVEM, cf. Span. Port. *ave*, and APĬCULA.

The further history of the words for 'bee' in French, though obviously extending far beyond the chronological borders of Vulgar Latin, may perhaps lay claim to our consideration as a concrete example of the kind of word-movement which must have been no less common during the Roman period. Perusal of the relevant map of the Linguistic Atlas will show that *e* is still in current use on the fringes of Normandy; elsewhere in the northern part of France this brief utterance has been treated as a phonetic casualty and replaced by various 'therapeutic devices': these form the principal theme of Gilliéron's book. In some patois, for instance, the bee is the *mouche-à-miel*, in others, quite illogically, the *mouchette*, in which Gilliéron sees an adaptation of *mouche-ep*. For historical evidence (which Gilliéron tended to neglect) one may turn to Littré's dictionary. There, under the rubric *abeille*, among the examples given in the historical section, we read: 'Il m'avironnerent aussi comme es' (thirteenth century); 'une multitude d'avilles, ce sont mouches qui font la cire et le miel' (fifteenth century); 'les abeilles ou avettes, les guespes, les freslons' (sixteenth century). Thus the thirteenth-century *es* had given way in the fifteenth century to an *aville*, which the author deemed necessary to explain as 'honey-fly', and the sixteenth-century author— in common with Ronsard—used indifferently *avette* (< AP-ĬTTA)[1] or *abeille*. All of these were dialectal developments, the one which the seventeenth century eventually preferred being the most characteristically southern—a truly remarkable example of the way in which a standard language could make good a lexical deficiency by borrowing from its humbler kindred.

This kind of competitive existence between a word and its derivative may be illustrated by many more examples chosen from Vulgar Latin. We have mentioned already SŌLEM (Span. *sol*, Ital. *sole*, Rum. *soare*) and SOLĬCULUM (Fr. *soleil*, Prov. *solelh*). Whereas in this instance Gaul alone preferred the diminutive, probably in order to avoid contact with SŌLUM (Prov. *sol*, Span. *suelo*, Ital. *suolo*), in the case of CAULEM, CAULĬCULUM (cf. p. 24, Pompeian *graffiti*), the diminutive prospered only in the east (Rum. *curechi(ŭ)*), but Fr. *chou*, Prov. *caul*, Span. *col*). With the meaning 'brother', most areas kept FRATER (Fr. *frère*, Old Ital. *frate*, Rum. *frate*), but a large part of Italy preferred FRATELLUM, whence the standard *fratello*. Northern France alone eventually opted for TAURĔLLUM (Fr. *taureau*) instead of TAURUM (Old Fr. *tor*, Prov. *taur*, Span. Ital. *toro*, Rum. *taur*). ACUS (Ital. *ago*, Log. *agu*, Rum. *ac*) was

---

[1] The diminutive suffix -ĬTTU, -ĬTTA (Fr. *-et*, *-ette*) enjoyed a remarkable popularity in all western parts of the Romance area; there is no trace of it in Rumanian. The Iberian Peninsula preferred a form with lengthened vowel (cf. Span. *-ito*, *-ita*). Also current though much less favoured were -OTTU and -ATTU, the latter applied in the first instance to the young of animals, cf. Fr. *louvat*, *verrat*. Though the first mentioned occurs in inscriptions in personal names, mostly feminine, e.g. Gallitta, Jul(l)itta, Pollitta, these suffixes in -TT- were otherwise unknown in Latin (except perhaps in SAGĬTTA) and they have no obvious Indo-European ancestry. The problem which they set has preoccupied many scholars, who have sought to explain them variously by Etruscan, Greek, Germanic, and Celtic. In a recent and detailed study (*La Formation diminutive dans les langues romanes*, Uppsala, 1957), B. Hasselrot argues strongly in support of the Celtic theory.

replaced in most of the Empire by *ACŪCULA (Fr. *aiguille*, Prov. *agulha*, Span. *aguja*, Ital. *agucchia*). It was left to northern France to prefer an affective *PISCIONEM (Fr. *poisson*, cf. Ital. *pescione*) to the simple PĬSCEM (Prov. *peis*, Span. *pez*, Port. *peixe*, Ital. *pesce*, Log. *piske*, Rum. *peşte*):[1] whether this originally meant a 'wee fish' or a 'great big fish' may be open to doubt, the suffix -ONEM being used in different parts of Romania as either diminutive (cf. *val—vallon*) or augmentative (cf. *balle—ballon*); in general it became diminutive in France and augmentative in Italy and Spain.

If the suffix played a major role in the exuberant word-building of Vulgar Latin, that of the prefix was scarcely less important. Verbs especially were liable to be enlarged in this way, usually by means of a common preposition—the favourites being AB, AD, CUM (CON), DE, EX, IN, PER, PRO, SUB, and TRANS—or by the repetitive RE. A familiar verb like PORTARE might be preceded by almost any one of these, thereby serving to give precise and dynamic expression, with no strain upon the lexical resources of the speaker, for a considerable variety of kindred but different meanings. All Romance languages comprise a large number of verbs, together with substantives derived by back-formation from verbs, of which the initial phoneme represents one of these prefixes, now more or less disguised in consequence of phonetic evolution, e.g. EX in Fr. *épouvanter*, Ital. *spaventare*, *spiegare* (< EXPLICARE), AD in Fr. *acheter*, *achat*, &c. (cf. p. 116). Like the suffix, the prefix could combine a therapeutic with a semantic value, the former sometimes becoming the more linguistically important. Thus FLARE 'to blow', though also adapted with the 'participial solution' to FLATARE (cf. Ital. *fiatare*), was more generally replaced in its original meaning by SUBFLARE (Fr. *souffler*, Prov. *soflar*, Span. *soplar*, Port. *soprar*, Ital. *soffiare*, Rum. *a sufla*). SUBFLARE having taken over the basic meaning, other such compounds acquired more specialized sense, e.g. INFLARE (Fr. *enfler*, Prov. *enflar*, Span. *hinchar*, Port. *inchar*, Ital. *enfiare*, Rum. *a umfla*); CONFLARE (Fr. *gonfler*, Ital. *gonfiare*, Old Ital. *cuffiare*, the last of these a dialectal variety meaning 'to eat', particularly of animals); and ADFLARE, AFFLARE (Span. *hallar*, Port. *achar*, Rum. *a afla*) 'to scent', 'smell out', which acquired new semantic impulses from its association with the hunt and in some

---

[1] PĬSCEM alone is not unrepresented in northern France, cf. Old Fr. *porpois*, lit. 'pig-fish', preserved in Eng. *porpoise* but now replaced in French by *marsouin* (see p. 267).

dialects became 'to attack', while in Spanish and Portuguese, as also in Rumanian, it has given the current word for 'to find'. Similarly, COMĔDERE was permitted by virtue of its prefix to survive the demise of ĔDĔRE, at least in the Iberian Peninsula, cf. Span. Port. *comer*, though elsewhere it too was displaced by MANDUCARE. The verb INITIARE is still to be found uncompounded in the dialects of northern Italy, e.g. Genoese and Milanese *insá*, Piedmontese *ensé*, &c., but as CUM INITIARE it was preserved much more widely in Italy and Gaul (cf. Fr. *commencer*, Prov. *comesar*, Ital. *cominciare*).

Local differentiation in Vulgar Latin vocabulary, both in the forms selected and in the meanings in which they were understood, must have been continuous from the earliest times of Roman colonization. The process was doubtless accelerated from the third century onwards, as the growing autonomy of the provinces expressed itself in a greater degree of linguistic independence. Some of the familiar words of Classical Latin are preserved only in southern Italy and Sardinia, e.g. CRAS 'tomorrow', cf. Sard. *cras*, South Ital. *crai*; this word was not unknown in the Iberian Peninsula, as is proved by Old Span. and Old Port. *cras*, but it was in early conflict with MANE and its compounds, by which it has been entirely replaced elsewhere (see below, p. 166). Next in archaism to Sardinian and southern Italian are Hispano-Romance and Balkan Romance, both of which have developed on very independent lines but nevertheless quite often coincide in their lexical choice. They, for example, have kept ROGARE (Span. Port. *rogar*, Rum. *a ruga*) in preference to PRECARE (Fr. *prier*, Prov. *pregar*, Ital. *pregare*), and HUMERUS (Span. *hombro*, Port. *ombro*, Rum. *umăr*) rather than SPATULA (Fr. *épaule*, Ital. *spalla*); together with Sardinian they still have ĔQUA (Span. *yegua*, Port. *égua*, Sard. *ebba*, Rum. *iapă*), obliterated elsewhere by an overlay of CABALLA, or—the 'beast of burden' being usually the mare—of JUMENTUM (Fr. *la jument*, S. Ital. *giumenta*). One cannot, however, draw from these examples of word-distribution any irrefutable inference concerning the stratification of Romance vocabulary. In the case of PLORARE and PLANGERE we have already seen French and Spanish agreeing upon the former, and Italy and Rumania opting for the latter. Other examples, as in morphological selection, will show France and Rumania united in opposition to Italy and Spain: the two latter, for instance, adopted as the word for 'uncle' the Greek θεῖος, latinized as THIUS (Span. *tío*, Port. *tio*, Sard. *tiu*, Ital. *zio*), whereas both France and Rumania have the Latin AVUNCULUS (Fr. *oncle*, Prov. *ouncle*, Rum. *unchi(u)*).

From any attempt at general classification one only returns with renewed faith in the principle that every word has its own history. As a detailed examination of the findings of linguistic geography would show, scarcely any two words in modern Romance idiom can be placed within identical frontiers. The frontiers of each word continually shift, advancing or receding. Some words how-ever are much more itinerant than others. Had we inherited lin-guistic atlases from the Middle Ages they would certainly have revealed a considerably different distribution of Vulgar Latin vocabulary from that which is observable today. The maps for 'bee' and 'mare', for example, would have shown APIS and ĔQUA (Old Fr. *ive*) still occupying a large area of northern Gaul. Yet despite this instability, it is quite possible to discern certain general directions in the movement of Vulgar Latin vocabulary, what we have elsewhere described as 'linguistic currents', corresponding to historical orientation. Perhaps the most clearly marked is the late Vulgar Latin current which reflects the community in evolution between the northern half of Italy and Gaul. Its effect on morpho-logy has already been observed. Its like effect upon vocabulary may be gauged from a comparison of the means of expressing a few common and well-defined concepts in the three major Romance languages of the west. With these examples, deliberately chosen to illustrate fundamental divergences between the Vulgar Latin of the Iberian Peninsula on the one hand, and that of Italy (north of Naples) and Gaul on the other,[1] we bring to a close our brief examination of the purely Latin sources of the Romance lexicon:

1. 'Table.' Fr. *table*, Ital. *tavola*, Span. *mesa*.

Lat. MENSA, attested as MESA in the *Appendix Probi*, is still the normal word for 'table' in areas of early Vulgar Latin, cf. Span. Port. *mesa*, Log. *meza*, Rum. *masă*; it is also found in Rheto-Romance (Engadine, *maisa*), in some parts of Italy, and in

---

[1] This subject has been examined in particular by J. Jud, Problèmes de géographie linguistique (*Revue de linguistique romane*, vol. i, 1925, pp. 181–236), and more recently by G. Rohlfs, *Die lexikalische Differenzierung der romanischen Sprachen* (see Bibliography). In selecting examples we have had recourse chiefly to the latter.

Vegliote (*maisa*). In these speeches TABULA still has its Latin sense of 'board', cf. Span. *tabla*. In later Vulgar Latin TABULA super-seded MESA as 'table', but without completely eliminating it; in French MESA has evolved with phonetic regularity to *moise*, rele-gated semantically to the technical language of carpentry, in which it means 'cross-piece'. A third Latin possibility was supplied by DĪSCUM: this became the *dais* of French, but *desco* is the usual word for 'table' in parts of northern Italy.

2. 'Bed.' Fr. *lit*, Ital. *letto*, Span. *cama*.

Here the difference arose in another way. Lat. LĔCTUS remained in western Romania as the one current word for 'bed', cf. Prov. *liech*, Cat. *llit*, Log. *lettu*, Engad. *let*. It was so used in the Iberian Peninsula where it developed to Port. *leito*, Span. *lecho*. These, however, gave way to a word *cama*, of uncertain origin, which must have been widely employed at a relatively early date, since it is attested in the south of Spain, before the Arabic invasion, in the *Etymologiae* of Isidore of Seville (A.D. 560–636). The author there writes (xix. 22. 29): 'Camisias vocari quod in his dormimus in camis'; and again (xx. 11. 2): 'Cama est brevis et circa terram: Graeci enim χαμαί breve dicunt' (Johan Sofer, *Lateinisches und Romanisches aus den Etymologiae des Isidorus von Sevilla*, p. 121). It goes without saying that Isidore's attempt to derive *cama* from a Greek word meaning 'on the ground' is entirely fanciful, and his suggestion of *cama* as the root of Span. *camisa* (see p. 183), though less improbable, does not command any support. The word is generally assumed to come from the pre-Indo-European sub-stratum in Spain.

3. 'Cheese.' Fr. *fromage*, Ital. *formaggio*, Span. *queso*.

CASEUS, the usual word for 'cheese' in Latin, survives not only in Spanish and Portuguese (*queijo*), but also in all of Italy south of the Spezia–Rimini line (Tuscan *cacio*, southern *caso*), and in Rumanian, as *caş*. The Rheto-Romance area uses a diminutive CASEOLUS (Grisons, *chaschöl*). FORMATICUS, originally the adjective in an expression CASEUS FORMATICUS, 'cheese made in a mould', was probably at first confined to Gaul, whence however it spread early into northern Italy, as also into the Catalan area (Cat. *fromatge*).

4. 'Lamb.' Fr. *agneau*, Ital. *agnello*, Span. *cordero*.

Latin AGNUS persists in the peripheral areas of southern Italy (Apulian *aine*, Calabrian *aunu*) and the north-western corner of the Iberian Peninsula (Galician *año*, north Port. *anho*). In the phonetic evolution of many regions, as the last examples indicate, AGNUS would have become a homonym of ANNUS, a fact which may help to explain the adoption in its stead of the diminutive AGNELLUS (cf. Cat. *anyell*, Rum. *miel*), attested already in the work of Plautus. This form was not generally favoured in Spain. Span. *cordero* (cf. Port. *cordeiro*) came into existence, like the Fr. *fromage*, through the predominance of the adjective in a combination of adjective and noun, in this instance the CHŎRDUS of AGNUS CHŎRDUS, used by writers on agricultural topics, notably Varro and Pliny, with the meaning 'late-born lamb' (cf. UVAE CHŎRDAE 'late grapes', FRUMENTUM CHŎRDUM 'late wheat', and FOENUM CHŎRDUM 'aftermath', whence the *rekor* used with that meaning in French-speaking Switzerland). A derivative *CORDARIUS must be postulated as the direct source of *cordero*.

5. (*a*) 'Brother.' Fr. *frère*, Ital. *fratello*, Span. *hermano*.

(*b*) 'Sister.' Fr. *sœur*, Ital. *sorella*, Span. *hermana*.

Latin FRATER and SŎROR were employed throughout Romania and have in general persisted, the latter more commonly in the form of the nominative (cf. Fr. *sœur*, Rum. *soru-mea*, *soră*, Old Span. and Port. *sor*, Old Ital. *sor*, *suoro*, *suora*); the accusative SŎRŌREM is found in Old Fr. and Old Span. *seror*. Of the diminutive forms used in standard Italian *fratello* is ancient and probably provided the model for *sorella*, located in the same geographical area, which includes central and northern Italy; *frate* too is found here but with the meaning 'monk', whereas in southern Italy, inversely, *fratello* is 'monk' and *frate* 'brother'. The early supplanting of FRATER and SOROR by (FRATER) GERMANUS and (SOROR) GERMANA over the whole Iberian Peninsula (cf. Port. *irmão*, *irmã*, Cat. *germà*, *germana*) seems to have been due to a desire to emphasize the blood-relationship, the original words having become semantically compromised on account of their wide use as terms of address (cf. Fr. *cousin germain*).

6. 'To arrive.' Fr. *arriver*, Ital. *arrivare*, Span. *llegar*.

While VENĪRE remained everywhere the usual verb for 'to come', two new terms conveying a more visual image were borrowed from maritime language. The older of these, which prevailed in Spain, was PLĬCARE, first used with reference to the folding of sails (cf. Port. *chegar*, Sicil. *chicari*). In Rumanian *a pleca* means inversely 'to go, to depart'; this is because the metaphor there was military, and referred to the folding up of tents (cf. Eng. 'to decamp'). AD-RIPARE 'to come to shore', was a somewhat later creation which found favour particularly in Gaul (cf. Prov. *arribá*). From Provence it spread to Catalonia, and during the Middle Ages was carried thence to Sardinia, as *arribare*. The *arrivare* now used everywhere in Italy appears from its intervocalic *v* to have been originally a northern development; more truly 'native' to Peninsular Italy is *giungere*, from JUNGERE, 'to join' and hence 'to reach'.

7. 'To boil.' Fr. *bouillir*, Ital. *bollire*, Span. *hervir*.

Romance distribution shows clearly that FERVĔRE was the earlier Vulgar Latin term for 'to boil'. It survives in Span. *hervir*, Port. *ferver*, and Rum. *a fierbe*; there is also an area of *ferve* in the heel of Italy, extending for some distance northwards along the coast. BULLĪRE meant in Latin 'to bubble' and its growth in favour at the expense of FERVERE again shows the popular tendency towards more picturesque speech (cf. Prov. *boulí*, Cat. *bullir*, Sard. *buḍḍire*). The word came as a useful borrowing from French to English: whereas we can both 'boil' and 'cook', Germans can only *kochen*.

8. 'To speak.' Fr. *parler*, Ital. *parlare*, Span. *hablar*.

Latin LOQUI disappeared in face of the competition of a series of more colourful verbs, each of which originally meant 'to tell a story'. Probably the first of these to be so used was NARRARE, now found with the attenuated sense only in Sardinia, where it was adapted to the proparoxytonic type of infinitive which that island favoured (Log. *narrere*, Campid. *nai*). In the Iberian Peninsula the originally deponent FABULARI became the usual word for 'to speak' (cf. Port. *falar*). This too must have been an early development in southern regions—the word was already employed in the same way by Plautus—but elsewhere the meaning 'to tell a story', supported by the noun FABULA, generally persisted (cf. Old Fr. *fabler*, Prov. *faular*, Old Ital. *favolare*). Christian influence fostered the expansion in the later Vulgar Latin of the west of the Greek PARABOLARE (Prov. *paraular*, Cat. *parlar*, see p. 201). Rumanian has little share in this, using for 'to speak' a verb *a vorbi*, of doubtful origin: although the form suggests a connexion with VERRUM.

it is more probably Slavonic. In passing, it may be noted that the kindred meaning of 'to say' was everywhere expressed by DICĔRE, except perhaps in southern Spain, where Mozarabic texts show a preference for GARRIRE (see p. 404).

9. (a) 'Morning.' Fr. *matin*, Ital. *mattina*, Span. *mañana*.
   (b) 'Tomorrow.' Fr. *demain*, Ital. *domani*, Span. *mañana*.

As already indicated (p. 161), the Lat. CRAS 'tomorrow'—in contrast to HŎDIE 'today', and HĔRI 'yesterday', which have generally survived—persists only in Sardinia and a restricted area of southern Italy. It was rivalled by MANE, which, as an adverb, meant primarily 'in the morning', but which even in the work of classical authors could sometimes mean 'tomorrow morning'. This word was kept in Romance, and in the medieval texts of the west it is similarly imprecise (Old Fr. *main*, Prov. *ma*, Old Span. and Old Ital. *mane*, Rum. *mîne*, *mîine*). The imprecision is paralleled in the German use of *Morgen*, as also in colloquial English 'in the morning'. In all the Romance languages except Spanish new linguistic resources have been invoked in a successful attempt to clarify this ambiguous situation. Latin having no word for 'morning' other than MANE used as an indeclinable noun, popular speech resorted to (HORA) MATUTĪNA (Ital. *mattina*), or (TEMPUS) MATUTĪNUM (Fr. *matin*, Prov. Cat. *mati*). Consistently with the general inclination to strengthen short adverbs by means of a prepositional prefix, MANE became DE MANE, thereafter specialized in sense as 'tomorrow' (cf. Prov. Cat. *demà*, Engad. *demaun*); in Old Italian the more current form was *dimane*, the modern prevalence of *domani* being due to a phonological peculiarity of Tuscan dialect, in which pretonic Latin E changed to O before a bilabial consonant, cf. *domandare*, *dovere*, *dopo* (< DE POST), &c. (cf. p. 464). Rumanian has achieved a similar clarification, but solely on the basis of MANE and DE MANE: in the modern speech *mîine*[1] is 'tomorrow', whereas a derivative of DE MANE, *dimineaţă*, has become 'morning'. Spanish, as usual, went its own independent way, but in this instance with less successful results. The *mane* of Old Spanish (as used in the *Poema del Cid*: 'Tras nocharon de noch, al alua dela man . . .' (l. 1100)) gave way to a fuller-bodied rival (HORA) *MANEANA, but the resultant *mañana* continued to be used with ambivalent

---

[1] Currently, *mîne* is Moldavian and *mîine* Daco-Rumanian, cf. *pîne* *pîine*, from PANEM.

meaning; hence 'tomorrow morning' is in Spanish *mañana por la mañana*, but in French *demain matin*, in Italian *domani mattina*. From the same equivocal basis Portuguese has established a distinction between *manhã* 'morning', and *amanhã* 'tomorrow'.

10. 'Summer.' Fr. *été*, Ital. *(e)state*, Span. *verano*.

In this instance it is the Iberian Peninsula which shows an unfamiliar Vulgar Latin origin, whereas French and Italian have preserved the AESTATEM of Classical Latin (cf. Prov. *estat*, Engad. *sted*). Both Spanish and Portuguese formerly used *estío*, from (TEMPUS) AESTIVUM, an adjectival creation like the (TEMPUS) HIBERNUM which everywhere replaced Classical HIEMS; 'summer' is still *estiu* in Catalan. The presence in Old Apulian of *stibo*, and in Logudorese of *istiu*, with the same meaning, proves that AESTIVUM came ready-made from Italy and that it is to be identified with an early current of Latinization. A third adjectival form (TEMPUS) VERANUM, was then created to replace the phonetically inadequate Latin VER (cf. replacement in Gaul by PRIMUM TEMPUS, Fr. *printemps*, and in Italy by PRIMA VERA, Ital. *primavera*). Eventually the resultant Span. *verano*, Port. *verão*, were transferred from 'spring' to the season which followed, ousting *estío* and making way for *primavera*. In Rumanian the Vulgar Latin VERA remained uncompounded, as *vară*, and has undergone an identical semantic transition from 'spring' to 'summer'; there too, *primăvară* is 'spring'.

11. As a final example we may appropriately quote here the names of week-days, which will again illustrate the lexical rift between French and Italian on the one hand, and Spanish on the other, though in a situation complicated by the intervention of Christian influences. These provoked a further rift within the Iberian Peninsula, now manifest in the different forms of Spanish and Portuguese. In order to explore the position more fully we append the names of week-days in six Romance languages:

| French | Italian | Spanish | Catalan | Rumanian | Portuguese |
|---|---|---|---|---|---|
| dimanche | domenica | domingo | diumenge | duminecă | domingo |
| lundi | lunedì | lunes | dilluns | luni | segunda-feira |
| mardi | martedì | martes | dimars | marţi | terça-feira |
| mercredi | mercoledì | miércoles | dimecres | miercuri | quarta-feira |
| jeudi | giovedì | jueves | dijous | joi | quinta-feira |
| vendredi | venerdì | viernes | divendres | vineri | sexta-feira |
| samedi | sabato | sábado | dissabte | sîmbătă | sábado |

These names became eventually settled only after a prolonged struggle between clerical reform and pagan tradition. The latter, so dominant in countries of Germanic speech, resisted strongly and on the whole successfully. The one great Christian triumph is the designation of Sunday as DIES DOMINICA, the Day of our Lord; but even as late as the sixth century Cassiodorus could still write: 'Dominica die, quem vulgo solis appellant.' Also due to Christian influence is the adoption of the Hebrew 'sabbath', in the various forms SAMBATA, SABBATA, SABBATUM, to designate 'Saturday' in Romance, though here again DIES SATURNI is still to be found on tombstones of the fourth and fifth centuries A.D. For the rest of the week the Christian system, likewise borrowed from the Jews, was to call each day a *feria* and give it a number. About A.D. 400 St. Augustine wrote: 'quarta feria, qui Mercurii dicitur a paganis et a multis Christianis.' In the seventh century Isidore of Seville omitted the Christians, writing simply: 'quarta feria, qui Mercurii dicitur a paganis.' This assumption, however, could only stem from the south and west of the Iberian Peninsula, where indignation against pagan deities was particularly intense; witness the caustic remarks of his Lusitanian neighbour, Martin of Bracara (Braga), late in the sixth century: '. . . ut nomina ipsa daemoniorum in singulos dies nominent et appellent diem Martis et Mercurii et Jovis et Veneris et Saturni, qui nullum diem fecerunt, sed fuerunt homines pessimi et scelerati in gente Graecorum.'[1] In fact, southern Spain before the Arabic invasion and after the conversion of the Visigothic kings to Catholicism (see p. 220) was one of the most uncompromising centres of Christian faith and to this persistent exclusion of the pagan element is due the retention in Portugal, continually drawing its Latin from the former region of Baetica (cf. p. 173), and in Portuguese alone among the surviving Romance languages, of the complete Christian system of nomenclature for the names of the week-days. The ordinal numeral being used alone in current speech, the sentence 'The boat leaves on Thursdays and Sundays' will be in Portuguese: *O navio parte as quintas e os domingos.*

A special effort to eliminate the 'day of Venus' may perhaps be seen in the Christian use of CĒNA PURA, yet another borrowing

[1] For these and further quotations see H. P. Bruppacher, *Die Namen der Wochentage im Italienischen und Rätoromanischen*, Romanica Helvetica, vol. xxviii. Berne, 1948.

from Jewish ritual, in which it was the meal consumed on the eve
of the sabbath. This has persisted only in Sardinia, where *kena-
pura* is still the current word for Friday in Logudorese. Since it
cannot belong to the older stratum of spoken Latin, one may
surmise that its adoption there was fostered by the many Christians and Jews, companions in misfortune, who were expelled
from Rome to Sardinia during the first two centuries A.D.

In the remaining pagan forms different preferences are clearly
apparent. The Latin basis of French and Italian is LUNAE DIEM,
&c.; that of Catalan, as of dialects in southern France, is DIEM
LUNIS, &c. In Spanish, on the other hand, as in Rumanian and
some of the dialects of Sardinia and Italy, DIEM has been allowed
to fall out: yet another example of an early popular tendency
common to southern Romania, against which the later Italo-
Gallic current of Latin reacted.

# II

# EARLY NON-LATIN INFLUENCES

*Latin and pre-Roman speeches*. From that first upsurge of Rome
which began with the expulsion of the Etruscan dynasty, usually
placed at about 510 B.C., until the political disintegration of the
western Empire at the end of the fifth century A.D., spoken Latin
continued to be diffused throughout the occupied lands, without
interruption, and in general with increasing momentum. The
process of linguistic assimilation is not difficult to envisage:
settlement of 'Romans' in a native township where they provided
administrative and legal offices, schools, markets, and by no means
least important, places of amusement; attraction of the local
population which acquired sufficient facility in the use of the
Roman norm to benefit from the services provided and to enjoy
the amenities; gradual spread of the new medium of speech from
the urban centres to the outlying hamlets, with in every region a
period of bilingualism during which the emphasis shifted from one
speech to the other, permitting the absorption of some common
terms from the dying language into the one by which it was
replaced. Where by the fifth century this process had been completed in all its stages, as in Spain and Gaul (with the exception of
the Basque country), the Latin vernacular remained. Where, however, Latin had not appreciably progressed beyond the towns, and
the country districts were still inhabited by a relatively dense
population, as in Britain and most of the Danubian lands, then
with the social decay of the towns the native idiom tended to flow
back and eliminate Latin. In either case, the speech which prevailed incorporated borrowings from the other.

The pre-Roman speeches ousted by Latin were many, and of
various linguistic affiliations. At the dawn of Roman history the
Italian Peninsula itself, in consequence of successive waves of
occupation, presented a most complex pattern.[1] We have the

[1] Detailed information concerning the ancient speeches of Italy may be found
in the following works: R. S. Conway, *The Italic Dialects*, Cambridge, 1897;
R. S. Conway, J. Whatmough, and S. E. Johnston, *The Prae-Italic Dialects of
Italy*, Cambridge, Mass., 1933; C. D. Buck, *A Grammar of Oscan and Umbrian*,
2nd ed., Boston, 1928; V. Pisani, *Le lingue dell'Italia antica oltre il latino*,
Turin, 1953.

authority of Quintilian, writing in the first century A.D., for the statement that by his time this complexity had been eliminated, that all Italy spoke the same language. From a purely philological standpoint, nothing could be more obscure than the stages by which this transformation came about: it can only be inferred as a consequence of the progress of Roman control. The overthrow of the Etruscans, a 'writing' people who handed down to the Romans the alphabet which they had borrowed from the Greeks and adapted to their own use, procured the disappearance of their pre-Indo-European tongue. Etruscan inscriptions, of which some 10,000 have been assembled to date, and which remain untranslated though their meaning can be partially inferred, peter out in the third century B.C.[1] Italic speeches closely akin to Latin, notably Umbrian (still preserved inscriptionally in the Iguvine Tablets), and Sabellic, from which Oscan developed as the speech of the southward-spreading Samnites, were finally doomed when the latter were defeated and their lands occupied. There is, however, evidence that Oscan lingered on in some regions until the first century: a few Oscan *graffiti* have been found at Pompeii, on walls decorated in the latest style of A.D. 79. This was the last non-Latin language to have been used during Roman times in the Italian Peninsula, with the exception perhaps of Greek in the extreme south, which Quintilian may have overlooked (see below, p. 197). Most of these speeches contributed words to the Latin lexicon (cf. *Appendix Probi*, p. 33), but at so early a date that they became absorbed into the Latin norm diffused throughout Italy. The linguistic substratum of Italian is thus, in the main, the substratum of Latin.[2]

Whereas the general acceptance of 'correct' Latin would seem in the Italian Peninsula to be a natural result of early linguistic unification, in remoter parts of the Empire, much farther removed from contact with Rome, one might expect the influence of well-defined native speeches to be much greater, affecting not only the vocabulary and syntax of Latin, but also lending a particular local colour to its pronunciation and thereby predetermining in some

---

[1] See M. Pallottino, *Etruscologia*, 3rd ed., 1954 (English translation by J. A. Cremona, *The Etruscans*, A Pelican Book, 1955); also V. Pisani, op. cit., pp. 290-303.
[2] For further study of the substratum of Latin, see in particular A. Ernout, *Les éléments dialectaux du vocabulaire latin*, Paris 1909; also L. R. Palmer, *The Latin Language*, 1954.

measure the future development of local Romance sound-systems. In fact, we come here upon one of the most abstruse and fiercely-debated problems of Romance philology. Since the past century, when the study of sounds in evolution was first seriously envisaged, hypotheses concerning the supposed phonological influence of the pre-Roman substratum have been repeatedly advanced by some scholars and contradicted with no less conviction by others. Even within Italy there is a classic example: the so-called *gorgia toscana*, a form of aspiration whereby $k > h$, $p > ph$, $t > th$, has been attributed to Etruscan speech habits.[1] In Gaul, a Celtic influence is commonly invoked to account for the passage of Latin u to [y] (see p. 192); a specific bone of contention in Spain is the supposed 'Iberian' origin of the change $F > h$ (see p. 423); and likewise with many more sound-changes which took place before the appearance of written Romance made positive evidence available. Such hypotheses have an air of probability, but it seems fair to say that not a single one of the many adduced can be safely removed from the sphere of controversy and presented in the form of established knowledge. The difficulty lies partly in a lack of evidence concerning the pronunciation of the submerged speeches, but above all in the fact that sound-changes of fundamentally similar character have occurred in the past in languages of quite different origin, with no discernible substratum, and indeed are still occurring in the present, in circumstances which do not permit one to assume the interference of another language. Such changes may be considered as 'spontaneous', in the sense that they have their origin in the speech-apparatus of the individual. They represent a natural state of language: it would indeed be much more surprising if sounds did not change! Since we can readily observe sound-changes taking place 'spontaneously' in recent times, there is no logical basis for the assumption that sound-changes which occurred in a remote past must have been 'conditioned' by outside causes; there is only a possibility that they may have been so 'conditioned'.

The question-mark which hangs over the supposed contribution of pre-Roman speeches to the sound-systems of Romance has no relevance to their lexical contribution. Many words from these

[1] See W. von Wartburg, *Die Ausgliederung der romanischen Sprachräume*, p. 6. The attribution has been opposed notably by G. Rohlfs and by Robert A. Hall, Jr. ('A Note on *gorgia toscana*', *Italica*, vol. xxvi (1949), pp. 65–71).

distant sources, and turns of expression commonly listed as 'syntax' though they have the same function as vocabulary, appeared in the medieval written languages. Many are still in everyday use. Others continue a fossilized existence in place-names. The only real problem to which they may give rise concerns the identity of the source.

*The Spanish enigma.* With reference to sources, it is perhaps the Spanish Peninsula, of all regions of Romance speech, which presents the greatest difficulty. Its spoken Latin absorbed a notable variety of pre-Roman elements from a most ill-defined substratum.

An early acquisition resulting from the victorious conclusion of the second Punic War (201 B.C.), Spain was latinized very gradually from the centres of first occupation: the north-east, which became the nucleus of Tarraconensis, and the southern area taken over from the Carthaginians, called Baetica after its river, the Baetis (Guadalquivir). Penetration into the interior from both areas was fiercely resisted. From Baetica the path of subjugation led north-westwards into the region afterwards known as Lusitania; there the Romans suffered heavy reverses in 148 B.C. at the hands of a local chieftain named Viriathus, celebrated by Camões in the *Lusiads*. In the course of the campaign which followed, the armies from Baetica became the first Romans to set foot in north-west Spain, the later Gallaecia. Meanwhile, the advance along the Ebro from the base at Tarraco proceeded still more slowly, ending only with the famous eight-year siege of Numantia, which capitulated in 133 B.C. In the Cantabrians, the region from which modern Spanish stems, some of the hill-tribes were not finally subdued until the reign of Augustus. But who were these people capable of opposing so stubbornly the progress of Roman military power?

Not long ago there would have been a ready answer: eastern Spain was occupied by the Iberians, whose language persists in Basque, and western Spain by the Celts; in the centre the two peoples had met and mingled producing the ethnic group conveniently known, already in Roman times, as Celtiberian. But these assumptions which had almost attained the status of 'acquired knowledge' have now been seriously challenged.

At the centre of the problem is the uncertainty concerning the presumed relationship between Iberian and Basque. The latter is still with us, fully available for investigation to all who are not daunted by its baffling complexity; spoken on both slopes of the western Pyrenees, in three principal dialects on the French side, and four in Spain, it projects from a remote pre-Indo-European past with all the fascination which zoologists find in the coelacanth. Iberian was once no less real. It is attested in inscriptions found along the Mediterranean coast of Spain and extending, as appears from the latest discoveries, as far into France as the region of Montpellier; written in a Greek-type script which seems to be part phonetic and part syllabic, these inscriptions, like those of Etruscan but with less certainty concerning the value of symbols, can be tentatively read but not understood. It is generally accepted that the Iberians reached Spain from Africa; they seem also at one time to have occupied Sardinia.

The long-standing identification of Basque with Iberian was mooted academically as early as 1821 by W. von Humboldt (*Prüfung der Untersuchungen über die Urbewohner Hispaniens*, Berlin, 1821); it appeared to have been confirmed by the researches of one of the most outstanding Romance philologists, Hugo Schuchardt, who even hazarded a reconstruction of Iberian declension (see W. J. Entwistle, *The Spanish Language*, p. 29). For inscriptional data, however, Schuchardt relied mainly upon the readings of E. Hübner (*Monumenta linguae ibericae*, Berlin, 1893), which further investigations—assisted by the discovery of new material, including the Alcoy lead-tablet, the longest surviving Iberian text—have shown to be unsound.[1]

The fact that Basque is of so little help in the translation of Iberian would seem to constitute an *a priori* argument against the assumption of an affinity between them. What is more, archaeologists have for some time maintained that Basque and Iberian represent two quite different cultures.[2] We might add in passing that anyone acquainted with the Basques, probably one of the most homogeneous peoples in Europe, would find it difficult to associate their ethnic type with the idea of African provenance. While neither of these latter considerations is in any way conclusive, since the Iberians might well have superimposed their language on a people of different speech and origin, just as Latin

[1] Notably the investigations of M. Gómez Moreno. See J. Caro Baroja, 'Sobre la historia del desciframiento de las escrituras hispánicas', *Actas y memorias de la Sociedad española de antropología, etnografía y prehistoria*, vol. xxi (1946), pp. 151–71.

[2] See P. Bosch Gimpera, 'El problema de los orígenes vascos', *Eusko-Jakintza*, vol. iii (1949), pp. 39–45. Bosch Gimpera accepts the possibility of a cultural influence of Iberian on Basque.

overlaid and eliminated Iberian, yet in the absence of more precise evidence it is difficult to believe that their political power and organization was such as to achieve for their language a widespread acceptance.

The doubts thus cast upon the postulated relationship between Basque and Iberian have prompted a return to a theory according to which Basque is akin to certain dialects in the Caucasus. The Caucasian area is a linguist's paradise: there, in a geographical space about half the size of France, is an extraordinary complex of different languages, of which one is attested, as Old Georgian, since the sixth century A.D. Some of these speeches are pre-Indo-European, and since the Caucasus has all the attributes of a place of refuge, one may surmise that they were crowded into their present confinement by successive waves of Indo-European expansion. If this is so, the 'Caucasian theory' would imply that the remote forbears of the Basques evaded the Indo-Europeans by a westerly migration, thus arriving before them in western Europe.

Some scholars are now prepared to accept the affiliation between Basque and Caucasian as definitely established.[1] A disturbing detail is the fact that the Greeks used the term *Iberes* in referring to the people of the Caucasus: even in ancient times this gave rise to discussion concerning their possible connexion with the *Iberi* of Spain. Though the coincidence of names may be quite fortuitous, one cannot exclude the possibility that Basque and Iberian share a distant Caucasian kinship. This might well be the key to the whole problem.

Even the other element in the Celtiberian concept is open to question. It is certain that there was a Celtic invasion of Spain,

---

[1] See A. Tovar, 'Hoy podemos afirmar, y ello es ya una verdad del dominio común, que en su íntima estructura, y en caracteres verdaderamente típicos, el vasco se parece a las lenguas del Cáucaso, lo cual supone un parentesco remotísimo en el tiempo, que nos traslada a varios milenios antes de Cristo. Las semejanzas con el Cáucaso son sustancialmente: la pasividad del verbo, rasgo importantísimo, y que arrastra consigo otras coincidencias fundamentales, como son la existencia del caso ergativo o agente, visible como en el vasco en el caucásico del norte, y la intercalación en el verbo mismo de elementos gramaticales que expresan el objeto y aun el término indirecto. . . . La relación vasco-caucásico, entrevista por nuestro Fita y confirmada con estudios sistemáticos por Schuchardt, Trombetti, Dumézil, Lafon y otros, es un hecho que ha de tenerse en cuenta y que por su mismo misterio es evidente que nos traslada a epocas muy remotas. Ultimamente K. Bouda ha clasificado varios centenares de correspondencias léxicas vasco-caucásicas; de ellas resulta la imagen de una cultura común ya con agricultura avanzada. . . .' (*La lengua vasca*, Monografías Vascongadas, No. 2, San Sebastián, 1950, pp. 23–24).

in about the seventh century B.C., which extended over the western area and into the modern territory of Portugal. The path of this invasion is marked by place-names with the termination -*briga* (see W. J. Entwistle, op. cit., pp. 37–41). But the relatively slight Celtic element to be found in Spanish seems to derive largely from later association with romanized Gaul.[1] This has prompted the inference that by the time of latinization the Celts had been absorbed by the earlier inhabitants and spoke the native tongues.

We are thus confronted with the hypothesis of a multi-lingual pre-Roman Spain. In the absence of inscriptional evidence the only avenue for further investigation into the geographical distribution of indigenous speeches is to be found in the study of place-names. In two recent articles G. Rohlfs has shown how this may be undertaken with no sacrifice of scientific method.[2] Both have their source in the analysis of suffixal elements. Abundantly represented and strictly localized on the Gascon side of the Pyrenees is the suffix -*os*, in such village names as *Angos*, *Anos*, *Arbos*, *Bernos*, *Urdos*; all of these five recur on the Aragonese side, with normal Hispanic diphthongization, as *Angüés*, *Anués*, *Arbués*, *Bernués*, *Urdués*, together with a variety of other names similarly formed, e.g. *Aragüés*,[3] *Arascués*, *Bagüés*, *Banagüés*, *Sigüés*, &c. The roots of these words are identical with the names of persons, of miscellaneous origin but predominantly Celtic, which are to be found in France and Italy in place-names formed with the

---

[1] In the words of W. J. Entwistle 'only one word of proved Celtic origin is peculiar to the Peninsula: Gal. Port. *tona* "rind", cf. Welsh *ton*, Irish *tonn*' (*The Spanish Language*, pp. 39–40). There may well be more: the subject calls for further investigation.

[2] The two articles are as follows: 'Sur une couche préromane dans la toponymie de Gascogne et de l'Espagne du nord', *Revista de Filología Española*, vol. xxxvi (1952), pp. 209–56; 'Le suffixe préroman -UE, -UY dans la toponymie aragonaise et catalane', *Archivo de Filología Aragonesa*, vol. iv (1952), pp. 129–52. Both have now been republished, the latter with slight modifications, together with other essays, in a separate volume: G. Rohlfs, *Studien zur romanischen Namenkunde*, Studia Onomastica Monacensia, vol. i, Verlag der Bayerischen Akademie der Wissenschaften, Munich, 1956. Here will be found yet a third essay concerning a pre-Roman suffix, *Un type inexploré dans la toponymie du Midi de la France et de l'Espagne du Nord*; this time the suffix in question is -ÈSSU, cf. Fr. *Alès*, *Argelès*, *Camarès*, *Camalès*, *Urdès*, *Belvès*, &c., and Span. *Aniés*, *Apiés*, *Arbaniés*, *Artiés*, *Banariés*, *Biniés*, *Ipiés*, *Lardiés*, &c. These are limited in the north by the Dordogne, whence they extend southwards to the department of the Hautes-Pyrénées; on the Spanish side they are almost entirely confined to the province of Huesca. In this instance Rohlfs refrains from attempting to identify them with a specific ethnic group.

[3] The etymology of *Aragüés* as Basque *ara-otz* 'cold plain', first postulated by Menéndez Pidal and afterwards repeated by many others (including W. J. Entwistle, *The Spanish Language*, p. 26), is definitely to be discarded.

Celtic suffix *-acum* (> *-ac*, *-ay*, *-y*, see p. 195), with the Latin suffixes *-anum*, *-ate*, and with the Ligurian *-ascu*, *-asca*. To the Latin and Celtic suffixes certainly, and presumably also to the Ligurian, can be attributed the meaning 'belonging to', 'property of'. One may, for instance, compare the Gasc. *Arnos* with Fr. *Arnac* (Drôme, Cantal), *Arnay* (Côte d'Or) and Ital. *Arnago* (Venezia), *Arnano*, *Arnate* (Lombardy); and Gasc. *Bernos*, Arag. *Bernués*, with Fr. *Bernac* (Hautes-Pyrénées), *Bernay* (Eure, Sarthe, Vienne), *Berny* (Aisne), and Ital. *Bernate*, *Bernaga*, *Bernasca* (all in Lombardy). All these names indicate the houses or estates of ARNUS and BERINUS respectively. It may thus be concluded that Pyrenean *-os*, *-ués*, originally possessed the same semantic value.[1] The suffix occurs in place-names in the Basque country, written as *-ots* on the French side and as *-oz* on the Spanish side, with a dental element due to a peculiarity of Basque phonology (cf. Lat. CŎRPUS > Basque *gorputz*, Lat. LAPIS > Basque *lapitz*). In Roman times it must have been *-ossu*, which is in fact attested in the inscriptions of Aquitaine. In the second article Rohlfs applies the same method to an examination of the suffixes *-ué*, common in eastern Aragon, e.g. *Bestué*, *Sercué*, *Senegüé*, *Chinagüé*, *Belsué*, &c., and *-úy*, or in reduced form *-í*, equally common in Catalonia, e.g. *Balastúy*, *Barnúy*, *Beranúy*, *Beraní*, *Bretúy*, *Senúy*, *Sensúy*, &c.; these are local dialectal developments of another suffix denoting 'property of', which in Latin documents is attested as *-odius* or *-oius*.

The region between the Basque country and the Mediterranean is in this way compactly defined, at least on the Spanish side, as the former habitat of two peoples, an '-ossu-suffix' people and an '-oius-suffix' people. But who were these peoples, and of what affiliation? In fact, the geographers of antiquity mention by name two tribes located in these regions, the *Jacitani*, whose name persists in *Jaca*, and the *Ilergetes*, similarly perpetuated in *Lérida*, the former *Ilerda*. The area of the *-ossu* suffix indicates a people living astride the Pyrenees as do the Basques. From the same geographers we know that the people living to the north were the *Aquitani*: the formal resemblance between *Jacitani* and *Aquitani* can scarcely

---

[1] This same conclusion was reached independently by J. Séguy and is expressed in an article which appeared at the same time as that of Rohlfs: 'Le suffixe toponymique "-os" en Aquitaine', *Actes et mémoires du Troisième Congrès International de Toponymie et d'Anthroponymie*, vol. ii (1951), pp. 218–22 (published in 1952).

be fortuitous; in all probability they were one and the same people. Other scholars than Rohlfs, notably R. Lafon,[1] in attacking the Basque–Iberian theory, have suggested that affinities with the Basques should be sought rather to the north, among the *Aquitani*. Thus the former abode of *Aquitani* and *Jacitani* may well correspond to the area of a submerged pre-Indo-European speech akin to Basque. The affiliations of the Ilergetes are probably quite different: Rohlfs, perceiving a connexion with Cisalpine Gaul, tentatively suggests that they were a branch of the Ligurians.

The two penetrating articles from which the matter of the above brief synthesis is extracted mark a notable advance in the study of the distribution of pre-Roman and pre-Celtic peoples, and constitute an invitation to further research conducted on similar lines. At the same time they serve to emphasize our ignorance of the demography of pre-Roman Spain. In these circumstances it would manifestly be unscientific to attach any label more precise in its implications than 'pre-Romance' to those non-Latin elements, other than Celtic, which were present in the spoken Latin of the Peninsula. Such elements may have come from various sources. Some have their cognates in Basque and may have been borrowed from speeches of a Basque type, but, Basque itself being a language replete with words borrowed from neighbouring speeches, the direction of loan cannot be certainly determined.

Probably to be associated with a particular substratum is a fairly compact group of words in which a stressed vowel is followed by *-rro*, *-rra*, or *-rdo*, *-rda*. Among them is *izquierdo*, surely the most commonly used pre-Romance word in Spain, cf. Basque *ezker(r)*, Port. *esquerdo*, Cat. *esquerre*, Prov. *esquer*, Gasc. *esquerr*. Its meaning of 'left' was still conveyed by *siniestro*, from Lat. SINISTER, in medieval Spanish, e.g. in the *Poema del Cid*, but *izquierdo* is early attested, and any suggestion that it might be a relatively recent borrowing from Basque is discounted by the widespread use of cognate forms in southern France and Portugal. Ill omens which placed a taboo on *siniestro* created opportunity for its diffusion: in Old French *senestre* was similarly replaced by the Germanic *gauche*. The same consonantal alternance of *rr* and *rd* is

[1] *Eusko-Jakintza*, vol. i (1947), pp. 507 ff. Lafon suggests that there is an etymological connexion between the name of the *Ausci*, who inhabited the region of *Auch*, and the name *Euskara* by which the Basques designate their own language.

apparent in *barro* 'mud', which in Aragonese is *bardo*, cf. Port. *barro*, Cat. Prov. Gasc. *bard* (the Ital. *barro*, a clay used in pottery, is borrowed from Spanish). The pattern recurs, *-ano* being a suffix, in Cast. *marrano* 'pig'; Arag. *mardano*, west Cat. *mardà* and east Cat. *marrà* mean not 'pig' but 'ram' (the common notion being 'male animal'), and in this acceptation the word is used over a considerable part of southern France (see G. Rohlfs, *Le Gascon*, p. 24). Similar to these in structure, and unexplained etymologically, are Cast. *perro* 'dog', and *zorro* 'fox', which have ousted the Lat. CANIS and VULPES. Quite a number of pre-Romance substantives contain a suffixal element constructed in like manner, e.g. *guijarro* 'pebble', *pizarra* 'slate', *becerro* 'calf', *cencerro* 'cow-bell', *cachorro* 'puppy'.[1]

The names of the mountain goat are usually pre-Romance. In different localities of Aragon, with the *rr/rd* alternance again appearing, it is *sarrio*, *sisardo*, *xixardo*, cf. Gasc. *isart*, whence the standard Fr. *isard*. Basque has no surviving indigenous word to convey this meaning and current Castilian is *gamuza*, identical in origin with the *chamois* of the Alps, another pre-Romance form which was latinized as CAMOX, CAMŌCEM.

Like Celtic words in French, the remnants of pre-Romance speech in Spain are particularly well represented in topographical terminology. The Cast. *vega* 'land beside a river' (for the meaning cf. Fr. *grève*, from Celtic), attested in medieval texts as *vaica*, *vaiga*, certainly appears to be cognate with Basque *ibaiko* 'bank', formed on *ibai* 'river'. To the same root belongs *ibón* 'mountain lake', which on the French side of the Pyrenees persists in such forms as *ioû*, *eoû*, *uoû*, *uoung*, *boum* (S. Palay, *Dictionnaire du béarnais et du gascon modernes*, and G. Rohlfs, op. cit., p. 27), cf. the *Lac d'Ôo*, near Luchon. Some localities south of the Pyrenees prefer in this sense the more widespread *basa*, in Castilian

---

[1] Some scholars would add to this list the adj. *bizarro* 'brave', which has been traditionally associated with Basque *bizarr* 'beard', and compared semantically with the French use of *poilu*. It has been recently pointed out, however, that Ital. *bizzarro* 'lively, spirited' (cf. Ital. *bizza*), previously looked upon as a loan-word from Spanish, was already current in Italy in the thirteenth century—it is used by Dante—whereas *bizarro* is not attested in Spain until late in the sixteenth century, the inference being that it then came as a loan-word from Italian (see A. Prati, *Vocabulario etimologico italiano*, Milan, 1951, and cf. p. 473). The type of suffix discussed above is not uncommon in Italian, cf. Ital. *ramarro* 'lizard', *tabarro* 'cloak' (the same word as Fr. and Eng. *tabard*): it also occurs in Latin borrowings from Etruscan (cf. J. Corominas, *Diccionario crítico etimológico de la lengua castellana*).

*balsa* 'pool', equally pre-Romance though probably of quite different provenance. Common in the mountains of Aragon with
the meaning 'limit, boundary-stone' (cf. the French adoption of
Celtic *borne*) is a word *muga*, adjacent to the Basque country, and
farther east *buega*, *buaga*; it is *muga* in Basque and *mugo* in neighbouring parts of Gascony. This seems to be strictly local, and one
is tempted to infer from it a pre-Romance dialectal variation as
between Old Basque *MŪGA and 'Jacitanic' ( ?) *BŎGA.

Some such topographic words, on the other hand, have been
identified in widely separate areas. None has been in the past more
generally claimed as 'Iberian' than *nava* 'plain in the mountains',
the presumed root of *Navarra*, but this has now been shown to
enjoy no less currency in the Dolomites than in the Cantabro-
Pyrenean region.[1] Equally widespread is the *garma* 'steep moun-
tain-slope' 'scree', of the Asturias, found in Pyrenean toponymy
as *garmo*, and in that of the Alps as *galm*.[2] Likewise shared with
the dialects of the Alps are Cast. *losa* 'flat stone', cf. Port. *lousa*,
Cat. *llosa*, Prov. *lausa*, Piedmontese *loza*, and Cast. *arroyo*
'stream', mentioned by Pliny as specifically Spanish in the form
ARRUGIAE 'channels used in mining', but which extends from Piedmontese to Friulan as *roia*, *rogia*, *roie*, &c.[3]

Other words of presumed pre-Romance origin include such
miscellaneous terms as *manteca* 'butter', *abarca* 'sandal', *ascua*
'embers', *brujo* 'sorcerer' (perhaps more familiar in the fem. *bruja*
'witch'), *cama* 'bed', and *sarna* 'mange'. The last two of these
attracted the attention of Isidore of Seville, who wrote of *sarna*:
'Impetigo est sicca scabies prominens a corpore cum asperitate et
rotunditate formae. Hanc vulgus sarnam appellant' (*Etymologiae*,
iv. 8. 6; for his comments on *cama* see p. 163).

Of presumed substratic influences in Spanish phonology, much
has been written, but little can be retained as established fact.
The Aragonese sonorization of voiceless plosives after nasal and
liquid consonants, which Menéndez Pidal, recalling the name of
Huesca (a doubtful identification), would explain as a consequence
of Oscan settlement (*Orígenes del español*, 3rd ed., p. 303), had

---

[1] Cf. J. Corominas, op. cit., under *nava*.
[2] For further details see our contribution to *Studies in Romance Philology
and French Literature presented to John Orr*, Manchester, 1953, p. 61.
[3] J. Hubschmid, *Zeitschrift für romanische Philologie*, vol. lxvi (1950),
pp. 34–35. Here, too, there is evidence of ancient dialectal variation as between
types *RŬGIA and *RŎGIA, cf. Leonese *arruoyo* (Corominas, op. cit., under
*arroyo*).

previously been attributed to 'Iberian':[1] it is indeed a feature of Basque (e.g. VOLUNTATEM > Basque *borondate*, TEMPORA > Basque *dembora*, CŬLTER > Basque *golde*) as well as of Pyrenean Romance. Most hotly debated is the origin of the evolution F > *h*, which Old Castilian shares with Gascon: arguing primarily from its geographical contiguity with the Basque country, Menéndez Pidal expresses the conviction that here we have a clearly recognizable influence of a native speech which possessed no *f* (op. cit., pp. 198–233); other scholars have pointed, however, to the well-attested presence of the phenomenon in Vulgar Latin, and in Romance dialects far removed from Spain, notably those of southern Italy, and have observed that in early borrowings from Latin the Basques replaced *f* not by *h* but by a bilabial consonant (e.g. FĔSTA > Basque *pesta*, *besta*, &c., cf. p. 424).[2] Another peculiarity which has been commonly related to the substratum is the Spanish pronunciation of *s*; the acoustic effect, which no foreigner in Spain can fail to observe, is due to an 'apico-alveolar' point of articulation, i.e. a positioning of the point of the tongue against the alveolar ridge. When the Moors came to Spain, they tended to confuse this sound with the alveolar [ʃ] (see p. 423). Curiously, a similar apprehending is perpetuated in many medieval English borrowings from French, e.g. *push*, *finish*, which seems to indicate that *s* was 'apical' in Old French too. If this were so, there is no valid reason for explaining apical *s* by the influence of a particular substratum; it was more probably a feature of spoken Latin.

There is indeed nothing in the sounds of Hispano-Romance which really requires to be explained otherwise than as a natural outcome of Latin, and nothing in its morphology.

*Celtic*. Various regions in Romania might be mentioned as having a pre-Roman element no less uncertain than that of Spain: Sardinia for example, where, in addition to Iberians, and probably preceding them, there lived a people known to the Greeks as *Ioalei*, whose speech is quite unknown; or Sicily, where the Siculi, speaking a language closely related to the Latin branch of Italic, shared the island with remnants of earlier inhabitants, the Sicani, almost certainly pre-Indo-European; indigenous speeches in the

---

[1] J. Saroïhandy, 'Vestiges de phonétique ibérienne en territoire roman', *Revue internationale des études basques*, vol. vii (1913), pp. 475–97.

[2] W. Meyer-Lübke, and more recently John Orr, 'F > h, phénomène ibère ou roman?' *Revue de linguistique romane*, vol. xii (1936), pp. 10–35 (reprinted in *Words and Sounds in English and French*, Oxford, 1953).

area of Balkan Romance also tend to be lost in obscurity. A very great part of Romania was, however, founded upon the territory of two well-known Indo-European speech-families: that of Celtic in the west, and of Greek in the east. The fate of these two presents a remarkable contrast. In the Greek-speaking lands of the east, Latin made little headway; in the west, Celtic became the foremost linguistic victim of Roman expansion.

The Celts had spread into Gaul between 900 and 600 B.C., from a point of departure probably located in the south of modern Germany. Thence part of their number moved into Spain, and further waves of migration brought them to the British Isles. Much of the Alpine territory became their habitat, and Italy as far south as the valley of the river Po. From this region some turned eastwards again, ravaging the lands of northern Greece, and ultimately founding, during the second century B.C., the Celtic kingdom of Galatia in the heart of Asia Minor. The Celts of northern Italy were in early contact with the Romans: to them is due the first recorded sack of Rome, a consequence of their victory at the battle of the river Allia (390 B.C.). Many years later they were finally defeated; it was in 222 B.C. that Roman armies carried hostilities north of the Po, captured Mediolanum (Milan), then the capital of the Celtic Insubres, and for the first time reached the foot of the Alps. Colonies of Latin settlers were planted at Placentia (Piacenza) and Cremona in 218 B.C., and shortly afterwards at Bononia (Bologna) and Parma. The territory thus acquired was organized as Gallia Cisalpina, a province beyond the recognized limits of Italy. To this day a line drawn roughly from Spezia to Rimini marks off the dialects of the Peninsula from those of 'Continental' Italy, sometimes referred to collectively as 'Gallo-Italian' on account of their apparent affinity with French. Under this heading are included the modern idioms of Piedmont, Lombardy, Liguria, and Emilia; Venetian tends to be in a class apart, but shares some of their most characteristic features. These features are primarily phonetic: in common with northern France they change accented Latin A to e (PORTARE > *porté*), diphthongize Ē and ō (HABĒRE > *aveir*, ODŌREM > *udour*), front U to [y] and also o to [ɸ] or [œ], nasalize vowels (PANE > **pã**), drop final vowels other than A, simplify double consonants, change -CT to -*it* (FACTUM > *fait*). At least one morphological peculiarity also reminds us of northern France: the use in some areas of a first person plural flexion of the finite verb of the same origin as French -*ons*, i.e. from a presumed -ŭMUS (see p. 121). The sum of these character-istics shared with French, though the continuity is partly broken by the strongly romanized area of Provençal, does indeed incline one's thoughts towards the plausibility of attributing them to the influence of a common Celtic substratum, but when one examines the evidence concerning each separate feature, its distribution and possible affinity with Celtic, doubts begin to arise.

To the period of Gallia Cisalpina, when the complementary Gallia Transalpina was merely a vague definition of the land which lay beyond, are probably due those Celtic words which have been carried over a wide area of Romania. Thus BRACAE and CAMĪSIA, designating the Celtic long trousers and shirt, though sparsely attested in Latin literature, in the case of the latter not until the closing years of the western Empire, were doubtless quite familiar to the toga-clad Romans long before one of them caused a scandal by appearing in Celtic attire in the streets of Rome. Both became 'common Vulgar Latin', cf. Fr. *braies*, Prov. Cat. Span. Port. *bragas*, Ital. *brache*, Rum. *brace*; Fr. *chemise*, Prov. Cat. Span. Port. *camisa*, Ital. *camicia*, Rum. *cămașă*. Equally widespread is CARRUM, the Celtic cart, cf. Fr. *char*, Prov. Cat. *car*, Span. Port. Ital. *carro*, Rum. *car*. Common to the west are CAMMĪNUS, the Celtic road, cf. Fr. *chemin*, Prov. Cat. *camí*, Span. *camino*, Port. *caminho*, Ital. *cammino*, and the verb CAMBIARE, originally 'to exchange' and sub-sequently the successful rival of Lat. MUTARE, cf. Fr. *changer*, Prov. Cat. Span. Port. *cambiar*, Ital. *cambiare*; so too is ALAUDA 'lark', cf. Old Fr. *aloe*, mod. *alouette*, Prov. *alauza*, Cat. *alosa*, *alova*, Old Span. *aloa*, mod. *alondra*, Ital. *lodola*, *allodola*. A borrowing less to be expected is BECCUS 'beak, snout', which probably had a slang value in popular usage, cf. Fr. Prov. Cat. *bec*, Span. *bico*, Log. *biccu*, Ital. *becco*. Also claimed for Celtic, but with less certainty, is CABALLUS: the word is not Latin in origin, but it has no obvious Indo-European affinity with any word in the surviving Celtic speeches (it does exist in modern Celtic, but as a loan-word from Latin, cf. Welsh *ceffyl*, Irish *capal*).

Such words are not numerous: most of the Celtic loan-words in Romance idioms are clearly to be identified with the original area of Celtic substratum, their not infrequent presence in Spanish and Italian being due to the later radiation of Gallo-Romance.

It is of some linguistic importance that Gaul was conquered for

Rome in historical stages. The acquisition of southern Gaul, from
the Alps to the Pyrenees, followed upon that of Gallia Cisalpina,
and also upon that of Spain, the primary objective of the Romans
being to secure firmly the land route between the two countries.
Astride the eastern end of the route was a people often mentioned
in ancient literature as Ligurian, a people whose language has left
little or no trace in inscriptions. Vestiges certainly persist in
toponymy, most noticeably in suffixes, and they seem to indicate
that Ligurian was once spoken over a considerable area, extending
perhaps even to the Pyrenees. It is generally believed to have been
pre-Indo-European, though some scholars have pointed to the
possibility of a connexion with Illyrian. The separate identity of
the Ligurians was brought to an end by Rome as the last stage in
the pacification of Gallia Cisalpina, largely by a wholesale transfer
of population to Samnium (180 B.C.). Farther along the coast were
a number of Greek maritime colonies, the largest and most important being Massilia. These were friendly to Rome, but Greek
citizens and Roman travellers alike were exposed to the depreda-
tions of the Celtic tribesmen living in the hinterland. In 125 B.C.
Massilia appealed to Rome for help. The call was answered and
the tribes repelled by Roman soldiers. In 118 B.C. a colony of
Roman citizens was founded at Narbo Martius (Narbonne) whose
mission it was to protect the western end of the route to Spain.
Meanwhile, the Roman armies, extending their operations inland,
completely defeated the Celtic Allobroges and Arverni, and the
area was temporarily pacified, with the Aedui accepted as official
allies of Rome. The whole stretch of territory from the Alps
to the Pyrenees was finally organized into a province; taking its
name from Narbo, as Hispania Tarraconensis was named after
Tarraco, it became Gallia Narbonensis. In later years this new
acquisition was referred to simply as 'Provincia' and therein lies
the origin of the name Provence in its wide medieval application.

This was the province assigned to Julius Caesar by the Roman
Senate in 58 B.C., probably in fact through the influence of members of that body who wished to discredit him, for at the time it
boded trouble. The 'allied' Aedui had engaged in a war against
the Sequani and the situation was complicated by an incursion
of Germanic tribes under the Swabian chieftain Ariovistus, upon
whom the Sequani had called for assistance. The westward surge
of Germanic tribes eager to settle in Gaul was already beginning.

Fresh from the experience of dealing with similar if less threatening circumstances in northern Spain, Caesar immediately launched upon the series of campaigns whereby he threw the Germans back across the Rhine and established his reputation in history as the conqueror of Gaul. The principal source of information concerning these campaigns is his own account of them, which he called *Commentarii*.

The brief but fierce resistance of the Gauls has immortalized the names of two of their chieftains. In 54 B.C. Ambiorix led a last unsuccessful revolt of Belgic tribes in the north. The other and more prolonged rebellion was that of Vercingetorix, chief of the Arverni, who lived in the central mountains of France and have given their name to Auvergne. Uniting different tribes under his leadership he so harassed the Roman armies by guerilla tactics that for a time their withdrawal seemed inevitable. Eventually Caesar succeeded in pinning him down in the fortress of Alesia, a place of uncertain location though nowadays tentatively identified with Alise-Sainte-Reine (Côte d'Or). There he was starved into submission (52 B.C.). The subsequent assimilation of the Gauls to a Roman way of life was made more easy by the fact that they were a lively and intelligent race, with a developing culture of their own, certainly more advanced than any which the Romans encountered in Spain. The early loanwords already mentioned testify to their use of vehicles and roads, as does also the speed with which Caesar was able to move his armies. Already familiarized to some extent with Mediterranean culture by the penetration of traders and by the Greek influence spreading from Massilia, later too by the well-established Roman provinces to the south, they soon learned to appreciate the benefits which a higher standard of living could confer. Moreover, although flashes of a Celtic national feeling had appeared, particularly in the support given to Vercingetorix, there was at the time of Roman invasion no permanent central authority around which such feeling could have crystallized. It rapidly ceased to have any significance, and the Gauls became proud to acquire Latin and to serve Rome, the more warlike from the beginning in her armies, and later the more ambitious in her affairs of state. Gaul was soon to become a favoured province, developed not only by the usual method of planting colonies in which could settle the veterans of the legions—first created on a long-service basis for use in Spain and by Caesar's time already a well-established institution—but also intellectually, by the founding of numerous schools for the native population. Here—at Narbonne, Arles, Toulouse, Bordeaux, Lyon, Autun—the sons of the Celtic nobility could absorb Roman culture, and learn the 'correct' Latin of Rome itself, with its literary standard so different in the prose of Cicero and his generation from the vernacular of those traders and soldiers who were the unconscious or semi-conscious tutors of the mass of the population. From the beginning there probably appeared in Gaul more clearly than in other provinces the division into two currents of 'learned' and 'popular' speech. Throughout the history of French this dichotomy which prevailed in Rome itself is continually apparent, and the interplay of these two forces, naturally divergent but brought to some extent into unison by the craft of writers and grammarians, is at every stage a vital factor in the formation of the linguistic norm. In the south, the later territory of Provençal, the cleavage is less manifest. There the influence of administrative Latin, already founded in an earlier province and continually fed from Rome, penetrated more deeply and directly into the whole population.

In accordance with their usual practice the Romans opened up the country with new roads, remodelling and reconstructing along the natural lines of communication. The great centre upon which all roads converged was Lugdunum (Lyon). This city became the administrative capital for all the three provinces into which Gaul was divided in the reign of Augustus: Aquitania in the south-west, Belgica in the north, and Lugdunensis extending between them to include all the north-west. Immediately to the south of Lugdunum the province of Gallia Narbonensis retained for a while its separate identity. The old Celtic townships, many of which had been razed, were revived and developed anew, and on their sites stand many of the more important modern French towns, still with their Celtic names. These became the centres for the diffusion of Latin. So close were relations with Italy, so excellent the communications, that throughout the period of the Empire linguistic changes innovated there seldom failed to reach Gaul, in what we have described as 'the current of late Vulgar Latin'.

Despite this intensity of colonization the Celtic tongue by no means disappeared overnight. In fact, its gradual elimination seems to have proceeded over a period of nearly five centuries, extending almost to the collapse of the Empire in the west. This helps us to understand why Britain, thoroughly occupied and administered by the Romans but less directly in contact with Rome, and held for less than four centuries, should have retained for the most part its Celtic speech. Celtic would naturally linger longest in the more remote areas. The latest and clearest testimony which we possess concerning its persistence in Gaul is contained in an epistle of St. Jerome to the Galatians (in Asia Minor), in which he compares the speech of the latter to that of the Treviri. From this it would appear that towards the end of the fourth century A.D. a Celtic idiom was still in use in the neighbourhood of Trèves (now the Germanized Trier, see p. 233, note), despite the fact that this town became the site of an important Roman school. The progress of Christianity, with Latin as its language, was the determining factor which finally suppressed the use of Celtic in outlying regions.

The immediate linguistic substratum in Gaul must have been fairly uniform. Except perhaps in peripheral Aquitanic and Ligurian areas, the Celts, by the time of Roman occupation, had obliterated the unknown speech of earlier inhabitants, presumably pre-Indo-European, whose traces linger in the dolmens and menhirs of Brittany, and from a still more remote epoch in the cave-paintings of Lascaux, though it is of course probable that some pre-Celtic words were adopted by the Celtic invaders and quite certain that many are preserved in the mysterious roots of place-names. Our knowledge of the Celtic speech of Gaul is very circumscribed. Some inscriptional evidence is available and toponymy is in this context a particularly useful source of information (see below), but in order to determine how much of current French is Celtic one must chiefly rely upon the method of comparing early French words which are neither Latin nor Germanic in origin with possible cognates in the insular Celtic languages which have survived.[1]

The total contribution of Celtic to the French lexicon, including many words which have persisted only in local dialects, has been computed by W. von Wartburg at *c.* 180 items. Invariably they are of domestic and rustic connotation: as the Gauls acquired

[1] See in particular G. Dottin, *La langue gauloise*, Paris, 1920. A recent scholarly work by J. Whatmough, *The Dialects of Ancient Gaul*, is as yet available only in microfilm. There has been no comprehensive study of the Celtic element in Romance to supersede R. Thurneysen, *Kelto-romanisches*, Halle, 1884, though much new material may be found in W. von Wartburg's *Franzö-sisches etymologisches Wörterbuch*, some of which is incorporated into his *Évolution et structure de la langue française*.

Latin they adapted to Latin form the names of certain objects which pertained to their most intimate daily life. Isolated examples of such adaptations have found their way into Latin texts, as for instance plant- and tree-names in descriptions of local vegetation, but for the most part they are unattested and in order to characterize them one must have recourse to hypothetical reconstructions.

An illustration of the way in which the partial resistance of Gaulish acted to the detriment of the Latin synonym may be found in the words for 'soot', an only too familiar element when the fire was situated in the middle of the floor, as it still is in the more remote parts of the Pyrenees. The Latin for 'soot' was FULIGINEM, which in the spoken Latin of some western areas was pronounced as FULLIGINEM, cf. Span. *hollín*, Port. *fuligem*, Ital. *fuliggine*, Rheto-Rom. (Engad.) *fulin*, Rum. *funingine*. But Gaul kept its native word, which persists in French as *suie*. This form, together with those still current in the modern dialects, including in this instance Walloon and Swiss French, leads us to postulate an original Gallo-Roman *SŪDIA. From Provençal the word has penetrated to Catalan, where it appears as *sutge*.

Similarly connected with the Celtic fireside are the *broche*, the spit on which meat was cooked, and the *landier*, a larger type of fire-dog (Fr. *chenet*), which derives from a Celtic ANDEROS, meaning 'young bull'. The cradle, which in spoken Latin was CUNA, cf. Ital. *cuna* and *culla*, the latter from the diminutive CUNULA, retained in Gaul its Celtic name, appearing in Old French as *berz*. This suggests a latinized form *BERTIUM, which travelled across the Pyrenees to give Port. *berço*, Old Span. *brizo*, though within the Pyrenean area it has a rival in a type *JUMPA, of uncertain origin. Southern France employs *bres*, which has passed in the same form into Catalan. From the Old French stem are derived the mod. *berceau* and the verb *bercer*.

Celtic dwellings were built of timber, and the carpenter, if such specialization had evolved, must have been the most prominent craftsman. The term 'carpenter' itself is in fact Celtic, Fr. *charpentier*, or more precisely its dialectal equivalents, Norman *carpentier* (> Eng. *carpenter*) and Prov. *carpentier* (> Ital. *carpentiere*, Span. *carpintero*, Port. *carpinteiro*) having attained during the Middle Ages a widespread diffusion; cf. also *charpente* and the verb *charpenter*. The debris of the trade still have a Celtic name as *copeaux*. A feature of house-construction, carried over from the

Celtic hut to the stone building learnt from the Romans, is the *auvent*, the broad eave unknown in countries of lesser rainfall.

The terminology of the household reveals a Celtic consumption of beer, honey, and milk. The first of these was the usual drink in Gaul before the introduction of the Roman vine. It is named in Latin texts as CEREVĪSIA, whence Old Fr. *cervoise*, which became Old Ital. *cervogia*; the Provençal form, *cerveza*, passed into the Iberian Peninsula, cf. Cat. *cervesa*, Span. *cerveza*, Port. *cerveja*. Its preparation has left another Celtic word in *brasser* 'to brew', restricted to France, together with the derivative *brasserie*. The term for 'dregs', Fr. *lie*, Prov. *lia*, also Celtic, has extended as *lía* to Spanish and Portuguese. Even the wooden barrel used to contain the liquid, the Fr. *tonneau*, is Celtic. Related to the taste for honey—which the Anglo-Saxons though perhaps not the Celts exploited for the preparation of mead—are Old Fr. *bresche*, Prov. *bresca* 'honey-comb', whence *bresca* in Catalan and Spanish, and Fr. *ruche* 'beehive', a word which also exists in Gallo-Italian dialects, but with rather different meanings: these pre-suppose Gallo-Roman *BRĪSCA and *RŪSCA. Milk was soon designated everywhere by the Lat. LACTE, but the whey, now *petit-lait* in standard French, is still widely known in country districts as *le mègue*, from a Celtic word latinized as *MESIGUM.

The ploughing of the Celts is represented in French by *charrue* from CARRŪCA, maintained in face of the Lat. ARATRUM which prevailed elsewhere, by *soc* 'ploughshare', and *raie* 'furrow', from words latinized as *SOCCUM and *RĪCA, peculiar to Gaul; their harvesting by *javelle* 'sheaf', cf. Prov. *gavela*, Cat. *gavella*, Span. *gavilla*, from *GABELLA, and by the verb *glaner*, cf. Prov. *glenar*, which is attested in the Latin of the sixth century as GLENARE. To confine their animals in pens they used the CLĒTA, cf. Fr. *claie*, Prov. *cleda*, which must have extended early to northern Aragon where it is *cleta* still. For the livestock, Latin names were generally adopted, though Fr. *mouton*, *bouc*, and *cochon* are all lacking in an obvious Latin counterpart: the two former have been claimed for Celtic, but with no certainty (*bouc* may well be Germanic); *cochon* remains a mystery. Unquestionably Celtic, however, is Old Fr. *veltre*, *veautre* 'hunting dog', found in latinized form as VERTRAGUS, cf. Ital. *veltro*; these dogs were much prized and indeed formed one of the principal exports of Roman Britain. A few fishes have retained Celtic names, notably *lotte* and *saumon*.

From the Celtic systems of measurement there remain *boisseau* 'bushel', a derivative of Old Fr. *boisse* (< *BOSTIA); *lieue* 'league', from a word attested as LEUCA, cf. Prov. *lega*, Cat. *llegua*, Span. *legua*, Port. *légua*, and *arpent* 'acre' from AREPENNIS, cf. Prov. *arpen*, Old Span. *arapende*.[1]

Especially persistent, in Gaul as in Spain, were the indigenous terms denoting prominent topographical features, together with names of common trees and plants. In the former category are *borne*, in Old French also *botne*, *bosne*, *bone* (< *BOTINA), further represented in the mod. Fr. *abonner*, of which the original meaning is 'to set a limit'; *combe* (< CUMBA), cf. Prov. *comba*, Cat. *coma*, which strongly resisted the Lat. VALLEM (cf. in English *Coombe Valley*, *High Wycombe*, &c.); *lande* (< LANDA), cf. Prov. Ital. Old Span. Port. *landa*; *boue* from BAWA, cf. Welsh *baw*, and probably *bourbe*, with its derivative *bourbier*; *breuil* 'copse' from a word attested as BROGILUM, cf. Prov. *brolh*, which passed into Italian as *broglio*, whence *imbrogliare* and *imbroglio*; *talus* from TALŪTIUM, formed on a Celtic TALOS; and *grève* (< GRAVA), cf. Prov. Cat. *grava*, which first meant 'stone' and was then applied to the pebbly or sandy ground beside a river: the original sense is preserved in the diminutive *gravelle*, cf. Eng. *gravel*. Among trees which retained their Celtic names are the yew, *if* (< *ĪVUS), the birch, *bouleau*, and the oak, *chêne*. The birch is mentioned by Pliny as BETULLA but it is a masc. BETULLUM which became Old Fr. *bëoul*, of which *bouleau* is a derivative, and which spread over the Pyrenees to give Cat. *bedoll* and Span. *abedul* (with an agglutinated Arabic article, see p. 280). Words for the oak, which among the Celts was the object of a religious cult, derive from a root CASS- with different suffixes: Aragonese has *caxico*, *caixico* (*x* with

---

[1] It has been usual to consider as Celtic the Fr. *pièce*, cf. Ital. *pezza*, *pezzo*; Old Span. *peça*, *pieça*; mod. *pieza*; Port. *peça*. A recent article by C. Livingston seems with good reason to cast doubt upon this attribution (*Neuphilologische Mitteilungen*, vol. iv, pp. 178–88; see also Gunnar Tilander, *Studia Neophilologica*, vol. xxvii, pp. 31–42). Here he suggests a Latin origin and attaches the word to the progeny of PĔDEM. According to this theory there must have existed beside PEDITARE a collateral *PEDITIARE (cf. p. 115), which, contracted to *PETTIARE, gave rise to a verbal substantive *PETTIA. The verb being used with the technical meaning 'to pace out (a piece of land)', *PETTIA would then have meant the piece of land so measured (not, as W. von Wartburg says, a 'piece of cloth'). As G. Tilander points out, this etymology is well supported by Span. *pedazo*, Port. *pedaço*, which continually recurs in medieval legal documents with precisely this meaning, and which corresponds to a Latin type *PEDATIUM. Eng. *patch* probably derives in the same way, via a Norman-Picard *peache*, from *PEDATIA.

the value of [ʃ]), whence Span. *quejigo*, a variety of evergreen oak; Fr. *chêne*, in Old French more commonly *chasne*, suggests *CASSI-NUS, and may have been influenced by *fresne*, from Lat. FRAXINUS. Lesser vegetation owing its nomenclature to Celtic includes the *balai*, originally the plant 'broom', *bruyère*, a derivative of *BRŪCUS, cf. Prov. *bruc*, Cat. *bruch*, and a BERULA mentioned in the fourth century by Marcellus Empiricus of Bordeaux, which persists in French as *berle*, but is more familiar in the *berros* 'water-cress', of Spanish, corresponding to a type *BERURO, probably closer to the Celtic form.

Two words denoting persons and related to the social order are of Celtic origin. One of these, *vassal*, in medieval Latin VASSALLUS, was destined to become universally employed with the later growth of feudalism. W. von Wartburg sees in its persistence from Celtic an indication of the development of serfdom already in the third century, consequent upon a decline in urban prosperity and a general tendency on the part of peasants to seek the protection of local landowners: 'Ce n'est pas par hasard que le mot de *vassal* est d'origine gauloise, non germanique' (*Évolution et structure de la langue française*, p. 25). The retention of *truand* 'vagrant, beggar', from a Celtic *TRŪGANT, may be due to the same social circumstances.

Words thus surviving from the Gaulish substratum have in general a very precise and concrete meaning. Abstract concepts are rarely represented. One colour-adjective remained as Old Fr. *bler* 'grey, dappled' from *BLARUS, cf. Prov. *blar*, often applied to horses; in modern French it exists only in the derivative *blaireau* 'badger', and by extension 'badger-hair brush', 'shaving-brush'. The few other Celtic epithets tend to express crudeness of quality: Fr. *rêche* 'rough' from *RESCUS; Prov. Cat. *croi*, north Ital. *crojo* 'hard, cruel' from *CRŌDIUS; Fr. *dru* 'thick', 'strong' from *DRŪTUS, which survives in the mod. *herbe drue*, and with adverbial usage in *tomber dru*, 'to fall thick and fast'. As is particularly apparent from the meaning of *dru*, *drudo*, in north Italian dialects, *DRŪTUS also conveyed the idea of fertility and in this context it is the root of the Old French word for 'love-making', *druerie*, whence *dru*, fem. *drue*, in the sense of 'lover'.

At least one abstract noun survived directly from Celtic: a word *BRIGUS or *BRIVUS 'strength', 'courage', cf. Old Fr. *brif*, Prov. *briu*, Span. *brío*, Port. Ital. *brio*. In Old French it occurs more commonly in the verbal derivative *abriver* 'to make speed', and especially as a participle used adverbially with the meaning 'at full speed', as in the line:

Uns veltres vint corant toz abrivez.

(*Couronnement de Louis*, ed. E. Langlois, l. 292)

To infinitives from Celtic already quoted in connexion with substantives may be added Fr. *briser*, also found in Old French as *bruisier*, which was borrowed into English as *to bruise*; it appears to derive from a root BRŪS- or BRĪS-, whence there may have developed alternative forms *BRŪSIARE and *BRĪSIARE.

When languages mingle it sometimes happens that curious hybrid forms are produced. There is evidence of this in the meeting of Gaulish and Latin. Thus *orteil* 'big toe', undoubtedly derives from Lat. ARTICULUM, but the initial vowel seems to be the relic of a Celtic word for 'toe': in the Kassel Glossary (see p. 318) the Bavarian *zaehun*, cf. Germ. *Zehen* 'toes', glosses a supposedly Romance word *ordigas*. Similarly, Fr. *craindre*, in Old Fr. *criembre*, represents Lat. TREMERE, but with a change of initial consonant which has been explained as due to a Celtic root CRET-. The habit of counting in scores, transmitted by the Celts if not Celtic in origin, has introduced an intrusion of the substratum into the French numeral system (see p. 74), though such purely Latin forms as *setante*, *uitante*, *nonante*, were known to Old French and have continued to be used in dialects, including those of Belgium and Switzerland.

Possible influence of Celtic on Gallo-Roman pronunciation remains, in the words of the late Professor M. K. Pope, 'a very vexed question'. Commonly attributed to Celtic are the development of Latin ū to [y], and of -CT- to -*it*- as in FACTUM > *fait*, LACTŪCA > *laitue*, &c. These, it is suggested, are due to a palatalizing tendency in Celtic articulation. The former phenomenon is common to all French dialects, except eastern Walloon, and also occurs in northern Italy and in parts of Portugal. Attempts to relate it to Celtic are largely based upon the fact that Celtic frequently shows an alternance between ī and ū (cf. above *BRŪS- and *BRĪS-); modern Welsh dialect, incidentally, reveals a similar alternance between a U-pronunciation in the north and an I-pronunciation in the south. There is, however, no direct evidence to support the hypothesis of an intermediate Gaulish pronunciation [y]; the sound is indeed more characteristic of Germanic than of Celtic. Various other objections have been raised against the attribution of this change to the influence of a Celtic substratum;[1] nevertheless, considering the coincidence of its geographical extension with that of former Celtic speech, it is perhaps of all such attributions the least improbable. Less worthy of acceptance, in our opinion, is the oft-repeated identification with Celtic of the passage of -CT- to *-it-*; in face of the arguments alleged in its favour one cannot ignore the fact that it is characteristic of the whole Iberian Peninsula (FACTUM > Port. Arag. Mozarabic *feito*, Cat. *feit*, *fet*; Cast. *hecho* probably developed through a similar intermediate stage). Here a similar result has been attained by the group -LT- (MULTUM > Port. Arag. *muito*, Cast. *mucho*). In at least one word of French the group -PT- has also become *-it-*, viz. CAPTĪVUM > *chaitif*, *chétif*. The most valid conclusion, we would suggest, is that in the spoken Latin of the west the dental consonant tended to attract preceding consonants towards a palatal point of articulation, in much the same way as velar plosives were attracted by front vowels (see p. 53). Again, one might point to a palatalizing tendency in the passage of Latin stressed A to *e*, common to northern France and northern Italy, but this too occurs in non-Celtic areas, cf. Neapolitan *nès* < NASUM. Briefly, a general tendency towards palatalization can certainly be detected, but as a common phenomenon it extends far beyond the limits of the Celtic substratum.

It is in French toponymy that the Gauls have left their most permanent mark. In this respect, France is still a predominantly Celtic country. Many of the more important French towns perpetuate the names of the tribes of whom we read in the *Commentarii de bello gallico*, and this despite the fact that in Roman times they were given a Latin name. On the present site of Paris was the Roman *Lutetia*, but the name of the Parisii who dwelt there has prevailed. Rheims was to the Romans *Durocortorum*, but the inhabitants never forgot that it was the home of the Remi. These names, it will be observed, all have a final *s* which survives from the Latin locative plural in -IS, -IBUS having been early eliminated from popular speech, cf. also Amiens (*Ambiani*), Angers (*Andecavi*), Beauvais (*Bellovaci*), Cahors (*Cadurci*), Nantes (*Namnetes*),

---

[1] Notably by W. Meyer-Lübke, 'Zur U-Ü Frage', first published in the *Zeitschrift für französischen Sprache und Literatur*, vol. xli (see also vols. xliv and xlv), and reproduced in *Meisterwerke der romanischen Sprachwissenschaft*, ed. L. Spitzer, Munich, 1929.

Poitiers (*Pictavi*), Soissons (*Suessiones*), Tours (*Turnones*), Trèves (*Treviri*), Troyes (*Tricasses*). A remarkable picture of the human geography of pre-Roman Gaul is in this way preserved.

Names which are not tribal in origin frequently contain common Gaulish words. Of these the most widespread is the term designating a fortified settlement, latinized as DUNUM, cf. Irish *dun* 'fortress'; its Germanic cognates include Anglo-Saxon *tūn*, whence Eng. *town* and the *-ton* of English place-names, cf. also Germ. *Zaun* 'fence'. Among the best-known examples are *Lugdunum* (Lyon) and *Virodunum* (Verdun), of which the latter has been translated to Spain as *Berdún*, situated near the Navarro-Aragonese border. Some of these names show divergent phonetic evolutions due to the loss of different unaccented vowels. This is explained by A. Dauzat as follows:

La série *Mel(o)dúnum* > *Meudon*, *Ebur(o)dúnum* > *Yverdon*, *Uxell(o)-dúnum* > *Issoudun* représente l'évolution phonétique populaire et régulière du latin vulgaire, tandis que *Melun*, *Embrun*, *Issolu* ne peuvent reposer que sur des formes restaurées, des formes littéraires sans syncope réintroduites par l'école et par les puristes, et dans lesquelles la voyelle contre-finale s'est conservée jusqu'à la chute des consonnes médianes : le *d* se trouvant ici entre deux voyelles est naturellement tombé. En face de \**Meldunum*, \**Eburdunum*, \**Uxeldunum*, formes populaires, on a donc eu, pour des noms de lieux similaires, *Melodunum*, plus tard \**Meloün* > *Melun*, *Eburodunum* > \**Ebroün* > *Embrun*, *Uxellodunum* > \**Uisseloün* > *Issolu*.

(La toponymie française, p. 170)

In consequence of its adoption into the spoken Latin of a fairly wide area DUNUM is sometimes found uncompounded, e.g. *Thun* in Switzerland, *Dun* (Creuse) and *Daun* in the Eifel. Spanish place-names formed with DUNUM are all concentrated in the Pyrenean area, cf. in addition to the *Berdún* mentioned above, *Navardún* in Aragon, and *Salardú*, *Besalú* (< *Bisuldunum*) in Catalonia.

Similar in meaning to DUNUM are two other Celtic terms, BRIGA and the less common DURUM, the latter as in *Altessiodurum* (Auxerre, pronounced Ausserre) and *Brivodurum* (Brieure), the former as in *Scaldobriga* (Escaudœuvres), and of more frequent occurrence in Spain and Portugal, cf. *Conimbriga* (Coimbra), *Mundobriga* (Munébrega), *Nemetobriga*, *Lacobriga*, *Caesarobriga*, *Augustobriga*. The two latter of these, in which BRIGA is attached to Roman names, indicate that, like DUNUM, it enjoyed a separate existence in spoken Latin. As a first element it occurs in *Brigantium*, cf.

*Bregenz*, on the Austrian shore of Lake Constance, probably the original *Brigantium*, and in Spain *Betanzos*, in Portugal *Braganza*. The Celtic word for 'victory', SEGO, cf. Germ. *Sieg*, is found in combination with BRIGA in *Segobriga* (Segorbe), cf. also *Segovia* (Segovia and Sigüeya). Northern France has preserved in its place-names the Celtic MAGOS 'field', cf. *Catomagus* (Caen), *Rotomagus* (Rouen), *Noviomagus* (Noyen and Noyon, cf. Nijmegen, in Holland), and various other words designating topographical features (e.g. NANT- 'valley', 'watercourse', VERN- 'alder') may be added from the evidence of place-names to our previous collection. In passing, we should mention that if some of the modern names seem rather far removed from the latinized original their authenticity as derivatives can usually be established by reference to the many medieval legal documents in which they are recorded: a veritable mine of information, invaluable and indeed essential for all who would engage in the study of European toponymy.

When considering the pre-Romance substratum of Spain we gave particular attention to certain suffixal elements in place-names with the meaning 'property of', and we mentioned in passing a Celtic suffix *-acum*, used with this function (see p. 177). In Gaul it was much favoured, producing such local terms as *Juliacum* 'property of Julius', *Sabiniacum* 'property of Sabinius', *Aureliacum*, *Luciacum*, *Flaviniacum*, &c. The owners were probably well-to-do Gallo-Romans of Celtic descent who had assumed Roman names: hence the frequency with which some of the more common names recur. Examining the distribution of these formations on a map, one discovers that they lie in the neighbourhood of large towns and along the sides of the ancient Roman roads. In the region of Paris and towards the east the ending *-iac(um)* became *-y*, by a normal process of phonetic evolution already accomplished in the ninth century, when the first written French appeared (cf. JACET > Old Fr. *gist*, mod. *gît*). Modern place-names corresponding in this northern area to the above-mentioned Gallo-Roman forms are found as *Juilly*, *Savigny*, *Orly*, *Lucy*, *Flavigny*. To the west and south, but still for the most part north of the Loire, the first palatal element was entirely absorbed into the preceding consonant and the result of *-iac(um)* was *-ay*, later reduced in pronunciation, though not always in orthography, to *-é*: hence the name of Madame de Sévigné. South of the Loire and north of Bordeaux, particularly concentrated in the region of Charente, there is an abundance of similar formations ending in -*ac*, cf. *Julhac*, *Aurillac*, *Savignac*, &c. Since the palatalization of the velar consonant which resulted in the endings -*y*, -*ay* is a characteristic feature of *langue d'oïl*, as opposed to *langue d'oc*, the presence of so many -*ac* forms in this area constitutes one of the principal reasons for supposing that a southern type of Gallo-Romance, the future *langue d'oc*, once extended as far north as the banks of the Loire. Another concentration of -*ac* endings is found within the confines of Brittany; in this instance the explanation would seem to be that when in the sixth century the territory was settled by Britons seeking refuge from the Anglo-Saxon invaders of England they found there a Gallo-Roman speech in which the ending -*ac* was still intact. Over a wide area of south and south-eastern France, the former Gallia Narbonensis, the Celtic -ACUM is rare or non-existent, its function being fulfilled by the Latin -ANUM: a further sign of more intense latinization.

*Greek*. Ranging from the most 'popular' to the most 'learned', and coming at different times through various channels, the contribution of Greek to the spoken Latin of Romania is much more difficult to assess comprehensively than that of Celtic.

Shades of Greece hung about Rome in its infancy. Before the expulsion of the Tarquins the Greeks successfully vied with Etruscans and Carthaginians for the domination of the western Mediterranean, and Greek culture had already secured its unique authority, an authority based on traditions of which the full antiquity is only now being revealed. Greek trading stations were scattered around the coast from Spain to the Black Sea: a pointer to their commercial undertakings may be seen in the fact that all the coinage minted during the fourth century B.C. by Celtic peoples, in Britain as in Gaul, is imitated from Greek models; the Roman currency which was later to sweep it away, likewise imitated from Greek, had not then been devised. In the wake of commerce came the civilization of Greece, and notably its alphabet, originally derived from Semitic: the earliest Gaulish inscriptions, like those of the Etruscans and the Iberians, are in Greek-type characters.

Not far from Latium, large Greek colonies were established in Sicily and southern Italy. After the defeat of the Samnites who dwelt in the intervening territory, these were to be the next victims of Roman expansion. Their political downfall, in 272 B.C., provided a Greek beginning for Latin literature: Livius Andronicus, a Greek taken as slave to Rome from the captured city of Tarentum (Taranto), there translated into Roman idiom the *Odyssey* and various Greek plays. Earlier attestations of Latin, like those of Etruscan, are confined to inscriptions of a religious or official character.

By comparison with the Celtic 'substratum' the Greek contribution to Vulgar Latin, a continuous accretion of new terminology from a language of superior civilization, can best be defined as an 'adstratum'. Yet there are at least two areas in Romania with reference to which the term 'substratum' is not inapplicable, areas of limited geographical extent where elements of a local popular Greek persist in the Latin overlay. On the southern coast of Gaul the prosperity of Massilia fostered the growth of a number of smaller colonies, many of which have kept their Greek name to the present day, e.g. Nice, Monaco, Antibes, and west of the Rhône, Agde, and over the Spanish border, Ampurias; here the Romance patois still incorporate a number of words left by the pre-Roman Greek inhabitants, words recalling their maritime pursuits, their agriculture, their building and art. A few of these were diffused into Provençal, and one at least has come via Provençal into standard French, viz. *gond* 'hinge', cf. Prov. *gofon* (γόμφος).[1] The second and more important area is southern Italy. To this day there are villages in Apulia, south of Lecce, and in the southern tip of Calabria, which are Greek in speech. The Greek-speaking area was much more extensive in the Middle Ages, as may be deduced from the fact that Petrarch, in 1368, suggested a visit to Calabria to one of his copyists whose Greek was inadequate. During the sixteenth century there were still in Calabria some twenty-two Greek-speaking localities, a number reduced in the nineteenth century to twelve, and now to four (Bova, Condofuri, Roccaforte and Roghudi). In the past it has been customary to suppose, accepting Quintilian's statement at its full value (see above, p. 171), that Latin did in fact eliminate the Greek of Magna Graecia and that the medieval Greek of southern Italy was the result of later Byzantine occupation. This supposition seems now to have been disproved by the researches of G. Rohlfs, according to whom the Greek lexicon of the south is Doric, and much more archaic than that of Byzantine Greek. The recession of Greek from its former frontiers with adjacent Romance has left literally hundreds of Greek words in the southern patois, so that in this

[1] W. von Wartburg, *Évolution et structure de la langue française*, pp. 9–11.

area alone in the Peninsula one may perhaps distinguish a sub-stratum to Italian.[1]

Concerning the Greek adstratum, in so far as it affected written Latin, there is no lack of easily available information. It is well known that Greek played a prominent role in the moulding of the literary medium and contributed on a generous scale to its vocabulary. Much of this contribution was early accepted into spoken Latin and diffused as such, entirely losing its Greek identity; its subsequent fate in Romance has never been the object of a separate and detailed examination. Research directed to this end might nevertheless prove rewarding: only thus could one determine how much of the Greek element was confined to the Roman intelligentsia and how much was received into popular speech, only thus distinguish the relative currency in the Empire of synonyms of Latin and Greek origin.

The most cursory survey reveals a remarkable capacity on the part of the ordinary Roman for absorbing the jargon of the *Graeculi*, even to the extent of abandoning many current words in his native tongue. One wonders when and under what circumstances some of the choices were made. How, for example, did Greek PĔTRA (Fr. *pierre*, Prov. *peira*, Span. *piedra*, Ital. *pietra*, Rum. *piatră*) acquire its ascendancy over Lat. LAPIS, now restricted in space to Italy, Sardinia, and Spain (Ital. *lapide*, Log. *labide*, Span. *laude*), and in meaning to 'tombstone'? Why, unless it be for purely phonetic reasons, should a word so un-Latin as COLAPHUS (Ital. *colpo*, Fr. *coup*, Prov. *colp*, whence Span. *colpe, golpe*) have been generally preferred to ICTUS? Why CHŎRDA (Fr. *corde*, Prov. *corda*, Span. *cuerda*, Port. Ital. *corda*, Rum. *coardă*) rather than FŪNIS (Old Fr. *fun*, Ital. *fune*, Rum. *funie*)? And why should PLATEA (Ital. *piazza*, Fr. *place*, Prov. *plasa*, whence Span. *plaza*) have become so characteristic of the Roman settlement? That SCHOLA should be Greek is less surprising, and the same may be said of CAMERA (Fr. *chambre*, Prov. Cat. *cambra*, Ital. *camera*, Span. *cámara*, Port. *câmara*) and CATHĔDRA (Fr. *chaire*, whence *chaise*, Prov. *cadiera*, Span. *cadera*, Port. *cadeira*, Log. *kadrea*), since both of these words

[1] G. Rohlfs, *Griechen und Romanen in Unteritalien. Ein Beitrag zur Geschichte der unteritalienischen Gräzität*, Geneva, 1924. See also by the same author *Dizionario dialettale delle tre Calabrie*, Halle–Milan, vol. i, 1932, vol. ii, 1934, and various other publications (listed in *An den Quellen der romanischen Sprachen*, Halle, 1952). Rohlfs's views gave rise to prolonged and lively controversy with Italian scholars, notably C. Battisti, who were reluctant to accept them.

designate refinements unknown to a primitive dwelling. On the other hand, it seems strange that butter should have come to a pastoral community as a foreign luxury-good, labelled BŪTȲRUM (cf. Old Fr. *burre*, mod. *beurre*, Ital. *butirro*, replaced by *burro*, from French); since Spain uses with this meaning the pre-Roman *manteca*, *mantequilla*, one is tempted to conclude that the early Romans were 'non-butter-making'.[1] In fact, at least the first four of these Greek words, together with a host of others related principally to building, furniture, food, amusement and vice, are to be found in the work of early Roman writers and may therefore be presumed to have been current in Rome during the second century B.C., suggesting that even at that early date the city was permeated by the influence of Greek artisans and slaves.

Whereas such miscellaneous terms betray a continuous pressure of Greek upon Latin from ill-defined sources, there is one more homogeneous influence, more easily traceable: that of Christianity, which reached the heart of the Roman Empire through the intermediary of the poorer Greek-speaking community in Rome, so increased by the first century A.D. that it formed a considerable part of the city's population. The technical vocabulary of the new religion was predominantly Greek. In essence, it was a learned type of Greek, but being acquired by simple people its words passed into Vulgar Latin and Romance with varying degrees of phonetic change. Many such words, when first they appear in the earliest Romance texts, conform only in part to the general pattern of popular evolution and in other respects show a 'semi-learned' character which must be due to the pronunciation heard at religious services. Had it developed in accordance with the 'laws' of phonology, the word EPĪSCOPUM, for example, should have given in French such forms as *\*evesve*, *\*eveve*, instead of which the *sc* is retained in Old Fr. *evesque*, and the rest of the word falls away (i.e. 'apocope' instead of 'syncope', a popular feature in southern Gaul but normally not so in the north, see p. 42); Span. *obispo*, on the other hand, shows the syllabic development which one would expect, but is 'learned' in its retention of the vowel *i*; Ital. *vescovo* differs from both in being entirely popular. This

---

[1] A view supported by the fact that in parts of northern Spain and southern Italy the use of butter is still rare, and it is not made locally. The practice of eating it seems to have reached Greece from the 'barbarians', probably the Scythians (see W. von Wartburg, *Französisches etymologisches Wörterbuch*, under BŪTȲRUM).

Church influence, it should be observed in passing, extends also
to Latin words which were caught up in the orbit of Christianity.
Thus SAECULUM, which in Christian usage acquired a new significance, appears as 'semi-learned' in Fr. *siècle* and in Span. *siglo*:
in each case the vowel has undergone popular development but
the consonant group C'L should have palatalized, giving λ in both
languages at the medieval stage, and ultimately j in the former
and 'jota' in the latter (contrast the popular development of
ŏCULUM).

By contrast, the word ECCLESIA (ἐκκλησία) itself has evaded the
Church. Gaining in the fifth century a marked ascendancy over
the rival word BASILICA (βασιλική), a much earlier borrowing into
Latin, it came to denote a building conspicuous in the landscape
and frequently referred to in conversation: it therefore developed
in the main with the popular trend, giving rise to a multiplicity of
forms in the different Romance languages, e.g. Fr. *église*, Prov.
*glieisa*, Cat. *esglesia*, Span. *iglesia*, Port. *igreja*, Log. *keya*, Ital.
*chiesa*. Within the areas of the standard speeches there are also
countless dialectal variants: the south-western corner of France
alone comprises *glèsio*, *glèyge*, *glèyse*, *gliji*, *glisie* (S. Palay, *Dictionnaire du béarnais et du gascon modernes*). While the Christianized
Germanic peoples adopted a different word formed on a Greek
etymon which meant 'House of the Lord', cf. Eng. *church*, Scot.
*kirk*, Germ. *Kirche*, ECCLESIA found its way into other non-
Romance speeches and survives in Basque as *eleiza*, in Albanian
as *kise*, and nearer home, in Welsh as *eglwys*. BASILICA, thus van-
quished in the west, though leaving some relics, was triumphant
in the east, cf. Rum. *biserică*.

Likewise Greek in origin are the names of many of the dignitaries, both natural and supernatural, who presided over the
Church's growth. Below the EPĪSCOPUS (ἐπίσκοπος) was the PRESBY-
TER (πρεσβύτερος): in consequence of the use of this word with
a shifting accent (PRÉSBYTER, PRESBÝTERUM) Gallo-Romance came
to possess a double series of forms, hence Old Fr. *prestre*, mod.
*prêtre* and *presveire*, Prov. *preire*, *preveire*, Cat. *prévere*, *prebére*;
Italian has *prete*, and Spanish the purely learned *presbítero*. Very
popular forms persist in the non-Romance languages of the Empire, e.g. Basque *bereter*, Albanian *prift*, and Welsh *pryfder*.
Scarcely less alive and personal to the medieval mind were the DIA-
BOLUS (διάβολος) and the ANGELUS (ἄγγελος). The former appears

in the *Cantilène de sainte Eulalie* as *diaule*, with a typically Picard vocalization of the *b*, but in general the Latin *b* has been preserved in western Romance, cf. Fr. Prov. Cat. *diable*, Span. *diablo*, Port. *diabo*, whereas in more easterly speeches it has remained intervocalic and passed to *v*, cf. Ital. *diavolo*, Rum. *diavol*; Basque has *deabru*, but Welsh *diafol*. In all of these there is a measure of popular development, but the learned influence of the Church is seen in the maintenance of the initial consonant plus yod; the evolution of DIABOLUS may be contrasted in this respect with that of the heathen DIANA, which was kept in the folk-lore of some regions with the meaning 'fairy', cf. Old Prov. and Old Ital. *jana*, Asturian *šana*, Rum. *zînă*, and as 'sorcerer', Old Fr. *gene*. The angel has similarly been handed down with varying degrees of 'popularization', cf. Fr. *ange*, Prov. Cat. *àngel*, Span. *ángel*, Ital. *angelo*, but also a more popular *agnolo*, Rum *înger*.

A few words which gained currency in this way, of similar Greek origin, have spread beyond the sphere of religion to become essential components of the most basic vocabulary of Romance. The most striking example is PARABOLARE: formed on the noun PARABOLA ($\pi\alpha\rho\alpha\beta o\lambda\dot{\eta}$) which meant in the first instance a 'comparison', then a 'parable', and then through Christian usage 'the word of God', PARABOLARE 'to preach' was semantically extended in the late spoken Latin of Italy and Gaul to become the usual word for 'to speak', cf. Fr. *parler*, Prov. *paraular*, Cat. *parlar*, Ital. *parlare*; thereby it completely replaced the Latin deponent verb LOQUI, though it failed to oust another Latin word, FABULARI, firmly entrenched in the earlier spoken Latin of the Iberian Peninsula, cf. Span. *hablar*, Port. *falar* (see p. 165). The noun PARABOLA, in its semantic development to the simple meaning of 'word', probably followed in the wake of the verb. Even a term so 'unpopular' in appearance as PROTHYRON ($\pi\rho\dot{o}\theta\upsilon\rho o\nu$, the place in a chapel allotted to the household gods), adopted into Church Latin as a technical expression designating the iron gate which separates the choir from the nave and beside which the preacher stood to deliver his sermon, by A.D. 1200 is placed in the mouth of one of the low-class characters, a crier of wine, imagined by the Picard writer Jean Bodel in his *Jeu de saint Nicolas*:

> Connart, or ne fai pas le prorne,
> Que tu n'aies ton peleïc!
>
> (Ed. F. J. Warne, ll. 621–2)

(Connart, don't blow your own trumpet, unless you want a good hiding!) Thus *faire le prorne*, after being a more colloquial expression for 'to preach', became 'to hold forth', 'to brag'. In the French of Paris the word underwent a consonantal dissimilation, giving *prosne*, and side by side with *faire le prosne* there developed a verb *prosner*, ultimately *prôner*. Dignified by incorporation into the literary language this provided a synonym for *vanter* (< VANITARE), as when Molière wrote:

> Qui d'une sainte vie embrasse l'innocence
> Ne doit point tant prôner son nom et sa naissance.

(Tartuffe, Act II, scene ii)

In addition to the positive contribution of Greek to spoken Latin one must also take into account its negative influence. But for Greek, the eastern parts of the Empire might well have come within the linguistic compass of Romance. There, as in the west, the Romans employed their own language for all administrative purposes and in inscriptions it is still abundantly represented, but it met with no success among populations who spoke Greek, or acknowledged Greek as the language of prestige. Only in the mountainous country to the north of Greece did Latin win acceptance, in the land of Illyricum, annexed as early as 168 B.C., though almost unheard of in Roman history until shortly before the dawn of the Christian era, when the Roman plan to complement the Rhine frontier with a frontier on the Danube suddenly endowed it with strategic importance. Later a Romance speech was carried thence to Dacia, north of the Danube, but in circumstances which remain somewhat mysterious (see p. 481).

Unwittingly, the Romans probably contributed in no small measure to the eclipse of Latin in the east by the founding there of a second capital city. In A.D. 330 it was established in the heart of the eastern Empire by that same Constantine who accepted for Rome the practice of the Christian religion; from him it acquired its name of Constantinople. By intention, it was to be a replica of Rome, with a Senate and all the paraphernalia of imperial government. Christianity was to be its religion and in the name of Rome it was to control all the eastern provinces and defend their frontiers. So well did it prosper that before the century was out it was the rival of Rome itself, and the means of splitting the Empire into two parts. The last Emperor to rule over the whole of Romania was Theodosius I, 'the friend of the Goths' (see p. 215). Upon his death in A.D. 395 the inheritance was divided between his two sons, Honorius ruling in the west, and Arcadius becoming the first Emperor of the East. The line of territorial division was drawn from Sirmium, on the river Save, southwards through Illyricum to the Adriatic, all of Greece proper thus coming within the eastern sphere; in Africa, Cyrenaica was allotted to the east, while Tripolitania remained with Rome.

The name of the ancient Greek colony of Byzantium, founded in 667 B.C., on whose pleasant and strategic site Constantine had chosen to build his new city, was restored to favour. For the conscious promotion of culture and learning a university was inaugurated there, more akin to our modern universities than anything the world had previously known. But culture in this part of Romania remained obstinately Greek. Thus while the new Rome was fully endowed with the imperial outlook, on the eventual disruption of the western Empire it became the stronghold of Greek tradition, its language 'Byzantine Greek'.

*Germanic.* Very different is the evidence for an early influence of Germanic. As Greek was gratefully accepted, so Germanic was spurned. Here we come upon a linguistic problem of fascinating complexity, a problem which must be examined in some detail, since the Germanic element in Vulgar Latin represents but a foretaste of what was to come, the beginning of the new phase which marks the passage from Latin to Romance.

Already under the Empire thousands of German soldiers and slaves lived a large part of their lives among the Romans. When the Romance languages first appear on record in medieval texts they contain some hundreds of words of Germanic origin. The question which here arises is: To what extent were Germanic words already present in Vulgar Latin before it disintegrated into the different Romance idioms?

Before attempting an answer it might be well to consider how much knowledge we possess of Germanic speech during Roman times; and incidentally, how much faith can be placed in the Germanic etyma given by etymological dictionaries, which for a newcomer to Romance studies may have a certain air of improbability. Apart from the Runic inscriptions of Scandinavia, which are said to date from the third century, there is one important source: the translation of the Bible into Gothic by the missionary bishop Ulfilas (or in Germanic form, Wulfila) who lived from

A.D. 311 to 383. At the time the Goths were still in Dacia, which province they had occupied after the Roman withdrawal in A.D. 271; it was in fact Ulfilas who led his Christian following southward across the Danube to live under Roman protection in Moesia (see p. 215). Considerable portions of his translation still survive, from copies made in about A.D. 500 in Italy, then under the rule of the Ostrogoths. Its unique linguistic value may be judged from the sample given below, where it is compared with the English revised version, both being translations from the Greek; the text is transliterated into Roman characters from the alphabet 'invented' by Ulfilas, who used Greek symbols, supplementing them when they proved inadequate by other symbols taken from Latin and possibly from the rudimentary Runic alphabet of the Goths:

### St. Mark, Chapter iii, vv. 1-5

1. Jah galáiþ aftra in synagōgēn, jah was jáinar manna gaþaúrsana habands handu.
2. Jah witáidēdun imma háilidēdiu sabbatō daga, ei wrōhidēdeina ina.
3. Jah qaþ du þamma mann þamma gaþaúrsana habandin handu: urreis in midumái.
4. Jah qaþ du im: skuldu ist in sabbatim þiuþ táujan aíþþáu unþiuþ táujan, sáiwala nasjan aíþþáu usqistjan? Iþ eis þaháidēdun.
5. Jah ussaíƕands ins miþ mōda, gáurs in dáubiþōs haírtin izē qaþ du þamma mann: ufrakei þō handu þeina! Jah ufrakida, jah gastōþ aftra sō handus is.

(J. Wright, *Grammar of the Gothic Language*, p. 220)[1]

1. And he entered again into the synagogue; and there was a man there which had his hand withered.
2. And they watched him, whether he would heal him on the sabbath day; that they might accuse him.
3. And he saith unto the man that had his hand withered, Stand forth.
4. And he saith unto them, Is it lawful on the sabbath day to do good, or to do harm? to save a life, or to kill? But they held their peace.
5. And when he had looked round about on them with anger, being grieved at the hardening of their heart, he saith unto the man, Stretch forth thy hand. And he stretched it forth: and his hand was restored.

Thanks to this document we possess an extensive knowledge of the grammar and vocabulary of Gothic during the Vulgar Latin period. But the Goths were by no means the only Germans to be

[1] Second edition, with a supplement to the Grammar, by O. L. Sayce, Oxford, 1954.

in contact with the Romans. No less close were the Franks, and other tribes of the upper and lower Rhine; and of their speech the earliest comparable records date from more than three centuries later. It therefore follows that the Germanic loan-words quoted here and in the next chapter, unless they are attested as Gothic in Ulfilas's Bible, are to be considered as hypothetical in relation to the time at which they were first adopted into Vulgar Latin or Romance, though most of them are later attested, and in a form which does not suggest that they had undergone much change in the interval. Having said this, we may perhaps be dispensed from introducing Germanic words with the conventional asterisk to which most of them are really entitled.

From a study of Latin literature one might be justified in concluding that Germanic influence during the time of the western Empire was negligible. Except on rare occasions, when a Germanic word is introduced with the apparent idea of creating 'local colour', Latin writers kept their style free from such barbarisms. The *Germania* of Tacitus contains only one Germanic word: FRAMEA 'spear', probably as exotic to the Romans as is 'assegai' to us; in no other work by the same author does it reappear. The elder Pliny employs the Germanic word SAPO, which originally designated a kind of cream—*fit ex sebo et cinere*—used in dressing the hair. Whereas FRAMEA left no trace, SAPŌNEM has given the word for 'soap' throughout Romania, viz. Fr. *savon*, Cat. *sabó*, Span. *jabón*, Port. *sabão*, Ital. *sapone*, Rum. *săpun*; Welsh took up a Romance form *sebon*; Anglo-Sax. *sāpe*, Eng. *soap*, is purely Germanic. Also used by Pliny is the word GANTA 'wild goose', found with the same meaning in Old Fr. *jante*, which has become transferred to the stork in Prov. Cat. *ganta*. A fourth-century writer, Palladius, composed a *De re rustica* in which he employed the Germanic word VANGA 'hoe', which persists with the same meaning in Ital. *vanga*. For the rest, the very few Germanic words found in the work of other obscure Latin authors have in general disappeared.

This paucity of documentary testimony concerning the Germanic element in Vulgar Latin is belied by the evidence of the Romance languages. Most Germanic terms in Romance are due to the various invasions which took place from the fifth century onwards (see next Chapter); but some are of such widespread usage that they cannot be identified with any particular tribal settlement and we therefore assume that they were adopted into Vulgar Latin at a time previous to the main invasions. Now comes the question: When? Here we find that somewhat divergent views are expressed by those German and Austrian scholars who have taken a leading part in discussion of the problem. The Viennese professor J. Brüch (*Der Einfluss der germanischen Sprachen auf das Vulgärlatein*, 1913) drew up a list of some hundred Germanic words which he believed to have been incorporated into Vulgar Latin by A.D. 400. But E. Gamillscheg (*Romania Germanica*, 3 vols., 1934–6) will have none of this. One word only will he allow, which, on account of its presence in Rumanian as well as in the west, can be deemed to have become part of the general vocabulary of Vulgar Latin by the end of the fourth century. It is the Visigothic MARRJAN 'to anger', 'annoy', a verb which survived in Old Fr. *marrir*—still current in the seventeenth century, as in the punning expression *mari très marri*—in Ital. *smarrire* 'to bewilder', 'lose', and in Rum. *a amări* 'to embitter'; as an adjectival past participle it is also represented by Prov. Cat. *marrit* and Old Span. *amarrido*. According to Gamillscheg, the term was generalized in military slang with a sense approximating to that of the Fr. *avoir le cafard*, and it conveyed the longing of the German soldier for home. All other Germanic borrowings he seeks to localize in particular areas, mostly on the outskirts of the Empire, where the military contingents were thickest. He concludes that at the end of the fourth century the 'common Vulgar Latin' speech was still almost entirely free from Germanic elements, which gained their wider currency only in the confusion of the century which followed.

In quoting examples of these early Germanic borrowings we shall not seek, as does Gamillscheg, to determine from the slender phonological evidence the precise Germanic source of each one. It is a difficult undertaking, complicated by the facts that the Germanic speeches of that period did not differ greatly one from another, and that the same word may have been borrowed at different times, in different localities, and from different Germanic idioms. Moreover, it is not always easy to determine from its geographical extension in Romance whether a word really dates back to this earlier phase of borrowing, or whether it would not be more correctly attributed to the later radiation of Frankish (see next Chapter). With all these reservations, we may now point to a number of terms of which the presence in the western Romance-speaking area seems to be previous to the full-scale invasions of that area by Germanic tribes. It will be observed that the flavour of the military camp is predominant.

In the first place, the camp itself: this was in Gothic the HARI-BERGO, a word formed in the usual Germanic way of two elements, meaning literally the 'army-shelter'. The Germanic *h* ceasing to be pronounced, this word became Span. Ital. *albergo*, Cat. *alberc*, Prov. *auberc*, and it changed in meaning, retaining its 'shelter' element but ultimately losing that of 'army', to become the common word for 'inn'. So firmly was HARI-BERGO entrenched that the subsequent overlay of Frankish HERI-BERGA was confined to northern France, where, retaining its *h*, it became Old Fr. *herberge*. It is likely, however, that the feminine Frankish form was responsible for the development in Provençal of an alternative, *auberga*, which, a thousand years later, was to oust *herberge* from the north.

The following Germanic substantives are of similarly wide diffusion: SUPPA 'soup', cf. Fr. *soupe*, Prov. Cat. Span. Port. *sopa*, Ital. *zuppa*; BANK 'bench', cf. Fr. Prov. Cat. *banc*, Span. Port. Ital. *banco*; HARPA 'harp', cf. Fr. *harpe*, Prov. Cat. Span. Port. Ital. *arpa*; FANIGS 'mud' (originally an adjective formed from Gothic FANI, cf. Eng. *'fen'*), cf. Old Fr. *fanc, fange*, mod. *fange*, Prov. *fanc, fanga*, Span. Ital. *fango* (Span. *fango* was probably borrowed from Catalan); SKUMS 'foam' (Germ. *Schaum*, Eng. *scum*), cf. Fr. *écume*, Prov. Cat. Port. *escuma*, Ital. *schiuma* (Span. *espuma*, Ital. *spuma*, Rum. *spumă* are from the Lat. SPUMA); BINDA 'bandage', cf. Fr. *bende, bande*, Prov. Cat. Span. Ital. *benda* (mod. Span. *banda* is the same word reintroduced from French); MARKA 'frontier territory' (cf. Germ. *Finmark, Dänemark, Ostmark*, &c.), cf. Fr. *marche*, Prov. Cat. Span. Port. Ital. *marca*; TRIUWA 'truce', cf. Fr. *trêve*, Cat. *treva*, Prov. Span. Ital. *tregua*, Port. *trégua*.[1]

The eclipse of BELLUM, the usual Latin for 'war', was complete. In the east, where borrowings from Germanic are almost entirely absent, it was replaced by a Slavonic word, Rum. *răz-boi*; and in the west by Germanic WERRA (cf. Germ. *Wirren* 'disorders', *Wirrnis, Wirrwarr* 'confusion', and Eng. *war*). This

---

[1] Another word commonly listed as Germanic is BRASA 'embers', cf. Fr. *braise*, Prov. Cat. Span. Port. *brasa*, North Ital. *braza*. There is, however, no clear affiliation with BRASA in early Germanic speeches and the provenance of the word must be considered as uncertain (cf. J. Corominas, *Diccionario crítico etimológico de la lengua castellana*, vol. i, under the rubric *brasa*).

disappearance is sometimes explained as being due to the homonymic clash between BELLUM 'war', and BELLUM, neuter adjective, 'beautiful'. Gamillscheg questions this explanation on the
ground that the coexistence of the two words during the Latin
period proves that the homonymic clash can have given rise
to no linguistic inconvenience. To this one may answer that
whereas the ambivalence of HOC EST BELLUM may not have in-
convenienced those Romans who were born to it, it may yet have
impressed the Germanic soldiery as being extremely odd.[1] But
when and where did the replacement of BELLUM by WERRA first
take place? It must have happened quite early, and Professor
Gamillscheg sees here an example of that overlay of one Germanic
dialect by another to which we have previously referred, a Gothic
WERRA (which in the fourth century would probably have been
adopted as *VERRA) having been supplanted by the forms deriving
from Frankish WERRA (> Fr. *guerre*), propagated after the Frankish
occupation of Gaul.

A similar overlay would seem to account for the different forms
of the word for 'spur', essentially a Germanic object. A Gothic
SPAURA, in which the diphthong was resolved as half-open ɔ, persisted in the Iberian Peninsula, cf. Span. *espuera*, *espuela*, Port.
*espora*, whereas a Frank. SPORO gave rise to Old Fr. *esperon* (whence
Ital. *sperone*) and Prov. *esporó*; the latter then crossed the Pyrenees,
cf. Cat. *esporó*, and appears in Spanish as *esporón*, *espolón*, rival
forms to the earlier representatives of Gothic.

Germanic WĪSA ('wise' as in Eng. 'likewise') must have been of
early diffusion to produce Fr. *guise*, Prov. *guiza*, Span. Cat. Port.
Ital. *guisa*; from this word Spanish and Portuguese have created
a verb *guisar* 'to prepare', and by specialization of meaning 'to
cook'.

A few Germanic adjectives denoting colour are of early adoption. BLANK generally replaced Lat. ALBUS, cf. Fr. Prov. Cat. *blanc*,
Span. *blanco*, Port. *branco*, Ital. *bianco*, though ALBUS remains in
Rum. *alb*, Rheto-Rom. *alf*; the feminine of the Latin adjective has
everywhere survived as a substantive meaning 'dawn', cf. Fr. *aube*,

---

[1] The incongruity is remarked upon in the fifth century by the Gallo-Roman
Sidonius (see p. 301): 'sicut ex adverso maiores nostri proelia, quibus nihil est
foedius, bella dixerunt...', 'just as our ancestors, going by contraries, called
wars, which are the foulest of all things, *bella*' (Sidonius, Poems and Letters, ed.
with an English translation by W. B. Anderson, Loeb Classical Library, Vol. 1,
p. 412).

Prov. *auba*, Cat. Span. Ital. *alba*, Port. Rheto-Rom. *alva*, Rum. *alba*. BRŪN (cf. Germ. *braun*, Eng. *brown*) became Fr. and Prov. *brun*, Span. Port. Ital. *bruno*; among the Franks of northern France this adjective gave rise to a verb *brunir*, whence Ital. *brunire*, both with the meaning 'to burnish'. The word for 'grey', Fr. Prov. Cat. *gris* (< GRĪSI) was diffused from the Gallo-Roman area to give Span. Port. *gris*, Ital. *grigio*. A Germanic FALWA gave Fr. *fauve* 'tawny', Prov. *falb* (> Ital. *falbo*), while the same root appears in the Iberian Peninsula with the Latin suffix -ARIA, cf. Span. *overo*, Port. *fouveiro*. It has been suggested that these four epithets owe their currency to the fact that they were widely used with special application to horses: this carries more conviction than an alternative theory according to which they were the distinguishing colours painted by the German soldiery on their shields.

A further adjective of colour, *BLUND, survives as Fr. *blond*, Prov. *blon*, Ital. *biondo*; it is generally assumed that the word was used to characterize a particular shade of Germanic hair, the *rutilae comes* described by Tacitus, but in fact, though it probably came into Romance via Frankish, it seems to have no affiliation in the Germanic languages and its ultimate source remains doubtful. We might also mention here, though with no certainty as to whether it might not be more appropriately placed among the borrowings subsequent to the Frankish invasions, the term BĪSI, similar in form and meaning to GRĪSI, which gave Fr. *bis*, as in *le pain bis*, Prov. and Cat. *bis*, Ital. *bigio*; the same word is also found in French as *beige*, apparently a dialectal development, attested in the thirteenth century and used in particular of wool in its natural state.

A number of common verbs of Germanic origin are widely employed in Romance. These too would appear to owe their diffusion to a Vulgar Latin current in the fifth century rather than to specific tribal settlements. Among the most familiar are the following:—BASTJAN (connected etymologically with Eng. 'bast', the fibre beneath the bark of trees, used in wattle-building) > Fr. *bâtir*, Prov. Cat. Span. Port. *bastir*, Ital. *bastire*. BRIKAN (cf. Germ. *brechen*, Eng. *to break*) > Fr. *broyer*, Prov. *bregar*, Cat. *bragar*, north Italian dialects, *zbregar*. SPARANJAN (cf. Germ. *sparen*, Eng. *to spare*) > Fr. *épargner*, Prov. *esparnhar*, Old Ital. *sparagnare*, *sparmiare*, whence mod. *risparmiare*. WARDŌN (cf. Eng. *to ward off*)

> Fr. *garder*, Prov. Cat. Span. Port. *guardar*, Ital. *guardare*.
WARNJAN (cf. Germ. *warnen*, Eng. *to warn*) > Fr. Prov. *garnir*,
Span. Port. *guarnir*, Ital. *guarnire*: the sense developed through the
concept of 'protect' to that of 'cover', 'clothe'. WARJAN (cf. Germ.
*wehren*, Eng. *ware* as in *aware, beware, wary*) > Old Fr. *garir*,
mod. *guérir*, Prov. *garir*, Cat. Old Span. Port. *guarir*, Ital. *guarire*;
the older French form *garir* persists with a change of conjugation
in *garer*, cf. also *gare* and *garage*. KRATTŌN (cf. Germ. *kratzen*, Eng.
*to scratch*) > Fr. *gratter*, Prov. *gratar*, Ital. *grattare*, Rheto-Rom.
*sgratter*: absent from the Iberian Peninsula which in this instance
remained true to Latin with RASICARE, cf. Prov. Cat. Span. Port.
*rascar*. LIKKŌN (cf. Germ. *lecken*, Eng. *to lick*) > Fr. *lécher*, Prov.
*lecar*, Ital. *leccare*, Rheto-Rom. *licher*; here again the Iberian Peninsula differs, using Lat. LAMBERE, cf. Span. *lamer*, Port. *lamber*.
FRONJAN (cf. Germ. *fronen*) > Fr. *fournir*, Prov. Cat. Span. Port.
*fornir*, Ital. *fornire*. RAUBŌN (cf. Germ. *rauben*) > Old Fr. *rober*,
Prov. *raubar*, Cat. Span. *robar*, Port. *roubar*, Ital. *rubare*. HRAUST-
JAN (cf. Germ. *rösten*) > Fr. *rôtir*, Prov. *raustir*, Cat. *rostir*, Ital.
*arrostire*. And of special interest for its semantic development, one
of the commonest verbs in Romance: WAIDANJAN (formed on
WAIDA, 'meadow', cf. Germ. *Weide*, Eng. *weed*) > Fr. *gagner*,
Prov. *guadanhar*, Cat. *guanyar*, Span. *guadañar*, Port. *ganhar*,
Rheto-Rom. *guadagner*, Ital. *guadagnare*. As its etymology indicates, this verb originally conveyed the idea of going out into
the fields in quest of food: thus Old Fr. *gaaignier* meant 'to till',
and the *gaaigneor* was the labourer; the concrete sense is preserved in mod. Span. *guadañar* 'to mow', whence *guadaña*
'scythe', whereas mod. Fr. *gagner* and Ital. *guadagnare* have acquired the abstract meaning 'to gain', 'to earn' (cf. the comparable
semantic development of Eng. *to earn*, cognate with the Germ.
*Ernte* 'harvest'). Spanish expresses the latter sense by means of
a different verb of Germanic origin, *ganar*, from the Gothic
GAINŌN 'to be open-mouthed' and hence 'to strive after' (cf. Germ.
*gähnen* 'to yawn', and see p. 222).

In conclusion we may record a curious instance of the German
soldiers' adaptation of their language to Latin by means of a
literal translation. The V. Lat. COMPANIO is formed from CUM
PANE, which corresponds exactly to the Gothic GA-HLAIBA (cf.
Eng. *loaf*). Many languages, like Gothic, contain words in which
the act of giving or sharing bread has come to express the notion

of friendship or hospitality, e.g. Eng. *lord*, from Anglo-Sax. *hlāford*, composed of *hlāf* and *weard* 'loaf-ward', and similarly *lady*, from Anglo-Sax. *hlǣfdige* 'loaf-maid'; the Russian for 'hospitality' is literally 'bread-salt'. Thus the COMPANIO was the soldier's 'pal', a sense retained in Fr. *copain*, deriving from the Old French nominative used as a vocative; the accusative COMPANIONEM has developed into the more literary *compagnon*, and an analogical feminine *compagne* was later created. The word survives in most other Romance languages of the west, cf. Prov. *companh*, *companhó*; Cat. *company*, *companyó*; Old Span. *compaño*, *compañón* (mod. *compañero*); Rheto-Rom. *cumpagn*; Ital. *compagno*.

Such was the linguistic vanguard of the invasions which were to bring about the final collapse of the Roman Empire in the west.

# III

## THE FORMATIVE PERIOD OF ROMANCE

THERE is, of course, no real dividing line between Latin and Romance. Vulgar Latin was differentiated into the various Romance idioms by a natural process of evolution, which became more rapid only in consequence of the weakening of the social and political cohesion which had formerly tended to hold it in check. But the close of the fifth century, marking the final collapse of the Roman Empire in the west, may be taken as the time when the use of the term 'Romance' begins to be apposite, with reference to the unrecorded utterance of the people. From this time onwards we may make a general distinction, using the conventional terms previously defined, between Gallo-Romance, Italo-Romance, Hispano-Romance, Rheto-Romance, and Balkan Romance. We may assume that thereafter, with the disappearance of Roman administration, the speakers of Romance vernacular from different parts of the former Empire, on account of local phonetic change and varied lexical and semantic choice rather than of any far-reaching modification of accidence and syntax, became increasingly unable to understand one another.

Arguments which have been advanced to suggest that the 'unity' of spoken Latin persisted until the age of Charlemagne can be accorded here no serious value: they are based upon an unimaginative interpretation of written evidence which is quite inapplicable to the ordinary illiterate inhabitant. The fact that a linguistic feature is not attested in writing until the eighth century constitutes no proof of its novelty at that time. Such features are usually of frequent occurrence in speech long before they appear as 'mistakes' committed by the literate minority. By the ninth century, when writing in the vernacular as opposed to Latin first became a conscious practice, most of those changes which serve to characterize the medieval Romance idioms had already taken place.

The four centuries which constitute the formative period of Romance, if we may now so term it, were known to an earlier generation of historians as the 'Dark Ages'. Research has now thrown much light upon the darkness, but the picture which emerges is one of confusion, of brigandage and local warfare, in which the efforts of individuals to re-establish a semblance of the civic order of Roman times met with repeated failure. The frontier of civilization, based for so long on the Rhine and the Danube, was obliterated, and the eastern bastion of Byzantium, though unconquered, was weakened and by-passed, as miscellaneous tribes of varied origin, coming from the north and the east, migrated at will through the length and breadth of the former Empire.

First among these, and most important for the story of Romance, were the different peoples of Germanic stock. Next in time, and still more effective as obliterators of Latin, were the Slavs; but besides these there came conquerors of non-Indo-European speech from a more remote east. Finally, the Arabs rolled up the Roman world in Africa and overran Spain. To these tribal movements is due not only, in large measure, the hastened fragmentation of Vulgar Latin, but also the delimiting of the areas which in the Europe of the future were to be Romance-speaking countries. And although their general influence as linguistic 'superstrata' on the speech-habits prevalent in those countries remains somewhat conjectural, and may easily be exaggerated, it is nevertheless certain that, with new implements and methods, new social and moral conceptions, the invaders made their own contributions, in some instances on a considerable scale, to the lexical resources of the Romance languages.

## GERMANIC INVASIONS

*The 'German problem'*. During most of its existence the Roman Empire had a 'German problem', under various guises, and in varying degrees of acuteness. Already in the first century B.C. Germanic tribes on the move had attempted to settle in Celtic-occupied Gaul, only to be decisively repelled by Julius Caesar. Thereafter they remained the foremost representatives of that outer world which the Rhine–Danube frontier was designed to contain. The one Roman attempt to reduce them to submission, and thereby shift the frontier eastwards to the Elbe, ended disastrously in the year A.D. 9, when three legions were annihilated at the *Teutoburgiensis saltus* (in the region of modern Osnabrück); with this battle the German leader Arminius succeeded in doing what Vercingetorix in Gaul had so narrowly failed to do. Of their customs and tribal organization during the first century A.D. we have a most valuable if somewhat idealized account in the *Germania* of Tacitus (*c.* A.D. 54–*c.*120), who sought by implication to give his fellow-Romans a lesson in virtue. That they engaged in commercial relations with Roman traders is apparent from the early borrowing of names of such commodities as CASEUM (> Germ. *Käse*) and VĪNUM (> Germ. *Wein*).

The second century witnessed one hostile clash, when, in A.D. 167, during the reign of the philosopher-Emperor Marcus Aurelius, the tribe of the Marcomans, impelled by pressure of other tribes, broke into the Roman province of Pannonia (the western part of modern Hungary), to be thrown out only after a struggle which lasted for fourteen years. Another hundred years elapsed before the two attacks which marked the first serious and permanent bites into Roman territory. In A.D. 260 the Alamans launched an assault on the Roman garrisons in the Agri Decumates (i.e. 'tithe-lands'), and drove them across the Rhine. The loss of this large wedge of land situated between the upper reaches of the Danube and those of the Rhine (comprising modern Baden and Wurtemberg) meant the severing of direct communications between Gaul and the provinces of Vindelicia (with its capital at Augusta Vindelicorum, modern Augsburg), Noricum, Pannonia, and others farther east: in philological terms, it marks a beginning of the isolation of Vulgar Latin in Gaul from more easterly developments. Shortly after this event, in A.D. 271, the menace of the Goths at the other end of the frontier compelled the Romans to evacuate their last-won province of Dacia, and withdraw their forces south of the Danube. But still they were safe behind the two great rivers.

Meanwhile, however, a kind of peaceful penetration was taking place with Roman consent. Small communities of Germans were permitted to settle within the territory of Gaul. Germans were enlisted in the Roman armies, to such an extent that the forces charged with defending the frontiers became progressively germanized. This may have been partly on account of the Christian aversion to war; a rapid decline of population at the heart of the Empire during the third century was another contributory factor.

Roman politicians of the day were thus confronted with the classic situation of a weakened centre and a menacing periphery, a situation in which some sought a pro-German and others an anti-German solution, the former envisaging a gradual absorption of the potential enemy. In this setting there occurred an unforeseen event of the kind which tends to disrupt such plans, the sudden appearance of another and more ruthless aggressor. Though the evidence of trade, in silk, for example, suggests some slight contact with the distant east, the Romans in general can have had little idea of what lay on the farther side of the plains of Scythia: that was literally the back of beyond. When therefore, in A.D. 395, a barbaric people of Mongolian origin, the Huns, came pouring through the Caspian Gates into the eastern provinces, the circumstance produced no little consternation, as may be judged from the vivid description contained in a letter of St. Jerome, then in Palestine:

As I was seeking a dwelling suitable for so great a lady (Fabiola) . . . suddenly messengers flew this way and that and the whole Eastern world trembled. We were told that swarms of Huns had poured forth from the distant Sea of Azov, midway between the icy river Tanais and the savage tribes of the Massagetae, where the gates of Alexander keep back the barbarians behind the rocky Causasus. Flying hither and thither on their swift steeds, said our informants, these invaders were filling the whole world with bloodshed and panic. At that time the Roman army was absent, being kept in Italy by reason of civil war. . . . May Jesus save the Roman world from such wild beasts in future! Everywhere their approach was unexpected, they outstripped rumour by their speed, and they spared neither religion nor rank nor age. . . .
        (*Select Letters of St. Jerome*, transl. F. A. Wright, The Loeb
                        Classical Library, p. 329)

Of all the Germanic tribes the most easterly at this time were the Goths, the overrunners of Dacia. These were the people whom Bishop Ulfilas had set out to convert in A.D. 341 to the Arian version of Christianity (Arius had maintained that the Son is not co-eternal with the Father in the Trinity), and for whose benefit he had translated the Bible into Gothic. At the moment of the Hunnish invasion the Visigoths (West Goths), settled under the Emperor Theodosius I as Roman *foederati* south of the Danube in Moesia and Thrace (at the instance of Ulfilas, see p. 204), had taken advantage of dissensions in Italy to revolt against Rome, and under their leader Alaric were doing their own share of plundering in the eastern provinces. The Empire had in fact been at grips for some time past with its German problem. Certain historians have for this reason denied the importance of the Hunnish invasion in provoking the migration of Germanic tribes, maintaining (with J. B. Bury) that

the idea of the 'wandering of the nations' and unproven speculations as to its connection with tremendous movements in the heart of Asia— an hypothesis which is as superfluous as it is undemonstrable—have led to unhistorical notions as to the nature of the break-up of the Empire. The facts do not warrant us in looking at the German movements in the fourth and fifth centuries as anything more than a continuation of the old war on the frontiers.

Yet it seems more than a coincidence that, shortly after the Hunnish onslaught, the Germanic tribes in the east of the Empire should have begun a movement which ultimately led them to the extreme west, and that subsequent incursions of the Huns into the heart of Europe should have been closely followed by further westerly migrations of the tribes in that area, seeking new homes within the Roman world.

*Vandals, Alans, and Swabians.* Interesting as the debate on causes may be, it is with the ensuing events that we are mainly concerned. Two principal tribes, the Visigoths and their northern kinsmen the Vandals, followed roughly similar directions. The latter, thwarted by the Roman army in an attempt to enter Italy from the north, turned westwards, and joined on the way by Alans[1] and Swabians, crossed the Rhine on 31 December, A.D. 406, thus arriving in Gaul some six years before the Visigoths. For the next three years they ravaged that country, and then passed on into Spain. There they settled in four groups, the Alans in Lusitania (modern Portugal), the Swabians and the Asding Vandals in Gallaecia (Galicia), and the Siling Vandals in southern Baetica (Andalusia). As in Gaul, their 'vandalism' made them the terror of the romanized populations living in the towns. In A.D. 416 they were attacked by the newly-arrived Visigoths, acting on this occasion in the interest of Rome (see below). The Alans were defeated and scattered and the Siling Vandals of the south completely wiped out. After the return of the Visigoths to Gaul, war broke out in the north-west between Gunderic, king of the Asding Vandals, and Hermeric, king of the Swabians. While the former was besieging the latter a Roman army appeared and drove off

[1] The Alans, though here acting in association with Germanic tribes, were not Germanic in origin. They appear to have come, like the Huns, from somewhere in Asia.

the Asding Vandals, who left their lands and retreated south. They were then allowed to settle in Baetica, thus taking the place of the other Vandal group which had been annihilated two years earlier. In A.D. 429, under Gaiseric, son of Gunderic, they crossed the straits into the province of Mauritania, and six years later made an agreement with Rome whereby this new settlement received official recognition. The agreement, however, was soon broken, and moving now eastwards they established a Vandal kingdom in the Roman province of Africa, in the Carthaginian territory of former days. From this base they occupied for a while the islands of Sicily, Sardinia, and Corsica, and in A.D. 455, still under the leadership of Gaiseric, they landed in Italy and emulated the Visigoths by pillaging Rome.

The kingdom of the Vandals in Africa endured for nearly a century, until A.D. 533, when they were attacked and utterly defeated near the site of Carthage by the Byzantines under Belisarius; that was the time when Justinian, the greatest of Byzantine emperors, was waging his campaign to restore the power of the Empire in the west (see p. 228). Their rule, in the record of history, was ephemeral. Never were they sufficiently numerous or well-organized to found a permanent nation. The memory of their brief sojourn in Baetica remains in the name of Andalusia, propagated during the time of Muslim occupation, as *Al-Andalus*, to include the whole province.

More frequent are the traces of the Swabians, whose kingdom in north-west Spain survived for a century and a half, until it fell before the Visigoths. Among the few words which they have left are the Port. *britar* 'to break' (< BRIUTAN, cf. Anglo-Sax. *brēotan*), and the Galician *laverca* 'lark' (< LAWERKA, cognate with the English, cf. Anglo-Sax. *lāwerce*, and with Germ. *Lerche*). No less than four localities in the province of Coruña preserve the name of *Suevos*. Traces of the passage of the Alans are still to be found in the *Puerta del Alano*, at Huesca, and *Villalán*, at Valladolid.

*Visigoths*. Much more important, from our standpoint, are the Visigoths. In closer contact with Rome and familiar with the Roman way of life, led by resolute and ambitious men who dreamed of founding a Gothic Empire, they played a large part in the final dismemberment of the Empire in decline and in the creation of new territorial divisions. When the decisive fifth century began they were prominently on the scene as defenders of the Roman frontier on the lower Danube, pledged to serve the policies of a Rome already half-germanized, in which the most powerful figure of the day was the general Stilicho (d. A.D. 408), himself of Vandal origin, father-in-law and protector of the young Emperor Honorius. But already they were on the move. Their restless king Alaric had acquired for himself the Roman title of *magister militum per Illyricum* and his forces were spreading through that country. Of Stilicho it has been aptly said that it was his misfortune 'to prove the unwisdom of the policy begun by the Emperor Valens in A.D. 376, the settlement of the Germans tribally and *en bloc* within the Empire' (Previté-Orton). Scarcely had he returned from deflecting in Rhetia the southward advance of the Vandals when he found that Alaric with his Visigoths had entered Italy (A.D. 401). Alaric being nominally an ally, he was able by diplomacy and bribery to persuade him to return to Illyricum, but seven years later, when Stilicho had been murdered by his own legionaries, Alaric promptly invaded Italy for a second time. For the next two years the Visigoths wandered through Italy at will, twice besieging Rome and forcing the inhabitants to pay ransom. On the second occasion Alaric set up the prefect of the city as a mock-Emperor, in opposition to Honorius, who had removed his court to Ravenna. In A.D. 410 he marched on Rome for a third time, and on this occasion allowed his soldiers to sack the capital of the Empire. Then he moved into southern Italy, with the apparent intention of migrating to Africa, the land of corn, but before the project could be carried into effect he died.

Alaric has been described as 'the Moses of the Visigoths', always seeking to establish his people in a promised land. It would have been possible for him to settle them in Illyricum, or even in Italy itself, but perhaps his quest was for a place less menaced by potential enemies. Although his final move was in the opposite direction, it was certainly he who prepared the way for the future Visigothic kingdoms in Gaul and in Spain.

The new orientation was determined by Alaric's successor, Athaulf. Turning his people north again, he led them into Gaul. There, at Narbo, he married Placidia, half-sister of the Emperor, whom he had abducted, though the marriage appears to have taken place with her consent. He was undoubtedly an admirer of Rome, and thus may have sought by a bond of kinship to strengthen the alliance. Tarrying but a short time in Gaul, the Visigoths moved in A.D. 415 into Spain, and there Athaulf was stabbed to death by a rival, who within a few days met a similar fate. The next king, Wallia, though probably elevated to power in order that he should reverse the pro-Roman tendencies of Athaulf, was destined to become a strong champion of the Roman cause. He it was who attacked and routed, as we have already told, the more primitive Germanic tribes then harassing the Ibero-Roman population. In return for this service, and doubtless in the hope of inducing them to settle down quietly, Honorius offered the Visigoths a permanent home in south-west Gaul, the seven cities of Toulouse, Agen, Bordeaux, Périgueux, Saintes, Angoulême, and Poitiers being specified for their occupation (A.D. 419). The offer was accepted, and six years later they declared themselves an independent kingdom, with Toulouse as capital. This kingdom in Gaul survived for eighty years, during which time the Visigoths were to render at least one outstanding service to the cause of the west. In A.D. 451 the Huns, under their leader Attila, by then the ruler of a considerable domain in central Europe, made an incursion into Gaul. Rome had not yet bowed to the inevitable, and one of her last great generals, Aëtius, hastened north to confront the threat, on his way persuading the Visigothic king, Theodoric, to join forces with him. The combined army came upon Attila as he was besieging Orleans, engaged him in a battle since known as that of the Catalaunian Fields, and compelled him to withdraw across the Rhine. Subsequently, after a savage invasion of northern Italy, from which he was obliged by famine and pestilence to desist, Attila died, and thereafter the Hunnish menace receded.

The end of the rule of the Visigoths in Gaul came in A.D. 507, with their defeat at Vouillé (in the modern department of Vienne) by the Franks (see p. 234). But this event was only the prelude to the establishment of a greater Visigothic kingdom in Spain, whither they withdrew. With their capital first at Barcelona and later at Toledo, the Visigoths developed Spain into the semblance of a modern nation. At the beginning there were rival authorities: the Swabians still ruled the north-west; in their present domains the Basques were still independent; Roman nobles still held extensive territories in the centre and south; and on the southern coast the Byzantines, following up their rout of the Vandals, had restored in A.D. 554 the rule of the Empire. Of these, the first three were subdued during the reign of Leovigild (A.D. 568–86), the kingdom of the Swabians being completely extinguished. It was left to King Sisebut, who reigned from A.D. 612 to 621, to conquer the Byzantine territories other than Algarve, the most southerly province of Portugal. Algarve finally fell in A.D. 629.

Under the Visigoths Spain thus became a politically unified country, but social unification was slow to follow. The Germanic element for a long time remained, as it had been in Gaul, an aloof military caste, devoutly Arian in religion, and forbidden to intermarry with the 'native' population; in this it was perpetuating a ban on intermarriage originally imposed by the Romans (see Menéndez Pidal, *Orígenes del español*, 3rd ed., p. 505). The Visigoths were the landowners, feared and shunned by the Catholic Spaniards of the towns, with their still superior civilization. The first real attempt to bridge the gap was made by King Recared, son of Leovigild, who in A.D. 589 abandoned the 'Arian heresy' to embrace Catholicism. Thereafter the Visigothic monarchy secured the support of the Roman Church. Eventually the ban on intermarriage was removed (c. A.D. 655), and King Receswinth (reigned A.D. 649–72) issued a code of mingled Gothic and Roman law, replacing the laws which had previously been quite different for the two peoples. With later revisions this became the *Forum Judicum*, the basis of the Spanish *Fueros* of the twelfth and thirteenth centuries, with their notable element of Germanic custom. The only written language throughout the Visigothic period was of course Latin, which in addition to serving Church and State was the medium of a certain amount of disinterested literature, including in particular the work of Bishop Isidore of Seville (A.D. 560–636, see p. 304).

This was the realm so swiftly overthrown, in A.D. 711, by a small force of Arabic invaders. The attempt at unification had come too late. Yet those of its survivors who found refuge in the mountains of the north were to maintain and hand down to their descendants the Christian fervour which eventually prevailed during the long centuries of the Reconquest.

*The Visigothic element in Romance.* Wherever the Visigoths went, in Gaul and more particularly in Spain, they have left their trace in place-names and personal names. The former usually derive from the latter, a fact which reflects the practice of taking possession of the land. Small clusters of Visigothic place-names in the French Pyrenees, e.g. *Adervielle, Estarvielle, Loudenvielle,* and

*Loudervielle*, all in the Louron valley,[1] suggest the persistence of colonies in those easily defensible regions, after the general withdrawal to the south. In the Iberian Peninsula, where, as is to be expected, such names are most numerous in the north-west, they frequently derive from a latinized genitive, in which one may perhaps detect the influence of the notary, e.g. *Guitiriz* (< Witerici), *Guimarães* (< Vimaranis). While many of these personal appellations survive only in toponymy, or in surnames, and now appear rather outlandish, others have gained in popularity and so come to count among the most familiar Christian names of modern Spanish, e.g. *Fernando, Ramiro, Alfonso,* and *Elvira*. The tribal name of the Goths, like that of the Swabians, was attached to a number of localities, e.g. *Godos, Revillagodos, Gudillos, Godojos, Godones,* &c.; contrasting these with the *Romanos, Romanillos, Romanones, Romancos,* &c., which are no less common in toponymy, we have a glimpse of the *apartheid* in which the two peoples lived (cf. Menéndez Pidal, loc. cit.).

Already half-romanized before their occupation of Spain, and using Latin as their written medium, the Visigoths had largely abandoned by the seventh century the use of their Germanic speech. For this reason, and in consequence of the lack of social contact to which we have referred, the direct influence of Visigothic on the Romance of the Peninsula is less considerable than one might have anticipated. Sifting from the Germanic element in Spanish those words which must owe their diffusion to the late Vulgar Latin period (see pp. 207–11), and also those which derive from the Frankish overlay embedded in Gallo-Romance—this latter an important factor from the time of Charlemagne, whose Empire included northern Spain—we find that there remains a residue of miscellaneous terms which can definitely be attributed to Visigothic. The vocabulary of administration, so prominent in the Frankish loan-words in French, is almost entirely absent. Of the few terms of legal connotation incorporated into medieval texts the only one which survives in modern Spanish is *lastar*, meaning literally 'to follow in the tracks of' and thence 'to stand

---

[1] To these may be added *Aranvielle* (Louron valley), and on the other side of the Col de Peyresourde, nearer Luchon, *Jurvielle* and *Cathervielle* (valley of Larboust), and *Saccourvielle* (valley of Oueil); see J. A. Cremona, *Une colonie visigothique dans les Pyrénées Centrales?*, Actes et Mémoires du premier congrès international de langue et littérature du Midi de la France, Avignon, 1957, pp. 289–296.

in for another' (< LAISTŌN from Gothic LAISTS 'track', cf. Germ.
*leisten*, now generalized in sense as 'to accomplish'). Among terms
denoting office, it seems certain, despite the contrary opinion of
Gamillscheg and others, that Span. *escanciano*, Port. *escanção* 'cup-
bearer', together with the verb *escanciar*, developed directly from
Visigothic and owe nothing to the Old Fr. *eschanson*, mod.
*échanson*: the Gothic was SKANKJA, gen. SKANKJANS, attested in
latinized form in the COMES SCANCIARUM of the *Lex Visigothorum*,
whereas the Old Fr. nom. *eschanz*, acc. *eschanson*, derives from the
Frank. SKANKJO; the word is cognate with Germ. *schenken* (see
J. Corominas, *Diccionario crítico etimológico* . . ., under *escanciar*).
In the military sphere, Port. and Old Span. *elmo* represent Gothic
HILMS; this was replaced in Spanish by *yelmo*, borrowed from
Gallo-Romance (< Frank. HELM, see p. 246). Also peculiar to the
Peninsula is Port. *aleive*, Old Span. *aleve* 'treachery', from the
Gothic verb LĒWJAN 'to betray' (this generally accepted etymology
is, however, rejected by Corominas, op. cit.); mod. Span. *alevosía*
is formed on the adj. *alevoso*. Other Visigothic terms pertain for
the most part to pastoral and domestic life, e.g. Span. Port. *ganso*
'goose' (< GANS, still the same word in modern German); most
probably—though a Lat. AVIA has been suggested—the Span. *aya*,
Port. *aia* 'governess' (< HAGJA, cf. Germ. *hegen* 'to preserve',
*Heger* 'keeper'); certainly Span. *ropa*, Port. *roupa* 'clothes'
(< Gothic RAUPA); Old Span. Port. *luva* 'glove' (< LOFA, cognate
with the English word), later largely replaced by *guante*, borrowed
from the north (see p. 246); and the verb *ganar* (< GAINŌN), with
the substantive *gana* 'wish, desire', preserving a meaning closer
to that of the original.

A few words are common to the Iberian Peninsula and the earlier
territory of Visigothic settlement in Provence, e.g. Prov. Cat.
Span. Port. *brotar* 'to bud' (< BRUTŌN, cognate with Eng. *sprout*);
Prov. Cat. Span. Port. *estaca* 'stake' (< STAKKA); and Prov. Port.
*agasalhar*, Span. *agasajar* 'to receive hospitably', from GASALJA
'companion' (cf. Germ. *Geselle*): the word appears in latinized
form in a document of A.D. 804 from Valpuesta, *meos gasalianes
mecum commorantes*.

Most probably due to Visigothic is the introduction into
Spanish of the common Germanic suffix -ING, as in *abolengo*
'ancestry', *realengo* 'royal', &c.

Several Peninsular words claimed as Visigothic have their

parallel in Italy, where they are presumably due to the very closely related Ostrogothic (see p. 226). Thus Span. Port. Cat. *aspa* 'reel' (< HASPA) is *aspa* in Italian too, and the difference in the quality of the tonic vowel in Span. *rueca* 'distaff', cf. Gasc. *arròco*, does not disguise its identity with Ital. *rocca* (< RUKKA, cf. Germ. *Spinnrocken*). The Span. Port. *espeto* 'spit' corresponds to Italian dialect forms, e.g. *spite* at Naples, *speto* at Rome (< Gothic SPIUTS; contrast Old Fr. *espiet*, from Frank. SPEOT). Similarly, Cat. Span. Port. *ataviar* 'to adorn' (< AT-TAUJAN) is paralleled in Ital. *taffiare*.

In giving these examples we have discarded some, quoted by Gamillscheg, Meyer-Lübke and others, of which the Gothic affiliation seems doubtful; yet even after the most rigorous selection there subsists a body of words sufficient in itself to show that the legacy of Germanic invasion in the Iberian Peninsula is by no means negligible. It is, however, less important than in Italy, and much less important than in northern France.

*Burgundians, Alamans, and Bavarians.* The scene now shifts to the Rhine. At the time when the Visigoths were but recently settled in their kingdom in south-western Gaul, three Germanic peoples inhabited its long valley: in the north the Franks, in its middle course the Burgundians, and in its upper reaches the Alamans. Some of these, the Franks in particular, were conglomerates of the various tribes mentioned by Caesar and Tacitus. The Burgundians, however, were comparative newcomers from the east who had occupied the former territory of the Alamans, when these, probably under Burgundian pressure, had moved south into the Agri Decumates. The two peoples were bitter enemies. In A.D. 437 the Burgundians, who had incurred the wrath of Rome by supporting the puppet emperor Jovinus, were attacked by a Roman army composed chiefly of Hunnish mercenaries under the command of Aëtius and all but exterminated. In this event lies the origin of the famous German epic of the *Nibelungenlied*; the Burgundian king Gundicar is the historical prototype of the Gunther of the poem. Those who survived the assault were removed by the Romans to the Gaulish territory of Sapaudia (Savoy), near the shores of Lake Geneva, where they became the nucleus of a new Burgundian kingdom. Meanwhile, part of the Alamans moved north into their former home on the middle Rhine, where later they were to be attacked and defeated by the Franks, and to see their lands incorporated into Frankish territory.

The Burgundians recovered and prospered in their new site. Humbled by defeat, they gladly accepted the position of Roman *foederati* and as such mingled with the Gallo-Roman population; intermarriage was permitted, and, previously Arian like the Visigoths, they were gradually converted to Catholicism. Like the other Germanic tribes within the Empire, with the weakening of Roman authority they soon extended their occupation, taking in most of the territory of modern French Switzerland and then moving along the upper valley of the Rhône to Lugdunum. From this former Roman capital they spread in all directions, encompassing to the north a part of the site of modern Burgundy whereby they laid the foundations of the medieval state which perpetuates their name, and proceeding southwards down the lower valley of the Rhône until they found their access to the sea blocked by the similarly expanding Visigoths. When, at the end of the century, both peoples were attacked by the Franks, the Burgundians offered a much sterner resistance than the Visigoths and finally succumbed to Frankish domination only in A.D. 534, after more than thirty years of war.

The territory which the Burgundians occupied in Gaul corresponds roughly to the area of modern Franco-Provençal dialect, so named because the patois of which it is composed in some features resemble northern French and in others Provençal. It is probable that these patois owe their community in evolution partly to the social cohesion which the Germanic tribe imposed, though later this was reinforced by the ever-growing influence of Lyon as a commercial, administrative, and ecclesiastical centre. The Burgundians, in consequence of their previous history, were of all Germanic settlers the most rapidly assimilated to Romance (with the possible exception of the Norsemen in Normandy). They have left their trace in place-names, but otherwise their linguistic influence was slight. Of words in the patois which have been claimed by various authors as specifically 'Burgundian' most are in fact of wider diffusion and come more probably from Visigothic or Frankish. One is perhaps worthy of retention: *fata* 'pocket', from a stem FATT- (cf. Germ. *Fetzen* 'tatter', 'rag'). The pocket seems to have been a Germanic innovation, cf. Fr. *poche* (< Frank. POKKA), Ital. *tasca* (< TASKA). In modern dialect *fata* is confined within the boundaries of the first Burgundian kingdom as it existed in A.D. 457.[1]

While the resettled Burgundians became champions of Latin civilization, their Alamannic neighbours to the east still clung to German custom and speech. They too spread southwards and in so doing drove a wedge of Germanic language, the source of modern Schwytzer-Dütsch, between the Romance-speaking lands of Gaul and Rhetia. In face of this advance the Rhetians withdrew and became increasingly confined to the less accessible regions of the Alps, where their Rheto-Romance has since evolved in isolation. Towards the year A.D. 600 another Germanic people from farther east, the Bavarians (Bajuvari), an off-shoot of the Marcomans whom we have previously encountered in Pannonia, moved into the eastern Alps, the modern Tyrol, and likewise pushing south they furthered the splitting of the Rhetic area into its present-day segmentation. The steady encroachment of Germanic dialects in the Alpine regions was to continue throughout the Middle Ages; many places with Rheto-Romance names now lie in German-speaking territory. Inevitably, modern Rheto-Romance has come to contain a large number of Germanic words, including both those of early penetration and later borrowings made from the neighbouring dialects. As an illustration, we might mention that, whereas to express the sense of 'own' (adjective) most Romance languages have recourse to the Lat. PROPRIUS, here one finds dialectal forms, *egen*, &c., corresponding to the Germ. *eigen*; in some areas the word sounds almost identical with the kindred Scot. *ain* (as in *my ain folk*). Certain phrases too would seem to have their origin in a literal translation of Germanic models, e.g. *clamer oura* (*oura* < FORAS), with the meaning 'to proclaim', suggests Germ. *ausrufen*, and *dir giù* 'to renounce', similarly recalls *absagen* (see C. Tagliavini, *Le origine delle lingue neolatine*, 2nd ed., p. 265); cf. also *der sü* (*aufgeben*), *esser pigliò aint* (*eingenommen sein*), *avair qualchün sül strich* (*jemanden auf dem Strichh aben*), quoted as Germanisms by A. Velleman (*Dicziunari scurznieu de la lingua ladina*, p. ix).

*Ostrogoths.* In Gaul the stage is now set for the invasion which was to have the most profound influence on future political, social,

---

[1] See W. von Wartburg, *Die Entstehung der romanischen Völker*, p. 120, and G. Rohlfs, *Germanisches Spracherbe in der Romania*, p. 12. The word *fata* has a cognate in Span. *hato* Port. *fato* 'clothes', presumably Visigothic.

and linguistic developments, that of the Salian Franks. But respect for chronology constrains us to turn back at this point to events in Italy, where the last emperors continued to play their enfeebled role.

By the middle of the fifth century Germanic invasions were an accepted fact, and the policy of those generals who, like Aëtius, still supported the imperial cause consisted of turning the Germans into corners of the Empire, in such a way that they should not menace the integrity of Italy itself. Thus might Rome have been spared another Alaric, and perhaps, with the Germans peacefully distributed and absorbed into the local romanized populations, the central authority might one day recover its former power.

Ultimately, the Germans were to a great extent absorbed, but only long after the central authority had vanished. From the time of the political division of Romania, in A.D. 395 (see p. 203), emperors in the west became largely a succession of puppets, continuing in office under the protection of dictatorial military leaders, most of whom, like Stilicho, were themselves of Germanic origin. The end of the line came finally in A.D. 475 with the deposition of the boy Emperor Romulus Augustulus. His deposer was an officer in the Roman army, Odovacar, of the Germanic tribe of the Heruli. 'Pitying his infancy, and because he was comely,' so a chronicler tells us, 'Odovacar gave him an income of six thousand solidi and sent him to live in Campania with his relations.'

The newcomer proclaimed himself king, though inviting the protection of Zeno, then Emperor in the East. Most of the provinces, including northern Gaul, which was still under the control of a Roman general, refused to recognize the rule of Odovacar. Thus with the final disruption of the western Empire we find the modern territory of Italy appearing for the first time in history as a single political unit, with its own sovereign. But the reign of Odovacar was not destined to last for long. After thirteen years, in A.D. 489, he was defeated in battle and slain by Theodoric, King of the Ostrogoths.

The exact time at which the Goths split into two distinct tribes is not known, but it appears to have been after their occupation of Dacia. Their separate existence in history dates from the time when Theodosius I, having settled the Visigoths in Moesia, similarly settled the Ostrogoths in Phrygia, in western Asia Minor

(A.D. 386). There the Ostrogoths soon became subjects of the Huns, in whose wake they moved into central Europe and in whose ranks they fought at the battle of the Catalaunian Fields. After Attila's death his subject peoples combined to throw off the Hunnish yoke, winning a decisive victory at the battle of Netad (A.D. 454). In this action the Ostrogoths played a leading part, and after the Hunnish withdrawal they made a pact with the Emperor of the West, then Valentinian III, whereby they were allowed to occupy Pannonia. They were probably established as *foederati*, but in this capacity they were no asset to Rome. In A.D. 455 Valentinian was assassinated, a year after he had treacherously murdered his loyal general Aëtius. For thirty years thereafter the Ostrogoths were continually engaged in plundering the provinces of Illyricum and Thrace, as the Visigoths had done before them, a thorn in the flesh of both the imperial powers. Then, like Alaric, they turned west.

The immediate motive of this westward turn was a pact between the Ostrogothic king and the Emperor Zeno. The latter, unwilling to accept the downfall of his counterpart in the west, proposed to Theodoric that if he could overthrow the usurper Odovacar he should rule in Italy until such time as he, Zeno, could reassert the imperial authority. After a prolonged struggle, in which both Visigoths and Burgundians joined, the former in support of the Ostrogoths and the latter in defence of Odovacar, Theodoric was eventually victorious, and coming upon Odovacar at Ravenna, he killed him with his own hand. Meanwhile, the Emperor Zeno died and was succeeded by Anastasius, with whom Theodoric had no pact. Thereupon, making Ravenna his capital, as Honorius had done, Theodoric established in Italy an Ostrogothic rule which was to last for fifty years. During this time he added to his domains the modern territory of Provence, possession of which was sought by the Franks, on whom he inflicted a heavy defeat near Arelate (Arles).

Theodoric was an admirer of Roman civilization, and, considered in general, his rule was benevolent. Though an Arian, he did not interfere in the conduct of Catholic affairs. He undertook the classic task of draining the Pontine marshes, repaired roads, and restored the walls of Rome. In contrast to other Germanic tribes, the Ostrogoths reserved for themselves only a third of the land. Their occupation was most dense in the northern half of the

Peninsula and the Po valley, where the memory of it is still perpetuated in numerous place-names, e.g. *Godego, Valgoda, Goderia,
Godi*, &c. There was, however, during this period no real fusion
of Ostrogoths with the Italian population, partly for religious
reasons, partly because the Ostrogoths practised the same policy
of racial separation as did the Visigoths in Spain. A few words
which would appear from a comparison with similar loan-words
in Spanish to be Gothic in origin have already been noted (p. 223),
but in general the contribution of Ostrogothic was obscured by
the subsequent and much heavier overlay of Langobardic. Words
of Germanic origin which have survived in Italy alone of the
Romance-speaking countries may be assumed to derive from one
or the other of these two sources. Occasionally it is possible to
distinguish between them on purely phonetic grounds, words of
Langobardic origin having undergone certain sound-shifts characteristic of High German which were unknown to Gothic as they
were to Low German. Thus, corresponding to Germ. *bloss* are
Lombard *biott* 'naked', and Emilian *bioss* 'simple', 'unadorned', of
which the latter seems to be definitely Langobardic and the former
no less surely Ostrogothic. Similarly, a 'clod of earth' is in Tuscan
*zolla*, cf. south Germ. *Zolle*; but in the peripheral areas of Elba
and northern Corsica the same word survives with the *t* of Gothic
as *tolla*. With the same meaning one finds in northern and eastern
Italy *zoppa* but in Umbria and the Abruzzi *toppa*. The word
*tasca* 'pocket', also appears from its *t* to be Ostrogothic, cf. south
Germ. (Bavaria) *Zäschen* 'train (of a dress)'.[1] The Ostrogothic
contribution to Italo-Romance vocabulary seems by no means to
have been completely eliminated, but the two Germanic speeches
resembled one another too closely to permit of more detailed disentangling from the Langobardic overlay.

The decline and fall of the Ostrogoths was brought about by
the Byzantines. When in A.D. 526 Theodoric died there was no
successor of the same calibre to continue his rule. The following
year witnessed the accession at Byzantium of the greatest emperor
of the East, Justinian, and the beginning of his determined attempt
to restore imperial fortunes in the west. In A.D. 535 Belisarius,
fresh from his conquest of the Vandals, set sail with an army from
Byzantium to Sicily. Received there with open arms, he landed
in Italy, and marching north took Naples and Rome in turn, with

[1] G. Rohlfs, *Germanisches Spracherbe in der Romania*, pp. 13 and 22.

little opposition. Then, however, he was besieged in Rome by an Ostrogothic army and kept there for more than a year (A.D. 537–8), during which time the population suffered considerable hardship. The Ostrogoths destroyed the fine system of aqueducts which provided the city's water-supply and Belisarius was reduced to setting up makeshift mills on the Tiber to grind corn; not until the sixteenth century was Rome's water-supply adequately restored. Eventually, Belisarius was relieved by the arrival of reinforcements from Byzantium. Thereafter the war dragged on until A.D. 552, but it ended with the complete Byzantine occupation of Italy and the disappearance from history of the Ostrogoths. Many of the survivors were enrolled in the Byzantine army. In the following year Byzantine forces reoccupied Sardinia, where Ostrogoths had but lately settled; thus, although briefly held by both Vandals and Ostrogoths, and later menaced by Langobards and Franks, Sardinia is the only geographical area in western Romania to have escaped a long-standing Germanic occupation, and of which the native Romance is almost entirely free from Germanic elements directly attributable to a superstratum.

Italy during this time lay devastated and untilled. No part of the Empire can have suffered more from its disintegration. The period is marked, however, by one notable Italian development of another kind, of incalculable significance for the future creation of literary standards in Romance: the founding by St. Benedict (d. A.D. 543) of a monastery at Monte Cassino, whence his monastic rule, with the initial blessing of Pope Gregory, was to spread over Europe.

*Angles and Saxons.* While the struggle between 'barbarians' and Byzantines continued in the south, other Germanic invaders spread over the north and west of the former Empire, including Britain, Roman since the occupation begun in A.D. 43 during the reign of Claudius.

The first people of Germanic stock to live in England were among the Roman soldiery, and it is quite probable that before the end of the fourth century isolated colonies of Germanic settlers had been planted in Britain as in Gaul. But the main influx came during the fifth century after the withdrawal of Roman legions which took place while Alaric was ravaging Italy. Archaeological evidence suggests that during the first half of that century the romanized Celtic population continued to lead a prosperous existence,

with large farmsteads and flourishing trade. The first enemy to
appear was the old foe of the Romans, the combination of Picts
and Scots living beyond Hadrian's Wall. According to the single
literary witness, the historian Gildas (*c.* A.D. 516–70), it was a
British chieftain, Vortigern, who invited the Saxons, then marauding in the Channel and inclining to settle on its Gallic coast rather
than to the north, to assist him in repelling this enemy. The new
guests soon proved too strong for their hosts and settled parts of
Britain on their own account. From the south coast they spread
over modern Sussex and Surrey and then westwards along the
Thames valley, eventually founding the kingdom of Wessex.
Meanwhile, the Angles landed at various points on the east coast
between the Tees and the Thames, and making their way inland
they too founded kingdoms, of which the chief were to be Mercia
and Northumbria.[1]

Germanic settlement seems to have met with much stronger
resistance in Britain than on the Continent. Both Gildas and the
later Nennius, in his *Historia Britonum* (early ninth century),
mention a great British victory won at Badon Hill, a locality as
yet unidentified. Nennius, but not Gildas, names the British
leader on this occasion as Arturus. For some time the country
remained divided between the two groups into approximately
equal halves, with the Celts occupying all the hillier western part.
Of subsequent contacts nothing certain is known; there is only
the obvious fact that Celtic speech receded, until by the tenth
century it was confined to Cumbric, Welsh, and Cornish.

After the landings in England, Angles and Saxons continued
their piratical association with Gaul, and the evidence of place-
names suggests that both tribes made later settlements in the
north-east, particularly in the Boulogne area. A few nautical terms
in French derive from this source: most important are the words

---

[1] According to the Venerable Bede (*c.* A.D. 670–735), and his account is
probably correct, the Angles came from the land now known as East Schleswig,
where there is still a district called Angeln. As for the Saxons, their original
habitat was the lower valley of the Elbe, where many remained, forming a
kingdom later to be conquered by Charlemagne; on account of their fierce
resistance they frequently appear in medieval French epic as the *Saisnes*, a
formidable enemy, ranking in this respect with the Saracens and often confused
with them. Their name was later conveyed through medieval alliances to the
Saxony of central Germany. The third tribe usually mentioned, though there
were probably contingents from others, is that of the Jutes, whose name persists
in Jutland; they are credited with two settlements, one in Kent and the other
in Hampshire and the Isle of Wight.

indicating direction, Fr. *nord, est, sud, ouest*. Carried from French ports to other maritime centres of western Europe, these were finally adopted into the common usage of Romance-speaking countries (cf. Span. *norte, este, sud* or *sur, oeste*; Ital. *nord, est, sud, ovest*), ousting the former Latin terminology of orientation, or living beside it in a dual system. Among other French borrowings from Saxon are *bateau* (Anglo-Sax. *bāt*, Eng. *boat*) and *rade* (Anglo-Sax. *rād* a 'riding', Eng. *road*).

In addition to the founding of a large new area of Germanic speech and the obliteration of the Vulgar Latin of Britain except in so far as it remains incorporated into Celtic, where the Latin lexical element is very considerable (see p. 298), these invasions had the effect of eliminating Latin in a small part of Gaul. Some Britons of the south-west, as Gildas tells us, took to the sea and settled in Armorica (Brittany), where their Breton language still forms one of the few non-Romance enclaves in Romance-speaking territory. The Celtic immigrants were soon to find in Gaul a new Germanic neighbour, the Franks.

*Franks.* At the time of their westerly migration the Franks were a conglomerate of the different west Germanic tribes mentioned by Tacitus as inhabiting the lower valley of the Rhine. The Salian, i.e. 'sea-dwelling', Franks took the lead. Spreading out from the region known to the Romans as Toxandria (south Holland and north Belgium), in A.D. 455 they reached the Somme. Thence they probably began very soon to filter into the valley of the Seine, but the decisive date of Frankish occupation must be reckoned as A.D. 486, when a Frankish army met and defeated near Soissons an army under the Roman general Syagrius, who, despite his isolation from Italy and the deposition of the Emperor ten years earlier, was still continuing to govern the territory between the Somme and the Loire in the name of Rome. This was the land which the Franks, under their youthful King Clovis, now made their own. This became Neustria, 'the new land'; with the inclusion of Austrasia to the east it was to form the original Francia, and Clovis became the first 'French' king, founder of the Merovingian dynasty.

The question of the density of Frankish settlement has been much debated. Historians have generally maintained that, like other Germanic invaders, the Franks were merely a military caste, small in numbers, and that by their martial qualities they succeeded in imposing their will on a much more numerous but passive population. The linguistic evidence, on the contrary, suggests that this movement differed radically from the earlier migrations. Though the Gallo-Roman speech of northern Gaul eventually prevailed, when first it appears as a literary language it is permeated with words of Germanic stock and even shows unmistakable Germanic influences in its pronunciation and word-formation. The inference to be drawn is that the Germanic settlement was here much heavier than in the case of other tribes who made no permanent impact on the evolution of Latin. It must above all be remembered that in this instance there was no breaking of bridges: the Franks remained linked to the country from which they came, from which they could draw reinforcements, and in whose surviving Germanic dialects one may still find the equivalents of the Frankish words adopted into Gallo-Romance. Nor had they undergone a previous period of romanization, as did both tribes of the Goths. We conclude therefore that the end of the fifth century saw the initiation in northern France of a long period of bilingualism, rather similar to that which prevailed in our country after the Norman conquest; though perhaps in Gaul the speech of the conquered people, in this instance that of a higher civilization, was less seriously menaced. How long this bilingualism lasted, by what stages it disappeared, can only be a matter of conjecture. We assume that during the sixth and seventh centuries the two speeches were gradually fusing into one, with Gallo-Romance, backed by the use of literary Latin, assuming the ascendancy. By the eighth century, before the advent of Germanic reinforcement with the new Carolingian dynasty from Austrasia, the process was probably complete.

Place-names serve to confirm our impression of the density of Frankish occupation and incidentally give us an idea of its distribution. In Picardy the great majority of place-names are Germanic and so are about half of those in the Île de France. South of the Loire, to which boundary the Visigoths had extended their control shortly before the arrival of the Franks, they almost cease to exist until we reach the Visigothic remnants of the deeper south. In general, the Frankish names are those of small villages and hamlets, while the names of important urban centres have remained Celtic. This suggests that the Franks, when not engaged in war, preferred a country life, and, as we shall see, many of the Germanic words in French have to do with pastoral pursuits. In the towns the local population seems to have continued its normal life, and since towns set the standards of fashion and of speech, this fact contributes to explain the survival of Gallo-Romance.

While the Salian Franks were moving into Gaul via the coastal plains, the Ripuarian Franks, a kindred branch whose home was then on the right bank of the Rhine in the hilly country that faces Bonn, crossed the river and took possession of the great Roman frontier town of Colonia Agrippina (Cologne). Thence they spread westwards into the Eifel, former Celtic territory—witness the name of Daun, situated in its centre—and southwards to the valley of the Moselle, access to which had hitherto been denied them by another Roman outpost, Confluentes (Coblenz). Moving farther south they came into collision with the northern branch of the Alamans (see p. 223), who in A.D. 456, after the death of Aëtius, had also at last succeeded in their many attempts to establish themselves west of the Rhine. The resultant battle was a victory for the Ripuarian Franks (A.D. 496). Thereafter, however, the mass of them turned east again, eventually extending their dominion to the central German province of Thuringia. Meanwhile Clovis, who had lent them military assistance in the fight against the Alamans, took advantage of the victory to seize the territory which has become modern Alsace.

From this time on, considerable tracts of land west of the Rhine were given over to Germanic speech, and the much fought-over linguistic frontier began to assume its modern shape. There remains, however, a salient of Romance located in the Ardennes and along the valley of the Meuse; it is the home of the Walloons, with Liège as its chief centre. Some linguists have supposed that Wallonia must have been reclaimed for Romance after a temporary germanization. Others incline to believe that it remained predominantly Romance-speaking throughout the period of Germanic invasions, by-passed by settlers. The archaic character of the Walloon dialects, which have kept a number of Latin words lost elsewhere, lends support to the latter view. So, incidentally, do the physique and temperament of the inhabitants, contrasting sharply with those of their German and Flemish neighbours.[1]

[1] In a recent article it is suggested that until the thirteenth century there was a similar prolongation of Romance speech along the valley of the Moselle, between Trier (Trèves) and Kochem, see W. Jungandreas, 'Ein romanischer Dialekt an der Mosel um 1200' (*Zeitschrift für romanische Philologie*, vol. lxxi

In northern Gaul the Salian Franks were destined to enjoy a prosperity and permanence beyond that of any other migrating Germanic tribe, except the invaders of Britain. Their fortune was, however, founded in alliance with the Gallo-Romans, with whom the Franks, rejecting in this the racialism of the Goths, freely and rapidly intermarried. In A.D. 496 Clovis embraced the Christian faith, in its Catholic form: an action which, whatever its motive, enabled him to gain the allegiance of the people whose lands he had but recently seized, and which helped to procure their support for his projected attack on the Arian Visigoths. Latin was therefore adopted by the Franks as the language of religion. It also remained the language of administration, the medium in which their customs were codified, in the so-called *Lex Salica* (see p. 308).

His position secured, Clovis lost little time in the execution of his plans for further conquest. One battle (Vouillé, A.D. 507, see p. 219) sufficed to assert Frankish supremacy over the Visigoths, who rapidly withdrew, most of their land from the Loire to the Pyrenees coming under Frankish control. Here, however, the Franks made no attempt to dispossess the Gallo-Roman inhabitants: deeds still survive showing that when they acquired land in the south it was normally by purchase. The resistance of the Burgundians in the eastern territory was, as we have seen, much more stubborn. Clovis died in A.D. 511, and it was left to his successors to complete the task which he had set himself. Burgundian opposition was finally overcome in A.D. 534. The temporary check to Frankish expansion administered by the Ostrogoths at Arelate (see p. 227) was soon redeemed when all the territory of modern Provence and Dauphiny was ceded to them as the price of their non-intervention at the time of the Byzantine invasion of Italy. Thus by A.D. 536 the Franks had reunited the whole of Gaul under one king. Despite the weakness of later representatives of the Merovingian dynasty, the *rois fainéants* of history, the principle

(1955), pp. 414–21). The inference seems to be that Gallo-Romans gathered most densely along the two main highways leading to the Rhine frontier and in the vicinity of the towns which served them. Trier, in a position similar to that of Aachen, was of outstanding importance, not only for its strategic situation but also as a centre of cultural life and later of religious activity; with its imposing Porta Nigra, it still has the richest collection of Roman monuments to be found in any town north of the Alps. Migrating Germanic tribes may have left relatively unmolested these riverside populations, by which in any event they were probably outnumbered. It is the less inhabited regions, the rocky Eifel and the Hunsrück, where Celtic seems to have lingered longest (see p. 187), which yielded most easily to Germanic.

of French monarchy remained, and within the space of a few centuries France was to emerge as the foremost political unit in the new Europe; it was also the first Romance-speaking country to create from its legacy of spoken Latin the linguistic media of new literatures.

*The Frankish element in Romance.* An obvious pointer to the influence of the Franks in Gaul may be seen in the fact that they gave their tribal name to the whole land. In the eighth-century Glossary of Reichenau the term *Gallia* is glossed by *Frantia*, a latinization based upon such models as *Italia*, *Hispania*, and *Gallia* itself (for the spelling of *Frantia*, see p. 53). The use of the word was, however, for a long time very imprecise, the area which it designated varying in extent according to the outlook of the people who employed it and with the fortunes of the Frankish dynasties. During decadent periods of kingship it came to be restricted to the territory surrounding Paris: hence the term *francien* by which the medieval dialect of this area is usually defined. Latinization of FRANKISK, in which the suffix is cognate with Eng. *-ish*, cf. Germ. *-isch*, produced FRANCISCUS, whence Old Fr. *Franceis*, which later underwent a twofold development of the tonic diphthong to become both *François* and *Français*. The fem. FRANCISCA evolved regularly in Old French, giving *Francesche*, cf. Old Fr. *Angleis—Anglesche*, *Daneis—Danesche*, but the analogy of the masculine form of the suffix, reinforced by coalescence with *-eis* from Lat. -ENSEM, eventually brought about the replacement of *-esche* by *-eise*, later *-oise*, *-aise*.

The general influence of Frankish on Gallo-Roman vocabulary was so extensive that one may take at random almost any medieval French text and a crop of Germanisms will leap to the eye. Thus in the sample of the *Chanson de Roland* given by A. Ewert in *The French Language* (p. 358), the first twenty-one lines contain— excluding the proper names, which, with the possible exception of *Oliver*, are all Germanic—eight words of Germanic origin, words which were obviously in current use, viz.

> Li empereres se fait e *balz* e liez:
> Cordres ad prise e les murs peceiez,
> Od ses cadables les turs en abatied:
> Mult grant *eschech* en unt si chevaler
> D'or e d'argent e de *guarnemenz* chers.
> En la citét nen ad remes paien
> Ne seit ocis u devient chrestïen.

Li empereres est en un grant verger,
Ensembl' od lui Rollant e Oliver,
Sansun li dux e Anseïs li fiers,
Gefreid d'Anjou, le rei *gunfanuner*,
E si i furent e Gerin e Gerers;
La u cist furent, des altres i out bien,
De dulce France i ad quinze milliers.
Sur palies *blancs* siedent cil cevaler,
As tables juent pur els *esbaneier*,
E as eschecs li plus saive e li veill,
E *escremissent* cil bacheler leger.
Desuz un pin, delez un eglenter,
Un *faldestoed* i unt fait tut d'or mer;
La siet li reis ki dulce France tient.

Translating this passage into modern French one would be obliged to dispense with all the Germanisms except *blanc* and *fauteuil*, and in the case of the latter the meaning would no longer be appropriate; with a little adaptation, *gonfanon* and *escrime* might be retained. Briefly, the number has been halved: a fair indication of a diluting of the Frankish element in French which has taken place since the Middle Ages, largely as a result of continual borrowing from Latin and of the sixteenth-century influx of Italianisms; it remains, nevertheless, quite considerable.

Most of the substantives adopted from Frankish fall readily into semantic categories. Many are of topographical, pastoral, and agricultural connotation, or relate particularly to the household; these represent the more static type of vocabulary, spreading slowly within a limited area. Others refer to property and administration: as the 'feudal system' developed these came to provide its technical terminology. Above all, the Franks introduced a new and dominant nomenclature concerning military matters. The latter categories comprise words of the 'travelling' type, many of which rapidly passed from northern France to the south and beyond into Italy and Spain, thereby introducing a new Germanic element into the speech of those countries.

As already indicated, it is sometimes difficult to separate what is specifically due to the Frankish invasion from the common Germanic stock of Vulgar Latin, but in the words quoted below an attempt is made to confine selection to the undeniably Frankish, and to trace briefly their subsequent diffusion from the northern centre of assimilation into Romance.

The forest received in northern France the Germanic name of

WALD, cognate with Eng. *wold* and *weald*. This appears in Old French as *gaut* and in the derivative *gaudine*: in *Aucassin et Nicolete*, a thirteenth-century story written in a markedly Picard dialect (e.g. *le* for the feminine article), we read that Nicolete, from her prison,

> Esgarda par le gaudine
> Et vit la rose espanie

(three Frankish words!)

but in the same text we also encounter the synonymous *forest*, the Latin word from (SILVA) FORESTIS, the 'wild wood' as opposed to the plantation, by which *gaut* and *gaudine* were eventually to be eliminated. The Frankish term for the 'wood', BUSK (cf. Germ. *Busch*, Eng. *bush*) has, on the other hand, remained, developing in French to *bois* and extending early to the south as *bosc*; with the later vogue of Provençal lyric it passed into both Italy and Spain, italianized as *bosco* and hispanicized as *bosque*.

Among trees the holly and the beech received Frankish names as *le houx* (< HULS, cf. Netherland *Hulst*, Rheinland Germ. *Hülse*) and *le hêtre* (< HESTR, cf. Netherland *Heester*). Both of these are typical examples of 'static' vocabulary: study of French dialectal distribution will show that, except in so far as they participate in the fortunes of modern standard French, they have never progressed south of the Loire. They are thus unknown in Provençal, Spanish, and Italian. Holly is of course a northern growth; the beech, on the other hand, is very common in southern countries, but there was a strong rival term in Lat. FAGUS, found all over the rest of Romania, cf. Prov. *fau*, Span. *haya*, Ital. *faggio*, Rum. *fag*, together with a rich variety of dialectal forms, and even Basque *bago*. In Old French FAGUS survived as the less successful competitor, developing normally to *fou*, still extant in the derivatives *fouet* 'whip', and *fouine* 'beech-marten'.

The swampy land which combined with the forest to form most of the northern landscape became the Old Fr. *mareis*, mod. *marais* (< MARĬSK, cf. Germ. *Marsch*, Eng. *marsh*); a derivative, Old Fr. *marescage*, mod. *marécage*, preserves more closely the original *maresc*. Frankish too is the 'reed', *roseau*, formed with a Romance suffix on RAUS; and in the same context one might note the names of the hornet, *frelon* (< HRUSLO), and of at least three common birds: the tit, *mésange* (< MAISINGA, cf. Germ. *Meise*), the sparrow-hawk, *épervier* (< SPARWARI, cf. Germ. *Sperber*), and the heron, *héron* (< HAIGIRON). Of these, the bird-names migrated most readily. All three passed into Provençal, cf. *mezengo, esparvier, aigrú*, and thence, though in the case of the last-named perhaps directly from French, still farther afield, cf. Port. *musango*, with similar forms in the northern dialects of Spain; Ital. *sparaviere*, Old Span. *esparvel*; Ital. *aghirone, airone*, Span. *airón*, Port. *airão*.

The meaning 'to gather in the crops' was expressed in Germanic dialects by the verb WAIDANJAN (> Fr. *gagner*, see p. 210): the original association is preserved to this day in *gagnage* 'pasturage', and in the verbal substantive *regain* 'aftermath'. A Frank. BLAT appears to be the source of *blé*, the name of the principal crop, but if Frankish the word must have passed early to the south, cf. Prov. Cat. *blat*, north Ital. *biado*; Lat. FRUMENTUM survived in French as *froment*, restricted in sense to designate a particular kind of wheat. A sheaf of corn is a *gerbe*, from GARBA, which persists as *garba* in southern dialects, including Basque. Domestic animals have kept their pre-Frankish names, though *herde* (< HERDA) and *troupeau* (formed on TROPP, the origin of Fr. *trop*) both seem to have come with the Franks; in Old French the word *fouc* (< FULK, cf. Germ. *Volk*, Eng. *folk*) was used with the same collective meaning. Among parts of the animal one may record as Frankish the Fr. *croupe* (< KRUPPA), *hanche* (< HANKA) and *échine* (< SKINA). The new contribution to the range of agricultural implements was slight, being limited to the hoe, Fr. *houe* (< HAUWA), and the axe, *hache* (< HAPPJA), of which the latter is not strictly 'agricultural'; the aspirate *h* of *herse* 'harrow', suggests a Germanic influence, but the word is generally assumed to derive from Lat. HIRPICEM. In the stable we find a Germanic manger, *crèche* (< KRIPPJA). The general impression created by these loan-words is of a people more accustomed to seek their livelihood in pastoral occupations than in laborious tilling of the soil; words relating to the latter are much more prominent in the lexical residue left by the Celtic inhabitants of Gaul.

The Frankish 'home' became in Picard *ham*, from HAIM, cognate with the *-ham* so familiar in English toponymy; it survives in the French derivative *hameau* 'hamlet'. For the actual dwelling-place no less than three different words were brought into Gallo-Romance. A hut was a *borde*, a feminine substantive derived from BORD, which in Frankish meant 'plank', a sense which persisted in Old Fr. *bort*; the form BORDA suggests adaptation to the type of

word with collective meaning which derived from the original
neuter plural of Latin (see p. 56). In the Pyrenees *borda* is still
in everyday use, applied in some localities to the shepherd's hut,
in others to the stable. Twelfth-century French possessed as
diminutives both fem. *bordele* and masc. *bordel*, still with the meaning 'small house', cf. 'qui veit le bordel son veisin alumé, Il ad poür
del suen. . . .' (cit. Littré); in its modern sense, already attested by
Joinville, *bordel* thereafter travelled far and wide, cf. Prov. Port.
*bordel*, Cat. *bordell*, Span. *burdel*, Ital. *bordello*. The two other
words pertaining to dwellings are Fr. *halle* (< HALLA) and *salle*
( < SAL, cf. Germ. *Saal*). Of these the former belongs specifically to France; the latter is found as *sala* in Italy, but there it may
well be Langobardic rather than Frankish. In Italy *sala* has the
original sense of 'house', as also in the toponymy of Gascony and
parts of northern Spain: on the southern side of the Pyrenees, in
Aragon, there is a place-name *Salamaña* (< SALA MAGNA 'big
house'), and a village divided into two parts, *Salas Altas* and *Salas
Bajas*; cf. also the Gascon personal name *Sallenave* 'new house',
identical in meaning with the equally common *Casenave*.

If not great agriculturalists, the Franks seem to have prized
their gardens: *jardin* is an early derivative of Old Fr. *jart* (<
GARDO), later adapted into Spanish as *jardín* and into Italian as
*giardino*. One of its features was the *loge* 'arbour', 'bower' (<
LAUBJA, cognate with Eng. *leaf*); mod. Fr. *loge* 'box in the theatre',
is the same word after its passage from France to Italy, where as
*loggia* it received its special architectural meaning, to be returned
to France in the sixteenth century. Protecting the garden was the
*haie* (< HAGA, cf. Germ. *Hag*), a static word this, which like *hêtre*
has remained within the limits of northern France. HAGA has
an interesting derivative in *hagard*, used in the Middle Ages of
a falcon too wild for the chase.

Within the household Old Fr. *gascher* (< WASKŌN, cf. Germ.
*waschen*, Eng. *to wash*) appears as the rival of *laver*. Ousted by the
latter from the general sense of 'to wash', it found a refuge in
technical terminology. In the fifteenth century one could still say
*gascher poissons* for 'to clean fish', but the mod. *gâcher* is a mason's
word, 'to mix plaster'; colloquially, it has received a new diffusion
as 'to make a mess of', 'to spoil'. The Franks provided the towel,
in Old Fr. *touaille* (< THWAHLJA), which passed into Provence as
*toalha*, and thence farther afield to give mod. Span. *toalla*, Port.

*toalha*, Ital. *tovaglia*. The *cruche* 'pitcher' (< KRŪKA, cf. Germ. *Krug*) remained in French and only there.

Of foods there is little trace in Frankish loan-words except for Old Fr. *bacon* (< BAKKO, cf. Germ. *Bache* 'wild sow'); the term *lard*, which serves to translate our 'bacon', is Latin from LARIDUM. The Frankish housewife may have been responsible for the confection of *gâteaux* (cf. Old Fr. *gastel*) and *flan* (Old Fr. *flaon*), though the early affiliations and point of entry into French of the Germanic WASTIL and FLADO are as yet ill defined. Furniture owes little to Germanic but the *banc* (see p. 207); true, Frankish has given the word *fauteuil*, but this is scarcely to be associated with the primitive Frankish household; it is the 'folding-stool' (< FALDESTOL), used, as in the passage from the *Chanson de Roland* quoted above, for the accommodation of distinguished persons on military campaigns. To both domestic and military spheres belong the *bière* 'bier' (< BERA, cognate with Eng. *to bear*).

The terminology of dress comprises a number of Germanic additions. A derivative of *garnir* (see p. 210) with a Latin suffix appears in the extract from the *Chanson de Roland* as 'equipment', 'clothing'; brought by the Normans to England it has remained in our language as 'garment', with the same meaning, but in France it has been forced by pressure of the Romance synonym *vêtement*, similarly constructed, into a corner of its former semantic orbit and survives only as *un (mauvais) garnement*, an ill-clad person, hence 'urchin'. The shirt retained its Celtic name, but for clothing of the lower parts the Franks had a word HOSA, and for many centuries changing fashions brought about an interplay of meaning between the Celtic *braies*, the Lat. *chausses*, and the Germanic *heuse*, all to be largely superseded in the sixteenth century by the Italian *pantalon*; modern French preserves of the Frankish word only the derivative *houseaux*. Undoubtedly, the most popular of borrowings from the Franks in this sphere has been the feminine *robe* (< RAUBA). To the lady they also brought the *écharpe* (< SKERPA, cf. Eng. *scarf*), possibly the *guimpe* 'wimple' (< WIMPEL), though this may have come at a later date from Anglo-Saxon, and certainly the *nosche* (< NUSKJA), the 'brooch' of medieval times. A Germanic measure of cloth is the *aune* (< ALINA, ELINA, cf. Eng. *ell*). To feminine adornment may be attributed the word *fard* (< FARWIDA, cf. Germ. *Farbe*), with its verb *farder*.

Family relationships have left their trace in *bru* 'daughter-in-law' (< BRUTIS, cf. Germ. *Braut*, Eng. *bride*). The disappearance of Lat. PUER, replaced in Romance by various obscure words for 'boy' (cf. Span. *muchacho*, Ital. *ragazzo*, Port. *rapaz*, all of doubtful origin) is made good in French by the Germanic *gars*, believed to derive from a Frank. WURKJO 'worker', and its accusative *garçon* (see p. 67); for 'girl' there is an analogical *garce*, still so used in the current parlance of southern France (e.g. *pauvre garce!*), but which in the north has undergone a familiar depreciation of meaning.

The form of amusement most favoured among the Franks is indicated by the verb *danser* (< DANSŌN) and by various words referring to different kinds of dance, e.g. *estampie*, a medieval dance-rhythm, from the verb *estampir* (< STAMPJAN, cf. Eng. *to stamp*); *trépigner*, preserved more closely in Prov. *trepar* (< TRIP-PŌN, cf. Eng. *to trip*); *tresche*, with its verb *treschier* (< THRISKJAN, cf. Germ. *dreschen*, Eng. *to thresh*), which extended to Provençal as *trescar* and thence to Italy as *trescare*; Old Fr. *espringuer* (< SPRINGAN, cf. Germ. *springen*, Eng. *to spring*); and *gigue*, from Frank. GIGA, in which one may recognize the mod. Germ. *Geige* 'violin'. Song and dance were accompanied by the music of the *harpe* (< HARPA, see p. 207).

Inevitably, the administrative system of the Frankish overlords brought in its quota of new terminology, though, rather surprisingly, the names of the highest authorities remained Latin: hence the *roi* (< REGEM), the *duc* (< DUCEM) and the *comte* (< CŎMITEM), words evidently much in use in Gallo-Romance though none of them corresponded to an official position in Imperial Rome. But at the Frankish court, as the new social structure became more settled, there evolved a number of domestic offices in which are foreshadowed the ministries of present-day governments, and here the nomenclature is almost entirely Frankish. Among the immediate servants of the king were his *chambellan*, in Old Fr. *chambrelenc* (< KAMERLING), his *sénéchal* (< SINI-SKALK, lit. 'elder servant'), and his *échanson* 'cup-bearer' (< SKANKJON, cf. Germ. *Schenk*). Designation of 'master of the royal horse' seems to have been disputed by two expressions, both of which have survived, the Lat. COMES STABULI, whence *connétable* (which in its Old French form gave our 'constable'), and the Frankish MARI-SKALK (from MARAH 'horse', cf. Eng. *mare*, and SKALK) which became *maréchal*. In the association with horses one sees the link between terms corresponding in modern French to widely different status, the 'marshal' of the army and the *maréchal ferrant*, the blacksmith. Both SINISKALK and MARISKALK are found in Italy and Spain: palatalization of K before A indicates clearly that Ital. *maresciallo* is a borrowing from French; its absence in *siniscalco* suggests that this form might be a legacy of the local Germanic stock, though more probably it reached Italy via Provençal, an explanation which seems to hold good for Span. and Port. *mariscal* and *senescal*. Under the influence of *senescal*, Catalan has changed *mariscal* into *menescal* and uses the word with the meaning 'horse-doctor'.

From its own linguistic resources Frankish produced the names of two other prominent figures: the *marquis* and the *baron*. The former is the defender of the *marche* (see p. 207) and in Old French is the *marchis*; the same word passed through Provence, without palatalization of the K in MARKA, to give Span. *marqués* and Ital. *marchese*, mod. Fr. *marquis* being due to a return influence of Italian in the sixteenth century. The Old Fr. *ber*, acc. *baron* (< BARO 'free man'), at first a term applied to the assistant of the *comte*, extended in meaning in such a way as to typify the French nobleman, rather as 'milord' has served his English counterpart, and not only was adopted into Spanish as *varón*, acquiring there the general sense of 'male', and into Italian as *barone*, but also gave the word for 'mister' among the faraway Armenians, Christian allies of the Crusaders.

Another Frankish word for 'free', LETHIK (cf. Germ. *ledig* 'unmarried') appears in Old French as *lige*. Since the nobility owed homage to the king, the word came, by an inversion of sense, and possibly influenced by Lat. LIGARE, to express the relationship between the vassal and his 'liege-lord', and is applicable to both. Meanwhile, the general concept of 'free' was attached to the word *franc* itself (< FRANK)—*libre*, by which the meaning of *franc* was later restricted, is a learned borrowing from Latin, attested only in the sixteenth century—and as *franco* this passed into Italian, Spanish, and Portuguese. The *serf* remained Latin (SERVUS).

The feudal term for 'possessions' in medieval France was *alleu*, from a Frank. AL-OD, lit. 'all property', first attested as ALODIS in the Salic Law. Much used in legal texts, the word passed through this learned channel to Italian as *allodio*, to Spanish and Portuguese as *alodio*. The nobleman's estate was his *fief*, from Frank. FEHU (cf. Germ. *Vieh* 'cattle'). In this instance the word developed with popular tradition, passing into Provençal as *feu*, and thence to Italy as *fío*; in English we have a comparable though not entirely similar semantic evolution of Anglo-Sax. *feoh* 'cattle' to the mod. *fee*. It is probable that FEUDUM and FEUDALIS derive from the same source, though they are not attested till relatively late (the former in A.D. 884, see Du Cange, *Glossarium ad scriptores mediae et infimae latinitatis*); a combination FEHU OD has been postulated as the etymon of FEUDUM, but this does not meet with general acceptance.

Many are the derivatives of the Frank. BANN (cf. Eng. *ban*, *banns*). As Old Fr. *ban* it meant at first any kind of proclamation but then acquired the special sense of 'interdiction publicly proclaimed'. Both these meanings are contained in the Old Fr. verb *banir*. Thus when we read of Roland urging Charlemagne to lead against the Saracens his *ost banie*, we understand not his 'banished' army, but his 'mobilized' army, his feudal levies summoned by proclamation; but in a twelfth-century text one may already read 'Et Sabine, a tousjours, de la terre est banie', where the verb is employed with its modern acceptation. From the notion of *ost banie* the word *ban* itself came to have the further meaning of 'feudal levy', and gave rise to *arrière-ban* the 'reserve': hence the expression *convoquer le ban et l'arrière-ban*, nowadays commonly used in humorous reference to family gatherings. Then the word was applied to the distinguishing flag of a particular levy, whence the derivative *bannière*. In yet another meaning *ban* designated the area under the jurisdiction of the authority which issued proclamations. This produced its own crop of semantic offshoots. Thus the baker's oven and the mill intended for the service of all the inhabitants of the area came to be known as the *four banal*, the *moulin banal*—and so a new epithet was created for the literary criticism of the future (cf. the development of *guindé*, p. 267). Under the same heading comes the Old Fr. *esbaneier* 'to go out of the *ban* for pleasure, for an excursion'; the extract from the *Chanson de Roland* given above shows that at the time of its composition the literal meaning of *esbaneier* had already been lost: when Charlemagne's more mature knights played chess and 'tables' *pur els esbaneier*, it was 'to amuse themselves, to pass the time'. A technical usage gave rise to the Old Fr. *mettre a bandon*, *bandon* being the giving over to common pasturage of a field from which the hay had been reaped: this was remodelled to become *abandonner*, which passed into Italian, with its much extended meaning, as *abbandonare*. The precincts of a territory, originally within a league, received the appellation *banlieue*. An outlaw was a *forban*. To the same Germanic root belongs *bandit*, but this is a borrowing from Ital. *bandito*, all Italian forms with a *d*, cf. *bandire*, *bandiera* pertaining to a Gothic infinitive BANDVJAN, and not to Frank. BANJAN; Span. and Port. *bandir*, and its cognates, were likewise borrowed from Italian.

In the art of war the Franks were supreme. The word WERRA itself was Frankish, though also Gothic (see p. 207). Nomenclature of the trappings of war offers a perfect illustration of the fusion of Frankish and Romance elements in Gaul. Side by side with the *bannière* and the *gonfanon*, the latter from GUNDFANON 'flag of battle' (cf. Germ. *Fahne*, Eng. *vane*), there remained the *penon*, formed on Lat. PINNA 'plume' and later influenced by *pendant*, and also, as the royal standard, the *oriflamme*, from AUREA FLAMBA. Among offensive weapons the Latin short-sword, SPATHA, originally Greek, survived as *espee*, but synonymous with this was the *brant* (< BRAND). The spear was variously designated as *lance* (< Lat. LANCEA), *hanste* (< Lat. HASTA, possibly influenced by a Frankish word), and *espiet* (< Frank. SPEOT, cf. Eng. *spit*), the last-named subsequently altered through contamination with a common suffix to *épieu*. These words are often used interchangeably in the Old French epic. At first, all could be employed as missiles—witness the meaning of *lancer*—but at a time roughly coincident with the composition of the first epics as we know them—this may perhaps be narrowed down to the forty years which elapsed between the Battle of Hastings and the First Crusade (A.D. 1098)—French knights developed the long lance as a fixed weapon, the arm of medieval chivalry. In the earliest texts this is the *hanste*, and later the *lance*, while *espiet* was generally reserved for the missile until it became quite outmoded, thereafter serving as a synonym of *lance*. We have elsewhere suggested that in this tactical evolution lies the explanation of the enigmatic *pleine sa hanste* which occurs seven times in the *Chanson de Roland*, and in other texts in the more usual form *plaine sa hanste*: we see in it a fossilized form of an original command PLANA (IP)SA HASTA! 'Lance at the level!', used in eleventh-century lance-drill and exercise; such alternative translations as 'with a full blow of the lance', 'a full lance-length', 'with lance unbroken'—all of them possible in different contexts—would therefore be due to confusion of *plaine* (<PLANA) with *pleine* (< PLĒNA), a confusion to which various expressions in modern French bear ample witness (*French Studies*, vol. vii, no. 1, 1953).

Yet more terms existed in the nomenclature of missiles, as may be seen from the veritable hail of them which the unknown author conjures up in the following lines from the *Chanson de Roland*:

> Il lor lancent e lances e espiez
> (E) Wigres e darz
> E museras e agiez e gieser.
>
> (Ed. Whitehead, ll. 2074–5*a*)

Of these, *wigres* is borrowed from the Norse VIGR, and *museras* is a Saracen term from the Arabic *mizrāq*. Frankish is *agiez* (<ATGER, see E. Gamillscheg, op. cit., vol. i, p. 177); in the singular it occurs commonly as *agier*, *algier*. For the provenance of *gieser* we can discover no suggestion; in the context it should be plural, which tempts one to wonder whether it is not the same Germanic root, perhaps with a Germanic plural flexion. Old Fr. *dard*, which spread to all the languages of the Spanish Peninsula and to Italy as *dardo*, is certainly Frankish, corresponding to a form DAROD, cf. Anglo-Sax. *daroth*.

With the development of the static lance the use of missiles declined, until the bow and arrow, always available for the hunt but despised by soldiers as 'ungentlemanly', were effectively brought back to the field of battle in the hands of the English bowmen at Crécy. The *arc* has remained consistently Latin; the arrow was in Old Fr. *saete* from Lat. SAGĬTTA, the usual word in Romance, cf. Prov. Span. *saeta*, Cat. *sageta*, Port. *seta*, Rum. *săgeată*, Ital. *saetta* (but cf. *strale*, of Langobardic origin, see p. 263, and *freccia*, borrowed from French): this was eventually replaced by *flèche*, probably a post-Frankish loan-word from a VLEKE of the Low Countries (from an original FLIUGIKA 'the thing which flies', see E. Gamillscheg, loc. cit.).

Yet another missile, the *javelot*, e.g.

> De loig li lance javeloz acerez
> (*Guibert d'Andrenas*, ed. Jessie Crosland, l. 741)

is a relic of the Celtic armoury.

Defensive equipment includes the shield, which remained Latin as Old Fr. *escu* (< SCUTUM) and *bouclier*, formed on *boucle* from Lat. BUCCULA, but again there is a Frankish alternative in the word *targe* (< TARGA), of which the northern form passed into Spanish and Portuguese as *tarja*, while the Prov. *targa*, taken from the north before the *g* had been palatalized, travelled to Italy without change. The long coat of mail—accurately portrayed in the Bayeux tapestry, a panoramic record of the Battle of Hastings—was a Frankish innovation and bore in Old French the name *broigne* (< BRUNNJA), a word borrowed into Provençal as *bronha*, but which thence proceeded no farther. The *cotte*, a 'coat' worn over the mail, is also Frankish (< KOTTA); and to this context belongs *gant* (< WANT), since the glove was in the first instance an article of military equipment rather than part of everyday clothing: as Old Fr. *guant* it travelled south to give Ital. *guanto*, Cat. *guant*, Span. Port. *guante*. As is indicated by the glossing of Lat. GALEA by HELMUS in the Reichenau Glossary, the helmet became entirely Germanic. The word is of particular interest in that it offers one of the relatively rare examples of perceptible phonetic variation in the Germanic forms adopted into Romance: a Gothic HILMS had given in Italian, Spanish, and Portuguese *elmo*, with a close *e* developing from the Gothic short *i*, but the basis of Fr. *heaume* is Frank. HELM with an open *e*, and this form made an early passage across the Pyrenees to give Span. *yelmo*, by which Old Span. *elmo* was displaced, though the Gothic form was retained in Italian and Portuguese; the same vocalic alternance is to be observed in Gothic SPIUTS > Span. *espeto* (see p. 223), whereas Frank. SPEOT > Old Fr. *espiet*. All the paraphernalia connected with the sword were Germanic: thus the 'hilt', Old Fr. *heut* (< HILT); the 'sheath', Old Fr. *fuerre* (< FODR, mod. *fourreau*); the 'belt' or 'baldric', Old Fr. *baudret* (< BALDR); and the 'rings by which the sheath was attached to the belt', the Old Fr. *renges de l'espee* (*renge* < HRINGA).

The Frankish origin of Old Fr. *herberge*, at first the military camp, has been mentioned in connexion with its replacement by the southern and Gothic *auberge* (p. 207); in the verb *héberger* the Frankish type persists. The sentry was the *gaite* (< WAHTA, cf. Eng. *watch*, *wake*, and from Norman dialect, *wait*), whence the Old Fr. verb *gaitier*, mod. *guetter*; or in longer form he was the 'troops-watchman', the *eschargaite*, a word often corrupted to *eschaugaite* or *eschirgaite* (< SKARWAHTA, cf. Germ. *Scharwache*). SKARA alone became in Old French *eschiere* 'troops', and in this military sense persisted for a long time after the word had become confused with *eschelle* 'ladder', from Lat. SCALA, e.g.

> De Franceis sunt les premeres escheles.
>> (*Chanson de Roland*, ed. Whitehead, l. 3026)

Another Frankish borrowing of similar connotation is Old Fr. *renc*, mod. *rang* (< HRING), as again in the *Chanson de Roland*:

> Turpins de Reins en est levét del renc.
>> (l. 264)

Booty was defined as *eschech* in the passage from the *Chanson de Roland* previously quoted (p. 235); this represents a Frank. SKAK, adopted into Provençal as *escac*, and thence into Old Italian as *schacho*. This word seems to have become involved with the *eschecs* found in the same passage, meaning 'chess', which derives from the Persian for 'king', the mod. *Shah* (cf. Ital. *scacchi*). From the terminology of this ancient game *eschec* came to mean a defeat, as in expressions like the mod. *subir un échec*. The presence in the language of two identical words meaning 'booty' and 'defeat' must have created a difficulty; the homonymic clash was ultimately resolved through the replacement of *eschech* by *butin*, another Germanic word (cf. Germ. *Beute*), apparently a post-Frankish borrowing since it is not attested in French before the fourteenth century. A payment of money was a WADI, which, latinized as WADIUS, occurs in the Reichenau Glossary as the gloss of Lat. PIGNUS: hence Fr. *gage* and the verb *gager*, and from Norman dialect the Eng. *wage* and *to wager*. In the same context one may note Fr. *garant* from WARAND, the source of the English doublets *warrant* from Norman, and *guarantee* from French.

A number of Germanic verbs, all of which are represented in French, have been tentatively attributed to the common lexical stock of late Vulgar Latin (*bâtir*, *broyer*, *épargner*, *gagner*, *garnir*, *gratter*, *guérir*, *lécher*, Old Fr. *rober*, *rôtir*, see p. 209). Of these, *rober* survives in modern French only in *dérober*; *garder*, while keeping its separate existence, produced two compound forms, *esgarder* and *regarder*, both meaning 'to look at' (for a similar semantic development cf. Old Span. *catar* from CAPTARE, see p. 116): *regarder* ultimately prevailed, *esgarder* leaving only a relic in the verbal substantive *égard*. In northern France the 'common stock' was considerably augmented with new Frankish forms as a result of the invasion. Frank. KAUSJAN, before *regarder*, meant 'to look at', a sense which it still retained in Old Fr. *choisir*; only

late in the Middle Ages did it give way before the competition of
other words, to acquire, via the meaning 'to descry', the more
specialized sense of 'to pick out', 'to choose'; in so doing it all but
ousted the medieval word for 'to choose', Old Fr. *eslire* from
EXLIGERE (Class. ELIGERE). KAUSJAN passed into Provençal as *causir*
and with further diffusion became Old Span. *cosir*, Old Port.
*cousir*. Other Frankish verbs specifically associated with northern
France are as follows: SPANNJAN > Old Fr. *espanir*, mod. *épanouir*;
HATJAN (cf. Eng. *to hate*) > Fr. *haïr*; HAUNJAN > Fr. *honnir*; ROTJAN
(cf. Eng. *to rot*) > Fr. *rouir*, a term much used in connexion with
the preparation of linen fibre from flax; SAZJAN > Fr. *saisir*, probably first used with the special sense of 'to confiscate'; BOTTAN >
Fr. *bouter*, now archaic though still preserved in such expressions
as *le boute-en-train*, i.e. *celui qui met en train* 'the life and soul of
the party', and *le boute-feu* the 'toucher-off' of a cannon, hence
metaphorically of a conspiracy; SKIRMJAN (originally 'to protect',
hence Germ. *Regenschirm*, a 'protection against rain') > Old Fr.
*escremir*, which survives only in the substantive *escrime* in French,
though it remains in Eng. *to skirmish* and in Ital. *schermire*;
BLETTJAN (cf. Eng. *to bleed*) > Fr. *blesser*, one of the two verbs for
'to wound' in Old French, the other being *navrer*, which seems
to have been formed on the Frankish noun NARWA (cf. Germ.
*Narbe* 'scar'): the former of these meant 'to wound with a blow'
and the latter, now confined to the expression of feeling (e.g. *Je
suis navré* 'I am sorry'), 'to wound with a cut'; FURBJAN > Fr.
*fourbir*, particularly applied to the polishing of arms and thus connected with military vocabulary; SPEHŌN > Old Fr. *espier* (whence
Eng. *to spy*), mod. *épier*: the Old French verbal substantive *espie*
was later replaced by *espion* through the influence of Ital. *spione*;
SKIUHAN (cf. Germ. *scheuen*, Eng. *to shy*, and the adjective, of
different dialectal origin, *askew*) > Old Fr. *eschiver*, which borrowed into English became *to eschew*, and in the sixteenth century
was altered in French to *esquiver* through contact with Ital.
*schivare*, the same Frankish verb adopted into Italian from the
Provençal form *esquivar*; DUBBAN > Fr. *(a)douber* 'to arm' or 'to
dub' a knight; WERPAN (cf. Germ. *werfen*) > Old Fr. *guerpir* 'to
abandon', preserved only in *déguerpir*; WENKJAN (cf. Germ. *wanken*
'to waver', 'to totter', and Eng. *to wink*, from Anglo-Sax. *wincian*) >
Old Fr. *guenchir*, cf. Eng. *to wince*; WALKJAN (cf. Eng. *to walk*) >
Fr. *gauchir* 'to turn aside', whence the adj. *gauche*: the same word

occurs in Italian as *gualcire*, but it may in this instance be of Langobardic origin. At least one common verb, Old Fr. *esfreer*, mod.
*effrayer*, was formed with Latin elements from a Frankish noun:
it is literally 'to put out of peace', the noun being Frank. FRIDA
(cf. Germ. *Friede*).

Adjectives are no less prominent than verbs in the Frankish
contribution to French. To the list of colour-adjectives previously
mentioned as pertaining to the 'common Germanic stock' (*blanc,
brun, gris, fauve*, &c., see p. 208), the newcomers added the words
which appear in Old French as *bleu* and *sor* (*saur*). The latter of
these, attested as SORA, glossing RUFA in the Reichenau Glossary,
was frequently applied to young falcons and still more often to
horses, as, for instance, in the *Chanson de Roland*:

> Li Marganices sist sur un ceval sor.
>
> (Ed. Whitehead, l. 1943)

English *sorrel*, similarly used of horses, came from across the
Channel as a derivative of the same word. In this context *sor* appears as closely associated with the more widespread Germanic
colour-adjectives, adding strength to the suggestion that they too
were propagated with reference to horses.[1]

Frank. BLAW probably had connexions quite different from those
of SAUR. Vulgar Latin, curiously, possesses no consistently-used
term to define the colour of 'blue', and the Romance languages
contain various terms, mostly of exotic origin, which seem to be
related to dyeing and the cloth trade: Old French has *pers* from
Lat. PERSUS 'Persian', while Span. *azul* and Ital. *azzurro* derive
from Persian through Arabic (see p. 290). The semantic affinity
between colour and cloth is well illustrated by the name in Old
French of a dark-coloured material, *isanbrun*, or *isembrun*, from
Frank. ISARNBRUN, in mod. Germ. *eisenbraun*, lit. 'iron-brown'.
Whether or no this circumstance made the fortune of Frank. BLAW,
it spread rapidly over Gaul and is still used in Provençal and Catalan as *blau*, fem. *blava*. From Provence it passed into Italy as *biavo*,
later to be superseded in the north by the French form borrowed as
*blu*, but neither of these has ousted *azzurro* from standard Italian.

Just as the blending of Anglo-Saxon and Anglo-Norman enriched the stylistic potential of English so the fusion of Frankish

---

[1] The original meaning of Frank. SAUR seems to have been 'dry', 'withered'
(cf. OHG. *sorēn* 'to dry', see E. Gamillscheg, *Romania Germanica*, vol. i, p. 228).
Thence it was applied to the colour of things which were withered, such as
leaves.

and Gallo-Romance rendered the same service to Old French. This is particularly noticeable in the use made of the adjective by Old French poets. One of their favourite devices was to link epithets which are almost synonymous, and not infrequently one of the two was Latin in origin and the other Germanic. An example of this may be found in the first line of the passage quoted from the *Chanson de Roland* (p. 235), in which Charlemagne is described as *balz e liez*, words which evoke for the translator a similar wealth of synonym in English. Lat. LAETUS is here linked with Frank. BALD, the cognate of Eng. *bold*. The concepts of 'bold' and 'merry' being psychologically akin, it is in the latter sense that the word evolved in Old French, as is further apparent from the derivatives *s'ébaudir* 'to make merry', and *ébaudissement* 'merry-making'; the verb *baudir* 'to excite (dogs to the hunt)' conveys a suggestion of both meanings. Borrowed from French into English *baud* became *bawd*, a substantive, with a corresponding adjective *bawdy*. Eng. *bold* and *bawd* are thus doublets: the sense of the latter has perhaps influenced that of the former in the expression 'a bold woman'. In Italy as *baldo*, the word was adopted with the original meaning of 'bold', cf. *baldanza* 'boldness', but when the derivative *balderie* followed the same route it had already acquired a different significance, for Ital. *baldoria* means 'bonfire', 'feu de joie'.

At the other end of the emotional scale one encounters the linking of *sur* with *amer*, i.e. of Lat. AMARUS with Frank. SUR (cf. Germ. *sauer*, Eng. *sour*), e.g.

> 'Fille,' ce dist li rois, 'ressemblez votre mere;
> Ne soiez vers les povres ne sure ne amere.'
> (Adenet le Roi, *Berthe aus grans pies*, ed. U. T. Holmes, ll. 138–9)
> La perte de Bertain li fu sure et amere.
>
> (Ibid., l. 2347)

The adjective *sur* still survives in French, together with the derivative *surelle*, the name of a sour-tasting plant which as a loan-word in English has become another 'sorrel'.

To the 'merry and bold' sphere belong the Germanic adjectives *gai* and *hardi*. The Frankish affiliation of the former is somewhat doubtful. It may represent Frank. WAHI, but if it does one would expect the original Old French form to be *\*guai*, and of this there is no trace; if, on the other hand, it corresponds to the dialectal variant found in Old High German as *gahi* 'quick', 'bold', the *g* would normally have palatalized in the proto-French of the north. A form with palatalized *g* is in fact found, in Old Provençal texts from the northern regions of the Provençal area, as *jai*, side by side with the usual *gai* (cf. Span. *gayo*, Port. Ital. *gaio*): the correct inference would seem to be that *gai* is a Provençal germanism which passed at an early date to the north, perhaps replacing there the Frankish type. Concerning *hardi* there is no doubt: it is the past participle of a verb *hardir* from Frank. HARD-JAN 'to make hard'. It spread rapidly abroad, to England as *hardy*, which is thus the Anglo-Norman equivalent of *hard* (from Anglo-Sax. *heard*), to Italy as *ardito*, to Spain as *ardido*, and with an *f* representing the Frankish aspirate, as *fardido* in the *Poema del Cid*.

Another adjective associated with the Frankish 'baron' is *riche* (< RIKI, cf. Germ. *reich*), which in Old French meant 'powerful', and came only by semantic extension to be 'rich'. Here there is some doubt concerning the point or points of entry of the Germanic word into other Romance languages: while it is probably the Frankish word which became Prov. and Cat. *ric*, whether Span. and Port. *rico* and Ital. *ricco* are due to the same Frankish overlay, or whether they derive respectively from Visigothic and Ostrogothic or Langobardic, seems almost impossible to determine.

On the other side of the semantic picture are old Fr. *grain* (< GRAM, cf. Germ. *Gram* 'grief', cognate with Eng. *grim*), which was synonymous with *triste* and *laid* (< LAID, cf. Germ. *Leid* 'sorrow', 'pain'). The latter passed into Old Spanish and Portuguese, as also into Italian, as *laido*; Cat. *lleig* must be explained by a metathesized form *ladio*, attested in Italian. In Old French *laid* produced the derivatives *laidir*, cf. mod. *enlaidir*, and *laidange* 'insult'. More closely confined to Gaul is Frank. MORNI (cf. OHG. *mornēn*, Eng. *to mourn*), the adjective of which became Fr. *morne*, Prov. *morn*. Also appropriate to this context is *blafard* from Frank. BLAIKFARO (cf. Germ. *bleich*, Eng. *to bleach*).

Commonly used in Old French, though it disappeared with the Middle Ages, is the adjective *isnel* 'quick', from Frank. SNEL (cf. Germ. *schnell*). It occurs in the curious adverbial expression *isnel le pas* 'immediately', due to popular adaptation of *en es le pas* (see p. 90), which, on account of the disappearance of *es*, from Lat. IPSUM, had ceased to be comprehensible. The word is also Provençal, and it is found in Italian as *snello*, nowadays with the complimentary meaning of 'lithe', 'lissom', but this is another instance

in which the Italian form may have been inherited from Langobardic.

It has often been observed that the adjectives left in Gallo-
Romance by the Franks seem almost designed to characterize
their own moral conceptions. Reflexes of the Germanic conscience
may also explain the wide currency of two abstract nouns, *honte*
from HAUNITHA (cf. Germ. *Hohn*), and *orgueil* from URGOLI. The
former of these is specifically Frankish: though introduced into
Italian as *onta* from Prov. *onta*, and also into Spain where it
appears in written form as *fonta* (cf. above, *fardido*), it never succeeded in ousting there its Latin synonym VERECUNDIA, which
survives in everyday usage as Ital. *vergogna* and Span. *verguenza*;
in northern France, too, *vergogne* has persisted, the two words
often being linked together by Old French poets, but *honte* has
predominated in popular favour. URGOLI passed into Provençal as
*orgolh* and thence into Italian as *orgoglio*, where it nowadays defines pride in the 'good' sense, contrasting with *superbia*. Thus far
the word is certainly Frankish. The suggestion has been made that
Span. *orgullo* and Port. *orgulho*, on account of the quality of the
stressed vowel, are more probably Visigothic, but it is by no means
certain that they too are not borrowings from Provence.

One common adverb, Old Fr. *guaire(s)*, mod. *guère*, is a loan-
word from Frankish. At first it meant 'much', the sense of WAI-
GARO, but like *rien* and *personne* it acquired the opposite meaning
in consequence of continual use with a negative (for the contrary
semantic evolution of the original WAIGARO, corresponding to
OHG. *unwaigaro* 'strong', cf. the modern cognate *unweigerlich*: see
E. Gamillscheg, *Romania Germanica*, vol. i, p. 225). The word
extended to Provence as *guaire*, and thence to Catalonia as *gaire*.
It gave rise to a further adverb in Fr. *naguère*, the Old French construction for 'il n'y a guère (de temps)', cf. Cat. *no hi ha gaire*,
with the same meaning.

The examples thus far adduced, though by no means exhaustive,
will perhaps suffice to convey an adequate impression of the tremendous impact of Frankish on the Gallo-Romance vocabulary.
It is significant that they comprise not only those words of concrete and easily assimilated meaning which pass so readily from one
language to another, but also the means of defining concepts more
abstract in kind, concepts of *Weltanschauung* such as normally
require a literary channel to facilitate their transfer.

Perhaps no less significant, in this respect, is the Frankish contribution to Gallo-Romance word-formation. Already noted is the currency of the suffix -ISK (see p. 235), which, incidentally, extended to Provençal, preserving there a form very close to the original Frankish in *francesc, espanesc, proensalesc, grezesc*, &c., and thence to Italian, as in *Francesco*. To this may be added three more suffixes which enjoyed considerable favour in Old French. The most productive was *-art*, with a feminine *-arde*, to which is due the modern spelling *-ard* of the masculine, a purely orthographical change since the final consonant had ceased to be pronounced. It appears first as -HART in proper names such as BERNHART, EBERHART, REGINHART, which, the aspirate in this position soon being eliminated, became in French *Bernard, Évrard, Renard*. Thence it spread to other words referring to persons, e.g. *vieillard, bâtard, gaillard, richard, couard*; in the last-named of these it has become attached to Old Fr. *coue*, mod. *queue*, from CAUDAM, the 'coward' thus being the one who shows the tail. The suffix has continued to flourish and is now added to the most miscellaneous stems, both nominal and verbal, e.g. *paillard, veinard, grognard, soûlard, montagnard, dreyfusard*, &c. Similarly deriving from Frankish names is *-ald* (*-alt, -aut, -aud*), e.g. *Guiraud, Renaud*, &c.; this was originally -WALD, from the verb WALDAN 'to govern', as in ANSWALD, GRIMWALD, HERWALD, &c. Rarely used nowadays in the formation of new words, the suffix survives in a number of adjectives, most of them applied to persons and of a derogatory nature, e.g. *lourdaud, finaud, noiraud, nigaud, salaud, saligaud*. The third suffix is -ING (-LING); though undoubtedly Frankish in northern France, this suffix seems to have been adopted into the common Germanic stock of Vulgar Latin, or perhaps to have been more favoured in both Gothic and Langobardic than in Frankish. Spanish and Italian words containing the other two suffixes are for the most part easily identified as borrowings from Gallo-Romance; thus Old Fr. *hiralt, hiraut*, mod. *héraut*, from HERIALT, became Ital. *araldo*, Port. *arauto*, Old Span. *haraute*, later *haraldo, heraldo*; cf. also Fr. *gaillard*, Prov. *galhart*, which travelled south to become Span. *gallardo*, Port. *galhardo*, Ital. *gagliardo*, or again Old Fr. *bastard*, which in the same three languages became *bastardo*. On the other hand, the Span. and Port. *-engo* (see p. 222) and the Ital. *-ingo* are found in quite different combinations. In French -ING was less productive than elsewhere and its modern survivals have been considerably disguised through confusion with similar suffixes from Latin sources. Thus Old Fr. *chambrelenc* (see p. 241) has been altered to *chambellan*, Old Fr. *loherenc* to *lorrain*, Old Fr. *flamenc* to *flamand*, while *cormoran* represents a former *corp marenc* in which the Germanic suffix had replaced the -INUS of CORVUS MARINUS 'sea crow'.

Widely represented in the place-names of northern France is a suffix -INGAS, in its modern form usually -*anges*, cognate with the -*ingen* so common in Germany, e.g. *Solingen*, *Tübingen*, &c.; like the toponymic suffixes already discussed, it has the meaning 'belonging to' (see p. 177): thus *Fouchanges* is 'the estate of Fulko'. The same type appears in the Franco-Provençal area as -*ens*, -*ans*, bearing witness to the former existence of a Burgundian alternative -INGOS.

Less certain is the Frankish influence on the prefix-system of Old French. Its presence has indeed been disputed. Yet it is difficult to refuse to see a parallel between the notions of excess contained in Old Fr. *for-* as in *forconseillier* 'to give bad advice', *se forfaire* 'to act wrongly', whence the substantive *forfait*, *se forjouïr* 'to enjoy oneself immoderately', and in the *ver-* of German, cf. *vertrinken* 'to spend in drink', *vernichten* 'to destroy utterly', *sich verlieben* 'to fall in love'. Lat. FORIS, the alternative etymology proposed, which is found in Old Fr. *forsbourg* (later corrupted to *faubourg*), may well have been confused with the original Germanic prefix, dialectically FUR-, FOR-, and FIR-, and have determined its final form. No less certainly Frankish appears the *mes-* of Old Fr. *mesfaire*, *mesaventure*, &c., cf. the *miss-* of Germ. *missbrauchen*, the *mis-* of Eng. *misuse*; suggestions that this might derive from MĬNUS can command little support.

Two Frankish contributions to the Gallo-Roman sound-system are beyond dispute: the reintroduction of the phoneme *h*, which had long since ceased to be pronounced in words of Latin origin, and the introduction of a bilabial *w*, which survived as such in the regions most densely settled but became *gu* in the home of the *francien* dialect. It is noteworthy that the *h* was preserved only when initial; examples are numerous among words already quoted (*heaume*, *hardi*, *héron*, *honnir*, *honte*, &c.). There are instances of its becoming attached to words of Latin origin: ALTUS, through contact with Frank. HOH (Germ. *hoch*), became Fr. *haut*; and HASTA became *hanste*. This Germanic *h* was to persist in French until the end of the Middle Ages, since when it has served only, as the so-called '*h* aspirate', to maintain a vocalic liaison, as in *la haine*; it is still heard in parts of eastern France, and especially in Belgium. Elsewhere in Romania, with the exception of the Rheto-Romance area, Germanic *h* received no currency whatever; thus Old Fr. *osberc* and *elme*, beside the usual *haubert* and *heaume*, are easily recognizable as borrowings from the armourers of Provence, cf. also *auberge* and *herberge*. The evolution of *w* to *gu* is likewise well illustrated by previously quoted examples (*guerre, gant, garnement, guetter, guère,* &c.). Simplification of the sound to *g* appears to have taken place in French by the end of the twelfth century, the spelling *gu* being thereafter retained before *e* and *i* in order to indicate that the phoneme was still velar, as in *gant*. Here it must be added that a number of Latin words with initial v, normally kept in French, as in VALĒRE > *valoir*, have become involved in the Germanic evolution. In most cases this can be explained by the fact that the Latin word was paralleled in Frankish by a similar word, of similar meaning, but beginning with a *w*, e.g. *gâter* < VASTARE+Frank. WOSTAN; *guêpe* < VESPA+Frank. WABSA (cf. WAPCES in the Reichenau Glossary); *gué* < VADUM+Frank. WAD (cf. Anglo-Sax. *wadan*, Eng. *to wade*); *guivre* < VIPERA+Frank. WIPERA (originally a Germanic borrowing from Latin); *goupil* (the Old French word for 'fox' before the popularity of the stories of *Renard le goupil* brought about its replacement by *renard*) < VULPICULUM+Frank. WULF. With less obvious Germanic counterparts, but probably induced in the same way, are *gui* < VISCUM and *gaine* < VAGĪNA (J. Brüch suggests in this instance the influence of Frank. WAGI 'shell', 'peel'). This phenomenon of coalescence belongs specifically to northern France, the languages of other parts of Romania having generally preserved in these words the v of Latin. Span. *gastar*, Ital. *guastare* appear to constitute an exception, but they are probably due to diffusion from the north, as are certainly Ital. *guado* and *guaina*: in the case of these latter the v remains intact in dialectal forms of present-day Italy.

A similar hybridism may be detected in the development of the so-called 'onomastic' declension of Old French, i.e. the declension of proper names. Latin documents of the period show a masculine type with nominative in -o (or -us) and acc. -ONEM, and a formally corresponding feminine type with nom. -A, acc. -ANEM. In Old French texts these types are represented by such names as the following, some of which are Latin in origin but the majority

Frankish: *Charles—Charlon, Eudes—Odon, Hues—Huon, Naimes —Naimon, Marsilies—Marsilion, Guenes—Guenelon, Guis—Guion, Samse—Samson, Pierres—Perron*; fem. *Eve—Evain, Aude— Audain, Berte—Bertain, Marie—Mariain, Dode—Dodain, Pinte— Pintain* (the name of the hen in the *Roman de Renart*). To the same types belong a few common nouns designating persons, e.g. Old Fr. *ber—baron, ledre—larron, gars—garçon*; fem. *ante—antain, nonne—nonnain, pute—putain*. Among these it will be observed that *ledre—larron* is an entirely normal Romance development of LATRO—LATRONEM, which might have afforded a model for PETRUS—PETRONEM. Yet in view of the predominance of Frankish names among those so declined, especially in the masculine, it seems impossible to exclude all influence of Germanic. Frankish had a declension in -O, -UN (e.g. HUGO—HUGUN), which, allowing for the analogical *s* of the nominative, is parallel to the Old French declension; it is true that the accent in Frankish fell in both cases on the stem, but that it should have shifted in the accusative to the flexion would not, in northern Gaul, provoke our surprise. The argument for a Frankish influence in the feminine is perhaps less strong. Types such as MARIA—MARIANEM are attested in Rumania, where Germanic influence was almost negligible, and are probably due, in the first instance, to a Greek influence on Vulgar Latin. The feminine forms of Frankish were in -A, -UN (e.g. BERTA— BERTUN). But it is easy to apprehend that a generalization of the vowel A in the accusative would result in a complete welding together of the two declensions, Frankish and Vulgar Latin. The onomastic declension of Old French seems to imply a perfect marriage.

Further attempts to seek the effects of this marriage in the evolution of the French sound-system must be left in the realm of hypothesis. It has been frequently argued that the heavy Germanic stress is responsible for the general diphthongization in Old French of accented vowels, and correspondingly for the weakening or elimination of unaccented vowels. But such tendencies were already present in Vulgar Latin: diphthongization of stressed vowels is a phenomenon encountered in many parts of Romania, and as for the elimination of unstressed vowels, we have already seen abundant evidence of their fall, not only in the third-century *Appendix Probi* but even in the first-century Pompeian *graffiti*. This cannot be laid at the door of Germanic. Frankish stress tended at most to accelerate a linguistic evolution already in progress; that is all one can state with confidence. More important perhaps than any direct influence on the sound-system was the effect of Frankish in breaking down the cohesion and prestige of 'correct' spoken Latin, never so strong north of the Loire as in the south, thereby leaving the path open for rapid change and local differentiation in the Gallo-Roman vernacular of the northern region. In this way the Franks undoubtedly played a large part in creating the rift between *langue d'oïl* and *langue d'oc*, as it was revealed by the first appearance of vernacular texts. Above all, they helped to fashion a new civilization with a new language, and to ensure the political and literary ascendancy whereby that language, replete with Germanisms, was subsequently to enrich the vocabulary of every other Romance idiom in the west.

*Langobards.* The story of the last large-scale Germanic invasion on the Continent brings us again to Italy. There, scarcely had the Ostrogoths been overthrown and the Byzantine Exarchate established, when yet another tribe came pouring in from the north. These were the Langobards, perhaps the most primitive and uncouth of Germanic migrants, but destined to have almost as large a share in the formation of modern Italy, though in a more negative fashion, as had the Franks in that of France.

Coming originally from northern Germany, of West Germanic affiliation and therefore little removed from the Franks in speech, they had passed first into the present territory of Silesia and then into Pannonia, newly vacated by the Ostrogoths. Two other peoples, however, had made for the coveted land of Pannonia: the East Germanic tribe of the Gepidae, and the Avars, new invaders from beyond Europe (see p. 268), who like the Huns before them were establishing a kingdom in the plains of the middle Danube. In the resultant collision a combination of Avars and Langobards defeated the Gepidae (A.D. 567) who thereafter disappear as a unit from tribal circulation. The Avars then applied pressure to the Langobards, making with them a curious 'gentleman's agreement' whereby the Langobards were to seek a foothold in Italy, and in the event of success cede to the Avars their territory in Pannonia. In the following year the Langobard king, Alboin, led a large host, including remnants of the Gepidae and elements from other tribes, into the plains of Venetia and Gallia Cisalpina. The town of Mediolanum (Milan) fell at once into their hands, and soon the

Langobards were masters of the province of Lombardy to which they have given their name. It is possible that survivors from the kindred Ostrogoths, then nominally in the service of Byzantium, assisted the newcomers in their occupation. Before the Roman Ticinum, modern Pavia, Alboin met with unexpectedly stubborn resistance, and he succeeded in reducing the town only after a siege lasting for three years; thereafter it became the Langobardic capital.

The Byzantines remained in control of the cities of central Italy. Their capital was at Ravenna, at that time more Greek than Roman, and while Alboin pressed southwards along the west coast to occupy Tuscany, they consolidated their hold on a belt of territory extending from Ravenna to Rome. Alboin himself remained in Tuscany, but certain of his nobles passed through the Byzantine lines and founded to the south and east the two large duchies of Benevento and Spoleto. The extreme south, including Apulia, Calabria and Sicily, remained Byzantine; so too did Naples, though almost cut off by Langobardic territory and linked at times to Rome, at times to Calabria. A further Byzantine area was left intact in the neighbourhood of Venice, forming a nucleus which was to develop into the prosperous state of later days. Throughout most of the two centuries of Langobardic occupation this patchwork division of Italy persisted.

In A.D. 573 Alboin was murdered at the instigation of his wife, Rosamund.[1] After the brief reign of his successor a period of eleven years elapsed before the appointment of another king, the territory occupied by the Langobards being divided during the interval into independent dukedoms. An attack by the Franks in A.D. 584 compelled the dukes to form a coalition and nominate a king as leader, but never after Alboin did a royal court form the hub of a centralized authority. In this Langobardic division may be found the historical reason for the long-continued political disunity of Italy, contrasting with the early centralization and growth into nationhood of France.

Byzantine power in the west, after the death of Justinian,

---

[1] A vivid account of the murder is given by Paulus Diaconus in his *Historia Langobardorum* (see p. 327). According to this, Rosamund was incensed by an incident which occurred at a banquet, when Alboin, making merry, challenged her to drink to her father's health from a cup which he, Alboin, had had made from her father's skull. By a trick, Rosamund procured for herself a lover and then blackmailed him into committing the deed.

rapidly waned. The Italo-Roman population, coming to look upon the Byzantines as foreigners, as Greeks, grew to resent their presence, and had the Langobards possessed any vision of a united Italy, they might at this stage have brought it into being. Instead, the decline of imperial authority made way for the increasing secular power of the Papacy: after Justinian, the leading personality of the Christian world became Pope Gregory I, ruling at Rome. There was no spectacular downfall of the Byzantines in Italy, only a gradual shift of the people's allegiance from Emperor to Pope, both of whom nominally represented the same cause.

Rather late in the day there appeared a Langobardic king, Liutprand, who saw the possibility of exploiting the political situation, but his attempts to convert Italy into a unified Langobardic kingdom were thwarted by the desire of the dukes of Benevento and Spoleto to preserve their independence, a desire in which they were naturally encouraged by papal diplomacy. After Liutprand's death in A.D. 743 his successor Rachis sought to abandon his plans and make peace with the Pope; but the followers of Liutprand, now imbued with the idea of unification and impatient with the pacific policy of Rachis, deposed him in favour of his brother Aistulf (A.D. 748), who adopted the aggressive policy with such enthusiasm that in A.D. 750 he seized Ravenna and turned his arms against Rome. The Pope, Stephen III, appealed for help to the nominal secular defender of Christendom, the Byzantine Emperor, then Constantine V, but in vain. With no answer coming from the east, he turned for assistance to the west, to the Franks. It was this event which marked the real and final break between Rome and Byzantium. The Pope went in person to France and there met and consulted Pépin, son of Charles Martel (see p. 275), at that time mayor of the royal palace. As a result, he deposed Childéric, last of a succession of decadent Merovingian rulers, and anointed Pépin as king of the Franks; and thus began the Carolingian dynasty in France, in intimate alliance with the Roman Church. The new pattern of Europe was beginning to emerge.

The commitment which Pépin undertook as his share of the bargain was naturally to defend the Papacy, in the first instance against the menace of the Langobards. In the course of two campaigns in Italy he subdued Aistulf and compelled him to pay tribute to the Franks. With the next generation of rulers, however, war broke out again. Desiderius, successor of Aistulf, renewed the attack on papal territory, and the new Pope, Hadrian I, followed precedent in appealing for aid to the Frankish monarchy, now represented by Pépin's son, Charlemagne. In A.D. 773 Charlemagne defeated Desiderius and deposed him in his capital town of Pavia, thereafter assuming for himself the title of king of the Langobards. The authority of the Pope was confirmed, and Langobardic domination brought to an end. The secular ascendancy of the Franks was consummated in A.D. 800 with the crowning of Charlemagne as Emperor of the West.

Thus for 200 years the Langobards had ruled large tracts of Italy, and they have certainly left their mark upon the social evolution of that country. Yet, like the Visigoths in Spain but for quite different reasons, they failed to make that early symbiosis with the native population which was the peculiar achievement of the Franks. Theirs was no self-conscious abstention; they were not haunted by pride of race and made no laws to forbid intermarriage with the Italo-Romans, from among whom indeed many took their wives. On the other hand, unlike the Goths, they had little previous familiarity with Roman civilization, or with the Latin tongue. They came to Italy as barbarians, intent only on the seizure of land in which to dwell, lacking in political leaders with sufficient foresight to have a care for 'public relations'. In consequence they were both despised and resented, and for the first hundred years of their occupation they lived in a state of permanent hostility with the Italo-Romans. Then, with the disdain of the natives turning rather against the remnants of Byzantium, they began slowly to come under the influence of the Roman spell, and, formerly half-pagan and half-Arian, little by little they embraced the Catholic faith; by the time of the final collision with the Franks they had produced at least one outstanding scholar, Paulus Diaconus, whom Charlemagne, the patron of learning, summoned to his court. But their social and political education had come too late. After the humiliation of Pavia they continued to inhabit the country as subjects of the Frankish Empire, mingling with the local population, though keeping for a while their Langobardic speech, which seems to have lingered on in some districts until nearly A.D. 1000. For this reason it is not surprising that many of the Langobardic words which have remained in Italy belong only to rural dialects, particularly those of the north, and have never been adopted into the Italian literary language.

Langobardic place-names serve to indicate the areas of most dense occupation. In the north, especially in an arc around Pavia, they abound. Particularly numerous are names with the suffix -*engo*, corresponding, like the Frankish and Burgundian equivalents already noted, to the Germ. -*ingen*, e.g. *Marengo, Massalengo, Dardengo, Odardengo, Pastrengo,* &c.; the last of these contains the Lat. PASTOR, while the others are based on Langobardic cognomina. Also of frequent occurrence is the Langob. FARA, which meant 'family', a word of which the ultimate Germanic affiliation remains doubtful, but which was in current use in the seventh century: in the *Edictus Rothari*, the first code of Langobardic law, formulated in A.D. 643 at the behest of King Rothari and of particular interest for its many Germanisms, one may read: 'Si quis liber homo potestatem habeat intra dominium regni nostri cum fara sua megrare ubi voluerit . . ., &c.' (cf. p. 311). This FARA (or *Farra* in modern Italian toponymy) is generally linked in place-names with a family name, e.g. *Farra d'Alpago* (district of Belluno), *Farra di Soligo* (district of Treviso), *Fara di Gera d'Adda* (district of Bergamo), *Fara Vicentina* (district of Vicenza), *Fara Novarese* (district of Novara), *Fara in Sabina* (district of Perugia), *Fara filiorum Petri* (district of Chieti), &c. (see E. Gamillscheg, op. cit., vol. ii, p. 62). As elsewhere with the Goths, the latinized name of the Germanic tribe was commonly used by the Italo-Roman population to designate their settlements: thus *Longobardi* near Cosenza, *Massalombarda* near Ravenna, *Lombardore* (in a text of A.D. 1019 *Castello Langobardorum*) near Turin (op. cit., p. 69). Among Langobardic names referring to the nature of the land one of the most commonly encountered is BRAIDA 'plain', as in *Braida, Breda, Brera,* &c. While the density of these place-names is certainly at its greatest north of the River Po, they are also scattered throughout central Italy and occur sporadically as far south as the region of Benevento: a distribution entirely coinciding with the evidence of Langobardic occupation revealed by archaeological research.

In view of this widespread distribution it is impossible to draw a parallel between the influence of the Franks in France and that of the Langobards in Italy in determining future dialectal areas. Whereas in France the line of linguistic cleavage between French and Provençal is roughly identical with the southern limit of the original Frankish settlement, the somewhat similar division which exists between the dialects of continental Italy and those of the Peninsula in no way coincides with the geographical distribution of Langobardic dukedoms: this division, approximately marked by a line drawn from Spezia to Rimini, must have its origin in the earlier circumstances of Roman expansion.

*The Langobardic element in Italian.* Discounting words which have survived only in the dialects, one can still discover in literary Italian a number of words of Langobardic stock, though Old Italian does not bristle with them as does Old French with Frankish. In seeking them out we are confronted by the same difficulty as with Visigothic in Spain: that of distinguishing them from Germanic words incorporated into Vulgar Latin, and also from the Frankish overlay due to Carolingian expansion. Added to this is the complication arising from the earlier presence of Ostrogothic. When all the sifting has been done, there remain a number of words showing no obvious identity with the Gothic of Spain or with the Frankish of France, which did not pertain to the common Germanic stock, and which are to be found in Italy alone of the Romance-speaking countries. These, whether or no they be attested in the medieval Latin of the Langobards, can generally be assumed to derive from their speech.

Noticeably absent from the Langobardic contribution to Italian is the large body of terms associated with administration which figures so prominently among Frankish loan-words in French. This does not mean that the Langobards were no administrators. On the contrary, to them is primarily due the organization of communal life in northern and central Italy which led to the development of new urban centres side by side with the old Roman towns: a development which did not extend to the non-Langobardic south, where the Roman system of the LATIFUNDIUM (Ital. *latifondo*), involving the control of large estates by a landlord, often absent, has persisted to the present day, providing modern Italian politicians with the acute agrarian problems of that region. Into the legislation codified in Latin during the seventh century were incorporated, sometimes latinized and sometimes not, several purely Langobardic words of administrative flavour. Thus, in the *Edictus Rothari*: MUNDIUM, e.g. 'Si quis mundium de puella libera aut muliere habens eamque strigam . . . clamaverit', i.e. 'If anyone having the protection of a free girl or woman shall have called her a witch . . .', cf. Germ. *Vormund* 'guardian' and *Mündel*

'ward'; GAHAGIUM 'enclosure', cf. Germ. *Gehege*, cognate with
Frank. HAGA, Fr. *haie*; ARIMANNUS 'free man', and FAIDA (< FAHIDA,
cf. Germ. *Fehde*, Eng. *feud*) 'the right to pursue a vendetta'. Reproduced in un-latinized form are MORGINGAB, lit. 'morning gift',
the husband's addition to the dowry presented on the morning
after marriage, and various compounds of GILD 'money', e.g.
ACTOGILD, WIDREGILD (> Ital. *guidrigildo*), WERGILD or WIRGILD, in
which the first element is a Germanic form corresponding to Lat.
VIR, the meaning being 'money paid in compensation for the killing
of another man's serf' (the word survives with the sense of 'man' in
Eng. *werwolf*, i.e. 'man-wolf'), and LAUNEGILD or LAUNIGILD (> Ital.
*lonigildo*), where the reader will recognize the equivalent of Eng.
*loan*.[1] The majority of these terms, however, disappeared from
use, supplanted by borrowings from Frankish when Langobardic
law was suppressed in favour of the Salic Law of Charlemagne's
Empire.

The sphere of armament is likewise poorly represented in
Langobardic loan-words, and, although there is not the same
wealth of documentary evidence to support the suggestion, it may
be assumed that the Langobardic armoury suffered in its terminology a similar fate. Only one Langobardic name of a weapon
remains, that of the arrow, Ital. *strale* (< STRAL, cf. Germ. *Strahl*,
Anglo-Sax. *stræl*) and this is doubtless because, as we have previously had occasion to remark, the arrow pertained to the apparatus of hunting rather than to that of warfare.

Activities of the Langobards which remained unaffected by their
submission were naturally those of a domestic nature, and here
it will be found that loan-words, though considerably less numerous, fall into very much the same semantic categories as do the
non-military, non-administrative borrowings of Gallo-Romance
from the Franks. A few are associated with the pastoral scene, e.g.
*melma* 'mud' (< MELMA, cf. Gothic MALMA), and *tonfano* 'deep
hole in a stream' (< TUMPFILO, cf. Germ. *Tümpel* 'puddle'). A
few bird-names are included, e.g. Old Ital. *scriccio*, mod. *scricciolo*
'wren' (< SKRIKKJO), and *taccola* 'jackdaw' (< TAHHALA); *gazza*
'magpie', has also been claimed as Langobardic, though its
affiliations and possible connexions with Port. *gaio* and Fr. *jai*

---

[1] The corresponding expression in Frankish law was *widerlōn* 'payment',
which, through popular etymology and consonantal assimilation, was latinized
as WIDERDONUM; this word, which became in Old French *guerredon* 'reward',
also passed into Italian, through later legal texts, to give *guiderdone*.

'jay', remain doubtful (all may be cognate with Fr. *gai*, see p. 250). Ital. *zecca* 'sheep-tick', survives from Langob. ZEKKA, and invites comparison with Fr. *tique* from Frank. TICKA.

One kind of humble dwelling owes its name to Langobardic, the *stamberga* 'hut' from STAINBERGA, in which STAIN is 'stone' and BERGA the same verbal substantive as in Old Fr. *herberge* and mod. *auberge*. A further glimpse of phonetic variation in the Germanic dialects of the time is afforded by the Italian doublets *balco* and *palco*, which in early usage meant respectively 'hayloft' and 'plank'. Both were made international by the Italian architecture of the Renaissance, the former in its derivative *balcone*, cf. Fr. *balcon*, and the latter with the meaning 'box in the theatre', cf. Span. *palco*. The initial consonant here distinguishes a Langobardic PALK from a BALK which is probably Frankish or Gothic. The same consonantal alternance is to be found in Ital. *panca* 'bench', and *banco*, *banca*, cf. the BANK of the 'common Germanic stock' (see p. 207). Again, a Langob. PALLA gave Ital. *palla* 'ball', whereas Frank. BALLA became Fr. *balle*, a type which also appears in Italian as *balla*, *ballone*, &c. A primitive feather bed was presumably the object originally designated by *federa*, from Langob. FEDERA, cf. Germ. *Feder*, Eng. *feather*, though in modern Italian the word means 'ticking for the bed', 'pillow-case', a change which may be due to confusion with *fodera* 'lining', also Germanic in origin (cf. Frank. FODR, Germ. *Futter*, see p. 246). Of kindred Langobardic origin are the three words *zaina*, an ancient measure (< ZAINA), *zaino*, and *zana* (< ZANA), the two latter referring to different kinds of wicker baskets. The water used for washing clothes is in Italian *ranno*, from Langob. RANNO, a verbal substantive cognate with Germ. *rennen*, Eng. *to run*. It will be noted that most of these words have undergone little or no change in form since they were first adopted.

A variety of tool, in modern Italian found in the alternative forms *borino*, *burino*, and *bulino*, now specialized as the instrument used by the artist for engraving, derives from another Langobardic verbal substantive, BORO from BORŌN (cf. Germ. *bohren*, Eng. *to bore*); the word eventually passed into French as *burin*, into Spanish as *buril*.

In the gastronomic sphere we can discover only one word which may be due to the Langobards, viz. *fiadone*, a kind of honey-cake, derived from FLADO, but this was also Frankish, cf. Old Fr. *flaon*, mod. *flan*.

Names of parts of the body are prominent in the Langobardic contribution; as in the case of similar Frankish terms in French, they were probably applied more frequently to animals than to human beings. To this source Italian is indebted for *stinco* 'tibia' (< SKINKO, cf. Germ. *Schienbein*, Eng. *shin*); *schiena* 'back' (< SKINA, also Frankish); *strozza* 'throat' (< STROZZA); *guancia* 'cheek' (< WANKJA; the Gothic form WANGO, cf. Germ. *Wange*, is found in Provençal as *gango*); *zanna* 'boar's tusk' (< ZANN, cf. Germ. *Zahn*).

Designating originally the head-dress of the Langobards, which made them conspicuous among the other inhabitants of Italy, is the word *zazzera* (< ZAZERA), now applied generally to flowing locks. There is little evidence of further addition to dress and ornament: a Langob. SKAUZ (cf. Germ. *Schoß* 'lap') gave the dialectal word *scos* 'apron', used in Lombardy and Emilia, and also in southern Italy as *scosso*: and the Old Ital. *nusca* 'brooch', may have been taken over from Langob. NUSKA and thus owe nothing to the Frankish word which gave Old Fr. *nosche*.

Finally, a few verbs and adjectives of standard Italian are Langobardic. In the former category may be counted *strofinare* 'to rub' (< STRAUFINŌN, cf. Germ. *streifen*), *bisticciare* 'to quarrel' (< BISKIZZAN, cf. Germ. *bescheißen*, and for the meaning, Fr. *enmerder*), *scherzare* 'to jest' (< SKERZAN, cf. Germ. *scherzen*), and *bussare* 'to knock' (< BAUZZAN). Langob. KRINGAN (cf. Anglo-Sax. *cringan*, Eng. *to cringe*) produced an Old Ital. *gringolare*, which passed during the sixteenth century into French and survives there as *dégringoler*. Ital. *spiare* probably developed from Langob. SPEHŌN independently of Old Fr. *espier*, from the same verb in Frankish. The few adjectives which have found general acceptance in Italian are mostly of the kind applicable to the person, e.g. *gramo* 'sorrowful' (< GRAM), probably separate from Frankish; *lesto* 'agile' (< LIST, cf. Eng. *listless*), later borrowed into French as *leste*; *lonzo* 'weak' (< LUNZ); the dialectal *tecchio* 'big' (< THICKI, cf. Germ. *dick*, Eng. *thick*); and *guercio* 'squinting' (< DWERH).

In concluding this selection of words which have been incorporated into the national language we should perhaps emphasize that they represent only a fraction of the number of Langobardic forms still in use in the various dialects of Italy. The sum total has been estimated at nearly 300.

*Norsemen.* There is a postscript to the story of Germanic invasions. Towards the end of the eighth century, when East German and West German tribes had long since ceased their wandering, the seafaring North Germans fell prey to the migratory urge. Coming to England as the Danes—who, together with the Swedes, speak the eastern variety of Norse—they occupied in the first half of the ninth century the greater part of the country until they were halted by the Anglo-Saxon population under the leadership of King Alfred. By the Treaty of Chippenham the land was then divided, the Danes receiving the London area and all that lay north and east of Watling Street, the so-called Danelaw. Meanwhile, the West Norsemen, from Norway, pursued their conquests along the Atlantic route, occupying the Faroes, the Hebrides, and parts of Ireland. In A.D. 874 they made their settlement in Iceland, whence, in the tenth century, long before Columbus, they almost certainly became the first Europeans to set foot in America.

From our Romance standpoint the chief interest of these latter-day North German migrations is that they brought the East Norsemen to France. During the ninth century they made repeated landings on the coast from the Scheldt to the Garonne and carried their raids far inland. The decadent successors of Charlemagne were unable to repel them decisively, and though on occasions the Norsemen were met and defeated—most notably by Louis III at Saucourt in A.D. 881—just as in England they always came back. Faced with this Norse problem, the French King Charles the Simple in A.D. 911 adopted the English solution on a smaller scale, offering to cede to the Norse chief Rollo (Hrolf) the town of Rouen and the lower valley of the Seine, with the hand of his daughter Gisela as a further inducement. After some demur Rollo accepted and the bargain was concluded by the Treaty of Clair-sur-Ept. Rollo thereafter settled down to live as a landed French duke, kept his promise to be baptized, and loyally supplied Charles with Danish levies when so required. As the arrangement became known, Danish bands from other coastal areas of France drifted in to join Rollo's followers and were allowed to settle. After the example of their chief, most of these Norsemen rapidly embraced Christianity, and with it, native wives. Within a few generations their heirs had adopted the Gallo-Roman speech.

The adj. *normand* and the name of Normandy are their most obvious contribution to Romance, but they have also left their mark in a number of terms connected with the sea. First and fore-most in common usage is the word *vague*, from Norse VAGR (cf. Anglo-Sax. *wæg*, modified by *wafian* 'to waver', to produce Eng. *wave*), which has largely replaced Fr. *onde* from Lat. UNDA, cf. Prov. Span. Port. Ital. *onda*. The 'creek' became *crique* in French from Norse KRIKI. To Old French they gave the names of certain small boats, but these disappeared with changes in naval design, so that the Norse terminology survives only in the names of parts of the boat, e.g. *tillac* (< THILJA), *bitte* (< BITA), *hune* (< HUNN), *étrave* (< STAFN), *étambot* (< STAFNBORDH), *guindas* (< VINDASS, cf. Eng. *windlass*). At least three Norse verbs survive in French: *cingler* 'to sail', in Old Fr. *sigler* (< SIGLA, cf. Germ. *segeln*), *équiper* (< SKIPA, cf. Eng. *skiff* and *ship*), whence the verbal substantive *équipe*, and *guinder* 'to hoist' (< VINDA), now a favourite word of literary criticism in the expression *un style guindé*, i.e. a 'stilted' style. The *décor* may be suitably completed with 'sea-weed', Fr. *varech* (< WRAEC) and a few fish-names: *marsouin* 'porpoise' (< MARSWIN, lit. 'sea-pig'), *turbot* (< TÖRNBUT), and *hommard* (< HUMARR, cf. Germ. *Hummer*).

Many place-names in Normandy recall the Norse settlers, e.g. *Le Torp* (< THORP 'village', as in English place-names of Danish origin: *Osgathorpe, Oakthorpe, Donisthorpe*, &c.); *Bolbec, Caude-bec*, the *bec* of which is identical with Eng. *beck* 'stream'; *Yvetot, Bonnetot, Lilletot, Tournetot*, where *tot* derives from TOFT 'hut', as in Eng. *Lowestoft*. Some contain the name of the Norse land-owner linked with the Lat. VILLA, e.g. *Trouville* (< THOROLF-VILLA), *Canouville* (< KNUTR-VILLA), *Carville* (< KARI-VILLA).

Descendants of the Norsemen thus wedded to the soil of Roma-nia were to become during the eleventh century the foremost pro-pagators of the newly emerging French language and civilization. Intrepid both as sailors and as soldiers, they conquered Britain, which thus for the second time in its history just failed to become a Romance-speaking country, and in a very different direction they expelled the Muslims from southern Italy and Sicily, creating there another Norman kingdom rich in historical consequence.

### SLAVONIC INVASIONS

'Invasion' is perhaps scarcely the correct word to describe the process whereby Slavonic dispossessed Romance in the Balkans. It was more in the nature of a continual infiltration. Very primitive, and with much less social organization than the Germans, Slavonic tribes during Roman times had drifted westwards and southwards gradually constituting the two groups of the West Slavs (later Poles, Czechs, Slovaks, and the Sorabians of the upper valley of the R. Spree) and South Slavs (later Serbs, Croats, and Slovenes). It was as the result of another oriental invasion, that of the Avars, that the South Slavs were either pushed or carried south of the Danube.

The Avars were an Altaian tribe, close kindred of the Turks. Pressure of the latter, then rulers of an empire extending from China to the Black Sea, the Turkestan now divided between China and Russia, had driven them westwards. In A.D. 558 they were north of the Black Sea, and by A.D. 565 had moved on into the Carpathians, whence they descended into the plains of Pannonia, the future Hungary. It was at this point that they came into collision with the Germanic Gepidae and Langobards (see p. 257). The Gepidae defeated and the Langobards persuaded to undertake their Italian enterprise, the Avars remained masters of Pannonia and the lower Danube valley. By this time the local population north of the river was predominantly Slav, and the Slavs, apart from small groups which had already sought refuge on the southern bank, now became the serfs of the Avars.

The year A.D. 565 is that of the death of Justinian. The Byzantine Empire had reached the full extent of its power and its northern frontier still lay on the Danube. In Byzantine counsels there had even been talk of bridging the river and reclaiming the lost Roman province of Dacia, a fact which lends colour to the suggestion that descendants of the Roman colonists still lived there (see p. 482). But scarcely had the nephew and successor of Justinian, Justin II, a ruler of doubtful sanity, ascended the eastern throne when he began to lose all the territory which under the reign of his uncle had been so arduously reconquered. To the east he became involved in a war with Persia which was to last for twenty years (A.D. 572–92). The Avars, having left Italy to the Langobards, now found the Byzantine Empire sufficiently weakened to invite their marauding enterprise. In A.D. 580 they laid siege to the frontier town of Sirmium, and after two years it was yielded up to them by Tiberius II, the successor of Justin. In the meantime they had been able to by-pass the beleaguered town and plunder at will through the neighbouring Balkan lands. On these expeditions they were accompanied by large bands of Slav retainers.

Temporarily checked by the next emperor, Maurice, the Avars, like the Persians in the eastern and southern territories of Byzantium, seized the opportunity to renew their assaults during the confusion which followed upon the murder of Maurice and his replacement by the usurper Phocas. Being themselves of limited numbers, they were on this occasion accompanied by greatly augmented hordes of Slavs and also found allies among the Bulgarians, then dwelling to the north of the Danube delta. In A.D. 617 the combined forces almost captured Byzantium, but the citadel held out. When they withdrew, large numbers of Byzantine captives were carried off beyond the Danube and large numbers of Slavs remained in the Balkan lands. The year A.D. 626 witnessed another siege of Byzantium by the Avars, their last attempt to reduce the eastern capital; but this time the siege was called off after eleven days, apparently on account of rebellion among the Bulgarian and Slav allies, the latter no longer so submissive to the will of the Avar Khagans as they had been in the past.

The Avars then withdrew to their Pannonian home, but once again large numbers of Slavs elected to remain south of the Danube, where the former predominantly Romance-speaking population had considerably declined and much of the land must have been quite deserted. From this time we can identify the settlement of Serbs and Croats in the ancient Illyricum. Their fellow participants in the assaults on Byzantium, the Bulgarians, in A.D. 679 recrossed the Danube from the north and made a permanent settlement in the former Moesia. Originally they were a Hunnish tribe, which during the reign of the Emperor Zeno (see p. 226) had migrated from the Volga region to take up an abode along the shores of the Black Sea, between the Dnieper and the Danube. Mingling with the more numerous Slavs, whom they too at first employed as serfs, they gradually adopted Slavonic speech. By the ninth century they constituted a powerful state, which seems to have furthered the spread of Slavonic at the expense of Romance. The same ninth century saw the bringing of Christianity to all these newly established populations: for purposes of evangelization St. Cyril and St. Methodius translated the Scriptures into the Slavonic speech of their native region. As Church Slavonic (or Old Bulgarian) this became the recognized medium of religion wherever Slavonic-speaking peoples were subsequently converted to Greek Orthodoxy: and so began Slavonic literature.

Meanwhile, in Pannonia, the Avars had had the misfortune to become neighbours of Charlemagne; having finally defeated the Saxons and occupied Germany, during the years A.D. 795–6 he overran and obliterated their kingdom. Its western part, the modern Carinthia, was rapidly germanized, and the Slavs to the east now became vassals in the new Empire of the Occident. Just a century later, in A.D. 896, the much-occupied land of Hungary was settled by yet another tribe of nomads migrating from Asia, the Magyars, called in by Arnulf of Germany from their resting-place on the northern shores of the Black Sea to assist him in his wars against the Slavs of Moravia. For a while they were to be another 'scourge', carrying out widespread raids into Italy, Germany, and Provence, until in A.D. 955 they were defeated at the battle of the River Lech by Otto the Great of Germany. By this time they too had become mingled with the local Slavs, who throughout this period of difficult survival seem always to have compensated in numbers for what they may have lacked in leadership. Many were sold by Otto into captivity, and from this event, as is generally believed, dates the identification of the word 'Slav' with 'slave'. Germanized as SKLAVE, latinized as SCLAVUS, it was borrowed into the Romance languages to give Ital. *schiavo*, Fr. *esclave*, Span. *esclavo*, Port. *escravo*; its Venetian form has been adopted into current Italian as *ciao*, lit. '(I am your) slave'. The bulk of the Magyar people, however, escaped the fate of the Avars and remained to form the nucleus of modern Hungary, where their language, cognate with Finnish and Esthonian, is still preserved as Hungarian. In the year A.D. 1000, under their king Stephen, they were converted to Christianity; later they are to be found playing a leading part in the European struggle to repel Turkish invasion.

Among all this Balkan medley it is most difficult to discover any trace of the Romance-speaking people in whom we are primarily interested. Yet they must have been there. Two seventh-century chroniclers, writing in Greek and both repeating the same original text, mention a soldier in the Byzantine army who said in his native tongue: *Torna, torna, fratre*. This phrase, related to an event which occurred during a campaign in Thrace in A.D. 587, is claimed to be the earliest sample of Balkan Romance. Thereafter in the history of Rumanian comes a blank of a thousand years. The Vlachs are occasionally mentioned in texts of the ninth and tenth centuries, some located as shepherds in the region of Epirus, the present habitat of the Arumanians (see p. 483). These are the people whom we know to have been Romance-speaking: the term *Vlach* was adapted by the Slavs from German and used to designate 'Romans'.[1] It is indeed surprising that there should be so little evidence of the fate of Romance in the province of Illyricum, held for so long by Rome, and no less surprising that its present persistence should be chiefly in the territory of Dacia, the last province to be occupied and the first to be abandoned. The present eighteen million speakers of Balkan Romance presuppose a fairly considerable Romance-speaking ancestry (see also pp. 481–5).

Late in the sixteenth century Rumanian at last appeared, in texts of a purely religious character. During the following century it was officially recognized in Wallachia as the language of the local Church and used in place of Church Slavonic. As is to be expected, the Romance language which thus emerged from obscurity is penetrated with Slav elements. The Germanic so prominent in the Romance of the west is almost entirely absent: a few words have been attributed to Gothic, but the attribution is in most cases doubtful. The process of Slavonic penetration must have been fairly continuous, and although the words thus absorbed come from different dialects, for the most part they belong to the South Slavonic group. It has been estimated that some two-fifths of the Rumanian vocabulary, as found in a dictionary, derives from Slavonic sources. But the grammar of Rumanian is entirely

---

[1] As *uualha* the term is so used in the Glossary of Kassel (see p. 319). At an earlier date it had been applied by the Germans to the Celts. This seems to have been due to a generalization of the name of the Volcae, a Celtic tribe who became the nearest neighbours of the Germans to the west (cf. the French generalization of the name of the *Alamanni*, to give *allemand*). Anglo-Saxon invaders brought the term to Britain: hence *Wales*, *Welsh*, and *Cornwall*. The name of *Gaule* also implies the influence of a Frank. WALHA, for Lat. GALLIA would normally have evolved to *\*Jaille*. When the Celts of Gaul had become identified with the Romans the term was applied by the Germans to the latter, and extended to all the Latin-speaking inhabitants of the Empire. It persists to this day in the German adjective *welsch*, used of the neo-Latin peoples with the derogatory sense already suggested by the Kassel Glossary, cf. *welsche Treue*. Another survival in western Europe is to be found in the name of the Walloons which derives from the *Waalsch* used by the Germanic tribes of the Rhine delta to designate the Romance-speaking people inhabiting what is now southern Belgium (see p. 233); yet again the term occurs in *Chur-wälsch* (see p. 479).

The ramifications of the word extended from German, with the later sense, through eastern Europe. It was not only used by the southern Slavs, as *Vlach* (Germ. *Wallach*), but also passed into western Slavonic: in modern Polish 'Italy' is *Wlochy* and 'Italian' is *Wloch* (cf. C. Tagliavini, *Le origini delle lingue neo-latine*, p. 124, note).

Romance (a few possible influences of Slavonic on morphological evolution have been mentioned in Chapter I); so too are most of the basic words of everyday speech. The effect of the infiltration of Slavonic has been to enrich the language, as Gallo-Romance was enriched by Frankish and Anglo-Saxon by Norman French, with a host of terms of near-synonymous character, thereby enlarging with subtle gradations the means of expression within any given semantic field. As an illustration we might perhaps quote from Grigore Nandris[1] the following comparison of Romance and Slavonic elements in the terminology of life and sustenance:

Of Latin origin: *viață* 'life'; *a viețui* 'to live'; *viețuitor* 'living'; *a mînca* 'to eat'; *merinde* 'provisions', 'food'; *a merinda* 'to rest', 'to eat'; *vipt* 'food'; *frupt* 'food not allowed in Lent'; *prînz* 'lunch'; *cină* 'dinner'; *a gusta* 'to taste'; *gustare* 'snack'; *a ajuna* 'to fast (in Lent)'; *ajun* 'Lent', 'eve'; *sec* 'food allowed in Lent', 'dry'; *foame* 'hunger'; *flămînd* 'hungry'; *comînd* 'funeral repast'.

Of Slavonic origin: *a trăi* 'to live'; *trai* 'life'; *trainic* 'durable'; *a se hrăni* 'to feed oneself'; *hrană* 'food'; *otravă* 'poison (food)'; *a otrăvi* 'to poison'; *post* 'Lent'; *a posti* 'to fast in Lent'; *pomană* 'funeral repast', 'commemoration'.

To the Romance philologist, whereas the Slavonic words in this selection sound no echo, those of Latin origin are familiar acquaintances, met long since in Spain and Italy, e.g. Span. *merienda*, Ital. *merenda* (< MERENDA); Ital. *pranzo* (< PRANDIUM); Span. Ital. *cena* (< CĒNA); Span. *gustar*, Ital. *gustare* (< GUSTARE); Span. *ayunar*, Ital. *(di)giunare* (< JEJUNARE; in Plautus, JAJUNARE). One cannot cease to wonder at the extraordinary tenacity of this Vulgar Latin of the east, so faithfully maintained by a people virtually lost to history and bereft of all that support of a Latin literary tradition which in the west counted for so much.

## ARABIC INVASIONS

*The rise of Islam.* During the times of the Roman Empire the Arabs dwelt in the traditional site of the kingdom of Sheba, along the eastern shores of the Red Sea. Like the Slavs, they were destined to be among the leading beneficiaries of Roman decline. Theirs was a more conscious and deliberate expansion, provoked perhaps in the first instance by the increasing infertility of their

[1] G. Nandris, 'The Development and Structure of Rumanian', *The Slavonic and East European Review*, vol. xxx (1951), pp. 7–39.

land but drawing its strength from the new religion preached by Mahomet.[1]

According to Arabic sources Mahomet (b. *c.* A.D. 570) was a trader in Mecca, a contemplative who espoused the doctrine of monotheism, together with belief in a future life, in which conduct on earth is punished or rewarded. In this he was undoubtedly influenced by Jewish and Christian teaching. After meeting with little recognition in his native town, he attracted to his faith a number of citizens of Yaṭrib, the later Medina, whither he migrated in A.D. 622. Being a person of some worldly consequence he was soon able to turn these few into a large following and within a short time he became the temporal lord of Yaṭrib. He then led an army against the 'infidels' of Mecca and in A.D. 630 took possession of that city, forcibly converting his fellow townsmen to 'Islam', i.e. 'surrender (to God)'; the followers of Mahomet were thereafter known as 'Muslims', or 'self-surrenderers'. Master of the whole territory, with a considerable army at his disposal, he seems to have been already planning a further expansion when he died in A.D. 632. The Muslims then elected his father-in-law, 'Abū-Bakr, as his 'representative', or 'Caliph', and it was he who consolidated the territorial gains of Mahomet, completing the unification of Arabia.

A new power thus suddenly appeared in the east, inevitably to engage in hostilities with the already existing powers of that area, Persia and Byzantium. The clash with the latter came quickly. In A.D. 634 Muslims and Byzantines met in battle at 'Aǧnādain, in Judaea, and the Muslims, under their general Ḥālid, were completely victorious. The next Caliph, 'Umar, continued the policy of conquest, and in A.D. 636 Ḥālid won another victory over a Byzantine army in the valley of the Yarmūk, beyond Jordan. Two years later Jerusalem fell to the Muslims; thence they were able to extend their control over all of modern Syria and Palestine. From Syria one branch of the army turned north-east to overrun the Byzantine territory of Mesopotamia. Then came the turn of Persia, weakened by its prolonged wars against Byzantium; after a stubborn resistance it finally succumbed in A.D. 652 and its ancient monarchy disappeared. Meanwhile, another of 'Umar's

---

[1] With the exception of the anglicized 'Mahomet' for 'Muḥammad', we have adapted the spelling of Arabic proper names, from whatever source they may have been taken, to the system of transcription used by the *Société asiatique* (see below, p. 280, note).

successful generals, 'Amr, had proceeded westwards from Palestine
to the Nile delta, where the Egyptian Babylon capitulated to him
in A.D. 641 and Alexandria, the chief stronghold of Byzantine
civilization in Egypt, in the following year. A new Muslim capital
was founded at Fusṭāṭ, near Babylon.

From Egypt the Muslims were soon pressing on along the north
African coast, driving out the Byzantines, subduing and converting
to Islam the native Berbers. Before Carthage the Byzantines held
them in check for some thirty years, but in A.D. 697 the city fell,
and the Emirate of Qairawān was founded in the former Roman
province of Africa, to be the point of departure, in the ninth century, for the Arab occupation of Sicily. By A.D. 708 the rule of
the Caliph had extended still farther westwards to include the
modern Algeria and Morocco, the Roman Mauritania, where the
population remained predominantly Berber, but was easily assimilated to the then relatively low cultural standards of the Arabs
and to the Muslim religion. Those Europeans who could withdrew to Europe before the tide of conquest, so complete in its
effects that the Roman and Byzantine culture of the previous 700
years, with its towns and civic government, vanished as though
it had never existed, leaving only ruins in the sand, those of Leptis
Magna and Sabratha among them, for the interest of the archaeo-
logist.

The assault on the Byzantine Empire had in the meantime continued in the east. Taking to the sea, Muslims occupied the island
of Rhodes and landed in Thrace, whence they made repeated
attempts, between the years A.D. 668 and 677, to take Byzantium
itself by storm. The discovery by a Syrian architect, Callinicus,
of the famous Greek fire, foreshadowing modern fire-arms, seems
to have played a decisive part in enabling the Byzantines to repel
them. Eventually, however, it was civil war among the Muslims
that gave Byzantium a respite.

A renewal of hostilities came with the following century. The
Muslim Empire having again been consolidated by the Caliph
Walīd I (ruled A.D. 705–15), his successor Sulaimān spent his brief
rule of two years in violent assaults upon the eastern capital. But
this time the Byzantines were fully prepared to meet them. Two
Muslim fleets in succession were destroyed by Greek fire: on the
second occasion a Muslim army, having lost all its supplies with
the fleet, was routed by a force of Bulgarians summoned to the

help of Byzantium. The next Caliph, 'Umar II, in A.D. 719 ordered a retreat. The threat of an Arabic advance into Europe from the east was thus averted, but most of the Christian Byzantine lands in Asia and in Africa had been lost to the new oriental faith, with its headquarters at near-by Damascus.

The vast Muslim Empire was not destined to endure for long as a single political force. Already in the mid-eighth century, the Persians, although converts to the new religion, which itself was assuming different forms in different regions, revolted against the Umaiyad dynasty in Damascus and defeated the Caliph, Mar-wān II. The seat of the Caliphate was thereafter removed to Baghdad and the supremacy of the Arabs declined.

*The Muslims in Spain.* At the western outlet of the Mediter-ranean the Muslim advance continued unchecked into Spain. In A.D. 711 an Arab general, Ṭāriq, landed with a small force of Ber-bers at the foot of the rock known as Caspe, since that time as Gibraltar, 'the mount (Ar. *ǧabal*) of Ṭāriq'. The Visigoths under their king Roderick, 'the last of the Goths', were met and defeated in battle near Jerez (Jerez de la Frontera, so-called because during the last centuries of occupation it stood on the boundary between Christian and Muslim states). Roderick was killed in the fight, the towns of Córdoba and Sevilla were quickly taken, and the advance proceeded northward as far as Toledo. The Muslim generalissimo Mūsā ibn Nuṣayr then came over from Africa to take charge, and by A.D. 718 the whole of the country, with the exception of the Cantabro-Pyrenean chain, had become a new dependency of Islam.

Such was the impetus of the invaders that within a few more years they had passed beyond the eastern Pyrenees to occupy the former province of Septimania, the modern Languedoc, extending to the Rhône. Thence, in A.D. 732, under the command of a new Arab governor of Spain, 'Abd-ar-Raḥmān (a different person from 'Abd-ar-Raḥmān I, see below), they traversed Aquitaine and ad-vanced north towards Tours. In the neighbourhood of Poitiers Muslims met Franks for the first time in battle. The result was a decisive victory for the Franks, led by Charles Martel, then the 'strong man' of France. With this reverse all Muslim hopes of a conquest of France were brought to an end: as the successful defence of Byzantium in A.D. 717 had checked the progress of Islam in the east, so now, in A.D. 732, it was contained in the west.

The Muslims withdrew to Septimania, whence they were later evicted by Pépin, son of Charles Martel and first king of the Carolingian dynasty (see p. 259). It was left to Charlemagne to carry the war into Spain and to establish as part of his Empire the Spanish March, a border country which for a long while became the scene of sporadic raids and fierce fighting. The memory of these events provided the motive for a whole cycle of poems in the Old French epic.

The ease with which the Muslims occupied Spain was due, as we have already inferred, to the aloofness of the Visigoths. They had still not blended with the Hispano-Roman population, which could thus regard with indifference what was a mere change of masters. Moreover, the many Jews who had settled in Baetica in Roman times probably welcomed the advent of the Muslims as a form of liberation. Under the Visigothic kings of the seventh century, ultra-zealous Catholics after their conversion from Arianism (see p. 220), they had become an object of persecution. Under the new régime they were destined to prosper, developing the high standard of culture to which the Hebrew literature of the region bears ample witness (see p. 401), until the end of the eleventh century when the deterioration of Muslim rule in the south drove them to the Christian north.

Muslim rule until that time was in fact remarkably tolerant. Christianity was not actively suppressed unless it assumed the form of political sedition. Manifestations of Christian resistance did at times occur, the most notable being that of the so-called Cordobese martyrs, led by St. Eulogius and Alvarus of Córdoba, but zeal in seeking martyrdom led to their rapid extinction. It is important to remember that both Arabic leaders and Berber followers came to Spain without women. Thus from the first there was produced a mixed stock from Muslim Arabic-speaking males and Christian Romance-speaking females, for which, incidentally, the son of Mūsā set a high-class precedent by marrying the widow of the defeated Roderick. There were probably other Visigothic widows available: not all escaped to the north. To the feminine element in the racial melting-pot may be attributed the persistence both of Christian religion and of Romance speech. That the latter did not die out, as philologists once supposed, has for long been apparent from the many references made to it in Arabic and Hebrew texts; its vitality has now been confirmed by the discovery and deciphering of Romance tail-pieces appended to Arabic and Hebrew poems (see p. 401). To the Arabs of Spain it was known as *latīnī*, with the suffix found in other Spanish words borrowed from Arabic (e.g. *jabalí* 'wild boar'); in more literary Arabic it was '*aǧamī*; since the local population living under Arabic rule acquired the designation of *mozárabes*, from a word meaning 'arabized', it is now called 'Mozarabic'. The chief linguistic casualty was literary Latin, which suffered a complete eclipse: in A.D. 1049 even the canons of the Christian Church were rendered into Arabic for their preservation. Thus bereft of the backing of literary prestige, Mozarabic tended to sink to the status of a popular jargon. It is perhaps simply in this association with the lower classes that one should seek the origin of the semantic development of Span. *ladino* to mean 'sly', 'roguish', though the supposed propensity for knavery of people who use more than one language has also been invoked in explanation. Most of the Mozarabic population must in fact have been bilingual, and this bilingualism served as a medium through which Arabic words could readily be incorporated into Romance, and through which the foreign sounds of those words were adapted to the Romance sound-system, which shows no tangible influence of the very different system of Arabic.

The civilization of Arabic Spain became within a short time remarkably advanced, comprising all the refinement which the Arabs had learnt from contact with Persian and Byzantine culture, a debt which we shall find fully reflected in the Arabic loan-words in Spanish. It was founded largely by the Umaiyad dynasty. The first ruler of this dynasty in the west came in A.D. 755 as a fugitive to Spain, raising there the standard of revolt after the downfall of his family in the east, when the Caliphate was transferred from Damascus to Baghdad. Quickly and ruthlessly he made himself master of the country, and as 'Abd-ar-Raḥmān I, he founded the Emirate of Córdoba, Muslim in character but politically independent.

The Christian states of the extreme north—León in the west, Navarre in the centre, and the Spanish March controlled by the Franks in the east—were able to recover during the ninth century some of the lost territory, but thereafter they were again thrown on the defensive by the greatest of the Umaiyads, 'Abd-ar-Raḥmān III (A.D. 912–61), under whose reign, while anarchy prevailed elsewhere in Europe, Córdoba attained its highest splendour. When in the eleventh century the Christian advance was resumed, it was with different leading states. León had become subordinate to Castile; Navarre, linked at times with Castile and at times with Aragon, had dwindled in importance; and Aragon was beginning to emerge as a new force. In the events of the reconquest which these states achieved lies the whole story of the political configuration of the Iberian Peninsula, and the cause of the ultimate crystallization of its Hispano-Romance into three different Romance languages (see pp. 398-9, 427-8, 436-7).

No part of the Peninsula remained quite unaffected by the influence of Arabic invasion. It even reached the court of León, to judge by the large number of Arabisms in the Latin documents of that court; Castile was rather more refractory. Aragon was heavily settled by *moros* (< Lat. MAUROS), as the newcomers came to be known on account of their identification with Mauritania. With its centre at Saragossa, this settlement extended its frontier to the foothills of the Pyrenees, to a line north of Huesca and Barbastro, the latter a scene of much fighting (cf. the Old French epic *Le siège de Barbastre*). The small town of Jaca, first nucleus of Aragon, which guards the approach to the Somport, shows, on the other hand, no trace of Moorish habitation. It seems highly probable that the formerly scant population of the upper Pyrenean valleys was considerably augmented by an influx of Christian refugees, unwilling to live under the alien faith. The resistance movement thus created sought bonds of alliance to the north, laying the foundations of a loosely-knit confederacy of Pyrenean states which promised during the later Middle Ages to evolve into a semblance of Switzerland, a situation still clearly reflected in the local mountain patois.

As the Moors were driven southwards they left in the reconquered cities a population scarcely less mixed than that of Andalusia. This is well illustrated by the Christian codes of law, which, drawn up in Latin, from the twelfth century onwards were adapted into Romance (see p. 412). For example, the thirteenth-century *Fuero de Teruel*[1]—Teruel was recovered for the Kingdom of Aragon by Alfonso II (reigned A.D. 1162-96)—deals at length with legislation for Christians, Moors, and Jews. In matters involving life and property all were entitled to equitable treatment, but there were social discriminations: thus Moors and Jews were allowed

[1] Ed. Max Gorosch, *Leges Hispanicae Medii Aevi*, No. 1, Stockholm, 1950.

to use the public baths only on Fridays, whereas Christians could bath on any other day of the week, with the sole restriction that on Sundays, 'for the reverence of our Lord', the bath must be cold. Since Christians were presumably the most numerous, the interdiction is perhaps less severe than it at first appears. Indeed, it represents a degree of tolerance that was not destined to last.

*The Arabic element in Hispano-Romance.* The contribution of Arabic to the Romance of Spain is much greater than that of the Visigoths and almost comparable in its extent with the Frankish impact on Gallo-Romance. Like the latter, it is predominantly a lexical influence: there is no appreciable trace of Arabic in the grammar of Hispano-Romance, or in its phonemic system. Yet in estimating its importance one should not overlook the fact that the borrowed lexicon contained words of quite different accentual pattern from that which western Romance had by this time established (see p. 42). Whereas the French have always adapted words from foreign sources to their own traditional rhythm, the Mozarabs of Spain showed a remarkable capacity for assimilating Arabic complete with the Arabic accent. The simple word-pattern inherited from Vulgar Latin, characterized by the paroxytone ending in a vowel (*bueno, digo,* &c.) thus underwent a revolutionary change. The number of oxytones was greatly augmented, and it included many with vocalic ending, e.g. *algodón, arrayán, azafrán, alguacil, marfil, albalá, jabalí, alfolí.* A new range of paroxytones was created, ending in a consonant, e.g. *almíbar, almófar, azúcar,* and proparoxytones, which the Vulgar Latin of the west had eliminated, again became a commonplace, e.g. *acémila, albérchiga, alcándara.* Nor were the Mozarabs in any way daunted by their previous lack of familiarity with the polysyllabic word, cf. *alcachofa, albaricoque, guadamacil, Guadalajara.* These 'mouthfuls' were destined, moreover, to set precedents; thereafter the Latin 'learned' word could similarly be digested whole: EXERCITUM, for example, could be hispanicized as *ejército.* Hispano-Romance thus emerged from Arabic occupation with a much greater diversity of rhythm and of rhythmic potential.[1] It would probably be true to say that in this respect Spanish, of all Romance languages, is the one which most closely resembles English—a strange consequence to be due to the Arabs!

[1] Cf. Y. Malkiel, in a review of the second edition of R. Lapesa, *Historia de la lengua española* (Romance Philology, vol. vi, no. 1, pp. 62–63).

The total number of words of Arabic origin in Spanish, including those which came through Arabic from other sources, has been estimated at the high figure of 4,000. Many of these, however, have now fallen out of use, or linger on only as recognized 'archaisms'. Since Arabic words usually end in a consonant, contrary to the habits of early Romance speech, such borrowings were adapted with the addition of a final vowel, *a*, *e*, or *o*, or in a few instances by changing the final consonant to one more acceptable to the Spanish ear, as from *b* to *d*; inversely, the Romance words of Mozarabic when incorporated into Arabic texts frequently show loss of the final vowel, e.g. *būn* for *bueno*, *ešt* for *este*, &c. Another peculiarity of these borrowings is that most of them, unless taken directly from literary sources, were incorporated together with the Arabic article *al*, of which the *l* was already in Arabic regularly assimilated to the initial consonant of the following noun when that consonant was one of the series *d*, *t*, *ḏ*, *ṭ*, *ḍ*, *ṯ*, *ẓ*, *n*, *r*, *l*, *z*, *s*, *ṣ*, *š*, and sometimes *ž* (< *ǧ*). The failure of a Romance-speaking people to recognize the article as a separate grammatical entity may be due in part to these various assimilations, but it is probably also to be explained by the fact that the general body of *moros* were, as the name implies, Mauritanian Berbers but recently arabized. Berber speeches have no definite article: in consequence, the innumerable Arabic loan-words in present-day Berber were taken over, almost without exception, with the article attached. The agglutinated article thus came into Romance as a characteristic feature of berberized Arabic. The lesser proportion of Arabic words adopted into current Mozarabic without the article may be assumed to have reached the people more directly from the genuinely Arab overlords.

Like the Frankish words in French, the examples quoted below fall readily into certain semantic categories; except in a few instances, we have refrained from giving Arabic etyma,[1] which,

---

[1] Transcription from Arabic gives rise to some difficulty. This is due both to the wide divergence that has long existed between written (Classical) and colloquial forms, and to the fact that the so-called Arabic 'alphabet' is a kind of syllabary in which, as a rule, consonants only are written. The three vowel-units of Classical Arabic are only regularly represented when associated with length. Any given consonant has the potential of one of the three or of zero-vowel, and familiarity with the grammar and vocabulary is necessary before the correct vowel or zero can be ascribed unhesitatingly to the consonant-letters of the text.

In addition to its three vowels (*a*, *i*, and *u*), Classical Arabic comprises twenty-eight consonants. In order to represent these, various systems of transcription have been devised. The one used in the text is that of the *Société*

unlike Germanic, could evoke no association for the great majority of English readers.

The Arabic contribution to the Spanish vocabulary is particularly noteworthy for its emphasis on the arts of peace. In the absence of any other source of information, it alone would suffice to demonstrate the refinement of Arabic civilization, beside which that of the Germanic invaders appears crude and materialistic. Coming from the east, with which they remained in contact, the Arabs absorbed much of the splendour of eastern courts and much of the learning of Greek schools, such as that of Alexandria; in consequence, many of the words which they have left in Spanish were originally Arabic borrowings from Sanskrit, Persian, Greek, and sometimes from Latin.

In their traditional existence the water-course was of paramount importance, more so than in countries which are deluged with rain, and thus the Arabic *wādī* occurs repeatedly in the river-names of the southern part of Spain: the Roman *Baetis* became the *Guadalquivir* 'big river'; in some instances a previous name was incorporated with *wādī*, as when the River Anas became the *Guadiana* and the River Lethe the *Guadalete*; other names show simply *wādī* with an appropriate epithet, e.g. *Guadasuar* 'the black river', *Guadalaviar* 'the white river', *Guadalajara* 'the stony river',

asiatique, which employs the consonants of the Latin alphabet, augmented by diacritic signs, as follows:

m (bilabial nasal), b (voiced bilabial plosive);
f (voiceless labio-dental fricative);
d (voiced dento-alveolar plosive), t (voiceless dento-alveolar plosive);
ḍ (voiced dental 'emphatic' or 'velarized' plosive);
ṭ (voiceless dental 'emphatic' or 'velarized' plosive);
ḏ (voiced interdental fricative), ṯ (voiceless interdental fricative);
ẓ (voiced interdental 'emphatic' or 'velarized' fricative);
n (alveolar nasal), r (alveolar trill), l (alveolar lateral);
z (voiced sibilant), s (voiceless sibilant);
ṣ (voiceless 'emphatic' or 'velarized' sibilant);
š (voiceless palato-alveolar fricative);
ǧ (voiced palato-alveolar affricate);
k (voiceless velar plosive), q (voiceless uvular plosive);
ġ (voiced uvular fricative), ḫ (voiceless uvular fricative);
‘ (voiced pharyngal fricative), ḥ (voiceless pharyngal fricative);
h (glottal fricative), ’ (glottal plosive);
w (labio-velar semi-vowel), y (palatal semi-vowel).

In some philological works the vowel *e* will be found to occur in transcriptions from Arabic, e.g. *Medina*. This is because many colloquial forms of Arabic, including no doubt the dialects previously used in Spain, akin to those of present-day Morocco, include an intermediate vowel-sound which Europeans have identified with *e*, and which may correspond to any one of the three vowels of Classical Arabic. For the sake of uniformity we have adhered to the Classical Arabic vowel-system.

*Guadarrama* 'the sandy river'. The Arabic *ar-ramla* 'strip of sand beside a river', which occurs in the last of these names, is also preserved in the *Ramblas* of Barcelona, now the main avenue which runs through the centre of the old city, and again in *Vivar-rambla* at Granada, 'the gate of the sandy way'.

In the exploitation of rivers to cultivate dry land the Arabs excelled, bringing to southern Spain a technique of irrigation which transformed it into a garden, since those days partially destroyed, though in the areas still under cultivation the old technique lives on with little change. The whole system is Arabic in its nomenclature: hence the *acequia* (Port. *acéquia*, Cat. *sèquia, siquia*), the narrow trench whereby water is distributed, and the *azud*, a small dam with a sluice which regulates the supply; hence too the *alberca* 'reservoir', and the *aljibe* 'cistern'. Whoever has travelled in southern Spain will have seen the horse or mule patiently treading round and round the draw-well, operating the wheel which brings up buckets of water: the bucket is the *arcaduz* and the well the *(a)noria*. With this image in mind, Spaniards have coined a popular expression *dar vueltas a la noria* 'to perform the daily round', most suggestive of monotonous toil. In this context it is perhaps appropriate to mention that *tarea*, the common word for 'task', is also Arabic.

Thus by their labours, on the not very fertile soil of ancient Baetica (as described in the first century A.D. by Columella, a native of Cadiz), the settlers produced rich harvests of fruit and vegetables, most of which still bear their Arabic name. Among the latter are the *alcachofas* (Port. *alcachofras*): borrowed directly from the Qairawān–Sicily region, without the article, the same Arabic word appears in Italian as *carciofo*; the Spanish form penetrated, however, into Provence, where it became *archichaut, arquichaut*, and thence into northern Italy as *articiocco*; the *artichoke* which reached England is an adaptation of this second Italian form, which also gave rise to the *t* of Fr. *artichaut*. In this way the two routes of Arabic influence, via Spain and via Italy, often converged.

Belonging more exclusively to Hispano-Romance are *zanahorias* (Cat. *safanories*, Port. *cenouras*) 'carrots', *chirivías* 'parsnips', *acelgas* (Port. *celgas*), a kind of beet of which the leaf is a very popular comestible in Spain, and two varieties of bean, *alubias* and *judías*. Other crops of Arabic provenance include *arroz* (Port. *arroz*, Cat. *arròs*) 'rice', for which Valencia is now famous, *alfalfa*, the lucerne used for fodder, *azafrán* 'saffron', *azúcar* 'sugar', and *algodón* (Port. *algodão*) 'cotton'. Each of the last three of these is involved in a history similar to that of the words for 'artichoke'. The Span. *algodón*, for example, passed into Provence as *alcotón*, and thence gave Old Fr. *auqueton*; but the same Arabic word took root in Italian as *cotone*, and when French supplies were drawn mainly from Italy this form, as *coton*, ousted Old Fr. *auqueton* and even travelled over the Pyrenees to give Cat. *cotó* and Port. *cotão*; for the Italian source of Eng. *saffron, sugar*, see below, p. 295.

Fruits with Arabic nomenclature include the *albérchiga* (Port. *alperche*) 'peach', *albaricoque* (Port. *albricoque*) 'apricot', the *naranja* (Port. *laranja*) 'orange', and the *limón* 'lemon'. The olive-tree retained its Latin name as *olivo* (< OLĪVUM, a loan from Greek), but the Arabic *az-zayt* became attached to its product, olive-oil, thereafter in Spanish *aceite*, and from this was derived a new name for its fruit, *aceituna*; in this instance Portuguese followed Spanish with *azeite* and *azeitona*, but Catalan, like Provençal and French, has remained faithful to Latin, and the fruit in Catalonia is still the *oliva*.

Many of the above terms provide good illustrations of the exotic element in Arabic itself. Thus *alubias, naranja*, and *limón* derive from Persian words adopted by the Arabs. Originally Greek are *acelga* (Arabic *silqa* from Greek Σικελός 'Sicilian'), and *arroz* (Arabic *ruzz* from Greek ὄρυζα); in Italy the word for 'rice' came from Greece without the intermediary of Arabic, to give Ital. *riso*, whence Fr. *riz*. From Latin through Arabic came *albaricoque* (Lat. PRAECOQUUS, the 'precocious', i.e. 'early' fruit) and *albérchiga* (Lat. PERSICA, the 'Persian' fruit). In native dialects of northern Spain the peach is still designated by words deriving directly from PERSICUM, with no influence of Mozarabic, e.g. Cast. *priesco, prisco*; Arag. *presiego, presieco*; Port. *pêssego*; Cat. *prèssec*. In modern standard Spanish both types have now been replaced by *durazno* (< DURACINUM, i.e. 'hard-berried'), or more commonly by *melocotón* (< MALUM COTONEUM).

Together with the names of agricultural products, those of outbuildings and other appurtenances of agriculture are frequently Arabic: hence the *alquería* 'farmhouse', the *alfolí* 'granary', the *almiar* 'haystack', the *aceña* 'water-mill', the *almazara* 'oil-mill', and the *tahona*, a mill operated by horses. The payment made to the miller in return for his services, the *maquila*, is also an Arabism.

Arab above all was the art of decorative gardening, and here the oriental delight in fragrance and colour, perceptions which are given much less prominence in the vocabularies of Latin and Germanic, finds its full expression and contributes a new element to Romance. The hotbed in which the plants were reared is the *arriata*. Among favourite plants were the *arrayán* 'myrtle', the *almezo* 'lotus tree', the *adelfa* 'rose-bay', the *azucena* 'water-lily', *alhucema* 'lavender', *almoraduj* 'marjoram', *jazmín* 'jasmine'. The blossom of the orange and lemon trees was *azahar*. Some of these words are again borrowings from other eastern languages; 'jasmine', for example, is originally Persian. Some appear in competition with names of Latin provenance, though these were applied to the plants in the wild rather than the cultivated state. Thus lavender grows abundantly in northern Spain and so that area kept *espliego*, from Lat. SPICULUM, which eventually triumphed over *alhucema* in standard Spanish. Marjoram, too, is nowadays known by a word propagated from the north, *mejorana* (cf. Fr. *marjolaine*, Ital. *maggiorana*), a derivative from Lat. AMARACUS, Greek in origin; presumably the same Greek word lies at the source of *almoraduj*. All these flowers bloomed in the Arabic pleasure-garden, of which the type is preserved at Granada in the *Generalife*: the *ǧannat al-'arīf* 'the architect's garden'.

Much of the Spanish terminology of building is a legacy from the Arabs. Their word for 'town' *madīna*, survives only in place-names, e.g. *Medina Sidonia*, *Medina del Campo*, *Medinaceli*, the Vulgar Latin use of CIVITATEM (> Span. *ciudad*, Cat. *ciutat*, Port. *cidade*) and VILLA (> Span. Cat. *villa*, Port. *vila*) having prevailed in current speech; but to the Romance terms designating smaller agglomerations they added *aldea* 'village', *arrabal* 'suburb', and *barrio* 'quarter (of a town)'.[1] In words which have their source in the particular skills of the *alarife* 'architect', and the *albañil* 'mason', the Arabic element predominates. To them are due the *azotea*, the flat roof of the southern type of dwelling, the *ajimez*, the arched window with a central pillar, the *taracea*, the marquetry of the floor, the *azulejo*, the glazed tile, and various words reflecting an improvement in sanitation, such as *albañal* 'sewer' and *alcantarilla* 'drain'.

Within the house the general term for furniture became *aiuar*,

---

[1] The Arabic origin of *barrio* has been disputed, but Corominas argues convincingly in its favour (*Dicc. crit. etim. de la lengua castellana*).

likewise borrowed from the Arabs; and there they introduced such luxuries as the *alfombra* 'carpet' and the *almohada* 'cushion', 'pillow', both of these being associated with their own earlier and more primitive existence, with the furnishing of their tents. The Arabic word for the tent itself was adopted as *alcoba*, which now came to designate the characteristic recess for the bed, to be transported in the seventeenth century into French, by writers in search of local colour, as *alcôve*. Kitchen utensils include the *alcuza* 'oil-bottle', and the *almirez*, a brass mortar still found in every Spanish household; also the wares of the *alfarero* 'potter': the *jarra* 'pitcher', and the *taza* 'cup'. The last-named of these words passed into Catalan and Provençal as *tassa*, and as *tasse* is first attested in written French in the fourteenth century. Dishes include *alcuzcuz*, still very popular in North Africa as *couscous*, and *albóndiga* 'forcemeat ball'. Among sweets were *almíbar* 'treacle', and *alfeñique* 'sugar paste': for all such confectionery we are primarily indebted to the Arabs, as propagators of the sugar-cane, which reached them by way of India from south-east Asia.

Then, as now, the Arabs dressed very differently from the Europeans. Their large outer garment became in Mozarabic the *aljuba*; this is cognate with Fr. *jupe*, one of the very few Arabic words in French which seem to have been borrowed directly as a result of the Crusades. Over the *aljuba* was thrown a cloak, the *albornoz*. The breeches were the *zaragüelles*; and on the feet were worn the *borceguíes* 'buskins', or in repose the *babuchas* 'slippers'. We have not been able to ascertain to what extent this eastern garb was favoured by the Mozarabic population: dress in medieval Spain appears to be a subject still in search of an author. The adoption of the words seems, however, to indicate that it was quite generally worn, at least among the upper strata of society, providing plenty of employment for the *alfayate* 'tailor'; the replacement of this word by *sastre*, of Latin origin (see p. 67), may have followed upon a change to more European types of costume, though in Portuguese the tailor is still the *alfaiate*. Among cloths which he used are *barragán* and *tiraz*, both Arabic. His fine workmanship has left the verb *recamar* 'to embroider'. Much decorative work was done, as it still is in both Spain and North Africa, with dressed sheepskin, the material of the pocket-books and purses hawked around the cafés of France by North African vendors; this is *badana*, a word which passed into Provence where it became *bazana*, and thence into northern France as *basane*, more familiar nowadays in the adjectival form *basané* 'tanned', used of the complexion.

Arabic craftsmen were particularly skilled in metal-work, and in Spain they found a country which had already been renowned for its mineral wealth under the Romans. Like the heavenly constellations (see below), the commonest minerals, such as iron, copper, and lead, retained their Latin names, but most of the less familiar received an Arabic appellation: hence *azogue*, the 'quicksilver' still mined in Andalusia, *azufre* 'sulphur', *almagre* 'red ochre', *albayalde* 'white lead', *alumbre* 'alum'. Together with the imported *marfil* 'ivory', these provided abundant raw material for the manufacture of *alfileres* 'pins', *ajorcas* 'bracelets', *arracadas* 'ear-rings', and other trinkets, as also for *ataujía* 'damaskeen'.

All these products gave rise to a lively commerce, with its own special vocabulary. Thence derive the *tarifa* and the *aduana*, both of which were to become international. The *arancel*, formerly *alanzel*, a 'fixed price' for commodities, remained local. Places for storage included the *almacén* 'warehouse', and nowadays 'store' in the English sense of 'large shop', and the *alhóndiga* 'public granary'. Also Arabic is the *arsenal*, but this term came to Spain, as to other parts of Europe, from Italy (see below). Arabic coinage was introduced, including the *maravedí*, so-called after the Almoravids (see p. 399), and an elaborate system of weights and measures. The latter was controlled by an inspector, the *almotacén*. It included the *quintal* 'hundredweight', from an Arabic form of which the root seems to be Lat. CENTUM, the *arroba*, which means literally 'fourth part' (of the *quintal*), the *cahiz* 'a measure of corn of about 12 bushels', the *fanega* 'a measure of about $1\frac{1}{2}$ bushels', and the *azumbre* 'a liquid measure of about half a gallon'. To these may be added the *almud*, where the second element appears to come from an arabized form of Lat. MŎDIUM (cf. Old Fr. *muid*). These measures are still in common use. In the Pyrenean locality of Benasque, a day's walk over the mountains from Luchon, the present writer recorded in local dialectal forms the following tables:

Measures for corn

6 *almuts*   = *1 quartal*
2 *quartals* = *1 faneca*
8 *faneques* = *1 cafís*

Measures for olive-oil

| | | |
|---|---|---|
| *1 lliura* | = | *2 quarterons* |
| *4 quarterons* | = | *1 arroba* |
| *4 arrobes* | = | *1 quintal* |

Measures for hay

| | | |
|---|---|---|
| *1 carga* | = | *10 arrobes* |

Thus is Arabic wedded to Romance, even in regions where the invaders had no foothold.

Though no ardent proselytizers, the Arabs maintained their own religion, and constructed beside the Christian churches their Muslim *alminares*. The *almuédano*, from the roof of the minaret, called the faithful to prayer, known by an Arabic word as *zala*. Like the Franks, the Arabs introduced their own funeral arrangements, and their word for 'coffin', as *ataúd*, has become general in Spanish. Catalan currently employs with this meaning the term *caixa*, a Provençal form from Lat. CAPSA (cf. Fr. *caisse*, also from Provençal); this usage has extended into Aragon, but in the very individual dialect of Benasque the Arabic word survives as *atabut*.

In lighter mood the Arabs were much attracted by music and the dance; popular music in Andalusia still leaves no doubt as to its oriental origin. Hence come the names of various musical instruments: the *laúd* 'lute', formerly *alaúd*, the *adufe* 'tambourine', and the *albogue*, a kind of shepherd's pipe. Like the knights of Charlemagne, the older and the wiser played the ancient game of chess, *ajedrez* (Cat. *aixedrés*, Port. *enxadrez*, *xadrez*), a word which ultimately derives from the same Persian root as Fr. *échec* (see p. 247).

Social and administrative terminology owes a great deal to Arabic influence. The head of the state was of course the Emir, whose title, as the result of Arabic seafaring, has given the word for 'admiral' (English borrowed from French) in all the western Romance languages: Span. Port. *almirante*, Fr. *amiral*, Ital. *ammiraglio*. In Old French it is the designation commonly given to the leader of a Saracen army, and it appears in various forms, e.g. *amirafle*, *amurafle*, *amiral*, *amiragon*, *amirant*, *amirauble*, *amuable*, &c., a selection from which one may deduce that to the French armies it sounded particularly outlandish. Its wide diffusion, its maritime meaning, and its early appearance in medieval Latin (as *amiratus* in the work of Einhardt) combine to suggest that it was backed by

other influences than that of Moorish Spain, most probably by
that of Byzantine Greek, in consequence of the initial hostilities
in the eastern Mediterranean.

More specifically 'Peninsular' are the *algalife*, the Spanish
adaptation of 'caliph', which occurs in the same form in Old
French; the *alcalde*, originally a magistrate, from the Arabic *al-
qāḍī* 'judge', and later the mayor; and the *alguacil*, a senior police
official. To the same administrative context belong *albacea*, the
executor of a will, and *albalá*, a legal certificate.

Inevitably, since they came as conquerors, the Arabs have left
in Spanish a certain legacy of military terms. The Arabic *ġāra* survives with little change in Span. Port. *algara* 'raid', 'foray', while
its derivative *algarada* is now 'battle-cry' in Spanish and 'battle'
in Portuguese. Arabic *dalīl* 'chief', became Span. Cat. *adalil*,
*adalid*, and Port. *adail*; another officer, the *qā'id* became the Span.
*alcaide* 'governor', 'jailor'. The 'sentry', and with extension of
meaning, the 'watch-tower', was the *atalaya*. The *zaga*, now often
the load packed on to the back of a carriage, seems to have acquired its currency as the rearguard of the Arabic army. Latin
CASTRA entered Spanish in an arabized form as *alcázar*, the usual
word for 'fortress'.

Arabic terms referring to military equipment frequently appear
in Spanish as near-synonyms of loan-words from Germanic, either
Frankish or Visigothic. The oval, leather-covered shield of the
Arabs has left in Spanish, as also in Catalan and Portuguese, the
word *adarga*, which coexists with the *tarja* imported from Gallo-
Romance. The Arabic 'helmet' is in Spanish the *almófar* or *almofre*,
Port. *almafre*. The 'scimitar' is the *alfanje* in both Spanish and
Portuguese; and the 'quiver' the *aljaba*, Port. *aljava*. The trumpet
and the drum, used as means of signalling, have both left Arabic
words: the former is the *añafil*, and the latter in Old Spanish the
*atamor*; in the modern languages of the Peninsula the drum is
now everywhere the *tambor*, a form which seems to have been
remodelled, like the Fr. *tambour* (Old French has always *tabour*,
whence the Eng. *tabor*), through the propagation at the time of the
Renaissance of the Ital. *tamburo*.

The Arabs were great horsemen, famous in battle for their
cavalry. One wonders whether the use of the lance at the level,
the arm of medieval chivalry which appeared in the French armies
towards the end of the eleventh century (see p. 244), was not

originally learnt from them; unfortunately there is little evidence concerning Arabic technique of assault before the twelfth century. To Old French they gave one of the commonest terms for a war-horse, the *auferrant*, borrowed through Prov. *alferan* from Span. *alfaraz*; the source of these words is the Arabic *faras* 'horse'. The corresponding Arabic for the rider, *fāris*, is preserved in Span. *alférez* 'ensign', 'scout', which later passed into Italian as *alfiere*. Through Mozarabic came the Spanish for 'rider', *jinete*, from the name of the Berber tribe of the Zenetes, renowned for their horsemanship; used also as the name of a type of small, swift horse, the word entered French as *genet* (whence Eng. *genet*, *jennet*). The Germanic word for 'spur' (see p. 208) met with an Arabic rival in *acicate*. Yet more Spanish words of like origin include *albarda* 'pack-saddle', *jaez* 'harness', *jáquima* 'halter', *alforja* 'saddle-bag', and *acémila* 'beast of burden', whence *acemilero* 'muleteer'.

The category of abstract words, fairly prominent in Gallo-Roman borrowings from Frankish, is less conspicuous in Hispano-Roman borrowings from Arabic. Perhaps because they were well represented in the language of the Church, words denoting strong emotions have remained generally Latin. One Arabic root has given rise to a few terms expressing pleasure: *alborozo* 'gaiety', *alboroto* 'noise', 'riot', and *alboroque* 'treat', 'celebration'. Sorrow seems to have played little part in the Arabic *Weltanschauung*: at least it was rigorously excluded from the harem, in and around which the cult of the beautiful evolved.

Adjectives which have survived are mostly of the derogatory kind, stemming from the language of abuse, and curiously akin in meaning to those which, in the sixteenth century, French was to borrow from Italian (see p. 471): thus *baladí* 'worthless', *baldío* 'uncultivated', *gandul* 'idle', *mezquino* 'small', 'paltry'. Of these *mezquino*, deriving from the Arabic *maskīn*—still the term with which an Arab beggar proclaims his poverty to the world—enjoyed a considerable diffusion. In Old French it was commonly used as *meschin*, meaning 'small boy', and likewise as *meschine* 'small girl', in which acceptance it still persists in many modern French patois. From standard French it disappeared with the Middle Ages, only to be replaced, etymologically speaking, by a form *mesquin* borrowed from Ital. *meschino*, with the original adjec-tival sense of 'poor', 'paltry', 'mean'.

The few words associated with colour left in Spanish by the occupation are mostly loan-words in Arabic and owe their wide currency to the cloth trade and the dyeing industry. Most common is *azul*, cf. Ital. *azzurro*, originally from Persian. Two words of particular interest which have remained as substantives are *carmesí* and *escarlata*. The former is semantically identical with Fr. *vermeil* (< Lat. VERMĬCULUM): Arabic *qarmaz* or *qirmiz* meant 'cochineal', and is formed on Persian *kirm*, 'worm', possibly an Indo-European cognate of VERMIS. The other term, *escarlata*, is from Arabic *siqillāṭ*, *siqirlāṭ*, taken this time from Byzantine Greek, from a σιγίλλατος which in turn is simply Lat. (TEXTUM) SIGILLA-TUM 'stamped cloth'. Yet another such term is *añil* 'indigo', origi-nally the name of the plant from which the dye is extracted: this again came to Arabic from Persian.

The Arabic contribution to Romance verbs is considerably less important than that of Germanic. Among those kept in Spanish one may note *acicalar* 'to polish', *halagar* 'to caress', and *ahorrar* 'to save'. The *Caja de Ahorros*, 'Savings Bank', is as familiar in modern Spain as is the *Caisse d'Épargne* in France or the *Cassa di Risparmio* in Italy: an example in which Germanic and Arabic loan-words meet, to the total exclusion of Latin.

Miscellaneous adverbial expressions, prepositions, and inter-jections were also taken over from Arabic. Among adverbs are Span. *marras*, from Arabic *marra*, meaning 'once', 'long ago', and the common phrases *de balde* 'for nothing', 'gratis', and *en balde* 'in vain', from the same Arabic root as the adj. *baldío*. Catalan adopted these latter as *de bades*, *en bades*, and thence they spread to Pro-vençal as *de badas*, *en badas*, and farther east to Genoese and other Italian dialects; with the extension of the Catalan maritime Empire *de badas* also became Sardinian. The one noteworthy contribution of Arabic to the Spanish system of prepositions is *hasta*; borrowed from *ḥattā*, and appearing in Old Spanish and Old Portuguese as *ata* (in the *Poema del Cid* as *fata* with a scribal *f* representing the sound *h*), in modern Portuguese as *até*, this word replaced all Vulgar Latin devices to convey the meanings 'until' (temporal) and 'as far as' (local). Among interjections are the Arabic vocative particle *yā*, as employed in the *Poema del Cid*:

Ya Canpeador, en buen ora cinxiestes espada!

(Ed. Menéndez Pidal, l. 175)

and *albricias*, which, although in the first place a substantive

meaning 'good news' (see p. 404) and then a reward for the
bringing of good news (cf. Port. *alvíçaras*), often comes to be
a simple 'Hurrah', e.g.

> Albricia, Albarffanez, ca echados somos de tierra!
>
> (op. cit. l. 14)

Arabic, too, is the much used *ojalá*, Port. *oxalá* 'would that . . .!',
from *wā šā allāh*, literally 'if it please God', and probably *he*, as in
*he aquí*, often used in Old Spanish with an ethic dative.

The majority of the words thus far quoted form part of the
vocabulary of everyday life, and as such, transmitted orally
through the Mozarabic population, they have become completely
integrated into that Castilian speech which is now Spanish. Many
of them, as we have seen, are also to be found in Catalan and
Portuguese, whether as the result of direct adoption from the
Mozarabic of those areas reconquered by Catalan and Portuguese
enterprise, or through subsequent borrowing from Castilian. Some,
particularly those of a travelling type, such as the names of weights
and measures, have entered into the local dialects of regions never
occupied by the Arabs; the still more peripatetic, names of products for the most part, penetrated into Provence and thence into
French and Italian, and even to English. Yet others had a limited
area of diffusion and never entirely ousted synonyms of Vulgar
Latin origin. Many which commonly occur in Old Spanish texts
have disappeared from the standard language but may well be
revealed as still extant by the further dialectal exploration of the
Peninsula, as yet far from complete.

There remains a last category of Spanish words deriving from
Arabic, of which the dialectal investigator would encounter but
few, and which we have grouped apart because by contrast with
the words adopted orally into Mozarabic they are 'learned': that
is, they were culled from the scientific literature of the Arabs
and diffused, with little change of form, through the medium of
translations, mostly from Arabic into Latin. During the Middle
Ages they became international, forming part of the vocabulary
of mathematics, of alchemy, the ancestor of modern chemistry,
of astronomy and the pseudo-science of astrology, of botany and
medicine.

The name of an outstanding Arabic mathematician, Al-Ḥwārizmī
(d. A.D. 820), influenced by a Greek word, gave rise to a medieval

Latin ALGORITMUS, which became the term for arithmetic; in Spain it was *algorismo* and *alguarismo*, in Old French *algorisme*, in Italian *algoritmo, algorismo*. From the title of one of this scholar' works an Italian mathematician, Leonardo Fibonacci, created and circularized at Pisa in A.D. 1202 the term *algebra*, adopted into both Italian and Spanish, and into French as *algèbre*. With the new development of these studies there came into general use the Arabic system of numerals, of Indian origin, which replaced the more cumbrous Latin system. It included a word for 'nought', *ṣifr*, originally an adjective meaning 'empty'. Latinized by Fibonacci as ZEPHIRUM, this became in Italian *zefiro, zefro, zero*, the last of these forms being ultimately borrowed into French as *zéro* and into Spanish as *cero*. In Spain, however, it had also been adopted locally as *cifra*, referring to any numerical sign; this was later propagated to Italy with the Spanish occupation of that country, as *cifra*, and thence it passed to France, where, reflecting the Italian pronunciation of the initial consonant, it became *chiffre*. Thus in all the western Romance languages, as in Eng. *zero* and *cipher*, the one Arabic word *ṣifr* gave rise to two different words, with different meanings.

Alchemy has given to the Romance languages its own designation (Fr. *alchimie*, Span. *alquimia*, Ital. *alchimia*), and the word for the 'still' (Fr. Prov. Cat. *alambic*, Span. *alambique*, Ital. *lambicco*), an essential part of the alchemist's equipment; both of these terms were in the first place adopted into Arabic from Greek. The word for alchemy originally designated the 'philosopher's stone', which was constantly sought as a means of converting the baser metals into gold. Another Arabic name for this stone gave Span. Port. *elixir*, Ital. *elisire*, Fr. *élixir*. To this Arabic terminology also belong Span. *alcohol* and *álcali*, likewise international.

Arabic astronomy provided names for many of the lesser constellations; the more conspicuous remained Latin. An Arabic word meaning 'direction' passed into Spanish as *azimut*, and a corrupted form of the same word as *cenit*, cf. Fr. *zénith*, Ital. *zenit*, while another word meaning 'opposite' became Span. *nadir*, which besides being English, is also Italian and French.

To the medicinal interests of the Arabs are due many names of herbs and also at least two terms for parts of the body: Arabic *nuḥā*, latinized as NUCHA, is the source of Fr. *nuque*, Span. Prov. Port. Ital. *nuca*; and Arabic *rāḥa* 'palm of the hand', nowadays attached to the sporting lexicon as Fr. *raquette*, Ital. *racchetta*, Span. Port. *raqueta*.

*The Muslims in Sicily and Italy*. Though Spain was the principal European theatre of Arabic colonization and bears its most indelible mark, other bands of Muslim adventurers, dominating the western Mediterranean with their ships, made landings and established settlements on various parts of its inviting coast. Their raids met at times with fierce local resistance, but the only organized opposition, until western Europe gathered strength for the Crusades, continued to be that of the Byzantine Empire. Early in the ninth century, after prolonged fighting against the Byzantines, the emirs of Qairawān succeeded in taking Sicily. Thence their fleets ranged far and wide. In A.D. 843 the suburbs of Rome suffered at Muslim hands yet another sack, while repeated incursions into southern Italy reduced that land to a state of complete disorder. On the coast of Provence the marauders seized in A.D. 894 the town of Frainet, from which base, for many years thereafter, they conducted plundering raids on both sides of the Alps, destroying all commerce in the region; this settlement was finally eliminated in A.D. 972 by an alliance of local nobles. North of Naples, a strong colony of Muslims was founded on the banks of the River Garigliano. It was here that they met with their first serious reverse in the Italian area: in A.D. 915 the colony was wiped out by another local league, organized on this occasion by the Pope, John X, but under the secular leadership of Byzantium; thereby southern Italy was restored for a while to Greek authority.

The island of Sardinia also suffered many Muslim attacks, though these came chiefly from the direction of Spain. Its inhabitants were still nominally subjects of the Byzantine Empire— the coinage in circulation in Sardinia continued to be Byzantine until the end of the eleventh century—but owing to the isolation consequent upon the cutting of sea-routes they had in practice developed a considerable measure of independence and with it such a spirit of resistance that they repelled raid after raid. Only for a very brief period at the beginning of the eleventh century did the Arabs, under a leader Muğāhīd, coming from the Balearics, succeed in obtaining a foothold; and then the Sardinians found allies in the nascent republics of Genoa and Pisa, whose combined fleets put an end to the enterprise by completely destroying that of Muğāhīd, while the Sardinians themselves settled accounts with such Arabs as remained ashore (A.D. 1016). Sardinia thus remained free from prolonged Arabic occupation, as it had largely escaped that of Germanic tribes, and the Vulgar Latin of Sardinia continued its Romance development with little outside interference until the beginning of the long Catalan and Spanish occupation (A.D. 1326–1714).

Faced with such local resistance, the Arabs of the central Mediterranean could only make really long-standing settlements in Sicily and Malta. The recovery of these islands for Christendom after more than two centuries of Muslim occupation was one of the decisive acts of a resurgent west. The Christian knights on this occasion were the distant Normans. Called in by the Byzantines, with the Papacy acting as intermediary, to assist in suppressing a revolt which had been stirred up in Apulia by the descendants of the Langobards, the Normans quickly overran a large part of southern Italy. Their leader, Robert Guiscard, was rewarded for his achievement, on Papal recommendation, with the title of Duke of Apulia (A.D. 1058). It was left to his younger brother, Roger, to bring about the downfall of Arab dominion in Sicily in a series of campaigns extending from 1061 onwards. In the same movement Malta became finally acquired for Christianity but not for Romance speech. After the death of the two brothers the lands which they had conquered were united into a single realm, the kingdom of Sicily and southern Italy, with Roger II as its first ruler: a realm which was destined to flourish and to play a notable part in the early development of the Italian language.

*The Arabic element in Italian.* From this brief account it will be anticipated that the influence of Arabic on the speeches of Italy is much less strong than its influence on those of the Iberian Peninsula. Except in Sicily, where the Arabic contribution remains quite considerable, there was no 'Mozarabic' population through which words could filter easily into Romance. The agglutination of the article, as in Spain, is quite absent: consequently, when an Arabic word beginning with *al-* is found in the Italian language, it can generally be assumed, except in the case of a few 'learned' words, to have come as a late borrowing from Spanish (e.g. *alfiere*, see p. 289). For the same reason, Arabic words in French and English, most of which travelled via Spanish or Italian, indicate by their form which of the two routes they followed.

The intimate terminology of settlement, that preoccupation with building, with household equipment and agriculture, so vividly reflected in Spain, is quite lacking in Italian arabisms.[1] For the most part, they are related to seafaring and trade. In the former category may be quoted the Ital. *cassero, cassaro*, which, like Span. *alcázar*, derives from an arabized rendering of Lat. CASTRUM; the Italian word, however, has a purely naval application, referring to the fighting part of a warship (cf. Eng. *forecastle, fo'c'sle*); with the disappearance of the raised poop it has now come to designate the quarter-deck. An Arabic *dār ṣināʿa*, meaning 'building-yard', is found in various dialectal forms in the different ports of Italy. In standard Italian it has been adopted as *darsena* 'wet dock', and also in its Venetian form as *arsenal*; the latter, taken over by the military, has now become international.

Among trading terms is the word for 'shop': the Arabic *maḫzan* 'shed', which with the definite article produced in Spanish *almacén* (see above, p. 286), became in Sicilian *magasenu*, in Italian *magazzino*; thence the word passed into French as *magasin*, of which the first mention recorded by Littré dates from the fifteenth century: 'Là estoient les boutiques des marchandises que ils (les Sarrasins) appellent magasins.' On account of the growth of commercial relations between Italy and France, at a time when Spain was still absorbed in the Reconquest, many of the commodities with which the Arabs enriched Europe entered the greater part of the Continent through Italy. Italian arabisms which thus proliferated include *zucchero, arancia, limone, safferano*, and the previously mentioned *cotone* (see p. 283). Arabic, too, is our 'syrup', through Fr. *sirop* from Ital. *sciroppo*.

As direct relics of the Arabic commercial system there still survive in Italian the word *zecca* 'mint'—curiously, the exact homonym of a word of Langobardic origin meaning 'sheep-tick' (see p. 264) and its derivative *zecchino*; the latter, formerly a coin, passed into French as *séquin*, whence Eng. *sequin*. For the 'customs', the Arabic loan-word from Persian which in Spanish gave *aduana* in Italian became *dogana*; at a later date the same word was to enter Italian again, this time via Turkish, in the form *divano*, whence Fr. *divan*.

Italian adjectives of Arabic origin are few in number, the most

---

[1] This does not, of course, apply to Sicilian, which includes a number of the Arabic terms of agriculture and irrigation familiar in Spanish, see A. Steiger, *Contribución a la fonética del hispano-árabe y de los arabismos en el ibero-románico y el siciliano*, Madrid, 1932.

noteworthy being *meschino* and *azzurro*. The colour terms *crèmisi* and *scarlatto* resemble their cognates in Spanish (see above, p. 290), but whether they entered Italian via Arabic, or by a more direct route from the east, seems open to question. Of the international 'learned' words propagated by Arabic science, Italian possesses, as we have already seen, a substantial share.

With this we conclude our brief examination of the Arabic contribution to Romance, remembering, as in previous instances, that it is in no sense complete.[1] The field is one which offers ample scope for further research: *Romania Arabica* awaits its author.

### THE NEW ROMANIA

In following the course of invasions within the frontiers of the Roman Empire to their ultimate stages and in exploring their contribution to the formation of Romance, we have come at times to the end of the first millennium and even passed beyond. If, however, a limit should be set to this formative period, to all that is implied by the 'Dark Ages', return to the ninth century is desirable, for by then the movement of peoples, except in the non-Romance north, had been largely completed, the geographical areas of the new languages basically determined, and in France the first written documents in a neo-Latin idiom were beginning to appear.

During the early years of this century Christian Europe experienced a moment of stabilization due to the ascendancy of the Carolingian dynasty. Charlemagne had realized the dream of a new Roman Empire in the west, which comprised at his death (A.D. 814) all of modern France, the Netherlands and most of Germany, a large part of Italy, and the north-eastern corner of Spain. Held together for a while under the reign of his son, Louis the Pious (d. 840), this Empire disintegrated in consequence of the quarrels concerning rights of succession between his three grandsons, Lothair, Charles (the Bald), and Louis (the German). After the alliance of the two younger brothers, sealed in the *Strassburg Oaths*, had procured the defeat of Lothair, a treaty was signed at Verdun (A.D. 843) in which the division of the Empire

For examples quoted we are chiefly indebted to the following: Menéndez Pidal, *Orígenes del español* (3rd edition); W. J. Entwistle, *The Spanish Language*; R. Lapesa, *Historia de la lengua española* (2nd edition); C. Tagliavini *Le origini delle lingue neolatine* (2nd edition); J. Corominas, *Diccionario crítico etimológico de la lengua castellana*.

was consummated. Lothair received the nominal title of Emperor and as his personal kingdom a strip of territory extending from Frisia southwards to Italy as far as the valley of the Po, including the modern Lorraine (Lotharingia), in which his name is perpetuated: this was *Francia media*. Charles obtained *Francia occidentalis*, and to Louis was left *Francia orientalis*. For ten years the three brothers kept the peace, all of them during this time being actively engaged in repelling, or failing to repel, the raids of the Danes. Then, in A.D. 854, war broke out between Charles and Louis, the latter having given support to an insurrection against Charles in Aquitaine. The following year saw the death of Lothair, and, their war having in the meantime produced little result, the two quarrelsome brothers (in fact, half-brothers) found a distraction in carving up his territories between them: Louis added Austrasia to his domains, together with the northern part of Burgundy, while Charles received Provence and the southern half of Burgundy. The son of Lothair, another Louis, was left with the kingdom of Italy. Louis the German was eventually the more successful, his work of consolidation laying the foundations of modern Germany, while the less diplomatic Charles initiated in France that era of weak kings and powerful barons which persisted until the fall of the Carolingian dynasty in A.D. 987. To the next dynasty, that of the Capetians, was left the difficult task of restoring prestige to the French monarchy.

Thus, politically, the most lasting result of Charlemagne's Empire was the inauguration of Germany. From the linguistic standpoint, one of its effects may be seen in a reinforcement of the prestige of German, which thereafter blocked the eastward extension of Gallo-Romance. Had Charlemagne's ambitions been limited to securing the traditional frontiers of Gaul, as established by the Romans and upheld, in so far as it lay within their power, by the Merovingians ruling from Neustria, it is possible that Romance speech would have eliminated Germanic west of the Rhine; instead, Germanic persisted and remains to this day from Flanders to Alsace. That Charlemagne did not identify his rule with Gaul is of course due in the first place to his belonging to the Germanic house of Austrasia, with the seat of his 'France', as we are constantly reminded in the *Chanson de Roland*, at Aix, the Roman AQUIS GRANI (so-called after a Celtic deity of healing). Among his Gallo-Roman subjects the period of bilingualism

induced by the Frankish invasions of the fifth century had almost
certainly drawn to an end under the Merovingians, and all the inhabitants of *Francia occidentalis*, whether predominantly Frankish
or Gallo-Roman in their ancestry, had come to use a Romance
form of speech. Apart from local changes of minor importance
(cf. p. 233), the eastern boundaries of Gallo-Romance cannot have
been very different in the ninth century from what they are now.

Elsewhere in Romania the limits of Romance speech were becoming similarly stabilized. Making due allowance for the confused situation in the Balkans, where Romance was losing ground,
and in Spain, where any lost ground was afterwards to be recovered,
and recognizing the continual recession of Romance before Germanic in the Rhetic area, one may state in general terms that the
delimitation of Romance-speaking countries had by the beginning
of the ninth century been largely accomplished.

Thus far had the tide of Latin fallen back. In so doing, it left
in the linguistically lost lands of Romania abundant traces of its
former presence. Not only the international vocabulary of Christianity, but also many words pertaining to the everyday life, commodities, and organization of Rome, words often belonging to an
early period in the diffusion of Latin, still remain within the
speeches of those peoples who had been 'natives' in the days of
Roman occupation. Welsh[1] and Breton, the various surviving

---

[1] The Welsh language, in particular, abounds in Latinisms, as is only to be
expected from its position as direct descendant of the native idiom of Roman
Britain. Appended is a short list of such borrowings, from which the reader may
deduce some of the essential sound-changes by which they are characterized.
Of particular note is the change of non-initial M to v (written in Welsh as *f*),
presumably through a phonological progression of **m** > **b** > **v**. Final vowels,
including the *a* which is generally so persistent in Romance, have been completely lost (cf. the Germanic treatment of Latin loan-words, as in CYMA >
Germ. *Keim*, see p. 34). There are close affinities with Romance in the treatment of Latin v, which was clearly a bilabial w in the Latin of Britain, and which
evolved to GW like the Frankish *w* in French; also in the retention of the Vulgar
Latin prothetic vowel before *s* 'impure' (see p. 25), &c.

The following examples are all taken from Henry Lewis, *Yr Elfen Ladin yn
yr Iaith Gymraeg* (Cardiff, 1943): ANCHORA > *angor*, ARMA > *arf*, ARTICULUS >
*erthygl*, ASINA > *asen*, AUCTORITATEM > *awdurdod*, AUGUSTUS > *Awst*, BAPTIZATI
> *bedysawd*, BARBA > *barf*, BESTIA > *bwyst*, CARITATEM > *cardod*, CATHEDRA >
*cadair*, CAULIS > *cawl*, CIVITAS > *ciwed*, CIVITATEM > *ciwdod*, CORONA > *corun*,
CORPUS > *corff*, CRUX > *crwys*, CRUCEM > *crog*, CUPA > *cib*, DE SUBITO > *disy-
fyd*, DISCO > *dysg*, DIURNATA > *diwrnod*, DOCTUS > *doeth*, ELEMENTA > *elfen*,
FATA > *ffawd*, FIRMUS > *ffyrf*, FOCUS > *ffoc*, FONTANA > *ffynon*, FORMA >*ffurf*,
FRUCTUS > *ffrwyth*, GENTEM > *gynt*, GERMANUS > *Garmon*, HABENA > *afwyn*,
HUMILITATEM > *ufylltod*, IMPERATOR > *ymherawdr*, INFERNUM > *uffern*, INI-
TIUM > *ynyd*, INTELLECTIO > *athrylith*, INTERVENIO > *athrywyn*, JOHANNES >
*Ieuan*, LACTIS > *llaeth*, LECTICA > *lleithig*, LIBER > *llyfr*, LITTERA > *llythyr*,
LUNAE > *Llun*, MALEDICO > *melltigo*, MALEDICTIO > *melltith*, MEMBRUM >

Germanic dialects, Basque, Albanian, and Berber, all have their share of Latin borrowings, bearing testimony no less than ruins and inscriptions to the former unity of the Roman world. Within the new Romania, the period of anarchy which followed, for a century and a half, upon the transient dominion of the Frankish Empire—anarchy everywhere except in Arab-occupied Spain, and nowhere more thorough than in France—brought no further inroads to the west. Socially, its effect was to stimulate the growth of the feudal pattern. Linguistically, it hastened the differentiation of Romance vernacular and gave shape to the dialectal groupings of the later Middle Ages and the present day, preparing the destiny whereby a chosen few were to become the nuclei of new national tongues.

*mymryn*, MEMORIA > *myfyr*, MENSA > *mwys*, MOLINA > *melin*, NUMERUS > *nifer*, OCCASIO > *achos*, OCCUPO > *achub*, OCEANUS > *eigion*, ORGANUM > *orian*, PAGUS > *pau*, PALMA > *palf*, PAPILIO > *pebyll*, PATER > *pader*, PECTINEM > *peithyn*, PENSUM > *pwys*, PISCATUS > *pysgod*, PISCIS > *pysg*, PONDUS > *pwn*, POPULUS > *pobl*, PORTA > *porth*, PRIMUS > *prif*, RETE > *rhwyd*, ROMANIA > *Rhufain*, ROMANUS > *Rhufawn*, SAGITTA > *saeth*, SCALA > *ysgol*, *ysgawl*, SCAMNUM > *ysgafn*, SCRIBO > *ysgrif*, SECURUS > *segur*, SEDES > *swydd*, SICCUS > *sych*, SOLIDUS > *swllt*, SOLIS > *Sul*, SPIRITUS > *ysbryd*, SPLENDIDUS > *ysblennydd*, STAGNUM > *ystaen*, STELLA > *ystwyll*, SUPERBUS > *syberw*, TABULA > *tafol*, TEMPESTAS > *tymestl*, TEMPLUM > *teml*, TEMPUS > *tymp*, UNITAS > *uned*, UNITATEM > *undod*, VAGINA > *gwain*, VENENUM > *gwenwyn*, VENERIS > *Gwener*, VESPERUM > *gosber*, VINUM > *gwin*, VIPERA > *gwiber*, VIRIDIS > *gwyrdd*, VIRTUS > *gwyrth*.

# IV

## MEDIEVAL LATIN AND ROMANCE VERNACULAR

A LANGUAGE is usually held to differ from a dialect in that it possesses a recognized standard, established by custom and consent, and recorded in literature. Its very existence depends upon learned influence, upon the conscious acceptance of a correct usage which the teaching and practice of writing help to determine. The term 'Romance language' thus becomes relevant from the time when scribes first took pains to make a record of Romance speech. Since those who did so were latinists, using the Latin alphabet, a form of Latin control presided over the initiation and growth of the new western standards, and Latin provided a storehouse of words from which the Romance lexicon could always be supplemented should its own resources appear inadequate, as was not infrequently the case when a writer wished to express ideas unfamiliar in daily conversation. It is indeed almost symbolic that the earliest surviving specimen of Romance, the *Strassburg Oaths* (see p. 334), should be contained in the framework of a Latin chronicle.

In the creation of literary Romance the north-western part of Romania, the Gallic area, has an undisputed primacy. The final purpose of the present chapter is to ascertain why this should have been so. Following briefly the course of literary evolution to the point of crisis, we shall attempt to show that the early ninth century must have known a *questione della lingua* not altogether unlike the one which later agitated the intellectuals of the Italian renaissance, associated in this instance with the Latin revival directly inspired by Charlemagne: and that the gradual spread of literary bilingualism in western Romania, a bilingualism not seriously compromised until the sixteenth century, was an immediate consequence of the Carolingian Empire.

*Latin continuity.* After the fall of Rome and throughout the period of invasions the tradition of literary Latin persisted in the west. In this respect there was no sudden upheaval. The schools of antiquity continued to function, though precariously and in a state of decline, until A.D. 529, when they were finally closed, not as a result of barbarian intervention but by a decree of the Emperor Justinian, acting in his capacity as leader of the Christian world. Meanwhile, the new 'church' schools had come into being under the patronage of the developing religious institutions. Here the spirit was quite different: in the mind of ecclesiastical authority pagan learning had become the legacy of a sinful past, and the moral problem of what to teach was resolved, at least in theory, by a strict adherence to Christian discipline.

Though authors as individuals may have suffered from the transition to barbarian rule, there was no immediate diminution in the output of Latin literature. In Gaul, for example, the times of imperial collapse coincided with the life of Sidonius Apollinaris (c. A.D. 430–c. 480), a poet with a most revealing biography. Born at Lyon, of Gallo-Roman nobility, he engaged in politics, paid frequent visits to Rome, and married the daughter of Avitus, one of the short-lived Roman emperors of those days. In about A.D. 470 he retired from political life to enter the priesthood, and within a very short time was Bishop of Clermont. Then came the Visigothic occupation of Auvergne, against which the new bishop organized a local resistance movement, stubborn but futile. For this he was thrown by the Visigoths into prison, but within a few years he was released and restored to his see. His poetry, written for the most part in the course of his earlier career, is still imbued with classical influence. In his letters, the literary work of the bishop, he avails himself of a classical model, the younger Pliny, to give a lively picture both of himself and of a somewhat melancholy decade.

More ill-fated was Boethius (c. A.D. 480–524), born in Rome during the rule of Odovacar to meet his death at the hands of the Ostrogoths. Steeped in the classical style of which he is the last outstanding representative, familiar with both Plato and Aristotle, the latter of whom he partially translated, he became with his *Consolatio Philosophiae* one of the greatest Christian writers and one of the most profound influences in medieval literature: in England he was translated by King Alfred for the edification of the Anglo-Saxon people, while his life-story forms the subject of the oldest surviving poem in Provençal (see p. 372). Like several other masterpieces the *Consolatio* was composed in prison, where Boethius had been consigned by order of Theodoric, charged with treason. At an early age he had attained high political office, including the consulship, which persisted under Ostrogothic dominion. In A.D. 523, at a time of increasing tension between Theodoric and his Roman subjects, a plot was devised whereby the king should be overthrown with the assistance of the Eastern Emperor. Theodoric believed Boethius to be implicated, and in the following year, though protesting his innocence in the *Consolatio*, he was executed, the victim of a political purge.

St. Benedict (*c.* A.D. 480–*c.* 544), founder of the monastery of Monte Cassino and of the Benedictine Rule, the *Regula Monachorum*, was a contemporary of Boethius. So too was Cassiodorus (*c.* A.D. 480–*c.* 570), who also founded a monastery and succeeded in living through difficult times to a ripe age. A native of southern Italy, he rose like Boethius to high office in Rome, being secretary to Theodoric and later consul. In literature he ranks as an historian, both by the letters written while he held political office and by the numerous works composed after his retirement in A.D. 537; unfortunately, what was probably the most valuable of these, a *History of the Goths*, has been lost: we know of its twelve books only from a summary given by another and less reliable writer of Gothic history, Jordanes (*c.* A.D. 516–73). Posterity has a very special debt to Cassiodorus, for it was he who made the copying of manuscripts a seemly occupation for Christian monks.

In addition to these outstanding figures, a number of minor poets, grammarians, and historians, remarkable for their diversity of origin—thus Orosius and Priscian in Spain, Rutilus and Salvianus in Gaul, Sedulius who spent most of his life in Athens, and Corippus in Africa—were engaged during the same period in composing Latin works which still partially survive. The times of invasion were in this way bridged, and the traditions of western literature preserved.

*The growth of medieval Latin.* From the mid-sixth to the mid-seventh century the flow of literary production did not seriously abate, but as the training of the pagan schools receded in memory, familiarity with classical writing diminished, and with it the tendency to use classical models. On the other hand, with the ever-increasing dominance of the Church and the conformity which it imposed, the new manner of writing inaugurated by St. Jerome and St. Augustine became universal. This Christian Latin, as we have seen, aimed in the first place at simplicity, drawing its inspiration from popular parlance; but inevitably, with the passage of time it too became a stereotyped standard, something to be learnt at school, into which the more ambitious stylist could introduce a new complexity.

It was through this medium that much of the learning of Greece, including its practical science, was transmitted to western Europe: the example given by Boethius was followed by men with a less metaphysical bent. Medicine in the Middle Ages thus derived from latinized versions of Greek texts, until that of the Arabs, originally inspired by the same Greek sources, became available. Among such texts may be noted the 'pharmacology' of Dioscorides, done into Latin in Italy during the time of Ostrogothic occupation; also the medical treatise of Oribasius, known as the *Oribasius Latinus*, and the 'dietetics' of the Greek doctor Anthimus, both of which date from the same sixth century. A manual of technology, the *Compositiones Lucenses*, so-called from the fact of its discovery at Lucca, in Tuscany, gives instruction in dyeing and metalwork, in the preparation of parchment and paint, and other similar crafts: though the manuscript is eighth-century, this too seems to have been put together in the sixth century, and again the sources are Greek.

The literature of travel, which had already left one monument in the *Peregrinatio ad loca sancta*, was continued in the *Itinerarium Antonini Placentini* (c. A.D. 570), describing a journey from Constantinople to Jerusalem. For purposes of pilgrimage, the medieval inspiration to travel, most of the itineraries of imperial Rome were still available. They are preserved in a twelfth-century text now at Vienna, the famous *Tabula Peutingeriana*, a veritable treasure-house of toponymy.

Works of a religious character continued to be written in large numbers, and deriving from these, didactic and moralizing works, later to be the cue for so much rather dull poetry and prose in medieval French. Only in its hymns does Christian literature preserve something of the pagan conception of lyrical beauty: here an exacting standard had been set within imperial times by Prudentius (A.D. 348–405), born in Spain, probably at Saragossa. Traces of classical quality persist in the Latin poetry of Venantius Fortunatus (A.D. 540–600), who, though born an Italian, became in later life the Bishop of Poitiers; but the prose of his more famous contemporary and fellow bishop, Gregory of Tours (A.D. 538–94), a native of Clermont, is characterized by a self-conscious inability to write in the elegant style of his predecessors (see below, p. 305). No writer of the sixth century was more prolific than Gregory: his output includes not only religious works, of which the best known is the *Liber in gloria Confessorum*, but also the still more celebrated *Historia Francorum*, which, while revealing him as historian and politician, forms the source of much of our knowledge of the early period of the Merovingian dynasty. Among ecclesiastical scholars must also be counted Isidore, Bishop of Seville (A.D. 570–636), the most prominent writer of the Visigothic kingdom in Spain, whose twenty books of *Etymologiae*, so called because of the fanciful etymologies in which they abound, formed a long-accepted encyclopaedia for the Middle Ages; his opinions concerning what is 'vulgar' are still of interest to the philologist. In Italy, at the same time, lived the man who, historically, is the most outstanding figure of all, Pope Gregory the First (A.D. 540–604). His literary remains are quite considerable. Naturally, they deal almost entirely with religious matters, in particular with Church organization. Most interesting to the layman are the fourteen books of letters, covering the fourteen years of his Papacy.

To the same period belong the first Latin 'lives of saints', beginning with the *Vita Patrum* (sometimes called the *Vitae Patrum*), a miscellany by various authors, to which Gregory of Tours contributed, and which consisted partly of original 'lives', partly of translations from Greek. This set a fashion in biography. Venantius Fortunatus composed a *Life of Saint Radegunda*, in honour of his patron-queen, while three other bishops, Cyprianus of Toulon, Firminius and Viventius, produced a *Life of Saint Caesarius*, a bishop of Arles famed as a preacher, who died in A.D. 524. Thereafter in medieval Latin such lives of saints abound. To mention but a few of the most popular: *Vita Vedastis* (Saint Vaast, Bishop of Arras, d. A.D. 538) written *c.* A.D. 650 and rewritten by Alcuin (see below, p. 325) at the end of the eighth century; *Vita Genovevae* (Sainte Geneviève, patrons aint of Paris, d. *c.* A.D. 500), text of *c.* A.D. 750; *Vita Memorii* (Saint Mémoire, deacon at Troyes at the time of Attila's invasion, who led a deputation to beg Attila to spare the city but was put to death), text early eighth century; *Vita Desiderii* (Saint Didier, Bishop of Vienne, d. early eighth century) written in Spain by the Visigothic king Sisebut; *Vita Leudegarii* (Saint Léger, Bishop of Autun, killed A.D. 679) written by order of his successor, Bishop Hermenarius; *Vita Wandregiseli* (Saint Wandrille, d. A.D. 762) written by a monk of the abbey founded by him at Fontenelle, near Rouen. Thus, with pious commemoration of the early heroes of the Church, largely an array of bishops, there began that tradition of hagiographical literature with which, a few centuries later, Romance vernacular was to break into the literary field.

On a different stylistic plane, Latin was also the language of law. Each of the Germanic tribes, once settled within the frontiers of the Empire, formulated its legislation, a mixture of Roman law and Germanic custom, in the Latin tongue. Most important is the *Lex Salica*, the code of the Salian Franks, first drawn up in A.D. 507, the year which marked the overthrow of the Visigoths in France and the occupation of their territory. This *Lex Salica* considerably influenced the codes of other Germanic peoples, particularly the *Lex Ribuaria* of the Ripuarian Franks; its influence is also apparent in the Langobardic *Edictus Rothari* (see p. 261). Of other peoples, the Visigoths had their *Lex Visigothorum*, the Burgundians their *Burgundionum Leges*, and beyond the limits of the new Romance-speaking area, though included in Charlemagne's domain, the Bavarians their *Lex Baiuvariorum*. In all these codes a simplified form of Latin, in which the syntax is close to that of the spoken language, was habitually used. Some, notably the *Edictus Rothari*, provide interesting examples of the way in which Germanic words could be incorporated into a Latin text, just as, at a later date, English words were to be embodied into the French legislation drawn up in England during Norman times.

*Evidence of the vernacular in medieval Latin.* When past philologists scoured medieval texts in an attempt to determine the so-called 'chronology of Vulgar Latin', considerable importance was attached to Gregory of Tours. This was because of his own assertion that he wrote as a man of the people. A scholar's attitude to the problem was liable to be dependent upon the degree of belief or disbelief with which he accepted this statement. It may therefore be of interest to reproduce a well-known extract from his preface to the *Liber in gloria Confessorum*, in which, addressing himself to a friend who is supposed to have been Venantius Fortunatus, he apologizes for the 'rusticity' of his style:

Liber in gloria confessorum incipit feliciter.
Pudet insipienti, reprobo imperitoque atque inerti illud adgredi, quod

non potest adimplere; sed quid faciam, quod oculi non patior, quae de beatorum virtutibus vel ipse saepius inspexi vel per relationem bonorum virorum et certae fidei evidenter gesta cognovi? Sed timeo, ne, cum scribere coepero, quia sum sine litteris rethoricis et arte grammatica, dicaturque mihi a litteratis: 'O rustice et idiota, ut quid nomen tuum inter scriptores indi aestimas? Ut opus hoc a peritis accipi putas, cui ingenium artis non subpeditat, nec ulla litterarum scientia subministrat? Qui nullum argumentum utile in litteris habes, qui nomina discernere nescis; saepius pro masculinis feminea, pro femineis neutra et pro neutra masculina conmutas; qui ipsas quoque praepositiones, quas nobilium dictatorum observari sanxit auctoritas, loco debito plerumque non locas. Nam ablativis accusativa et rursum accusativis ablativa praeponis. Putasne: videtur, ut bos piger palaestrae ludum exerceat, aut asinus segnis inter spheristarum ordinem celeri volatu discurrat? Aut certe numquid poterit corvus nigredinem suam albentium columbarum pinnis obtegere aut obscuritas picis liquoris lactei colore mutari? Nempe, ut ista fieri possibile non est, ita nec tu poteris inter scriptores alios haberi.' Sed tamen respondebo illis et dicam, quia: 'Opus vestrum facio et per meam rusticitatem vestram prudentiam exercebo. Nam, ut opinor, unum beneficium vobis haec scripta praebebunt, scilicet ut, quod nos inculte et breviter stilo nigrante describimus, vos lucide ac splendide stante versu in paginis prolixioribus dilatetis.[1]

The passage might be translated into English as follows:

Here, with God's blessing, begins the book to the glory of the Confessors.

An uneducated man, awkward, uncultured and inept, is ashamed to embark on an enterprise which he cannot carry through to completion. What then, am I to do? For I cannot allow clear evidence of the supernatural powers of the Saints to remain hidden from the world—either what I have myself frequently seen or what I have learnt from what good men of unquestionable integrity have told me. But, since I am untrained in the devices of rhetoric or in the art of grammar, I am afraid that when I begin to write it may be said to me by scholars: 'Poor simple soul, why do you imagine that your name will win a place among the (great) writers? Why do you imagine that this work, devoid of all stylistic refinement and aided by no conscious literary skill, will win acceptance with men of culture? You have no experience of literary composition to stand you in good stead; you do not know how to discriminate between nouns. Quite often you confuse feminine with masculine, neuter with feminine and masculine with neuter. And even actual prepositions, the rules for whose usage are based on the authority of the most famous authors, you frequently put out of their rightful place. You assign to them accusative instead of ablative cases, or again ablatives in place of accusatives. Do you not consider it as if a lumbering ox were to train for the sport of

[1] From W. Arndt and B. Krusch: *Gregorii Turonensis opera*, in *Monumenta Germaniae Historica, Scriptores rerum merovingicarum*, tome I, Hanover, 1885, quoted by Studer and Waters, *Historical French Reader*, p. 6.

the wrestling-ring, or a slow-moving ass to run in swift course between the ranks of the ball-players? Or can it be (that you expect) that the crow will be able to conceal the dark colour of its plumage beneath the feathers of white doves; or that the darkness of pitch can be changed by the colour of milk? Assuredly, even as these things cannot occur, so too you will not be able to take your rank among other writers.' But nevertheless, I will answer these critics and say: 'I am doing your work, and because of my own lack of culture, I will give you an opportunity to display your learning. For, in my opinion, these writings of mine will confer this service on you, namely, that what I write about in my obscure style, and in my crude and cursory fashion, you will be able to enlarge upon in a clear and elegant style, extending over more pages.'

Such were the literary preoccupations of the sixth century! Judged by classical standards Gregory's prose is not entirely 'correct', but it is certainly not characterized by elementary mistakes of case and gender, as he suggests.[1] Its peculiarities are largely syntactical and semantic. He uses *ut quid* (l. 7), recalled in the following sentence by *ut* alone (l. 8), as 'why?', cf. the Vulgate, 'Deus meus, ut quid dereliquisti me?' (Matt. xxvii. 46); the construction appears to have been suggested by Gr. ἵνα τί, of which in the Vulgate it is a literal rendering. In his vocabulary, he employs classical words with non-classical meaning, e.g. *feliciter* which acquired its Christian sense of 'with God's blessing' from the fourth century onwards; *reprobus* which, originally 'spurious', has now come to be 'inept'; and *iners* 'lazy' in Classical Latin, here meaning 'stupid'. But these are not words of the popular type which Romance has preserved. Nor is his syntax that of the 'common man'; it is indeed much less revealing than that of the fifth-century author of the *Peregrinatio ad loca sancta*.

Scholars have perhaps been prone to take too seriously Gregory's protestations of linguistic innocence. Far from being popular, his language seems to show a conscious but rather awkward striving for literary effect. Despite his disclaimers, he was by intellectual formation a man of letters. Yet the very fact of his artifice implies the existence of a considerable gulf between the literary style and an everyday speech in which the solecisms which he mentions must have been of quite usual occurrence.

Much of the evolution which the writing of medieval scholars obscures is made plain in the Latin of the growing army of scribes,

[1] In this category there is the single mistake *pro neutra*, which may not be due to Gregory; one manuscript has the correct *pro neutris*.

of all those whose business it was to make an accurate record, with no thought of style, no desire to emulate the great. Legal documents, from the sixth to the eighth centuries, are often little more than a latinized vernacular, in which the common trends of western Romance are clearly apparent. Typically informative is the text of the Salic Law. Though originally of the sixth century, it survives only in Carolingian handwriting, and since it was probably recopied many times one cannot assign to a precise period the many 'vulgarisms' which it contains. They seem to have escaped the eye of the learned Latinists of the early Carolingian court, unless, as has been suggested, they were deliberately left without correction in order that the text might remain easily comprehensible for the people. The Law consists of a series of articles, each defining a crime or misdemeanour, and laying down the penalty which it incurred, as shown in the following examples:

1. Si quis porcello de inter porcos furaverit, DC dinarios, qui faciunt solidos XV, culpabilis judicetur.
2. Si quis maiale votivo furaverit et hoc testibus quod votivus fuit potuerit adprobare, DCC dinarios, qui faciunt solidos XVII, culpabilis judicetur, excepto capitale et dilatura.
3. Si quis sigusium canem magistrum imbulaverit aut occiderit, DC dinarios, qui faciunt solidos XV, culpabilis judicetur.
4. Si quis servo aut caballo vel jumentum furaverit, MCC dinarios, qui faciunt solidos XXX, culpabilis judicetur.
5. Si quis in napina, in favaria, in pissaria vel in lenticlaria in furtum ingressus fuerit, CXX dinarios, qui faciunt solidos III, culpabilis judicetur.
6. Si quis prato alieno secaverit, opera sua perdat.
7. Et si fenum exinde ad domam suam duxerit et discaregaverit, excepto capitale et dilatura, MDCCC dinarios, qui faciunt solidos XLV, culpabilis judicetur.
8. Si quis vinea aliena in furtum vindimiaverit, et inventus fuerit, DC dinarios, qui faciunt solidos XV, culpabilis judicetur.
9. Si quis alterum vulpe clamaverit, solidos III culpabilis judicetur.
10. Si quis alterum leborem, solidos III culpabilis judicetur.
11. Si quis baronem ingenuum de via sua ostaverit aut impinxerit, DC dinarios, qui faciunt solidos XV, culpabilis judicetur.
12. Si quis caballum carrucaricium involaverit, cui fuit adprobatum, excepto capitale et dilatura, MDCCC dinarios, qui faciunt solidos XLV, culpabilis judicetur.
13. Si quis ingenuo Franco aut barbarum qui legem salega vivit, occiderit, cui fuit adprobatum, VIIIM dinarios, qui faciunt solidos CC, culpabilis judicetur.
14. Si quis hominem ingenuum in poteum jactaverit, et vivus inde exierit, IVM dinarios, qui faciunt solidos C, culpabilis judicetur.

With texts such as these we find fully incorporated into the official written language that 'incorrectness' previously observed, from an earlier date, in scratchings on walls and in the engraving of tombstones. Here is the collapse of declension, *-em* being reduced to *-e*, and *-o* serving equally with *-um* to indicate the accusative singular masculine, as in No. 1, 'Si quis porcello . . . furaverit'; No. 2, 'Si quis maiale votivo furaverit . . .; No. 4, 'Si quis servo aut caballo vel jumentum furaverit . . ., &c. The *m* of the accusative feminine is also liable to disappear, as in No. 8, 'Si quis vinea aliena . . . vindimiaverit'. Popular phonetic developments have also crept in: notably, the voicing of the intervocalic voiceless occlusives, as in *leborem* (LEPOREM), *salega* (SALICA), and *discaregaverit* (formed on CARRICARE); elsewhere in the Salic Law are to be found many more examples of this phenomenon, e.g. *abis* (APIS), *cabra* (CAPRA), *erbex* (HIRPEX), *vodivus* (VOTIVUS), *pradum* (PRATUM), *segare* (SECARE), &c. The change in quality whereby the Latin short close vowels, ĭ and ŭ, became the half-close E and O (see p. 43), here illustrated by *salega* and *poteum* (for PŬTEUM, No. 14), is another common feature of the Salic Law, cf. *edoneus* (ĪDONEUS), *pesaria* (PĬSARIA), *cobitum* (CŬBITUM), and *docarius* (DŬCARIUS). On the other hand, a Latin Ē is sometimes represented by *i*, as in *dinarios* (DĒNARIOS) and *vindimiare* (VINDĒMIARE). This is a rather puzzling feature of medieval orthography: it occurs both where the vowel is stressed and where it is unstressed (for stressed forms, cf. *rigni*, *habyre*, in the text of A.D. 716 quoted on p. 325), and sets a minor problem in the *savir et podir* (SAPĒRE ET POTĒRE) of the vernacular *Strassburg Oaths* (see p. 340).

In its vocabulary the Salic Law abundantly illustrates the exuberance of popular 'word-building', particularly in the definition of objects closely related to the soil, as for instance in the series (No. 5): *in napina, in favaria, in pissaria vel in lenticlaria*, i.e. 'in the turnip-plot, in the bean-plot, in the pea-plot, or in the lentil-plot'. Noteworthy too are the formations based on CARRUM, *discaregaverit* (No. 7), the source of the French verb *décharger*, and *caballum carrucaricium* (No. 12). In the case of the latter the word-building instinct appears to have exceeded the acceptable limits, so much so that another scribe has substituted *caballum qui carrucam trahit*: and *carrucaricium* has left no trace in Romance.

The Romance terminology of animals, since clauses dealing with their theft are so numerous, is well represented in the Salic

Law. Beside the *porcus* and the *porcellus* is the *maiale* (No. 2), a term unfamiliar though not unknown in Latin. M. Terentius Varro (116–27 B.C.), a native of Reate, defines it precisely in the following sentence: 'castrantur verres commodissime anniculi, utique ne minores quam semestres, quo facto nomen mutant atque e verribus dicuntur maiales' (*De re rustica*, ii. 4. 21). Although present in the Salic Law the word has left no progeny in Gallo-Romance; on the other hand, still as *maiale*, it has survived as the most current word for 'pig' in Italian. Its apparent connexion with the month of May has prompted the theory that in the first place it was the fattened pig sacrificed to the earth-goddess Maia.[1] Besides pigs, dogs find a frequent mention, and a careful distinction was made between watch-dogs, hunting-dogs or 'retrievers', and sheep-dogs. The *sigusium canem* (No. 3)—the adjective also occurs as *secusius, seusius*, and *siutius*—was a hunting-dog, undoubtedly deriving its name, like many other species of dog, from its reputed place of origin: in this case probably Segusio, nowadays Susa, in Piedmont. In common with *maiale*, the word persists in modern Italian as *segugio* or *seügio*; in Old French it is *seüs*.

The Germanic element in the vocabulary of the Salic Law is less prominent than one might perhaps have expected. It is largely confined to titles of rank—thus, apart from the obvious *Franco* and *salega*, the only Germanic term in the fourteen articles quoted above is *baronem* (No. 11)—and to a few terms associated with Germanic law and custom, e.g. *faidus* 'feud'. This paucity of germanisms may be explained by the fact that the text was originally composed within the lifetime of Clovis, before any real fusion of Frankish elements with Romance could have taken place; and it was probably the work of a Gallo-Roman 'drafting committee'.

Langobardic texts, formulated at a longer interval from the initial occupation, show a livelier picture of the integration of Germanic vocabulary. To examples already quoted from the

---

[1] See F. Schramm, *Sprachliches zur Lex Salica*, Marburg, 1911. The author casts doubt on the etymology of *maiale* given above: 'Mir scheint diese Etymologie zwar sehr volkstümlich zu sein, aber der Richtigkeit zu entbehren. Denn einmal wurde das Schwein ursprünglich fast zu allen Opfern benutzt, dann aber finden wir, daß der Erdgöttin Maia ein trächtiges Schwein—sus praegnans, quae hostia propria est terrae (*Macrobius*, i. 12. 20)—geopfert wurde, als symbolisches Zeichen der Fruchtbarkeit. Dazu wäre eine sus maialis, das unfruchtbare Tier, wenig geeignet' (p. 58). The fact that the pregnant sow should have been replaced by a castrated pig (probably much fatter!) does not seem to us to invalidate the proposed etymology: symbolic detail in such rites may be rapidly forgotten.

*Edictus Rothari* (see p. 262) may be added the *snaida* and *plovum* of the following clauses from the same code:

1. Si servus extra iussionem domini sui ticlatura aut snaida (var.: sinaidam) fecerit in silva alterius, manus ei incidatur.
2. Si quis plovum aut aratrum alienum iniquo animo capellaverit, componat solidos tres. . . .

In No. 1, *snaida* (cf. mod. Germ. *Schneide*, OHG. *sneida*) means 'path cut through a wood'; by extension of meaning it came to be 'boundary' and it is still used in the Abbruzzi as *seneide* 'boundary-stone'. In No. 2, the linking of Germ. *plovum* with Lat. *aratrum* was perhaps intended to include two different types of plough, representing the two different cultures. The Latin of the *Edictus Rothari* is very similar to that of the *Lex Salica*, as may be judged from the remarkable collection of accusatives in the following:

3. Si quis castanea, nuce, pero aut melum inciderit, componat solido uno.

A perfect example of a Romance genitive occurs in the phrase: 'Si quis mundium de puella libera aut muliere habens . . .' (cf. p. 262). Yet both texts still embody features of the written tradition, e.g. the use of the future perfect with its classical meaning, which the vernacular had almost certainly discarded. We can still only guess at what was actually being spoken and await confirmation from the Romance texts which were soon to appear.[1]

*Glosses and glossaries.* Among the clergy, as acquaintance with the structure and vocabulary of Classical Latin became increasingly remote, even the Christian texts of the fourth and fifth centuries, including above all the Vulgate, began to require some measure of linguistic commentary to make them fully comprehensible to readers and learners. Thus the Scriptures, like the Sanskrit Vedas before them, gave rise to their own literature of philological interpretation. This commentary, from the seventh century onwards, appears in the form of the *gloss*, an annotation, marginal or

[1] The Latin of this period may be further studied with the help of the following anthologies: G. Rohlfs, *Sermo Vulgaris Latinus*, 2nd ed. Tübingen, 1956, from which the above quotations from the *Lex Salica* and the *Edictus Rothari* are taken (the original editions are respectively J. M. Pardessus, *Loi salique*, Paris, 1843, and F. Bluhme, *Monumenta Germaniae Historica*, Legum tom. iv); H. F. Muller and P. Taylor, *A Chrestomathy of Vulgar Latin*, New York, 1932; and Manuel C. Díaz y Díaz, *Antología de latín vulgar*, Madrid, 1950. It will be noted that the above authors follow a tradition in which the term 'Vulgar Latin' is applied to the written word, a usage which we have not admitted.

interlinear, whereby a difficult word in the manuscript was explained by another word, or sometimes by a whole phrase. Then, in certain instances, an anonymous clerk collated these glosses, usually the work of different hands and inserted at different times, and arranged them in roughly alphabetical order, thus creating a *glossary*, the rudiments of a dictionary. Where Latin is glossed by Latin, it may be inferred that the word glossed had disappeared from the popular speech of a particular region, while the word given as a gloss had survived, in an evolving but still recognizable form, to become part of the vocabulary of the local medieval Romance.

The best-known collation of Latin glosses, certainly the most informative for the student of Romance philology, is the so-called Reichenau Glossary. The rediscovered manuscript, now at Karlsruhe, formerly belonged to the Abbey of Reichenau, one of the most famous of medieval monastic institutions, founded by the Benedictines in A.D. 724 on the fertile island of Reichenau, off the German side of one of the north-westerly reaches of Lake Constance. But its place of composition, as may be judged from internal evidence, was certainly northern Gaul. Its most recent editor attempts to situate it more exactly at the monastery of Corbie, in Picardy.[1]

The Glossary, intended primarily as a companion to the Vulgate, consists of two parts: a series of 'notes' following the order of the text, and an alphabetical arrangement (here one sees the origin of modern editorial techniques). The first part, which comprises no less than 3,152 glosses, begins with the Book of Genesis, explaining the name—'Genesis dictus eo quod tenet exordium generationis'—and then proceeding to give equivalents for words which might not be understood, e.g.

> subicite: subponite
> producat: germinat
> callidior: vitiosior
> perizomata: succintoria
> auris: tenuis ventus

and so on, through the books of the Old Testament until the middle of the second Book of the Maccabees, at which point it

[1] A. Labhardt, *Contributions... à l'explication des Gloses de Reichenau*, Neuchâtel, 1936, pp. 27–28. The same scholar has published the text as *Glossarium biblicum codicis Augiensis CCLVIII*, Neuchâtel, 1948. Most of the glosses quoted in anthologies are drawn from the *Corpus glossariorum Latinorum*, 7 vols. (five of texts and two of indexes), by G. Loewe and G. Goetz, Leipzig, 1889–1923. More are to be found in the *Glossaria Latina* by W. M. Lindsay, Paris, 1926–31.

suddenly breaks into the New Testament with the Gospels and the Acts of the Apostles; it then returns to the second Book of the Maccabees, at the point of interruption, and ends with the Books of Daniel, Jonah, and Jeremiah, and the Psalms. This curious order may be taken to indicate that the manuscript is not autographic, but is a copy made by a scribe, probably from another copy in which the leaves had been displaced. The alphabetical part contains words not only from the Bible but also from various Lives of Saints and other religious writings, from which one may infer that it began life as a quite different work. In the Reichenau MS., however, both texts are in the same handwriting. According to a majority among palæographers the script is northern French and dates from approximately A.D. 800. The work is thus a compilation, put together some time in the eighth century.

For the linguist, not all the glosses are of equal interest, some being much more 'Romance' in character than others. This is doubtless due to their diversity of origin. One of the principal sources was Isidore of Seville, from whose *Etymologiae* the compiler has sometimes borrowed directly and some of whose definitions have reached the Reichenau Glossary via another and more vast compilation of glosses, the *Abavus maior* (so-called after its first word in alphabetical order), now at Munich and as yet unpublished except for extracts; according to Labhardt (op. cit., p. 43) the Reichenau Glossary owes some 700 glosses to the *Abavus maior*. Of the greatest significance, however, is the fact that the glosses which from the Romance standpoint awaken the liveliest interest are in general those for which no source has been discovered. These are presumably the personal contribution of the unknown Gallic lexicographer, revealing the Latin basis of the vernacular current in his day and in his native region.

Not only does the Glossary show with remarkable clarity how much of Latin vocabulary was dead in the Gallo-Romance of the eighth century and how much lived on in oral tradition, but also, for the first time, indications of local selection are quite unmistakable. For example, ARENAM is glossed by SABULO (a popular accusative in -o), cf. Fr. *sable*; UVAS is glossed by RACEMOS, cf. Fr. *raisins*; CASEUM is glossed by FORMATICUM, cf. Fr. *fromage* (see p. 163); VOMERE is glossed by CULTRO, cf. Fr. *coutre*. Had the Glossary been composed elsewhere than in Gaul, none of these would have been necessary, because all four of the words glossed were still in current use in Spain and Italy, as they are to this day, cf. Span. *arena, uva, queso*; Arag. *guambre*; Ital. *arena, uva, cacio* (in the south and centre), *vomero*. Among the verbs, there are at least two examples of the glossing of DARE by DONARE, cf. Fr. *donner*; this again would have been quite superfluous in Spanish or Italian territory where DARE has been retained as the normal verb for 'to give', cf. Span. *dar*, Ital. *dare*. Among specifically Gallic peculiarities one may point to three examples of the mysterious verb ALARE (see p. 127), quite unknown in other parts of Romania. Equally pertinent is the glossing of VESPERTILIONES by CALVAS SORICES, the antecedent of Fr. *chauve-souris*. To designate the bat Italian has kept VESPERTILIO, somewhat disguised by the accidents of phonetic evolution, as *pipistrello*. Spain has turned the species into 'blind mice', cf. Old Span. *murciego* (mod. *murciélago*), from MUREM CAECUM. No other people but the Gallo-Romans had the curious thought of turning them into 'bald mice'. In fact, bats are not noticeably bald, and one is tempted to infer that CALVAS SORICES is a product of 'popular etymology', hiding a quite different word. In most French patois bats are called 'flying mice' or 'bird-mice'; it may well be that CALVAS is in reality *KAWAS, the Germanic word which survives as the root of Fr. *chouette* 'owl', and that the *chauve-souris* is not a 'bald mouse' but an 'owl-mouse', which would be much more appropriate.[1]

In the examples given below we have confined our choice to those which do show a particularly Romance character, grouping them in such a way as to illustrate the morphological and lexical tendencies discussed in the first chapter. The words recorded as glosses will be recognized as pertaining to the terminology of everyday life—domestic, pastoral, and agricultural. With the brief indication that cases and tenses were intended by the compiler to correspond with those of the Biblical text, we refrain from further commentary:

| | |
|---|---|
| ager: campus | vomere: cultro |
| umo: terra | sagma: soma vel sella |
| arenam: sabulo | passer: omnis minuta avis |
| amne: fluvio | coturnices: quacoles |
| litus: ripa | vespertiliones: calvas sorices |
| plaustra: carra | oves: berbices |

[1] Cf. A. Dauzat, *Le français moderne*, 1951, pp. 23–24. M. Dauzat describes Old Fr. *choue* as 'Gaulish' but it might equally be Germanic, cf. Cast. *chova*, 'jackdaw', Visigothic according to U. T. Holmes (*Studies for S. E. Leavitt*, 1953, p. 58), cf. also Eng. *chough*, Danish *kaa*.

aper: salvaticus porcus
catulus: catellus
uvas: racemos
caseum: formaticum
viscera: intralia
iecore: ficato
de gremio: de sinu
in ore: in bucca
pueros: infantes
anus: vetulae
spadones: castradi
sexus: generis
mares: masculi

forum: mercatum
hiems: ibernus
grando: pluvia mixta con petris
favillam: scintillam
machinas: ingenias
rerum: causarum
calamus: penna unde litteras scribuntur
in scelere: in peccato
nefas: peccatum
crimine: peccato
Gallia: Frantia
Italia: Longobardia

Among these echoes of peaceful existence are a few words of more martial connotation:

> milites: servientes
> ensis: gladius
> framea: gladius bisacutus
> ictus: colpus
> castra: castellum

Further, and here is an additional reason for assigning the text to northern France, scattered amid the Latin terms are a number of latinized borrowings from Frankish:

> scabrones: wapces
> galea: helmus
> pignus: wadius
> ocreas: husas
> turmas: fulcos
> castro: heribergo

A few pronouns aptly illustrate the reduction of the classical system:

> id: hoc
> is: ille vel iste
> ab his: ab istis
> cuncti: omnes
> nemini: nulli

Adjectives, while showing the same process of lexical selection as nouns, also exemplify a point of morphological interest, viz. the decay of the synthetic comparison of Classical Latin:

saniore: plus sano
optimos: meliores
optimum: valde bonum
obesis: crassus

pingues: quae naturaliter grassi sunt
arefacta: sicca
infecunda: sterelis

pulcra: bella  
venusto: pulchro vel onesto  
vorax: manducator  
vorax: manducans  

pronus: qui a dentes iacet  
levam: sinistram  
precoce uve: qui ante maturescunt  
    vel solis calore vel ubertate terre  

Again the Frankish element appears:

rufa: sora

Verbs show, in particular, the elimination of anomalous and irregular forms:

dem: donem  
da: dona  
si vis: si voles  
flare: suflare  
pollicitus est: promisit  
cecinit: cantavit  

tetigit: tangit  
ceciderunt: caderunt  
iacere: iactare  
serunt: seminant  
minatur: manatiat  
sepulta: sepelita  

and a further rich choice of Romance vocabulary:

sublata: subportata  
segregat: seperat  
transgredere: ultra alare  
transilivit: trans alavit  
transfretavit: trans alaret  
transfretare: trans fretum ire, id est trans mare  
onerati: carcati  
stabilivi: firmavi  
vituperant: blasphemant  
non hesitaveris: non dubitaveris  
ludebant: iocabant  
poto: do tibi bibere  

cave: provide  
obviare: incontrare  
emit: comparavit  
meditare: cogitare  
isset: ambulasset  
submersi: dimersi, necati  
concidit: taliavit  
vinxit: ligavit  
transgrediuntur: trans vadunt  
ingredi: intrare  
oportet: convenit  
transmeare: transnotare  

Among verbs, too, there is a Frankish contribution:

non pepercit: non sparniavit  
respectant: rewardant  

Adverbs reveal a general rejection of the rich variety to be found in Classical Latin:

deinceps: postea  
olim: antea  
dudum: antea  
vicessim: per vices  
semel: una vice  

iterum: alia vice  
ita: sic  
ibidem: in eodem loco  
furtim: per furtum  
singulariter: solamente  

Prepositions in the language of the Glossary, as in that of the Laws, show a similar restriction, and in consequence a greatly extended use of such simple forms as *in, ad, per, de,* and *trans*; *contra* also gains in currency, e.g.:

> adversum: contra
> in occursum eorum: in contra illos

It is now easy to understand why Gregory of Tours should have experienced difficulty in using prepositions according to 'the authority of the most famous authors'!

Occasionally a word employed as a gloss is elsewhere glossed, a fact which may be due to the diversity of source to which we have previously referred; thus:

> callis: semita parvula
> semitas: vias

and

> specum: speluncam
> spelunca: concavata saxa

and the already quoted:

> venusto: pulchro vel onesto
> pulcra: bella

Sometimes, too, a rustic misconception creeps in, as when the scape-goat, the 'bouc emissaire', gives rise to the gloss:

> emisarius: qui non est castradus (No. 440)

though in a following gloss we find quite correctly:

> emisarius: ab emitendo ad vindictam dictus (No. 1070)

If the Reichenau Glossary may be described as the forerunner of the modern dictionary, then the Glossary of Kassel, of the same period, merits no less aptly the title of a medieval antecedent of the bilingual phrase-book, as used by the present-day tourist. Conventionally named in this instance after the town to whose civic library it belongs, the manuscript was originally discovered in the monastery of Fulda, in the German province of Hesse-Nassau; like Reichenau, this was a famous Benedictine foundation, dating from A.D. 744. The text consists of two parts, in both of which Latin (or Romance) words are translated into a form of German characterized by features of a Bavarian dialect. The first and longer part contains 180 items, arranged in the manner adopted by the modern dialectologist in framing his questionnaire; thus:

> 1. The human being  (items   1–61)
> 2. Domestic animals  (  „    62–90)

| | |
|---|---|
| 3. The house | (items 91–100) |
| 4. Clothing | ( „ 101–119) |
| 5. Tools and utensils | ( „ 120–50) |
| 6. Miscellaneous | ( „ 151–80) |

In the selection of the following examples the above order has been preserved:

| | | | |
|---|---|---|---|
| homo | man | aucas | cansi |
| caput | haupit | auciun | caesincli |
| capilli | fahs | pulli | honir |
| oculos | augun | pulcins | honchli |
| facias | uuangun | callus | hano |
| mantun | chinni | galina | hanin |
| collo | hals | pao | phao |
| tundi meo capilli | skir min fahs (i.e. cut my hair) | paua | phain |
| radi me meo colli | skir minan hals (i.e. shave my neck) | casu | hus |
|  |  | mansione | selidun |
| radi meo parba | skir minan part (i.e. shave my beard) | stupa | stupa |
|  |  | bisle | phesal |
| labia | lefsa | keminada | cheminata |
| coxa | deoh | furnus | ofan |
| innuolo | chniu | caminus | ofan |
| talauun | anchlao | furnax | furnache |
| pedes | foozi | segradas | sagarari (probably means 'latrine') |
| ordigas | zaehun |  |  |
| uncla | nagal | stabulu | stal |
| putel | darm | pridias | uuanti |
| putelli | darma | mediran | cimpar ('beam') |
| figido | lepara | trapes | capretta ('smaller beam') |
| pecunia | fihu |  |  |
| cauallus | hros | capriuns | rafuun ('rafters') |
| equm | hengist | camisa | pheit |
| iumenta | marhe | pragas | próh |
| equa | marhe | mufflas | hantscoh |
| boues | ohsun | uuanz | irhiner |
| uaccas | choi | siccla | einpar ('bucket', cf. Germ. *Eimer*) |
| armentas | hrindir |  |  |
| pecora | skaaf | sedella, sicleola | ampri |
| pirpici | uuidari | calice | stechal |
| fidelli | chalpir | hanap | hnapf |
| ouiclas | auui | caldaru | chezil |
| agnelli | lempir | caldarola | chezi |
| porci | suuinir | cramailas | hahla |
| ferrat | paerfarh | implenus est | fol ist |
| troia | suu | saccuras | achus |
| scruua | suu | manneiras | parta |

| siciles | sihhila | puticla | flasca |
| falceas | segansa | laniu uestid | uullinaz |
| fomeras | uuaganso | lini uestid | lininaz |
| martel | hamar | albioculus | staraplinter |

The second part is a kind of conversational manual comprising a further sixty-five items, many of them in the form of questions. Here the Latin is much more 'correct' than in the first part, and consequently of less interest. The longest phrase, coming after the glosses of *sapiens homo* and *stultus*, and no doubt suggested by them, runs as follows:[1]

| Stulti sunt | Tole sint | sapienti(a) | spahe |
| romani | uualha | in romana | uualhum |
| sapienti sunt | spahe sint | plus habent | mera hapent |
| paioari | peigira | stultitia | tolaheiti |
| modica est | luzic ist | quam sapientia | denne spahi |

It must be supposed that in the Latin text *in romana* represents *in romano* or *in romanis*; the translation then reads: 'The Romans are stupid, the Bavarians are wise; little wisdom is there in the Romans, they have more stupidity than wisdom.'

Of late the Kassel Glossary has been somewhat neglected. To the scholars of fifty years ago its Latin vocabulary appeared most enigmatic: some considered it to be Gallo-Romance, some opted for Rheto-Romance, while yet others declared it to be Italian. In his work published in 1923, M. Titz seems only to deepen the mystery.[2] Observing, quite correctly, that a few orthographical features are insufficient to permit of localization of the whole, he set out to localize individual words by comparing the vocabulary with that of modern and medieval Romance. In passing, it should be noted that he was preponderantly better-informed for the Gallo-Romance area on account of the then recent publication of the *Linguistic Atlas of France*. Not surprisingly, his system led him to the conclusion that the Glossary is a compilation from many sources; how many is best illustrated in his own words:

Il y a, dans les Gloses de Cassel, un groupe de mots français et réto-français d'une part, et de mots provençaux et italo-provençaux de l'autre côté. Tout pesé, nous sommes convaincu que la présente rédaction de notre monument a été compilé à deux sources, à deux glossaires

[1] For the translation of *romani* by *uualha*, see p. 271, note.
[2] Karel Titz, *Glossy Kasselské*, Prague, 1923 (written in Czech, with a long summary in French).

dont l'un contiendrait les gloses latines, romanes, gallo-romanes, françaises et réto-françaises et proviendrait d'un monastère franco-suisse, l'autre contiendrait les gloses latines, romanes, gallo-romanes, provençales, italo-provençales et proviendrait d'un monastère provençal de l'Est.

This seems a perfect example of the way in which a scholar can become bemused by his own erudition. That the lengthy Reichenau Glossary, inspired by a highly serious purpose, should have been elaborated from various sources, copied and circulated from one monastery to another, is not difficult to apprehend; but that a brief list of household words, of no intrinsic value at the time, and in such barbarous form, should have been so compiled, penned by scribe after scribe, and circulated across Europe, is much more than we can readily accept. Moreover, M. Titz completely ignores the German part, which for his thesis has no significance, and which he considers to be a late addition. But if we do that, what did the glossary gloss? Without the German translations it has no *raison d'être*. Discounting the short second part, which has all the appearance of a postscript, is it not much more feasible that the whole thing was written down one evening by the fireside in a Bavarian monastery, fruit of the converse of one of the monks and a passing traveller of Romance speech?

That the words were taken down by a Bavarian from oral dictation seems quite certain. No manuscript from Gaul could contain such 'barbarisms' as *putel, putelli* (Lat. BOTĔLLUM, cf. Ital. *budello*, Old Fr. *boele*, whence Eng. *bowel*), *pirpici* (Lat. VERVECES, cf. Fr. *brebis*), *fidelli* (Lat. VITELLI), *ferrat* (Lat. VERRES, -ATTUM,[1] cf. Fr. *verrat*), *callus* (Lat. GALLUS), *trapes* (Lat. TRABES), *pragas* (Lat. BRACAS, see p. 183), *fomeras* (Lat. VOMERES), and *puticla* (Lat. BUTTICULA, cf. Fr. *bouteille*). In all of these words the unvoicing of the voiced consonants is due to the speech-habits of the Bavarian, as evinced in his own *part* (Germ. *Bart*), *lepara* (Germ. *Leber*), *cansi* (Germ. *Gänse*), *hapent* (Germ. *haben*), and *paioari* for *Baiu-vari*. It also seems most improbable that the word-list derives, as M. Titz suggested, from the classroom, from the exercise of novitiates learning Latin: neither master nor pupil could unconsciously turn Latin dictation into words containing so many prominent Romance features. In some examples the attempt to

---

[1] For the suffix -ATTUM, see p. 159, note.

give phonetic representation to Romance words seems quite deliberate. To postulate as their source a Romance-speaking in-
formant, who must have been quite illiterate, is therefore not
unreasonable. Concerning the provenance of such a person, one
is first tempted to entertain a preference for the Rheto-Romance
area,[1] on account of its geographical location near the frontier of
Romance and Bavarian; support for this theory might be sought
in the xenophobic remark of the second part, typical of the kind
of derogatory comment which one frequently hears in such regions,
were it not for the dubious nature of the attachment of the second
part to the first. Yet distance in space does not invalidate the
possibility of Gallo-Romance. The date tentatively put to the
work by M. Titz, to which no scholar would take serious exception, is *c.* A.D. 802; this coincides with the time when Charlemagne
was consolidating his rule in Bavaria and Austria (see p. 270), and
it is by no means improbable that soldiery from Gaul were lodged
in the vicinity of a Bavarian monastery (M. Titz suggests Freising
as the place where the copy was made). We therefore incline
towards the vision of a monk with some intellectual curiosity
conducting a brief linguistic investigation of their speech,
noting in Latin the simple words which he recognized, latinizing others, and attempting a phonetic representation of words
which failed to suggest any Latin origin; but visions may be de-
ceptive!

Despite all this uncertainty, the Kassel Glossary remains a
document of the highest interest. The much more important
Glossary of Reichenau provides a rich display of Gallo-Romance
vocabulary, but in latinized form, with only occasional glimpses of
popular phonetic evolution. In the Kassel Glossary, on the other
hand, mingled with Latin words, are recorded for the first time
words which are purely Romance in sound, some of them indeed
almost identical with their equivalents in modern French. In the
spelling of *mantun* and *talauun*, for example, one can detect an
attempt to represent nasalized vowels, cf. Fr. *menton* (< MEN-
TONEM) and *talon* (< TALONEM). Allowance being made for the
faulty transcription of the initial consonant, *ferrat* is Fr. *verrat*
(see above). The linguistic feature which contributes most to give

---

[1] This was the opinion most widely held before the appearance of the study
by M. Titz; see in particular P. Marchot, *Les gloses de Cassel. Le plus ancien
texte réto-roman*, Fribourg, 1895.

to the words of the Kassel Glossary their character of northern Romance is of course the loss of post-tonic vowels; this is further exemplified by many other items, e.g. *putel* (see above), *auciun*, cf. Fr. *oison*, *pulcins*, cf. Fr. *poussins* (<PULLICĪNOS), *mediran*, cf. Fr. *merrain* (< *MATERIAMEN), *capriuns*, cf. Fr. *chevrons* (< *CAPRE-ONES), and *martel*, which is Old Fr. (< MARTELLUM). A Romance diphthong occurs in *manneiras*, which, deriving from MANUARIAS, 'used by hand', here designates a kind of axe, cf. Ital. *mannaia*, Rheto-Rom. *manera*. In *cramailas*, cf. Old Fr. *cramail* (< CREMA-CULUM) and mod. Fr. *crémaillère*—a long adjustable chain suspending the cauldron over the fireplace—the spelling *il* is already used to represent one of the new consonants of Romance, the so-called *l mouillé* (see p. 364). Another strikingly popular form is *bisle*, probably written through ultra-correction for *pisle*: if we take the tonic *i* as a graphy for the Romance diphthong *ei* (cf. the *Strassburg Oaths*, p. 340), here is Old Fr. *peisle* (< PENSILE), anomalously spelt *poêle* in modern French. Still more surprising is *pridias*, in which, but for the Bavarian translation, one would scarcely recognize a Romance word for 'walls'; it must derive from Lat. PARI-ĒTES, presumably through an intermediate *P(A)RĒTIES, for which there is elsewhere no evidence. Finally, the list contains a characteristic non-Latin element, represented by the Germanic *mufflas* (cf. Fr. *moufles*), *uuanz* (cf. Picard *wanz*, Fr. *gants*), and *hanap*, from HNAPP, cf. Germ. *Napf*; also by the Celtic root of *ordigas* which seems to have combined with ARTICULUM to produce *orteil* (cf. p. 192). This foreign element constitutes perhaps the strongest argument for attributing the Romance of the Kassel Glossary to northern France.

From the whole of western Romania there survives an abundance of linguistic commentary of the kind illustrated by the Glossaries of Reichenau and Kassel. In each country a proliferation of glosses heralded the appearance of texts written in the local vernacular. Some, by their very nature, indicate their geographical origin, as for instance the Greek–Latin glosses of southern Italy. But for the most part they permit of no precise location: thus Latin texts containing glosses of an apparently Spanish character have been discovered in Italian monastic libraries. In Spain, the most important glosses by far are those which came from the monasteries of Silos and San Millán; dating from the tenth century, they are almost entirely Romance, the first tangible examples of Spanish (see p. 405). In France, however, the output was checked by more radical measures, by a sudden revival of scholarship, which, so far as Latin texts were concerned, made the practice of glossing unnecessary.

*The Carolingian Renaissance.* The period extending from the mid-seventh to the mid-eighth century was on the Continent a rather barren time for literature and learning. The inspiration to study and to write seems temporarily to have lost its force. Yet, as often happens in the spiritual movements of mankind, it was not entirely lost, but had taken refuge in those peripheral areas which it had reached only late, and whence it was to flow back with a renewed vitality. Ireland and Britain, Celts and Anglo-Saxons, lent much of the impetus which resulted in a revival of learning in the Carolingian Empire.

This development was, of course, due to the fact that where Christianity went, there went Latin. The Irish Church was primarily the creation of St. Patrick (*c.* A.D. 373–463). Born in Britain, most probably in Wales, he was carried away captive by Irish raiders as a youth of sixteen, but escaped from slavery to Gaul, to return later as a missionary. It may be that in the Irish schools which were subsequently founded the reading of classical authors for purposes of exercise was to some extent practised, but in the main the language there used and taught as the key to the Scriptures was the typical Church Latin of the fifth and sixth centuries. In Ireland, however, where from the first it was completely foreign and therefore immune from the disintegrating influence of Romance vernacular, it underwent none of the deterioration of standards which afflicted the literary Latin of Gaul.

It was now the turn of Ireland to send missionaries to the Continent. Of these the most famous was Columbanus (*c.* A.D. 540–615), a monk from the monastery of Bangor, who conducted in Gaul and Germany missions which left lasting memorials in the form of monasteries, among them that of Luxeuil founded by Columbanus himself, and the still more celebrated Swiss monastery of Saint-Gall due to one of his disciples: at Saint-Gall, centuries later, the scholars of the Italian Renaissance were to discover their richest harvest of the lost texts of classical antiquity. The work of the Irish was afterwards continued by Anglo-Saxon monks, culminating in the activities of Boniface in Germany, from A.D. 715 until his martyrdom in Frisia in A.D. 755.

In England itself, after the Augustine missions at the end of the sixth century, there was a partial return to paganism. Reconversion in the south came as the result of a direct appeal to Rome, whence Theodore of Tarsus was sent to become Archbishop of Canterbury from A.D. 669 to 690; a Greek scholar, he founded a school which inaugurated the study of that language in our country. The return of Christian and Latin tradition to the north was largely due to the Irish monks of Iona: invited by King Oswald of Northumbria to convert his country they sent Aidan, later Bishop of Lindisfarne. In this area, at the monastery of Jarrow, lived the outstanding representative of Anglo-Latin literature, the Venerable Bede (c. A.D. 670–735), in the judgement of the present day the greatest literary figure of the time. No mere retailer of legends after the usual medieval manner, but an historian in the modern sense, careful to check the accuracy of his sources and to ensure the truth of his statements, Bede has left in his *Historia ecclesiastica gentis Anglorum* by far the most reliable account of events in England after the Anglo-Saxon occupation. Besides being a scholar, he was a teacher. One of his pupils, Egbert, became Archbishop of York and founded there another active centre of Latinism. Ultimately, this promising revival of culture in England, though to some extent kept alive in the south by the efforts and example of King Alfred, was in the north obliterated by the Danes. Lindisfarne was sacked in A.D. 793 and York itself in A.D. 867, with the total destruction by fire of a library which by then was widely renowned. But before this happened the Cathedral school of York had produced a number of distinguished alumni, among them Alcuin (A.D. 735–804). Upon Alcuin rests the immediate relevance of the Irish and Anglo-Saxon movements to the Carolingian Renaissance.

Literary standards in Gaul had in the meantime considerably deteriorated, as the 'Dog Latin' of everyday practice gained an ascendancy over the 'Church Latin' of scholarly circles. A Reichenau Glossary might assist the clergy in reading the Scriptures, but this in itself was not enough. With the accession of Pépin, the first Carolingian, one finds already an attempt at reform, at least in the eradication of vernacular influences upon orthography. The measure of improvement which this achieved is well brought out by a study of documents written at the court during the eighth century; compare, for instance, the following two versions of the same text:

| A.D. 716 | A.D. 768 |
|---|---|
| *(reign of Chilpéric II)* | *(reign of Pépin)* |

| | |
|---|---|
| Oportit climenciae princepale, inter citeras peticionis, illut que pro salute adescribetur, et pro divine nominis postolatur, plagabile auditum suscipere, et, procul dubium, ad aefectum perducere, quatenus de caduces rebus presente secoli aeterna conquiretur, juxta preceptum Domini dicentis: 'Facetis vobis amicis de mamona iniquetatis' … et dum sacerdotum congrua inpertemus beneficia, retrebutorem Domino ex hoc habyre meriamur in eterna tabernacola. Igetur venerabelis … abba de baselica peculiaris patronis nostri domni Dionisii marthyris, uby ipse preciosus domnus in corpure requiiscit, climenciae rigni nostri supplecavit. … | Oportet climentiae principali, inter citeras petitiones, illud quod pro salute adscribitur et pro divine nominis postulatur, placabile auditum suscipere, et procul dubium ad effectum perducere, quatenus de caducis rebus praesentis saeculi aeterna conquiritur, juxta praeceptum Domini dicentis: 'Facite vobis amicos de mammona iniquitatis' … et dum sacerdotum congrua impertimur beneficia, retributorem Domino ex hoc habere mereamur in aeterna tabernacula. Igitur venerabilis … abba de basilica peculiaris patroni nostri Domni Dionysii Martyris, ubi ipse pretiosus domnus in corpore requiescit, climentiae regni nostri supplicavit. … |

(Mario Pei, *The Language of the Eighth-Century Texts in Northern France*, p. 387)

Yet this was a mere correction of grammar and spelling, undertaken for a practical purpose. The real restoration of literary Latin was brought about through the personal interest and energy of Charlemagne, and it was carried into effect by the group of scholars with whom he surrounded himself at his court at Aix. Foremost among these was Alcuin. The meeting between the two men appears to have taken place at Parma, on the occasion of one of Alcuin's Italian journeys. Invited by Charlemagne to the imperial court, Alcuin joined him there, having first obtained the sanction of his Archbishop at York, in A.D. 782. From then until A.D. 796 he remained as head of the palace school and adviser to Charlemagne on educational and religious matters. In this capacity he became the guiding genius of the new intellectual movement. Even during the last few years of his life, after he had been granted permission to retire to the Abbey of Saint-Martin at Tours, he still continued the work of reform, developing a school of copyists which eliminated Merovingian script, grown almost unintelligible, and replaced it by Carolingian, a form of writing based on capitals, later to be the model for printed characters.

At the court of Aix there prevailed a spirit of erudition, at once serious and playful, which one instinctively likens to that of the Pléiade in sixteenth-century France. One is tempted to compare the role of Alcuin with that of Daurat, convener of poets and scholars: it would perhaps be dangerous to push the analogy too far. In the playfulness Alcuin certainly had his share. His sense of humour, which nowadays would probably attract the epithet 'donnish', found expression in his letters and also in his habit of bestowing nicknames on his friends. He himself was Flaccus, the Emperor was David, and the poets Angilbert and Theodulf were respectively Homer and Pindar. However inappropriate such sobriquets may now seem when applied to these men, they nevertheless serve to show the direction of their interests, the range of their ambitions. If Alcuin chose to call himself Flaccus (Horace to us), it was presumably because he had read and admired the work of the Roman poet, though where and in what circumstances he developed such an 'un-Christian' taste we have not been able to ascertain. At some point he had gone beyond the limits of the theological treatises on which he had been nurtured and the Christian Latin in which they are couched, and was himself practising that deliberate cult of the Classics which has characterized every European renaissance. Rather surprising, at first sight, is the orientation towards Greek, but it should be remembered that Charlemagne, in gathering together scholars from every corner of his Empire, had enlisted an important contingent from Italy, where Byzantine influence was still strong. Alcuin may also have been in contact with scholars from the school of Greek at Canterbury.

All the personalities of the group were poets after their manner, but in literary inspiration they are somewhat disappointing. Alcuin himself has left in particular two long poems, the one entitled *De patribus, regibus et sanctis Eboricae ecclesiae*, a history of the see of York, and the other *De clade Lindisfarnensis monasterii*, a lament for the sack of Lindisfarne. Both are generally considered to be rather dull: the genius of Alcuin was expressed in his deeds and direction of studies rather than in literature. Of Angilbert, one of Charlemagne's favourite diplomatic envoys, a man greatly esteemed by his colleagues, little has survived, and that little is of no outstanding quality; in history he finds a niche as the lover of Charlemagne's daughter Bertha and father by her of Nithard, to whom we are indebted for his preservation of the text of the *Strassburg Oaths* (see below, p. 331). If the lyrical vein does appear, it is chiefly in the work of Theodulf of Orleans (the place of his bishopric). A native of northern Spain, of Visigothic descent and hence sometimes known as Theodulf the Goth, he reached Charlemagne's court in about A.D. 781, and quickly winning favour he eventually succeeded Alcuin as chief educational adviser when the latter retired to Tours. To his misfortune he survived most of the others, and shortly after Charlemagne's death he was falsely accused of conspiracy and thrown into prison at Angers. While in captivity he beguiled the time by writing hymns, one of which is said to survive in the English hymnal as 'All glory, laud, and honour'.

Among prose-writers Paulus Diaconus (c. A.D. 725–c. 799) is outstanding for his *Historia Langobardorum*, which recounts the whole story of the Langobards from the time of Alboin's invasion until their downfall at the hands of Charlemagne (see p. 257). A Langobard himself, brought up at the court of Pavia, Paulus became the close friend of Adelperga, the reputedly beautiful and certainly cultured daughter of King Desiderius. When, in A.D. 757, she contracted a political marriage with Arichis, Duke of Bene-vento, Paulus accompanied her, and thereafter lived for nearly twenty years at the southern court. Then came the Langobardic defeat, in consequence of which Desiderius and his queen were dispatched to the monastery of Corbie, and Paulus followed his sovereign's fate by retiring to the monastery of Cassino. His fame as a scholar, however, had come to the notice of the Emperor, who summoned him to Aix, where he remained as a leading member of the literary circle until he was allowed to return to Monte Cassino, to spend there his declining years.

A late-comer to the circle was Einhardt (c. A.D. 770–840), a German from the valley of the Main, and a product of the monas-tery of Fulda. As a young man of twenty-one he was admitted to a position at the palace school, probably with the help of Alcuin, whose special protection he seems to have enjoyed. After Charle-magne's death he remained in favour at court, the close companion of the Emperor Louis, a man of his own age, until about A.D. 830, when he retired to the monastery of Mulinheim (the present-day

Seligenstadt). By that time the court had lost much of its attraction, having become a centre of fierce political intrigue through the feebleness of Louis and the quarrelsome disposition of his sons. Probably in this retirement he completed his masterpiece, the *Vita Caroli*, a work destined to be one of the most widely read of the Middle Ages, as the eighty or more surviving manuscripts well testify.

In his munificent and enlightened patronage of scholarship lies the most enduring greatness of Charlemagne. His Empire soon collapsed, but, despite all the anarchy and disruption which followed, standards of literature and learning never again fell so low as they had been in France during the years which preceded the Carolingian dynasty. As an illustration of the change which had come over written Latin we can perhaps do no better than quote an extract of the *Vita Caroli*, in which Einhardt's fluent and lucid prose takes us back beyond the time of Gregory of Tours. In fact, the style is closely imitated from that of the Roman historian Suetonius, of whose *Lives of the Caesars* the monastery of Fulda possessed the only copy then known; the *Life of Augustus* formed an obviously suitable model for a biographer writing in the heroic vein. What passage could be more fitting to our purpose than the description of the battle of Roncesvaux, with its first mention of Roland?

Cum enim assiduo ac poene continuo cum Saxonibus certaretur, dispositis per congrua confiniorum loca praesidiis, Hispaniam quam maximo poterat belli apparatu adgreditur; saltuque Pyrinei superato, omnibus quae adierat oppidis atque castellis in deditionem acceptis, salvo et incolomi exercitu revertitur; praeter quod in ipso Pyrinei iugo Wasconiam perfidiam parumper in redeundo contigit experiri. Nam cum agmine longo, ut loci et angustiarum situs permittebat, porrectus iret exercitus, Wascones, in summi montis vertice positis insidiis—est enim locus ex opacitate silvarum, quarum ibi maxima est copia, insidiis ponendis oportunus—extremam impedimentorum partem et eos qui novissimi agminis incedentes subsidio praecedentes tuebantur desuper incursantes, in subiectam vallem deiciunt consertoque cum eis proelio, usque ad unum omnes interficiunt, ac direptis impedimentis, noctis beneficio, quae iam instabat, protecti, summa cum celeritate in diversa disperguntur. Adiuvabat in hoc facto Wascones et levitas armorum et loci in quo res gerebatur situs, et contra Francos et ars morum gravitas et loci iniquitas per omnia Wasconibus reddidit impares. In quo proelio Eggihardus regiae mensae praepositus, Anshelmu-comes palatii et Hruodlandus Brittannici limitis praefectus cum aliis conpluribus interficiuntur. Neque hoc factum ad praesens vindicari poterat, quia hostis re perpetrata ita dispersus est, ut ne fama quidem remaneret, ubinam gentium quaeri potuisset.[1]

(*Scriptores rerum Germanicarum, Einhardi Vita Karoli Magni, Editio Quarta*, Hanover, 1880, p. 9)

Thus were the cadences of the classical sentence restored and all the tricks of composition as taught throughout the centuries in schools, down to the present day. But, inevitably, so far as Gaul was concerned, this was at a price: the restored Latin was so removed from vernacular usage that no Romance-speaking person without an advanced classical training could hope to understand it. There is one clear testimony to the linguistic crisis of the times. The Council of Tours assembled in A.D. 813, the year before Charlemagne's death, issued in its seventeenth canon an order whereby the clergy were required to translate their sermons: 'et ut easdem omelias quisque aperte transferre studeat in rusticam romanam linguam aut theotiscam, quo facilius cuncti possint intellegere quae dicuntur'.

This marks a crucial point in the genesis of literary Romance. But how, exactly, should the evidence be interpreted? It is commonly taken to imply that the recognition of Romance as a language was a direct consequence of the Latin revival. But, pondering the matter, we incline to suggest a somewhat different perspective. The real cause of the literary priority of French seems to lie not

---

[1] The material of this passage was borrowed by Einhardt from the Royal Annals of which it retains some of the phrases. We append a translation:

While the war against the Saxons was being prosecuted constantly and almost continuously, he (Charlemagne), having placed garrisons at suitable places along the frontiers, attacked Spain with all the military forces which he could muster. He crossed the Pyrenees, received the submission of all the towns and fortresses which lay in his path, and came back with his army safe and intact, except that, on the return journey, in the heart of the Pyrenees, he had occasion to experience a little of Basque treachery. For, as the army was proceeding stretched out in a long file, as the character of the place with its narrow passage required, the Basques, having prepared ambushes up in the mountain—the position is most suitable for laying ambushes on account of the darkness of the woods which there abound—rushed down and threw into the valley below the last part of the baggage-train and those who were acting as a rear-guard; then they engaged them in battle, killed them to the last man, seized the baggage, and sheltered by the help of nightfall dispersed as quickly as possible. The Basques were favoured on this occasion by the lightness of their arms and the situation of the place in which the battle was fought; the Franks, on the other hand, were on unequal terms with the Basques on account of the weight of their arms and their disadvantageous position. In this battle Eggihard, the royal seneschal, Anselm, count of the palace, and Roland, prefect of the march of Brittany, were killed, together with many others. Nor could this deed be straightway avenged, for once it was perpetrated the enemy so dispersed that there remained no indication of where they could be sought out.

so much in the Latin revival itself as in the bilingual character—
Romance and Germanic—of Charlemagne's Empire, of which the
Latin revival was another and parallel consequence. A first Germanic influence, that of the Salian Franks, had been absorbed,
without involving a direct threat to the continued use of medieval
Latin as the sole literary language; throughout the Merovingian
period scribes continued to write in a Latin which incorporated
Germanisms and made increasing concessions to popular Romance
usage, just as they did in other countries of Romance speech.
But then came the accession of a dynasty which shifted the centre
of power to the linguistic perimeter, and the ruling members of
which were again Germanic. Of Charlemagne, Einhardt tells us:
'not satisfied with his native tongue, he applied himself to the
study of foreign languages, and learnt Latin so well that he could
express himself as well in that language as in his native tongue'
(*Vita Karoli*, chap. 25). Apparently, he took a considerable interest
in this native tongue, and Einhardt leaves us in no doubt as to its
affiliation when, a little farther on (op. cit., chap. 29), he tells how
the Emperor gave new Germanic names to the months and the
winds. The third ruler of the Austrasian house, Louis the Pious,
is said to have uttered on his death-bed the words *huz, huz* (i.e.
'out, out'), which implies that he died a good German; not until
Charles the Bald and the decline of the court of Aix was there
a Carolingian monarch identified with France and Romance
speech. Like Charlemagne, nearly all the leading scholars who
created the Latin revival were men who spoke Germanic dialects
as their native tongue and Latin as their acquired medium. It was
not unnatural that, being scholars, they should question the standards of their acquisition, literary Latin, and seek to reform them
by reference to a past tradition: for this there is a parallel in the
fact that, a few centuries later, the first books of French grammar
were to be composed in England. Concurrently with the elevation
of Latin, written German was being used as a medium of communication, particularly for religious instruction, in the German-
speaking part of the Empire. With this precedent, the employment
of written Romance in the Romance-speaking part of the Empire
became an obvious counterpart.

Mention of *lingua theotisca* in the canon of the Council of Tours
prompts one further reflection. Why should the prelates have
seen fit to prescribe the use of German in Germany? It is most

improbable that the inhabitants of the eastern half of the Empire were at any time capable of understanding a sermon in Latin. Only during the eighth century was much of this territory brought within the bounds of Christendom. Boniface and his fellow monks from England, when among the continental Saxons and the Frisians, must certainly have found in their native English a more practical medium than Latin for preaching the Gospel. In fact, far from initiating a revolutionary reform, the Council of Tours in this instance was merely bestowing its official recognition upon a state of affairs which already existed. If this were so with reference to German, it could equally be true of the situation in the Romance-speaking area: the element of crisis would then be less acute than is commonly inferred. Yet an official sanction is not to be despised. From A.D. 813 the knowledgeable man in France was to be consciously bilingual; and the priest was credited with two languages to use and confuse, as in the satirical picture given by the author of the *Roman de Renart*, where Renart is 'confessed' by his cousin Grinbert, the badger:

> puis le baisa et si l'asout,
> moitié romanz, moitié latin.

*(Première branche*, ed. M. Roques, ll. 1124–5)

*The emergence of written Romance.* It is to be expected that once Gallo-Romance had attained such degree of recognition as was granted by the Council of Tours, some record of it in writing should within a short time appear. The earliest surviving specimen of written Romance, coinciding with an historical event, can be exactly dated at A.D. 842. On 14 February of that year Charles the Bald and Louis the German met at Strassburg to conclude their alliance against Lothair. The circumstances are described in detail in a Latin chronicle known to later historians as *De dissensionibus filiorum Ludovici Pii*, composed by Nithard (d. A.D. 844). The author here tells how the two kings harangued their men in *romana* and *teudisca lingua*, and proceeds to quote verbatim the terms of the oaths taken by the soldiers of each camp and by the kings themselves: in all, two oaths in Gallo-Romance and two in German. These are the *Strassburg Oaths*, of which the Romance 'dialect' has set for scholars a long-debated problem. That it cannot be satisfactorily located may be partly due to the fact that both the Romance and the Germanic versions were translated from an original scribal draft in Latin: the scribe of the Romance version, lacking the written precedents which by that time had been established for the Franconian dialect of German, would then, not unnaturally, have been much influenced in the orthography of his rendering by that of the Latin draft (see A. Ewert, 'The Strasburg Oaths', *Transactions of the Philological Society*, London, 1935, pp. 16–35). From some forty years later, however, there survives a poem of twenty-nine lines, the *Cantilène de sainte Eulalie*, composed in a vernacular which leaves no doubt as to its origin in Picardy. Court and monastery appear from the outset as centres for the forging of the new literary standards, but the monastery predominates.

From the evidence of these ninth-century texts the tradition of writing in the vernacular appears as created in northern France. Other centres in western Romania followed the example at a distance, almost as though reluctantly. In the courts of Provence, whose ruling nobles owed a nominal allegiance to the decadent French monarchy but lived in virtual independence, a prolific and spectacular outburst of secular verse began at the end of the eleventh century, but two works of religious inspiration, the *Boecis* and the *Chanson de sainte Foi d'Agen*, as also the provençalized 'Clermont poems', all of them difficult to date with any accuracy (late tenth to early eleventh centuries), show that before this time the clergy of the south had become aware of the practical advantages of literary composition in *langue d'oc*. In Spain the first continuous passage in a local dialect occurs in the *Glosas Silenses*, dating from the mid-tenth century, but this is scarcely more than a foreshadowing of the literary standard. Much of early Spanish writing has certainly perished; not until the mid-twelfth-century *Poema del Cid* is there a surviving literary text of any amplitude. Earlier than this are some of the Mozarabic fragments appended as ḫarǧa's to the two types of Arabic and Hebrew lyric, muwaššaḥ and zajal, composed in the south. The end of the twelfth century saw the emergence of prose vernacular in both Portuguese and Catalan, the former in legal texts, and the latter first attested in the so-called *Homilies d'Organyà*, a collection of six short sermons discovered at Organyà in the diocese of Urgel. Italian came still later, slowly disentangling itself from the medieval Latin which it continued to resemble so closely: there is no substantial Italian text until well into the thirteenth century, by which time both the *langue d'oïl* and the *langue d'oc* of France were fully established as the media of abundant literatures.

The twilight of the Romance languages in the west thus comes to an end, their prehistory merging into separate histories. Yet Latin remained everywhere their literary rival until it was finally subordinated in consequence of the convulsions of the sixteenth century. The pressure of new intellectual and spiritual demands, assisted by print, then gave literary status to other Romance dialects. Rheto-Romance, represented earlier in a few twelfth-century fragments, at length came to the light; so too did that Cinderella of the Romance languages, Rumanian, though masked in a Cyrillic script which until the nineteenth century effectively concealed from scholars its Romance identity.

# THE CREATION OF ROMANCE STANDARDS

From the pattern of unrecorded Romance as it must have been in the ninth century, certain local speeches, widely separated in the limited geographical concepts of the time, were to assume the role of standard languages. Their gradual development in the west, adumbrated in the previous chapter, will here be examined in more detail, in a roughly chronological sequence. As late-comers, with little or no medieval tradition, the standards forged from Rheto-Romance and Balkan Romance will be relegated, though with regret, to a position of minor importance in the general scheme.

## GALLO-ROMANCE

### (a) Langue d'oïl

*The Strassburg Oaths.* Shortly after the successful outcome of the alliance between Charles the Bald and Louis the German, the chronicler Nithard was killed in a battle near Angoulême fought by the forces of Charles against the rebellious vassal, Pépin II of Aquitaine (14 June, A.D. 844). His account of the events which he witnessed is thus closely contemporary, and the oaths sworn at Strassburg were recorded as he heard them, indeed as he may have helped to draft them. There is, however, a gap of some 150 years between A.D. 842 and the date of the single surviving manuscript; it is therefore very probable that a difficulty of interpretation in the French version is due to scribal corruption.

The relevant excerpt from Nithard's text is as follows:[1]

Ergo xvi kal. marcii Lodhuvicus et Karolus in civitate quę olim

---

[1] Editions of the *Strassburg Oaths* are numerous. The extract given here is from Nithard, *Histoire des fils de Louis le Pieux*, éditée et traduite par Ph. Lauer (Classiques de l'histoire de France au moyen âge, Paris, 1926).

The text of the French Oaths (for an examination of the discrepancies between these and the German Oaths, see above, p. 331) may be translated in the following terms:

1. For the love of God and the salvation of the Christian people and our common salvation, from this day forward, in so far as God gives me knowledge

Argentaria vocabatur, nunc autem Strazburg vulgo dicitur, convenerunt et sacramenta quę subter notata sunt, Lodhuvicus romana, Karolus vero teudisca lingua, juraverunt. Ac sic, ante sacramentum circumfusam plebem, alter teudisca, alter romana lingua, alloquuti sunt. Lodhuvicus autem, quia major natu, prior exorsus sic coepit:

'Quotiens Lodharius me et hunc fratrem meum, post obitum patris nostri, insectando usque ad internecionem delere conatus sit nostis. Cum autem nec fraternitas nec christianitas nec quodlibet ingenium, salva justicia, ut pax inter nos esset, adjuvare posset, tandem coacti rem ad juditium omnipotentis Dei detulimus, ut suo nutu quid cuique deberetur contenti essemus. . . .'

Cumque Karolus haec eadem verba romana lingua perorasset Lodhuvicus, quoniam major natu erat, prior haec deinde se servaturum testatus est:

'Pro Deo amur et pro christian poblo et nostro commun salvament, d'ist di in avant, in quant Deus savir et podir me dunat, si salvarai eo cist meon fradre Karlo et in ajudha et in cadhuna cosa, si cum om per dreit son fradra salvar dift, in o quid il mi altresi fazet, et ab Ludher nul plaid nunquam prindrai, qui, meon vol, cist meon fradre Karle in damno sit.'

Quod cum Lodhuvicus explesset, Karolus teudisca lingua sic hęc eadem verba testatus est:

'In Godes minna ind in thes christianes folches ind unser bedhero gehaltnissi, fon thesemo dage frammordes, so fram so mir Got geuuizci indi mahd furgibit, so hald ih thesan minan bruodher, soso man mit rehtu sinan bruher scal, in thiu thaz er mig so sama duo, indi mit Ludheren in nohheiniu thing ne gegango, the, minan uuillon, imo ce scadhen uuerdhen.'

Sacramentum autem quod utrorumque populus, quique propria lingua, testatus est, romana lingua sic se habet:

'Si Lodhuuigs sagrament que son fradre Karlo jurat conservat et Karlus, meos sendra, de suo part lo fraint,[1] si io returnar non l'int pois,

and power, I will support this my brother Charles in aid [i.e. feudal 'aide'] and in everything, as one ought by right to support one's brother, provided that he does likewise to me, and I will never enter into any agreement with Lothair which, with my consent, may be harmful to this my brother Charles.
2. If Louis keeps the oath which he swore to his brother Charles, and Charles my lord for his part breaks it, if I cannot deter him therefrom, neither I nor anyone whom I can deter therefrom will be of any assistance to him against Louis.

[1] We have changed here the *non l'ostanit* given by Lauer to the more usually accepted *lo fraint*; both are attempts to make good the difficulty arising from the manuscript reading *ñ lostanit*, which has been variously interpreted. Earlier editors, from F. Diez onwards( Diez read *non lo se tanit*) thought that *stanit* must represent either SE TENET or EX TENET, and translated the phrase as 'does not keep it' (see also A. Tabachovitz, *Étude sur la langue de la version française des Serments de Strasbourg*, Uppsala, 1932, who considers *tanit* to be a dialectal form from Lorraine). In the version given by Lauer *ostanit* is held to be the same word as Old Fr. *obstenir* 'to defend', 'maintain'. The chief objection to all these renderings is that the German text employs the word *forbrihchit* (mod. Germ. *verbricht*) 'breaks'; since the French text is in most respects a close

ne io ne neuls cui eo returnar int pois, in nulla ajudha contra Lodhu-
uuig nun li iv er.'

Teudisca autem lingua:

'Oba Karl then eid then er sinemo bruodher Ludhuuuige gesuor
geleistit, indi Ludhuuuig min herro then er imo gesuor, forbrihchit,
ob ih inan es iruuenden ne mag, noh ih noh thero nohhein, then ih es
iruuenden mag, uuidhar Karle imo ce follusti ne uuirdhit.'

Quibus peractis Lodhuvicus Renotenus per Spiram et Karolus juxta
Wasagum per Wizzunburg Warmatiam iter direxit.

Concerning the version of the *Strassburg Oaths* in German there
is no problem: it is a straightforward piece of simple prose in the
Rhenish-Franconian dialect which at that time was coming into
use in the great monasteries and is of no particular significance for
the study of the German language. But our first specimen of
'French', if we may call it such, presents various difficulties. These
are partly textual; as A. Ewert writes (loc. cit.):

If the French and German Oaths be read through without any
palaeographical or philological preoccupations, one cannot but be
struck by the fact that the French version reads awkwardly, presents
a number of obscurities and stylistic blemishes, and, in a word, does
not read as if it were all of a piece, whereas the German version shows
not the slightest blemish from beginning to end. In the French Oaths
we have the awkward repetition of *salvar*, we have the addition of the
phrase *et in aiudha et in cadhuna cosa*, which comes oddly after *salvarai*,
however we may try to justify its presence, and we have finally, apart
from minor blemishes, the crucial passage *de suo part ñ lostanit*.

Still more fundamental than textual problems is that of the language itself. If we judge from our knowledge of the evolution of
French as gleaned from other sources, in particular from the
*Cantilène de sainte Eulalie*, the language of the Oaths seems, for
A.D. 842, to be most archaic. As regards its place of origin, scholars
have suggested a remarkable range of possibilities. For some it
comes from the Rhône valley and for others from Lorraine, for
some it is Picard while others have opted for Poitevin—this last
suggestion being less improbable than may at first appear to be

---

parallel, one would expect to find there too a word for 'breaks'. Normally this
would be Old Fr. *fraint* from FRANGIT; in the Oaths such a word could conceivably be written *franit*. Hence the favourite theory according to which a
copyist wrote *stanit* instead of *franit*, a mistake easy to make since *st* and *fr*
look very similar in Carolingian handwriting, and that a further lapse brought
in the abbreviation *ñ* for *non*, obviously out of place if the verb means 'breaks'.
Since this is not entirely satisfying, we have reproduced above (p. 339) the much
more drastic explanation advanced by Ewert.

the case, since Charles the Bald had established his court at Poitiers. The four regions, however, could scarcely be more widely removed from one another within the area of French, and from this diversity of opinion it seems permissible to conclude that the Oaths contain insufficient data to allow of localization in any given speech area.

Professor Ewert's approach to these questions merits further attention. It may be assumed, he observes, that both versions are translated from an original draft in Latin, Latin being then, as for long afterwards, the common language of all notarial documents. He then attempts a hypothetical reconstruction, employing the phraseology of like documents, in particular that of the Oaths taken at Coblenz in A.D. 860 by the same two protagonists with the sons of Lothair, oaths recorded in a Latin which contains terms closely resembling those of the *Strassburg Oaths*. Since the result of the experiment is illuminating, we reproduce his text in full, recalling, as he does, that in any Latin original the names of Charles and Louis would have to be represented in the conventional notarial manner by *nomen*, or more probably by its abbreviation $\bar{n}$:

1. *Ad Dei voluntatem et ad populi christiani
   In Godes minna ind in thes christianes folches
   Pro Deo amur et pro christian poblo
2. *et nostrum commune salvamentum,
   ind unser bedhero gehaltnissi,
   et nostro commun salvament,
3. *de isto die inantea, in quantum mihi Deus
   fon thesemo dage frammordes, so fram so mir Got
   d'ist di in avant, in quant Deus
4. *scire et posse donaverit, $\left\{ \begin{array}{l} \text{adjutor ero} \\ \text{sic salvabo} \end{array} \right.$
   geuuiczi indi mahd furgibit, so hald ih
   savir et podir me dunat, si salvarai eo
5. *isti fratri meo $\left. \begin{array}{l} \\ \end{array} \right\} \bar{n}$
   *istum fratrem meum
   thesan minan bruodher,
   cist meon fradre Karlo et in ajudha et in cadhuna cosa
6. *sicut homo per drictum esse debet fratri suo,
   soso man mit rehtu sinan bruher scal,
   si cum om per dreit son fradra salvar dift,
7. *in hoc ut ille mihi similem promissionem faciat,
   in thiu thaz er mig so sama duo,
   in o quid il mi altresi fazet,

8. *et ab Lodhario nullum placitum inibo
   indi mit Ludheren in nohheiniu thing ne gegango,
   et ab Ludher nul plaid nunquam prindrai
9. *quod, per meam voluntatem, isti fratri meo ñ
   the, minan uuillon, imo
   qui, meon vol, cist meon fradre Karle
10. *in damno sit.
    ce scadhen uuerdhen.
    in damno sit.
11. *Si ñ sacramentum, quod fratri suo ñ juravit,
    Oba Karl then eid, then er sinemo bruodher Ludhuuuige gesuor,
    Si Lodhuuigs sagrament, que son fradre Karlo jurat,
12. *conservat, et ñ meus senior,
    geleistit, indi Ludhuuuig min herro
    conservat, et Karlus meos sendra
13. *quod suo fratri ñ juravit, infrangit,
    then er imo gesuor, forbrihchit,
    de suo part ñ lostanit,
14. *si ego illum inde retornare non possum,
    ob ih inan es iruuenden ne mag,
    si io returnar non l'int pois,
15. *nec ego nec nullus quem ego inde retornare possum,
    noh ih noh thero nohhein then ih es iruuenden mag,
    ne io ne neuls cui eo returnar int pois,
16. *auxilio contra ñ illi non ero.
    uuidhar Karle imo ce follusti ne uuirdhit.
    in nulla ajudha contra Lodhuuuig nun li iv er.

With reference to the few points in which the French text differs from the German, Ewert makes the following commentary:

It is surely a striking fact that these divergent readings in the French Oaths are the very readings which have always puzzled commentators and have called forth the most varied emendations, and I think there is good reason for regarding them as spurious. In at least two cases they have the effect of rendering the oath taken by Louis more explicit or binding: I refer to the addition of *et in ajudha et in cadhuna cosa* and the strengthening of the negation in *nulla ajudha* by the addition of *nunquam* or its substitution for *nun* (*non*). It is unlikely that the oath was taken in this form, for the essence of the pact was the imposition of absolutely equal obligations on both sides. It is much more probable that the oath was retouched by a later hand, and I suggest that the hand was that of Nithard, who wrote his history in a large measure as a justification of Charles the Bald and whose desire to bolster up the case of his sovereign may have been responsible in the first instance for the preservation of the full text of the Oaths in his book.

The passage *de suo part ñ lostanit*, so completely different from the German text and the easy rendering of the latter into Latin, is held to be 'spurious from beginning to end'. A quite new and apparently convincing theory is put forward to explain the cause of the spuriousness:

> The emendation which has hitherto enjoyed the greatest favour is that which regards *lostanit* as a misreading of *lo fraint*, but this has always encountered a stumbling-block in the presence of the preceding *ñ*, which would appear to negative what should be affirmative. But I would hold that in the original French version this *ñ* denoted *nomen*, not *non*, and that its misinterpretation as *non* was responsible for the recasting of the whole phrase. The original version was, in my opinion, a literal translation of the Latin, the *ñ* being allowed to stand or to slip into the French text instead of being replaced by the proper name *Lodhuwig*. We would thus have as the original French version *que suon fradre ñ jurat infraint*, with the accented form *suon* as a pendant to the accented *meos*.

The ease with which the French version slips back into notarial Latin is most impressive. Therein perhaps lies the clue to its mystery. It seems almost to be a Latin consciously vulgarized by adaptation to the most common features in the vernacular of the day, features which were widespread over northern France. Adopting an opinion previously expressed by others, Ewert says of it: 'I believe with M. Muret that "l'aspect archaïque des Serments de Strasbourg reflète peut-être une langue de cour . . . un usage de la langue vulgaire qu'on pourrait qualifier, en des termes empruntès à Dante, *aulicum et curiale vulgare*", and further, that the regular orthography of the Oaths in those portions which may be regarded as authentic presupposes a tradition whose roots are to be found in the scribal practice of the preceding age.' This is the opinion which places least strain upon our credulity, for other countries, Italy in particular, show a similar development of the standard language as a composite literary form, closely following the usage of medieval Latin. Such a chancery French could, more-over, have been helped into existence both as a consequence of the instructions given to priests to use the vernacular and as a pendant to the growing employment of a written vernacular in the German area. But how far it enjoyed any general currency is impossible to say: apart from the *Strassburg Oaths*, it has left no relic.

To whatever difficulties they may give rise, the *Strassburg Oaths* remain the first specimen of continuous prose in a Romance language, and as such they call for a detailed linguistic examination. We have described their language as 'archaic'. In what respects is it archaic? Chiefly, apart from obvious Latinisms, by the preservation of *a* in the stressed position and in an open syllable (see below, p. 356), e.g. *fradre, salvar, returnar,* and by the apparent absence of any diphthongs resulting from the spontaneous segmentation of a stressed vowel. In later texts the vowel *a*, stressed and free, has closed to *e*, as in the *Cantilène de sainte Eulalie*: *presentede, spede,* &c. This is a French development which must have become general by the time of the Oaths. With reference to diphthongs, the *Eulalie* shows for half-open vowels the evolutions ɛ > *ie* (*ciel*) and ɔ > *uo* (*buona, ruovet*), and for the half-close vowels, e > *ei* (*concreidre, sostendreiet*) and o > *ou* (*bellezour*). In the Oaths there is no trace of the earlier of these diphthongizations, that of the half-open vowels—though in fact they are lacking in fully acceptable examples, since *Deo* (Fr. *Dieu*) and *poblo* (Fr. *peuple*) were subject to learned influence, *meon* (Fr. *mien*) was liable to be affected as in the feminine (Old Fr. *meie, moie*) by the half-close vowel of Lat. ME (Fr. *moi*), while *vol* is a back-formation from the verb VOLĒRE (Old Fr. *voleir*), in which the vowel was originally pretonic. By contrast, the notation of half-close vowels, stressed and free, does seem to indicate a change, in that, corresponding to the Latin Ē, the scribe has written *i* (*savir* from SAPĒRE, *podir* from POTĒRE, *dift* from DĒBET, and possibly *sit*, though this may be pure Latinism) and for ō he has *u* (*amur* from AMŌREM, *dunat* from DŌNAT). These graphies, however, set a problem. Far from being peculiar to the Oaths, they are abundantly represented in Latin texts written in France during the earlier part of the eighth century, before the Carolingian reforms. Reference to the sample of these texts given on p. 325 will show *habyre* and *rigni* (reign of Chilpéric II) corrected to *habere* and *regni* (reign of Pépin). Mario Pei further records, in texts dating from A.D. 700 to 717, such forms as *dibio* for *debeo, plina* for *plena, mercide* for *mercede, vinit* for *venit, tuttum* for *totum, nubis* for *nobis, negucia* for *negotia, rispunsis* for *responsis,* &c. (*The Language of Eighth-century texts in Northern France,* pp. 20–21 and 30–31). Thus, while this use of *i* and *u* in the eighth century may well reflect the development of diphthongs *ei* and *ou* in current speech, its occurrence in the Oaths appears as no more than a reversion to traditional scribal practice. One may wonder why a scribe who could record accurately the diphthong *ei* in *dreit* did not record in the same way what was presumably the same sound in *savir* and *podir*. On the other hand, to argue from his failure to do so that the sound of *ei* in *dreit* must have been different from the sound of *i* in *savir* and *podir* would be to assume in the scribe a greater degree of consistency than he elsewhere displays.

The Oaths do indeed contain diphthongs, but they are all of the 'agglutinated' type, i.e. formed by the combination of a Latin vowel with another vocalic element, in this instance always the yod (see p. 25), e.g. the afore-mentioned *dreit* (< DIRECTUM), together with *plaid* (< PLACITUM), *pois* (< \*POTEO), and the future flexion *-ai* (< HABEO). When this new growth of diphthongs had come into being, the sole diphthong which survived in Vulgar Latin, AU (see p. 44), became a pure vowel, here attested in *cosa* (< CAUSA). With these developments we are entirely in the realm of Old French.

Another aspect of the vowel system which is fully French is to be observed in the treatment of post-tonics. In the majority of words in the text, any post-tonic vowel other than *a* has disappeared. From those which remain it is possible to draw an inference of particular significance: comparing *Karlo* and *Karle*, *fradre* and *fradra*, one observes that the letters *o*, *e*, and *a* are all called upon to represent what must be the same sound, and this sound can be only the so-styled '*e* mute' of French (phonetic symbol ə). This is the first positive evidence of the development in French of a vowel quality unknown to Vulgar Latin and for which the Latin alphabet possessed no symbol. In later texts, as for instance the *Vie de saint Alexis*, the mute *e* continued to be sometimes represented by *a* until the orthography of Old French was stabilized. In passing, it may be noted that the identification of *a* as a symbol for ə permits of the assumption that the unstressed *a* in such words as *salvament*, *salvarai*, *sagrament*, &c., corresponded in reality to this sound. By the same token, the verbs *dunat* and *jurat*, in the absence of any indication of stress— the spelling of *dunat* with *u* cannot be unreservedly accepted as such—might be present tense or perfect: only from the sense of the passage can we infer that *dunat* is present (< DŌNAT, Fr. *donne*) whereas *jurat* is perfect (< JURAVIT, Fr. *jura*), an interpretation which is substantiated by the German Oaths. Yet a further point of interest is the introduction of a post-tonic '*e* mute' after a group of consonants where in Latin there was either no vowel at all or one which would normally have ceased to be pronounced, e.g. *fradra* (< FRATER), *sendra* (< SENIOR); this is the so-called 'supporting vowel', an Old French innovation.

Among consonantal features, the preservation of *c* [k] before **a** is noteworthy, e.g. *cadhuna* (< CATA UNA), *cosa* (< CAUSA). This appears at first sight to be another example of 'archaism', since the French development of CA- to *cha* (Old Fr. tʃa) had certainly been initiated before this time. On the other hand, it may be a dialectal feature, or more precisely, an indication that the language is not that of the Île de France. Palatalization of **k** before *a* is an evolution pertaining specifically to the *francien* speech of that area, not affecting in the Middle Ages the Norman–Picard territories, or those of southern France, and it is probable that in the ninth century its geographical extent was still very limited (cf. p. 364).

More striking is the development of the intervocalic plosive consonants, all of which are here represented in a Romance form. The intervocalic *p* of SAPĒRE has completed its French evolution to become the *v* of *savir*. The *b* of IBI has lost its plosive character to become the *v* of *iv*, sole testimony in France to an intervening stage in the passage of IBI to *y*, while the *b* of DĒBET, having first undergone a similar change to *v*, here appears as the voiceless *f* of *dift*, an assimilation due to the loss of the unstressed vowel. Latin dental *t* when intervocalic occurs as *d* in *podir* and *fradra* (*r* following a consonant acts as a vowel, see p. 355), and as *dh* in *ajudha*, *cadhuna*. In each case the sound actually used at the time must have been the same: we can therefore conclude that inter-vocalic *t*, having first sonorized to *d*, had by the ninth century ceased to be a plosive and had acquired the value of ð, the fricative *d* as used in modern Spanish; it had thus reached the penultimate stage of the French evolution: -t- > -d- > -ð- > -. The attempt to convey the continuous nature of the consonant by the graphy *dh*, which may have been suggested by such words as *bruodher* and *Ludhuuuig* in the German Oaths, is not found again in French; in the *Vie de saint Alexis* the same sound is represented by *th*. Inter-vocalic **k** occurs in the Oaths only in the one word *sagrament* (< SACRAMENTUM); in fact, pronunciation had probably gone a stage further towards the Old Fr. *sairement*.

Final consonants show the maintenance of *t* in such verb forms as *dunat*, *fazet*, *jurat*, *conservat*. This *t* also occurs regularly in the French texts which followed, and was presumably still pro-nounced during the ninth and tenth centuries, but the evidence of scansion confirms that it had ceased to be articulated by the end of the eleventh.

Another new sound in French—in addition, that is, to the mute *e* and the fricative *d*—and a consequent orthographical problem for the scribes, arose from the group *k* plus yod. This was the so-called affricate **ts**, traces of which are discernible in earlier Latin texts, as in the spelling *Frantia* for *Francia* (Reichenau Glossary), and in the frequent confusion of *ci* and *ti*, as in *peticionis, preciosus* (see text, p. 325). In the *Strassburg Oaths* the difficulty is met by the use of *z*, as in *fazet* (< FACIAT); to represent the same sound the later scribe of the *Eulalie* had recourse first to *tc* (*manatce*), then to *cz* (*czo*), and finally to *zs* (*lazsier*). A further French feature is the introduction of the so-called 'glide consonant' in the interior of a word between two consonants which are both so open that they do not create a firm syllabic frontier, as in *sendra* (cf. Fr. *cendre* < CĬNĔREM, *moindre* < MĬNOR, *pondre* < PONERE, *chambre* < CAMERA, *sembler* < SIMULARE, *poudre*, Old Fr. *poldre* < PŬL-VERE, &c.); this, incidentally, is the only example of the word which shows a normal evolution of SENIOR, French having favoured an anomalous *sire*, presupposing an earlier *SEIOR (see p. 70). Since glide consonants do not occur in the dialect of Picardy, the word *sendra* alone would seem to eliminate the possibility of a Picard origin for the Oaths.

In its general morphological and syntactical aspects, the language of the Oaths presents no enigma. It displays all those features which the evidence of Vulgar Latin would lead one to expect and which were to become the commonplace of Old French. The two-case declension of masculine nouns is regularly observed (nom. *Deus, Karlus, Lodhuuigs*; acc. *Deo, Karlo, Lodhu-uuig*). Genitive and dative, where the reference is to persons, are conveyed simply by the use of the accusative form without a preposition (gen. *Pro Deo amur et pro christian poblo . . . salvament*; dat. *cist meon fradre Karle in damno sit*); the absence of preposition is here a relic of classical usage which was to persist for some time in Old French, cf. *Vie de saint Alexis*:

> Al tens Nöé et al tens Abraham
> Et al David . . .

Personal pronouns are frequently employed: EGO appears as both *eo* and *io*, in which the spelling of the former is probably influenced by Latin, whereas the latter is nearer to popular pronunciation; MIHI is reduced to *mi*, which survived as dative in the eastern dialects of France, but not in *francien* (cf. p. 78); and the third person occurs as nom. *il*, acc. *l'* (Old Fr. *lo*) and dat. *li* (see p. 80). An indefinite pronoun *om* has developed from HOMO, equivalent here to the *man* of the German Oaths. Among demonstratives, uncompounded *ist* is found side by side with *cist*, from ECCE *ĬSTĬ (cf. p. 87), and *o* still stands alone to represent HOC. The possessives are worthy of note: *meos* (< MEUS) occurs in this form only in the Oaths, while *meon* is the sole example of an intermediate stage between MEUM and *mien*; it is probable, however, that in each case the spelling is influenced by Latin and affords no true guide to the usage of the day. Relatives show a normal nom. *qui*, acc. *que*, and an excellent example of *cui* employed as a strong form of accusative (see p. 96).

Tenses represented are the present, both indicative and subjunctive, the perfect and the future; the last-named of these exhibits the new Romance construction (*salvarai, prindrai*) side by side with a specimen of the one future tense which survived into Old French from Classical Latin, viz. *er* (< ERO). Of syntactical interest is the use of *si* (< SIC) introducing a finite verb which is not preceded by a personal pronoun (*si salvarai*); this again was to be a feature of Old French (cf. p. 149). Other new forms of conjunction are to be observed in *si cum* (< SIC QUOMO), and *in o quid* 'provided that', followed by the subjunctive. Adverbs include both *int* (< INDE) and *iv* (< IBI), which seem already to have acquired something of the pronominal function ('from it' and 'in it') of their derivatives *en* and *y*. The vocabulary is very simple and apart from the proper names it contains not a trace of Germanic, a fact which may be due to translation from Latin and opposition to the German Oaths. Noteworthy as first appearances are *di*, the direct survival of DIEM, still used in *midi* and the names of weekdays; *ajudha*, a verbal substantive from the V. Lat. verb ADJUTARE; and *cadhuna*, compounded from CATA UNA (see p. 98). Of all the lexical elements in the Oaths only *sendra* was never to appear again in written French.

*The beginnings of French literature.* The *Strassburg Oaths*, though constituting a unique linguistic monument, cannot be called 'literature' in the conventional sense of the word, and are scarcely 'French', but the first text which entirely fulfils the conditions

implicit in both these terms was to follow shortly after: the previously mentioned *Cantilène de sainte Eulalie*. In it, as in suc-
ceeding works, one finds a prolongation into the vernacular of that
hagiographical tradition established by the latinizing authors of
preceding generations (see pp. 304–5). How much popular literature of this kind was actually produced during the ninth and tenth
centuries is impossible to say. It may have been quite abundant.
Once the practice of giving religious instruction in the tongue of
the people had been generally adopted, it should have given rise,
so one would expect, to translations of prayers, the Creed, and
other parts of the liturgy, as in German; but such writing was no
serious employment for the French scribe.

The *Eulalie* is a short hymn, or to give it the technical name,
deriving from its place in the service, a *séquence*. Intended to be
sung on the saint's day, its twenty-nine lines tell in brief phrases,
with a lack of adornment which heightens the effect of pathos,
of her martyrdom, and end with a request that she may intercede
on behalf of the singers. The substance of the poem is taken from
a Latin hymn composed in honour of the saint by Prudentius.
Born at Mérida, she had met her death on 10 December, A.D. 304,
a victim like St. Fides (see p. 380) of Diocletian's final attempt to
stamp out Christianity. In A.D. 878 her cult was revived by the
supposed discovery of her bones at Barcelona, an event which led
to many pilgrimages. This suggests a tentative dating for the
French composition, and one which is, moreover, confirmed by
the evidence of the single manuscript in which it survives. Belonging now to the municipal library of Valenciennes, where it was
found in A.D. 1837, the manuscript contains in addition to the
*Eulalie* a poem written in German to celebrate the victory of
Saucourt (3 August, A.D. 881), in which the victor, Louis III, is
spoken of as though still alive. Since Louis died on 5 August of
the following year, the German composition can be almost exactly
dated, and it may be assumed with a high degree of probability
that the *Eulalie* was written roughly at the same time, i.e. between
A.D. 880 and 882, or some forty years after the *Strassburg Oaths*.
Since the manuscript came originally from the Benedictine monastery of Saint-Amand-les-Eaux, near Valenciennes, and since the
language of the *Eulalie* contains features which are characteristic
of the Picard area, it seems reasonable to assume that this monastery was also its place of composition.

The dialectal features of the text, as compared with the Old French which followed, though sufficient to give an approximate localization, are not very numerous. They include *diaule* (< DIA-BOLUM, with Picard vocalization of the *b*), the popular *seule* (< SAE-CULUM), and words showing the preservation of **k** before *a*, e.g. *cose* (< CAUSA), and also *chielt* (< CALET) and *chieef* (< CAPUM), where, as in *chi* for *qui*, the graphy *ch* before *i* is made to correspond to **k**, a practice later to be adopted by Italian scribes. Another Picardism is probably to be detected in the line:

Enz enl fou lo getterent com arde tost

in which *lo* refers to Eulalie and thus appears to be a spelling of what in later Picard is the fem. *le* from ILLAM. Among features which confirm the early dating are, in particular, the diphthong *uo*, and possibly the *ae* of *maent* (< MANET). With these few exceptions, the language is very much the same as that of the literary productions which followed and can be considered as 'early French'. Thus the text already shows a certain linguistic standardization. The considerable divergences between this usage and that of the *Strassburg Oaths*, upon which we have already remarked, probably derive from a difference of milieu rather than one of time: the language of the Oaths developed as an administrative standard while that of the *Eulalie* was a monastic standard. That the *Eulalie* should present a much more faithful recording of popular speech is perhaps due to the fact that the monks were in closer contact and sympathy with the people and, indeed, by origin were of the people. Moreover, the spiritual inspiration of their writing required a pondering, however subconscious, over the aesthetic possibilities of the new language, which notarial records did not. So it comes about that of the two great influences of monastery and court, Church and State, it is rather the monastery which first determined the mould of literary French. Only some time later, with the growth of secular power which resulted from the founding of the Capetian dynasty, with its capital at Paris, did the court take charge.

The two literary texts which survive from the tenth century shed rather more mystery than light on the evolution of the language. They are the so-called 'Clermont poems', the *Passion du Christ* and the *Vie de saint Léger*, both preserved in an eleventh-century manuscript found at Clermont-Ferrand and first published in A.D. 1848. The manuscript is that of a Latin glossary, into the blank pages of which the two Romance poems were written by a later hand. It is impossible to date their composition with any certainty: indeed, after the *Strassburg Oaths* and the *Eulalie*, no work earlier than A.D. 1130 can be securely dated; but they are generally believed to be late tenth-century, a time suggested by an allusion in the *Passion* to the approaching end of the world, which was confidently expected by Christians for the year A.D. 1000. Both are texts of some literary value and sustained composition: in all, the *Passion* has 516 lines, and the *Vie de saint Léger* 240. Both are written in octosyllabic verse—the first regular metre to appear in French, for the *Eulalie* permits of no scansion—divided into stanzas each containing two assonanced couplets. Thus each displays a conventional literary craftsmanship. The *Passion*, drawn from the Gospels of Matthew, John, and Mark, begins with the entry into Jerusalem, then tells of Christ's crucifixion, resurrection, and ascension, and continues with the works of the apostles. The *Vie de saint Léger*, roughly translated from a Latin *Vita* (see p. 304), recounts how the good Bishop Leodegar was put to death by his wicked enemy Ebroïn after a number of deferments provoked by divine intervention: even when dead, with his head cut off, the saint remained standing for several days.

The mystery of these texts lies in their language, which appears to be a mixture of French and Provençal. While some scholars have suggested that this may be an early form of Franco-Provençal, others have decided that both texts must have been composed originally in northern France and then copied and altered by a Provençal scribe: thus E. Koschwitz, in his anthology *Les plus anciens monuments de la langue française* (4th ed., Leipzig, 1930) accompanies them with reconstitutions in *francien* made by G. Lücking (A.D. 1877) and Gaston Paris (A.D. 1872) respectively. This procedure of reconstitution, much favoured by early editors, has now been abandoned, for, interesting though it may be as an exercise, the texts thus created are of a purely hypothetical character. The northern origin of the *Vie de saint Léger* does seem, however, to have been definitely established; J. Linskill (*Saint Léger, étude de la langue du manuscrit de Clermont-Ferrand, suivie d'une édition critique du texte*, Paris, 1937), after a searching examination of the language, and in particular of the assonances, upholds the view previously expressed by the German scholar

H. Suchier, according to which the poem as we know it is a provençalized version of a text composed in the Picard–Walloon area,
the same region to which we have ascribed the *Eulalie*. There is no
recent study of the longer *Passion du Christ*; the latest seems to be
that of P. Dreyer, *Zur Clermonter Passion*, Erlangen, 1901. The
handwriting of the two texts, according to Linskill, is apparently
not the same; and certainly the Provençal element in the *Passion* is
much stronger than in the *Vie de saint Léger*. Nevertheless, it must
have a similar history: inspection of its assonances reveals many
couplets which in fact, in the Provençal, do not assonance, but
which would assonance perfectly in *francien*, e.g. *diz : forsfez*
(fr. *diz : forsfist*, ll. 289–90), *vestit : retrames* (fr. *vestit : retramist*,
ll. 219–20), *perveng : criz* (fr. *pervint : criz*, ll. 313–14), *felluns : van*
(fr. *fellons : vont*, ll. 357–8), *primers : pecchiad* (fr. *primiers : pechiet*,
ll. 377–8), &c.

The only remaining document in the vernacular attributed to
the tenth century, though its date within that century cannot be
determined, is a brief prose abstract of a priest's sermon on the
prophet Jonah, in which the French is mingled with Latin phrases.
Discovered in the binding of a Latin text, it has come to be known
as the *Fragment de Valenciennes*. It is not only fragmentary, but
also difficult to read; yet slight though it may be, it holds our
interest as a relic bearing witness to what must have been the
common practice of priests throughout French territory after the
time of the Council of Tours. The following is a brief extract from
the Koschwitz edition, in which the Latin words and phrases are
placed in italics:

si escit foers de la *civitate* e si sist *contra orientem civitatis* e si avardevet *cum Deus per* . . . fereiet u ne fereiet. *et preparavit dominus
ederam super caput Ione, ut faceret ei umbram. laboravit enim* . . . dunc,
co *dicit, Ionas profeta habebat* mult laboret e mult penet a cel *populum*;
e *faciebat* grant jholt, et eret mult las et *preparavit dominus* un edre sore
sen cheve, quet umbre li fesist e repauser s'i podist. *et letatus est Ionas
super ederam letitia magna.* dunc fut *Ionas* mult *letatus*, co *dicit*, por
que *Deus* cel edre li donat a sun soveir, a sun repausement li donat.
*et precepit dominus* vermi *ut percuteret ederam, et exaruit. et paravit
Deus ventum calidum super caput Ione, et dixit: melius est mihi mori
quam vivere.* dunc, co *dicit*, si *rogat Deus* ad un verme que percussit cel
edre sost que cil *sedebat*, e *cum* cig eedre fu seche, si vint grancesmes
jholt *super caput Ione, et dixit: melius est mihi mori quam vivere.* (Cf.
Book of Jonah, chap. iv, verses 5–8.)

The language of this curious text again points clearly to the

Picard–Walloon area. In *avardevet*, the first *v* probably represents the Germanic *w* which Picard preserved, while the ending *-evet*, from Lat. *-ABAT*, is also characteristic (cf. p. 135). Picard, too, is the weakened form of possessive *sen*, here used side by side with *sun*. Whether the graphy *jholt*, for which some editors read more plausibly *cholt* (Fr. *chaud*), is designed to indicate a non-Picard palatalization, is difficult to assess.

To the mid-eleventh century belongs one poem, the *Vie de saint Alexis*, a story inspired by the ideals of Christian teaching, in which the hero renounces wife and family and all material comforts, in order to attain the holy condition of poverty and chastity. The theme must have made a deep if somewhat bewildering impression on medieval listeners: here, for the first time, is a vernacular text preserved not by the chance survival of a single manuscript, but in a number of copies. In all there are six versions extant, the oldest of which were penned in England by the scribes of that new society which emerged from Norman occupation. These are at least a hundred years posterior to the original composition, which must have come from the Continent, probably from the region where Normandy adjoins the Île de France. Besides being the most 'literary' work in French thus far encountered, the *Alexis* is the most sustained, consisting of 125 stanzas each with five assonanced lines. The lines are decasyllabic, with a caesura after the fourth syllable, the metre of the secular epic which was to follow.

Epic marks in France the break with hagiographical tradition. Of the eighty or so epic poems which have been preserved the finest by far, the *Chanson de Roland*, is probably the oldest. Like the *Alexis*, in its earliest-known form it was copied in England and contains characteristically Anglo-Norman features; the manuscript, unadorned and 'pocket' size, may be seen at Oxford in the Bodleian Library. According to the French palæographer, Ch. Samaran, its handwriting is that of the second quarter of the twelfth century, but concerning its origins, and the date of the continental poem of which the Oxford version must be a copy, countless pages have been committed to print and controversy still continues. The opinion of J. Bédier, according to which the 'continental poem' was the work of a single author taking his cue directly from the passage in Einhardt's *Vita Caroli* quoted above (p. 328), no longer meets with general acceptance. Perhaps more satisfying, though this by no means affords a solution to the problem, is the view that the poem as we know it was indeed composed in the first place in the Île de France during the last quarter of the eleventh century, but as a modernization—witness the use of the lance, then the new arm of the nascent medieval chivalry—of a legend well known and widely circulated before, in oral tradition if not in the form of a written text.

*The French standard.* Thus we reach the end of the eleventh century, and as yet, among the texts encountered, there is not a single one which can be precisely located in the Île de France, the home of the *francien* dialect, the source of modern French. The first which can be so placed is the *Pèlerinage de Charlemagne*, written some time during the first half of the twelfth century to be sung at the Fair of Saint-Denis. Yet, from the *Eulalie* through the *Alexis* to the *Chanson de Roland*, despite dialectal features, there is discernible a common tongue. Had each author sat down to compose his piece in his native patois, without reference to the writing of others, the results would surely have been much more different from one another than in fact they are. The common feature is apparently *francien*, and to explain this we must again have recourse to the monasteries, remembering the close ties which bound them, and the fact that the above-mentioned Saint-Denis was the site of one of the most important of all. From its central situation, Saint-Denis played a preponderant part in the general organization of monastic life; and if the cloisters, in France as in Germany, saw the growth of a vernacular standard usable for religious instruction, it may be assumed, despite the absence of texts, that the monks of Saint-Denis had a large share in its creation.

When in A.D. 987 the Capetian dynasty came into being, with a royal capital fixed at Paris for the first time since the decline of the Merovingians, it was a creation of the Church, dependent upon the good will of the Church. How close were the links between Church and Monarchy is shown by the fact that the first Capetian king, Hugues Capet, besides being Count of Paris, was a titular abbot of the monastery of Saint-Denis, as also of Saint-Germain-des-Prés and of Saint-Martin of Tours. Throughout the *Chanson de Roland*, indeed almost as its motive force, there echoes a strong plea in support of this alliance between secular and ecclesiastical powers. Nor did the Church easily relinquish its grip. During the twelfth century we still find an abbot of Saint-Denis, Suger, acting as chief adviser to Louis VII, as he had acted to his father before him. It is therefore in no way surprising that the literary standard of the monastery should have become that of the court with no apparent discontinuity.

During the long reign of Louis VII, who came to the throne in A.D. 1137 and died in A.D. 1180, the monarchy began to recover the importance which it had lost in the ninth century in consequence of the ill-fated policies of Charles the Bald and the weakness of his Carolingian successors. By his marriage, in the year of his accession, to Eleanor of Aquitaine, Louis once again brought the extensive territory south of the Loire under the rule of France. This, however, was a short-lived success. Granddaughter of the first known troubadour, used to the more sophisticated pleasures of the southern courts, Eleanor did much to foster in the north a liking for more worldly literature, in particular for the love-lyric, but her tastes and conduct alienated the Church protectors by whom the king was still dominated, and in A.D. 1152, with their connivance, he divorced her. By her subsequent marriage to Henry Plantagenet, later Henry II of England, the territory of Aquitaine became an English possession. It was left to Philippe-Auguste, Louis's son by his third wife, Adèle de Champagne, to make good the loss and set the French throne upon a really firm foundation. During his reign, from A.D. 1180 to 1223, the English were defeated; after the battle of Bouvines (A.D. 1214) they retained in France only a part of Poitou. At the same time the success of the Albigensian Crusade (see below, p. 389) finally established the supremacy of the north over the south, and gathered most of France into the modern nation.

Only by this worldly success of the people who spoke it could the popular tongue be elevated to the dignity of a national literary language. For the authorities of the Church it had never been more than a convenient medium of approach to the illiterate; throughout the Middle Ages their language was Latin. Once the court had begun to flourish, with all the intercourse of an everyday non-ecclesiastical life, it rapidly became the arbiter both of the manners which it created and of the speech which it used. During the last thirty years of the twelfth century poets were ceasing to be anonymous and the literature of those years contains abundant testimony to the cult of *francien*. The poet born within the territory of the Île de France could boast of writing correctly, as does Garnier de Pont-Sainte-Maxence, who, introducing his *Vie de saint Thomas de Cantorbéry*, written in A.D. 1173 when the 'murder in the cathedral' was still fresh in memory, sees fit to give us this assurance:

Mis langages est buens, car en France fui nez.

Similarly, Bertha, mother of Charlemagne, is described by Adenet le Roi as speaking French so well that one would have thought her born 'au bourc à Saint Denis': a stretch of the poet's imagination which nevertheless serves to illustrate our point. On the other hand, poets who were not born in the Île de France tend to apologize for the 'uncouthness' of their attempts to write French—though a nobleman of the standing and the virile temper of the Picard poet, Conon de Béthune, when laughed at for his strange 'accent', could afford to utter an indignant protest against the assumption of linguistic superiority which he found at court:

La roïne n'a pas fait que cortoise
Qui me reprist, ele et ses fiz li rois;
Encor ne soit ma parole françoise,
Si la puet on bien entendre en françois,
Ne cil ne sont bien apris ne cortois
Qui m'ont repris se j'ai dit moz d'Artois
Car je ne fui pas noriz à Pontoise.

It is to be noted that the complaint is lodged in excellent *francien*; and this dates from about A.D. 1182.[1]

While the growing power of the court under Philippe-Auguste, and with it the increasing centralization of the country, must be placed first among those causes which favoured the supremacy of *francien*, there were contributory factors tending in the same direction. A rapid development in the system of education culminated in the founding of the University of Paris, which received its charter from the Pope in A.D. 1231. This, of course, was an ecclesiastical enterprise, but students in their conversation used French, and coming from many districts would require a common norm. Also, the courts of law were established at Paris, and from the thirteenth century onwards played a large part in the unification of French, to which they contributed, incidentally, many words and phrases of purely legal origin. And, finally, on a humbler plane, the entertainers of the day, the *jongleurs*, who sang at the fairs their own

[1] For the quotations we are indebted to K. Nyrop, *Grammaire historique de la langue française*, vol. i, pp. 22–23.

verse and that of others, united in corporations, and during Lent, when forbidden to practise their art, they held 'holiday courses', schools of *jonglerie*: yet another potent force making for linguistic centralization.

As the country unified the language, so the language unified the country, and by the end of the thirteenth century France had become the strongest and most centralized of all European states. Its rich literature, in which prose was at last coming into its own beside verse—the first outstanding prose work was Villehardouin's account of the fourth crusade, written *c*. A.D. 1210—rapidly penetrated to every court in Europe, creating there new fashions in composition, leaving on all sides its trace in lexical borrowings, and achieving the status of a second international language, the medium of travel and diplomacy. For French medievalists the thirteenth is the *grand siècle*.

This brilliant progress was much hampered during the two centuries which followed by the miseries of the Hundred Years War; the European primacy in letters and the arts passed to Italy. But if the flow of popular inspiration, except in a few instances of irrepressible genius such as that of François Villon, tended to respond unfavourably to adverse conditions, this was nevertheless a time when the learning of the cloister, forced back upon itself, played an important part in the evolution of the language. The fourteenth century was above all an age of translation from Latin, of a new wedding between French and the older language, which the prestige acquired by French during the previous century had made possible. It was the age of the 'mot savant', when Latin words were freely adopted into the national idiom. One has only to glance at the historical sections of Littré's dictionary to see how many are the learned words first attested in French in the translation of Livy by Bersuire, and that of the Latin version of Aristotle by Oresme. On the debit side, the etymologizing instinct of fourteenth-century Latinists was at the same time responsible for a thoroughgoing corruption of French orthography, as evinced in such monstrosities as *aultre*, *doubter*, *sçavoir* (false association with SCIRE), and *poids*, in which last-named the *d*, introduced as a result of false association with PONDUS, has persisted to this day.

It was left to the impact of humanism and the Italian Renaissance to raise again the standard of French literature, and incidentally to enrich French vocabulary with the greatest influx of foreign borrowings since the time of the Frankish invasions (see p. 231). The sixteenth century was one of linguistic exuberance, a philologist's paradise, as any reader of Rabelais will know. Thereafter, with the swing of the pendulum towards 'order', it became the task of seventeenth-century pundits to prune and to standardize. However much they pruned, and however many good words of Old French were eliminated, the vocabulary of French continued to grow. The oft-commented verbal economy of Racine affords no true picture. The *Dictionnaire de l'Académie* (A.D. 1694), and even more so the rival dictionary of Antoine Furetière (A.D. 1690), reveal an ever-increasing importation of learned terms, designed to meet the needs of medicine and the developing sciences, of which many now came from Greek. With its grammar at the same time rigorously codified on a basis of court usage, and a strong check applied to the natural tendencies towards phonetic divergence, the sophisticated medium of the seventeenth century differs little in its essentials from the standard French of today.

*Sounds and spelling.* In reaching this pre-eminent position, French underwent perhaps less modification of its general structure than is commonly supposed. As we have seen in the first chapter, its accidence and syntax do not radically differ from thos of Vulgar Latin. What did change, and indeed startlingly change, to the extent of creating the impression of a quite different language, is the sound-system. The Old French of the ninth century appears in this respect already much farther removed from Latin than do Provençal, Italian, and Spanish some centuries later. For this reason, and in order to have available a study in sound-change which may serve as a term of comparison in a less detailed reference to other Romance languages, we have thought it desirable to summarize briefly the more remarkable features of French phonology.

We observed, when examining the earliest texts, that the scribes who first committed the new language to writing were confronted with the task of contriving a phonetic representation with the range of symbols available, those of the Latin alphabet. The result shows that their labours were undertaken with care, and with such degree of collaboration as was necessary in order to ensure that the more unsuitable devices were eliminated, and a practical norm established. The written French of the twelfth century is thus a fairly close record of the spoken tongue. Thereafter, speech continuing to evolve while spelling became a fixed tradition, the gulf between the two gradually widened, with the effect that in modern French, as in modern English, spelling is an archaic survival far removed from the reality of the sounds employed.

Our chief guide to the pronunciation of Old French is therefore its spelling; the evidence of rhyme forms a useful corollary. Comparing a passage written in this language with one in the Latin from which it derives, one is immediately confronted with certain aspects of phonetic change. With reference to vowels, there is the obvious loss of the post-tonics upon which we have already commented (p. 341), but above all Old French impresses by its abundance of diphthongs and even triphthongs. These call for further explanation.

The diphthongs of Old French arose in two different ways. Some were 'conditioned', that is, formed by the agglutination of two originally separate vowel sounds; some were 'spontaneous', the result of the progressive lengthening of a single stressed vowel, followed by a 'segmentation' into two perceptibly different sounds as the tongue failed to hold its first position.

Segmentation occurs only when the vowel is pronounced with a heavy stress, that is, where it is the 'tonic' vowel in a word or group of words. For this kind of diphthongization to take place in the Gallo-Romance which became French it was also essential that the vowel should be 'free', which means in practice that it should be followed by only one consonant (or by a plosive consonant plus *l* or *r*). To put the matter more theoretically: syllabic division required that where possible each syllable should begin with a consonant, but where two consonants were grouped the first of them belonged to the preceding syllable; thus the syllabic division of NASUM was NA|SUM, the syllable NA being 'open' and the vowel A 'free', whereas in PARTEM the division was PAR|TEM, the syllable PAR being 'closed' and the vowel A 'blocked' (or in another terminology 'checked'). An exception to this general rule occurred when a very close consonant was followed by a very open consonant, as in the words PĔTRA and CAPRA: the modification of the stressed vowel of these words, as it appears in *francien*, points to a syllabic division PĔ|TRA and CA|PRA. It should be remembered that the syllabic division implied by *francien* is not of universal application in the Romance area (cf. p. 47).

The propensity of the free vowel to diphthongize, as contrasted with the stability of the blocked vowel, is strikingly evident in the following summary:

| Tonic vowel free | | Tonic vowel blocked | |
|---|---|---|---|
| NĪDUM | > Old Fr. *nid* | VĪLLA | > Fr. *ville* |
| | Mod. [ni] | | |
| PĬLUM | > Old Fr. *peil, poil* | MĬTTERE | > Fr. *mettre* |
| | Mod. [pwal] | | |
| TĔLA | > Old Fr. *teile, toile* | | |
| | Mod. [twal] | | |
| PĔDEM | > Old Fr. *pied, piet* | SEPTEM | > Old Fr. *set* |
| | Mod. [pje] | | |
| MARE | > Fr. *mer* | PARTEM | > Fr. *part* |
| CŎR | > Old Fr. *cuer* | PŎRTA | > Fr. *porte* |
| | Mod. [kœ:ʀ] | | |
| FLŌREM | > Old Fr. *flour* | | |
| | Mod. [flœ:ʀ] | | |
| GŬLA | > Old Fr. *goule* | PŬLLA | > Fr. *poule* |
| | Mod. [ǵœl] | | |
| DŪRUM | > Fr. *dur* [dy:ʀ] | NŪLLUM | > Fr. *nul* [nyl] |

This shows in the first place that of all Latin vowels only ī has remained unchanged in quality whether free or blocked; the back vowel ū appears in orthography as unchanged, but we know that in pronunciation it had been fronted to [y]. A close point of articulation accounts for their relative stability. In the development of free half-open vowels, as in that of free half-close vowels, diphthongization occurred with a certain regularity of pattern. The front half-open ɛ lengthened and via a stage \*eɛ became iɛ, an opening and rising diphthong; similarly, the back half-open ɔ lengthened and via a stage \*oɔ became uɔ, attested in the *Eulalie*, and then uɛ: again, an opening and rising diphthong. Since this treatment of Latin ĕ and ŏ is found over a considerable part of Romania, it may be assumed to have been inherent in the pronunciation of Vulgar Latin before the collapse of the western Empire (see p. 46). The half-close vowels e and o show a similar parallelism, and a result which is in direct opposition to that of ɛ and ɔ : both lengthened to give closing and falling diphthongs, ei and ou; this is a later and more restricted evolution, common to northern France and northern Italy (cf. p. 182). As for the passage of free A to ɛ, likewise characteristic of northern France and northern Italy, that too was presumably the final result of a process of diphthongization, viz. a > aɛ > ɛ. The single graphy with *ae*, *maent* (< MANET) in the *Eulalie*, may be a correct phonetic appreciation; here, however, the diphthong is followed by a nasal, and in this situation, the second element closing still further under the influence of the nasal, it continued to be a diphthong, MANET becoming eventually Old Fr. *maint*, cf. MANUM > Fr. *main*, &c.

Diphthongization by agglutination is a more diverse phenomenon since it may take place through the coalescence of a variety of sounds. The most familiar of the agglutinating phonemes is the so-called yod: this sound, already present in Classical Latin in such words as JAM, MAJOR, PEJOR, &c., became more common in Vulgar Latin as a result of the closing of unstressed *i* and *e* when placed between consonant and a following vowel, as in VINEA, TIBIA, PALATIUM, &c. (cf. p. 25 and p. 30), and still more so in Romance through the palatalization of the velar plosives **k** and **g** (see pp. 52–55). The yod is a somewhat unstable phoneme, liable to be pronounced with varying degrees of aperture, so that, on the one hand, it readily becomes completely consonantal, while on the other it attaches itself to vowels assuming a certain vocalic quality. Old French diphthongs formed in this way are as follows:

**ai** < **a** plus yod, e.g. *maire* < MAJOR, *aire* < AREA, *faire* < FACĔRE

**ei** < **e** (pretonic) plus yod, e.g. Old Fr. *neiier* (later *noyer*) < NECARE, Old Fr. *leisir* (later *loisir*) < LĬCĒRE

**ie** < yod plus a, e.g. *moitié* < MEDIETATEM, Old Fr. *chier* < CARUM

**oi** < **o** plus yod, e.g. *dortoir* < DORMITŌRIUM, *voix* < VŌCEM, *noix* < NŬCEM; also < AU plus yod (AU having been reduced to O), e.g. *joie* < GAUDIA

**yi** < **y** plus yod (at first, like *oi*, a falling diphthong), e.g. *truite* < TRŪCTA, *fruit* < FRŪCTUM.

These are straightforward examples of the combination of two sounds; a more complicated situation arose when the yod combined with a stressed free vowel which had spontaneously diphthongized. If it was in immediate contact with the *i*-sound of a diphthong, it had no apparent effect upon the evolution of that diphthong: thus the Ē of RĒGEM, eventually followed by a yod due to the palatalization of G, produced exactly the same result as did the Ē of TĒLA. But where the immediate attachment of the yod was to the other element of such a diphthong, the outcome, in the period preceding the appearance of French texts, seems to have been a triphthong. So we may postulate:

$$\text{yod plus e} > \text{*}i\widehat{ei}$$
$$\varepsilon \text{ plus yod} > \text{*}i\widehat{\varepsilon i}$$
$$\text{ɔ plus yod} > \text{*}u\widehat{ɔi}$$

Only by supposing that these triphthongs once existed and were then reduced by absorption of the middle element can one logically explain the Old French result of the given combinations. In fact, ɔ plus yod appears as *ui* [yi], e.g. *nuit* < NŎCTEM, *cuisse* < CŎXAM, *cuir* < CŎRIUM, while the other two both produced the pure vowel *i*, e.g. *cire* < CĒRA, *merci* < MERCĒDEM, and in the second instance, *lit* < LĔCTUM, *pis* < PĔCTUS, &c. A similar development is to be observed in the case of the few examples of the vowel *a* both followed and preceded by a yod, as in JACET > Old Fr. *gist*, mod. *gît*, CACAT > *chie*, and in the -IACUM ending of numerous place-names, e.g. AURELIACUM > *Orly*, &c. (see p. 195). The net result was therefore to increase in French the incidence of the front close vowel.

A further agglutinating element in Old French developed in consequence of the vocalization of *l* before another consonant. Latin grammarians of the fourth century inform us that in this position *l* was pronounced *pinguius*, from which it may be understood that, as in similar circumstances in modern English, the *l* had a velar articulation, i.e. it was produced with the back of the tongue lifted towards the velum. By pronouncing first *altre* and then *autre* one may easily perceive that a slight depression of the tongue suffices to change a velar *l* into the vowel *u*, and that is precisely what happened in French. Manuscript evidence suggests that by the tenth century the change had already taken place; by the eleventh it was certainly an accomplished fact, though many scribes continued to write such words with *l* for some time thereafter. Three diphthongs came into being in this way: **au**, whereby was restored to Old French a sound-combination, the last diphthong of Vulgar Latin, which in northern France had been lost through reduction to *o* by the end of the eighth century; e.g. *autre* < ALTER, *aube* < ALBA, *taupe* < TALPA, &c.; **eu**, e.g. *eux* < ĬLLOS, *cheveux* < CAPĬLLOS (the *x* of the French words is merely an orthographical variant for *s*); **ou**, e.g. *coup* < \*COLPU (from COLAPHUM, see p. 198), *pouce* < POLLICEM, *poumon* < PŬLMONEM, &c. It will be observed that since the *l* plus consonant had previously constituted a block, none of the vowels with which this *u* combined had been diphthongized; and further, that the *u* could become attached to a pretonic vowel, as in *poumon*, just as to one that was tonic. In combination with the half-open ɛ, the *u* had the unusual effect of producing a triphthong, an *a* emerging as a kind

of glide vowel between the two phonemes, e.g. *chapeaux* < CAP-
PĚLLOS, *beaux* < BĚLLOS, *oiseaux* < AVICĚLLOS, &c.; all these have
original singulars in *-el* (< -ĚLLUM), Old Fr. *chapel, bel, oisel*, the
modern singulars having been created during the later Middle
Ages by back-formation from the plural. The appearance of a non-
etymological glide vowel, resulting in a triphthong, is a phenomenon which has no parallel in standard French, though in
southern dialects there is a similar passage of *iu* to *ieu*. When *ieu*
developed as the second triphthong of Old French, it was in a
different and more familiar way: through combination of the diphthong *ie* with a following *u*; this came about where ε had diphthongized before an *l mouillé* [ʎ], which subsequently vocalized
before *s*, e.g. *mieux* < MĚLIUS, *vieux* < VĚCLUS, and also in a few
words through the survival of a post-tonic *u*, e.g. *Dieu* < DEUM,
Old Fr. *Grieu* < GRAECUM, *lieue* < LĚGUA, and *lieu* < LŎCUM (presumably resulting from vocalic dissimilation of *\*lueu*).

The number of French words containing diphthongs was still
further increased by the ending of a condition of hiatus due to the
loss of intervocalic consonants. Groups of phonemes so affected
developed in different ways, with different shiftings of stress within
the group; compare, for instance, TRADĪTOR > Old Fr. *traître* >
*traître*, and VAGĪNA > Old Fr. *guaïne* > *gaine*, with CATĒNA > Old
Fr. *chaeine* > *chaîne*, and yet again with CATHĚDRA > Old Fr.
*chaiere* > *chaire*. The effect of these resolutions of hiatus was
to bring the sounds in question into line with the system of diphthongs already established, and not to create new ones.

So it came about that eleventh-century French was characterized by an extraordinary wealth of diphthongs and triphthongs;
adding them up we find: falling diphthongs **ai, au, ei, eu, oi, ou,
yi**, rising diphthongs **iε, uε**, and triphthongs **eau, iεu**. The impression which such a language created upon the ear must have been far
removed from that of Latin, as also from that of modern French.
Indeed, the parallel which leaps to the mind is modern English,
with its kindred system, cf. **ai** as in 'by', **au** as in 'bough', **ei** as
in 'bay', **oi** as in 'boy', and **ou** as in 'bow': an English propensity
which has permitted the retention in our language, almost unchanged, of such borrowings from Old French as 'faith' and 'joy'.
As the *Eulalie* bears witness, most of this sound-system was already
present in French in the ninth century. Its creation had taken place
in the preceding centuries. And yet some scholars would have us

believe that the 'unity of Vulgar Latin' was preserved until the time of Charlemagne!

From the beginning of the twelfth century the number of diphthongs was gradually reduced. Probably the first to go was **ai**, passing via a stage ɛe to ɛ; the scribes who in the latter half of the twelfth century recorded the works of Chrestien de Troyes followed this change, writing *fet* for *fait*, *tret* for *trait*, *sohet* for *souhait*, &c., but in general the older spelling persisted. At about the same time, in the Île de France region, but not in Normandy, the diphthong **ei** changed its character, continuing an evolution from Ē which is the most complicated in the history of the development of French vowels from Latin. First of all, the diphthong widened from **ei** to **oi**, the stage perpetuated in French orthography, which seems to have been reached by the middle of the century. During the following century the accent shifted from the first element to the second, which thereafter underwent a progressive opening in quality: thus ói > oé > oɛ, and the first element becoming more closed, eventually the sound became wɛ. This stage, reached by the end of the thirteenth century, became stabilized as 'correct' pronunciation for some five centuries thereafter: thus for Molière and his contemporaries the pronunciation of *roi* was rwɛ, as it still is in Canadian French. But no evolution could better illustrate the tendency for sounds to change in quality in the speech of the uneducated. Already at the beginning of the fourteenth century Parisians were eliminating the **w** and pronouncing a pure vowel ɛ, a change which became permanently accepted in certain words, e.g. *craie* (< CRĒTA) and *monnaie* < MONĒTA), and in the termination denoting nationality, in Old Fr. -*ois* (< -ĪSCUM or < -ENSEM): compare, on the one hand, *Français, Anglais, Irlandais, Écossais*, and on the other, *François, Suédois, Danois, Chinois*. The final passage of wɛ to wa was again a popular development, already attested in the fifteenth century, particularly in the rhymes of Villon, but which did not make serious inroads into the accepted standard until well into the eighteenth century. Grammar books of French written in England during this time show the prevalent hesitation, their authors instructing the learner to pronounce wɛ in some words and wa in others. The rejection of wɛ was probably consummated by the disappearance of the court.

Other diphthongs were reduced in the course of a similar

process of evolution, ending with the consonification, and in some instances complete disappearance, of the part of the diphthong which carried no stress. In this way *ou*, from tonic free ō, *eu*, and *ue*, all converged, the two former presumably via a stage øw, at which point they became identical, and *ue* via a stage wø; loss of the w, in circumstances similar to the reduction of wɛ to ɛ, left French with the two new 'abnormal' vowels ø and œ, which, coming from the same sources, depend for their different acoustic effect upon the position of the sound in the word: where the sound is final, as in *peut*, the vowel pronounced is ø, but where it is not final, as in *douleur*, then the vowel is œ (an exception to this rule is found in the case of adjectives with feminine in -*euse*, e.g. *précieuse*, where the ø:z pronunciation is due to the influence of the masculine). To put an exact chronology to these changes is scarcely possible; they took place gradually in the capital and slowly spread to surrounding districts and to the large towns with which the capital was in closest contact. But for the Parisian area it may be assumed that the vowels ø and œ had attained their modern qualities before the end of the Middle Ages. In orthography both came to be represented by the combination *eu*, though when they were preceded by a *c* recourse was had to other devices, e.g. *œu* as in *cœur*, and the archaic *ue*, as in *cercueil*.

The surviving diphthong of Vulgar Latin, AU, first developed presumably to **ou**, a stage attested in Portuguese (Port. *ouro* < AURUM), and thereafter became **o** (AURUM > Fr. *or*). The beginning of this development must have been relatively late in northern France: the fact that a **k** which precedes the AU is palatalized (see below, p. 364), as in CAUSA > *chose* and CAULEM > *chou*, indicates that the AU must still have been so pronounced until about the end of the eighth century; in parts of the Provençal area it persists to this day (see p. 44). The diphthong **ou** from other sources, notably from a pretonic or a blocked tonic ō or ŭ (e.g. Fr. *poumon*, *double*), developed with emphasis on the second element to become [u], thereby filling a position in the vowel-scheme which had long previously fallen vacant in French in consequence of the fronting of Latin ū to [y].

The triphthong **eau** was reduced to əo and by the seventeenth century had become the simple vowel of *beau*. Thus, of all this sound-system only *ieu* [jø], *ie* [je], *ui* [ɥi], and *oi* [wa], retain in modern French anything of the diphthong quality of Old French, and since j, ɥ, and w are more consonantal than vocalic, even these cannot be considered as true diphthongs. Much of the story of vocalic development in the French which became standard is therefore contained in two phases: one of intensive diphthongization which has its origins in a period probably as early as the collapse of the Roman Empire in the west and which reaches a climax in the eleventh and twelfth centuries; and one of gradual reduction of diphthongs, by the seventeenth century almost complete.

There is an additional factor which in French, as in Portuguese, has appreciably contributed to change the character of the vowel-system: the phenomenon of nasalization. In orthography this influence remains unrecorded. But when, already in the *Chanson de Roland*, a word such as *vent* is found to assonance with a word such as *tant*, it is clear that the vowels of these two words had become identical. We must assume that they had acquired a pronunciation similar to that of modern French: in both cases, an anticipatory movement of the velum had permitted an escape of breath to the nasal cavity during the articulation of the vowel, and in course of this process the tongue position of *e* had been lowered to that of *a*; thus they coalesced as [ɑ̃]. In the above examples the vowels are blocked: when the same vowels were free they likewise converged, but only after the normal process of diphthongization had taken place, with the result that in modern French both have become [ɛ̃], e.g. VANUM > *vain* [vɛ̃], and PLĒNUM > *plein* [plɛ̃]. Nasalization occurred only when the nasal consonant followed the vowel and belonged to the same syllable. When, as in the feminine of the above adjectives, the nasal consonant was followed by a Latin A, persisting in Old French as [ə], the syllabic division was VA/NA, PLĒ/NA, and in consequence the tonic vowels show no trace of nasalization in modern French, e.g. VANA > *vaine* [vɛːn] and PLĒNA > [plɛːn]. The nasalization of other vowels in Old French, producing the evolutions *in* > ɛ̃, *on* > ɔ̃, and *un* > œ̃, and thereby bringing the total of nasalized vowels to four, took place in exactly similar circumstances, but, as is evident from assonance and rhyme, at a later date.

Among features of consonantal development, the weakening of intervocalic plosives (see p. 24 and pp. 49–50) contributed much towards the distinctive character of French. The incidence of intervocalic *v* was greatly increased by the merging of both bilabials, when intervocalic before a front vowel, including the open

A, with the original v of Latin, e.g. RĪPA > *rive*, SAPĒRE > *savoir*; BA > *fève*, CABALLUM > *cheval*; LAVARE > *laver*, VĪVA > *vive*. Complete elimination of the intervocalic consonant was most perturbatory, since the resolution in Old French of the state of vocalic hiatus thereby created has often left modern French words with only one syllable, as contrasted with the two or more syllables of their equivalents in other Romance languages. This invariably happened when the consonant was dental, e.g. VĪTA > *vie*, VIDĒRE > *voir*, &c. Before a back vowel the velars produced a similar result, e.g. SECŪRUM > Old Fr. *seür* > *sûr*, A(U)GUSTUM > Old Fr. *aoust* > [ut] > [u]; so, too, in a few words, did B and V, e.g. TABŌNEM > *taon* > [tã], PAVŌNEM > *paon* > [pã], PAVŌREM > Old Fr. *peör* > *peur*.

Another voiceless intervocalic consonant which participated, in France as in northern Italy, in the early tendency to voicing is the Latin s, e.g. PAUSARE > poze (Fr. *poser*), CAUSA > ʃoːz (*chose*); the Gallo-Romance sound-system thereby acquired a new phoneme [z], of which the incidence came to be augmented by the palatalization of intervocalic k before a front vowel, in such evolutions as PLACĒRE > *plaisir*, LĬCĒRE > *loisir*, VICĪNUM > *voisin*, &c.

The upheaval in the consonant system brought about by the palatalization of velar plosives before a front vowel has already been examined in its initial stages, in its general application to the Romance area (see p. 53). The outcome in Old French, of which spelling takes no account, was as follows:

k (plus *e* or *i*) > kj > tsj, e.g. CĒRA > *[tsjeirə]* > Old Fr. [tsirə] > *cire* [siːʀ]

g (plus *e* or *i*) > gj > dʒ, e.g. GENTEM > Old Fr. [dʒã] > *gent* [ʒã]

The sounds ts and dʒ, known as affricates, persisted until the thirteenth century, when they were reduced to s and ʒ respectively. English has kept the affricate dʒ in such borrowed words as *gentle*, *general*, *giant*, and, with an attempt at phonetic rendering, *budget*, from Old Fr. *bougette* (a diminutive of Old Fr. *bouge* 'bag', 'sack', from BŬLGA, probably a loan from Celtic). As the last example shows, the result was the same when the velar plosive was initial to a syllable, after another consonant, as when it was initial to a word.

Before the open vowel a palatalization of velar consonants seems *a priori* unlikely to occur, and in the greater part of the Romance area it did not. In *francien*, however, such palatalization took place, though at a later date, probably not until towards the end of the seventh century. Again, Latin ǵ became dʒ, reduced in the thirteenth century to ʒ, e.g. GAMBA > *jambe*, GAUDIA > *joie*, GALBINUM > *jaune*, cf. Eng. *joy, jaundice*, &c.; but the k on this occasion developed more consistently to the corresponding voiceless affricate tʃ, later reduced to ʃ, e.g. CAPUM > *chief* > *chef*, CARA > *chiere* > *chère*, CARRICARE > *chargier* > *charger*, CATHĔDRA > *chaiere* > *chaire* (*chaise*), cf. Eng. *chief, cheer, charge, chair*. The k, it will be noted, again produced a yod, which combined with the following tonic free vowel but was later absorbed. This palatalization before **a** is one of the most specific features of *francien*, distinguishing it both from the Provençal dialects of the south and from the Norman and Picard dialects of the extreme north. When in modern French a word is encountered beginning with a *ca-* or *ga-* which corresponds to the same sounds in Latin, it may generally be assumed to have come as a borrowing either from one of these dialects, or from Spanish or Italian, or as a 'learned' word of relatively late adoption.

In some circumstances a k or ǵ has simply palatalized to yod, leaving no other consonantal element. This is what happened to ǵ in the intervocalic position before a front vowel, e.g. PAGENSE > *pays*, MAGIS > *mais*, and subsequently in *francien* to ǵ and k, the latter having in the interval voiced to ǵ, before the vowel a, e.g. PAGANUM > *paien*, PACARE > *payer*. Both velars were also palatalized before a following consonant, e.g. FACTUM > *fait*, NŎCTEM > *nuit*, LACTEM > *lait*, LAXARE (i.e. LACSARE) > *laisser*, DĬGITUM > *doigt* (the g is a scribal addition), FRIGIDUM > *froid*. If the second consonant was N or L, the yod combined with it giving rise to new consonants ɲ and λ, which, in the scribal devices of northern France, were represented by gn and il (*ill-*) respectively, e.g. AGNELLUM > *agnel, agneau*, DIGNARE > *daigner*, SOLĬCULUM > *soleil*, MACULA > *maille*.

In all, the palatalization of k and ǵ contributed five new consonants to Old French—ts, tʃ, dʒ, ɲ and λ—now reduced to three—ʃ, ʒ, and ɲ—the λ having in recent times become a simple j. The incidence of the new consonants is due also to certain combinations of consonant with an earlier yod: P, B, and V plus yod produced alveolar fricatives with which the affricates became identical after their thirteenth-century reduction, e.g. SAPIENTE >

*sachant*, SEPIA > *sèche*, APPROPIARE > *approcher*; TIBIA > *tige*, RABIA > *rage*, ABBREVIARE > *abréger*; SERVIENTE > *sergent*, ALVEUM > *auge*; and with the earlier yod the consonants L and N gave the same result as with a yod derived from a velar plosive, e.g. MIRA-BILIA > *merveille*, CONSĪLIUM > *conseiᵤ*; VINEA > *vigne*, CASTANEA > *châtaigne*.

*Dialectal variety.* During the thirteenth century, while French influence was extending to other countries, there still remained within the Gallo-Romance area certain centres of resistance. Of the manner in which French asserted its supremacy in the south we shall have more to say later. There it was in conflict with the highly developed literary medium formed in the tradition of *langue d'oc*. In the north, much nearer to the Île de France, the Picard–Walloon area retained and even fostered a certain linguistic autonomy. Largely on account of the wool trade, this region had witnessed the growth of a wealthy bourgeois class, with a taste for the lighter forms of literature. Many of the masterpieces of the medieval period, such as the *Jeu de saint Nicolas* and *Aucassin et Nicolete*, are Picard in origin, the former of these being associated with Arras, and the latter more probably with the territory of Hainault. The language used in these texts shows many local features. As we have previously suggested, it is not to be considered as an entirely independent record of local speech, but rather as a common written medium adapted to local conditions, and hence, a kind of Franco-Picard. The power of the Counts of Flanders, to whom the greater part of Picardy belonged, though with ever-changing frontiers, gave political backing. This seems to account for the extreme 'Picardism' of the chronicler Jean Froissart (1337–c. A.D. 1404), a native of Valenciennes who worked in the service of Flanders and spent five years of his life at the English court among the enemies of France (see, for example, his account of Wat Tyler's rebellion, reproduced by A. Ewert, *The French Language*, pp. 380–4). Later he changed political sides, and unless the peculiarities of his idiom are to be attributed to scribes rather than to the author, which seems unlikely, his subsequent writing reflects a conscious attempt to follow the new allegiance. Describing his travels in Béarn, he tells how his host, Gaston Phébus, receiving him at Orthez (cf. p. 394), listened as he read his works and sometimes interpolated: 'quant il cheoit aucune chose ou il vouloit mettre debat ou argüement, trop volontiers en parloit a moy, non pas en son gascon, mais en bon et beau françois' (*Voyage en Béarn*, ed. A. H. Diverres, p. 66). Thus the last great 'Picard' writes in elegant French and pays homage to its universality.

One of the most noticeable aspects of Picard is its opposition to *francien*, and incidentally its accordance with Italian speeches, in the treatment of the velar plosives. Before E and I the voiceless **k** palatalized to tʃ, hence such typically Picard spellings as *chelle* (Fr. *celle*), *chité* (Fr. *cité*), *rachine* (Fr. *racine*), *merchi* (Fr. *merci*), &c., whereas **k** and **g** before A remained intact, e.g. *caut* (Fr. *chaud*), *cartre* (Fr. *chartre* < CARCEREM 'prison'), *cose* (Fr. *chose*), *ganbe* (Fr. *jambe*), *gardin* (Fr. *jardin*), *gaune* (Fr. *jaune*). Other features common in Picard texts are as follows: absence of glide consonants, e.g. *tenre* (Fr. *tendre*), *ensanle* (Fr. *ensemble*); development of the triphthong *iau* corresponding to Old Fr. *eau* (hence the Picard form, adopted by French, of *fabliau*); extension of the same triphthong to words ending in -ĬLLOS, e.g. *chiaus* (Fr. *ceux*), *caviaus* (Fr. *cheveux* < CAPĬLLOS); opening to *au* of the diphthong produced by blocked ɔ and vocalized *l*, e.g. *caup* (Fr. *coup*), *saus* (Fr. *sous* < SOLIDOS), *faus* (Fr. *fous* < FOLLES); instances of diphthongization before a block, e.g. *tierre* (Fr. *terre*), *fieste* (Fr. *fête*); reduction of the triphthong *ieu* to *iu*, e.g. *mius* (Fr. *mieux*); retention of Germanic *w*, e.g. *warder* (Fr. *garder*), *wage* (Fr. *gage*), *waires* (Fr. *guère*); a feminine article *le*, cf. Anglo-Norman *Mary-le-bone*; feminine possessive adjectives *me*, *te*, *se*, and masculine possessive adjectives *men*, *ten*, *sen*; plural possessive adjectives *no* and *vo*, created by back-formation from *nos* and *vos*; infinitives from -ĒRE ending in -*ir*, e.g. *caïr* (Old Fr. *cheoir* < CADĒRE), *veïr* (Fr. *voir* < VIDĒRE). The sum of these features, and the above list is by no means exhaustive, points to a dialect which must have been almost incomprehensible to the average thirteenth-century Parisian. Eventually this literary 'Picard' gave way, as at an earlier date most other local varieties of *langue d'oïl* had given way, before the ascendancy of *francien*. Further east, however, the Walloon dialect, which in its early stages had much in common with Picard, developed a separate existence. Protected by the fact that it lay for most of its history outside the political frontiers of France, it has come in modern Belgium to have almost the status of a language. Its chief cultural centre, Liège, has a theatre devoted to the performance of plays in Walloon and a lively Walloon literature.

Medieval texts from other parts of the area of *langue d'oïl* reveal a willing conformity with the *francien* standard, though the occasional dialectalism will often suffice to indicate their approximate place of origin. Those of Champagne, for example, are easily identified by the continuing evolution of the diphthong *ei* before a nasal, e.g. *poine* (Fr. *peine*), as also by the use of the verbal flexion *-eiz*, *-oiz*, from -ĒTIS, which in *francien* had been replaced by *-ez*, from -ATIS. Most important, after Picard, especially in view of its contribution to Anglo-Norman, is the dialect of Normandy, to which region various of the typically Picard features extended. Notable among these is the preservation of **k** and **g** before **a**, reflected in many English loan-words, e.g. *car* (Fr. *char*), *cape* (Fr. *chape* < CAPPA), *caitiff* (Fr. *chétif* < CAPTĪVUM), *gammon* (Fr. *jambon*), &c. Not infrequently the twofold source of English borrowings, from Norman and from *francien*, has given rise to doublets, e.g. *cattle* and *chattel* (Old Fr. *chatel* from CAPITALEM), *catch* and *chase* (Norman–Picard *cachier* and Old Fr. *chacier*, mod. *chasser*, from CAPTIARE).

*The extension of French to England.* From the time of its constitution as a literary language, Old French owes comparatively little to foreign sources. A further and continual trickle of Germanisms entered in consequence of the growth of close commercial relations with the Low Countries, a few more through military contacts, but the movement of lexical influences was largely in an outward direction. Medieval German and Flemish are rich in borrowings from French: in German they even gave rise to a new verbal suffix *-ieren*, compounded of Old Fr. *-ier* and Germanic *-en*, as in *marchieren*. So far afield was this radiation felt that even in distant Norway, beyond the limits of the Roman world, the thirteenth-century author of an encyclopaedia of pedagogy makes a father say to his son: 'And if you wish to be perfect in knowledge, learn all languages, but above all Latin and French, because they are the most widely used.'[1] Scandinavia also added to its own famous epics a *Karlomagnussaga*, derived from the French epic, while in Bavaria a monk known to us as Konrad translated an early version of the *Chanson de Roland* as the *Ruolantes Liet*.

No other Germanic country, however, experienced the full force

---

[1] Quoted by K. Nyrop, *Grammaire historique de la langue française*, vol. i, p. 34. For Anglo-Norman see in particular, J. Vising, *Anglo-Norman Language and Literature*, London and Oxford, 1923; M. K. Pope, *From Latin to Modern French, with especial consideration of Anglo-Norman*, Manchester, 2nd ed. 1952; D. M. Legge, *Anglo-Norman in the Cloisters*, Edinburgh, 1950.

of French impact, or underwent its linguistic influence to the same extent as did England. Even in A.D. 1051, Duke William of Normandy, paying a visit to the court of his cousin Edward the Confessor, discovered that French was spoken fluently there. When, fifteen years later, he occupied the country and distributed it as fiefs to his barons, the language of the conquerors soon became everywhere supreme, Anglo-Saxon remaining in use only among the churls. In a number of works written by Englishmen the author informs us that he writes in French in order that all may understand. Thus, for a space of 300 years, after some six centuries of Anglo-Saxon and Danish settlement, England was again to be reckoned as a partially Romance-speaking country.

This new extension of Romance has come to be known as 'Anglo-Norman'. The term covers a considerable linguistic variety. During the first hundred years or so, while the new dynasty still held its continental possessions and before *francien* had become fully established as the national language of France, Anglo-Norman was very much the same as the dialect spoken in Normandy and in it is discernible a similar evolutionary trend. From the middle of the twelfth century, however, a cleavage developed between the spoken tongue and the literary language. The many Anglo-Norman writers came to aspire, like their contemporaries in France, to write 'French of Paris'; those who were French by birth, like Marie de France, took pains to state the fact:

> Marie ai num, si sui de France.

Meanwhile, the spoken language was deviating considerably from any form of speech in use on the Continent: declension broke down; final mute *e* ceased to be pronounced (e.g. *sir* for *sire*); the 'abnormal' vowel [y], which the English had never properly assimilated, became mixed with [u] (hence *dour* for *dur*), a fact which gave rise to much confusion; and in the verbal system analogy ran riot, producing such novelties as *diser* for *dire*. As English gradually returned to general use, knowledge of French became more and more an accomplishment of the educated; cut off from Paris, they tended to set their own standards, and so began the long tradition of 'Stratford-atte-Bowe'. The kind of French still used in England during this later period, as a medium for light literature, can best be illustrated by example; the extract which follows is taken from *Fouke Fitz Warin* (ed. L. Brandin, *Classiques français du moyen âge*, Paris, 1930), an historical romance written, in its present form, early in the fourteenth century, and treating the favourite theme of the wronged and noble outlaw:

> La dame e ces fyles en la tour veient lur seignour si demené q'a poyne pussent ester: crient, palment e grant duel demeynent, quar ja mes ne quident ver lur seignour en vie. Fouke le fitz Waryn fust remys en le chastel, quar yl ne fust qe dis huit anz. Si oy le cry en la tour, monta hastivement, si vist sa dame e tous les autres plouré. Yl s'en ala a Hawyse e demaunda quey ly fust e pur quoy fesoit si mourne chere. 'Tes tey, fet ele, poy resembles tu ton pere q'est si hardy e si fort, e vous estes coward e tous jours serréz. Ne veiéz vous la mon seignour, qe grantment vous ad chery e suefment norry, est en peryl de mort pur defaute de ayde? E vous, maveys, aléz sus e jus seyntz, e ne donéz ja garde.' Le vadlet, pur la repreofe qe ele avoit dyt, tot enrouy de yre e de maltalent, e s'envala meintenant de la tour e trova en la sale un vieil roynous haubert e le vesty meyntenant a mieuz qu'il savoit e prist une grose hasche denesche en sa meyn, si vynt a une estable qe ert delees la posterne par ount home vet vers la ryvere, e trova la un somer. Yl mounta meyntenant le somer e s'en issist par la posterne e passa bientost la ryvere e vynt al champ ou son seignour fust abatu de son destrer e en poynt de estre ocys, s'yl ne ust survenu.

Such are the inconsistencies of this passage that it appears at first sight to contain elements from all the dialects of northern France; they must, however, be largely orthographical. First the writer gives *quey* and then in the same sentence *quoy*: the former is 'correct' Norman dialect, since in Norman the diphthong *ei* remained: the latter is the spelling made familiar by *francien*, in which the diphthong had evolved to *oi*; in *ver* (Fr. *voir*) there is evidence of the Anglo-Norman levelling of the diphthong. Similarly, we read *demeynent* but *poyne*, the latter a spelling which might be phonetic in the dialect of Champagne, but here the pronunciation must obviously be as in *demeynent*, as is indeed confirmed by the English *pain*. A specific feature of Anglo-Norman is to be observed in the treatment of *a* and *o* before a nasal, as in *demaunda, ount, mounta*; compare, in modern English, *aunt, staunch, taunt, gauntlet, Maundy,* and *mount, fount, sound, round, noun,* all borrowed words of which the French equivalent may easily be recognized. Another and less common feature is revealed in the form *vadlet*, replacing Old Fr. *vaslet*; elsewhere in the same work there occurs *idle*, for 'island' (Old Fr. *isle*). This is not an orthographical fantasy: before disappearing, when before another consonant, the *s* seems first to have become a fricative ð, which thereafter developed in England, in a few words, to implosive *d*, e.g. *meddle*, from Old Fr. *mesler*, and *medlar*, from Old Fr. *meslier* (< \*MESPILARIUM).

The gradual return of English to general prestige and the unavailing efforts of those who favoured the maintenance of French find many an echo in contemporary literature and legislation. Towards the end of the thirteenth century Robert of Gloucester wrote a verse chronicle in English, which begins:

> Engeland is a right good land, I ween of all lands the best.

Continuing in this patriotic vein, Robert deplores the fact that if a man does not speak French he is despised, but finds encouragement in the tenacity with which the lower classes still were clinging to English; in conclusion, he remarks that there seems to be no country in the whole world, except England, which does not insist upon the use of its own native speech. During the first half of the fourteenth century these sentiments came to be those of the majority. A reactionary decree of the University of Oxford, issued in A.D. 1340, which bade students use either French or Latin in conversation, serves chiefly to show that in fact they were tending to prefer English. Indeed, so strong was the movement in this direction that a few years later, in A.D. 1348 we find a Fellow of Stapledon Hall (now Exeter College), John of Cornwall, requiring his pupils to construe in English instead of in French. His example was followed by others, and thus began at Oxford the educational reform by virtue of which, within forty years, all the schools in the country had replaced French by English as the medium of instruction. Thereafter French was learnt as a foreign language, and an interesting consequence of the change is to be seen in the fact that the study of French grammar began on this side of the Channel: the first grammar book of French was John Barton's *Donait français* (c. A.D. 1400), so named after the *Donatus*, the popular textbook of Latin known to every medieval schoolboy.

The use of English in public affairs developed rapidly as the pupils of the 1340's reached maturity, and as the brotherhood in arms of the Hundred Years War opposed England as a nation to France. In A.D. 1362, during the reign of Edward III, on account of 'les grantz meschiefs' caused by the use of French ('la lange Franceis, q'est trop desconue en dit realme'), a decree was passed whereby English was made the official spoken language of legal proceedings; in the same year Parliament was opened with a speech in English. The decisive break with French tradition at court came in A.D. 1399 with the accession of Henry IV, the first monarch since the Conquest to speak English as his native tongue. Thus the century witnessed a complete linguistic revolution, consummated in literature by the genius of Chaucer. Anglo-Norman was thereafter a dead language. It did not, however, entirely disappear. On the contrary, taking over the functions of that other dead language, medieval Latin, it persisted for a long time in use as the technical idiom of legal documents: only in A.D. 1731 did Parliament pass a Bill to the effect that records of the law should be made in English and even then the Bill met with considerable opposition. As in the case of similar documents in medieval Latin, the influence of the vernacular was liable to make itself felt, and hybrid forms of the 'nous givons' type are not uncommon. On the other hand, many French phrases attained through this medium a wider currency and passed into the English language: the sovereign still assents to Bills in Parliament with the formula 'le Roy le veult'.

The promising new Romance language thus petered out, but from the fusion of the two peoples the Anglo-Saxon grammatical basis of English emerged profoundly modified, with many of its flexions lost; and the vocabulary of English was so changed and enriched that in this respect our language can still be described as half-Romance. The extent to which our syntax is indebted to French constitutes a problem which still leaves scope for investigation. Many are the phrases which, though Germanic in content, are very suggestive of Old French idiom. Our most current salutation, 'How do you do?', somewhat bizarre when judged from an Anglo-Saxon standpoint, appears to be a rendering of Old French 'Comment le faites vous?', superimposed on 'How do you fare?', the replacement of *fare* by *do* having been induced by confusion of the former with the French verb *faire*. (See John Orr, *The Impact of French on English*, Taylorian Lecture, Oxford, 1948.)[1]

### (b) Langue d'oc

*Early Provençal*. For those whose interest is primarily centred in general European literature, the term 'Provençal' connotes

[1] For a recent and more detailed study of this subject, see A. A. Prins, *French Influence in English Phrasing* (The Hague: Martinus Nighoff, 1954, 326 pp.).

above all lyric poetry and the dominant theme of courtly love. In its beginnings, however, the vernacular writing of the extensive territories to the south of the Loire is religious in character, just as to the north, and its inspiration is no less obviously that of the monastery. Of texts which still survive the one which may be presumed to be earliest is the fragment known as the *Boecis*: presumed, because there is no external evidence to suggest even an approximate date and opinions expressed on the subject are in consequence considerably at variance. On palæographical grounds the manuscript can be attributed to the eleventh century, and consideration of the linguistic features of the *Boecis* has induced most scholars to place its composition at not much later than A.D. 1000.

The first notice of this text goes back to the eighteenth century, when a bibliophile, the *abbé* Leboeuf, mentioned it under the heading 'Ce que j'ai vu en 1727 dans un des volumes de la fameuse bibliothèque de l'abbaye de Fleury ou St-Benoît-sur-Loire', in a work entitled 'Dissertations sur l'histoire civile et ecclésiastique de Paris' (A.D. 1738). In A.D. 1813 it was rediscovered at the municipal library of Orleans, some twenty miles away, by one of the pioneers of Romance studies in France, F. Raynouard, who published it for the first time. The text comes at the end of a long Latin manuscript containing extracts from the Bible and sermons, of which the final page, and with it the last part of the poem, had previously been lost. What remains is a work of 257 decasyllabic lines, with a regular cæsura after the fourth syllable, arranged in laisses of unequal length: a poetic form closely resembling that of the later French epic, but with the surprising and perhaps significant difference that in the *Boecis* assonance has already given way to rhyme. After some initial moralizing in a misanthropic vein (cf. the beginning of the *Alexis*), the author proceeds to tell the life-story of Boethius (see p. 301), whom the Middle Ages turned into a Christian martyr. Following the medieval confusion of CONSUL with COMES, he makes Boethius, like Alexis, a 'count of Rome', a landed vassal owing homage to the Emperor; but despite this anachronistic overlay it is clear that he had the *Consolatio Philosophiae* close at hand.

A short extract will suffice to show how widely the language differs from *langue d'oïl*:

V. Coms fo de Roma e ac ta gran valor
   Aprob Mallio lo rei emperador:

El era-1 meler de tota la onor,
De tot l'emperi-1 tenien per senor.
Mas d'una causa nom avia genzor:
De sapiencia l'apellaven doctor.

VI. Quan venc la fis Mallio Torquator,
Donc venc Boecis ta granz dolors al cor
Ne cuid aprob altre dols li demor.

VII. Morz fo Mallios Torquator dunt eu dig:
Ec vos e Roma l'emperador Teiric;
Del fiel Deu no volg aver amig. . . .

X. El Capitoli l'endema, al di clar,
Lai o solíen las altras liz jutjar,
Lai veng lo reis sa felnía menar.
Lai fo Boecis, e foren i soi par.
Lo reis lo pres de felni'a reptar:
Qu'el trametía los breus ultra la mar,
Roma volía a obs los Grex tradar.
Pero Boéci anc no venc e pensar.
Sal en estant e cuidet s'en salvar:
L'om no-1 laiset e salvament annar.
Cil li faliren qu'el soli aiudar,
Fez lo lo reis e sa charcer gitar.[1]

(R. Lavaud et G. Machicot, *Boecis*; Toulouse, Institut d'études
occitanes, 1950)

In many respects the treatment of vowels is typically Provençal:
tonic *a* remains, as in the rhymes of the laisse last quoted; there
is no spontaneous diphthongization, cf. the half-open vowels in
*era, meler* (< MĔLIOR), *breus* (< BRĔVES), *Grex, cor, dols, obs*
(< ŎPUS), and the half-close vowels in *aver, valor, onor, senor,*

[1] *Literal translation*:
He was a count of Rome and had very great standing with the king-emperor
Manlius: he was the best of the whole domain. They held him as lord of the
whole Empire. But for one reason he had a more noble renown: they called
him 'doctor of knowledge'.
    When the end of Manlius Torquator came, then very great grief came to
Boethius' heart: beside it, methinks, no other grief remains to him.
    Manlius Torquator, of whom I speak, was dead: behold in Rome the
Emperor Theodoric; he did not wish to have a friend in the faithful man of
God. . . .
    In the Capitol, the next day, at full light, there where they were wont to
try other cases, there came the king to practise his felony. There was Boethius
and there were his peers. The king began to accuse him of felony: that he
was sending letters across the sea, and wished to betray Rome for the benefit
of the Greeks. But to Boethius, never did it come to his mind. He leaps to his
feet, and thought to defend himself. He was not allowed to go safely away.
Those whom he was wont to help abandoned him. The king had him thrown
into his prison.
    *Note*: the Emperor Manlius Torquator is entirely fictitious, the name having
been borrowed from the full name of Boethius himself, viz. Anicius Manlius
Torquatus Severinus Boethius; see Lavaud and Machicot, op. cit., p. 50.

*genzor* (< \*GENITIOREM), &c.; the Vulgar Latin diphthong AU is preserved in *causa*. The few other diphthongs here recorded are due to combination with the yod, e.g. *cuid, lai* (< ILLAC), *reis, laiset*. A feature of Provençal which the *Boecis* does not reveal, possibly because in the tenth century it had not yet become general, is the 'break' of the half-open vowel in contact with a palatal element, and sometimes with a neighbouring *u*, the final result frequently being a triphthong, e.g. LĔCTUM > *liech, lieit,* PĔCTUS > *pieitz,* VĔCLUM > *vielh,* ĔGO > *eu, ieu,* LĔVEM > *leu, lieu;* FŎCUM > *foc, fuoc, fuec,* NŎCTEM > *nuoit, nuoch, nuech,* FŎLIA > *fuolha, fuelha,* ŎCULUM > *uolh, uelh,* &c. To discover these forms, which sometimes reflect dialectal variation, in their full florescence, one must await the lyric.[1]

Of the unstressed vowels, post-tonic *a*, which in modern dialects has become variously ə, e, and most commonly o, seems here to retain its original quality: this may be deduced from the fact that when a final vowel occurs as 'supporting vowel' it is recorded as *e*, e.g. *altre*, and elsewhere in the same text, *entre, essemple*.

Consonantal evolution shows in particular the loss of *n* where it had become final, e.g. *ta* (< TANTUM), *endema* (< IN DE MANE), elsewhere *bo, be, passio, razo,* &c., and also before final *s*, e.g. *fis* (< FINIS). This is a feature of northern Provençal, one respect in which the *Boecis* may be contrasted with the *Chanson de sainte Foi* (see below). Failure to indicate the new sounds of palatalized *l* and *n*, as in *meler, senor*, must be due to scribal practice: therein lies another clue to the relative antiquity of the text, for in later Provençal these are regularly represented, either, as in *francien*, by *il* and *gn*, or more characteristically, by *lh* and *nh*. Treatment of k before *a* is inconsistent; cf. *causa* but *charcer* (< CARCEREM), and elsewhere in the text, *carcers, kadenas, cadegut* 'fallen', but *chastia* < CASTIGAT) and *chaitiveza* 'captivity'. Similarly, intervocalic *d*, though the poem shows examples of its retention, e.g. *credet, veder*, is here lost in *fiel* (< FIDĒLEM), also in *creessen, traazo, veüt*. Such fluctuating usage seems to point to a meeting place of *langue d'oc* with *langue d'oïl*. Certain features appear to situate the text more precisely in the *limousin* area, particularly the generalization of *-en* as the flexion of all third person plural forms, whether they

---

[1] For the complicated vocalic development of the modern idioms, see J. Ronjat, *Grammaire istorique des parlers provençaux modernes*, 4 vols., Montpellier, 1930–41.

correspond to Lat. -ENT, -ANT, or -UNT, cf. *tenien, apellaven, foren, faliren,* &c. A form *auvent,* from AUDIENTEM, shows the filling of a hiatus by *v,* a procedure not unknown in *francien* (cf. POTĒRE > Fr. *pouvoir*), but which is noticeably of frequent occurrence in the dialect of Limoges. The retention of *p* in derivatives of IPSE (*eps, epsa, epsament*), where later Provençal texts have *eis,* &c., may be simply an archaism, but since the form *meeps* (< *METĬPSE) is still encountered in a document from Limoges of A.D. 1140, it is probable that this too was local. The abbey of Saint-Martial of Limoges has been suggested as place of origin of this earliest Provençal text.[1]

In its morphology the *Boecis* displays all those features of Provençal already mentioned in the first chapter, e.g. persistence of the two-case declension, cf. *méler,* nominative, and *genzór,* accusative (see p. 70); the perfect tenses, with strong forms ending in *c* or *g,* cf. *ac, volg, venc* (see p. 141), and weak forms of the first conjugation with the 'DĒDI' flexions, cf. *cuidet, laiset* (see p. 137).

The second Provençal text of any substance is yet another monument of hagiographical literature, the *Chanson de sainte Foi d'Agen.* Again the date is difficult to determine. The author appears to have known a Latin *Liber miraculorum sanctae Fidis* composed between A.D. 1010 and 1020 by one Bernard d'Angers; this gives a *terminus a quo.* The single manuscript in which the *Chanson* has been preserved has been placed on palæographical grounds as between A.D. 1030 and 1070. In the absence of any other clue one can only estimate the time of composition as 'mid-eleventh century'.

The history of the manuscript is such as to stir anew one's wonder at the almost miraculous survival of so much medieval literature. It was known already to an outstanding scholar of the sixteenth century, Claude Fauchet. In his *Recueil de l'origine de la langue et poesie françoise, ryme et romans* (A.D. 1581), Fauchet puts forward the thesis that the French were the inventors of rhyme, and continues: 'Ce que je pense prouver par deux couples tirees d'un livre escrit à la main, il n'y a guieres moins de cinq cens ans, lequel le dit sieur Pithou m'a presté, contenant la vie de sainte Fides d'Agen.' There follow strophes 2 and 3 of the *Chanson de sainte Foi,* accurately reproduced, with the comment: 'J'estime que ce langage est vieil Espagnol, pour le moins Cathalan, par le

[1] Vladimir Rabotine, *Le 'Boèce' provençal, étude linguistique,* Strassburg, 1930; see also Lavaud and Machicot, op. cit.

vers *Que fo de razon espanesca.*[1] Fauchet's tentative dating corresponds remarkably with that of modern opinion; of his suggestions concerning language and rhyme, more anon.

Thereafter the manuscript disappeared. When in A.D. 1817 Raynouard published his collection of early Romance texts, he included, together with an expression of regret at the loss, the two strophes given by Fauchet. In A.D. 1901 came the sensational news of the rediscovery of the complete text at the library of the University of Leyden. Leite de Vasconcelos, a Portuguese scholar well known to students of Romance philology, had asked the librarian for information concerning any manuscripts which might be of interest for research in Portuguese or Spanish. Among them he found a work, catalogued in A.D. 1716 as being by the fifteenth-century Valencian poet, Ausies March, which in fact was the lost *Chanson de sainte Foi.* On the manuscript was the signature 'P. Pithou', proving that it was the same text which had been lent to Fauchet. Beneath the signature, and in the same hand, was a note: 'Monsieur Daniel me l'a donné à Paris, 1577.' A different hand had written on the same page: 'Liber ignotae mihi linguae'; while yet another hand had made use of a blank space to copy out in large letters the title of an edition of the works of Ausies March: 'Les obres del Valen cavaller et elegantissimo poeta Catalan Ausies March, imprimida en Barcelona en casa de Claud. Bornal, 1562'; the erroneous classification is thus explained.

The full manuscript, as discovered, consists of four parts, of which the *Chanson de sainte Foi* is the second, the others being in Latin. An ex-libris shows the place of origin of the first Latin text to have been the monastery of Saint-Benoît-sur-Loire. Although we cannot tell at what date the four texts were put together, it is by no means unlikely that they were already in company in the library of that monastery. An added weight is given to this supposition by Pithou's mention of a M. Daniel, for Pierre Daniel was a scholar known to have acquired some of the remains of the library of Saint-Benoît-sur-Loire after the monastery had been sacked by the Huguenots, during the Wars of Religion. Our two most ancient Provençal texts, the *Boecis* and the *Sainte Foi*, seem thus for a period of the Middle Ages to have lain side by side under the shelter of the same monastic roof. Yet, as we shall

---

[1]  Fauchet here writes *razon*, though in reproducing the text he gives the form in the manuscript, which is *razo*.

see, they really belong to quite different parts of the Provençal domain.

The *Chanson de sainte Foi* consists of 593 lines of octosyllabic verse, divided into laisses of unequal length, of which the first five are as follows:

I. Legir audi sotz eiss un pin
Del vell temps un libre Latin;
Tot l'escoltei tro a la fin.
Hanc non fo senz q'el nonl declin;
Parled del pair' al rei Licin
E del linnadg' al Maximin.
Cel meirols saintz en tal traïn
Con fal venairels cervs matin:
A clusals menan et a fin;
Mortz los laissavan en sopin.
Jazon els camps cuma fradin;
Nolz sebelliron lur vizin.
Czo fo prob del temps Constantin.

II. Canczon audi q'es bella 'n tresca,
Que fo de razo Espanesca;
Non fo de paraulla Grezesca
Ne de lengua Serrazinesca.
Dolz' e suaus es plus que bresca
E plus qe nulz pimentz q'om mesca;
Qui ben la diz a lei Francesca,
Cuig me qe sos granz pros l'en cresca
E q'en est segle l'en paresca.

III. Tota Basconn' et Aragons
E l'encontrada delz Gascons
Sabon quals es aqist canczons
E ss' es ben vera 'sta razons.
Eu l'audi legir a clerczons
Et a gramadis, a molt bons,
Si qon o monstral passions
En que om lig estas leiczons.
E si vos plaz est nostre sons,
Aisi conl guidal primers tons,
Eu la vos cantarei en dons.

IV. Totz temps avez audid asaz
Q'Agenz fo molt rica ciutaz,
Clausa ab murs et ab vallaz;
Garonnal corr per cell un laz.
La gentz d'achi fo mal' assez;
En oz esteron et en paz;

Nons pars neguns dels granz peccaz,
Plus cel q'es folz qetz melz membraz,
Entro en pres Deu pietaz,
Et en la croz los ag salvaz
E de Diable deliuraz.

V. Bella foil gentz, si fosson san;
Enferm soll cor, quar son pagan;
Guerpiron Deu, corron al fan,
Cubergrol tot d'aur Cordoan;
Profergl unsquegs l'anel del man;
Qui mais non pod, pecza de pan;
Melz estera, qil dess az can.
Tota lur obra fant en van;
E! quar nons foron Cristian![1]

(*La chanson de sainte Foi d'Agen*, ed. A. Thomas, Classiques
français du moyen âge, Paris, 1925)

As Fauchet observed, the text is rhymed throughout, usually
with a masculine rhyme, though occasionally with the feminine
rhyme ending in post-tonic *a*, as in the second laisse. The first
laisse contains a straightforward reference to a Latin original, but
the second sets a number of problems. What did the author mean

---

[1] *Translation:*
Beneath a pine-tree I heard read a Latin book of ancient times; I listened
to it right to the end. Never was there wise counsel which it does not expound.
It told of the father of the king (i.e. Roman Emperor) Licinius, and of the
lineage of the king Maximian. They pursued the saints (lit. 'put the saints
to such flight') as does the hunter the stags in the morning. They bring them
to prison and to their end; they left them lying on their backs, dead. They
lay in the fields like beggars; their neighbours did not bury them. That was
towards the time of Constantine.
I heard a song which is beautiful as a dance, which was on a Spanish theme.
It was not in Greek words, nor in Saracen tongue. It is more sweet and suave
than a honeycomb and than any spiced drink one may mix. I think that great
profit will accrue to whoever declaims it well in the French fashion, and that
he will gain a reputation in this world.
All the country of the Basques and of Aragon, and the country of the
Gascons, know what this song is, and whether this theme is really true. I
heard it spoken by clerks and lettered men of good standing, just as it is told
in the story of martyrdom in which one reads of these matters, and if our tune
pleases you, as the first tone guides it, I will sing it to you for nothing.
For long past you have often heard say that Agen was a very strong city,
enclosed by walls and ramparts; the Garonne runs along one of its sides. The
people of that place were very wicked; they lived in idleness and in ease; not
one of them abstained from great sins, the foolish still less than the most wise,
until God was seized by pity for them, and on the Cross He had saved them,
and delivered them from the devil.
Handsome were the people, had they been healthy. Their bodies are ailing,
because they are pagans; they abandoned God, they ran to the shrine, they
covered it all with gold of Córdoba; each one offered the ring from his hand,
and he who could not do more, a piece of bread. Better had it been given to the
dog. They do all their work in vain. Ah! why did they not become Christians!

by *a lei Francesca*? According to Fauchet, 'in the French way' means 'in rhyme', and this is the sole evidence which he adduces in support of his contention that the French were the inventors of rhyme. But, as we now know, French poetry at that time was assonanced and continued to be so for another century; to Provençal, among all Romance languages, goes the primacy in rhyme. Fauchet's theory being thus unacceptable, one may speculate concerning further possible interpretations. For our part, we are tempted to suggest that 'in the French way' means 'in the vernacular, as opposed to Latin': the fashion of vernacular writing, based in the north on Germanic precedent, first attested in Provençal in the areas of Clermont and Limoges, which were most obviously exposed to northern influences, thus at length reached the southernmost limits of Gallo-Romance.

In the same breath the southern poet speaks of 'profit', in terms which seem to imply that he is thinking of profit not in the form of spiritual reward, but as hard cash, and almost as though this source of income were his personal discovery. If this be so, he is the first example in Romance literature of the professional minstrel, of exploitation by the laity of themes which were dear to the Church, marking a point of transition from the ecclesiastical to the purely secular.

No less enigmatic in this laisse is the mention of a *razo Espanesca*: the theme is certainly not Spanish, and even if the poem were composed, as has been mooted,[1] in Catalan-speaking Roussillon, that scarcely justifies such a use of *razo*. That the sombre theme of the poem should be set to a tune suitable for dancing is even more surprising.[2] One is tempted to surmise that the laisse may have been originally composed for a different purpose. The fact that *razo* is the only example in the whole poem of the fall of final *n*, a phonetic feature previously noted as typical of the *limousin* flavour of the *Boecis*, may perhaps be an indication of its extraneous character.

[1] See *La chanson de sainte Foy*, ed. E. Hoepffner and P. Alfaric, 2 vols., Paris, 1926. In the second volume, due to M. Alfaric, it is suggested, though on slender evidence, that the place of composition may have been the monastery of Cuxa, situated to the south of Prades, in the diocese of Elne, now that of Perpignan (p. 13). In the first volume M. Hoepffner writes: 'Notre texte n'est certainement pas catalan. Mais il est né dans le voisinage immédiat de cette langue, près de la frontière linguistique qui la séparait du parler languedocien' (p. 207).

[2] According to M. Alfaric (op. cit.) the reference is to a *danse sacrée*; but is *tresca* the right word for such a dance?

The story proper begins with the setting of the scene in Agen, in the fourth laisse. From the Latin text the author learnt that the young saint had met her death at the hands of one Dacian, a governor sent to rule the province by Diocletian and Maximian, joint emperors from A.D. 286 to 305. Saint Fides, in common with Saint Eulalia (see p. 345), is among the reputed victims of their campaign of persecution directed against the Christians. Her 'passion', i.e. martyrdom, was for long celebrated at Agen on 6 October, the earliest evidence of the cult dating from early in the seventh century. In the Latin *Vita*, from which the *Chanson* was adapted, the story of Saint Fides had become mixed with that of another saint, St. Caprais, and this mixture is perpetuated in the poem, where St. Caprais is introduced as sole witness of the descent of an angel who blew out the fire upon which Saint Fides was burning. This intervention was of little practical avail, since one of the attendant Basques—'qui sont d'Aran', as the author erroneously tells us—thereupon cut off her head. Later, two monks carried her body to Conques, where, says the author, it is still kept 'sainte et pure'. The poem continues with invective against the Roman emperors, and ends, logically enough, with the author's declaration that he is too disgusted to sing of them further.

Whatever the literary worth of the *Chanson de sainte Foi*—though vividly told in parts, the story as a whole is rather confused—its importance as a linguistic document is outstanding. Before its rediscovery scholars tended to believe that the *limousin* area was the cradle of the Provençal literary standard. Here, however, is a text almost as early in date as the *Boecis*, written in the same language, but containing none of the peculiarities which enabled us to associate the *Boecis* with that area. Thus the final *n*, except in the word *razo* mentioned above, is maintained throughout the poem, e.g. *pin, fin, declin, pagan, fan, man*, &c. (see the rhymes of laisses Nos. I and V); so too is *n* before final *s*, e.g. *canczons, razons, bons*, &c. (see the rhymes of laisse No. III). The velar plosives are unchanged before the vowel *a*, e.g. *camp, canczon, cantar, gaudir, pagan, engan*, &c.; in the few instances in which the graphy *ch* occurs it seems to have the value of *k*, cf. *achi* and *aqi*. The flexion of the third person plural of verbs of the first conjugation is regularly *-an* (Lat. -ANT) in the *Sainte Foi*, e.g. *ausan, eran, laissavan*, &c., whereas the flexion *-en*, characteristic of the *Boecis*, is here entirely absent, both -ENT and -UNT being represented by

-*on* (sometimes written -*un*), e.g. *corron, corrun, esteron, feiron,* and with an enclitic pronoun, *cubergrol, meirols, menerols*; in later texts the ending -*on* is generalized to include even verbs of the first conjugation. Yet another peculiarity of the *Sainte Foi* is the passage of the ending of the first person singular of the future tense from *ai* to *ei*, e.g. *dizer vus ei, farei, pregarei*, &c.; the -*ai* ending, of which the *Sainte Foi* contains a single example, *prometrai*, is usual in Provençal. These features indicate that the work was originally composed in the southern part of the Provençal area, most probably in the region of Narbonne.[1]

A few distinctive features of the language of the *Sainte Foi*, as compared with that of later texts, are to be explained by its antiquity rather than by its geographical localization. Most striking are the final voiced consonants of words such as *jag, plag, pag, pod, prob, saub*, &c.; these had been voiced while still intervocalic, but later texts show them to have become voiceless again, just as happened in northern French, when the fall of the final vowel left them in a final position; the *Sainte Foi* thus records an intermediate stage of development. Another peculiarity is the preservation of the etymological group *stz* in such forms as *audistz, estz, gardistz*, &c. The group *dr* likewise persists in *considrar* (later Prov. *cosirar*), though the typical Provençal evolution of this group to *ir* is also found, as in *veirez*. Noteworthy, too, is the preservation of an etymological consonant in such words as *antpar* (< ANTE PARET), *biscbat* (< EPISCOPATUM), *marmre* (< MARMOR), where later texts have *ampar, bisbat, marbre*. Finally, the text contains a rare form of definite article, which occurs alone as *czo*, and combined with prepositions in *detz* (for *del*), *az* (for *al*) and *enz* (for *enl*); other texts occasionally show a fem. *za*. It has been suggested that this is the Lat. IPSE, but IPSE occurs in more regular forms, and the spelling here points to a combination with ECCE; the ECCE EUM, ECCE EA, suggested by A. Thomas, is perhaps the most acceptable etymon.

After the *Sainte Foi* there is no work written in Provençal which can be said with certainty to precede the secular lyric. It is true that one important poem, a fragment of a life of Alexander the Great and the first of many Romance compositions devoted to that subject, has both Provençal connexions and a strong claim to antiquity (see p. 396), but there is no justification for placing it

<hr>

[1] This is the localization suggested by A. Thomas, op. cit., p. xxxviii.

much earlier than the beginning of the twelfth century. The same remark applies to two short religious poems, one of them a Christmas carol, preserved in a manuscript now at Paris which came originally from the monastery of Saint-Martial of Limoges (published by P. Meyer, *Anciennes poésies religieuses en langue d'oc*, Bibliothèque de l'Ecole des Chartes, 1860). Writing in prose, earlier in the south than in northern France, appears during the first years of the twelfth century, in legal documents. The large collection of such documents assembled by M. Clovis Brunel (*Les plus anciennes chartes en langue provençale*, 2 vols., Paris, 1926) shows Latin to have been in general use until that time, though a Latin which frequently contained words and phrases of the vernacular. The first complete prose text deliberately written in Provençal, an act of donation, dates from A.D. 1102 and comes from Rodez, in the province of Rouergue; thereafter such texts abound in all parts of the Provençal area. But before the eleventh century ended, the first of a galaxy of troubadour poets had already begun his literary career: he was none other than the most powerful nobleman south of the Loire, William, seventh Count of Poitiers and ninth Duke of Aquitaine (A.D. 1071–1127).

*The lyric.* No literary problem, unless it be that of the origins of northern French epic, can have given rise to so much speculation as has the mystery of the Provençal lyric. Since the poems of Guillaume de Poitiers which survive, eleven in all, display the attributes of a practised technique, it is generally assumed that such verse must have been composed before his day, that the first record of versifying in the vernacular was preserved on account of the great worldly prestige of the author. There is, in fact, in the Provençal area one slight previous indication of a secular lyric. A manuscript now at the Vatican library, which formerly belonged to Saint-Benoît-sur-Loire, contains a Latin dawn-song dating from some time early in the eleventh century, possibly even from the tenth, in which a vernacular refrain is inserted between each three lines of Latin. This refrain, three times repeated, is unfortunately almost illegible. It appears to run as follows:

> Lalba par umet mar atra sol
> Poy pas abigil miraclar tenebras.

Whatever it may mean, this is certainly Provençal (for a summary of attempted interpretations, see C. Tagliavini, *Le origini delle lingue neolatine*, 2nd ed., pp. 434–5). Comparing this couplet with the recently discovered Romance refrains in the Hebrew and Arabic poetry written during the same period in southern Spain (see p. 400), one inclines to suppose that popular Romance verse assumed literary form under the tutelage of the established literary languages; but there remains an unexplained hiatus between these early vestiges and the polished lyric of the troubadours.

The example set by Guillaume de Poitiers was followed by lesser noblemen in all the courts of the south and by *jongleurs* of humble birth who sought their patronage. By the mid-twelfth century lyrics were being composed in every estate of the Provençal domain. This literary outburst was the accompaniment to great social changes. During the eleventh century the south had emerged from the period of chaotic conditions consequent upon the collapse of Charlemagne's Empire and the continual threat of Moorish incursions. In Spain, the Reconquest, in which many southern French noblemen had taken part, had met with success and carried the menace away. Then, at the end of the century, came the call to the First Crusade and the south responded in full measure. There can be little doubt that the experiences of this Crusade, the sight of different and richer forms of civilization, played a large part in changing feudal mentality. Thereafter the local lord, who had previously hoarded his considerable wealth in coffers and turned his closely-guarded fortress into a museum, suddenly revealed a taste for luxury and ostentation, purchased rich clothing, and, in a word, 'went gay'. In relatively peaceful conditions there developed a social habit of reception and entertainment, setting a pattern for the whole of Europe, including northern France, which in its essentials is still followed. One court vied with another in lavishness. Manners were cultivated and codified; women acquired a much higher status, and under their influence the relations between the sexes became sentimentalized as never before. Song had a large part in all this, and the poems of the troubadours—a fact which must always be borne in mind if one seeks to pass judgement on their literary worth—were written expressly to be sung. Thus in the Provençal lyric the harmony of the words is of greater significance than their logical content. The troubadour was at once poet and composer, and of his two crafts, musical composition came first.

Though the subject-matter may at times grow monotonous, these lyrists reveal a great diversity of temperament. Guillaume de

Poitiers, irreligious and anti-clerical, the imprisoner of bishops, excommunicated by the Pope, launches the flood of love-poetry with a rather crude eroticism, though on occasion he unexpectedly sounds a gentler note, and in one poem, presumably among his latest, he repents for his sins and seeks divine forgiveness. Marcabrú and Cercamon, both Gascon by birth and of humble condition, appear from the outset as the satirists of courtly love, motivated by a deep concern for the effects of its relaxed morality upon social conditions. The vehement condemnations of Marcabrú probably have a psychological origin in the fact that he himself was a foundling; but he too could write with sympathy, portraying the loneliness of the constant woman whose husband or lover had departed for the Crusade. Such voices in the wilderness had little effect upon the aristocracy, which remained consistently amorous. But in the work of Jaufré Rudel, 'prince of Blaye' (at the mouth of the Garonne), there appears all the yearning of a visionary imagination, a sublimation of sentiment which created the legend of the distant princess so beloved of later poets, as expressed in the following verses:

I.  Lanquan li jorn son lonc en may
    m'es belhs dous chans d'auzelhs de lonh,
    e quan mi suy partitz de lay
    remembra.m d'un'amor de lonh:
    vau de talan embroncx e clis
    si que chans ni flors d'albespis
    no.m platz pus que l'yverns gelatz.

II. Be tenc lo Senhor per veray
    per qu'ieu veirai l'amor de lonh;
    mas per un ben que m'en eschay
    n'ai dos mals, quar tan m'es de lonh.
    Ai! car me fos lai pelegris,
    si que mos fustz e mos tapis
    fos pels sieus belhs huelhs remiratz!

III. Be.m parra joys quan li querray,
     per amor Dieu, l'alberc de lonh:
     e, s'a lieys platz, alberguarai
     pres de lieys, si be.m suy de lonh:
     adoncs parra.l parlamens fis
     quan drutz lonhdas er tan vezis
     qu'ab bels digz jauzira solatz.

IV. Iratz et gauzens me'n partray,
    s'ieu ja la vey, l'amor de lonh:

mas non sai quoras la veyrai,
car trop son nostras terras lonh:
assaz hi a pas e camis,
e per aisso no.n suy devis. . . .
Mas tot sia cum a Dieu platz![1]

(Ed. Martín de Riquer, *La lírica de los trovadores*, vol. i,
Barcelona, 1948, p. 105)

This is the first half of a poem composed *c.* A.D. 1147. It seems
scarcely credible that such polish and musicality could have been
attained so soon in a language so new to literary tradition.

Rather before Marie de France, first poetess in *langue d'oïl*,
troubadour verse revealed a feminine talent in the Countess of
Die: nothing is known of her, and only five of her poems have
survived, but they are sufficient to unveil a poetic personality, an
ardent disposition which inevitably calls to mind her sixteenth-
century near-compatriot, Louise Labé. In her writing, and in that
of the lover whose faithlessness she laments, Raimbaut d'Orange
(d. *c.* A.D. 1173), the valley of the Rhône first comes within the
scene as a centre of lyrical composition. But the poet of greatest
lyrical genius during this exciting twelfth century brings us back
to the land of Limoges: none surpasses Bernard de Ventadour
(*c.* A.D. 1120–*c.* 1180). Son of a servant at the castle of Ebles III
of Ventadour, Bernard became so well versed in *Fin' Amor* that his
lord's wife fell in love with him; in consequence he was expelled
and the wife later repudiated, but within a short time we find him
at the court of Eleanor of Aquitaine, reputedly her lover too. He
himself anticipated the verdict of posterity by declaring that he
was the best *cantador* of all: his heart, so he tells us, was more

---

[1] *Translation*:
  When the days are long in May, I delight in the sweet song of birds in the
distance, and when I have turned away, I remember a distant love. I go in
sombre, pensive mood, so that neither birdsong nor mayflower pleases me
more than the frozen winter.
  I hold the Lord as true, through whom I shall see the distant love, but for
one blessing which befalls me I endure two ills, for she is so far away. Ah!
would that I were a pilgrim there, so that my staff and my cape might be seen
by her beautiful eyes!
  Great joy will come to me when I ask of her, for God's love, a place in
the distant abode. And if it pleases her I shall dwell by her side, although I
am from afar. Then there will be true converse when the distant lover is so
near that he will enjoy with beautiful words the solace of love.
  If ever I see her, the distant love, sad and happy shall I leave her. But I do
not know when I shall see her, for our lands are very far apart. There are
many paths and byways, and therefore I cannot foretell. . . . But may it all
be as God pleases!

strongly drawn than that of others towards love and hence towards song. We reproduce the first four verses of one of his best-known variations on a single theme, in which his technique in the use of the new idiom invites comparison with that of Jaufré Rudel:

I. Can vei la lauzeta mover
de joi sas alas contra.l rai,
que s'oblid'e.s laissa chazer
per la doussor c'al cor li vai,
ai! tan grans enveya me'n ve
de cui qu'eu veya jauzion,
meravilhas ai, car desse
lo cor de dezirer no.m fon.

II. Ai, las! tan cuidava saber
d'amor, e tan petit en sai!
car eu d'amar no.m posc tener
celeis don ja pro non aurai.
Tout m'a mo cor, e tout m'a me,
e se mezeis'e tot lo mon;
e can se.m tolc, no.m laisset re
mas dezirer e cor volon.

III. Anc non agui de me poder
ni no fui meus de l'or'en sai
que.m laisset en sos olhs vezer
en un miralh que mout me plai.
Miralhs, pus me mirei en te,
m'an mort li sospir de preon,
c'aissi.m perdei com perdet se
lo bels Narcisus en la fon.

IV. De las domnas me dezesper;
ja mais en lor no.m fiarai;
c'aissi com las solh chaptener,
enaissi las deschaptenrai.
Pois vei c'una pro no me'n te
vas leis que.m destrui e.m cofon,
totas las dopt'e las mescre,
car be sai c'atretals se son.[1]

(Op. cit., p. 271)

[1] *Translation*:
When I see the lark beating its wings with joy against the sunbeam and, forgetful, letting itself drop away, on account of the sweetness which goes to its heart, alas! there comes over me such great envy of one whom I see rejoicing that I wonder my heart does not melt with desire.
Woe is me! I thought I knew so much about love, and I know so little. For I cannot refrain from loving her who will never grant me her favour. She has stolen my heart, and stolen me, and herself and all the world; and

Some forty-one poems can be attributed to him with certainty; of these, some seven or eight, according to Carl Appel, were probably composed in England, whither he is believed to have come in the following of Eleanor. His last days, so we are told in an ancient *Vida*, were spent in a Cistercian monastery.

The latter half of the century saw these poets ever increasing in number. A contrasting personality appears in Bertrand de Born (*c.* A.D. 1140–*c.* 1210), a most truculent poet, who, besides writing more than vigorous love poems, specialized in the political song, the *sirventés*, largely devoted to fomenting between different nobles the warfare in which he took such delight. Arnaut Daniel, developing a technical virtuosity already foreshadowed by Raimbaut d'Orange, became the leading poet of *trobar clus* (closed poetry), as opposed to *trobar leu* ('light' or easy poetry), and the protagonist of a new tradition of mystification in European verse. Raimbaut de Vaqueyras, a wandering *jongleur* of versatile gifts, is of particular philological interest on account of his bilingual poem in which he debates with a Genoese lady (see p. 453), and especially for the multilingual poem, written between A.D. 1190 and 1203 when the author was in Italy, which includes verses written in Provençal, Italian (Genoese type, see p. 453), French, Gascon (see p. 390), and Portuguese (see p. 433): the supposed purpose of the mixture was to convey a state of mental perturbation provoked by love, though an unkind critic might suspect that the poet was more intent on displaying his wide knowledge of the Romance languages.

Among other 'characters' is Folquet de Marseille, a merchant who entered the Church and became Bishop of Toulouse, where he died in A.D. 1231, after distinguishing himself by his cruel treatment of the Albigenses (see below, p. 393). Peire Vidal, a native of Toulouse, who travelled round the courts of Italy and Spain and passed in his day for a great eccentric, has left some forty not very original poems. For almost the full course of the thirteenth century lived and rhymed the satirist and moralist Peire

when she took herself away, she left me nothing but desire and a yearning heart.

Never more did I have power over myself. I was no longer mine from that moment when she let me look into her eyes, into a mirror which charms me. Mirror, since I saw myself in thee, deep sighs have slain me, for I lost myself, just as the handsome Narcissus lost himself in the fountain.

I despair of ladies. Never again will I put my trust in them. Just as I was wont to be their champion, henceforth I will be their detractor. Since I see that not one lends me help against her who destroys and confounds me, I fear and disbelieve them all, for I know they are all alike.

Cardenal, born at Puy-en-Vélay, who, with some seventy poems still extant, is the most abundantly represented of all troubadour poets.

These are but a few of the best known: in addition to anonymous material, the *Bibliographie der Troubadours*, by A. Pillet and H. Carstens (Halle, 1933), lists no less than 460 names of troubadours whose work has partially survived. Never before or since has a country been so swept by the lyrical urge.

*The Provençal standard.* In whatever region they may have been born, the troubadours conform to a fairly well stabilized linguistic standard. The question of its origin has been no less hotly debated than that of the origin of the lyric itself. In the course of discussion, the two problems involved have frequently been merged into one; this, as we have seen, is a fallacious approach: before the composition of the first-known lyric, a Provençal literary language had come into existence as a medium for the didactic and hagiographical literature conceived in clerical circles. Up to this point, the literary beginnings of the *langue d'oc* are very similar to those of the *langue d'oïl*. But there the parallel ends. Whereas in the north the standard speech rapidly became associated with a particular area—the Paris basin—in the south there was no one region which enjoyed a comparable political supremacy.

There were in fact two regions with which, had their prosperity endured, a local secular standard might have become identified. In his day, the greatest power in the south was Guillaume de Poitiers, who ruled over lands more extensive than those of the King of France. To the latter he owed a nominal allegiance; this he acknowledges in one of his poems, the poem of repentance, where, before leaving for Spain to fight with Alfonso the 'Batallador' against the Moors (A.D. 1117–20), he expresses concern for the fate of the son whom he left behind:

> Si Folcos d'Angieus no.l socor,
> e.l reis de cui ieu tenc m' onor,
> faran li mal tut li plusor,
> felon gascon et angevi.

In reality, however, he was quite independent. Moreover, by his marriage in A.D. 1094 to Felipa of Toulouse, he established a link with the only court in the south which could in any way rival his. Turning this connexion into a claim, he twice attempted to seize the territories belonging to the house of Toulouse, on the first occasion during the absence of his brother-in-law, Count Raimon de Saint-Gilles, on the First Crusade; but on both occasions the citizens of Toulouse frustrated his plans. After his death in A.D. 1127 his son ruled for ten years as Guillaume, eighth Count of Poitiers and tenth Duke of Aquitaine. When he died there was no male heir, and so in A.D. 1137 the vast succession passed to a woman, Eleanor of Aquitaine, with consequences which we have already described (p. 351). Aquitaine now being a bone of contention between England and France, Toulouse came into the ascendant, and under the rule of Count Raimon V (A.D. 1148–94), to whom the viscounts of Carcassonne, Narbonne, and Béziers owed allegiance, Languedoc became the political centre. This was the land in which troubadour civilization attained its greatest heights of splendour and frivolity. Its independence, however, was always somewhat insecure. For some time past the kings of Aragon and Catalonia had taken a proprietary interest in the southern fiefs; but open hostilities were avoided by a series of matrimonial alliances: Raimon VI of Toulouse, who succeeded in A.D. 1194, was married to a sister of King Pedro II of Aragon, and in A.D. 1204 Pedro himself married the Viscountess of Montpellier. When in A.D. 1209 the armies of Philippe-Auguste appeared in Languedoc, massacring the inhabitants of Béziers and laying siege to Carcassonne—all this ostensibly in answer to the Pope's appeal for an extirpation of the Albigensian heresy—it was natural that Pedro II should rally to the support of the Count of Toulouse. In A.D. 1213, Count Raimon being hard pressed by the French under Simon de Montfort, King Pedro went to his assistance at the head of a large army containing the flower of Aragonese and Catalan nobility. When the two armies met at Muret, on 12 September, the much larger forces of the south were utterly routed and King Pedro killed. Thereafter all territories east of the Garonne came under French control, and the ambitions of the house of Aragon and Catalonia were bounded by the northern limits of Roussillon. The courtly life of the south was shattered.

During its brief prosperity this courtly life thus had its focus first in the central part of the domains of Guillaume de Poitiers, and then in the Languedocian possessions of the counts of Toulouse, more particularly in western Languedoc. It is within these areas that the home of medieval Provençal must be sought. All other regions can be excluded: the lands west of the Garonne and east of the Rhône exercised no perceptible influence. Although some of the earliest troubadours were Gascon by birth, they did not write in Gascon. The first sample of this very individual speech occurs in the poem of Raimbaut de Vaqueyras (see above, p. 387), where it is represented as a language different from Provençal:

> Dauna, io mi rent a bos
> coar sotz la mes bon'e bera,
> q'anc hos, e gaillard'e pros
> ab que no.m hossetz tan hera.
> Mout abetz beras haissos
> e color hresqu'e noera.
> Boste son, e si.bs agos
> no.m destrengora hiera.[1]

(V. Crescini, *Nuovi studi medievali*, i, 1923, p. 73)

The text already shows such typically Gascon features—upon which the author seems to dwell with relish—as the passage of Latin F to *h*, e.g. *hos* < FUISSET, *hossetz* < FUISSĒTIS, *hera* < FĔRA, cf. Fr. *fière, haissos* < FACTIONES, cf. Fr. *façons, hresqu'* < FRĬSKA, *hiera* < *FIBĔLLA (for FIBŬLA, cf. Prov. *fivela*, Span. *hebilla*), and the development of intervocalic -LL- to -*r*-, e.g. *bera* < BĔLLA, *noera* < NOVĔLLA, and *hiera*. Noteworthy, too, is the Gasc. *sotz*, which derives from an analogical *SUTIS, whereas Prov. *etz*, like Fr. *êtes*, remains true to Lat. ESTIS (cf. p. 128). As for the idiom of modern Provence, east of the Rhône, a troubadour from that region, Raimon Feraut, assures us that his native tongue is not *dreg proensales*. Among the French, the term *poitevin* gained some currency as a synonym for 'Provençal', but this was chiefly because for them the territory of *langue d'oc* began with Poitou.

That many scholars should have sought to identify Provençal precisely with the dialect of Limoges is due to the early and continued literary productivity of the *limousin* area. The assumption appeared to be supported by the fact that a Catalan troubadour, Raimon Vidal of Besadún (A.D. 1160–1210), author of a 'poetic art' intended to instruct his compatriots in the craft of lyrical composition, the *Rasos de Trobar*, always refers to Provençal as

---

[1] *Translation*: Lady, I surrender to you because you are the best and most beautiful that ever was, and gay and honest—if only you were not so cruel to me. You have most beautiful features and a fresh and bright (lit. 'new') complexion. I am yours, and if I had you, I would suffer no constraint (lit. 'no clasp would constrict me').

'Lemosi'; but he himself is careful to explain that he understands 'Lemosi' in the widest possible sense: 'Totz hom que vol trobar ni entendre, deu primierament saber qe neguna parladura non es naturals ni drecha del nostre lengage mais acella de Franza e de Lemozi, o de Proenza o d'Alvergna o de Caersin; per qe ieu vos dic qe, quant ieu parlarai de Lemosy, qe totas estas terras entendas et totas lor vezinas et totas qe son entre ellas', i.e. 'Whoever wishes to write in Romance (*nostre lengage*) must choose as his standard either French or Lemosi, this latter being the language of Provence, Auvergne or Quercy, &c.' This constitutes a remarkable testimony to the widespread use of Provençal, but it does not help in localizing the sources of the literary medium. Undoubtedly, *limousin* played an important part, but not an exclusive part. The origin of the medium lies in its employment for religious instruction. The *Boecis* and the *Sainte Foi* survive to indicate the geographical extremes of the area which saw its birth: the ecclesiastical centres of Limoges and Narbonne, with Toulouse as the connecting link. Both the *Boecis* and the *Sainte Foi* contain dialectal features which can be approximately localized: once the language came to be moulded by the troubadours, these peculiarities tended to be accepted as alternative forms, without reference to their geographical origin (see, for example, in the extract from Jaufré Rudel, *gauzens* but *jauzira*). In view of this latitude Provençal may be described, though in a restricted sense, as a *koine*: a language, that is, which grew as a common literary medium and comprised different dialectal elements; literary Italian was to develop in the same way, with still less normalizing rigour.

*The influence of Provençal.* A century of song-writing in Provence has left its mark on all the literatures of western Europe. To the Germanic languages this influence was conveyed partly through the medium of French, though there are many instances of direct contact; connexions with the *Minnesänger* of southern Germany were probably established as a result of the Crusades.[1] After the destruction of the Provençal courts at least one well-known troubadour, Peire Vidal, travelled as far afield as Hungary. Both Marcabrú and Bernard de Ventadour are believed to have visited the Anglo-Norman court of England. But it is south of the

[1] See István Frank, *Trouvères et Minnesänger, recueil de textes pour servir à l'étude des rapports entre la poésie lyrique romane et le minnesang au xiie. siècle,* Saarbrücken, 1952.

Pyrenees and in Italy that Provençal influence had its greatest and most lasting effect.

Some time before the Albigensian Crusade there had developed a Catalan group of troubadours writing in Provençal. The earliest to have left a poem to posterity is again the most powerful ruler in the land, King Alfonso the first of Catalonia and the second of Aragon (A.D. 1162–96), father of the Pedro II killed at Muret. At the Catalan courts there was always a welcome for the troubadours of Provence, and many found refuge there after the catastrophe which befell them. Following the advice given to them in the *Rasos de Trobar*, the poets of Catalonia continued to write in Provençal until well into the fourteenth century, though the linguistic peculiarities of Catalan appear increasingly in their work. The debt of literary Catalan to Provençal is certainly considerable; it is not easy, however, since the two areas had been very closely linked ever since Roman times, to distinguish between what is borrowed and what developed on the native soil.

Some troubadours seem to have made their way to Galicia and Portugal, where again there appeared a lyric form written in the troubadour manner, but in the native dialect (see p. 434). It was, however, in Italy, then beginning to evolve its own courtly civilization, that the dispossessed poets of Provence found their principal refuge; some indeed, like Raimbaut de Vaqueyras, whose patron was the Marquis of Montferrat, had either settled there or made prolonged visits at an earlier date. The result was that in Italy, as in Catalonia, there grew up a school of native poets writing in Provençal, of whom at least one, Sordello, born near Mantua, is to be reckoned among the greatest of the troubadours: some forty of his poems survive, composed between A.D. 1220 and 1260. The lyrical inspiration also became manifest in Sicily, at the court of Frederick the Second, where, as in Portugal, poets wrote in the Provençal manner but in the native idiom, and thereby played a part in the founding of the Italian language (see p. 461). Thus the Italian vocabulary was enriched with borrowings from *langue d'oc*, as also from *langue d'oïl*.[1] Both Petrarch and Dante owe much to the prompting of Provençal; and the fact that the work of the troubadours was restored to a place of honour in the realm of

[1] See, in particular, G. Baer, *Zur sprachlichen Einwirkung der altprovenzalischen Troubadourdichtung auf die Kunstsprache der früheren italienischen Lyriker*, Zürich, 1939; and R. Bezzola, *Abbozzo di una storia dei gallicismi italiani nei primi secoli (750–1300)*, Heidelberg, 1925.

literary appreciation is due in the first instance to those Italian
scholars of the sixteenth century who sought to discover the
sources used by their two great national poets. They had not far
to seek: in Italy the troubadours had never fallen into the same
oblivion as in France; collections of their songs, *canzonieri*, had
continued to be prized and copied, and it is for this reason that
Provençal poetry, as we know it, is preserved largely in manuscripts of Italian origin.

*The decline of Provençal.* The nature of the heresy to which the
small town of Albi gave its name—though the chief centre was
Toulouse—still remains somewhat obscure. It may have embraced
elements gathered from various sects then active in southern
Europe: in particular, the Albigenses appear to have been kindred
spirits of the Cathari (the 'pure') of northern Italy. That it was
undermining the authority of the established Church over a large
part of southern France is quite certain, but that courtly circles
were deeply involved seems improbable: the general tone of
troubadour poetry suggests a complete indifference to religious
mysticism. For some time past, however, the Papacy had looked
askance at the phenomenon of courtly manners, and although
there is no concrete evidence to confirm the oft-repeated allegation
made in the last century—by a French historian, F. Samazeuilh—
that Provençal was actually condemned as the language of heresy,
there is ample testimony to the fact that song-writing was held
by the Church to be a shiftless and sinful occupation. This is not
surprising, since the inspiration of the Provençal lyric is essentially
pagan, glorifying all the impulses which the Church held in ab-
horrence; not until after the Albigensian Crusade, in the work of
Peire Cardenal in the first instance, was the love-cult transformed
into adoration of the Virgin. Thus the Pope could not have been
greatly perturbed if the King of France, while suppressing a
popular deviation in the name of religion, should also have found
it expedient, in pursuit of his own ends, to destroy the Languedocian courts.

Destroyed they were, and in the collapse of the social conditions
upon which the structure was based, the aristocracy found itself
burdened with new and non-lyrical preoccupations, excluding the
patronage and upkeep of minstrels. It may well be argued that
before these events took place the Provençal lyric had lost its
freshness and was already in a decadent state, but the curtain, in

the Provençal homeland, was certainly brought down by the Albigensian Crusade. So ended what had been the most original and spontaneous expression of the genius of southern France: not that the natives of Provence ceased abruptly to write in their own language, but the literature of the thirteenth and fourteenth centuries shows an increasing subservience to models imported from the north, and above all to the moralizing and didactic tendencies which met with clerical approval.

Meanwhile, the use of the French language was penetrating the south and gaining ever wider acceptance. Only west of the Garonne, in Béarn, did a new political centre of some importance arise, maintaining its independence, with a capital first at Orthez and then at Pau, and using its own standardized Bearnese—a pleasant kingdom which came to an end when Henry, then sovereign of both Béarn and Navarre, deemed Paris to be 'worth a mass' (A.D. 1594); shortly before its absorption it produced two poets of some note, Pey de Garros and Guillaume Ader, the latter of whom sang Henry's praise in an epic entitled *Lou gentilome gascoun*. Elsewhere, the majority of those possessed by literary aspirations soon began to wield the pen in French. Already in the early fifteenth century a 'méridional', Antoine de la Salle (b. A.D. 1380) was established as one of the foremost writers of French prose. Clément Marot, born at Cahors (c. A.D. 1496) was the first in a long line of French poets hailing from the south. Du Bartas (A.D. 1544-90), though he could write excellent Gascon verse in honour of Henry IV, before the latter's apostasy, belongs essentially to French literature.

As often happens under such circumstances, literary Provençal became the pastime and rallying point of an eclectic circle, artificially cultivated and surrounded by the bedside solicitude due to a language in decline. In A.D. 1323 a society was founded at Toulouse for the purpose of renewing its lyrical tradition; since Provençal poetry had then come to be known as 'lo gay saber', the society assumed the name of 'sobregaya companhia'. Under its auspices literary competitions were held, and in A.D. 1356, its president then being Guillem Molinier, it produced a book of Provençal grammar, the *Leys d'amors*, intended for the guidance of competitors. The society ultimately became the *Académie des jeux floraux de Toulouse*, a model for many others of its kind, and as such it still functions; but in A.D. 1694—a significant date in the later history of French, since it was that year which saw the first appearance of the *Dictionnaire de l'Académie française*—the *Académie des jeux floraux* belied the intentions of its founders by admitting poems in French as well as in Provençal, thereby bringing the cult of the southern language to its lowest ebb.

More recently, many attempts have been made to revive the use of Provençal as a literary medium. Best known is that of Frédéric Mistral, who succeeded in raising considerable local enthusiasm and a large band of followers, including some of undisputed talent. A native of Arles, and a poet in the lyrical tradition, Mistral is also remembered by scholars on account of his two-volume dictionary, the *Tresor dou felibrige* (A.D. 1878–86). There is at present a similar group of *felibres* in Gascony, led by Simin Palay, who has emulated Mistral by producing an equally valuable dictionary, the *Dictionnaire du béarnais et du gascon modernes* (2 vols., Pau, 1932). Such movements, however, lack political backing and have only a limited measure of popular support; in consequence, there is no longer any one form of standard which really corresponds to a currently spoken tongue. Yet the *langue d'oc* lives on, in all the diverse patois of the Midi, where every peasant is bilingual, speaking his native idiom to his fellows and to strangers his acquired variety of 'regional French'.

*Franco-Provençal.* The territories of *langue d'oc* and *langue d'oïl* correspond quite closely to those which were first occupied by the Visigoths and the Franks. Each language, in its literary form, evolved from the centre of a former Germanic kingdom. In post-imperial Gaul there was a third area, which as yet has found no significant place in our account of the growth of new languages: that of the Burgundians, comprising the lands later controlled by the ducal houses of Savoy and Burgundy, and including the present *Suisse romande*. The inhabitants of this region of mountains and valleys speak nowadays a number of very diversified patois which in some of their features resemble French and in others Provençal, whence they have come to be traditionally grouped under the generic heading of 'Franco-Provençal'. The very isolation of the region, separated from the two principal centres in literary tradition no less than in history and geography, leads one to wonder whether it may not have witnessed an attempt, ultimately abortive, to create from the heritage of Gallo-Romance yet a third literary norm.

Two texts at least survive which seem to point in this direction.

The earlier is the so-called 'Alexander fragment'. Discovered on two folios of a twelfth-century manuscript at the Laurentian library at Florence, it consists, unfortunately, of a mere 105 lines of octosyllabic verse, the beginning of a much longer poem. The substance of the poem is known from a Middle High German adaptation, running to 7,302 lines, by the priest Lamprecht, who names the author of the original as 'Elberich von Bisenzûn'. He is therefore known in French as Albéric, but the identification with Besançon has on linguistic grounds long since been doubted; instead, it has been suggested that Albéric's abode was Briançon, and more recently, with much more probability, a locality near Valence called *Pisançon*.

To date the fragment with any accuracy is impossible. The fact that Lamprecht's adaptation was completed by A.D. 1130 does, however, provide a *terminus ad quem*, from which we may deduce that the composition of Albéric's poem, still heavily marked by Latin, was roughly contemporary with that of the Oxford version of the *Chanson de Roland*. Its vernacular certainly appears no less archaic, but in the absence of a Franco-Provençal term of comparison it is difficult to say what was 'archaic' in the Franco-Provençal area. In its subject-matter, as the first of a series of Romance poems recounting the exploits of Alexander the Great, it breaks new ground: as northern France created the secular epic, and Provence the lyric, so the Franco-Provençal area gave birth to the *roman d'antiquité*, the source of courtly romance.

The more important text from this region, preserved in full in a manuscript now in the Bodleian library, is a *chanson de geste* of 10,002 lines which conforms entirely to the epic tradition of northern France. Known as *Girard de Roussillon*, it tells of a prolonged feud between Girard and the French king. Girard's fief is not the Pyrenean province which we have previously mentioned: the name, in the text *Rossilho*, seems to have been that of a castle situated in the Rhône valley, near Vienne. It is now generally accepted that the hero of the poem has an historical antecedent in a personage of some note associated with that region, in Latin texts *Gerardus*, Regent of Provence. This Gerard had been Count of Paris during the reign of Louis the Pious. On the latter's death he espoused the cause of Lothair, whose defeat cost him his title and estates. He was, however, recompensed by Lothair with the titles of Count of Lyon and Count of Vienne, places which nominally remained within the central kingdom. His regency of Provence derived from his official protection of Lothair's infant son, on whom the title of 'King of Provence' had been conferred. When, after Lothair's death, Charles the Bald and Louis the German shared out between themselves his inheritance, the Kingdom of Provence was claimed by Charles, a claim which Gerard resisted, seeking to maintain its independence: hence the hostilities. The poem reflects very little knowledge of this historical background, so little indeed that Charles the Bald has become Charles Martel, and Girart is the type of wronged and rebellious vassal encountered in other French epics.

In the form in which it survives, which may not have been its earliest form, the work dates approximately from between A.D. 1160 and 1170. It is therefore a good half-century later than the 'Alexander fragment', and its language appears much more 'mixed': scrutiny of the following lines (6572–84) will show how its linguistic features are divided between those of the north and those of the south:

> Dun Bos d'Escarpion vent per lo cant.
> Grant a la forcheure, doljaz per flant;
> Ja gencor chevaler om ne demant.
> E out elme e oberc perclar e blant,
> E a ceinte une espede veila trencant;
> Son escut a son col, d'os d'olifant,
> Anc non vistes tan fort ne meins pesant.
> E chavauge un chaval corser ferant,
> E at lacat en s'ast un aurebant.
> 'Marestun! Marestun!' vai escridant,
> L'enseine de Girart fort essaucant,
> E la Carlon Martel vai abaissant,
> E maint franc chevaler mort crabentant.[1]

(Ed. W. Mary Hackett, Société des anciens textes français, 3 vols., Paris, 1953–5)

Two works do not in themselves suffice to establish a linguistic norm; in fact, any possible growth of a third language was

---

[1] *Translation*: Sir Boson of Escarpion comes to the field. He is well-forked, and slender in his loins; never could one ask to see a nobler knight. His helmet and hauberk were shining white, and he has girt on an old well-cutting sword. The shield hanging from his neck was of elephant bone; never did you see one so strong or so light. He rides a swift warhorse and has an oriflame tied to his lance. 'Mareston! Mareston!' he goes shouting, raising aloud the battle-cry of Girard and making that of Charles Martel grow fainter, as he kills many a bold knight.

frustrated by the expanding use of French. For proof of this one has only to turn to the legal documents of the region, recently examined by M. Paul Aebischer (*Chrestomathie franco-provençale*, Berne, 1950). Here one discovers that, although many a local dialectal feature is recorded, there is no evidence of a consistently used vernacular standard. We quote M. Aebischer's conclusion:

> Le plus grand ennemi de la littérature—je prends ce terme dans son acception la plus vaste—franco-provençale a été le français: qu'ils soient de Forez ou de Fribourg, de Grenoble ou de Genève, nos premiers textes en sont déjà marqués. Mais elle en a eu un autre: le latin. Dans toutes les terres soumises à la juridiction de la maison de Savoie, ou à son influence, l'usage s'est maintenu très tard de rédiger les chartes en latin: et du latin on a passé directement au français.
>
> (Op. cit., p. 6)

Here, as elsewhere, it is not until the sixteenth century, with its sudden awakening of interest in dialects other than the conventional standard, that one encounters the figure of the local poet, defiantly writing in his own cherished patois in opposition to the alien language of officialdom.

## HISPANO-ROMANCE

*The ascendancy of Castile.* Compared with other modern Romance languages, both Spanish and Portuguese are remarkably homogeneous. Only in the north, from Galicia to Catalonia, do Hispano-Romance dialects show the same degree of local differentiation as is normally encountered elsewhere in countries of Romance speech. Only there, in fact, does one find the direct continuation of Vulgar Latin relatively undisturbed by historical cataclysms. The origin of this situation must be sought in the Reconquest, achieved primarily by Castile, in alliance with León, and to a lesser extent by Aragon, allied with Catalonia (cf. p. 278).

Aragon came into being as a new power when its first king, Ramiro I (d. 1063), united the small state around Jaca, a former dependency of Navarre, with the counties to the east, Sobrarbe, Ribagorza, and Pallars. In Alfonso I, 'El Batallador' (reigned A.D. 1104–34), this kingdom produced an outstanding conqueror of Moors, who extended its limits to the south at their expense. Farther east the Spanish March developed into the County of Barcelona (see p. 436). In A.D. 1137 the whole area was united under one ruling house by the marriage of Petronila, daughter of

Ramiro II of Aragon, with the Count of Barcelona, Ramón Berenguer IV. The Kingdom of Aragon and Catalonia was thereafter to become famous in history, but its interests turned to the sea, and it was left to Castile, from its dominant central position, to take the lead in furthering the recovery of the southern territories.

The great victory of the eleventh century was the recapture of Toledo, in A.D. 1085, by an army of Castilians and Leonese, under the command of Alfonso VI of Castile. The Christians were then held in check for a while by the arrival of successive Moorish reinforcements from Africa. The Almoravids, a tribe of Berbers who had founded a Muslim state in Morocco, called in after the fall of Toledo, defeated the Castilians in battle but could not retake the town. Subsequently another tribe, the Almohades, Berbers settled in the Atlas region, having attacked and overcome those of the Almoravids who had remained in Africa, proceeded in A.D. 1146 to carry out an invasion of Spain on their own account. They rapidly overran Andalusia and stemmed the Christian advance for two generations more. Eventually they were overwhelmed by a confederated Christian army, under Alfonso IX of Castile, at the battle of Las Navas de Tolosa (A.D. 1212). This battle was decisive. Under Ferdinand III, the Castilians were at last able to reoccupy the great cities of the south, Córdoba (A.D. 1236) and Seville (A.D. 1248), where Arabic invasion had begun more than five centuries earlier. Within forty years of Las Navas de Tolosa all that was left to the Moors in Spain was the Kingdom of Granada. There they remained, developing a learned and artistic society, the last florescence of Arabic culture in Europe, until their final expulsion in A.D. 1492, the year in which Columbus landed in America, a year in which the Inquisition reached its height,[1] in a fateful decade of Spanish history.

*Mozarabic.* Until very recently the Castilian *Poema del Cid*, of the mid-twelfth century, was considered to be the first literary text in a Spanish idiom. While it still remains the first work of any ample scope, its absolute priority as a text has been compromised

---

[1] The Inquisition itself had an important linguistic consequence in that its victims, the Spanish Jews, were driven to find new homes in North Africa, the Balkans, and the Near East. Until the recent war their communities were particularly strong in the Balkans, and their language, Judeo-Spanish, preserves features of the Spanish in use in the Iberian Peninsula at the time of their expulsion. See C. M. Crews, *Recherches sur le judéo-espagnol dans les pays balkaniques*, Paris, 1935. A Judeo-Spanish newspaper is now published in Israel.

400 THE CREATION OF ROMANCE STANDARDS

by the discovery of brief Spanish verses composed in Mozarabic Spain, many of which are certainly of earlier date. Preserved in Arabic and Hebrew characters, their Spanish replete with Arabic words, they present the usual problem of transliteration (see p. 280, note) and as yet have been only partially deciphered; nevertheless, they suffice to show that from the eleventh century to the thirteenth there existed in this region a lyrical poetry in Romance vernacular. It is thus conclusively proved that Mozarabic Spanish, for which the previous evidence came only from isolated words in Arabic and Hebrew texts (particularly from the work of botanists who quoted local plant- and flower-names), was in current use in Muslim Spain and was submerged only by the southerly flow of Castilian. The discovery has also given rise to renewed speculation concerning the possible influence of Arabic poetry in the development of the Provençal lyric, but the point of contact, if any, remains concealed.

The Mozarabic verses, usually four lines in all, occur each as a tailpiece, rather like the French 'envoi'. They are known as _ḫarǧa_'s, and the type of poem to which they were usually attached was called in Arabic a _muwaššaḥ_.[1] This was a genre much practised in the Arab world; it forms the subject of a treatise written towards the end of the twelfth century by an Egyptian author, Ibn Sanā' al-Mulk, in which we are told: 'The _ḫarǧa_ is the last strophe of the _muwaššaḥ_. One of its rules . . . is that it should be composed with the help of vulgar idioms and words from the popular speech. If it is written in classical language, in the same way as the other strophes, the _muwaššaḥ_ is no longer a _muwaššaḥ_ in the true sense of the word.' He then goes on to say that the _ḫarǧa_ may be written in '_aǧamī_—the word meaning 'foreign speech' by which the Muslims of Spain designated Romance—and insists that it should have a lively and piquant flavour. In Spain there was a second Arabic genre with _ḫarǧa_ attached, known as the _zajal_, which differed slightly in structure from the _muwaššaḥ_ and was composed in the variety of Arabic dialect in use in the Peninsula, whereas the _muwaššaḥ_ was traditionally written in

---

[1] For what follows we are principally indebted to S. M. Stern, _Les chansons mozarabes_, xxviii+63 pp., Palermo, 1953. See also F. Cantera, _Versos españoles en las muwaššaḥas hispano-hebreas_, Sefarad, vol. ix (1949), pp. 197–234; and Dámaso Alonso, _Cancioncillas 'de amigo' mozárabes_, Revista de filología española, vol. xxxiii (1949), pp. 247–394. The transcriptions have been taken over from Stern without modification.

classical Arabic. The fact that the same *ḫarǧa* is to be found with different *muwaššaḥ*'s, whether they be Arabic or Hebrew, suggests that the *ḫarǧa* was often borrowed from a song which had previously been a separate entity in Romance.

Collections of Hebrew poems containing Romance *ḫarǧa*'s are in fact no new discovery: they have been published by Hebrew scholars from A.D. 1851 onwards. Many are by named poets, as, for instance, the *Dīwān* of Abraham ibn Ezra (ed. J. Egers, Berlin, 1868), Browning's Rabbi ben Ezra, who died in A.D. 1167. On account of difficulties of interpretation, however, they remained unscrutinized until S. M. Stern, then writing a thesis on the *muwaššaḥ*, brought them to the attention of Romance scholars in an article entitled: 'Les vers finaux en espagnol dans les muwaššaḥs hispano-hébraïques. Une contribution à l'histoire du muwaššaḥ et à l'étude du vieux dialecte espagnol "mozarabe" ' (*Al-Andalus*, 1948, pp. 299–346). This was the signal for a general awakening of interest, particularly among Spanish scholars. While his article was still in the press, Stern discovered for the first time a *ḫarǧa* in an Arabic poem. More Arabic poems with *ḫarǧa*'s quickly came to light, in particular an anthology acquired in Morocco and compiled by a certain Ibn Bushra towards the close of the fourteenth century; these latter were published by E. García Gómez under the title: 'Veinticuatro kharjas romances en muwaššaḥs árabes' (*Al-Andalus*, 1952, pp. 57–127). More are still being discovered in manuscripts belonging to the libraries of Tunisia and Morocco.

It is now apparent that the *muwaššaḥ* with a Romance *ḫarǧa* is an Arabic creation, which found early imitators among the Hebrew poets of Spain. According to tradition, the genre was invented by a poet who lived at Cabra, near Córdoba, at the beginning of the tenth century. Unfortunately, no tenth-century *muwaššaḥ* is still extant, but those which have survived from early in the eleventh century are quite numerous, both in Arabic and in Hebrew. Thus far, those written in Hebrew have been the more successfully deciphered.

The *ḫarǧa*, always intended to be spoken by a woman, was introduced by the last strophe of the Arabic or Hebrew poem. In the examples given below a translation of the linking strophe precedes the text of the *ḫarǧa*:

1. Yehuda Halewi (d. *c.* A.D. 1140), *Dīwān*, i. 157–8 (Stern, No. 3).
   Poem written in honour of Yosef ibn Ferrusiel, known as Cidello.

Torrents of aromatic oil have flooded the Valley of Stones (Wādi 'l-Ḥijāra, i.e. *Guadalajara*) with the news of the lord who gives his good care to God's people. 'Long live the prince!' they say, 'Amen!', and rejoicing they cry:

dš knd mw sdylh bnyd          tn bwnh 'lbš'rh
km r'yh dšwl 'šyd             'n w' d 'lḥj' rh

Des cand meu Cidello venid    tan bona 'l-bišāra
Com rayo de sol esid          en Wādi 'l-Ḥijāra

Since my Cidello comes, so good is the news; he rises like a ray of sunshine at Guadalajara.

## 2. Yehuda Halewi, *Dīwān*, i. 163–4 (Stern, No. 4). Poem written in honour of Ishaq ibn Qrispin.

The graceful gazelle, this young girl who told her story, would give her life for thee; when her cherub rose and flew away from her, she could not withhold her tears. She cried out in a stricken voice and confessed her love before her companions:

gryd bš 'y yrmnl'š            km kntnyr 'mw m'ly
šn 'lḥbyb nn bbr' yw          'dbl'ry dmnd'ry

Garid vos ay yermanellas      com contenir a meu male
Sin al-ḥabib non vivireyu     advolaray demandare

Tell me, little sisters, how to contain my grief. Without my lover I shall not live; I shall fly away to seek him.

## 3. Ibn Bushra anthology, p. 161 (García Gómez, No. XVIII; Stern, No. 7). Anonymous.

For long since she has been seized by folly and caught in the snares of love; because of the solitude in which I left her she sang and wept:

km s flywl 'lynw              nwn mš 'drmš 'mw šynw

Com si filyol alyenu          non mas adormis a meu senu

As though (you were) an alien son, you sleep no longer on my breast.

## 4. Todros Abulafia (d. *c.* A.D. 1285; Stern, No. 16). To Don Isaac ibn Sadoq, counsellor of King Alfonso the Wise.

When he comes, the town is clothed in his glory; for so long as he stays, it feels transported to heaven with pride. That is why it exclaims on the day of his departure:

ky fr'yw 'w ky šyr'd dmyby    ḥbyby nwn tytwlgš dmyby

Que farayo o que serad de mibi    ḥabībī non te tolgas de mibi

What shall I do, or what will become of me? My love, do not leave me.

5. Muḥammad ibn 'Ubāda, Ibn Bushra anthology, p. 17 (García Gómez, No. I, Stern, No. 22).

The young girl did not cease lamenting to one who is unjust. Oh wind! Who can become attached to someone who will not help? When she saw him free, while she was caught by love, she sang and had no hope but to turn towards him:

| my sydy 'br'hym | y' tw' mn dlj | b'nt myb | dy nḫt |
| 'n nwn šnwn k'rš | yrym tyb | ġrmy 'wb | lġrt |

| Meu sīdī Ibrāhīm | yā tu omne dolje | vent' a mib | de noḫte |
| In(?)non si non queris | yireym'a tib | gar me a ob | legarte |

My lord Ibrahim, oh, man so dear, come to me in the night. If (?) not, if you do not wish, I shall go to you; tell me where I shall find you.

These few poems will suffice to indicate the nature of the new discovery. While adding considerably to the known stock of Mozarabic vocabulary, the ḫarğa's serve to confirm such conclusions as had already been reached concerning the evolution of Latin in Mozarabic Spain (see Menéndez Pidal, *Orígenes del español*, 3rd ed., pp. 415–40). With regard to phonology, consonantal development provides the more reliable evidence since the vowels have to be supplied by the transcriber: thus No. 1 above is quoted by Menéndez Pidal with a verb-form *viened* (op. cit., p. 430), in place of Stern's transcription *venid*, but with *exed*, where the stressed vowel is apparently undiphthongized, corresponding to Stern's *esid*. It is difficult, in these circumstances, to make any pronouncement concerning diphthongization in Mozarabic. On the other hand, the Semitic script clearly reveals that the final consonants of the Latin present indicatives vĕnit and ĕxit were still pronounced, though with the relaxed tension of the voiced form. Of particular interest is the evidence of palatalization, as shown in such forms as *dolje* (< dulcem), *noḫte* (< nŏctem), and *yermanellas* (< *germanĕllas, cf. Cast. *hermana*). The spelling of *noḫte* implies an intermediate stage in the evolution of the group -ct- to -it- which took place over the greater part of the Peninsula, cf. Port. *noite*, Cat. *nit*, Arag. *nueyt* (*Fueros de Aragón*, ed. G. Tilander, *passim*): an inference substantiated by the plant-name *lahtaira* 'yellow goose-grass' (< lactaria, Cast. *cuajaleche*), as found in a botanical text; the passage of -ct- to -ch-, as in the current Span. *noche*, is thus one of the peculiarities of the originally eccentric Castilian dialect. Another Castilian eccentricity is the passage of F to *h* (see p. 423), for Mozarabic consistently shows the preservation of Latin F, e.g. *fareyo, filyolo* (< FILIOLUM, cf. Cast. *hijuelo*), as do Portuguese, Catalan, and Aragonese, and indeed all the other dialects of Spain. Prominent among morphological features is the form *mibi*, a MIHI adapted to the series of TIBI and SIBI; this, however, is not specifically Mozarabic: it also occurs in the medieval Latin documents of northern Spain (cf. p. 79). The future forms in -*ayu* (or -*eyu*, the different transcriptions being given solely on account of rhyme), e.g. *vivireyu, farayo, advolaray*, show an early stage in the usual development of this tense. Among lexical features the most remarkable is a much-used verb *garir*, e.g. *gar, garid*, &c.; common enough in Latin as GARRĪRE, whence the adj. GARRULUS, and still used as *garrire* in Italian, this word is not otherwise known in Hispano-Romance, though it is still to be found in the tenth-century Latin documents of San Millán (see below), e.g. 'Sunt enim plurime, et precipue mulieres, qui in ecclesia garriunt.' But here the meaning is rather different: only in Baetica does GARRIRE represent the choice made from the many possible ways inherent in Latin of conveying the sense 'to say, tell, affirm'. Of the Arabic words incorporated into the *ḫarǧa*'s, *'l-bišāra* (No. 1) appears again as *albricias* in the *Poema del Cid* (see p. 290).

The new documentation thus affords a glimpse both of the process whereby Arabic words were adopted through Mozarabic into Spanish, and also of the kind of Hispano-Romance which might have become the national language, had there been no Muslim occupation and no Castilian-led Reconquest.

*The earliest Romance in northern Spain.* As we have now inferred, the long line of Christian strongholds from which the Reconquest began formed nurseries for all the modern varieties of Hispano-Romance. Ultimate concentration of political strength in a central area, just as in northern France, gradually brought about the creation of Spanish; but, again as in northern France— the parallel is remarkably close—the earliest traces of Romance in written documents are slightly anterior to the ascendancy of the power which was to predominate, and they show characteristics somewhat at variance with those of Castilian. For the origin of these documents we must look to the monasteries, in this instance during the tenth century.

Two monasteries are particularly prominent: that of San Millán,

situated in the west of the modern province of Logroño, in territory then under the growing influence of the Kingdom of Navarre,
which reached its apogee under Sancho el Mayor (A.D. 1000–35);
and that of Silos, lying farther west, in Castile. Each of these has
left Latin documents with Romance glosses, known respectively
as the *Glosas Emilianenses* and the *Glosas Silenses*: the *Glosas
Emilianenses* contain in addition two glosses in Basque, an indication of the very close proximity of San Millán to Basque-speaking
country.

The Latin documents of San Millán are the earlier: their Visigothic script can be dated as early tenth-century. They consist of
a miscellaneous collection of religious works: *ejemplos*, which are
stories of asceticism borrowed in part from the *Vita Patrum* (see
p. 304); litanies, mass, and prayers; a *Liber Sententiarum*; and
sermons attributed to St. Augustine. The glosses, which are both
marginal and interlinear, appear to have been written in towards
the middle of the same century. They include one passage of
continuous prose, the first in Spanish; with the Latin which it
glosses it runs as follows:

Latin:
    . . . adjubante domino nostro Jhesu Christo cui est honor et imperium
cum patre et Spiritu Sancto in secula seculorum.

Gloss:
    cono ajutorio de nuestro dueno, dueno Christo, dueno Salbatore,
qual dueno get ena honore, e qual duenno tienet ela mandatione cono
Patre, cono Spiritu Sancto, enos sieculos delos sieculos. Facanos Deus
omnipotes tal serbitio fere ke denante ela sua face gaudioso segamus.
Amem.

Translation:
    With the help of our Lord, Lord Christ, Lord Saviour, which Lord
is in Heaven (lit. 'in the honour'; the word had probably acquired its
feudal sense of 'estate') and which Lord holds the power with the Father,
with the Holy Ghost, in the ages of the ages (i.e. 'world without end').
May Almighty God make us do such service that we may be joyful
(i.e. 'blessed') before His face. Amen.

Most striking in this passage is the popular use of the definite
article: where it stands alone ILLA has become *ela* (*ela mandatione,
ela sua face*), and the masculine form with the *l* retained occurs in
*delo*(*s*), but where it follows the prepositions *con* and *en* (*cono, ena,
enos*), the *l* has been elided giving forms masc. *o, os,* and fem. *a;*

these articles are still in current use in the local patois of western Aragon and Navarre, and also at the western end of the Cantabrians, where they have given rise to the standard forms of modern Portuguese. Diphthongization of the half-open vowels has taken place generally, as in *tienet* (< TĔNET), *sieculos* (< SAECULOS), *dueno* (< DŎMINUM), and even before an original consonant group, as in *nuestro* (< NŎSTRUM, see p. 86). This is a feature common to Castilian and Navarro-Aragonese; the diphthongs widened in the latter to *ia* and *ua*, e.g. *uamne* (< HŎMINEM), in the glosses quoted below: in the valleys of Aragon it is still possible to hear *tiambo* (< TEMPUS) and *guano* (< BONUM), and in local toponymy the suffix *-ués* alternates with *-uás* (see p. 176). The diphthongization of the vowel of EST, represented by the spelling *get* (cf. below *dulce jet*), pertains, however, more specifically to the Navarro-Aragonese area, for EST became *es* in Castilian. The infinitive FACĔRE has been reduced through *\*faire* to *fere*, as in French: again the modern patois preserve *fer*, contrasting with Cast. *hacer*. Among consonants, intervocalic voiceless plosives are preserved (*salbatore, patre, faca, sieculos*), as they still are in certain localities (see p. 50). Thus, in this earliest specimen of northern Hispano-Romance the stamp of the region of Navarre is quite unmistakable.

More general features worthy of note include: absence of declension, all nouns and adjectives deriving from the Latin accusative, singular and plural; the use of *segamus* (as in *get*, *g* is for **j**), which, coming from SEDEAMUS, shows how parts of the verb *\*ĔSSERE* were replaced by the more resistant verb SĔDĔRE; the maintenance of the Classical FACIEM in *face* (cf. Cast. *haz*), whereas both Fr. *face* and Ital. *faccia* derive from a V. Lat. FACIA, adapted to the Latin first declension (see p. 61); on the other hand, a popular *faca* (cf. Cast. *haga*), which presupposes a V. Lat. subj. *\*FACAT*, instead of the FACIAT which became Fr. *fasse* and Ital. *faccia*.

Of the many single glosses which further reveal the type of Romance which was here evolving, with its special vocabulary and characteristic morphology, we quote the following selection:

repente: lueco (Cast. *luego*)
suscitabi: lebantai, lebantaui
et tertius ueniens: elo terzero diabolo uenot
uix: ueiza
indica: amuestra

diuisiones: partitiones
beneficia: elos serbicios
caracterem: seingnale (Cast. *señal*)
inueniebit: aflaret (from AFFLARE 'to breathe upon', 'to scent', whence
    Cast. *hallar*)
incolomes: sanos et salbos
solliciti simus: ansiosu segamus
nos . . . precipitemur in geenna: guec ajutuezdugu (Basque), nos non
    kaigamus
diuersis: muitas
adtentius: buena mientre
occupare: parare vel aplecare
adtendat unusquisque: katet quiscataqui (see p. 98)
non se circumueniat qui talis est: non se cuempetet elo uamne en siui
    (cuempetet < COMPUTET)
insinuo: jo castigo
candidis: albis
inermis: sine arma
galea: bruina
sentiat: sepat
exteriores: de fueras
et tu ibis: e tu iras
multitudo tormentorum: penas
asperius: plus aspero mas
terribilem: paboroso vel temeroso
donec: ata quando (Cast. *hasta cuando*)
gesit: fezot
galea: gelemo (Cast. *yelmo*, see p. 246)
sustinuit: sufriot
suabe est: dulce jet
ubi: obe
repleuimur: nos emplirnos amus
unicuique: quiscataqui huamne
audite: kate uos (cf. above, katet quiscataqui; the verb is *catar*, as used
    in the *Poema del Cid*, from CAPTARE, see p. 116)
siquis: qualbis uemne
flos: flore
feni: jerba
crimine: peccato
tu ipse es: tu eleisco jes (eleisco < ILLE *ICSU for ILLE IPSU)
manes: tu siedes
quid agas: ke faras

The manuscript containing the *Glosas Silenses*, now in the
library of the British Museum, dates from the second half of
the tenth century, and is thus slightly later than that of the
*Glosas Emilianenses*. In this instance both the Latin text and the

glosses appear to be in the same handwriting, a fact which suggests that the scribe was copying a text in which the glosses were already present. The matter of the text is again religious; it includes in particular a lengthy *Penitencial*: a catalogue of misdeeds similar in form to that of the *Lex Salica* and the later Spanish *Fueros*, but in which, instead of the fine to be paid, we are given the penance to be observed. The examples which follow will show that these glosses, while adding to our repertory of tenth-century Hispano-Romance, are very similar in character to the *Glosas Emilianenses*:

relinquens: elaiscaret
deuenerit: aflaret
(sacrificium) sordidatum: nafregatu
comburatur: kematu siegat
abluantur: labatu siegat
ignorans: qui non sapiendo
caste: munda mientre
catholicus: christianus
si ignorans: si non sapet
iudicio damnetur: desonoratu siegat judicatu
strages: occisiones, matatas
ceteris: con os altros
negat: non quisieret dare
sine . . . uel testibus: o sen tiestes, testimonio
sortilegos: qui dat sortes
auguria: agueros
non liceat: non conbienet
ad tendere: scuitare (< AUSCULTARE, cf. Cast. *escuchar*)
omnia exercere: manda pro fere totas cosas
respuit: laiscare saket
accedant: aplekan (< ADPLICANT, cf. Cast. *llegar*)
per semed ipsum: per sibi eleiso (cf. above *Glos. Emil.*, eleisco)
sterelis: infecunda, sine fruitu
prius: anzes
semel: una uece
fuerit lapsus: kadutu fuere
exercuerit: facet, andat
usque in finem: ata que mueran
hii: estos
femora: campas (cf. Old Cast. *cama* 'leg')
uti: ke aiat usuale lege
consobrina: cusina (this appears, like Ital. *cugina*, to be a borrowing from Old French; cf. Prov. and Cat. *cosí*, but Cast. *sobrino* 'nephew')
abunculi: tio
matertere: tia

fraternitatis consortio: ad una kaza jermano gasaillato (cf. Cast. *agasajar*,
   see p. 222)
(filios) alat: pasceret, gobernaret
(baselicam) fundaberit: firmaret, ficieret
nec audeat: non siegat osatu
ad nuptias: a las uotas (cf. Cast. *bodas*)
euntes: qui ban ido
ballare: cantare
saltare: sotare
in saltatione: ena sota
monstruose (fingunt): qui tingen lures faces (i.e. 'who stain their faces';
   lur < ILLORUM, is Navarro-Aragonese)
fingunt: simulant
nasceretur: naisceset
emersise: ke cadiot
quamuis: macare ke siegat (cf. Old Cast. *maguer*, Ital. *magari*)
secum retinere uoluerit: consico kisieret tenere
abscissus est: monaco taillatu abieret a so menbra
proibeatur: betatu lo ajat tolitu
proibuit: betait
relabuntur: tornare
eos: akelos
accipiter: acetore (cf. Cast. *azor*)
post circulum anni: por lo anno pleno
femus: stiercore (cf. Cast. *estiércol*)
satiabiliter: por fartare (cf. Cast. *hartar*)
inedie: de la famne (cf. Cast. *hambre*)

A study of these examples will show that the *Glosas Silenses*, although they come from a Castilian monastery, contain the same Navarro-Aragonese features as the *Glosas Emilianenses*. Indeed, there is obviously a very close connexion between the two sets of manuscripts. The same Latin word in the one set is frequently glossed by the same Romance word in the other, in many instances not a particularly appropriate choice; thus in both PRIUS is glossed by *anzes*, EXERCERE by *facere*, ADULTERIUM by *fornicatione, fornicio*, PUDOR by *uerecundia, uergoigna*, &c. The link is confirmed by at least one curious mistake: UOTA is glossed by *promissione* in the Silos text, while the glosser of San Millán, wrongly reading DEUOTOS as DE UOTOS, wrote into the margin *promissiones*. One is therefore tempted to wonder whether the original glossers had in each case access to a lost glossary, locally compiled. As we know from the evidence of the Reichenau Glossary, the practice of using such lexical compilations had already begun in Gaul in the eighth century, and two centuries later they were probably in general circulation in all the monastic schools of the west. Most of these glossaries, like that of Reichenau, with its scrupulous observance of the grammatical forms of the original text, were Latin–Latin; but whoever first recorded the glosses of San Millán and Silos was making a deliberate attempt to write in Romance, explaining the Latin, on a stylistic level so different as to preclude accuracy, by words and phrases from popular parlance. Thanks to an unknown monk, the morphological and phonological features of Romance as it developed in the Rioja region are attested from the tenth century; setting aside such of those features as are not shared with Castilian, we may look upon the glosses as a first glimpse of the language that became the national idiom of Spain.[1]

Nearly 200 years separate these documents from the *Poema del Cid*; and not until the end of the twelfth century did the deliberate writing of prose vernacular become an accepted notarial practice: in this respect Castilian was a century later than Provençal. The interval seems to have been partly due to a revival of Latinism in the monasteries, as the ripples of the Carolingian Renaissance spread (see below, p. 426). But the area of Latin culture was limited, and the pressure of the vernacular so strong that the language of local notarial documents, which have survived in plenty from this time, became a kind of mixture of Latin and Romance: or more precisely, a Romance thinly disguised by the effort of the clerk to maintain an appearance of Latin. One may observe, for example, in the following short extract from a late-eleventh-century text of Aragonese origin: the characteristic diphthongization, as in *nietu* (Cast. *nieto* < NĔPTU), and *spuenna* (< SPŎNDA, which designates in Spanish toponymy a marginal piece of land); the general use of accusative forms; *illo* and *illa* consistently employed as definite articles; the Romance perfect ending *-od*, later *-o* (< -AVIT), as in *matod*; the development of QUĬD to *ket*, whence Span. *que*; the metathesis of *padule* (< PALU-DEM), whence Arag. and Old Cast. *paúl*, still very common in toponymy; and *illores*, obviously the *lures* of the *Glosas Silenses* in a latinized (!) version:

Hec est karta de illa binea de illa padule ket dedit donna Blasquita

---

[1] In common with all writers on early Spanish we are much indebted to Menéndez Pidal's *Orígenes del español* (3rd ed., Madrid, 1950). The text of the manuscripts of San Millán and Silos is there given in full. The morphological and phonological aspects of the glosses are exhaustively studied; their vocabulary still leaves some scope for further investigation.

et Garcia Azenarez cum suos germanos ad senior Sancio Galindiz et ad illa donna Urracka in Salamagna per .C. solidos per illo kaballo de seniore ket matod Garcia Azenarez. Et sunt fermes . . . senior Garcia Sanci suo nietu. . . .

Hec est karta de conpara ket conparabit senior Sancio Galindiz et illa duenna donna Urracka: in Uno Kastiellu illo malguelo in Aba denante Sancti Mames; tutu illo precio pryso abent illores donnos. . . .
. . . bindimus ad bobis .II. terras . . . et illa binea de illa spuenna de Nuaçola, et alia binea de Munocio Asnari.

(Menéndez Pidal, *Orígenes del español*, pp. 41–42)

Almost in Aragonese dialect is another text of *c*. A.D. 1090, particularly noteworthy for its testimony to the evolution of the definite article to *ero*, *era*, forms still preserved as *ro*, *ra* in a few remote villages of Sobrarbe, the central part of northern Aragon, a region with which the document is identified by the place-names which it contains (e.g. *Bregoto*, the mod. *Broto*). As the following extracts show, it consists of a series of bequests:

De illa particigon que feci senigor Sango Garcece. Ad Galino Acenarece era lorika, ero kabalo, era espata. Ad Sango Scemenones ero kabalo, era mulla, era espata, ero ellemo. Ad Scemeno Fertungones, si tene illa onore, tiega ero kabalo per mano de Cosnelga; e si lesca era onore, ero kabalo segat suo engenobo; e .II. elmos. . . . A Scemeno Garcece ero pullero bago. . . . Ad Eneco ero pullero kastango. . . . A Rrapun e Sango pascanlos e bestanlos, tanto usque pan poscan deredemere. Ad illos mancepos de sua masonata a kien .IIII. mesuras, ad kien .U. mesuras; ad Sango d Arbaniese mes de illos alios; aro mancipo de Bregoto faca lo suo per jodicio, sega tuto ero de Monteson suo. Eros meskinos d Erbise demannelos senigor Fertungo Acenarece; eras bertutes kede aduscomos da Roma, e son en Alkecar, demanelgales senigor Fertungo Acenarece; quano erit fraucato Sancte Nicolagi, tornelas ad Albaruala.[1]

(Op. cit., p. 43)

---

[1] *Translation*: Concerning the division (of property) made by Sr. Sancho García: To Galino Acenarez the cuirass, the horse, the sword. To Sancho Jiménez the horse, the mule, the sword, the helmet. To Jimeno Fertuñez, if he retains the estate, let him keep the horse by the hand (i.e. intermediary) of Cosnella; and if he leaves the estate, let the horse be his freely; and two helmets . . . . To Jimeno García the bay foal. . . . To Iñigo, the chestnut foal. . . . As for Rapún and Sancho, let them be fed and clothed until they can pay for their bread. To the servants of his household, to some four measures, to some five measures; to Sancho of Arbaniés more than to the others; to the servant from Broto, let his be done (i.e. transacted) legally, let all the (property) of Monzón[a] be his. Let Sr. Fertuño Acenarez look after (lit. ask for) the children of Arbisa; the relics which we brought from Rome, and which are at Alquézar, let Sr. Fertuño Acenarez look after them; when (the Church of) St. Nicholas[b] shall be built, let him send them to Albaruela.

[a] Monzón was reconquered in A.D. 1088.

[b] The Church of St. Nicholas of Bari still stands at Albaruela, north-west of Parbastro.

Spanish scribes, like their French counterparts, were confronted with a problem of sound and spelling, and the outlandish appearance of many words in this document is the result of rather clumsy attempts to represent the new non-Latin phonemes. For the palatal [j] one finds both *g*, as in the glosses, and *ig* (e.g. *particigon = partición*, *senigor = señor*, *bago = bayo*, &c.); the palatalized sounds [ɲ] and [ʎ] are recorded by *ng* and *lg* respectively (e.g. *kastango = castaño*, *Fertungo = Fertuño*, *Cosnelga = Cosnella*, *demanelgales = demandellelas*, mod. *demándeselas*). The spelling *sc* corresponds to the alveolar fricative [ʃ], which later became the *jota* in Castilian (e.g. *Scemeno* = Cast. *Jimeno*; *lesca*, with a change of the initial consonant apparently due to the prefix *de*, became Cast. *deja*; *aduscomos*, a perfect typical of Aragonese— in which the flexion of the third person singular, *ó* <-AVIT, influenced the flexions of all the other persons—corresponds to the mod. Span. *adujimos*. The curious *engenobo* (< INGENUUM) illustrates another Aragonese characteristic, viz. the tendency to fill any vocalic hiatus with a consonant, cf. the name of the hamlet of *Bubal*, which in medieval documents is always *Bual*.

To discourse further upon the popular features of this text is perhaps unnecessary: the reader will have observed how thin is the camouflage of Latin. It seems quite clear that, by the end of the eleventh century, the general practice was to read out such a document in Romance, for the benefit of the illiterate who formed the mass of the population; the notary, in the circumstance usually the parish priest, then placed it on record according to his lights.

In the official chanceries, where the *Fueros* were elaborated, the standard of erudition was higher, and the Latin more consciously 'correct', in the medieval tradition. Thus, when in the following century the *Fueros* began to be rendered into Romance, it was as a deliberate act of translation, which involved the setting of new standards: therein lies the creation of Spanish prose. Many of these remarkable documents, long neglected by linguists, have now been published.[1] In so far as it is possible to date them, the earliest appears to be *Los Fueros de la Novenera*, which contains

---

[1] Most noteworthy is the Swedish series of *Leges Hispanicae Medii Aevi*, directed by Prof. Gunnar Tilander. To date it comprises: *El Fuero de Teruel*, ed. Max Gorosch, 1950; *Los Fueros de la Novenera*, ed. Gunnar Tilander, 1951; *Vidal Mayor: Traducción aragonesa de la obra 'In Excelsis Dei Thesauris' de Vidal de Canellas*, ed. Gunnar Tilander, 1956. Before the series as such was inaugurated Tilander had also published the *Fueros de Aragón*, 1937.

numerous references to King Sancho 'el bueno', later known as Sancho el Sabio, King of Navarre (A.D. 1150–94). The *Novenera*, a name no longer in use, was a district to the south of Pamplona; as one would expect from this localization, dialectal features in the text again point to Navarro-Aragonese. With the indication that *nuyll* is used positively, meaning 'any', we give as a sample the following items:

69. De diluuio d'agoa que faze daynno.

Por diluuio de agoa que uienga et faga daynno un uezino a otro, uayan lo veer bonos hombres el logar et saquen carrera por dont uaya el agoa que menos enoio li faga.

70. De casamiento.

Todo hombre o toda muyller que prenga bendictión, si's quisiere fillos de hermanos sean, del día que prengan bendición, si quiere sea iurada con otro, de quoanto que ganen su meatat deue auer de mueble et de heredat.

76. De pastor, cómo deue catar oueillas.

Nuyll ombre qui oueillas cate de seynnor et sea pastor, ha se de leuantar de nueytes tres uezes et ha de leuantar las oueillas tres uezes, et con su iura ha de seer creydo; et si non lo faze, ha a peytar la oueilla.

77. De qui dize a otro que li pude la boca.

Nuill hombre que dize uno a otro 'la boca te pude', ha a iurar en Sant Esteuan et deue pagar LX sueldos de calonia; et si non lo podiere prouar, ha a iurar en las Ribas esta uerdat, es assaber en dos hombres o en dos bonas muilleres. (Las Ribas, elsewhere in the text Las Arribas, is the name of the place where oaths were taken.)

This particular penal code is marked by a clemency which presumably reflects the goodness of King Sancho. Most of the other *Fueros*, with much harsher penalties, date in Romance translation from the thirteenth century.

*The Castilian standard.* By the end of the twelfth century French was already the medium of a mass of literature including hagiographical poetry, epic, and courtly romance; in Provence most of the best-known lyrics had already been written; Spain until that time is represented by a solitary surviving work: the epic *Poema del Cid*, of which the composition is tentatively placed at *c.* A.D. 1140. Written in what is obviously popular Castilian, though with sporadic traces of Navarro-Aragonese, the poem is a landmark in the history of Spanish.

By A.D. 1140 Castilian hegemony extended over a large part of north-central Spain. It was in the newly-conquered territory, according to the opinion of Menéndez Pidal, that the epic was composed: at Medinaceli, in the extreme south of the present province of Soria. But this is only a hypothesis: it is true that the author reveals a close familiarity with the topography of that region; on the other hand, all the fundamental associations of the story are with the old Castilian capital of Burgos, whence the Cid was banished, and with the village of Vivar—he was Don Rodrigo de Biuar (in the spelling of the text)—some six miles north of Burgos, from whose Franciscan monastery comes the single manuscript in which the poem is preserved. During the Cid's lifetime, this was on the frontier between the kingdoms of Castile and Navarre.[1]

The manuscript, now in the possession of the Pidal family, was first published as early as A.D. 1779.[2] It is in a somewhat dilapidated state and the first sheet has been lost; what remains comprises 3,735 lines of verse. Like the Oxford *Chanson de Roland*, it bears a signature: near the end one may read: 'Per abbat le escriuio en el mes de mayo, En era de mill. e. CC.XL.V. anos.' Since the handwriting seems quite clearly to be that of the fourteenth century, the date here given sets a problem: 1245 of that time corresponds to 1207 in our calendar; it is generally assumed that a C has been accidentally omitted and that the real date is A.D. 1307. This places the manuscript more than a century and a half later than the date of the original composition, as conjectured from internal evidence, and its many corrupt forms may have been due to the hands of scribes who had copied it before it reached those of Per Abbat. But should we be justified in attributing to scribal carelessness the fact that its lines will not scan? As the following sample shows, they vary in length:

> En su conpaña .Lx. pendones leuaua; exien lo
>   uer mugieres e uarones.
> Burgeses e burgesas por las finiestras son,
> Plorando delos oios, tanto auyen el dolor.
> Delas sus bocas todas dizian una Razon:
> 'Dios, que buen vassalo, si ouiesse buen Senor!'
>
> (Ed. Menéndez Pidal, ll. 16–20)

[1] See Menéndez Pidal, *La España del Cid*, vol. i, pp. 165 ff.
[2] By T. Sánchez, in his *Colección de poesías castellanas anteriores al siglo XV*, vol. i, Madrid, 1779. The standard edition is now: Menéndez Pidal, *Cantar de mio Cid. Texto, gramática y vocabulario*, 3 vols., Madrid, 1908–11.

Some scholars believe that originally they were Alexandrines, others that they represent a ballad metre with alternating lines of seven and eight syllables; while a different school of thought would exonerate the scribes, maintaining that such irregularity was a characteristic feature of the earliest forms of epic poetry.[1] Whatever their length, it is clear that the lines were intended to assonance, as in Old French.

One need not seek far into the past for the sources of the story, for its hero is a well-known historical personage who died only in A.D. 1099, a contemporary, that is, of William the Conqueror. In real life he was a turbulent figure, fighting sometimes against the Moors and sometimes against Christians; his chief exploit was the capture from the Moors of Valencia, in A.D. 1092. In legend he has become the noble outlaw, the kind of person of whom people say 'What a good vassal, if only he had a good lord!', and thereby presents a close affinity with the heroes of certain French epics, with characters like Girard de Roussillon. The tone of the poem, its humour and familiarity, also recalls French treatment, as, for example, in the *Charroi de Nîmes*; but never does it attain the lofty idealism of the Christian knights of the *Chanson de Roland*, in their fight against the infidel.

That the output of this kind of poetry in medieval Spain was not confined to a single composition is quite certain. Later prose chronicles contain much 'epic material', retailing again the story of the *Cid*, and other stories which the authors must have drawn from similar poems: lines of verse from the original works can often be detected embedded in the prose. Some of these, as, for instance, the tenth-century tale of the *Siete Infantes de Lara*, have their roots much deeper in Spanish history than has the *Poema del Cid*. But of the primitive verse-forms there remains, in addition to the *Cid*, only a fragment of a hundred lines discovered some forty years ago in the cathedral of Pamplona: christened *Roncesvalles* by its first editor, Menéndez Pidal, it is part of a Spanish adaptation of one of the French versions of the *Chanson de Roland*. In date it is a relative late-comer: Menéndez Pidal places it in the first third of the thirteenth century, but for its most recent editor, J. Horrent,

---

[1] The metre of the *Cid* is analysed in detail in the edition of Menéndez Pidal. See also Janet H. Perry, *The Harrap Anthology of Spanish Poetry. With an Introductory Essay on the Development of Metrical Forms*, London, 1953. As Miss Perry remarks (p. 34), the much later *Roncesvalles*, though imitated from French, shows the same metrical irregularity as the *Cid*.

it belongs to the end of that century, at the earliest estimate.[1] Its language contains features which locate it as Navarro-Aragonese.

The *Poema del Cid* thus looms out of the mist as a lonely twelfth-century monument to a lost epic literature. Writing inspired by religious themes comes next in order of survival: it inaugurates Spanish drama, with a verse fragment consisting of the first 147 lines of a mystery play, the *Auto de los Reyes Magos*, discovered at Toledo. The date of this work has been much discussed and widely differing opinions on the subject expressed, but there seems to be little reason for placing it earlier than the end of the twelfth century; its language is Castilian.[2] Strictly in the religious tradition is the first-known poet of Spain, Gonzalo de Berceo (d. *c*. A.D. 1250), a priest brought up in the monastery of San Millán, whose work includes both a *Vida de San Millán* and a *Vida de Santo Domingo de Silos*, adapted into rhymed stanzas from earlier Latin 'lives'. In the work of Gonzalo we find Spanish literature evolving, as did French, from something to be recited by a *jongleur* (the *mester de joglaría*) to suitable matter for the reading circle (the *mester de clerecía*). His Castilian, if we again draw a comparison with the French of the time, seems quite remarkably modern: so much more slowly has Castilian changed between the thirteenth century and the present day. A mid-thirteenth-century *Libro de Alixandre*, introducing another theme from France (see p. 396), is attributed in a fifteenth-century manuscript to Gonzalo de Berceo, but the style differs so much from his as to make the attribution suspect. From this time onwards anonymous poems of religious inspiration are fairly numerous, some, like the *Vida de Santa Maria Egipciaqua*, being obvious adaptations from French.

The prose which had developed in legal usage during the latter part of the twelfth century came fully into its own during the thirteenth. Following upon the *Fueros*, the municipal franchises granted by the kings, the *Forum Judicum* itself (the 'Forum of the Judges', hispanicized as *Fuero Juzgo*), the basic legal code of Spain deriving from the old *Lex Visigothorum*, which compilers of local statutes used as their model, was turned into Castilian in A.D. 1241

[1] Menéndez Pidal, '*Roncesvalles*', *un nuevo cantar de gesta del siglo XIII*. Revista de filología española, iv, 1917, pp. 105 ff.; J. Horrent, *Roncesvalles. Étude sur le fragment de cantar de gesta conservé à l'Archivo de Navarra (Pampelune)*, Paris, Les Belles Lettres, 1951.
[2] Edited by Menéndez Pidal, *Revista de archivos, bibliotecas y museos*, Madrid, 1900.

by order of King Ferdinand III. This was at the time when the Kingdom of Castile and León reached its summit of power. During the no less remarkable reign of Alfonso X, 'el Sabio' (A.D. 1252–84), scholarship received royal patronage, and under his direction began the compilation, by a number of collaborators, of the encyclopaedic *Crónica general*. Castilian prose thus became the medium of history, and literary activity was centred at the court, thereafter the final arbiter of the linguistic norm.

Such is the development of a Castilian standard as it appears in the literature which has survived. It must, however, be admitted that the picture which emerges, in the earlier stages, is not very coherent: too much of the evidence has been lost. By the time of the *Poema del Cid*, the use of Castilian speech must have already extended far beyond the folds of the Cantabrians, following the rapid success of Castilian leadership in war, particularly during the period A.D. 1050–1100. To the south there was not, as in France, the Romance speech of another flourishing civilization to delay its progress. Mozarabic, unsupported by literary Latin, enjoyed no prestige, and the Mozarabic population, while contributing much to the growing fund of vocabulary, quickly adapted their Romance to the Castilian model. Such peculiarities of pronunciation as characterize Andalusian, commonly referred to as a 'dialect' though not in direct descent from Vulgar Latin, are probably the result of a local 'spontaneous' evolution of Castilian rather than a 'conditioned' persistence of Mozarabic speech-habits. Most noticeable, and particularly so to a foreigner, are the *seseo* and the *ceceo*, modifications of the sibilants which produce a slurred effect (see W. J. Entwistle, *The Spanish Language*, pp. 218–20).

In the north, as we have seen, Navarro-Aragonese seemed at first to rival Castilian, rather as Picard rivalled *francien*, but it was drawn into the central literary orbits of Castilian and Catalan at an earlier date, producing nothing which could compare with the lively output of thirteenth-century Picardy. During the initial phases of the Reconquest both Leonese and Aragonese dialect made a limited advance on the flanks of Castilian. The former survives in Miranda, the north-westerly corner of Portugal, where it is protected from Castilian infiltration, and in local varieties is still alive in the Asturias, which came early under Leonese dominion. In Aragon, the persistent dialectologist may still coax from the oldest inhabitants of the remoter villages forms which sound very much as they must have done in the mouths of the tenth-century monks of San Millán: it is their last refuge, a striking contrast to the situation on the northern side of the Pyrenean frontier, where one descends into the midst of a patois-speaking people.

*Characteristics of Castilian.* Unlike that of French and Provençal, the vocalic system of Castilian is remarkably simple. The effect of such changes as took place, completed for the most part by the time of the earliest texts, was to turn the seven vowels and one diphthong of Vulgar Latin back into the five pure vowels recognized in Classical Latin. The stressed half-open vowels diphthongized, whether free or apparently blocked, to become *ie* and *ue* (see p. 46), of which the second element, though opening in some regions to *a*, retained in standard Castilian a close quality. Latin AU fell into line by becoming *o* (e.g. AURUM > *oro*, THESAURUM > *tesoro*, &c.). The diphthong *ai* which developed from the combination of *a* with yod, becoming first *ei*, had by the eleventh century been reduced to *e* (e.g. BASIUM > *beso*, AREA > *era*, and the suffix -ARIUM > -*ero*). A diphthong *oi* of Old Castilian evolved like the same combination in Old French to *ue* (e.g. AUGŬRIUM > *agüero*; and the suffix -TŌRIUM, which became Old Cast. -*doiro*, -*duero*, but was then altered to -*dero* under the influence of -*ero* < -ARIUM: the normal evolution is still very common in Aragonese toponymy, e.g. *Labatuero* < LAVATŌRIUM, *Pasatuara*, *Picatuero*, &c.). In modern Spanish slight variations in the quality of these vowels, resulting from position in the word and the influence of neighbouring consonants, may certainly be perceived, but, as compared with those to be observed in other Romance speeches, they are scarcely such as to warrant a general classification embracing more than the five phonemes traditionally represented in Spanish orthography; only these five, with the two diphthongs, have significant value as vocalic symbols.

The post-tonic vowels *a*, *e*, and *o* have persisted throughout the history of Castilian, though there is some evidence during the medieval period of a tendency to drop final *e* (cf. *noch*, in the *Cid*). The tendency may have been propagated from the east, since Aragonese place-names reveal a frequent disappearance of post-tonic *e* and *o* (e.g. *Morcat*, *Monclús*, which in medieval documents are *Morkato* and *Monte cluso*; compare also such forms in minor toponymy as *Fuanz* < FONTES, which has given rise to a double plural *Fuances*). This development is typical of Catalan. But in

Castile a learned reaction succeeded in maintaining the post-tonics, and the effects of this reaction seem to have extended to Aragon after the union of the two dynasties under Ferdinand and Isabella (A.D. 1469).

A peculiarity of Castilian development, which in this respect shows a complete contrast with Old Provençal (see p. 374), lies in the fact that a palatal element prevented the diphthongization of the Vulgar Latin stressed half-open vowels, apparently by raising ɛ to e and ɔ to o (e.g. MATĔRIA > *madera*, SĔDEAT > *sea*, LĔCTUM > *lecho*; HŎDIE > *hoy*, PŎDIUM > *poyo*, FŎLIA > *hoja*, NŎCTEM > *noche*, &c.). There is one notable exception to this general rule: VĔTULUM, in Vulgar Latin VECLU, became *viejo*, with a diphthong probably to be accounted for by the influence of Old Cast. *viedro* < VETEREM. Where the palatal element was itself a medieval development, as was the λ coming from -LL- (see below), diphthongization had already taken place, so that in Old Castilian one finds *castiello* < CASTĔLLUM, *siella* < SĔLLA, &c.; but the palatal then exercised an influence similar to that of the earlier period, raising *ie* to *i*, and thus producing *castillo*, *silla*, &c. It is to be noted that this is a specifically Castilian phenomenon, breaking through a continuity in evolution which formerly extended from Aragon to León: in both Aragonese and Leonese the palatal had no such effect, diphthongization occurring normally even when it was present, cf. Arag. *pueyo*, *fuella*, *nueite*, *castiello*, *betieto* (< VITĔLLUM), &c. The half-close vowels of Vulgar Latin also tended in Castilian to be raised by a palatal, e.g. VINDĒMIA > *vendimia*, PLŬVIA > *lluvia*, ŬNGULA > *uña*, &c. A feature which Castilian shared with the dialects was the elision of the semi-vowel of *ue* after the consonant groups *fr* and *fl*, e.g. FRŎNTEM > *fruente* > *frente* (cf. the common Aragonese toponymic *Frande*), FLŎCCUM > *flueco* > *fleco*.

Consonants have displayed in Castilian a greater propensity to change than have vowels. While the latter remained relatively stable, the former continued to evolve, and the two most prominent features of the Spanish consonantal system as compared with that of other Romance languages, the 'jota' and the 'zeta', are of sufficiently recent development to have been absent from the Castilian carried to the New World. The sound in earlier Castilian which became the jota was ʃ, still heard in the local pronunciation of Mexico (**meʃiko**, Cast. *Méjico*), and in the French *Don Quichotte* (Cast. *Quijote*). The zeta arose from an earlier affricate **ts**, reduced elsewhere, as in the Argentine, to a pure sibilant. Thus neither of these sounds enters into a consideration of medieval Castilian.

From the earliest times *b* and *v* were confused in the bilabial fricative β, pronounced with varying degrees of tension according to its position in the word. This confusion is apparent in the *lebantai*, *lebantaui* of the *Glosas Emilianenses*, the Castilian verb being *levantar*, formed on LEVANTE; the mistake is still very common in the writing of the semi-literate. Modern distinctions between *b* and *v* are purely orthographical, the work of etymologists.

Intervocalic voiceless plosives soon became assimilated to their voiced equivalents, and then lost their plosive quality, giving the fricatives β, ð, ɣ. This is the stage attested in Old French for -T- by the spellings *dh*, *th*. In modern Spanish they are tending to weaken further, with the dental disappearing as it disappeared in French (see p. 363): the pronunciation -*ao* for -*ado* is generally accepted. The geographical progress of the tendency to voice intervocalic plosives would appear to have been very slow; although it is complete in the earliest recorded Castilian, in northern Aragon, as also in Bearnese valleys to the north of the Pyrenean chain, there are places where they are still voiceless (see p. 50).

Before ɪ and ᴇ the velar **k** followed the usual Romance development, becoming **ts**, the later zeta, e.g. CERTUM > *cierto*, CAELUM > *cielo*, &c. The same result comes from the Romance groups **tj** and **kj**, e.g. PŬTEUM > *pozo*, MINACIA > (*a*)*menaza*, RATIONEM > *razón*, FURNACEUM > *hornazo*.

The evolution of **ǵ** before ɪ and ᴇ follows in Castilian a somewhat different path. If the vowel was stressed, it became presumably first **dj** and then **j** (written variously *g*, *j*, or *y* in medieval texts, *y* in modern Castilian), e.g. GENERUM > *yerno*, GYPSUM > *yeso*, GELUM > *yelo* (*hielo*). In this way it came to coincide with the Latin ᴊ before ᴀ, e.g. JACET > *yace*. A peculiarity is the fact that if the following vowel was not stressed the consonant entirely disappeared, though it is usually represented in modern spelling by an *h*, e.g. GERMANUM > *hermano*, GELARE > *helar*; the same fate befell Latin ᴊ before an unstressed ᴀ, e.g. JACTARE > *echar*, JANUARIUM > *enero*; similarly JUNIPERUM became *\*JENIPRU*, whence Cast. *enebro*. These developments again show Castilian individuality: in most northern dialects the evolution was to **dʒ**, which then unvoiced to **tʃ**; thus in Aragonese 'chalk' is *cheso*, 'January' is *chiner*, 'brother' is *chirmán*, and the 'juniper' *chinipro*.

While J before a front vowel was thus linked with G, a J before a back vowel followed in Castilian its own course of development, this time similar to that of Aragonese as described above; from tʃ, however, it became ʃ, and then the jota, e.g. JŬVENEM > *joven*, JŬNCUM > *junco*, JŎCUM > *juego*, JUDÆUM > *judío*. In Aragonese, where the jota is known only as a recent importation brought with Castilian, 'young' is *choben*, 'game' is *chuego*, and 'rush' is *chungo*.

The palatalization of Latin L in consonantal groups played a large part in the evolution of the Castilian sound-system. Before the appearance of texts, initial CL-, PL-, and in some instances FL- had become kλ, pλ, and fλ, after which they lost the first element to converge as λ, e.g. CLAVEM > *llave*, CLAMARE > *llamar*, PLĒNUM > *lleno*, PLANUM > *llano*, PLORARE > *llorar*, PLĬCARE > *llegar*, PLŬVIA > *lluvia*, FLAMMA > *llama*. This development shows an affinity with Italian (cf. *chiave*, *chiamare*, *piano*, *fiamma*, &c., see p. 467), a fact which suggests that the tendency to palatalize L in these circumstances may go back to Vulgar Latin. Catalan, however, concords with French in retaining the Latin groups; so, too, does Aragonese, though in the valley of the Ésera, a region of very individual speech extending from Benasque to Graus and lying between Aragonese and Catalan, groups pλ, kλ, and fλ, representing the intermediate stage, are still currently used. To the west of Castile there is another area of palatalization, with a different ultimate result (cf. Port. *chamar*, &c., see p. 432).

The same sound λ also resulted from the internal combination of L with a yod; but by the twelfth century the λ from this source underwent a further development to the affricate dʒ, which thereafter lost its dental element and in the course of the sixteenth century became the jota, e.g. ŎCULUM > *ojo*, FŎLIA > *hoja*, AURĬCULA > *oreja*, FĪLIUM > *hijo*, GENŬCULUM > *hinojo*, TĔGULA > *teja*, APĬCULA > *abeja*, OVĬCULA > *oveja*, &c. This again was a trend which the northern dialects in general did not follow: in Aragonese 'sheep' is *güella*, 'bee' is *apella* or *abella*, 'eye' is *güello*.

Some time after the λ from the above groups had changed in Castilian to dʒ, probably in the thirteenth century, the -LL- of Castilian was palatalized to λ, thereby filling the place vacated in the internal consonant system; it underwent no further change until recent times, when, like the same sound in French, it has tended to be reduced to j: the current pronunciation of *calle* is now **kaje**. In this instance the dialects display a greater differentiation than Castilian, the Latin -LL- having become in some places in Aragon, and also in the Asturias, either the dental **t** or the affricate tʃ: thus VITELLUM has given Arag. *betieto, betiecho*, comparable with Gasc. *bedèt, betèt, betètch* (orthography of the *Dict. bearn. gasc.*, see p. 395). The stages by which this change took place remain somewhat mysterious: one cannot assume that the -LL- was first palatalized to λ, as would seem normal, because at that stage it would in these dialects have become linked with the λ from L plus yod; in fact, the results of L plus yod (λ) and the results of -LL- have been kept quite apart in Gascon as in Aragonese. There must therefore have been a direct passage from lateral to dental with no palatalization, similar perhaps to the Sicilian -LL- > -*dd*- (cf. p. 28).

Another palatalization of L occurs where it is followed by T, as in MULTUM, which became the widespread *muito*, and AUSCULTARE becoming *scuitare* (*Glosas Silenses*). At this stage the group -LT- linked up with -CT-, cf. FACTUM > Arag. *feito*, NŎCTEM > Arag. *nueyt(e)* (see p. 403). The result of these groups in Castilian is tʃ (*mucho, hecho, noche*); the sound was probably in an earlier stage of development the same as in Aragonese and Mozarabic, but by the eleventh century it had already become that of modern Spanish: in a text of A.D. 1090 it is represented by -*gg*-, the spelling -*ch*- being finally adopted during the course of the following century. In much the same way, the group -CS- (usually written x) developed to ʃ, which thereafter joined with the same phoneme from other sources to become the jota, e.g. MAXILLA > *mejilla*, MATAXA > *madeja*, EXEMPLUM > *ejemplo*, DIXISTI > *dijiste*, &c.

The group N plus yod developed as in French to a palatalized N, the sound [ɲ], and so it remained, e.g. VINEA > *viña*, SIGNA > *seña*, SENIOREM > *señor*, &c. Later, the incidence of this phoneme in Spanish was reinforced in consequence of a palatalization of -NN-, occurring at the same time as the similar development of -LL-, e.g. ANNUM > *año*, PĬNNA > *peña*. In Aragonese, but not normally in Castilian, it was further reinforced by an evolution: -ND- > -*nn*- > -*ñ*-, cf. the name of a village *Laspuña*, and the toponymic *Espuañas*, from SPŎNDA; Catalan, in common with Gascon, shows a like assimilation of the D, but then reduced -*nn*- to -*n*-: thus in Catalan toponymy SPŎNDA became *Espona*.

The second element of the group -MB- was commonly assimilated to the first, in Castilian as in other dialects, e.g. PALUMBUM >

*palomo*, LUMBUM > *lomo*. Learned reaction succeeded, however, in maintaining the *b* of many such words, e.g. *cambiar, ambos,* though corresponding forms without *b* are to be found in Old Castilian texts, including the *Poema del Cid*. A document from Ribagorza of A.D. 913 shows that the reduction of -MB- to -*m*- had at that time already taken place in Aragon; in it we read: 'In locum ubi dicitur Intramas Aquas' (*Orígenes del español*, 3rd ed., p. 286). AMBOS in its reduced form is still of frequent occurrence in Aragonese toponymy: in addition to *Tramasaguas* (< INTER AMBAS AQUAS, cf. *Tramezaygues*, in the Gascon *Vallée d'Aure*), there is *Endramos* (< INTER AMBOS, attested as *intramos* in A.D. 1076, loc. cit.), and the name of a village *Tramacastilla*, which appears to preserve the Latin neuter plural, INTER AMBA CASTELLA (also preserved in the name of Castile, 'the place of many castles').

In modern Spanish the consonant *s* has a pronunciation which to the foreigner seems rather peculiar: it is 'apico-alveolar', i.e. articulated with the apex of the tongue pressed towards the teeth-ridge (cf. p. 181). This pronunciation is of ancient date: for the Moors such an *s* sounded identical to the alveolar ʃ, and this is undoubtedly the reason why, in a few words, the initial *s* has become involved in the passage of ʃ to the jota, e.g. SAPŌNEM > *iabón*, SŪCUM > *jugo*, SYRINGA > *jeringa*. Similarly, a few words in which Latin C was followed by I or E, and which should therefore have evolved with an initial **ts**, appear instead with **tʃ**, and so have escaped the subsequent passage of **ts** to the zeta, e.g. CICCUM > *chico*, CĪMICEM > *chinche*.

Of all Spanish sound-changes none has provoked so much comment and controversy as has the evolution of F to *h*, as in FABA > *haba*, FABULARE > *hablar*, FACĔRE > *hacer*, FATA > *hada*, FĪLIUM > *hijo*, FUMUM > *humo*, FĬLĬCTUM (from FILICEM) > *helecho*, &c. This *h* is a feature which Castilian shares with Gascon; in the latter speech, however, it appears in the earliest texts (see Raimbaut de Vaqueyras, p. 390) and is still strongly pronounced, whereas in Castilian it became usual in the written language only in the fifteenth century, and little more than a century later it had been eliminated from standard pronunciation.

In the *Poema del Cid*, not only is Latin F consistently maintained, but also *honte* and *hardie*, Old French words with an aspirate *h* of Germanic origin, appear as *fonta* and *fardida*, while Arabic *ḥatta* is rendered as *fata*. What can be deduced from this? Either that the symbol *f* was being used to represent the sound *h*, which is improbable, or that the scribe was 'correcting' the *h* of the loan-words to the *f* of Castilian. If the latter explanation were the true one, the forms *fonta*, *fardida*, and *fata* being regarded as 'hyper-correct', then the scribe must have been aware of the existence, in the popular speech, of what for him was the 'incorrect' pro-nunciation of *f* as the aspirate. Considering this fact, and also adducing from the toponymy of medieval texts some examples of F > *h* dating back to the eleventh century, Menéndez Pidal came to the conclusion that the phenomenon, in the original Castile which bordered upon the Basque country, was of much earlier date than most scholars, in particular Meyer-Lübke, would at that time allow. In the absence of further evidence one might easily suppose that it dated back to the latinization of that region. Pointing then to the similar contiguity of Gascony with the Basque country, and to the absence of the phoneme *f* in Basque, Pidal argued (without questioning the identification of Basque with Iberian) that here was a clear indication of the influence of the Iberian substratum on the sound-system of Romance.

Many objections have been raised to this theory. As Meyer-Lübke pointed out, in some of the earliest words borrowed from Latin into Basque, *f* was rendered not by *h* but by *p* or *b*, e.g. FĔSTA > Basque *pesta*, *besta*, FABA >Basque *baba*, FATUM > Basque *patu*, FĪCUM > Basque *biku*, &c. Moreover, if Basque could have this influence on its western and northern frontiers, it is strange that there should be no similar result to the east and the south, where *f* was consistently maintained. The discussion was given a new turn by John Orr, in an article entitled 'F > h, phénomène ibère ou roman?' (*Revue de linguistique romane*, vol. xii, 1936, pp. 10–35). Orr produced a third suggestion: agreeing with Pidal, against Meyer-Lübke, that the phenomenon might well go back to the Vulgar Latin period, Orr disagreed as to its origins; for him, the *h* owed nothing to Iberian influence, but was simply a rustic alternative to *f* in common Vulgar Latin. The presence of such alternances in Latin has long since been known, e.g. HABA (FABA), FORDEUM (HORDEUM), FAEDUS (HAEDUS), HANULUM (FANULUM), FOSTEA (HOSTEA), &c. (W. M. Lindsay, *The Latin Language*, p. 56); by some scholars the forms with H are attributed to the influence of Etruscan. The phenomenon is also widespread in the present-day dialects of southern Italy, e.g. in Calabria, *hilu*, *higliu, hava, harina, humu, huocu, hierru,* &c. (cf. G. Rohlfs, *Le Gascon,* p. 97, note). To this we may add that it occurs in Arumanian (S. Puşcariu, *Die rumänische Sprache,* translation H. Kuen, p. 283) and dialectally in Daco-Rumanian, though only before a front vowel, e.g. *a hi, hier,* 'iron', corresponding to the standard *a fi, fier.* Orr further sets out, recalling the unexplained (or inadequately explained!) Fr. *hors,* side by side with Old Fr. *fors* (< FORIS), to demonstrate its presence in French toponymy. This, the major part of his article, has not, in our opinion, received from linguists the attention which it deserves. A few of the examples quoted for north-east France may, as has been objected, owe their *h* to Frankish; but between the Seine and the Loire there are various place-names which can scarcely derive their *h* from anything but a Latin F: *Hamars,* as compared with *Famars,* near the Belgian border, seems quite certainly to be FANUM MARTIS; *Houssemagne,* cf. *Fossemagne,* farther south, is surely FOSSA MAGNA; the many names with initial *Hon-* (*Hondouville, Honvault,* &c.) suggest as their most probable etyma the Lat. FONTEM and FUNDUM; and forms such as *La Heugrie, Les Heugues, La Heuzerie,* side by side with similar names beginning with F-, imply that one need not seek their origin farther afield than in the derivatives of the Lat. FILICEM. Yet even if these proposed etymologies were entirely rejected, Orr's theory of a Latin origin for F > *h* remains none the less valid: so abundant are the incontrovertible examples of F > *h* in territory far removed from the 'Iberian' substratum.

Spanish scholars almost without exception, and many others, still adhere to the theory of Menéndez Pidal: so extremely suggestive of 'substratic' influence is the presence of the phenomenon in two Romance speeches, both of which evolved in the immediate neighbourhood of a pre-Romance idiom which knew no *f*. We incline towards a solution involving a compromise: the Latin nature of the phenomenon is, to our mind, undeniable, but that the absence of *f* in the local speech should have favoured the adoption of Latin forms with *h* seems well within the bounds of linguistic probability. In this view, the effect of the substratum was to determine a choice rather than to initiate a change.

In conclusion, it should be noted that the adoption of *h*-forms is by no means universal in Castilian. Many words have retained the *f*, e.g. FONTEM > *fuente,* FORTEM > *fuerte,* FŎCUM > *fuego,* FĔSTA > *fiesta,* FĪDEM > *fe,* FOEDUM > *feo,* FRONTEM > *frente,* &c.

The fact that the diphthong *ue* appears to have impeded the passage of F to *h* was adduced by Meyer-Lübke in support of his contention that F > *h* was a late phenomenon, but this argument is of little weight, since the diphthongization itself probably dates back to Vulgar Latin. Professor W. von Wartburg, favouring the 'Iberian' theory, suggests that under the influence of the substratum Latin labio-dental *f* became a bilabial *f*, which thereafter became *h* in a weak position and returned to labio-dental *f* in a strong position (*Die Ausgliederung der romanischen Sprachräume*, pp. 9–12). This is ingenious, but there is no clear-cut division into strong and weak positions, and the theory which supposes a period of hesitation between *f* and *h*, with learned influence favouring the former, impresses us as more plausible. Gascon, incidentally, shows no such hesitation: in that dialect an F in any position has become *h*, e.g. FĔSTA > *hèsto*, FATA > *hàdo*, FABRUM > *hàure*, FRŪCTUM > *herùto*, FRIGIDUM > *herét*, FEBRUARIUM > *herewè*, FORMATICUM > *hourmàdye*, FLAMMA > *halàmo*, PROFUNDUM > *prehoùn*, &c.

In its morphology and syntax Castilian has evolved from Vulgar Latin with relatively few idiosyncrasies (see Chapter I). Its vocabulary was enriched not only by the oriental words of Mozarabic, but also by borrowings from French and to a lesser extent from Provençal. Contacts with the civilizations to the north were many and varied. During the Reconquest, from the time of Charlemagne onwards, knights with their followers frequently came from both northern and southern France to fight side by side with the Spaniards of the Christian states. The inclination of Spanish monarchs to wed French princesses brought Gallic influence to the court. Perhaps more important, the monks of the Benedictine monastery established in A.D. 910 at Cluny, on the banks of a tributary of the River Saône, during the eleventh century acquired a reputation for learning and founded new establishments far and wide: among these were the monastery of San Juan de la Peña and various other monastic centres in Spain. Heirs to the Carolingian Renaissance, they replaced the Visigothic script of Spain by the Carolingian, and it is doubtless due to their teaching that the 'Romancing' tendencies apparent in the Latin of Spain during the ninth and tenth centuries, culminating in the glosses, quite abruptly vanish; monastic texts of the eleventh century are written for the most part in a fairly standard medieval Latin. The same period saw an ever-increasing influx of pilgrims making for the shrine of Saint James of Compostela, in Galicia. Most of them crossed the Pyrenees either via the Somport to Jaca, or further west, via the Port de Cize and the Basque valley of Roncesvaux to Pamplona; the two routes met at Puente La Reina, south of Pamplona, whence the *camino francés* continued through Logroño, Burgos, and León to Santiago. Along this route Frenchmen who ministered to the needs of their fellow countrymen were allowed to settle, and the *barrio franco* became a common feature both there and in reconquered towns.

All of these elements are reflected in the many loan-words from the north which are present in the earliest Castilian: the knightly: *linaje, coraje, homenaje, mensaje, barnax* (Old Fr. *barnage* < \*BARO-NATICU), *palafré* (Fr. *palefroi* < PARAVERĒDUM); the courtly: *dama, doncel, doncella, deleyt, balada, trobar, roseñor* (later *ruiseñor*), *cosiment* (< Prov. *causimen* 'choice', from the verb *causir* < KAUSJAN); the monastic: *monje* (Prov. *monge*), *fraile* (Prov. *fraire* < FRATER); the peregrinatory: *manjares, viandas, mesón, hostal* (Prov. *ostal* < HOSPITALE, cf. Old Fr. *hostel*). A considerable number of such words were later ousted by semantic equivalents from the native Castilian stock.

*Portuguese.* West of León, in the extreme corner of the Iberian Peninsula, where the Cantabrians in a series of ranges splay out to the sea, was the home of the Pre-Roman Gallaeci and of the post-imperial kingdom of the Swabians. After the Muslim invasion it became one of the chief places of Christian refuge, untouched by the occupier. The frontier of Mozarabic Spain was established for a while, towards the end of the tenth century, along the line of the River Douro. To the north of this line evolved the variety of medieval Romance traditionally known as Galician-Portuguese.

Historically, the split between Galicia and Portugal had its origins in events which followed upon the capture of Toledo in A.D. 1085 (see p. 399). The victorious Alfonso VI of Castile gave two of his daughters in marriage to two brothers, Raymond and Henry, noblemen from Burgundy, and then conferred upon the brothers the fiefs of Galicia and Portugal respectively. The boundary between the two fiefs was marked by the River Minho, which is still the northern frontier of Portugal. In addition to the narrow strip of Christian territory between this river and the Douro, Henry received the freshly-conquered lands to the south, extending as far as the River Mondego; Coimbra, on the Mondego, had been retaken in A.D. 1064. Thus to Henry and his heirs fell the area of battle and with it the task of prosecuting the Reconquest. This they did with vigour. Henry's son, Alfonso, in A.D. 1143 obtained from Alfonso VII of Castile the title of King of Portugal, thereby founding a Burgundian dynasty which was destined to endure until A.D. 1383. The fortunes of the new kingdom were secured by Alfonso's success in delivering the great port of Lisbon from Muslim rule (A.D. 1147). By A.D. 1250, aided by the progress of the Castilians in Andalusia, the Portuguese had extended their control to include the Algarve and all the present limits of the country. The seat of the monarchy was normally at Coimbra; only under the following dynasty of the house of Aviz was it shifted to Cintra, in the neighbourhood of Lisbon.

Like the Catalans in the east of the Peninsula, the Portuguese turned their attention to the sea and soon became a great maritime nation. Meanwhile, the frontier on the Minho hardened, the Galicians having thrown in their lot with Castile. Not, however, until the mid-fourteenth century was there any marked difference between the speeches of the two regions. Thereafter, the speech of the central territory between Coimbra and Lisbon became gradually accepted as a Portuguese standard, though it was left to the sixteenth century to consolidate it as such, to the great national poet Luís de Camões (A.D. 1525–80) and to those grammarians who 'defended' Portuguese—in particular João de Barros (*Dialogo em louvor da nossa linguagem*, A.D. 1540) and Pedro de Magalhães de Gandavo (*Dialogo em defensam da lingua portuguesa*, A.D. 1574)—and who, in doing so, sought to make it as different as possible from Spanish. Galician, in the meantime, degenerated to a patois status; it is still widely spoken and practised as a literary cult by local enthusiasts.

The literary origins of Galician-Portuguese bear some resemblance to those of Provençal, as the latter developed at the end of the eleventh century, though with no previous evidence of hagiographical texts: the prose of notarial usage appeared almost simultaneously with vernacular lyric poetry. In this part of Romania, however, literary recourse to the vernacular occurred a century later; until then a fairly consistent standard of Latin was maintained. Probably the earliest specimen of Galician-Portuguese to have survived is an act of partition dated 1230; as in the case of the dating given by Per Abbat to his copy of the *Cantar de mio*

*Cid*, we must here deduct thirty-eight years to arrive at the corresponding date in the present-day Gregorian calendar: this places the text in A.D. 1192. Now kept in the national archives at Lisbon, the document came originally from the monastery of Vairão; the properties to which it refers are situated in the valley of the Minho, near Braga. It was first edited by J. Leite de Vasconcelos (*Dois textos portugueses da idade media. Festgabe für A. Mussafia*, Halle, 1905). The following is the text in full:

In Christi nomine amen. Hec est notitia de partiçon e de deuison que fazemus antre nos dos herdamentus e dus cout[us e] das onrras e dous padruadigus das eygreygas que forum de nossu padre e de nossa madre en esta maneira: que Rodrigo Sanchiz ficar por sa partiçon na quinta do couto de Uiiturio, e na quinta do padroadigo dessa eygreyga en todolus (us) herdamentus do couto e de fora do couto; Uaasco Sanchiz ficar por sa partiçon na onrra d'Ulueira e no padroadigo dessa eygreyga, en todolus herdamentus d'Olueira e en uu casal de Carapezus que chamam da Uluar e en outro casal en Agiar que chamam Quintaa; Meen Sanchiz ficar por sa partiçon na onrra de Carapezus e nus outrus herdamentus, e nas duas partes do padroadigo dessa eygreyga, e no padroadigo da eygreyga de Creysemil e na onrra e no herdamento d'Arguiffi, e no herdamento de Lauoradas e no padroadigo dessa eygreyga. Eluira Sanchiz ficar por sa partiçon nos herdamentos de Centegaus, e nas tres quartas do padroadigo dessa eygreyga, e no herdamento de Creyximil, assi us das sestas com'en outro herdamento.

Estas partiçoens e diuisoes fazemos antre nos, que uallam por en secula seculorum amen. Facta karta mensse marcii era m. cc xxx. Uaasco Suariz testis, Uermuu Ordoniz testis. Meen Fanrripas testis. Gonsaluu Uermuiz testis. Gil Diaz testis. Dom Martio testis. Martim Periz testis. Don Stepham Suariz testis. Ego Iohannes Menendi presbiter notauit.[1]

(R. M. Ruggieri, *Testi antichi romanzi. Trascrizioni*, pp. 98–100)

[1] *Translation*:
In Christ's name, amen. This is to give notice of the partition and division which we make between us of the possessions and hunting-reserves and estates and patronages of the churches which belonged to our father and mother, in this way: that Rodrigo Sanchiz shall retain for his share a fifth of the reserve of Vitorinho and a fifth of the patronage of that church, and all the possessions of the reserve and from outside the reserve; Vasco Sanchiz shall retain for his share the estate of Oliveira and the patronage of that church, all the possessions of Oliveira, and a farmhouse of Carapeços which is called Olivar, and another farmhouse at Aguiar which is called Quintãa; Mendo Sanchiz shall retain for his share the estate of Carapeços and the other possessions and the two parts of the patronage of that church and the patronage of the church of Creixomil and the estate and the possessions of Argufe, and the possessions of Lavoradas, and the patronage of that church; Elvira Sanchiz shall retain for her share the possessions of Santagões and three quarters of the patronage of that church, and the possessions of Creixomil,

Elvira, the daughter of this well-to-do family of Sanchiz, was abbess of the convent of Vairão, to which she left all her share of the property upon her death in the following year. Her will, which has also survived among the documents of Vairão, is as follows:[1]

In Christi nomine. Amen. Eu Elvira Sanchiz offeyro o meu corpo áás virtudes de Sam Salvador do monsteyro de Vayram, e offeyro con o meu corpo todo o herdamento que eu ey en Centegaus e as tres quartas do padroadigo dessa eygleyga e todo hu herdamento de Crexemil, assi us das sestas como todo u outro herdamento: que u aia u moensteyro de Vayram por en secula seculorum. Amen.

Fecta karta mense septembri era MCCXXXI. Menendus Sanchiz testes. Stephanus Suariz testes. Vermúú Ordoniz testes. Sancho Diaz testes. Gonsalvus Diaz testes.

Ego Gonsalvus Petri presbyter notavit.[2]

From these two texts the principal features of the Romance which was spoken during the twelfth century in the Minho valley are already apparent: they include many of the peculiarities of modern Portuguese.

The definite article from ILLA, ILLUM, has lost its *l*, as in Aragon and Navarre, giving rise to a series: fem. *a, as*, masc. *u, us*; in the orthography which came to be accepted the masculine forms are *o, os*, but the *u*-sound is preserved in current pronunciation. These forms serve both as definite article and as pronoun, e.g. *que u aia u moensteyro* (contrast Cast. *que lo haya el monasterio*).

both those of the sixths(?) and the other possessions. These partitions and divisions we make between us that they may be valid for ever after. Amen.
 This document was made in the month of March, in the year 1230. (Signatures of eight witnesses.) I, Iohannes Menendi, priest, was notary.
 *Note*: We assume that *sestas* 'sixths', refers to divided property, cf. the Italian use of *sesto*, and the semantic development of *quinta* in both Portuguese and Spanish.
 [1] Likewise first published by Leite de Vasconcelos. For both texts see also Angelo Monteverdi, *Manuale di avviamento agli studi romanzi*, pp. 189–192, and J. Huber, *Altportugiesisches Elementarbuch*, pp. 291–3.
 [2] *Translation*:
 In Christ's name, amen. I, Elvira Sanchiz, offer my body to the safe keeping(?) of Saint Salvador of the monastery of Vairão, and I offer with my body all the possessions which I have in Santagões and the three quarters of the patronage of that church, and all the possessions of Creixomil, both those of the sixths(?) and all the other possessions: may the monastery of Vairão have this for ever after.
 This document was made in the month of September, in the year 1231. (Signatures of five witnesses.) I, Gonsalvus Petri, priest, was notary.
 *Note*: Monteverdi, op. cit., suggests that the *virtudes* of Saint Salvador may be the virtuous nuns, but we prefer to look upon them as the abstract virtues of the saint; alternatively, the word might well have the more concrete sense of 'relics', which we have attributed to it in translating the Aragonese *eras bertutes kede aduscomos da Roma* (see above, p. 411).

In its phonology, Portuguese concurs with Provençal and Catalan in not diphthongizing the stressed half-open vowels, e.g. *nossa, fora, corpo, sesta* (contrast Cast. *nuestra, fuera, cuerpo, siesta*). The tendency towards spontaneous diphthongization being here rejected, the seven stressed vowels of Vulgar Latin have normally remained without change. Even where a yod is present, it tends in general to combine with a consonant, and only joins with a vowel to produce a diphthong when the consonant is of such a nature that it will not readily absorb it. Thus FŎLIA and HŎDIE have given in Portuguese *folha* and *hoje*, but CŎRIUM and NŎCTE became *coiro* and *noite*; similarly, CERĔSEA > *cereja*, VENIO > *venho*, VĔCLUM > *velho*, but MATĔRIA > *madeira*, LĔCTUM > *leito*. The incidence of the *ei* diphthong was increased by the fact of its being the normal result both of Ē plus yod, as in *moensteyro* above (cf. MYSTĒRIUM > *misteiro*, FĒRIA > *feira*), and of A plus yod, via a stage *ai*, e.g. LACTEM > *leite*, BASIUM > *beijo*, PRIMARIUM > *primeiro*, and as in the above texts, MAN(U)ARIA > *meneira*, OLIVARIA > *Ulveira, Olveira*. Vulgar Latin's surviving diphthong AU remained in Portuguese at the stage *ou*, as in *outro* < ALTERUM and *couto* < CAUTUM (a 'protected place', hence the specialization as 'hunting-reserve'), cf. AURUM > *ouro*, CAUSA >*cousa*, AMAVIT > *\*amaut* > *amou*, SAPUIT > *\*saupit* > *soube*, etc. Thus in the twelfth century the speech of the area was already characterized among Romance idioms as one of falling diphthongs, with a predominance of *ei*.

The impression was at the same time heightened as a consequence of nasalization. This phenomenon has played a most important role in the evolution of Portuguese and is another feature which served in medieval times to mark it off as a language apart. Hesitancy on the part of the scribes in spelling any word which in Latin had contained a nasal consonant is visible in our texts: *partiçon* (< PARTITIONEM) is followed by *partiçoens*, this being linked with *divisoes* (< DIVISIONES), while the *oen* spelling occurs again in *moensteyro*(< \*MONESTERIUM); an attempt to represent nasalization also explains the *m* of *chamam* (< CLAMANT) and *uallam* (< VALEANT); *Martio* and *Martim* are different graphies for the same name. Where the Latin N was intervocalic it disappeared entirely, nasalizing the preceding vowel; if the second of the two vowels thus brought together was similar in quality to the first, it was readily absorbed, e.g. LANA > *lãa* > *lã*; but if the tonic vowel came into contact with a different post-tonic vowel, in the sequences A–O, O–E, and A–E, the result was a nasal diphthong, again of the falling type, e.g. MANUM > *mão*, GERMANUM > *irmão*, LECTIONES > *lições*, PONES > *pões*, CANES > *cães*, RATIONES > *razões*.

Among vowels other than tonic, final *o* and *a* have remained, as in Castilian, but final *e* has disappeared, except when used as a supporting vowel, e.g. *casal* (< CASALEM), but *antre* (< INTER) and *padre* (< PATER). Atonic *o* has tended to close to *u*, e.g. *herdamentus* (formed on *herdar* < HEREDITARE) side by side in our texts with *herdamento*, and *padruadigu* (< PATRONATICUM) together with *padroadigo*. An unstressed *e* has similarly become more closed in the pronunciation of modern Portuguese.

Consonantal development presents little difficulty. The intervocalic voiceless plosives of Latin have regularly sonorized. The groups tj and kj have been reduced to a single phoneme, as in *partiçon* and *fazemos*. A yod combined with *l* and *n* to produce the palatalized consonants represented in later spelling by *lh* and *nh*, following Provençal practice. Initial CL-, PL-, and FL- developed at first, as in Castilian, to λ, and thereafter followed an evolution: λ > tj > tʃ > ʃ; during the medieval period the sound in use was tʃ, reduction to ʃ being as late as the seventeenth century, e.g. CLAMARE > *chamar*, CLAVEM > *chave*, PLORARE > *chorar*, PLĒNUM > *cheio*, FLAMMA > *chama*, FLAGRARE > *cheirar*. Another distinctive feature is the loss, which occurred during the twelfth century, of intervocalic *l*, e.g. CAELUM > *céu*, SALŪTEM > *saude*, VOLARE > *voar*, COLŌREM > *coor*, *côr*; some of the words which dwindled in this way were later replaced by learned equivalents, e.g. DOLORŌSUM > *doroso*, replaced by *doloroso*, SILENTIUM > *seenço*, replaced by *silêncio*. The combined effect of the fall of both *l* and *n* in the intervocalic position, together with the series of diphthongs due to vocalized *l* and the yod, has been to endow Portuguese with a very vocalic character, most noticeable when one contrasts it with the neighbouring Castilian, and especially with Catalan.

A peculiarity of Portuguese morphology illustrated in the above texts is the persistence of the Latin imperfect subjunctive (or future perfect), as in *ficar* (< *FIGICARET); identity in form between this and the infinitive gave rise to the 'personal infinitive' (see p. 144). The meaning of *ficar*, cf. Fr. *ficher*, is in Portuguese and Provençal 'to remain'; hence *ficar em* (with the definite article, *ficar no, na*) 'to remain in', 'to abide by', or as we have translated it, 'to retain'.

Such are the more prominent features of the language which, during the later Middle Ages, was to attain literary distinction as the medium of a rich lyrical poetry, a medium accepted in other parts of the Peninsula as the appropriate standard for the writing of songs. Among the most prolific of Galician-Portuguese poets was Alfonso X of Castile, the protector of Castilian letters: his verse, collected as the *Livro das Cantigas de Santa Maria*, is largely of religious inspiration, as the title indicates. At the time there was a general feeling that Galician-Portuguese was more suited to the lyric and Castilian to epic and historical matter: a division of function probably imitated, consciously or unconsciously, from France, where a similar distinction was held to exist between *langue d'oc* and *langue d'oïl*, though there it was fact rather than fancy; it has its parallel in the ancient literature of Greece.

The full flowering of this lyric came during the thirteenth century and lasted almost till the end of the fourteenth. No specimen could be much earlier than the Portuguese strophe in the multilingual poem of Raimbaut de Vaqueyras (see p. 387); following immediately upon the Gascon strophe, it reads as follows:

> Mas tan temo vostro preito
> todo.n son escarmentado.
> Por vos ei pen' e maltreito
> e meo corpo lazerado:
> la noit, can jaç'en meu leito,
> so mochas vetz resperado;
> e car nonca m'aprofeito
> falid'ei en meu cuidado.[1]

One may well suspect that Raimbaut's knowledge of Portuguese was limited: his *mochas* (for *muitas*) inclines towards Spanish, and a number of features suggest his own native Provençal. On the other hand, his strophe is sufficiently Portuguese to imply that contacts did exist, although there is little or no record of them,

---

[1] *Translation*:
But so greatly do I fear your scorn that I am much distressed thereby. For you I suffer pain and torment, and my body is racked: at night, when I lie in my bed, I am often wide awake; and since I never enjoy any reward, I have failed in my intent.

between the poets of Provence and those of the western seaboard
of the Iberian Peninsula: a conclusion to which one would in
any event be led by a consideration of the numerous echoes of
Provençal lyric in the themes and forms employed in Galician-
Portuguese. While none would deny the existence in Galicia of
a native lyrical gift, Provençal influence is quite obvious in the
love-poems, the *cantigas de amor*, and the *cantigas de amigo* which
differ from the former only in that the words are supposed to
be spoken by a woman, and also in the satirical poems, the *cantigas de maldizer* and *cantigas de escárnio*, recalling the Provençal
*sirventés*.

Briefly, it is a poetry transferred from one court to another, in
which kings and great rulers found their pleasure. One of the first
short poems is traditionally attributed, though with no certainty,
to King Sancho I of Portugal (A.D. 1154–1211); it is a *cantiga de
amigo*:

> Ay eu coitada, como vivo en gram cuydado
> por meu amigo que ei alongado!
>       Muyto me tarda
>     o meu amigo na guarda!
>
> Ay eu coitada, como vivo en gram desejo
> por meu amigo que tarda e non vejo!
>       Muyto me tarda
>     o meu amigo na guarda!

Such simple verse scarcely calls for translation. The verb *coitar*,
'to oppress, trouble', familiar in the same form in Provençal (cf.
Old Fr. *coitier*, Old Cast. *cochar*), derives from a popular *COCTARE,
from Class. COGERE; *desejo* similarly represents a popular *DĒSĒ-
DIUM, apparently a reduced form of DESIDERIUM (cf. Cast. *deseo*,
Cat. *desig*). The only difficulty lies in the interpretation of *na
guarda*, which might refer to the fortress in which King Sancho
had his abode. Most famous of these poets is another royal personage, King Denis (Diniz) of Portugal (A.D. 1279–1323), who
founded the University of Lisbon and played in his country the
same role of patron as did Alfonso the Wise in Castile. Many have
remained anonymous and to date their work with accuracy is
impossible. Like the poetry of the troubadours, it was for a long
time lost and was rediscovered chiefly in Italian manuscripts.
Indeed, the not inconsiderable body of Galician-Portuguese verse
is preserved almost entirely in three *cancioneiros*, the two longest

being the *Cancioneiro da Vaticana* (1,205 poems) and the *Cancioneiro Colocci-Brancuti* (1,675 poems, only 470 of which are not in the Vatican *Cancioneiro*). Both of these were copied in Italy during the sixteenth century, the latter for the well-known humanist Angelo Colocci (d. A.D. 1549); both were first published by E. Monaci (Halle, 1875 and 1880 respectively). At Lisbon, in the Biblioteca da Ajuda, is the much smaller *Cancioneiro da Ajuda*, containing only *cantigas de amor*, in all 286 complete poems and some fragments (first published by Carolina Michaelis de Vascon-celos, Halle, 1904).

Imitation of Provençal was naturally responsible for an early contribution of that language to Portuguese, but much more im-portant, as in Spain and for similar reasons, was the influence of medieval French. Contacts with France have indeed been con-tinuous almost throughout Portuguese history and have resulted in the adoption of a large number of French words into the lan-guage in more recent times. Castilian exercized some influence during the fifteenth and sixteenth centuries: in A.D. 1578 Portugal became subject to the Spain of Philip II; but after the recovery of independence, achieved in A.D. 1640 under the leadership of the house of Braganza and with French assistance, the Portuguese tended to turn more and more away from their eastern neighbours. A traveller in Portugal today will find French much more widely known than Spanish. Pronunciation has in the meantime con-tinued to evolve on very individual lines, thereby widening the gap between the two adjacent speech-areas which formerly were so closely related: nasalization has progressed to include even the close vowels, e.g. *sim* [sĩ] 'yes', and *um* [ũ] 'one'; unstressed vowels, converging towards a central point of articulation, have lost their clear quality to become what are sometimes known as 'whispering vowels'; and the consonant *s*, except where initial or intervocalic (in which latter case it voiced to *z*), has acquired the sound of alveolar ʃ or ʒ, e.g. *as suas mãos* 'his hands', pronounced as aʃ suaʒ mãuʃ (the vowel a being 'whispered'). In consequence of all these changes, the student who approaches Portuguese after having learnt Spanish will find that, whereas reading the language is relatively a simple matter, in its pronunciation it is at first most disconcerting.

*Catalan.* The question whether Catalan should be considered as a language has at times given rise to debate, much of it ill-informed and coloured by political partisanship. From the standpoint of the linguist there can of course be no doubt concerning its status. During the later medieval period it came to rank as one of the 'great languages' of western Europe. The individuality which it had developed was certainly no less marked than that of Portuguese, and its abundant literature is perhaps more original and more varied in scope. As the chancery language of the prosperous Kingdom of Aragon it was carried far over the Mediterranean area, by military, maritime, and commercial enterprise. Its decline set in only at the end of the fifteenth century, after the union of Aragon and Castile. By then it was so firmly rooted in tradition that it has maintained a strong cohesion to the present day.

Modern Catalonia has its origins in the *Marca Hispanica* established by Charlemagne and Louis the Pious in order to block the route of Muslim invasion. Within the March were various counties, each with a local ruler, dependent at first on Frankish protection. The largest was that of Barcelona, situated to the south, facing the Moorish Kingdom of Tortosa. To the west were the counties of Pallars and Urgel, adjoining the Moorish Kingdom of Lérida. To the north, along the coast, lay Gerona and Ampurias, while the central area was occupied by Besalú, Ausona, and Cerdaña. Finally, between the two ranges into which the wall of the Pyrenees divides as it approaches the sea, were the counties of Conflent and Rosellón, later to be merged in the French province of Roussillon. Of all these, Pallars alone, joining with Ribagorza, became part of the original Kingdom of Aragon. The remainder were welded together under the leadership of Barcelona.

The union was effected largely by Ramón Berenguer III (A.D. 1096–1131) by means of inheritances and marriage settlements in the first instance: Besalú was acquired in A.D. 1111, Cerdaña in A.D. 1117, and in A.D. 1123 his overlordship was acknowledged by the Count of Ampurias. An ambitious third marriage to Douce of Provence—his first was with a daughter of the Cid—brought him nominal possession of all the coastal lands of southern France as far as Nice, a later basis for Catalan claims on Languedoc. Meanwhile, he waged war upon the Moors and captured from them the frontier town of Balaguer (A.D. 1106), though he failed in his attacks upon Lérida and Tortosa. A counter-attack by the Moors of Valencia brought them to Martorell, within a few miles of Barcelona, but there they were decisively repelled. He also

launched, in A.D. 1115, a first attack on the Balearics, in alliance
with the Republic of Pisa, and thus began a long association between Catalonia and the growing maritime republics of Italy.
Incidentally, it is in a Latin poem composed by an Italian, Lorenzo
Vernes, to celebrate this undertaking, that the term 'Catalan'
appears for the first time.

Under the rule of Ramón Berenguer IV (A.D. 1131–62) the work
of expansion continued. To him fell the Moorish strongholds
which had defied his predecessor: Fraga (A.D. 1134), Tortosa
(A.D. 1148), and Lérida (A.D. 1149); thus the south-westerly flank
of the new state was secured along the line of the Ebro and its
tributaries. Most important, in A.D. 1137 he married Petronila,
daughter of King Ramiro II of Aragon, and heiress to the crown,
thereby uniting the County of Barcelona with the Kingdom of
Aragon: the maritime state had acquired a hinterland, and being
itself much more wealthy and thickly populated it had no difficulty
in remaining preponderant, though the name of Aragon became
associated with its history. By the same act all prospect of the
union of Aragon with Castile was for some centuries deferred.
Ramón Berenguer IV's successors, Alfonso II (A.D. 1162–96) and
Pedro II (A.D. 1196–1213, battle of Muret) were the kings of
Aragon and Catalonia whom we have already encountered pursuing their interests north of the Pyrenees (see p. 389). It was left
to Jaume I, 'James the Conqueror', to continue Catalan expansion
in a more profitable direction. Supported only by Catalans, the
Aragonese having refused to take part, he led the expedition which
in A.D. 1229 succeeded in occupying Majorca; by A.D. 1235 Minorca
and Ibiza had been captured. But perhaps his greatest exploit was
the final reduction of Valencia (A.D. 1238), which, after having
been seized by the Cid, had been lost again to the Almoravids in
A.D. 1102. The occupation of the country to the south to include
Alicante marked the limit of the Catalan contribution to the
Reconquest.

Much of the remainder of James's reign was spent in pursuit
of his claims in the north, and in seeking to bolster up Provençal
noblemen in their futile resistance to the French monarchy. The
latter, with some audacity, produced a counter-claim, based upon
Charlemagne's creation of the Spanish March, to all the territories of the house of Barcelona. The outcome of this was the
treaty of Corbeil (A.D. 1258), by which the various claims were

abandoned and the northern frontier of Catalonia was established to include Cerdaña, Conflent, and Rosellón. Thereafter, the Kingdom of Aragon and Catalonia turned to the sea, and during the latter part of the thirteenth century and the fourteenth built up an empire which at its greatest extent comprised Corsica and Sardinia, Sicily and the Kingdom of Naples, and even, governed from Sicily, the Duchy of Athens (A.D. 1311–87).

This brief summary of the early history of Catalonia shows how close were the links between that country and southern France. Ever since Roman times the territories of the coastal strip had been intimately connected, the eastern extremities of the Pyrenees forming no serious barrier to communication and commerce. Thus Catalan and *langue d'oc* evolved during the formative period with similar tendencies; and when Provençal, the *Lemosí* of Raimon Vidal of Besadún (see p. 390), emerged as a language backed by literary and courtly prestige, it was quite natural that aspirant troubadours born in the Catalan area, in the absence of any other recognized standard, should associate themselves with the Provençal school and adopt its medium. In so doing, moreover, they were following a royal example set by their king, Alfonso II, of whose poetic composition, highly esteemed by his contemporaries, there remains only one specimen, and that of somewhat doubtful attribution. Among the best known, in addition to Raimon Vidal, are Guillem de Bergadà (1140–1213), Guillem de Cabestany (1160–1220?) and Guerau de Cabrera (living between 1145 and 1179). The last one of any consequence, usually referred to in the older anthologies as Cerveri de Gerona, has recently been identified, by Martín de Riquer, as Guillem de Cervera (living between 1250 and 1280); his work is still written in a fairly conventional Provençal, though with the addition of a number of Catalan features. It was left to one of the greatest literary figures of the age, Ramón Llull (see below), to show that the *pla catalanesc* of his prose could also be used as a medium for verse.

With the poets of Catalonia thus composing in a foreign tongue almost until the end of the thirteenth century, it is to prose that we must look for the first specimens of authentic Catalan. The earliest is a fragment containing six short sermons, discovered in the archives of the parish of Organyà,[1] in the diocese of Urgel,

---

[1] By Joachim Miret i Sans, who first published it in an article, 'El mes antig text literari escrit en català, precedit per una colecció de documents dels segles

whence it has come to be known as the *Homilies d'Organyà*. This relic which chance has preserved bears witness to the growth of the ecclesiastical practice of preaching in the vernacular, and recalls in its form the older Picard relic, the *Fragment de Valenciennes* (see p. 348). From palæographical evidence the manuscript may be approximately dated as late twelfth century, contemporaneous, that is, with the first appearance of Romance texts in other parts of the Peninsula; it is now kept in the Central Library of Barcelona. The second sermon, a commentary on a very well known passage of the Gospel according to St. Luke, is as follows:

*Dominica in LXa. In illo tempore, cum turba plurima convenirent et de civitatibus properarent ad Iesum, dixit per similitudinem: Exit qui seminat seminare semen suum.* Seinor, nostre Seinor dix aquesta paraula per semblant, et el esposa per si el ex. Aquel qui ix seminar la sua sement, e dementre que semenava, la una sement cadeg prob de la via e fo calzigad, e.ls ocels del cel mengaren aquela sement: aquest seminador dix nostre Seinor que son los maestres de sent' eglesia . . . de la predicacio de Iesu Christ. Los auzels del cel qui mengaren aquela sement son los diables qui tolen la paraula de Deu de coratge d'om per mal e peccatz e per males obres. *Et aliut cecidit supra petram et natum aruit, quia non habebat humorem.* Aquela sement qui cadeg sobre la pedra fo seca per zo car no i avia humor, demostra la paraula de Deu qui cad el cor del om e ven diable e la tol del cor per zo car no a humor de caritad en si. *Et aliut cecidit inter spinas, et simul exorte spine sufocaverunt illud.* E aquela sement qui cadeg en les espines demostra la paraula de Deu qui cad entre .ls. . . . dels rics omens d'aquest segle, qar pensen de lurs riqezes e no segexen la paraula de Deu e amen les terenals coses e meins preden les celestials. *Et aliut cecidit in terram bonam, et ortum fecit fructum centuplum.* Dix: aquela sement qui cadeg en la bona terra demostra lo cor del bon cristia, qui reten be la paraula de Deu e la ment en obra, co es, senes avareza e senes adulteri e senes escarn e senes neguna oreeza. Primerament no entenien los apostols de que nostre Seinor o dezie. E ia dixeren ad el. *Interrogabant autem discipuli eius que esset hec parabola.* Seiner trastot poderos, si a tu platz, fes.nos entendre aquesta paraula. E nostre Seinor dix ad els: *Vobis datum est nosse misterium regni Dei, ceteris autem in parabolis*: A vos es donad a conoxer lo mester del regisme de Deu, pus qe aqels qui . . . crezen per paraules. Donces, frares cars, rezebam la paraula de la predicacio de Iesu Crist en goig e retingams.la en nostre cor, que diable no la pusca gitar de nostre cor, et aixi farem fruit en paciencia senes nulla oreeza. Sapiats, seinor, que qui mas se trebalara dels afans de Deu en est segle,

XI, XII, XIII' (*Revista de bibliografía catalana*, iv, 1904). It has also been published by A. Griera, *Les Homilies d'Organyà* (*Vida Cristiana*, 1917). The text is difficult to read and has given rise to some doubtful transcriptions. We have therefore preferred to reproduce the text of the second sermon as recently checked from photostats by A. Monteverdi (op. cit., pp. 177–8).

maior gazardo n'aura el seu regisme. Donces, fraires cars, esforcem.nos
que.ls pecatz en qe somo nos lexen, e nostres penitencies prenam per
zo que Iesu Crist nos deu portar denant los angels el cel. *Quod ipse
prestet.*

There is nothing difficult or obscure in this homely exegesis of
a familiar theme. The symbol *x* represents the non-Latin sound [ʃ],
as in the orthography of the modern language; *ex*, from ĪPSE, is
nowadays *eix*, while *ix*, from ĔXIT, is still written in the same way.
In the vocabulary, *calzigad* 'trampled underfoot', is the past participle of a verb *calzigar*, which would appear to derive from a
*CALCICARE formed on the common V. Lat. *CALCEARE (Cast. *cal-
zar*, Cat. *calsar*, Prov. *causar*, Fr. *chausser*, &c.); *escarn* 'mockery',
the word which we have already encountered in the Port. *cantigas
de escárnio*, is a verbal substantive from *escarnir*, identical in Provençal, and corresponding to Old Fr. *escharnir* from Frank.
SKIRNJAN; *oreeza* 'squalor', 'debauchery', is a substantive formed
by the addition of *-eza* (< -ĬTIA) to the adj. *ore*, in Provençal orthography usually *orre*, from Lat. HORRIDUM (cf. Old Fr.
*ord*, whence the noun *ordure*); *gazardo* 'reward', is another migrating Germanism, obviously borrowed from Prov. *gazardo(n)*
(< Frank. WIDERLŌN, which French corrupted to *guerredon*, see
p. 263, note).

The influence of literary Provençal is still very marked, even in
this medium of local preaching. One might, in particular, pick out
a multitude of points of resemblance between the language of the
*Homilies d'Organyà* and that of the *Chanson de sainte Foi d'Agen*.
But this does not prove either that the latter is Catalan or that
the former is Provençal. In addition to the points of resemblance,
the *Homilies* are characterized by a few features, absent from the
*Chanson de sainte Foi*, which are specifically Catalan. Thus the
two-case declension which Provençal preserved in common with
Old French is here quite lacking, except for the vocative forms
*seiner* (sing.) and *seinor* (pl.), and these are most probably due to
the Catalan practice of adopting Provençal modes of address.
Prominently Catalan is the weakening of post-tonic *a* to *e* (ə in
eastern Catalan) where it is followed by a consonant: this gave rise
to feminine plurals in *-es* side by side with singulars in *-a*, e.g.
*males obres, espines, coses, paraules*, &c., and to plural verbal
flexions in *-en* corresponding to singulars in *-a*, e.g. *pensen, amen*
(< AMANT), but *demostra, semenava*. Yet another Catalan feature is

the reduction of the primary AU of Latin to *o* as in *coses*, and as in *goig* (< GAUDIUM, Prov. *gaug*). As for the treatment of the secondary AU of Vulgar Latin, our text, containing both *ocels* and *auzels* from the same AVICĔLLOS, reveals a hesitation which in fact persisted for a long time in Catalan; the language finally opted for *ocell*, which doubtless represents the popular tendency as opposed to the 'learned' influence exerted by Provençal, but it still keeps the *au* in *paraula* (< PARABOLA). The use of the series of conjunctive pronouns as disjunctives, a feature which links Catalan with Aragonese, is well illustrated by the phrase *si a tu platz*. Of what was probably the most striking acoustic difference between Catalan and Provençal, the maintenance in the former of unpalatalized Latin ū, the orthography gives, of course, no indication.

The standardization of Catalonia's national language was largely the work of her greatest king, James the First. In addition to developing the chancery use of vernacular prose, he was himself responsible for the first of the four 'great chronicles', the *Llibre dels feyts del rey En Jaume*. Perhaps it was this royal example and encouragement which induced Ramón Llull (1233?–1315?), born in Majorca where his father had settled in the wake of conquest, to write his copious works in Catalan rather than in Latin: by so doing he became the foremost among the authors of medieval Catalonia and may indeed be truthfully claimed as the first to have composed in a Romance tongue the serious literature of science and philosophy. Contemporary with Llull was Ramón Muntaner (1265–1336), a Catalan Villehardouin, who wrote the second of the 'great chronicles', the other two being those of Bernat Desclot, *Crònica del rey En Pere* (Pedro III), and of Bernat Descoll, *Crònica de Pere el Ceremoniós* (Pedro IV). These chronicles differ much in style, some revealing the personality of the author while others remain quite objective, but all are motivated by an intense patriotic fervour. By the end of the fourteenth century Catalonia was thus endowed with a full record of her achievements, a body of historiographical literature excelling that of any other country. The same period also saw the creation of a mass of political, religious, and juridical writing, among which might be mentioned the speeches of the *Corts*, the Catalan Parliament, and the *Llibre del Consolat de Mar*, which formed a basis for the later maritime codes of all Europe. Another great individual writer appeared during the latter half of the fourteenth century in the person of Bernat Metge (1350–1410), whose masterpiece, *Lo Somni*, is described by all critics as 'the purest model of Catalan prose'.

Increasing literary production culminated in the fifteenth century in a brief but brilliant 'Golden Age', insidiously accompanied by the social and political changes which presaged eclipse. In 1412 the strong dynasty of the Counts of Barcelona came to an end; the new ruler, Fernando de Antequera, was a Castilian whose favour inclined rather to Aragon than to Catalonia. Contact with the manners and literature of Italy brought new influences which penetrated Catalonia and thereafter Castile; and it is perhaps symptomatic of a decline in the authority of Barcelona that three of the outstanding Catalan writers of the age are Valencians: Joanot Martorell (b. between 1410 and 1420, d. after 1462, author of *Tirant lo Blanch*), Jaume Roig (d. 1479, author of the satirical *Llibre de les Dones*), and the poet Ausies March (1397–1459). The change in dynasty made possible the marriage of Ferdinand of Aragon and Isabella of Castile (1479), which, by uniting the two crowns, inflicted upon Catalonia, the predominant partner of the earlier union, a loss of independence from which she was never to recover. Thereafter Castile was in the ascendant, and Catalans abandoned their literary language for Spanish. The long period of effacement came to a partial end with the Romantic movement, when the scholars of Catalonia began to rediscover the literature of the past and to reveal it to a people which had never ceased to speak Catalan. There followed a revival of creative writing, producing a number of talented poets, among whom the priest Jacinto Verdaguer (1845–1902) is usually accorded the first place. During the present century the local philologists have elaborated the language, pruning, polishing, and enriching, to a degree of flexible standardization reminiscent of French. The Civil War brought a setback, from which Catalan as a literary medium is now beginning to recover.

Whatever political misfortunes befell Catalonia, the common tongue which took such firm root during the Middle Ages has always continued to be the only one known to the mass of the peasant population. Its boundaries are still those of the medieval county. In Aragon, although it certainly exercized a passing influence, it was never assimilated to replace the Aragonese dialect, already strongly marked by Castilian at the time of the union of Aragon and Catalonia; Muntaner, at the height of Catalan expansion, remarked upon the difference: 'si ben catalans e aragonesos són d'un senyor, la llengua llur no és una, ans és molt departida.' To the west the frontier is marked by the first Aragonese valley, that of the Ésera, an area of mixed speech which inclines in some of its features to Catalan and in others to Aragonese, the former element being perhaps the stronger. Within the compact linguistic territory of Catalan it is possible to distinguish an eastern and a western variety, the latter being due in the main to the attraction of Lérida, the site of an important medieval university. Roussillon, despite its cession to the French by the Treaty of the Pyrenees (1659), has remained obstinately Catalan, preserving many of the more archaic forms of the medieval language and creating within France a linguistic frontier which was certainly not so well defined in the time of the troubadours: no present-day traveller can fail to sense the change in atmosphere between Perpignan, on the one hand, and the Languedocian centres of Béziers and Narbonne, on the other. The small Pyrenean state of Andorra is also Catalan in speech. Only in the reconquered territory to the south, where Valencia dissociated her fortunes from those of Barcelona, has the local idiom tended to lose ground. The introduction of Catalan was in fact confined to the coastal strip, the hilly hinterland having been occupied during the Reconquest by the Aragonese, who readily accepted Castilian. Valencian does, however, continue to be spoken by the people, with an articulation distinguished by the term *apitxat*, and it has its literary devotees. Overseas, Catalan has persisted in the Balearics, with certain archaic features of which the most notable is the use of the definite article deriving from IPSE, *es* and *sa*, formerly much employed on the mainland and still surviving there in a few places (see p. 88). It has also left its mark in Sardinia, where the Catalans ejected the native inhabitants from Cagliari, to make it their administrative centre until in the sixteenth century it was taken over by the Castilians. The southern Campidanese dialect of Sardinia still contains numerous borrowings from Catalan, propagated from Cagliari (see p. 475). In the north-west of the island the more isolated settlement of Alguero, founded in 1355, has remained Catalan in character, a consequence of the rigorous policy of exclusion practised by the occupiers; its 12,000 inhabitants still speak an archaic type of Catalan, increasingly influenced by the neighbouring Sassarese dialect.

Modern standard Catalan, not greatly different from the norm of medieval literature, impresses the hearer, in contrast to Castilian and especially to Portuguese, by its very consonantal quality; this is apparent in print, as may be judged from the following sample:

Ha estat un dia deliciós, d'una vagarositat esponjosa, d'un silenci de meravella. De tant en tant, he tret el cap a fora. Tot era gris i somort; si de cas el cel s'obria, tot semblava tocat d'un color d'estany oxidat, lleugerament blavís. Com ahir, la mar ha semblat tot el dia adormida en la seva eterna indiferència.

(Josep Pla)

A brief scrutiny of this passage quickly reveals that the consonantalism of Catalan is due primarily to two features of vocalic evolution: the loss of post-tonic vowels other than *a* (*e* is sometimes to be found as a supporting vowel, e.g. *pare* < PATREM), and the relative absence of vocalic combination in diphthongs and triphthongs. In common with Provençal and Portuguese, Catalan eschewed spontaneous diphthongization: thus PĬLUM > *pèl*, CAELUM > *cel*, PRŎBA > *prova*, NEPŌTEM > *nebot*. Conditioned diphthongization took place as elsewhere, but by the time of the appearance of a native literary language many of the resultant combinations had already been reduced to pure vowels, e.g. *fet* (< FACTUM, cf. Prov. *fait, fach*), *llet* (< LACTEM, Prov. *lach*), *ix* (< ĒXIT, Prov. *eis, ieis*), *pit* (< PĔCTUS, Prov. *pieitz*), *nit* (< NŎCTEM, Prov. *nueit, nuech*). Moreover, as in Portuguese, a yod tended where possible to combine with a consonant rather than with a vowel, e.g. *vell* (< VĔCLUM, Prov. *vielh*), *ull* (< ŎCULUM, Prov. *uelh*), *fulla* (< FŎLIA, Prov. *fuelha*), &c. In this context it may also be noted that orthography sometimes creates the impression of diphthongs where in the modern language none exist, e.g. *vaig* < *VADEO, pronounced **batʃ**, *puig* < PŎDIUM, pronounced **putʃ**, and *mateix* < *METĬPSE, pronounced **məteʃ**. Vowel combinations do, nevertheless, occur in Catalan. If it lacks both the spontaneous diphthongization which characterizes Castilian and in large measure the diphthongs due to a yod which abound in Provençal and Old French, it compensates, as it were, by creating its own series, deriving from the agglutination of a stressed vowel with a *u* which may come from a variety of sources, including—an ancient peculiarity of Catalan—the vocalization of a voiced dental, e.g. *ou* < ŌVUM, *breu* < BRĔVEM, *viure* < VĪVERE, *palau* < PALATIUM, *clau* < CLAVUM, *niu* < NĪDUM, *peu* < PĔDEM, *veure* < VĬDĒRE, *creure* < CRĒDĔRE, *caure* < CADĒRE. Modern Catalan has even developed a *u* from the earlier *-ts* ending of the second person plural of verbs (< -TIS), e.g. pres. indic. *canteu, temeu, sentiu*; imperf. indic. *cantàveu, temíeu, sentíeu*, &c.

In its consonantal system Catalan accords with French and Provençal in maintaining intact the initial groups CL, FL, and PL, e.g. *clau* (masc. < CLAVUM, fem. < CLAVEM), *cloure* (< CLAUDERE), *flama* (< FLAMMA), *ple* (< PLĒNUM), *plorar* (< PLORARE). It also preserves L before T, as in *molt* (< MULTUM) and *escoltar* (< AUSCULTARE). On the other hand, it has created a new and very distinctive feature by palatalizing a single initial L, e.g. *llet* (< LACTEM), *llur* (< ILLORUM), *lluna* (< LŪNA), *lluny* (< LONGE, the graphy *ny* representing palatalized *n*). The fall of final *n*, already apparent in the *Homilies d'Organyà* (*gazardo, predicacio*, &c.), is general after a stressed vowel, and this fact gives a particularly Catalan character to a multitude of learned words, e.g. *traducció, compilació, versió, narració, intenció*, but plural *traduccions*, &c. Nasalization is quite absent.

Among morphological features are to be noted: the possessive plural *llur*, also found as *lur* in Aragonese; the persistence of INDE and IBI as *en* and *hi*, and of HOC in the commonly used neuter pronoun *ho* (the *h* of *hi* and *ho* is merely orthographical); the creation of a series of feminine possessive adjectives—*meva, teva, seva*, on the analogy of the masc. *meu*, &c.—in which the original *u* of Old Cat. *meua*, &c., has been consonified to β (cf. p. 85); and a new type of interrogative adjective—*quin, quina, quins, quines* (e.g. *Quina hora es?*)—which arose in consequence of the popular interpretation of the etymological *quina*, from QUI(S)NAM, as a feminine (see p. 97). Most of the above characteristics are, however, shared with the speeches of southern France. Something more specifically Catalan, which most strikes the foreigner on his first acquaintance with the language, is the so-called 'periphrastic perfect'. This tense, which in everyday conversation has now almost entirely replaced the perfects deriving directly from Latin, consists of the infinitive of the required verb preceded by the present tense of *anar* 'to go', but by a form of that tense in which the usual first and second persons plural—*anem, aneu*—have not

ousted the original *vam*, *vau* from the verb VADERE. Thus the full
periphrastic perfect is as follows:

vaig cantar, temer, sentir, &c.
vas    „    „    „
va     „    „    „
vam    „    „    „
vau    „    „    „
van    „    „    „

Appearing occasionally in texts of the fourteenth century, gaining
ground in the fifteenth, this tense looks and sounds as though it
should convey the same aspect of time as does the French *je vais
chanter*, &c. When first employed, it probably did. But in medieval
narrative, as indeed in dialectal conversation in our country, past
meaning is frequently expressed by the graphic 'historic present';
a typical example may be found in the recurring *il va ferir* of Old
French epic. As a result of this confusion the periphrastic tense
emerged in Catalan as a perfect tense, the parts of the verb *anar*
serving as flexions, and in this function it became a simple and
convenient substitute for the diversity of perfects which had
developed etymologically from the weak and strong forms of
Vulgar Latin. Once the mind has been adjusted to the apparent
absence of logic, this constitutes a most desirable concession to
the non-Catalan who wishes to converse in the language: but the
Catalan purist still clings in writing to the original tenses.

## ITALO-ROMANCE

*Italian disunity.* The Italian language developed in circumstances
quite unlike those which attended the growth of other Romance
languages, with the possible exception of Provençal. There was
in Italy no sudden response of the vernacular to the Carolingian
Renaissance, no startling appearance of a text written in a language
considerably different from Latin, and above all no one political
centre which, achieving a spectacular supremacy, compelled an
early acceptance of its standardized speech.

After the collapse of Frankish dominion Italy was soon involved
in a revival of the Germanic dream of an imperial west. Emulating
Charlemagne, Otto the Great of Germany succeeded in A.D. 936
in re-establishing the ties between the two territories in the Holy
Roman Empire, a political concept thereafter pursued with varying
degrees of achievement, most notably in the twelfth century by

the Emperor Frederick I, 'Barbarossa'. During the thirteenth century, when German preponderance declined, attempts were made to create a united Italy from its largest single realm, the Kingdom of Sicily, founded by the Normans (see p. 294). This kingdom had become attached to the Empire by the marriage of Henry VI, the successor of Barbarossa, to Constance, daughter of Roger II of Sicily. Frederick II (A.D. 1197–1250) received the joint inheritance, but after his death the kingdom again acquired a separate ruler in the person of Manfred, Prince of Taranto, an illegitimate son of Frederick, who, by the terms of his father's will, was to govern as representative of the legitimate heir to the whole succession, the Emperor Conrad IV. Assuming full authority, Manfred appeared as a national Italian leader and for a while had all the central area of Italy pledged to his support, but his efforts were ultimately frustrated, largely through the opposition of the Papacy. After his death in A.D. 1266 the southern throne passed to the House of Aragon through the marriage of his daughter, another Constance, to Pedro III.

More significant for the future of Italy than the universal aspirations and complicated manœuvres of Empire and Papacy, which being frequently in conflict created for the people a problem of divided allegiance, was the steady growth during this period of the larger cities, especially in the north. Indifferent to the pretentions of high authority, hostile to any attempt to curb their independent activity, they conducted their own policies of local expansion, the stronger seeking to absorb the weaker. Many came under the control of 'despots', powerful families such as the houses of Visconti in Milan, of Este in Ferrara, of Della Scala in Verona, of Gonzaga in Mantua, of Carrara in Padua. Those of central Italy, notably Florence, Perugia, and Siena, evolved into 'republics', the nobility being eliminated from government and replaced by the merchant class: this in response to the idea of the sovereignty of the people which was being propagated at the time, though, as the historian Guicciardini remarks of Florence, the passion for equality went hand in hand with the ambition of every family to be first, and the path of democracy thus led to social strife and new forms of tyranny. The maritime cities also developed into flourishing republics, in the west Genoa and Pisa, the latter to be subjugated by Florence in A.D. 1406, and in the east Venice, most prosperous of all.

As certain of these medieval states gained in strength at the expense of others, Italy in the fifteenth century had come to be largely partitioned between five seigniories of very different character: Milan and Venice in the north; Florence, dominated by the Medici, in the centre; to the south the former kingdom whose capital had been transferred from Palermo to Naples, with a consequent decline in Sicilian participation; and finally the Papacy, which recovered a lost authority after the Council of Constance (A.D. 1417) had eliminated three rival Popes and secured the unanimous recognition of Martin V. With the balance of power thus evenly distributed, there remained little possibility of national cohesion, and the land became an easy prey for French, Spanish, and Austrian invaders; only in A.D. 1859 was a unified kingdom of Italy finally established.

*First traces of the vernacular.* The relatively late appearance of any recognizable Italian standard was due in large measure to political circumstance, but also to the fact that Italy was the homeland of Latin. The spoken language evolved slowly from the late Vulgar Latin of the Empire, in close contact with the universal standard of medieval Latin, with the result that the problem of non-intelligibility presented itself less acutely and with less urgency than elsewhere. The conscious identification of new types of speech different from Latin was preceded by a long period of unconscious bilingualism. Each important centre then discovered its 'municipal' idiom, a fact which accounts for the vitality of local dialect to the present day.

Until the end of the twelfth century the surviving written evidence of Italo-Romance is very fragmentary and often difficult to interpret. Usually claimed as the earliest sample is the so-called 'Veronese riddle', two lines inscribed in an Italian handwriting of the late eighth or early ninth century, probably Veronese, on a Latin manuscript of Spanish origin, still preserved at Verona in the Biblioteca Capitolare. The early date would seem at first to give the lie to our remarks concerning the lateness of Italian, but in fact the 'riddle' comes nearly two centuries before any more substantial text, and it is too slight, too close to medieval Latin, to be of more than passing interest. As read by A. Monteverdi (*Studi medioevali*, 1937, pp. 304 ff.) it is as follows:

> Se pareba boves, alba pratalia araba,
> & albo versorio teneba, & negro semen seminaba.

A doubt subsists concerning the affiliation of the first verb: according to some scholars it is the imperfect of PARĒRE, and should therefore be read as 'it seemed' (cf. Ital. *pareva*), whereas for others, including Monteverdi, it is a dialectal form corresponding to PARABAT, and as such an indication of the place of origin of the couplet, since PARARE is still used in the region of Verona with reference to driving animals. If we adopt this latter suggestion the text may be translated: 'He drove oxen and ploughed a white field, and held a white plough and sowed black seed.' This is not, as was at first mooted, a fragment of a Georgic poem, but a typical medieval conundrum in which oxen, field, plough, and seed represent respectively the fingers of the hand, parchment, pen, and ink.[1]

Of the popular features here evinced, accusatives in -*o*, though indeed Italian, and the *e* of *negro* corresponding to Latin ĭ, are already familiar in the medieval Latin of the time. More noteworthy is the fall of final *t* in the forms of the imperfect tense; current usage also appears in the reflexive *se*, which Monteverdi takes as a dative corresponding to SIBI, and in the flexion of *pareba*, if this is correctly construed as PARABAT. The vocabulary contains two words of some significance, *versorio* and *pratalia*: the former shows a local choice of Lat. VERSORIUM instead of ARATRUM which is confirmed by the evidence of modern dialects, *versor* being still the normal word for 'plough' in the area of Verona, Padua, and Venice; the latter, a popular derivative of PRATUM, which should here be taken as feminine singular rather than neuter plural, persists in place-names, e.g. *Prataglia*, *Praglia*, &c., from Tuscany to Venice and beyond. Despite such apparent Latinisms as *boves* and *semen*, and the preservation of intervocalic *b*, the 'riddle'—presumably a relic of some scribe's 'doodling' or trying out his pen—has a certain flavour of Romance, but little more.

The next traces of Italian vernacular occur in Latin legal texts, and in consequence are more positive evidence, almost exactly dated. They consist, like the *Strassburg Oaths*, of brief attestations transcribed as spoken. Four such passages, similar in content,

---

[1] A riddle in similar terms is still current among the peasants of Aragon:

> Campo blanco
> simién negra,
> cinco güéis,
> e una rella.

(White field, black seed, five oxen, and a ploughshare; see A. Badía Margarit, *El habla del Valle de Bielsa*, p. 357.)

survive from the years A.D. 960–3, all belonging to the archives of Monte Cassino. They are as follows:

1. Capua, March, A.D. 960.

Sao ko kelle terre, per kelle fini que ki contene, trenta anni le possette parte sancti Benedicti.

This formula is used four times in the Latin text.

2. Sessa Aurunca, March, A.D. 963.

Sao cco kelle terre, per kelle fini que tebe mostrai, Pergoaldi foro, que ki contene, et trenta anni le possette.

This formula also occurs four times, with the slight difference that on the last three occasions *kelle terre*, plural, is replaced by *kella terra*, singular, and *contene*, third person singular, by *conteno*, third person plural.

3. Teano, July, A.D. 963.

Kella terra, per kelle fini que bobe mostrai, sancte Marie è, et trenta anni la posset parte sancte Marie.

4. Teano, October, A.D. 963.

Sao cco kelle terre, per kelle fini que tebe mostrai, trenta anni le possette parte sancte Marie.

The purpose of each of the four Latin documents is to confirm the claims of a particular monastery to certain lands: in the first the monastery is Monte Cassino, in the second San Salvatore di Sessa, and in the last two Santa Maria di Cengla. The witness is required to testify in each case, except the second, that the monastery has held the land for thirty years in undisturbed possession; in the second case it is a private individual, Pergoaldo, who has held the land for thirty years, and either left or sold it to the monastery. In making his attestation the witness held in his hand a plan of the land, described in the Latin text as an *abbrebiatura*, in which the boundaries were indicated. Elsewhere, similar formulae are recorded in Latin: thus in a document of A.D. 964 one finds, in almost identical terms: 'Scio quia illae terrae per ipsos fines et mensuras quas tibi, Paldafrit comes, mostravi, per triginta annos possedit pars sancti Vincencii.'[1] By having these terms rendered into Italo-Romance vernacular the monks doubtless sought to ensure that no possible counter-claimant could plead ignorance

[1] See A. Monteverdi, *Manuale di avviamento agli studi romanzi*, p. 134

of their meaning. That such a precaution should have been deemed necessary constitutes the first clear indication in Italy that peasants experienced some difficulty in following a text read out in medieval Latin, even in the 'advanced' medieval Latin which the clerks of the time employed. The earliest surviving scraps of Italian were thus prompted by the same consideration as was the French of the *Strassburg Oaths*.

Apart from a concession to notarial tradition in the use of Latin genitives to indicate possession, the texts are almost entirely vernacular. Typical of general Italo-Romance development are the preservation of post-tonic vowels and the fall of final consonants. Among the latter is -*s*, whence the adoption of Latin nominative forms as the customary plural (see p. 64), e.g. *kelle terre, trenta anni, kelle fini*; by the tenth century this was such an established feature that it even appears in the medieval Latin of Italy, as when, in the first of our documents, the clerk describing the line of the boundary writes: 'descendit super ipsi monticelli de Marri, et vadit ad ipsi pleski' (a word of doubtful origin meaning 'rocks'). Italian, too, is the development or maintenance of lengthened consonants, as in *anni, possette* (for *possedette*), and the completely popular *trenta*, from TRIGINTA (see p. 74). The passage of SAPIO to *so* is represented at an intermediate stage in the form *sao* (cf. FACIO > *fao, fo*; VADO > *vao, vo*). Some features point specifically to southern dialect. The reduction of **kw** to **k**, as in *kella* < ECCU ILLA, *ki* < ECCU HIC, is definitely non-Tuscan, but is still characteristic of Neapolitan. Also southern is the persistence of TIBI as *tebe*; and the unusual *bobe*, which might be VOBIS but is more probably due to the analogy of *tebe*, betrays its southern origin by the change of initial v to a *b*, in pronunciation almost certainly fricative. The absence of spontaneous diphthongization in *contene* (Ital. *contiene*) is consistent with the vocalism of the south.

After these brief but revealing formulae one encounters no further text written in vernacular on the Italian mainland until towards the end of the eleventh century (for the Sardinian *Privilegio logudorese*, see p. 475). Popular tradition then comes again to the surface in a piece of fairly sustained prose, the so-called *Formula di confessione umbra*, a stereotyped confession of a penitent followed by a form of absolution: this is in fact but a vulgarized adaptation of a Latin text of the kind which had been used in the Church for centuries before. Though so strongly marked by Latin influence as to be almost a mixture of the old and the new, it shows the typical features of Italian, together with a few local peculiarities consistent with its having formerly belonged to the monastery of Sant' Eutizio, near the Umbrian town of Norcia. Among these are the flexion -*ao* for the third person singular of the perfect tense, and the distinction between post-tonic -*o* and -*u*, as in the following extract: 'Me accuso de lu genitore meu et de la genitore mia, et de li proximi mei, ke ce non abbi quella dilectione ke mesenior Dominideu commandao,' i.e. 'I repent on account of my father and my mother, and my near relations, since I did not have for them that love which my Lord God commanded.'

During the twelfth century and the early part of the thirteenth, still in the absence of an Italian literary movement, the evidence becomes rather less scant but no less scattered. It includes such items as the fragments of a Florentine banker's account-book, discovered in the fly-leaves of a manuscript at the Biblioteca Laurenziana and bearing the date A.D. 1211; and the inscription recorded as having once been visible in the cathedral of Ferrara, giving its year of foundation as A.D. 1135, though whether the inscription itself was preserved in a twelfth-century form is doubtful: two versions are current (see Dionisotti and Grayson, *Early Italian Texts*, pp. 50–51), of which the following seems the more authentic:[1]

> Li mile cento trenta cenque nato
> fo questo templo a S. Gogio donato
> da Glelmo ciptadin per so amore
> e tua fo l'opera Nicolao scolptore.

Composed late in the twelfth century, if not in the thirteenth, is the first surviving relic of a vernacular poem of any substance due to an Italian, forty lines written on the last folio of another manuscript in the Biblioteca Laurenziana, and commonly known as the *Ritmo Giullaresco Toscano*. The text contains many lacunae and is difficult to read: one can gather little more than that the poet is singing the praises of a bishop and asking him for a horse, a theme of some interest in that it shows the begging *jongleur* to have existed at this time in Italy as elsewhere.

[1] All the texts here quoted have been edited many times. They are conveniently accessible in C. Dionisotti and C. Grayson, *Early Italian Texts*, Oxford, Blackwell, 1949. See also E. Monaci, *Crestomazia italiana dei primi secoli. Nuova edizione riveduta e aumentata per cura di F. Arese. Presentazione di A. Schiaffini*, Rome, 1955.

To find at last a lucid passage of sustained metrical verse in an Italian idiom one must turn again to the Provençal troubadour, Raimbaut de Vaqueyras. In his multilingual poem (see p. 387) the Genoese strophe, second in order, is as follows:

> Io son quel que ben non aio
> ni jamai non l'averò,
> ni per april ni per maio,
> si per madona non l'ò;
> certo que en so lengaio
> sa gran beutà dir non so
> chù fresca qe flor de glaio;
> per qe no m'en partirò.[1]

More than this, Raimbaut has left a *Contrasto bilingue*, an amusing composition in which the poet, applying all his conventional amatory technique, pays court in Provençal to a Genoese lady unversed in the code of gallantry, who rebuffs him in her native tongue with an asperity apparent from the two strophes which follow:

> Jujar, voi semellai mato,
> qe cotal razon tegnei.
> Mal vignai e mal andei!
> Non avei sen per un gato,
> per qe trop me deschasei,
> qe mala cosa parei;
> nè no faria tal cosa,
> si fossi fillo de rei.
> Credi voi q'e'sia mosa?
> Mia fe, no m'averei!
> Si per m'amor ve chevei,
> oguano morrei de frei:
> tropo son de mala lei
>             li Proenzal . . .
> Jujar, to proenzalesco,
> s'eu aja gauzo de mi,
> non prezo un genoì;
> no t'entend plui d'un toesco,
> o sardo o barbarì,
> ni non ò cura de ti.
> Voi t'acaveilar co mego?
> Si lo sa lo meu marì
> mal plait averai con sego.
> Bel messer, ver e' ve di':

[1] *Translation*:
I am he who has no vantage, and never will have, in April or in May, if it is not by my lady; true that in her language I cannot tell her great beauty, fresher than a sword-lily; wherefore I shall not leave her.

no vollo questo latì.
Fraello, zo ve afì.
Proenzal, va, mal vestì,
       largaime star.[1]

Although this verse undoubtedly contains Provençalisms, in general it typifies the local 'municipal' standard which the poet must have found in use in Genoa between A.D. 1190 and 1203. As in the Gascon strophe (see p. 390), he seems to dwell on those features which to his ear were most remarkable. The early part of the poem contains various examples of the passage in Genoese of PL- to *ch-* (tʃ), e.g. *chù* < PLUS, *deschasei*, in which the root verb is PLACĒRE (cf. Ital. *dispiacete*), and *chevei*, from the Germanic verb which became Old Fr. and Prov. *plevir* 'to pledge'; this is forgotten in the latter part, where one finds *plui* < PLUS, another Italian evolution, and *plait* < PLACITUM. More consistent is the reproduction of Genoese second person plural flexion, in which the -TIS of Latin is reduced to *-i*, e.g. *semellai* (Ital. *somigliate*), *tegnei* (Ital. *tenete*), *vignai, andei, avei, deschasei*. Whether consciously or not, Raimbaut de Vaqueyras in composing this poem provided Italian lyrists with a lesson, showing how their own idiom could be adapted to elegant verse in just the same way as Provençal; the example was ultimately followed, though at a distance.

*Dante and the Italian standard.* Italian literature came rather suddenly into its own from about the year A.D. 1225. This is the approximate date of composition of the *Laudes Creaturarum* of St. Francis of Assisi, whence there derived a tradition of *Laudi*, and an Umbrian school of poets in which the outstanding name is that of Jacopone da Todi (*c.* A.D. 1230–1306). Undatable, but certainly of the same period, are two longer religious poems, resembling one another in structure: an Italian life of St. Alexis, the *Ritmo di S. Alessio*, preserved in a text with Umbrian

---

[1] *Translation*:

*Jongleur*, you must be drunk to make such proposals. A plague on your comings and goings! You have not the sense of a cat, for you displease me greatly, and you seem nasty; I would not do such a thing even if you were a king's son. Do you think that I am mad? By my faith, you shall not have me. If you pledge yourself for my love, you will die of cold this year: the Provençals have very bad ways. . . .

*Jongleur*, if I am in my right mind, I give not a farthing for your Provençal. I do not understand you any more than a German, or a Sardinian, or a Barbary Coast man, and I am not interested in you. You wish to quarrel with me? If my husband knows of it, you will have a bone to pick with him. Fine sir, I tell you in truth, I do not want this language. Brother, of that I assure you. Go away, ill clad Provençal, let me be.

characteristics, and a rather enigmatic, mystical composition found at Monte Cassino, whence its conventional title, the *Ritmo Cassinese*. With their mixture of Latinism and dialectal peculiarity, and above all their homespun versification, these poems have a certain quality in common: like their earlier counterparts in French and Provençal, they breathe the atmosphere of the monastery. At the same time an entirely different kind of poem, the secular lyric, was beginning its florescence. While poets of the north such as Sordello (see p. 392) imitated the Provençal song in its own medium, those of the south, favoured by the protection of the most enlightened literary patron of the time, the Emperor Frederick II, became the first natives of Italy who are known to have employed an Italian vernacular for similar ends. They include some twenty-nine named poets, writing with all the technical skill of the troubadours. Though of diverse origin, on account of their association with the court they became 'Sicilian'. Yet their verse is for the most part written, at least in the form in which it has been preserved, in a standardized language which owes little to Sicilian dialect. It is a *koine* based on the usage of central Italy.

How did this *koine* come into being? Fundamentally, the problem of its genesis is very similar to that of Provençal, indeed almost identical, but in Italy it has acquired an added piquancy from the fact that it preoccupied the greatest literary genius of the age, the poet Dante (A.D. 1261–1321). In a Latin treatise, *De Vulgari Eloquentia* (c. A.D. 1303), he examined the whole problem at length, thereby initiating the debates on the *questione della lingua* which were to be taken up by later generations of Italians, and in their wake by Frenchmen, Spaniards, and Portuguese.

Dante's contribution to linguistics is almost the prototype of a university thesis. First he defines his subject, explaining what he understands by *vulgaris eloquentia*: it is the speech which 'sine omni regula nutricem imitantes accipimus'; to this is opposed *grammatica*, the secondary or acquired speech, which for Italians was Latin. Of the two, the *vulgaris eloquentia* is the more 'noble', because (a) it is the first to have been used by the human race, (b) it is universal, though divided into many different forms, (c) it is 'natural', whereas the other is 'rather artificial'. It is this 'more noble' speech which he, Dante, proposes to examine; to the best of his knowledge the subject has never been studied before.

Confronted with the age-old problem of the origin of speech,

Dante begins in true medieval fashion, finding the answer in the Book of Genesis, though he inclines to cast doubt upon the implication that the first person to speak was a woman, the *presumptuosissima Eva*, in her conversation with Satan; it would be more reasonable to suppose that so noble an act first came from the lips of man, and that the first word to be pronounced was 'God'. The original language was of course Hebrew. After the diversification resulting from the Tower of Babel, three different types of speech came to Europe: a northern type, the unity of which is shown by the common use of the affirmative particle *Jo* (i.e. Germanic *Ja*), an eastern type, and a south-western type. Thus from fundamentalist interpretation of the Bible he passes in a bound to a scientific recognition of the existence in Europe of the three groupings now identified as Germanic, Greek, and Romance. Still using the word for 'yes' as his criterion, he subdivides the third group: 'nam alii oc, alii oïl, alii sì affirmando locuntur' (ed. A. Marigo, p. 52; cf. p. 62, 'nam alii oc, alii sì, alii vero dicunt oïl'). Concentrating then upon *lingua di sì*, in what is perhaps the most remarkable part of the treatise, he proceeds to make a summary analysis of the linguistic state of Italy in his day.

Everywhere he sees diversity:

Quare autem tripharie principaliter variatum sit, investigemus, et quare quelibet istarum variationum in se ipsa varietur, puta dextre Ytalie locutio an ea que est sinistre, nam aliter Paduani, et aliter Pisani locuntur; et quare vicinius habitantes adhuc discrepant in loquendo, ut Mediolanenses et Veronenses, Romani et Florentini, nec non convenientes in eodem genere gentis, ut Neapolitani et Caetani, Ravennates et Faventini; et quod mirabilius est, sub eadem civilitate morantes, ut Bononienses Burgi sancti Felicis et Bononienses Strate Maioris. (op. cit., p. 66),

i.e. 'But let us investigate why it (Romance) should have been diversified principally in three different ways, and why each of these varieties should in itself be diversified, for example the speech of the right side of Italy from that of the left, for Paduans speak in one way and Pisans in another; and why those who live more close to one another yet differ in their speech, as do Milanese and Veronese, and Romans and Florentines, and even those who are gathered together in the same ethnic type, as the people of Naples and Gaeta, of Ravenna and Faenza; and what is still more remarkable, those who dwell in the same municipality, as the Bolognese of the Borgo di San Felice and the Bolognese of Strada Maggiore.'

For this situation he finds—how rightly!—a single reason: the volatile nature of the human being, *instabilissimum atque varia-bilissimum animal* (op. cit., p. 68). He recognizes, moreover, that linguistic investigation must be conducted not only on a geo-graphical plane, but also historically (or in present-day termino-logy, it must be both synchronistic and diachronistic):

Nam si alia nostra opera perscrutemur multo magis discrepare videmur a vetustissimis concivibus nostris quam a coetaneis perlonginquis. Quapropter audacter testamur quod, si vetustissimi Papienses nunc resurgerent, sermone vario vel diverso cum modernis Papiensibus loquerentur (op. cit., p. 70),

i.e. 'For if we examine other works of mankind, we seem to be much farther removed from the early inhabitants of our own town than from contemporaries in distant countries. Wherefore I make bold to say that if the ancient people of Pavia could now come back to life, they would converse with the modern Pavians in a different or diverse manner of speech.'

The terms of reference of modern linguistic geography could scarcely be stated more aptly. The only essential point which Dante seemingly fails to apprehend is that all these varieties are but later developments of spoken Latin.

Within Italy he recognizes the existence of dialectal groupings, and ranging from Istria to Sicily he distinguishes 'at least fourteen' different dialects (*vulgaria*), though continuing to insist upon the fact that none is entirely homogeneous. In addition to these local forms of speech there exists in his day a literary Italian, a kind of ideal norm which all good writers seek to make their own. The problem of the relationship between dialect and standard language being thus fairly planted, Dante asks himself, as does the modern philologist: Whence comes this norm, this *volgare illustre*? Is it basically one of the various dialects? He then surveys them all in turn, suggesting illustrations of their distinc-tive features and dwelling with particular attention upon those for which a reasonable claim might be put forward. Roman dialect is summarily dismissed as being of all the most ugly (here there is perhaps a hint of political prejudice). As for Bolognese, which calls for special consideration, Dante would not oppose those who hold it to be the most beautiful of municipal speeches: it has gained lustre by borrowing the best from its neighbours, i.e. by a certain local standardization. But it is not 'quod aulicum et illustre voca-mus'. If it were so, famous Bolognese poets such as Guido Guini-celli, the greatest, and others whom he names, would never have departed from their native idiom, whereas on the contrary they are most discriminating in their choice, using words never heard in the centre of Bologna. And what of the Tuscans . . . 'qui titulum sibi vulgaris illustris arrogare videntur?' Their pretentions, it is true, are upheld not only by the populace but also by several famous men, e.g. Guittone d'Arezzo, 'qui nunquam se ad curiale direxit'. In fact, these Tuscans do not write in the best Italian, and their rhymes, closely examined, prove to be 'municipal'. Tuscans need to be taken down a peg!

Whatever his predecessors wrote, he tells us, has come to be called 'Sicilian': 'quia regale solium erat Sicilia, factum est, ut quicquid nostri predecessores vulgariter protulerunt, sicilianum vocaretur' (op. cit., p. 100). This is a tribute to the 'illustrious heroes', the Emperor Frederick and his son Manfred, but when one examines the dialect spoken in Sicily one soon perceives that this is no *volgare illustre*.

The quest is thus deliberately brought to a negative conclusion. No specific part of Italy can claim to have nurtured the Italian literary standard. It partakes of all local speeches, and is therefore superior to all. Seeking to define its usage and characteristics, Dante describes it as *illustre*, because it has a certain sublime quality; as *cardinale*, because it is the hinge upon which the municipal speeches move, i.e. it represents the common factor; as *aulicum*, because if the Italians had a royal court, as other countries have, it would be the language of the Palace; and as *curiale*, because it is the language used for official purposes.

What can modern scholarship add to Dante's analysis of the pre-Dante standard? In truth, it can do little more than amplify. In one particular direction, various writers, notably E. Monaci, have laid greater stress upon the importance of Bologna. Its schools, already famous by the end of the tenth century, evolving into the corporations of students and teachers thereafter known as 'universities', at the time of the appearance of the first secular lyrics were attracting alumni from all parts of Italy. Many of the poets of the 'Sicilian school' are known to have studied there, many in fact were jurists: among the earliest are three who seem to have been companions, Pier della Vigna (c. A.D. 1180–1249), a native of Capua, the Sicilian Giacomo da Lentino, and the Tuscan Jacopo Mostacci. For the writing of lyrics, elegantly turned as befitted their academic training, they would naturally require an accepted linguistic practice. The one secular patronage which could provide suitable scope for their abilities, offering employment and sympathetic protection, was that of Frederick II. Like Charlemagne before him, the Emperor was unstinting in his encouragement of learning and the arts. Since Bologna lay outside his domains, he founded for the higher education of his subjects a new University at Naples (A.D. 1224), and a medical school at Salerno, which, with that of Montpellier, was to become the most celebrated in Europe. To these various cultural meeting-places the standard would seem to owe its elaboration, a *koine* based, like Provençal, upon the common features of linguistic usage in a central area.

In another direction, recent inquiry envisages the possibility that the use of the term 'Sicilian' may be of greater significance than the surviving evidence would imply. From the thirteenth century comes one complete lyric written in an almost pure Sicilian vernacular, by a poet known as Stefano Protonotaro da Messina (alive in A.D. 1261, died before A.D. 1301). It is preserved not in a *canzoniere* but in the *Arte del Rimare* of a sixteenth-century author, Giammaria Barbieri (A.D. 1519–74), who quotes it as an example of Sicilian, saying that it was taken from a 'libro siciliano'. No such 'libro siciliano' is extant, but Barbieri's original manuscript has now come to light, and modern scholarship, which tended at first to regard the poem as a later fabrication, is now disposed to accept its authenticity. It comprises in all sixty-six lines, beginning as follows:

> Pir meu cori alligrari,
> Chi multu longiamenti
> Senza alligranza e joi d'amuri è statu,
> Mi ritornu in cantari,
> Cà forsi levimenti
> Da dimuranza turniria in usatu
> Di lu troppo taciri.
> E quandu l'omu à rasuni di diri,
> Ben di' cantari e mustrari alligranza,
> Cà, senza dimustranza,
> Joi siria sempri di pocu valuri:
> Dunca ben di' cantar onni amaduri.[1]

[1] *Translation*:
In order to lighten my heart, which for a very long time has been without pleasure and joy of love, I return to song, for delay would perhaps turn easily into a habit of being too silent. When a man has something to say,

If genuine, this poem implies the former existence of a literary standard which was fully Sicilian, and none could point more obviously to the importance of Provençal precedent. Not only do the tone and subject-matter recall the Provençal conventions, but here is the word *joi*, with the technical meaning 'joy of love', a form of northern Provençal origin; here, too, is a repeated use of the Provençal ending -*anza*, as in *alligranza* (Ital. *allegria*), *dimuranza*, and *dimustranza*.

Even without Stefano's poem, one can still infer from rhymes that some of the best-known lyrics were originally composed in an idiom more southern than the *volgare illustre* in which they have survived, that their present form is due to 'correction' by the copyists of the *canzonieri*. In the typical specimen of pre-Dante verse which follows, the opening of a *canzone* attributed to Rinaldo d'Aquino and tentatively dated A.D. 1227, the unusual *li sospire* suggests a Sicilian rhyme *diri–suspiri*:

> Giamai non mi conforto,
> né mi voglio ralegrare;
> le navi so(no) giute al porto
> e vogliono colare,
> vassene lo piu giente
> in terra d'oltre mare:
> (ed io) oi me lassa, dolente,
> como degio fare?
> Vassene in altra contrata
> e no lo mi manda a dire,
> ed io rimagno ingannata:
> tanti sono li sospire,
> che mi fanno grande guerra
> la notte co' la dia![1]

Taking into account all the theories advanced, one may perhaps tentatively envisage the crystallization of an Italian standard as

he should indeed sing and show pleasure, for unless displayed, joy would always be of little avail: so it is right that every lover should sing.

[1] *Translation*:
Never more do I find comfort, nor do I wish to know pleasure. The ships are gathered in the harbour and are ready to set sail. The noblest of men is going away, to a land beyond the sea; and I, alas, poor wretched one, what should I do?

He goes away to another country, and does not send to tell me, and I stay behind, deceived. So many are the sighs that wage war upon me night and day!

*Note.* The reading *giute* (line 3) should perhaps be emended to *giunte*, i.e. 'arrived', but it could be a southern form of the past participle of *gire* 'to go', due to forms of IRE preceded by a yod, as EAMUS, cf. mod. Ital. *gita* 'excursion.'

follows: the Norman court of Sicily became a first focus of lyrical composition in the vernacular, in imitation of the courts of Provence with which it maintained close contacts. The latter part of the twelfth century is the appropriate time for such a beginning. In the absence of any *langue de prestige* on the Italian mainland, poets would find their standard in the local speech of Palermo, a standard destined to be submerged as the extension of Sicilian interests to the northern part of the kingdom brought it into contact with the *koine* then being forged in the schools of central Italy; with stronger backing, this latter became the *volgare illustre*, the medium for composition in verse, though the name 'Sicilian' remained. A final modification, a definitely Florentine stamp, was given by Dante himself. The *De Vulgari Eloquentia* contains no suggestion of a break with the past, no flamboyant proclamation of revolutionary reform such as characterizes Du Bellay's *Deffense et illustration de la langue française*. Dante recognized the standard of his day; but when one examines his use of the *volgare illustre*, as adapted in the *dolce stil nuovo*, one finds that, although it comports a few lexical elements from neighbouring speeches, it is predominantly the dialect of his own native city, embellished with book-words, Latinisms and Gallicisms. The great prestige which Dante's literary genius conferred upon the Tuscan of Florence, soon to be reinforced by the influence of other pre-eminent Florentine writers, notably Petrarch (A.D. 1304–74) and Boccaccio (A.D. 1313–75), ensured that this should be the basis of the standard Italian of the future.

In consequence of this late literary development, the Romance of Italy, unlike that of Gaul and Spain, produced only one recognized language; yet as another consequence, in the long absence of an overriding nationalism, Italian dialects have persisted in current use, never seriously menaced by enforced centralization until the present century. The standard itself, though codified during the Renaissance by various authorities, the most notable of which is the Florentine *Accademia della Crusca* (founded in A.D. 1582), has never been so repugnant to the use of alternative dialectal forms as have French and Spanish.

The Gallo-Italian speeches of northern Italy, though certain of their general features seem to have filtered southwards, remained during the early period somewhat apart, each pursuing its own separate 'municipal' development. Piedmontese is well attested from the end of the twelfth century, thanks to a manuscript containing the text of twenty-two sermons, now lodged in the Biblioteca Nazionale at Turin: as is consistent with the history of the region, the language appears more Gallic than Italian. Epic poems, adapted or imitated from French, were composed in a kind of Franco-Italian, among them a version of the *Chanson de Roland* preserved in a fourteenth-century manuscript now in the Library of St. Mark, at Venice. Venetian became widely used as a spoken standard: the *lingua franca* employed during the later Middle Ages in all the ports of the eastern Mediterranean included a considerable Venetian element. It also formed the basis of a north Italian *koine*, a literary standard represented in the work of a group of thirteenth-century didactic poets, in particular Uguccione da Lodi, Fra Giacomino da Verona, and Fra Bonvesin de la Riva, about whom very little is known. The outstanding Venetian of the times, Marco Polo (A.D. 1254–1324), preferred, however, to write the account of his travels in French. With no author or literary movement strong enough to confer upon its local *koine* the prestige of a language, northern Italy stood at a linguistic cross-roads, where the problem of which vernacular medium to use was ultimately solved only by the emergence of a worthy Italian competitor to French and Provençal.

Since the fifteenth century the invention of printing and the spread of literacy, accompanied by a universal interest in the different forms of Romance vernacular, have engendered new dialectal literatures sometimes comprising works of considerable literary merit. In this context the Neapolitan lyric calls for special mention: made world-famous in song as a result of the growth of Naples during the eighteenth century to be the musical capital of Europe, it continues to find poets of unusual talent, including, for instance, in recent years Salvatore di Giacomo (A.D. 1860–1934). But such manifestations of local linguistic vitality have never seriously impinged since the time of Dante on the recognized supremacy of Florentine Tuscan as the Italian standard. Academic debates concerning the *questione della lingua* became narrowed down to contention between the supporters of *italianità*, which meant observance of the standards set by the great writers of the past, and those of *fiorentinità*, who preferred to follow trends of later Florentine development.

*Characteristics of Italian.* As perusal of the *Linguistic Atlas of*

*Italy* would quickly show, local Italo-Romance dialects have evolved in various ways, but the norm with which we are primarily concerned has remained since the Middle Ages quite remarkably conservative. Some consideration having already been given (in Chapter I) to the shaping of its typical morphology, we shall here examine those features, sound-changes in particular, which thereafter contributed most conspicuously to create its individuality among the Romance languages.

The pure vowels present no difficulty: when tonic, the seven of Italian are virtually identical with the seven of western Vulgar Latin (see p. 43); when not tonic they are five, again as in Vulgar Latin. The diphthong AU, though retained as in Provençal in some southern dialects, including Sicilian, was in Tuscan reduced to ɔ, e.g. CAUSA > *cosa*, AURUM > *oro*. Spontaneous diphthongization produced no further result than the early change of the half-open tonic vowels, ɛ becoming iɛ and ɔ becoming uɔ, e.g. PĔDEM > *piede*, FŎCUM > *fuoco*; this did not, however, occur regularly in proparoxytones, where the time spent in the articulation of the tonic vowel is relatively less than in shorter words, e.g. HĔDERA > *edera*, PŎPULUM > *popolo* (contrast Fr. *lierre, peuple*). As in French, diphthongization took place only when the vowel was free.

Medieval Italian is nevertheless rich in diphthongs, which, in contrast to those of medieval French, have persisted with little change to the present day. They are mostly of the conditioned type, due to combination of another vowel with *i* or *u*, which have come to have the value of semi-consonants (**j** and **w**). The *i* may be Latin in origin, as in *lei, lui, rabbia, abbia*; it may derive from final -S (see p. 51) as in *poi* < POS(T), *noi* < NOS, *stai* < STAS; or it may be due to Romance palatalization of L after a consonant (see p. 467), as in *più* < PLUS, *pieno* < PLĒNUM, *chiave* < CLAVEM, *piove* < PLŎVIT (for PLUIT). The *ie* of *pieno* is now identical in pronunciation with the spontaneous diphthong of *piede*, the half-close vowel of PLĒNUM having been opened in quality to change the unusual **je** into the **jɛ** which Italian already knew. The back semi-consonant survives in Tuscan from Latin QU before A, e.g. *quale, quattro, uguale* (< AEQUALEM), though not before other vowels, cf. QUID > *che*, QUAERERE > *chiedere* (Old Ital. *cherere*; for the dissimilation of *r . . . r* to *d . . . r*, cf. *fiedere* < FERERE for FERĪRE). It also survives from GU, e.g. LĬNGUA > *lingua*, SANGU(IN)EM > *sangue*, and occurs in the derivatives of compounds formed with

ECCU, e.g. *questo, quello, qui.* The rendering of Germanic initial w by *gu-* increased its incidence still further, cf. *guardare, guerra, guida.* Popular development has not normally created words in which the back semi-consonant occurs as the second element in combination with a vowel, though this inverse order is to be found in some learned borrowings such as *rauco, Europa,* &c. Triphthongs, not generally in favour, have in a few instances resulted from the fusion of a semi-consonant with a diphthong of spontaneous origin, e.g. *miei, suoi.* Unlike French in that it has created no noticeably new vowels and totally rejects nasalization, Italian seems nevertheless to exploit most of the vocalic possibilities inherited from Vulgar Latin.

In the evolution of tonic vowels there is one Florentine peculiarity which calls for mention: a tonic half-close vowel (e or o) tends to become the corresponding close vowel (i or u), before the group formed of nasal plus velar consonant, whatever vowel may follow, or before the palatals λ and ɲ, e.g. LĬNGUA > *lingua,* EXPĬNGERE > *spingere,* VĬNCTUM > *vinto,* ŬNGULA > *unghia,* JŬNCUM > *giunco,* CONSĬLIUM > *consiglio,* PŬGNUM > *pugno,* &c. This seems to be a kind of metaphony, or *Umlaut,* similar to the effect of the yod on Castilian vowels (see p. 419). So far is it from being a phenomenon of wide diffusion that even other parts of Tuscany show in such words the more usual development, and this doubtless accounts for the numerous exceptions to the general rule which are customary in the standard language, e.g. *degno* < DĬGNUM, *legno* < LĬGNUM, *vergogna* < VERECŬNDIA, *tronco* < TRŬNCUM, and *spegnere,* a doublet of *spingere* said to have been introduced from Sienese by Dante.

Of pretonic vowels, E closed to *i,* e.g. SECŪRUM > *sicuro,* NEPŌTEM > *nipote*; followed by a labial consonant, both E and I have passed to *o,* e.g. DEBĒRE > *dovere,* DE MANE > *domani,* SIMILIARE > *somigliare.* Pretonic O has usually closed to *u,* e.g. OBEDĪRE > *ubbidire,* COQUĪNA > *cucina,* HOC ANNO > *uguanno,* BOTĔLLUM > *budello*; in this instance, however, exceptions in which O remained intact are quite numerous and point to a period of hesitant usage, still perpetuated in some words, e.g. CULTĔLLUM > *cultello* or *coltello,* OLĪVA > *uliva* or *oliva.* Pretonic AU was early reduced to *u,* e.g. AUDĪRE > *udire,* AUCELLUM (for AVICĔLLUM) > *uccello.* Pretonic A remains unchanged.

Unchanged, too, are the four post-tonic vowels, *a, e, i,* and *o,* except that the last of these has assumed a more open quality; the fifth vowel, *u*, was assimilated in Tuscan to *o* at an early date. As the lines quoted from Stefano Protonotaro show, Sicilian and other dialects of the south, combining post-tonic *e* and *i* as *i*, and post-tonic *o* and *u* as *u*, are in this respect notably different. The regular persistence of vowels at the end of every word, elision being permissible only within the phonetic group, e.g. *siam per-duti, lasciar tutto*, &c., is one of those features which serve most obviously to characterize Italian.

Examining the consonantal system in quest of what is most characteristic, we can with some justification single out two of its tendencies: gemination and the proliferation of affricates.

Standard Italian differs from all other Romance languages, as also from Gallo-Italian, in that it not only retained in general the geminated (i.e. lengthened or 'double') consonants of Latin, e.g. *secco, anno, fiamma, mettere, villa*, but also doubled many of those which were formerly 'single'; this occurs notably after the accent, e.g. *acqua, doppio, occhio, femmina, macchina, collera*, but also on occasion before the accent, as in *cammino, sollazzo*, and in many words formed with a prefix, e.g. *allora, innamorare*. The tendency was probably stimulated by the example of geminated consonants due to various consonantal assimilations, e.g. FACTUM > *fatto*, NŎCTEM > *notte*, CIVITATEM > *città*, IPSUM > *esso*, OBSERVARE > *osservare*, DUBITARE > *dottare*, APTUM and ACTUM > *atto*, ET PURE > *eppure*, AUT VERO > *ovvero*, AUT *SIAT > *ossia*, and combinations of consonant with yod which produced geminated affricates, as in PALATIUM > *palazzo* (see below). Gemination having become a habit there seems in modern Tuscan to be no end to it, and in the case of consonants which are etymologically 'single', no fixity of usage: from the standpoint of the purist, gemination in many words may be considered as 'optional'!

Non-Latin consonants which appear in Italian, where all Latin consonants except H were retained, include a z due to the voicing of intervocalic s (as in *usare*, though the voicing is not general, see below, p. 468), the palatal λ and ɲ, the alveolar fricative ʃ (its voiced counterpart ʒ occurs only in a variety of pronunciation which reduces tʃ and dʒ to ʃ and ʒ respectively), and most conspicuously the affricates, dental ts and dz, and alveolar tʃ and dʒ.

The alveolar affricates arose in the first instance from the palatalization of velar plosives k and ɡ before i and e (see p. 53);

at some stage in its development initial g̑ was joined by initial j, e.g. CAELUM > *cielo* (tʃɛlɔ), GENTEM > *gente* (dʒɛnte), JŬNCUM > *giunco* (dʒunkɔ). When intervocalic, these consonants palatalized in the same way, e.g. PACEM > *pace*, LEGEM > *legge*, SIGILLUM > *suggello*, PEJUS > *peggio*, PEJOREM > *peggiore*, though before the accent g̑ has often disappeared, e.g. PAGENSE > *paese*, MAGISTRUM > *maestro*. The incidence of affricates in the language was then greatly augmented by the evolution of certain internal groups in which the second element was a yod. This was the Vulgar Latin yod due to closing of ı or ᴇ between consonant and following vowel, the sound which had such decisive effects on the vocalic system of French, but which in Italian left the vowels unaffected, its only influence in this respect being conservative, since in combination with a consonant it created a block. After some consonants the yod remained as in Vulgar Latin, e.g. HABEAT > *abbia*, SAPIAT > *sappia*, VINDĒMIA > *vendemmia*; the groups which produced affricates, incidentally setting orthographical problems for the scribes, are as follows (to simplify, we ignore gemination):

| | |
|---|---|
| T plus yod > **ts** | e.g. PŪTEUM > *pozzo*, PRĔTIUM > *prezzo*, PLATEA > *piazza*, PALATIUM > *palazzo*, STATIONE > *stazzone*,*ALTIARE > *alzare*, MARTIUM > *marzo*, ABSENTIA > *senza*. |
| but also > **dʒ** | e.g. RATIONEM > *ragione*, PRETIARE > *pregiare*, STATIONE > *stagione*. |
| and preceded by a plosive consonant > **tʃ** | e.g. CAPTIARE > *cacciare*,*TRACTIARE > *tracciare*, *GUTTIARE > *gocciare*. |
| D plus yod > **dz** | e.g. MĔDIUM > *mezzo*, RADIUM > *razzo*, MŎDIUM > *mozzo*. |
| but also > **dʒ** | e.g. HŎDIE > *oggi*, PŎDIUM > *poggio*, VĬDEO > Old Ital. *veggio*, -ĬDIARE > -*eggiare*, RADIUM > *raggio*, MŎDIUM > *moggio*. |
| C plus yod > **tʃ** | e.g. FACIA (for FACIES) > *faccia*, GLACIA (for GLACIES) > *ghiaccia*, *ghiaccio*, BRACHIUM > *braccio*, ECCE HOC > *ciò*, -ACEUM > -*accio*, as in *popolaccio*. |
| G plus yod > **dʒ** | e.g. EXAGIUM > *saggio*, PLAGIA > (*s*)*piaggia*, CORRĬGIA > *correggia*, REMĬGIUM > *remeggio*. |
| S plus yod > **tʃ** | e.g. CASEUM > *cacio*, BASIUM > *bacio*, CAMĪSIA > *camicia*. |
| but also > **dʒ** | e.g. OCCASIONE > *cagione*, PRESIONE (for PREHENSIONEM) > *prigione*, SEGŪSIUM (see p. 310) > *segugio*, CERĒSEA > *ciriegia, ciliegia*. |

The twofold developments observable in this table have been explained in various ways. In the case of s plus yod Meyer-Lübke suggested that the resultant affricate was voiceless after the accent and voiced before the accent; but as with the development of voiceless intervocalic plosives, for which he supplied a similar explanation (see p. 50), there are many exceptions to disprove the rule. The inconsistencies are more probably of geographical origin, again pointing to the relatively composite nature of Italian. Resultant doublets are differentiated semantically, e.g. *stazzone* 'shop', and *stagione* 'season' (the learned *stazione* provides a third Italian representative of the same word); *moggio*, a measure for grain (cf. Old Fr. *muid*, Span. *almud*, see p. 286) and *mozzo* 'hub' (cf. Fr. *moyeu* < MODIOLUM); *raggio* 'ray', and *razzo* 'spoke'. G. Rohlfs suggests that the *-zz-* forms, *mozzo* and *razzo*, came from dialects to the north of Tuscany with the technical vocabulary of vehicle-building, though admitting that this will scarcely account for *mezzo* < MĔDIUM (*Historische Grammatik der italienischen Sprache*, vol. i, p. 455).

Apart from the complications induced by the Vulgar Latin yod, the history of Italian consonants shows few major changes. All initial consonants other than C, G, and J remained intact. So, too, did most initial groups, though in the case of consonant plus L the latter phoneme was palatalized, as in the Iberian Peninsula, and indeed more consistently, the final result in Italian being j, e.g. PLANUM > *piano*, PLĒNUM > *pieno*, BLANCUM > *bianco*, CLAVEM > *chiave*, GLACIA > *ghiaccia*, FLAMMA > *fiamma*; internally these combinations developed in the same way, e.g. DUPLUM > *doppio*, FIBŬLA > *fibbia*, ŎCULUM > *occhio*, VECLUM (for VĔTULUM) > *vecchio*, ŬNGULA > *unghia*. The new consonant ʃ evolved from SC followed by E or I (whence the traditional spelling *sc*, *sci*), from ST plus yod, and from initial EX or intervocalic X, e.g. PĪSCEM > *pesce*, (DE)SCENDERE > *scendere*, ANGŬSTIA > *angoscia*, POSTEA > *poscia*, EX-ELIGERE > *scegliere*, EXAMEN > *sciame*, LAXARE > *lasciare*, MAXILLA > *mascella* (though intervocalic x sometimes became s, e.g. SAXUM > *sasso*, DIXI > *dissi*).

Voiceless intervocalic consonants were sonorized in the north but retained in the south, with the mixed results in the standard language which we have already noted: hence *nipote* but *povero* (< PAUPERUM), the b due to voicing of Latin P having become involved in the normal evolution of intervocalic B to V, as in HABĒRE > *avere*, TABULA > *tavola*; similarly, *mutare* but *strada*, *amico* but *lago*. In accordance with the tendency attested in the *Appendix Probi* (see p. 31), the original intervocalic v of Latin has in some words completely disappeared, particularly before a back vowel, e.g. RĪVUM > *rio*, *PAVURA > *paura* (but PAVŌREM > *pavore*), PAVŌNEM > *paone* (but also *pavone*); on the other hand, a non-etymological v has sometimes been introduced, sporadically as in Gallo-Romance, between vowels in hiatus, e.g. RUINA > *rovina*, VIDUA > *vedova*, GENUA > *Genova*. Intervocalic D was in general unchanged, as was also intervocalic G when followed by a vowel other than E or I, e.g. VIDĒRE > *vedere*, AUGŬSTUM > *agosto*. Intervocalic s, like the voiceless occlusives, was voiced in the north and retained in the south, with resultant varying usage in Tuscan: thus *cosa*, *casa*, *naso* are normally pronounced with s, whereas z is the rule in *caso*, *viso*, *usare*.

The new consonants λ and ɲ, written *gli* and *gn* respectively, both derive from internal groups. The former is the outcome of L plus yod, including L plus palatalized G, e.g. FŎLIA > *foglia*, FĪLIUM > *figlio*, MŬLIER > *moglie*, MĔLIUS > *meglio*, EX-ELIGERE > *scegliere*, COLLIGERE > *cogliere*; as in Spain, and as happened earlier in France, λ is frequently reduced to j in current speech. The groups GN and N plus yod, including MN plus yod, are the principal sources of ɲ, e.g. LĬGNUM > *legno*, CASTANEA > *castagna*, VINEA > *vigna*, SOMNIUM > *sogno*, BALNEUM > *bagno*.

Final consonants were completely eliminated, all at an early date, as the evidence of the first Italian texts has shown. There seems to have developed thereafter among the population of central Italy a subconscious conviction that all words must end in a vowel. Thus the third person plural of verbs, e.g. SUNT, PORTANT, having lost its T to end in -*n*, cf. Old Ital. *son*, *portan*, became adapted to the general scheme through the acquisition from the first person of an analogical -*o*, whence *sono*, *portano*. Foreign words borrowed into Italian, even the most recent, almost invariably undergo this process of acclimatization: 'jeep' is *gippe*, 'penicillin' is *penicillina*. Though the accentual pattern evolved from Latin has been modified by the admission of a few oxytones such as *città* and *virtù*, due to haplological reduction of *cittade de* and *virtude de*, the typical Italian word may be described as a paroxytone or proparoxytone beginning usually with a consonant and ending with a vowel. This is in marked contrast both with the oxytonic system of French and the accentual variety of Spanish (see p. 279).

The continuing resemblance of Italian word-rhythm to that of Latin made the enrichment of the literary language by the incorporation of Latin loan-words an obvious and easy undertaking. Many of the Latinisms first employed by Dante, Petrarch, and Boccaccio found root in the spoken language, and with the following centuries the number of such words steadily increased, creating a lexicon in which the division into 'learned' and 'popular' is much less apparent than in French. The fact that a word entered the language more probably through learned channels can often be detected only by the quality of a vowel. For example, *crudele* (< CRUDĒLEM) seems to be 'learned' because its stressed vowel is normally pronounced as the half-open ɛ; in the case of *fedele* (< FIDĒLEM), on the other hand, a 'correct' pronunciation requires the half-close vowel, the quality of which is consistent with popular evolution. Reference to other Romance languages will confirm that FIDĒLEM belonged essentially to the spoken idiom (cf. Old Fr. *feeil*), whereas CRUDĒLEM was 'bookish'. Yet in listening to present-day Italian one may well hear **fedέ:le** instead of **fedé:le**; such fluctuations between the half-open and half-close vowels in the stressed syllable are by no means uncommon and are due in large measure to the uncertainties consequent upon the merging of 'learned' words into the stream of popular evolution.

The extent to which a popular form differs from a corresponding learned form necessarily depends upon the susceptibility to change of its component phonemes; not all have remained in the traditional development of Italian so close to the Latin as has *fedele*: no difficulty arises in distinguishing, for example, between 'popular' *credevole* and 'learned' *credibile*.

Accretions to the Italian lexicon from sources other than Latin, both literary and non-literary, have been continuous and extremely varied, though no single event has provoked an avalanche of new words as did the Frankish invasion of Gaul, or the Arabic occupation of Spain. The linguistic residue of similar occurrences in Italy was, as we have seen, on a lesser scale. Greek elements, already so numerous in Latin, continued to enter the language from various directions, difficult to disentangle; among the few words commonly attributed to Byzantine rule is *paggio*, a young servant, already current as *page* in thirteenth-century French. Above all,

Provençal and Old French have left their mark. The former contributed many terms associated with courtly life and behaviour,
e.g. *losenga* or *lusinga*, *miraglio*, and words in *-anza* (cf. p. 460),
of which *accordanza* and *baldanza* have persisted in present-day
usage, and in *-aggio* (Prov. *-atge*), e.g. *coraggio*, *linguaggio*, *van-
taggio*, *viaggio*. The full number of words of Gallic provenance is
difficult to assess on account of the completeness with which they
have been assimilated, but some are clearly stamped as Old French
by the palatalization of c and g before A, e.g. *marciare*, *mangiare*
(the Old Italian form was *manicare*), *gioia*, *gioiello*: in the case of
the two latter the diphthong *oi* from the AU plus yod of GAUDIUM
is another unmistakable pointer. Gallo-Romance sound-change is
also apparent in the suffix *-iere*, corresponding to -ARIUM, as in
*cavaliere*, *barbiere*, *carpentiere*, *parrucchiere*, &c.; in Tuscan the
same suffix evolved to *-aio*, e.g. *calzolaio* (< CALCEOLARIUM) 'shoe-
maker', *carbonaio* (< CARBONARIUM), and in the south to *-aro*, e.g.
*calzolaro*, *carbonaro*. Spanish occupation also brought its lexical
quota, e.g. *alcova*, *mantiglia*, *negro*, *ginnetto*. Meanwhile, the standard language continued to absorb elements from various Italian
dialects, e.g. *lido* (< LĪTUS) from Venetian, *prua* (< PRŌRA) from
Genoese, *cavolo* (< CAULUM, for CAULEM) and *fanciullo* (< IN-
FANTEOLUM) from Naples, the last-named having ousted Old Ital.
*fancello* (< INFANTICELLUM). Its present capacity for neologisms,
chiefly from English, is quite remarkable.

*Italian influence.* Reciprocal borrowing between the Romance
languages during the final period of standardization concerns
above all France and Italy, the participation of Spain and Portugal
being by no means negligible but less important.

Until the end of the thirteenth century the preponderant factor
was the radiation of Gallo-Romance, but the rapid emergence of
cultural centres in Italy provoked thereafter an inverse trend which
culminated in the Italianism of the French Renaissance. The details of this period in Franco-Italian history are too well known to
be repeated here. We need only recall its linguistic effect upon
French, an influx of new lexica almost comparable in importance
with the aftermath of Frankish invasion, though different in character, its impact being apparent not in the rustic terminology of the
country-side but in the social jargon of the court and the large
towns. The Italian contribution to French is primarily the language of 'specialists', of those who dealt in the technicalities of the

arts and sciences, of war and politics, or of the growing 'big business' of the day, with its banking and seafaring. To the first category belong such words as *artisan, balcon, bronze, cabinet, carrosse, costume, façade, mosaïque*; to war, many terms of which the following are but a few: *alerte, attaquer, barricade, bastion, bataillon, caporal, cavalerie, colonel, escalade, escorte, espion, parapet, pistolet, révolte, sentinelle*; to banking: *banque, banqueroute* (Ital. *bancarotta*), *crédit, douane, faillite, million, trafic*, and probably *réussir* (Ital. *riuscire*); to seafaring: *boussole, bourrasque, frégate, galère, pilote, proue*; to courtly circles might be attributed *caresse, courtisan, cortège, intrigue, gazette, mascarade, pédant*.[1]

Despite their specialist character, many of the Italian loan-words gradually penetrated to every social milieu. Witness, for example, the success of the Italian *pantalon*, which, from small beginnings as a nickname applied to the long-trousered Venetians whose patron was San Pantalone, came to France with Italian comedy and eventually solved a long-standing problem of masculine attire and its nomenclature (cf. p. 240). In a different sphere the Old Fr. *soldier* (< SOLIDARIUM), or *soldoier*, and later with a Germanic suffix, *soudard*, now became the Italianate *soldat* (Ital. *soldato* < SOLIDATUM); he doubtless played his part in the diffusion of the new military terms. Words of abusive implication, always quick to spread (cf. p. 289), include *charlatan, baladin, bouffon, intrigant, poltron, poltronnerie, forfanterie, spadassin*—all quoted by Henri Estienne (see below) who contends that such notions were unknown to the French before their contact with the Italians, and for that reason unrepresented in the language.

Italian loan-words were invariably adapted to the pattern of French. Thus acclimatized, most of them have persisted, some as doublets of French words of similar origin, e.g. *cadence* (Ital. *cadenza*), side by side with *chance*, both from CADENTIA: in medieval French *cheance* had assumed its present meaning on account of its association with the falling of dice, a semantic change well illustrated in the following thirteenth-century lines quoted by Littré:

> Tornee lor est la cheance
> Du dé en perte et mescheance;

*médaille* (Ital. *medaglia*), from \*MED(I)ALIA, which in Old French

---

[1] Cf. A. Ewert, *The French Language*, pp. 297–8, and B. H. Wind, *Les Mots italiens introduits en français au XVIe siècle.*

had become *meaille* and as the designation of a small coin persists in the expressions *avoir maille à partir avec quelqu'un*, and *n'avoir ni sou ni maille*; *escale* (Ital. *scala*), the French development of SCALA being *échelle*; here the Italian word was borrowed only in its special reference to disembarkation, in the expression *faire escale*, already used by Rabelais in a half-assimilated form: 'je retourne faire scale au port dont je suis issu.' In a few instances an Italian word modified its French cognate, particularly when the principal difference lay in the Italian retention of a k which in French had been palatalized, e.g. Old Fr. *marchis, eschiver, meschin, embuschier* (cf. Eng. *ambush*), were replaced by *marquis, esquiver, mesquin, embusquer*. Fundamental changes of meaning due to Italian influence are reflected in the present use of *loge*, originally Germanic (cf. p. 239), also in *mesquin*, nearer to the sense of the original Arabic, since *meschin* in Old French was chiefly used as a common term for 'small boy', 'servant' (cf. p. 289).

Of primary importance, at this stage in the history of the Romance languages, was the spread of the Italian-inspired idea of deliberate cultivation of the vernacular standards. By writing *De Vulgari Eloquentia* Dante had provided his compatriots with a cue for endless speculation on this score, and it was from an Italian, Sperone Speroni, that Joachim du Bellay borrowed, without acknowledgement, the essential material of *La Deffense et illustration de la langue française* (1549), the commonly recognized starting-point of French classicism. Less than thirty years later, in the work of Henri Estienne,[1] the defence of the French language had become a matter of highly nationalistic interest, its superiority over Italian being asserted with vehemence, and with a satirical denial of the indebtedness of the French lexicon to Italian with which the facts do not accord. Both by immediate influence and through the creative reaction which this influence stimulated, Italy contributed largely to the conscious moulding of the literary language which produced the 'modern French' of the seventeenth century.

A Spaniard living in Italy, Juan de Valdés, was similarly inspired to enrich his native tongue after the Italian manner, though with less practical effect. In his *Diálogo de la lengua*, written *c.* A.D. 1535—some time, that is, before Du Bellay's more famous

---

[1] *Deux dialogues du noveau langage français italianisé*, 1578; *Projet du livre intitulé: De la précellence du langage françois*, 1579.

treatise—but not published until A.D. 1737, he states his plans for the improvement of Spanish and envisages borrowing from other languages, among them Italian:

> De la lengua italiana desseo poderme aprovechar para la lengua castellana destos vocablos: *facilitar*, *fantasía*, en la sinificación que lo tomáis acá, *aspirar* por tener ojo, como quien dice: *Cada cardenal aspira al papado*; *dinar*, *entretener*, *discurrir* y *discurso*, *manejar* y *manejo*, *deseñar* y *deseño*, *ingeniar* por inventar con ingenio, *servitud*, *novela* y *novelar*, *cómodo* e *incómodo*, *comodidad*, *solacio*, *martelo* porque no parece que es lo mismo que celos, *pedante* y *assasinar*.

> (Ed. *Clásicos castellanos*, pp. 138–9)

Certain of these terms appear to come directly from Latin rather than from Italian, but most count among the recognized Italianisms of Spanish: a result which can scarcely have been procured by an unknown manuscript. The author seems in fact to have been compiling a list of neologisms which he knew to have been used by Spanish translators and imitators of Italian literature. This was the chief medium of entry for Italianisms into Spanish and Portuguese, and for the most part they have remained literary, though the military and commercial relations of the time brought to the Iberian Peninsula a few of the kind which are more or less international, e.g. Span. *centinela*, *escopeta*, *parapeto*, *piloto*, *banca*.

Through popular channels came Span. *bisoño* 'raw', 'undisciplined', from Ital. *bisogno* 'I need', which seems to have been applied as a nickname to the Spanish soldier in Italy. With due reservation we venture to suggest that Span. *bizarro* 'brave', recalling Ital. *bizzarro* 'irascible', 'quarrelsome' (cf. p. 179, note), may have followed a similar route, a circumstance which would account for the semantic transition; as for its French equivalent *bizarre*, it is of interest to note that of the first two examples recorded by Littré the *bigearre* employed by Des Periers has the Italian meaning, whereas the *bisarre* applied to soldiers by Lanoue no less clearly means 'brave', whence one can perhaps infer that the word reached France both directly from Italy and via Spain.

*Sardinian.* The fortunes of standard Italian were slow to exert any influence in the island of Sardinia. For considering Sardinian as a language apart we have all the authority of the Middle Ages. The Genoese lady of Raimbaut de Vaqueyras's *Contrasto bilingue* (see p. 453) tells the poet that his Provençal is as incomprehensible to her as if he were a German, a Sardinian, or a *barbari*: a remark which probably has the value of first-hand testimony since Sardinia at the time was enjoying a period of independence marked by close ties with Genoa and Pisa. A later witness is Dante, who, in the *De Vulgari Eloquentia*, rejects any pretention on the part of Sardinians to provide a *volgare illustre*, because, imitating Latin as monkeys imitate men, they alone seem in fact to have no vernacular of their own: 'Sardos etiam, qui non latii sunt, sed latiis associandi videntur, eiciamus, quoniam soli sine proprio vulgari esse videntur, grammaticam, tanquam simie homines, imitantes' (ed. Marigo, p. 94). In thus perceiving that the 'outlandish' character of Sardinian speech lay in its approximation to Latin the poet-philologist had almost divined the truth concerning the origin of the Romance languages, and it seems strange that his linguistic insight should not have led him to draw the inference which now appears obvious.

If we ask why thirteenth-century Sardinian sounded to contemporary ears so like Latin, the *grammatica* of the literate, the answer must lie primarily in the early date of Roman presence in the island. When it was annexed, in 238 B.C., as a result of the successful First Punic War, current Latin idiom still provided the basis for the developing literary standard. By the Greeks and the Carthaginians it had been prized solely for its harbours, and since Roman interest for a long time went no farther, there is no indication of heavy settlement there by the lower strata of Roman society: the rugged and inhospitable interior offered no inducement. Historical knowledge of the phases of romanization is extremely scanty. Here, as in Italy, the initial Roman disasters of the Second Punic War provided the inhabitants with an opportunity to reassert their independence. A punitive expedition led by Tiberius Gracchus in 177 B.C., as a result of which he claimed to have captured or killed 80,000 Sardinians and the Roman market was glutted with low-price Sardinian slaves, marks their final and decisive subjugation. Local insurrections occurred again in A.D. 19, during the reign of Tiberius. By that time the first great Roman overseas acquisition after Sicily had become little more than a backwater in a far-flung Empire, and during the second century A.D. Sardinia appears in history chiefly as a place of deportation for 'undesirables' (cf. p. 169). It is true that the island is crossed by a few Roman roads, but the urban development which characterizes Roman rule in Gaul and Spain is significantly absent.

Nevertheless, the natives acquired Latin, and so completely that in the modern Romance of Sardinia the surviving elements of pre-Roman speech are much less considerable than in French or Spanish: linguistic as well as physical resistance must have been greatly reduced by the savage campaign of 177 B.C. The Latin which penetrated to the interior, in addition to being of an early date, was probably the relatively 'correct' and conservative standard of Roman administrators and their families. Since the later linguistic innovations of Roman traders remained confined to the coastal fringe, the modern dialect which most impresses by its Latinism is the Logudorese of the centre. Some of the 'archaic' features of this dialect have also survived in the Campidanese of the south, though the resistance of the latter to outside influence was undermined by the Catalan and Castilian occupation, based upon Cagliari (cf. p. 443). It is to be supposed that a similar type of early administrative Latin was at first established in Corsica, which, annexed together with Sardinia, shared during Roman times its rather obscure destiny, but there, on account of the greater proximity of Italian ports, any confraternity in archaism has been largely obliterated by continuous italianization; this has also affected in some measure the Sassarese and Gallurese dialects of northern Sardinia.

Thanks to its isolation and autonomy, Logudorese is one of the first branches of Italo-Romance to be attested in literary form: while notaries in Italy were entirely committed to Latin, the paucity of learned notarial tradition in Sardinia gave rise to an early practice of the vernacular for local legal purposes. Hence the popular character of the well-known *Privilegio logudorese*, or *Carta consolare pisana*, an original document preserved in the state archives of Pisa, of which the date can be fixed, from its reference to Gherardo, bishop of Pisa, as between A.D. 1080 and 1085. It is a brief missive addressed from Sardinia to the Pisans, of some historical interest in that it reflects diplomatic action taken by the latter, rivals of the Genoese, to establish a foothold in the island. We give below the text of the manuscript as it survives, a small portion at the end having been lost:

In nomine Domini amen. Ego iudice Mariano de Lacon fazo istâ carta ad onore de omnes homines de Pisas pro xu toloneu ci mi pecterunt; e ego donolislu pro ca lis so ego amicu caru e itsos a mimi: ci nullu inperatore ci lu aet potestare istû locu de non apat comiatu de

levarelis toloneû in placitu; de non occidere pisanu ingratis; e ccausa
ipsoro ci lis aem levare ingratis, de facerlis iustitia inperatore ci nce
aet exere intu locu. E ccando mi petterum su toloneu, ligatarios ci mi
mandarum homines ammicos meos de Pisas fuit Falceri e Azulinu e
Manfridi, ed ego fecindelis carta pro honore de xu piscopû Gelardo e
de Ocu Biscomte e de omnes consolos de Pisas; e ffecila pro honore de
omnes ammicos meos de Pisas: Guidu de Vabilonia e lLeo su frate,
Repaldinu e Gelardu, e Iannellu, e Valduinu, e Bernardu de Conizo,
Francardu e Dodimundû, e Brunu, e rRannuzu, e Vernardu de Garu-
lictu, e tTornulu, pro siant in onore mea ed in auitoriû de xu locû meu.
Custu placitu lis feci per sacramentu ego e domnicellu Petru de Serra,
e Gostantine de Azzem e Voso Veccesu e Dorgotori de Ussam e nNiscoli
su frate [e n]Niscoli de Zor[i e] Mariane de Ussam. . . .[1]

Reading this text aloud one quickly appreciates its closeness to
Vulgar Latin: it seems to resolve itself into a series of Latin words
in a Romance word-order, e.g. *ego donolislu* (EGO DONO ILLIS
ILLUM), *ego fecindelis carta pro honore de xu piscopû* (EGO FECI INDE
ILLIS CARTAM PRO HONORE DE IPSUM EPISCOPUM), &c. Yet in fact
it is a faithful record of eleventh-century Logudorese, containing
only a few scribal latinisms. Among these latter are the occasional
use of a diacritic sign over post-tonic -*a* and -*u* to recall the final
-*m* of the Latin accusative, and the retention of Latin spelling in
the *h* of *homines*, *honore* (also written *onore*), in the -*ti*- of *iustitia*,
and in the *p* of *ipsoro* (cf. *su*, *xu* < IPSUM, and *itsos*, in which the

---

[1] We have here followed the text given by A. Monteverdi, *Manuale di
avviamento agli studi romanzi*, pp. 145–6. *Translation*:
    In nomine Domini amen. I, the magistrate, Mariano de Lacon, compose
this letter in honour of all men of Pisa with reference to the tax (understand:
'exemption from tax') about which they made their request to me; and I
grant it (i.e. exemption) to them because I am a dear friend to them and they
(are dear friends) to me: Let no ruler who shall govern this place have power
to levy the tax upon them, as has been agreed, or to kill a Pisan arbitrarily;
and (as for) property belonging to them which shall be taken away arbitrarily,
let the ruler who shall be in the place do them justice. And when they made
their request to me about the tax, the ambassadors whom my friends the
citizens of Pisa sent me were Falcheri and Azzolino and Manfredi, and I
composed the letter for them concerning this matter in honour of the bishop
Gherardo, and of Ugo Visconti, and of all the councillors of Pisa; and I did
it in honour of all my friends of Pisa: Guido di Babilonia and Leo his brother,
Repaldino and Gherardo, and Giannello, and Baldovino, and Bernardo di
Conizzo, Francardo and Dodimondo, and Bruno and Ranuccio, and Bernardo
di Carletto, and Tornolo, because they do me honour and help my country.
This agreement I made with them upon oath, and (with me) sir Pietro di
Serra, and Constantino di Azzem, and Buoso Vecceso, and Torchitorio di
Ussam and Niscoli his brother, and Niscoli di Zori and Mariano di Ussam. . . .

*Note.* Sardinia at the time was divided into four 'magistracies' (*giudicati*),
those of Cagliari, Arborea, Torres, and Gallura, distributed between four
branches of the Laccon de Gunale family (see M. L. Wagner, *La lingua sarda*,
pp. 25–26).

scribe, pronouncing *issos*, from IPSOS, has apparently recalled Latin by inserting the *t* of ISTOS!); a scribal recollection of the equivalence of *notte* to Lat. NŎCTEM, *fatto* to FACTUM, &c., is responsible for the spelling *pecterunt*, where *ct* represents the lengthened *t* of the verb PETERE, and comparing this spelling with the vernacular representation of the same word as *petterum*, one observes that the final *-nt* of verbs is also a Latinism (cf. *siant*, but *mandarum*, and *aem* from HABENT).

A sprinkling of latinisms in no way conceals the characteristic features of Logudorese. Most obviously, it accords with Peninsular Italian in its partiality for lengthened consonants, e.g. *ammicos, petterum, e ccausa, e ccando, e ffeci, e lLeo, e rRannuzu*, and *xu, exere*, where *x* is a graphy for *ss*. It preserves intervocalic voiceless occlusives more regularly than does the Italian standard: hence not only *frate, amicu*, but also *locu* (Ital. *luogo*) and *piscopû* (Ital. *vescovo*, cf. p. 199); in his insistence upon the voiceless form the Logudorese scribe has even turned a Pisan *Ugo* into *Ocu*. Final *-s* remains, as in *omnes homines, ammicos meos*, &c., and the early tendency to confuse initial B and V, well attested in the *Appendix Probi* and a feature of Spanish, is here shown to be no less characteristic of Sardinian, cf. *Bernardu, Vernardu, Biscomte, Valduinu, Vabilonia*. The archaism of the vowel system (see p. 45) is illustrated most aptly: tonic Ĭ (cf. *piscopû*) continues to be different from tonic Ē (cf. *feci*), and tonic Ŭ (cf. *Dodimundû*) from tonic Ō (cf. *onore*), and the Latin distinction between post-tonic *-o* and *-u* is similarly maintained, cf. *ego, ccando, ammicos, meos*, but *amicu, caru, locu, toloneu*. The semi-consonant retained in Tuscan (see p. 463) has been eliminated from *ccando* and *ca* ( < QUIA). From the spelling of *ci* ( < QUI, cf. Ital. *chi*) one may assume that *c* was the velar consonant of Latin in *placitu, feci*, and *iudice*, as it still is in modern Logudorese.

In its morphology, having retained final *-s*, the dialect agrees with western Romance in deriving its plural substantives from the accusative (cf. p. 52); its definite article comes from IPSUM (cf. p. 88); IPSORUM instead of ILLORUM is used as a possessive pronoun (cf. p. 83); it has a dative plural of the personal pronoun *lis* from ILLIS (cf. p. 82), and a dative singular *mimi* from MIHIMET; the demonstrative ECCU ISTU appears as *custu* (cf. p. 91); the relative *ci* is used as an accusative (cf. p. 97); and in the periphrastic future the parts of HABĒRE precede the infinitive, e.g. *aet* *potestare, aem levare, aet exere* (cf. p. 106). Noteworthy in the syntax is the use of the singular verb *fuit* where in the context it should be plural.

In the absence throughout history of a centralized Sardinian nation the interesting features here attested have never become conjointly those of a standard Romance language. The occupation of the island by the King of Aragon in A.D. 1322 brought to an end its independence and native administration and thereafter the official language became Catalan, subsequently Spanish after the union of the houses of Aragon and Castile. By the Treaty of Utrecht (A.D. 1714) Sardinia came back into official contact with the sphere of Italo-Romance. Since then its writers, despite the efforts of local enthusiasts to create a literary 'Sardinian', have preferred to avail themselves of the prestige of Italian. But the dialects have lost nothing of their vitality and have undergone relatively little change: the Logudorese peasant can still claim to speak the variety of Romance most closely approximating to Latin.

## RHETO-ROMANCE

Rhetia, Vindelicia, and Noricum, the three Roman provinces which roughly correspond, in modern times, to Switzerland, Bavaria, and Austria respectively, were acquired for the Empire from 15 B.C., during the reign of Augustus. Such mountainous areas, as we have observed in the case of Sardinia, were not highly prized, but they were essential to the strategic concept of a Rhine–Danube frontier which evolved as a consequence of the subjugation of Gaul. Archaeological evidence shows the provinces to have been quite extensively romanized during their four to five centuries under Roman administration. Noricum was evacuated only in A.D. 487 after Odovacar's usurpation of power: we are told that the whole population moved southwards and obtained from Odovacar a settlement in Italy, leaving the land deserted (see C. Oman, *Europe, 476–918*, p. 14).

Until this time Latin must have been commonly used as far north as the Danube. Its recession, as place-names show, has been gradual but continuous from the first onset of Germanic incursions. During the Middle Ages the pressure of Germanic dialects was matched from the south by that of Italian dialects, notably

Venetian, and latterly both groups have been reinforced by the prestige of standard German and Italian. Only in the less accessible parts of Rhetia, and a small corner of Noricum, has the original Latin survived to the present day as an individual type of Romance speech.

The geographical area of what may be termed comprehensively 'Rheto-Romance', in reality a complex of much diversified patois, is now split into three principal fragments. One of these is contained in the Swiss canton of Grisons, in German *Graubünden*, a name which perpetuates the memory of the *Grey League*, created in the fifteenth century by the Romance-speaking people in successful resistance to Austrian attempts to absorb them. Now some 40,000 in all, these people are concentrated in and around two large valleys, formed by the upper waters of the Rhine and the Inn. Correspondingly, they have two principal types of dialect: in the Rhine valley *Romansh*, subdivided into *Surselvan* and *Subselvan*, with the forest of Flims between them; and in the Inn valley Engadinish, similarly divided into 'upper' and 'lower'. A further type is found in a small isolated valley to the south-east, the *Val Müstair* (Germ. *Münstertal*). The Roman capital of the province, Curia Rhetorum (Fr. *Coire*, Germ. *Chur*), has since the sixteenth century lost to German Swiss its Romance speech, formerly known as *Chur-wälsch* (see p. 271, note), a term which remains in the name of the suburb across the river, *Wälschdörfli*, where Romance lingered on. Despite this defection of the natural centre, the Rheto-Romance of the Grisons, having attained literary status with the Reformation, has in more recent times held its ground, particularly since the adherence of the Grisons to Switzerland as the fifteenth canton (A.D. 1803). As a language it profited from the general increase in literacy and tended to become the object of a patriotic cult, symbolic of local autonomy. This tendency came to a head in 1938, when the inhabitants, alarmed by the extravagant territorial claims of Fascist Italy, backed by the gratuitous assertion that Rheto-Romance is an Italian dialect, successfully brought pressure on the Federal Government to secure its recognition as the fourth national language of Switzerland.[1]

---

[1] The bibliography associated with this revival is considerable. Special mention should be made of the excellent *Dicziunari rumantsch grischun*, now appearing in fascicules; its present editor-in-chief is A. Schorta, to whom we are also indebted for a study of the *Val Müstair* (*Lautlehre der Mundart von Müstair*, Zürich, 1938).

It is now widely used for instruction in schools and as the language of school textbooks, but standardization remains uncertain. There are in fact two principal standards, one for the Catholic population speaking Surselvan Romansh (chief town Disentis), and one for the Protestant Engadine (chief town Samaden). The latter enjoys an advantage in that the Engadine has possessed its own printing presses and devotional books since the sixteenth century, the earliest printed works being Jacob Bifrun's *Christiauna Fuorma* (1552), a kind of catechism, and the same author's translation of the New Testament (1560). On account of the stabilizing influence of this religious literature, Engadinish is markedly more conservative than Romansh.

Prior to the sixteenth century the only substantial attestation of Romance in this region is an interlinear translation of a pseudo-Augustinian sermon, belonging to the monastery of Einsiedeln, which from the handwriting may be dated as early twelfth century. Although only a fragment, fifteen lines in all, it suffices to reveal a western type, which at this stage has much in common with the Romance of Gaul. Most notably, final -s remains, and with it a two-case declension, though certain inconsistencies of usage suggest that this was already breaking down. There is no indication of the spontaneous diphthongs which characterize later texts: SAPĒRE appears as *savir*, as in the *Strassburg Oaths*. Treatment of intervocalic consonants is almost identical with that to be observed in Gallo-Romance. Of particular interest are the first traces of local selection from Latin vocabulary: DECET, lost elsewhere, persists as *des*, and for 'to speak' the favoured verb is PLACITARE, here *plaidar*, in modern idiom *plidar*, *pledar*.

The two other regions of Rheto-Romance have no comparable linguistic fortune. The Ladin of the Dolomites—usually classified as Rheto-Romance though the Dolomites came within the frontiers of Noricum—is in process of gradual extinction. It continues to be spoken in four valleys radiating from the central mountain core: to the south those of the rivers Avisio and Noce, where it has long since been penetrated by Venetian and is now surrounded by Italian; to the north the Gadera and Gardena valleys, Austrian until 1919, where, enclosed by the more alien German, it has resisted more strongly. A few further islets survive to the east. Ladin is not attested in written form until the eighteenth century, and even before the cession of the whole area to Italy, and subsequent intensive italianization, its remaining speakers numbered only some 12,000.[1]

The third area, the largest and by far the most populous, is that of Friulan, the local speech of the province of Udine, with some 400,000 inhabitants. During the Middle Ages Friulan prospered, and extending along the banks of the Tagliamento to the Adriatic, it became at one time the current speech of Trieste, but its expansion was then checked by the rise of Venice. The earliest Friulan texts, dating from the end of the thirteenth century, already show a marked influence of Venetian. Subjected ever since to a continuous infiltration of extraneous elements, Friulan is now the least representative of the Romance idioms which perpetuate the spoken Latin of Rhetia.

## BALKAN ROMANCE

Balkan Romance confronts the philologist with an enigma, in that its strongest representation lies north of the Danube in the former Roman province of Dacia. Conquered during the reign of Trajan, in the course of two campaigns (A.D. 101 and A.D. 105–6), Dacia was abandoned under Aurelian, in A.D. 271, and was thus the least enduring of all the territories held by Rome. If the Latin language failed to become permanently established north of the Alps, or in a country such as Britain, occupied for four centuries and much more intimately related to the life and customs of Rome, how can one explain its apparent survival in an outpost so remote and so precarious?

A writer of the fourth century A.D., Eutropius, referring in his *Breviarium Historiae Romanae* to the Dacian campaigns, relates that many of the native Dacians were slain and that the survivors chose to leave their lands and settle beyond the confines of the Empire rather than submit to Roman rule; in consequence, he continues, Dacia was settled with colonists brought from far and wide: 'Traianus victa Dacia ex toto orbe Romano infinitas eo

---

[1] Recent studies of the southern valleys of the Dolomites include W. Th. Elwert, *Die Mundart des Fassa-Tals*, Heidelberg, 1943, and C. Tagliavini, *Il dialetto del Livinallongo*, Bolzano, 1934. The northern valleys had received earlier attention from Th. Gartner, one of the pioneers of Rheto-Romance studies, author of a *Rätoromanische Grammatik*, Heilbronn, 1883, and a *Handbuch der rätoromanischen Sprache und Literatur*, Halle, 1910.

The islets of Ladin farther east have been studied by C. Tagliavini, *Il dialetto del Comelico*, Geneva, 1926; see also the same author's *Le origini delle lingue neolatine*, 2nd ed., pp. 325–37.

copias hominum transtulerat ad agros et urbes colendas.' Drawing support from this testimony, some scholars, notably those of Rumanian origin, conceive a fully 'Rumanian' solution to the problem. The Latinity of Dacia, according to these, derives from Trajan's mass transfer of people, whose progeny thereafter succeeded, throughout the Middle Ages, in preserving a concealed Roman identity of speech in the fastnesses of the Carpathians and Transylvanian Alps, while the tides of Asian and Slavonic invasion flowed around. From their primitive homes they later spread south and east to the plains of the lower Danube, where they may well have been reinforced by migrations of the Romance-speaking minority still living in the lands of Slavonic speech on the right bank of the river. In favour of this theory it is argued that the complexity of Rumanian dialect in the mountainous region of Transylvania, its differentiation into many patois, indicates an area of ancient settlement, whereas the much greater syntactical and grammatical uniformity of Rumanian speech in the plains, and the high proportion of recent loan-words from Slavonic and Turkish, point to subsequent diffusion of the Romance-speaking population. If this were so, then the modern standard of Daco-Rumanian derives in unbroken tradition from the earliest Roman settlers of Dacia.

Other scholars, and they seem to include a majority of non-Rumanians, view with some scepticism the idea that Latin north of the Danube could have survived the medieval turmoil (see pp. 267–70). For them, modern Rumanian was cradled south of the Danube, in the Roman provinces of Illiricum and Moesia, and carried north by later migrations. The southern character of the earlier corpus of Slavonic loan-words in Rumanian is adduced as linguistic evidence in support of this counter-theory. There, at present, the problem remains.

Roman colonization south of the Danube was of ancient date. It first began with the Illyrian Wars (229 and 219 B.C.). The Istrian promontory was acquired in 221 B.C., and the whole territory of Illyricum came under Roman control as a result of the successful conclusion of the Third Macedonian War (168 B.C.), though not until 35 B.C., with the expansion of Empire under Octavian, does it appear as an organized province playing a significant role in Roman policy; with the same impulse, Roman rule was carried farther east along the banks of the Danube by the creation, in 29 B.C., of the province of Moesia, comprising the northern part of modern Bulgaria.

The original territory of Balkan Romance proper thus extended between the Adriatic and the Black Sea, bounded by the Danube to the north and Greek-speaking lands to the south. Where Greek did not oppose it, Latin can have met with little resistance. The most obvious identifiable substratum, though very little is known of it, was Illyrian. This was presumably the Indo-European language which has persisted in a restricted area as Albanian; it is therefore in Albanian that scholars seek affinities for such features of Balkan Romance as seem to call for explanation by a pre-Latin influence. Yet there is little in 'proto-Rumanian', as it may be inferred from the modern idioms, which does not clearly proceed from the same spoken Latin as Spanish, Sardinian, and the remoter dialects of southern Italy: its characteristics are, in fact, 'early Vulgar Latin'.

Nearest to Italy, extending along the eastern seaboard of the Adriatic, there persisted until comparatively recent times the Romance idiom now known as Old Dalmatian. Continual pressures of Venetian from the west and Croatian from the east combined during the Middle Ages to reduce its area until it finally died out in the island of Veglia (cf. p. 54, note). Sharing many features with the Italian dialects, Old Dalmatian seems to have possessed an individuality which marked it off from the inland Romance of Illyricum and Moesia. The latter, sometimes known collectively as Macedo-Rumanian, is closely akin to the modern language of Rumania and still persists in widely-scattered remnants. One small group of people of this linguistic affiliation, some 3,000 strong, inhabits the eastern part of the Istrian promontory, inland from Fiume; as their 'Istro-Rumanian' shows, they are not indigenous, their ancestors having probably sought refuge there to escape from the Turks. The direct linguistic representatives of Roman Illyricum, still in their original sites, are the Arumanians. According to Th. Capidan,[1] they number about 300,000, their most compact agglomerations being in northern Greece on the border of Epirus, in Albania, and in the south-west corner of Jugoslavia, near lakes Ochrida and Prespa. They are said to take a prominent part in local commerce and culture, all the innkeepers

---

[1] See Th. Capidan, *Aromânii—Dialectul aromân*, Bucharest, 1932, and *Meglenoromânii*, Bucharest, 1928.

of the region being Arumanian, though this happy situation may have been changed since the 1939–45 War. Recent political circumstances (according to our unofficial information) have uprooted the Meglenites, in their own language *Vlaši* (see p. 271, note), another branch of Macedo-Rumanians who lived farther east in the upper valley of the River Vardar and who knew none of the relative prosperity of the Arumanians. It is noticeable that all these peoples are concentrated in mountainous areas, not easy of access, where their Romance speech has evolved in isolation, unaffected by the Latin culture of the west. Scantily attested in the past, it has produced no significant literary norms.

The only standard forged from Balkan Romance is that of Daco-Rumanian, of which the earliest surviving specimen dates from A.D. 1521. It is a letter addressed to a local officer in Brașov, in the Carpathians, informing him of a movement of Turks from Sofia along the Danube valley. This presupposes a nascent literary tradition, which probably had its origin in local departures by members of the Orthodox Church from the strict use of Slavonic; but, as in the case of Rheto-Romance, the tradition was stabilized by the Reformation, reaching Transylvania from Hungary at the same time as the printing-press from Venice. From 1559 there remains a Protestant catechism, translated from Hungarian and printed at Brașov in the Cyrillic alphabet, in which the Lord's Prayer, transliterated, is as follows:[1]

Tatăl nostru (*Our Father*) ce ești în ceri (*which art in Heaven*), sfințească-se (*hallowed be*) numele tău (*Thy Name*), să vïe (*come*) împărăție ta (*Thy Kingdom*), fïe (*be done*) voia ta (*Thy Will*) cum în ceri (*as in Heaven*) așà și (*so also*) pre pămînt (*on earth*). Pită noastră (*Our bread*) sațïosă (*satisfying*) dă-ne noao (*give us*) astăzi (*this day*), și iartă noao (*and forgive us*) greșalele noastre (*our trespasses*), cum ertăm (*as we forgive*) și noi (*we too*) greșițilo(r) noștri (*those who trespass against us*), și nu-ne duce (*and lead us not*) în năpaste (*into temptation*) ce ne izbăveaște pre noi (*but deliver us*) de hitleanul (*from the evil*), că a ta e împărăție (*for Thine is the Kingdom*) și putere (*and Power*) în vecïe (*in eternity*), Amin.

This is typical Rumanian, but with a high proportion of loan-words. Of Slavonic origin are: *pită*, a kind of coarse bread; *greșală* 'sin', 'error', and the verb *a greși* 'to err', of which the past participle, *greșit*, is here used as a substantive; *năpastă*, pl. *năpaste* 'misfortune'; *a izbăvi* 'to save', and *vecïe* 'eternity'. The verb *a se*

---

[1] Quoted by C. Tagliavini, *Le origini delle lingue neolatine*, 2nd ed., p. 477.

*sfinți*, which appears in the third person singular of the present subjunctive, *sfințească-se* (see p. 129), is a hybrid form deriving from *sînt* (Romance) and *sfînt* (Slavonic). One word is Hungarian, viz. *hitlean* 'cunning'. Among the less obvious words of Romance origin *pămînt* is the Lat. PAVIMENTUM, the 'pavement' having become the 'earth', as opposed to heaven; for *tată*, see p. 156.

For the sake of comparison, we append the modern version of the same prayer, from which some of the non-Latin words have been eliminated, though others remain:

Tatăl nostru care ești în ceruri, sințească-se numele tău; vie împărăția ta; facă-se voia ta, precum în cer și pe pămînt. Pînea noastră cea de toate zilele dă-ne-o nouă astăzi; și ne iartă nouă greșelile noastre, precum și noi iertăm greșiților noștri; și nu ne duce în ispită ci izbăvește-ne de cel rău. Căci a ta este împărăția și puterea și mărirea în veci, Amin.

A fragment of another religious text printed in Transylvania in 1570 is in Roman letters, but the attempt to replace Cyrillic by Roman was not destined to succeed until the union of Moldavia and Wallachia in A.D. 1859. After numerous similarly fragmentary translations, a literary standard was established during the seventeenth century by the translation of the whole Bible, printed at Bucharest in A.D. 1688, and by chronicles composed in Moldavia. During the nineteenth century Rumanian became the medium of more creative writing, of authors seeking models from the kindred Romance literatures of France and Italy, whence they incorporated many new words. The accepted modern standard is the variety of Daco-Rumanian spoken at Bucharest; a conscious authority, the Rumanian Academy, after the pattern of the *Académie française*, legislates upon correct usage. Moldavian, the northern variety which extends over a considerable part of Bessarabia, now attached to Russia, has of late been claimed as a 'language' of the Soviet Union, but from a purely philological standpoint there is little justification for this new status.

## GREATER ROMANIA

A survey of the linguistic legacy of Rome can scarcely be concluded without some mention, however brief, of the remarkable turn in its fortune which came with the Age of Discovery. Portuguese, Spanish, and French, emerging from the Middle Ages as *langues de prestige*, widely used and relatively well standardized, rivalled English and Dutch in a struggle for acclimatization in the vast non-European world, each reproducing in some measure the earlier process of Latin expansion, with results as curious as they are informative.

First contacts between Romance-speaking adventurers and aboriginal populations produced linguistic media of the kind known as 'pidgin', some of them embracing the most diverse elements. Among the earliest was Portuguese-Malay, which became the *lingua franca* of the east, used even by the British and the Dutch. A recent study of the surviving Romance pidgin of the Philippines[1] provides an historical reconstruction of the kind of further development to which this Portuguese-Malay could give rise. The story begins in the Moluccas, with the small island of Ternate, now a backwater but once the centre of a large sultanate born of the eastward spread of Islam. The empire of this sultanate was disputed by that of the twin island of Tidor. These were the original 'Spice Islands', the home of the clove, and therefore a centre of interest for the Portuguese. In A.D. 1522 they succeeded in establishing a fort on Ternate, assisted by the quarrel between the two rival sultans, each of whom promised to recognize Portuguese suzerainty in return for support against the other. Half a century later the natives drove the Portuguese away, but the temporary union of the crowns of Portugal and Spain in A.D. 1578 brought the islands within the sphere of Spanish interests. After a prolonged struggle for possession against the Dutch, the Spaniards gained a footing in Ternate in A.D. 1606. In A.D. 1655 a Dutch reprisal destroyed all the clove-trees. Since these had now been transplanted to other localities, the Spaniards thereafter began to withdraw, evacuating 200 Christianized families, presumably of mixed blood, to the safety of Manila. From the descendants of these 200 families comes the 'Spanish contact vernacular' of the Philippines, now located in four distinct areas, two in Luzon, and two in the southern island of Mindanao, whither it was carried by soldiers during the subsequent Spanish campaigns: it is thus an hispanicized Portuguese-Malay grafted on to a native Tagalog substratum.

The complex human history which lies behind present-day manifestations of Romance in some of its strangest forms and most

[1] K. Whinnom, *Spanish Contact Vernaculars in the Philippine Islands*, Hong Kong and Oxford, 1956.

distant byways is aptly revealed in this well-documented study. Many of them await a thorough investigation. An equally remarkable mixture is to be found on the other side of the globe, in the island of Mauritius, where the French of settlers has become diversified among a coloured population with elements of Malagasy, Bantu, Swahili, and Indian dialects. No less strange-sounding are the French *creole* speeches of certain West Indian islands— St. Lucia, St. Vincent, Dominica and Grenada—removed for some time past, like Mauritius, from French control. These idioms recall the problem of the substratum, putting the old question in a modern context: To what extent does the structure of such predominantly Romance speeches reflect the speech-habits of non-European populations? Many scholars would see in them an adaptation of Romance vocabulary to exotic language-patterns. This may be a true appreciation; yet, on the other hand, there is a sameness in their peculiar features—generalized use of the infinitive of verbs, suppression of distinctions of gender, frequency of repeated forms, e.g. Philippine *buenong-bueno*, &c.—which seems more suggestive of the familiar 'baby-talk' affected by European occupants in their attempts at communication.

All these marginal varieties are doomed to extinction. None has become the basis of a new standardized language and indeed they persist only in territories somewhat removed from the modern routes of commercial development, principally in islands. Elsewhere, as fraternizing soldiers and sailors were followed by administrators and priests, the standards cultivated in Europe were enforced and established as 'correct'. Countries such as those of Central and South America, like the United States, though rejecting political ties yet remained intimately bound by language to the colonizing powers of Europe. Even where pronunciation has considerably evolved, as in the Portuguese of Brazil, the standard languages of Europe retain their prestige and characteristic local variations can usually be traced to archaic and dialectal phenomena in European development; little can be attributed with certainty to the influence of native substrata. In the rather exceptional instance of the French now used in Canada and Louisiana, where the imported language became well established as that of the homeland, but was then cut off and surrounded by areas of foreign speech, features of the continental French of the seventeenth and eighteenth centuries are abundantly preserved. The picture which emerges from a study of the linguistic outcome of European colonization seems in fact to confirm our impression of the fate of Latin in the conquered lands of the Roman Empire.

Language in nearly all areas of Greater Romania, whether in Europe or overseas, has been increasingly subjected during the past two centuries to a foreign influence: that of English, latterly receiving powerful reinforcement from its American variety. The age-long jostling of Romance and Germanic appears in different places and in different guises, but it never reaches an end.

# BIBLIOGRAPHY

The following bibliography is designed solely as an indication of the principal works consulted and an expression of acknowledgement to their authors; some publications to which passing reference has been made in the text, chiefly editions and articles contributed to reviews, are not included.

## (a) HISTORICAL

J. B. BURY, *A History of the Later Roman Empire*, 2 vols., 2nd ed., London, 1923.

J. CALMETTE, *L'effondrement d'un empire et la naissance d'une Europe*, Paris, 1941.

H. J. CHAYTOR, *A History of Aragon and Catalonia*, London, 1933.

P. COURCELLE, *Histoire littéraire des grandes invasions germaniques*, Paris, 1948.

A. GIMÉNEZ SOLER, *La edad media en la corona de Aragón*, 2nd ed., Barcelona, 1944.

C. HALPHEN, *Charlemagne et l'empire carolingien*, Paris, 1947.

E. M. JAMISON, C. M. ADY, K. D. VERNON, and C. SANDFORD TERRY, *Italy, Medieval and Modern*, Oxford, 1919.

F. LOT, *La fin du monde antique et le début du moyen âge*, 2nd ed., Paris, 1951.

C. W. C. OMAN, *Europe, 476–918*, 8th ed., London, 1923.

C. W. PREVITÉ-ORTON, *Outlines of Medieval History*, 2nd ed., Cambridge, 1929.

R. SETON-WATSON, *A History of the Roumanians*, Cambridge, 1934.

J. M. WALLACE-HADRILL *The Barbarian West, 400–1000*, London, 1952.

## (b) LITERARY AND LINGUISTIC

P. AEBISCHER, *Chrestomathie franco-provençale. Recueil de textes franco-provençaux antérieurs à 1630*, Berne, 1950.

D. ALONSO, 'Cancioncillas "de amigo" mozárabes', *Revista de filología española*, xxxiii (pp. 247–394), Madrid, 1949.

M. ALVAR, *El dialecto aragonés*, Madrid, 1953.

J. ANGLADE, *Grammaire de l'ancien provençal*, Paris, 1921.
—— *Histoire sommaire de la littérature méridionale*, Paris, 1921.

C. APPEL, *Provenzalische Chrestomathie*, 6th ed., Leipzig, 1930.

M. ASÍN PALACIOS, *Contribución a la toponimia árabe de España*, 2nd ed., Madrid–Granada, 1944.

A. BADÍA MARGARIT, *Gramática histórica catalana*, Barcelona, 1951.

W. A. BAEHRENS, *Sprachlicher Kommentar zur vulgärlateinischen Appendix Probi*, Halle, 1922.

M. BARTOLI, *Das Dalmatische, altromanische Sprachreste von Veglia bis Ragusa und ihre Stellung in der Apennino-balkanischen Romania*, 2 vols., Vienna, 1906.

R. Bezzola, *Abbozzo di una storia dei gallicismi italiani nei primi secoli*, Heidelberg, 1925.

P. Bosch Gimpera, *Etnología de la Península Ibérica*, Barcelona, 1932.

E. Bourciez, *Éléments de linguistique romane*, 4th ed., Paris, 1946.
—— *Précis historique de phonétique française*, 8th ed., Paris, 1937.

J. Brüch, *Der Einfluss der germanischen Sprachen auf das Vulgärlatein*, Heidelberg, 1913.

C. Brunel, *Les plus anciennes chartes en langue provençale*, 2 vols., Paris, 1926.

F. Brunot, *Histoire de la langue française des origines à 1900*, Paris, 1905– (recent volumes by Ch. Bruneau).

H. P. Bruppacher, *Die Namen der Wochentage im Italienischen und Rätoromanischen*, Berne, 1948.

Th. Capidan, *Aromânii—Dialectul aromân*, Bucharest, 1932.
—— *Meglenoromânii*, Bucharest, 1928.

A. Carnoy, *Le latin d'Espagne d'après les inscriptions*, Brussels, 1906.

J. Caro Baroja, *Materiales para una historia de la lengua vasca en su relación con la latina*, Salamanca, 1946.

H. J. Chaytor, *The Troubadours*, Cambridge, 1912.

R. S. Conway, *The Italic Dialects*, Cambridge, 1897.

R. S. Conway, J. Whatmough, and S. E. Johnston, *The Prae-Italic Dialects of Italy*, Cambridge, Mass., 1933.

J. Corominas, *Diccionario crítico etimológico de la lengua castellana*, 4 vols., Berne, 1954–7.

A. Dauzat, *La toponymie française*, Paris, 1946.

O. Densusianu, *Histoire de la langue roumaine*, 2 vols., Paris, 1901, 1938.

G. Devoto, *Storia della lingua di Roma*, 2nd ed., Bologna, 1944.

M. C. Díaz y Díaz, *Antología del latín vulgar*, Madrid, 1950.

C. Dionisotti and C. Grayson, *Early Italian Texts*, Oxford, 1949.

G. Dottin, *La langue gauloise*, Paris, 1920.

G. Ehrismann, *Geschichte der deutschen Literatur bis zum Ausgang des Mittelalters*, Munich, 1918.

W. Th. Elwert, *Die Mundart des Fassa-Tals*, Heidelberg, 1943.

W. J. Entwistle, *The Spanish Language*, London, 1936.

A. Ernout, *Les éléments dialectaux du vocabulaire latin*, Paris, 1909.

A. Ewert, *The French Language*, 2nd ed., London, 1943.
—— 'The Strassburg Oaths', *Transactions of the Philological Society* (pp. 16–35), London, 1935.

Th. Frings, *Germania Romana*, Halle, 1932.

E. Gamillscheg, *Romania Germanica*, 3 vols., Berlin–Leipzig, 1934–6.

V. García de Diego, *Diccionario etimológico español e hispánico*, Madrid, 1954.
—— *Manual de dialectología española*, Madrid, 1946.

E. García Gómez, 'Veinticuatro kharjas romances en muwaššaḥs árabes', *Al-Andalus*, Madrid, 1952 (pp. 57–127).

Th. Gartner, *Handbuch der rätoromanischen Sprache und Literatur*, Halle, 1910.

—— *Rätoromanische Grammatik*, Heilbronn, 1883.

J. GILI, *Catalan Grammar*, 2nd ed., Oxford, 1952.

J. GILLIÉRON, *Généalogie des mots qui désignent l'abeille*, Paris, 1918.

—— *Pathologie et thérapeutique verbales*, Paris, 1921.

—— (with E. EDMONT), *Atlas linguistique de la France*, Paris, 1903–10.

M. GOROSCH, *El Fuero de Teruel*, Stockholm, 1950.

C. H. GRANDGENT, *An Introduction to Vulgar Latin*, Boston, 1907.

—— *From Latin to Italian*, 3rd ed., Cambridge, Mass., 1940.

A. GRIERA, *Gramàtica històrica del català antic*, Barcelona, 1931.

G. GRÖBER, *Grundriss der romanischen Philologie*, Strassburg, 1888–; 2nd ed., 1904–.

E. HERAEUS, *Silviae vel potius Aetheriae Peregrinatio ad Loca Sancta*, 4th ed., Heidelberg, 1939.

E. HOEPFFNER and P. ALFARIC, *La chanson de sainte Foy*, 2 vols., Strassburg–Paris, 1926.

J. B. HOFMANN, *Lateinische Umgangssprache*, 2nd ed., Heidelberg, 1936.

U. T. HOLMES, *A History of Old French Literature from the Origins to 1300*, New York, 1948.

J. HUBER, *Altportugiesisches Elementarbuch*, Heidelberg, 1933.

J. HUBSCHMID, *Sardische Studien*, Berne, 1953.

I. IORDAN, *Introducere în studiul limbilor romanice*, Iaşi, 1932 (English adaptation by J. ORR, *An Introduction to Romance Linguistics. Its Schools and Scholars*, London, 1937).

K. JABERG, *Aspects géographiques du langage*, Paris, 1936.

—— (with J. JUD), *Sprach- und Sachatlas Italiens und der Südschweiz*, Zofingen, 1928–40.

—— *Der Sprachatlas als Forschungsinstrument*, Halle, 1928.

K. JACKSON, *Language and History in early Britain*, Edinburgh, 1953.

A. JEANROY, *Histoire sommaire de la poésie occitane*, Toulouse–Paris, 1945.

—— *La poésie lyrique des troubadours*, 2 vols., Toulouse–Paris, 1934.

J. JUD, 'Problèmes de géographie linguistique', *Revue de linguistique romane*, vol. i (1925), pp. 181–236.

A. KUHN, 'Der hocharagonesische Dialekt', *Revue de linguistique romane*, vol. xi (1935), pp. 1–312.

—— *Romanische Philologie. Erster Teil: Die romanischen Sprachen*, Berne, 1951.

A. LABHARDT, *Contributions à la critique et à l'explication des Gloses de Reichenau*, Neuchâtel, 1936.

R. LAFON, 'L'état actuel du problème des origines de la langue basque', *Gernika, Eusko-Jakintza (Études basques')*, vol. i, pp. 37–49, 151–63, 505–24, Bayonne, 1947.

R. LAPESA, *Historia de la lengua española*, 2nd ed., Madrid, 1950.

H. LAUSBERG, *Die Mundarten Südlukaniens*, Halle, 1939.

—— *Romanische Sprachwissenschaft: 1. Einleitung und Vokalismus. 2. Konsonantismus*, Berlin, 1956.

R. LAVAUD and G. MACHICOT, *Boecis. Le plus ancien texte occitan réédité, traduit et commenté*, Toulouse, 1950.

W. M. LINDSAY, *The Latin Language*, Oxford, 1894.

J. LINSKILL, *Saint Léger, étude de la langue du manuscrit de Clermont-Ferrand, suivie d'une édition critique du texte*, Paris, 1937.

E. LITTRÉ, *Dictionnaire de la langue française*, Paris, 1882.

E. LÖFSTED, *Philologischer Kommentar zur Peregrinatio Aetheriae*, Uppsala, 1911.

G. LOEWE and G. GOETZ, *Corpus glossariorum Latinorum*, 7 vols., Leipzig, 1889–1923.

A. LOMBARD, *Le verbe roumain, étude morphologique*, 2 vols., Lund, 1954–5.

F. LOT, 'A quelle époque a-t-on cessé de parler latin?' *Bulletin Du Cange, Archivum Latinitatis Medii Aevi*, vol. vi (1931), pp. 97–159.

Y. MALKIEL, *Studies in the Reconstruction of Hispano-Latin Word Families*, Berkeley–Los Angeles, 1954.

M. MANITIUS, *Geschichte der lateinischen Literatur des Mittelalters*, 3 vols., Munich, 1911–31.

P. MARCHOT, *Les gloses de Cassel*, Fribourg, 1895.

A. MARIGO, *De Vulgari Eloquentia, ridotto a miglior lezione, commentato e tradotto*, Opere di Dante, vol. vi, 2nd ed., Florence, 1948.

A. MEILLET, *Esquisse d'une histoire de la langue latine*, 5th ed., Paris, 1948.

R. MENÉNDEZ PIDAL, *Cantar de mio Cid. Texto, gramática y vocabulario*, 3 vols., Madrid, 1908–11.

—— *La España del Cid*, 2 vols., 4th ed., Madrid, 1947.

—— *Manual de gramática histórica española*, 9th ed., 1952. Madrid.

—— *Orígenes del español*, 3rd ed., Madrid, 1950.

—— *Toponimia prerrománica hispana*, Madrid, 1952.

W. MEYER-LÜBKE, *Grammatik der romanischen Sprachen*, 4 vols., Leipzig, 1890–1902 (French translation, *Grammaire des langues romanes*, Paris, 1890–1906).

—— *Romanisches etymologisches Wörterbuch*, 3rd ed., Heidelberg, 1935.

B. MIGLIORINI, *Fra il latino e l'italiano. Primordi della lingua italiana, 476–960*, Florence, 1953.

E. MONACI, *Crestomazia italiana dei primi secoli. Nuova edizione riveduta e aumentata per cura di F. Arese. Presentazione di A. Schiaffini*, Rome, 1955.

A. MONTEVERDI, *Manuale di avviamento agli studi romanzi. Le lingue romanze*, Milan, 1952.

—— *Testi antichi italiani*, Modena, 1948.

H. F. MULLER and P. TAYLOR, *A Chrestomathy of Vulgar Latin*, New York, 1932.

G. NANDRIS, *Colloquial Rumanian*, London, 1945.

—— 'The Development and Structure of Rumanian', *The Slavonic and East European Review*, vol. xxx (1951), pp. 7–39.

J. J. NUNES, *Compêndio de gramática histórica portuguesa*, 3rd ed., Lisbon, 1945.

K. NYROP, *Grammaire historique de la langue française*, 6 vols., Copenhagen, 1899–1930.

J. ORR, *Words and Sounds in English and French*, Oxford, 1953.

M. DE PAIVA BOLÉO, *Introdução ao estudo da filología portuguesa*, Lisbon, 1946.

S. PALAY, *Dictionnaire du béarnais et du gascon modernes*, 2 vols., Pau, 1932.

M. PALLOTTINO, *Etruscologia*, 3rd ed., Milan, 1954 (English translation by J. CREMONA, *The Etruscans*, London, 1955).

L. R. PALMER, *The Latin language*, London, 1954.

M. PEI, *The Italian Language*, New York, 1941.
—— *The Language of the Eighth-Century Texts in Northern France*, New York, 1932.

J. PIRSON, *La langue des inscriptions latines de la Gaule*, Brussels, 1901.

V. PISANI, *Le lingue dell'Italia antica oltre il latino*, Turin, 1953.

S. POP, *Grammaire roumaine*, Berne, 1947.
—— *La dialectologie*, 2 vols., Louvain, 1950.

M. K. POPE, *From Latin to Modern French, with especial consideration of Anglo-Norman*, 2nd ed., Manchester, 1952.

A. PRATI, *Vocabulario etimologico italiano*, Milan, 1951.

R. PRIEBSCH and W. E. COLLINSON, *The German Language*, 4th ed., London, 1958.

S. PUŞCARIU, *Limba română*, Bucharest, 1940 (German translation by H. KUEN, *Die rumänische Sprache*, Leipzig, 1943).

V. RABOTINE, *Le 'Boèce' provençal, étude linguistique*, Strassburg, 1930.

F. J. E. RABY, *A History of Christian-Latin Poetry, from the beginnings to the close of the Middle Ages*, Oxford, 1927.
—— *A History of Secular Latin Poetry in the Middle Ages*, 2 vols., 2nd ed., Oxford, 1957.

L. REMACLE, *Le problème de l'ancien wallon*, Paris, 1948.

H. RHEINFELDER, *Altfranzösische Grammatik*, 2nd ed., Munich, 1953–5.

E. RICHTER, *Beiträge zur Geschichte der Romanismen*, Halle, 1934.

M. DE RIQUER, *La lírica de los trovadores, antología comentada*. Tomo 1, *Poetas del siglo XII*, Barcelona, 1948.

G. ROHLFS, *An den Quellen der romanischen Sprachen*, Halle, 1952.
—— *Die lexikalische Differenzierung der romanischen Sprachen*, Munich, 1954.
—— *Estudios sobre geografía lingüística de Italia*, Granada, 1952.
—— *Germanisches Spracherbe in der Romania*, Munich, 1947.
—— *Griechen und Romanen in Unteritalien*, Geneva, 1924.
—— *Historische Grammatik der italienischen Sprache und ihrer Mundarten*, 3 vols., Berne, 1949–54.
—— *Le Gascon, études de philologie pyrénéenne*, Halle, 1935.
—— *Romanische Philologie*, 2 vols., Heidelberg, vol. i, 1950; vol. ii, 1952.
—— *Sermo Vulgaris Latinus*, 2nd ed., Tübingen, 1956.
—— *Studien zur romanischen Namenkunde*, Munich, 1956.

J. RONJAT, *Grammaire istorique des parlers provençaux modernes*, 4 vols., Montpellier, 1930–41.

R. M. RUGGIERI, *Testi antichi romanzi. 1. Facsimili. 2. Trascrizioni*, Modena, 1949.

J. RUIZ I CALONJA, *Història de la literatura catalana*, Barcelona, 1954.

J. SAROÏHANDY, 'Vestiges de phonétique ibérienne en territoire roman', *Revue internationale des études basques*, vol. vii (pp. 475–97), Paris, 1913.

F. SCHRAMM, *Sprachliches zur Lex Salica*, Marburg, 1911.

F. SCHÜRR, 'La diphthongaison romane', *Revue de linguistique romane*, vol. xx (pp. 107–44, 161–248), Paris, 1956.

S. SILVA NETO, *História da lingua portuguesa*, Río de Janeiro, 1952.

J. SOFER, *Lateinisches und Romanisches aus den Etymologiae des Isidorus von Sevilla*, Göttingen, 1930.

F. SOMMER, *Handbuch der lateinischen Laut- und Formenlehre*, 3rd ed., Heidelberg, 1914.

A. STEIGER, *Contribución a la fonética del hispano-árabe y de los arabismos en el ibero-románico y el siciliano*, Madrid, 1932.

S. M. STERN, *Les chansons mozarabes*, Palermo, 1953.

G. STRAKA, 'La dislocation linguistique de la Romania et la formation des langues romanes à la lumière de la chronologie relative des changements phonétiques', *Revue de linguistique romane*, vol. xx (pp. 249–67), Paris, 1956.

—— 'Observations sur la chronologie et les dates de quelques modifications phonétiques en roman et en français prélittéraire', *Revue des langues romanes*, vol. lxxi (pp. 247–307), Montpellier, 1953.

K. STRECKER, *Einführung in das Mittellatein*, 3rd ed., Berlin, 1939 (French translation by P. van de Woestijne, *Introduction à l'étude du latin médiéval*, 3rd ed., Geneva, 1948; English translation by R. B. Palmer, *Introduction to Medieval Latin*, Berlin, 1957).

P. STUDER and E. R. G. WATERS, *Historical French Reader*, Oxford, 1924.

C. TAGLIAVINI, *Il dialetto del Comelico*, Geneva, 1926.

—— *Le origini delle lingue neolatine*, 2nd ed., Bologna, 1952.

A. THOMAS, *La chanson de sainte Foi d'Agen, édité d'après le manuscrit de Leide*, Paris, 1925.

R. THURNEYSEN, *Kelto-romanisches*, Halle, 1884.

G. TILANDER, *Los Fueros de Aragón*, Lund, 1937.

—— *Los Fueros de la Novenera*, Stockholm, 1951.

K. TITZ, *Glossy Kasselské*, Prague, 1923.

A. TOVAR, *La lengua vasca*, San Sebastián, 1950.

V. VÄÄNÄNEN, *Le latin vulgaire des inscriptions pompéiennes*, Helsinki, 1937.

A. VELLEMAN, *Dicziunari scurznieu de la lingua ladina*, Samaden, 1929.

M. L. WAGNER, *La lingua sarda*, Berne, 1951.

W. VON WARTBURG, *Die Ausgliederung der romanischen Sprachräume*, Berne, 1950 (Spanish translation, *La fragmentación lingüística de la Romania*, Madrid, 1952).

—— *Die Entstehung der romanischen Völker*, Halle, 1936 (French translation, *Les origines des peuples romans*, Paris, 1941).

—— *Einführung in Problematik und Methodik der Sprachwissenschaft*, Halle, 1943 (French translation, *Problèmes et méthodes de la linguistique*, Paris, 1946).

—— *Évolution et structure de la langue française*, 5th ed., Berne, 1958.

—— *Französisches etymologisches Wörterbuch*, Bonn–Leipzig–Bâle, 1922–.

K. WHINNOM, *Spanish Contact Vernaculars in the Philippine Islands*, Hong Kong–Oxford, 1956.

E. B. WILLIAMS, *From Latin to Portuguese*, Philadelphia, 1938.

F. A. WRIGHT, *Select Letters of St. Jerome*, London, 1933.

—— and T. A. SINCLAIR, *A History of later Latin Literature*, London, 1931.

J. WRIGHT, *Grammar of the Gothic Language*, 2nd ed., Oxford, 1954.

N ZINGARELLI, *Vocabolario della lingua italiana*, 6th ed., Milan, 1938.

# SUBJECT INDEX

# WORD INDEX

## A. ROMANCE

### 1. GALLO-ROMANCE

#### (a) *Langue d'oïl*

## 2. HISPANO-ROMANCE

peu 445
pit 444
pla 438
plànyer 113
platz 441
ple 445
plorar 113, 445
poc 102
predicació 445
prèssec 33, 283
prévere, prebére 200
prova 444
puig 444

quin, quina, quins, quines 97, 445

rascar 210
ric 251
robar 210
rostir 210

sa, ses 88
sabó 205
safanories 282
sageta 245
seiner, seinor 440
sem, seu 129
semenava 440
sentíeu 445
sentiu 445
sèquia, siquia 282
serp 68
serpent 68
seu, seva 85, 445
si 150
só, sóc, ets, &c. 128
sopa 207
sus 149
sutge 188

tassa 285
temeu 445
temíeu 445
tenir 114
teu, teva 85, 445
traducció, traduccions, 445
treva 207
tu 441

ull 444
us 79

vaig 444
vaig cantar, &c. 446
vam, vau 446
vell 444
venir 113
versió 445
veser 113
veure 113, 445
villa 284
viure 445

*Galician*

año 164
laverca 217
tona 176n.

*Leonese*

arruoyo 180n.

*Mozarabic*

advolaray 404
dolje 403
esid, exed 403
farayo, fareyo 404
feito 193
filyolo 404
gar, garid, garir 404
lahtaira 403
mibi 79, 404
noḅte 403
venid, viened 403
vivireyu 404
yermanellas 403

*Portuguese*

a, as 81, 88, 430
abelha 158
acéquia 282
achar 160
adail 288
adarga 288
agasalhar 222
agosto 48
agouro 48
agradar 124
agradeça 124
agradecer 124
agradeço 124
aia 222
airão 238

al (< ALID) 97
albricoque 283
alcachofras 282
aleive 222
alfaiate 285
alfanje 288
algara 288
algarada 288
algo 100
algodão 283
alguém 100n.
algum 100
alheio 98
aljava 288
almafre 288
almirante 287
alodio 242
alperche 283
alva 209
alvíçaras 291
amanhã 167
amou 431
anho 164
antre 432
aquele 92
aquesse 92
aqueste 92
arpa 207
arroz 282
árvore 59
aspa 223
ata, até 290
ataviar 223
ave 158
azeite 283
azeitona 283

baixar 115
banco 207
bandir 244
barro 179
bastardo 253
bastir 209
bater 40
beijo 431
bem 146
berço 188
bordel 239
bragas 183
branco 208
brasa 207n.
brio 191
britar 217

## 3. ITALO-ROMANCE

[1] The letter *k* is used in transcription of modern Sardinian as a symbol for the voiceless velar plosive, usually represented in literary Sardinian, as in Italian, by *c* (*ch*).

## 4. RHETO-ROMANCE

## 5. BALKAN ROMANCE

# B. SOURCES OF ROMANCE[1]

## 1. ARABIC

## 2. CELTIC

[1] In the lists which follow Celtic words are given for the most part in latinized form, whereas Germanic words, being better attested (see p. 205), are given in Germanic form except when quoted from Latin texts.

# 3. GERMANIC

# 4. GREEK

# 5. LATIN (including Medieval Latin and hypothetical forms)[1]

[1] Latin words quoted in the text from Glossaries (pp. 312, 314–19, 406–9) have not been listed here unless singled out for special comment.

# 560

WORD INDEX

FLĒRE 154
FLŎCCUM 419
FLŌREM, -ES 44, 52, 60, 356
FLOREO 114
FLORĒRE 114, 115
FLORESCERE 114
FLORĪRE 114, 115
FLORISCERE 115
FŎCUS, -UM 298n., 374, 425, 463
FOEDUM 425
FOENUM 164
FŎLIA 57, 354, 419, 421, 431, 444, 468
FOLLES 366
FONTANA 298n.
FONTEM, -ES 418, 425
FORAS 225
FORDEUM (HORDEUM) 424
FORESTIS 237
FORIS 147, 254, 425
FORMA 298n.
FORMATICUS, -UM 163, 313, 426
FORMOSUS 26, 29, 30, 153
FORTIOREM 70
FORTIS, -EM 68, 425
FOSTEA (HOSTEA) 424
FOVEA 58n.
FRAMEA 205
FRANCISCUS, -A 235
FRANGIT 335n.
FRATELLUM 159
FRATER 63, 159, 164, 342, 427
FRAXINUS, -UM 42, 58, 191
FRIGIDUM, -A 29, 364, 426
FRŎNTEM 419, 425
FRŪCTUS, -UM 298n., 357, 426
FRUMENTUM 164
FUERAM 144
FUGĒRE 114
FUGIO 114
FUGĪRE 114
FUI 140, 142
FUISSET 390
FUISSĒTIS 390
FULIGINEM, FULLIGINEM 188

FUMUM 423
FUNDUM 425
FŪNIS 198
FURNACEUM 420

GALBINUM 364
GALEA 246
GALLITTA 159n.
GALLUS 320
GAMBA 154, 364
GANTA 205
GARRĪRE 166, 404
GARRULUS 31, 404
GAUDEO, GAUDĒRE 114
GAUDĪRE 114
GAUDIUM, GAUDIA 57, 357, 364, 441, 470
GELARE 420
GELUM 420
GENERUM 54, 420
GENITIOR, -EM 70, 374
GĒNITUS 70
GENTEM, -ES 37, 54, 101, 298n., 363, 466
GENTILIS 57
GENŬCULUM, -A 58, 421
GĔNUS 101
*GERMANĔLLAS 403
GERMANUS, -UM, -A 55, 164, 298n., 420, 432
GLACIES, GLACIA 61, 466, 467
GLIS 31
GRAECUM 359
GRANDIOR, -IOREM 70
GRANDIS 22, 68
GRANUM, -A 57
GRATUM 124
GROSSUS 154
GRUNDIO 33
GRUS, GRUIS 31, 62
GŬLA 44, 45, 46, 356
GUSTARE 272
GUTTA 101
*GUTTIARE 466
GYPSUM 420
GYRUS 29

HABA (FABA) 424
HABEAM 131
HABEAT 25, 108, 466
HABENA 298n.
HABENT 477

HABEO 106, 107, 108, 109, 341 (see also 128)
HABEO (AD) CANTARE 106
HABEO COMPARATUM 108, 109
HABĒRE, HABYRE 107, 108n., 109, 113, 128, 132, 182, 309, 325, 340, 468, 477
HABERE CANTATUM 110
HABITUM 117
HABUI 140, 141
HABUIT 108
*HABŪTU 117
HAC 87, 90, 147
HAC NOCTE 87
HAEC 86, 89
HAEDUS (FAEDUS) 424
HANC 87
HANC HORAM 87
HANULUM (FANULUM) 424
HASTA 244, 254
HELMUS 246
HERCULES 30
HEREDITARE 432
HĔRI 166
HIBERNUM 167
HIC 38, 86, 87, 89, 90, 91, 93, 147, 451
HIRPEX, HIRPICEM, ERBEX 238, 309
HOC 86, 87, 89, 90, 91, 344, 445
HOC ANNO 87, 464
HŎDIE 166, 419, 431, 466
*HOM, *HOMCE 90
HOMINEM NATUM 101
HŎMO, HŎMINEM, -ES 42, 66, 67, 99, 103, 344, 406
HOMO DICIT 104
HORA, -AM, -AS 87, 99, 147
HORDEUM (FORDEUM) 424
HORRIDUM 42, 440
HORTO 111
HORTUM 58n.
HOSPITALE 427
HOSTEA (FOSTEA) 424
HOSTIAE 30
HUMERUS 161
HUMILITATEM 298n.
HUNC 90

Nn

## 6. PRE-ROMANCE (Unidentified)

## PLACE-NAMES

# C. OTHER LANGUAGES

## ALBANIAN

kise 20
prift 200

## ANGLO-SAXON

bāt 231
brēotan 217

cringan 265

daroth 245

feoh 243

heard 251
hlāf 211
hlāford 211
hlǣfdige 211

lāwerce 217

rād 231

sāpe 205
strǣl 263

tūn 194

wafian 267
wǣg 267
weard 211
wincian 248

## BASQUE

baba 424
bago 237
bereter 200
besta 181, 424
biku 424
bizarr 179n.
borondate 181

deabru 201
dembora 181

eleiza 200
eskerr 178

garba 238
golde 181

gorputz 177
gura 45

ibai 179
ibaiko 179

lapitz 177

muga 180

patu 424
pesta 181, 424
phike 45

## GERMAN
### (Old High)

gahi 250
mornēn 251
sneida 311
sorēn 249n.
unwaigaro 252

## GERMAN (Modern)

absagen 225
aufgeben 225
ausrufen 225

Bache 240
Bart 320
bescheissen 265
Beute 247
bleich 251
bloss 228
bohren 264
braun 209
Braut 241
brechen 209
Busch 237

Dänemark 207
Definition 53
dick 265
dreschen 241

eigen 225
eingenommen sein 225
eisenbraun 249
Ernte 210

Fahne 244

Farbe 240
Feder 264
Fehde 263
Fetzen 224
Finmark 207
Friede 210
fronen 210
Futter 264

gähnen 210
Gans 222
Gänse 320
Gehege 263
Geige 241
Geselle 222
Gram 251

haben 320
Hag 239
hegen 222
Heger 222
hoch 254
Hohn 252
Hülse 237
Hummer 267

Ja 456
jemanden auf dem Strich
    haben 225

Kaiser 35
Käse 214
Keim 35
Keller 34
Kirche 200
Kirsche 34
Kiste 34
kratzen 210
Krug 240

Leber 320
lecken 210
ledig 242
Leid 251
leisten 222
Lerche 217

manch 102
marschieren 367
Marsch 237
Martius 53

# INDEX OF AUTHORS